THE FRENCH ARMY
A Military-Political History

✝

PAUL-MARIE DE LA GORCE

*

George Braziller, New York

THE FRENCH ARMY
A MILITARY-POLITICAL HISTORY

✠ ✠

TRANSLATED BY KENNETH DOUGLAS

CONTENTS

✠

vi   CONTENTS

THE FRENCH ARMY
A Military-Political History

✠

✠

Scarcely any reportorial assignment in France is more difficult than coming to grips with the Army, its personnel and problems. The secrecy that veils an important part of its activity; the atmosphere, so unlike any other, particular to military circles; the marked distrust that officers of all ranks feel for any outsider, however well intentioned, who takes an interest in Army life—all this conspires to make it an exceptionally delicate and, at times, impossible task simply to recount the history of the military establishment.

Yet it is a fact that for some years now, as every political development shows, the history of the Army is inseparable from that of the Nation. The Army has in its own way experienced the effects of social metamorphosis, economic evolution and political revolution. Like every human group it has its own laws which may be altered, under the influence of time or external transformations, but not entirely abrogated. Its own recruitment and hierarchy, its goals and internal discipline ensure that political, economic or social change will have on it certain precise effects, integrating it more thoroughly into society at large or keeping it apart from the general trend. The whole history of the relations between Army and Nation is made up of this dual evolution, simultaneous but not always parallel, harmonious at times and sometimes discordant.

In the most recent period French politics has become the setting for a new relationship between the Nation and its Army. The latter, far from remaining merely a social milieu in which the changing times are mirrored, has entered the arena of political conflict. On some occasions the whole military hierarchy has been involved. On others, only a group of officers or a few regiments have been affected. As-tounded, Frenchmen no longer recognized the Army, of which they had preserved a traditional though far from unified image that was based on the splendid myths of military history, on incidents of garri-son life, or on the customary symbols of antimilitarism. The Army has indeed traveled a long way. This book will endeavor to retrace the path it followed.

There is nothing arbitrary about choosing as an approximate start-ing point the year 1890. The French Army had just passed through a period of its history when, perhaps more than at any other time, it was in rapport with public sentiment, enjoyed the support of all social classes and was regarded with a warmth of feeling that precluded all risk of a crisis. Yet this period provides the best example of the various developments that, almost invisibly, were preparing the way for those clashes, and even ruptures, that later would explode in full public view.

The underlying significance of the Dreyfus Affair, grave as it ap-peared at the time, is that nevertheless neither the Army nor the Nation had any serious thought of challenging the basis of their rela-tionship. Not a trace can be found in military circles at that time of any attempt to overthrow the regime. And the men who em-bodied the regime and set its course did all they could, along diverg-ing but finally parallel paths, to solve the crisis without casting doubt on the importance of the Army.

The First World War, by refuting everything that the General Staffs and governments had expected to occur, once again raised the issue of the relative functions of political and military power. Yet at no time, for all their authority and the means at their disposal, did the Chiefs of Staff at General Headquarters attempt to supervise or even influence the over-all prosecution of the war. The only major problem, apparently, involved distinguishing political responsibility from military operations at the highest level, and since the problem arose in an unexpected context and on an unforeseen scale, three years were spent in solving it.

Victory gave the military leader quite exceptional authority. The drafting of a peace treaty posed essential questions both for the future of the country and for its military security. In this vital matter the highest military authority disagreed with the government. On the actual scene, in the Rhineland, the Army had all the means needed to force the hand of the government, and some Army leaders were making ready to use them. But this situation did not last more than a few months, and had almost no echo in Parliament. Fifteen years later (in the early 1930's), the Army appeared ready to involve itself in new political preoccupations; networks were being formed in the officers' corps. French society, for its part, seemed on the verge of revolutionary changes, heralded by the coming to power of the Popular Front in 1936. Many Army men appeared to be contemplating violent opposition, and only the collapse of the government coalition eliminated this danger. The crisis blew over, but the deep-seated reasons for its existence remained.

Some military leaders lent the whole weight of their authority to the most solemn decision made in our own day, the capitulation to the German forces in 1940. A considerable part of the Army appeared to be closely identified with the Vichy regime. But those who continued the struggle by joining the Free French, and the larger forces that later resumed combat, helped, in the atmosphere of the Liberation and of victory, to cast a veil over the 1940–1942 period which otherwise might have brought about a grave schism between the country and its defenders. Once more the crisis was reabsorbed, disguised or simply left to languish in a very necessary oblivion. But its roots had not been extirpated.

Finally the cold war and the Atlantic Alliance made official, so to speak, the opposition between a fraction of public opinion and the duty of the Army: henceforth, the enemy was to be found within as well as without. The conflict had become permanent and universal. One of the theaters of operation was Indochina, where for the first time in history all branches of the Army had to serve thousands of miles from Paris. But, in a sense, French politics was another battleground. And this takes us to the threshold of the Algerian War, to within a few years of the uprising of May 13, 1958.

Thus two epochs appear to confront each other. One provides only instances of crisis and conflict. The other suggests the notion of an endemic crisis masked over with ever-greater difficulty by a series of political expedients which, while delaying the final explosion, are unable to contribute to a solution. At last the day arrives when everything concurs to shake the Army out of its restraint and cause it to intervene openly and vociferously in the conduct of political affairs.

Every historical line of demarcation is based on an arbitrary choice. The Army of 1935 was not essentially different from that of 1920, and the events of 1940 would be inexplicable without a process that originated in the period immediately following the 1918 victory. Nevertheless, an examination of the facts does reveal a division. Before this is traversed the Army, apart from an occasional convulsion, appears not to be tempted to take political action, whereas afterward this temptation has become permanent, and is frustrated only by the precise turn of events. One day it is frustrated no longer.

The principal aim of this book is to determine where this historical turning point can be identified. Consequently, every stage of Army history has had to be situated with respect to its political, intellectual, economic and social setting. In other words, a position had to be adopted that lies on the confines of general history and military history. This constitutes, perhaps, the originality of our undertaking. It certainly explains its difficulty, if not its defects.

At some moments the general conditions of Army history seemed simple; they might be said to define themselves and so to remove all mystery from the problem of the relationship between the Nation and its Army. Yet at other times there seemed to be no way of dealing with the trials that shook military society except by making a detailed analysis of the evolution of French society as a whole and, more especially, of political society.

Such was the case, for example, when examining the initial symptoms of the Dreyfus Affair and the solution of the crisis which it precipitated. But it was particularly true for the years that preceded the Second World War. Then, indeed, the perturbations of French society affected the military establishment; the revolution in men's minds impinged on the Army cadres; and this picture of widespread crisis suggested that some convulsion of the state and social order was close at hand. We have left far behind the political or moral controversies aroused by the condemnation of Captain Dreyfus or by the terms of the military occupation of the Rhineland. The reaction of the officers' corps bore little resemblance, in 1936, to what it had been in 1898 or in 1918.

Thus it follows that the investigation of the real connections between Nation and Army, in a historical context, may take one rather far afield in the exploration of causal sequences. Such an investigation leads to conclusions that sometimes are simple and sometimes highly complex but which, I hope, will never appear arbitrary. This book may as a result seem remarkably ambitious since, while examining the history of the Army, it becomes involved in the history of society and of international relations, as well as of ideas and feelings. But at the same time it sets itself a much more modest goal than that of constituting a general history of the Army. It contains neither the recital of the great military episodes that mark the two World Wars and operations overseas, nor any systematic analysis of doctrines, whether these apply to strategy or to tactics, nor a history of armaments and their suggested utilization. Since it is concerned with the interrelationship of general history and military history, this book would have overshot the mark and fallen into irrelevancy if it had sought to become a historical encyclopedia of the French Army in the modern world. Besides, the time surely is not ripe for such an enterprise. For most of the years between 1890 and 1962, the official archives are still unavailable. As for what has occurred since 1945, the controverted and controversial avowals of politicians and military personages must be classed among those having a minimal historical value, while the general surveys, with a few (and hence all the more noteworthy) exceptions, are works of journalism.

I fell prey to one last scruple—perhaps the most serious of all. Whatever rigor historical research may achieve, it remains strangely cold in its treatment of the men at grips with the circumstances it endeavors to analyze. This coldness is an almost universal fault in the writing of history. In this particular instance, however, it appears especially unbearable because here we have to do with men whose lot it is to kill or be killed, with men indescribably close to us, many of them still alive and most of whom, in their physical being or their hearts, have actually undergone the trials that are treated in these pages as so many historical episodes. Some of these men, as they read this book, may have difficulty finding any echo of their own inner drama.

This danger is all the more acute since the conclusions that are drawn will no doubt seem harsh or pessimistic. Yet I am anxious to convince them that at no stage of the historical epoch here evoked did I feel myself estranged or indifferent. My familiarity with the world of the soldier has been sufficiently close and sufficiently prolonged for me to realize, quite concretely, what a particular political decision, moral conflict or drama of conscience signified for the individuals involved.

Yes, I thought of the trials that these men had passed through, as I pondered their history. I thought above all of the untold mass of suffering undergone by the humblest soldiers and the most modest officers, at every turning point, and in exchange for every victory and every defeat. Their sufferings loom up behind this book. May its readers, like its author, preserve them from forgetfulness.

CHAPTER ONE

BEFORE 1890

✠

"Every day he spends hours on the parade ground, drilling recruits, training noncoms and specialists, marching with the men, riding, and busying himself with all the details of food, clothing and maintenance. He must also take part in officers' training, appear on ceremonial occasions and carry out the special missions necessitated by life in a community. Furthermore, he loves his profession, which allows him to act and to exercise authority. Though his pay is meager, the officer is compensated by the exceptional prestige he enjoys. In the garrison, everyone treats him with respect. Tradespeople extend him credit. He is at the center of every activity. People admire his bearing. Women are favorably disposed. Families would be glad to have as a son-in-law this man of honor who, they say, 'has a future' or, at all events, a steady income and a pension for later on."

This picture of military life painted by Charles de Gaulle in *La France et son armée* represents the army that had fascinated him as a child, and the setting in which he looked forward to spending his life. It is a portrait valid for a long period of French military history, and covers, at the very least, the final quarter of the nineteenth century. For some twenty-five years, from just after the Franco-Prussian War to the century's closing, the Army molded itself in the image of what it wanted to be and of what the state required.

At the end of this quarter century occurred the first of those tempests that were to convulse the Army and transform it, sixty years later, into something entirely unimaginable at the outset. History has ordained that the same man who described so faithfully the ordered, active, studious existence, no less honorable than honored, of the French officer between 1871 and 1895, should later become the occasion and the instrument of crises that would wreck the Army's unity, sap the very foundations of military society and provoke the most violent political eruptions of twentieth-century France.

When the first of the Army's great trials was about to begin, on the eve of the Dreyfus Affair, the military establishment was all that twenty-five years of labor, of intellectual, financial and concrete effort could make it. Every officer familiar with the period would later gaze back on it nostalgically—for, after the defeat of 1870 and the Commune, the Army became the object of a profound fervor. The source of this emotion lay in the disaster that had just befallen the country, and in the desire to avoid for all time any similar catastrophe. The memory of the Prussians in Paris, of the invaders making their way down the valleys of Loire and Seine to occupy almost one-quarter of the national territory, continued to keep alive more or less consciously, for a whole generation, the French people's passion for their reborn Army.

On the plain of Longchamps, July 29, 1871, a few short weeks after the close of hostilities, 120,000 men with Marshal MacMahon at their head filed past Thiers, chief of the Provisional Executive. When the march past was over, the two men embraced. Thiers, that old politician who had already witnessed the death throes of so many regimes, is said to have sobbed aloud. Terrific applause rose from the dense crowd present at the parade. It was a moment that gave full public expression to the collective fervor which for twenty-five years would bind together the Army and the entire Nation.

This was the atmosphere that reigned in the National Assembly when, in 1872, the debate began on the new military measures intended to modernize the French Army. It was a period of intense struggle for and against the monarchy, for and against the bicameral legislature, for and against the restoration of a system harking back to the constitutional monarchy that had preceded the Revolution of 1848, as contrasted with the gradual evolution toward a republic that would finally become a democracy. But when the National Assembly took up military matters, a kind of national unity appeared to have arisen.

The spokesman of the Right, the Duc d'Audiffret-Pasquier, de-

clared that the Conservatives accepted the principle of compulsory
military service. This was a complete departure from their previous
viewpoint. For many, it was not only the defense of the Nation that
justified the new law. Their examination of the reasons for the defeat
of 1870 had convinced many deputies and journalists, moralists and
military men alike, that the causes were above all intellectual and
moral. The frivolousness of government and high command, was
traced back to the thoughtless existence of many members of the upper
bourgeoisie, to the neglect of studies and the contempt for science
that was openly proclaimed, during the last years of the Second Empire, in military and governmental circles. What was envisaged, after
the defeat, was a return to austerity, discipline and gravity, to a
passion for study, labor and exertion.

While the Right was shedding its former distrust of compulsory
military service—based on its fear of familiarizing the bulk of the
population, and more particularly the working classes, with the handling of arms—the Left remained faithful to the attitude it had adopted
during the latter part of the war (that is, after the collapse of the
Second Empire on September 4, 1870) and made national defense
the first article on its program. The Left had rediscovered the Jacobin
tradition of the revolutionary wars, when patriotism, the Republic
and the Revolution were fused into one great passion.

Among them was Jules Ferry, who later would become one of
the most important figures of the Third Republic. "Do you recall," he
wrote at the time, "that during the Empire we had little to say in
favor of militarism? Do you recall the vague longings for general
disarmament, the manifest detachment from any military spirit, and
the tendency to favor a kind of universal national guard that characterized the democracy of that day? These ideas had their adherents;
some among ourselves professed them, inclined toward them, or let
themselves be convinced. But today is there even one man, I ask you,
who has not been converted by events? This country has witnessed
the War of 1870; it turns its back forever on these perilous and disappointing utopias." In intellectual circles Michelet, Quinet and
Renan had the same attitude.

In July, 1872, the National Assembly adopted the first law prescribing the military organization of the country, and embodying
the principle of compulsory service.

This law dealing with manpower was followed by two others. One
determined that the Army, in time of peace, should have the same

organization it would maintain throughout a war. The other established the principle of the permanency of the cadres, their number being so calculated that, in case of mobilization, they would correspond to a total strength twice that of peacetime.

The military organization with which France thus equipped herself after the defeat of 1870 was to stand stoutly until 1914. The rigor, logic and simplicity involved bear witness to the seriousness and intellectual stature of the men who had elaborated it. On this basis the high command could get down to work, unconcerned with party quarrels, and fully conscious both that public opinion remained passionately attached to the Army and that the sole mission was to prepare France against the eventuality of a new conflict with the German Empire.

Thanks to the solidity of the Army's over-all organization and the nature of its mission, the military potential of France was no longer dependent upon political vicissitudes. Between 1870 and 1888, nineteen governments replaced each other, and sixteen War Ministers were installed in the Rue Saint-Dominique, only to depart before they could accomplish anything whatever. It was the permanency of the General Staff that mitigated the drawbacks caused by ministerial instability. The necessary intellectual implement of the military effort was set up in 1875, with the creation of the École Supérieure de Guerre under Colonel Lewal, and received its definitive form in 1880. From this point on, subaltern officers were admitted to the competitive entrance examination. The final examination qualified them to receive the General Staff diploma. The officers thus certificated—originally they numbered three hundred—were specially employed (*hors cadre*), but each remained attached to his own branch of the service for advancement and for the supervision of his career. Everywhere in the Army a veritable passion sprang up for military studies, for the history of warfare, and for the problems of strategy, tactics and matériel. There was a mighty reaction against the outlook that had prevailed under the Second Empire. "I eliminate from the list of promotions," Marshal MacMahon declared, "any officer whose name I have read on the cover of a book." Several periodicals were founded that specialized in military questions (*La Revue d'Histoire, Progrès, Spectateurs*), and the general press began to publish regular accounts of military matters.

The high command was anxious, also, to make sweeping changes in military equipment. "There was not a tool, a wagon or a boat,"

Charles de Gaulle could write, as historian of the Army, "for which new models were not adopted between 1897 and 1900."

In 1888 Freycinet became Minister of War and almost simultaneously General de Miribel rose to the highest Army post. They carried out the last and by no means least significant step required in the over-all modernization of the Army. This was to constitute a large General Staff to match the recent revolution in military ideas. On May 6, 1890, the "Army General Staff" was officially implemented, and General de Miribel was put in charge. His duty was twofold: to insure that the totality of France's armed strength would be made ready for war, and to provide the high command with all requisite information. In the event of mobilization, the head of the General Staff would become Major General in charge of the main group of armies in the field. The Army General Staff was itself divided into two sections, one forming General Headquarters and Army Headquarters, and the other, under the War Minister, supervising the execution of the main directives.

Meanwhile, a new Army Council had been set up to replace both the old Council and the "Committee of Defense." The number of members was set at a maximum of twelve. It was to be presided over by the War Minister, and the head of the General Staff was an ex officio member. It had to be consulted on all matters pertaining to national defense and its members were chosen, while peace still reigned, to command the armies in the field, with the obligation to prepare forthwith to carry out their duties. Finally, it devolved upon them to discharge all missions of inspection and to organize Army maneuvers in their entirety. These regulations were so logical, efficacious and adaptable that, with the introduction of a few reforms, they remained in force throughout World War I and beyond.

Freycinet and de Miribel sought, finally, to apply the lessons learned in the fifteen years that had elapsed since the new military laws had first been voted, particularly insofar as the rules governing military service were concerned.

Once again debate brought to light the traditional clash between two differing conceptions of what the Army should be. Several spokesmen for the Right were terrified at seeing the "professional army" lose its sharpness of definition, for in its traditional isolation from the Nation, and with its habits of discipline and its permanent officering, it constituted the ideal instrument for "maintaining order." (In conservative circles, the recollection of how the Army had

crushed the workers' revolt of 1848 and, later, the Commune, was
still vigorously alive.) On the extreme Left, voices were raised in
favor of a militia, which would draw more widely on the population
by summoning to arms, for a short period, every citizen of military
age. The advantages of an army that would "constantly mingle
with the people" were bolstered by the argument that any future
war would require such enormous forces that the permanent training
of the reserves would henceforth exceed in importance the size of the
contingent currently on active service.

Impassioned though these debates became, their scope was restricted, in actual fact, to points of detail such as the military obligations of members of the liberal professions or of seminarists. There was
unanimity, throughout the whole spectrum of public opinion, on
everything essential: on the principle of compulsory service, the importance of maintaining a Regular Army strong enough to withstand the first assaults in case of war, the training of more numerous
reserve officers, and the vital matter of "keeping the Army out of
political quarrels."

At the same time the General Staff set out to renew its conception
of warfare, launching out on a systematic study of all the theories
developed concerning modern war. Staffs and Intelligence were
passionately interested in problems of organization, transportation,
mobility, supplies and revictualing. This was the time when the
management of an army in the field came to be looked on as
an immense industrial undertaking. The silent labors of the officers
who pursued these researches represented the greatest military revolution that France had known since Napoleon. Filing cabinets, records
and graphs belonged henceforward to the military arsenal on an equal
footing with sabers and cannon. For the French Army, the reign
of the "Plan" had begun.

Relations with the German Empire dominated France's whole
foreign policy up to 1914. Every French government reached a
decision on the basis of the intentions attributed to Germany, and
on the danger that German political initiatives represented for
France. Franco-German relations were themselves dominated by the
question of Alsace-Lorraine. The territorial annexation carried out
under the Treaty of Frankfort (1871) had inflicted such a wound
on France that nothing could exceed in urgency the desire to avoid
a repetition of the German invasion. The lost provinces had belonged

to France since the days of Louis XIV and Louis XV, and the question of national sovereignty had not been raised even after the collapse of Napoleon. The touching protests of the deputies from Alsace-Lorraine before the National Assembly of 1871 were to awaken a profound and undying echo throughout the country. Only time would weaken the idea of *revanche* which now took hold of French popular feeling.

Yet the relative strength of the armed forces of France and Germany was such that no French government, during the last quarter of the century, could have envisaged the notion of any aggression directed against Germany. French and German diplomatic archives leave no doubt on that score. From 1875 on, when the French General Staff elaborated its first plans for mobilization in the event of war, the ruling idea was entirely defensive. It was provided that the armies would concentrate well behind the frontier. The plan aimed, essentially, at preventing the crossing of the Meurthe and the Meuse by the German armies. The defensive character of the French plan was even more heavily underlined by the construction, from 1874 on, of a fortified system whose main points were at Toul, Verdun and Épinal. Military recovery proceeded so well that the General Staff subsequently revised its plans. Beginning in 1889, the concentration of forces provided for in mobilization plan No. 10 envisaged, in the most favorable circumstances, a French offensive in the direction of Metz and Strasbourg. But this was altogether dependent on the estimate held by the General Staff of the relative strength of French and German forces at the moment that hostilities would begin. It was only for a very brief period that the French Army could consider snatching the initiative from the enemy and carrying the war into German territory.

After 1893, the relative strength of forces once more turned in favor of Germany. Since the German population was growing much more rapidly than the French, the contingent mobilized every year was much more numerous, and the reserves at the disposition of the Regular Army were far larger than those the French high command could count on. So the high command, after 1898, returned to its "defensive" concept.

The search for alliances, incumbent on France after the defeat of 1870, failed to create any major difference between government and high command. Italy had no common frontier with the German Empire and was also militarily and economically weak, so that it could not be a strong ally for France. Austria-Hungary, with which Napoleon III had vainly sought a rapprochement in 1868 and 1869, was now definitely turning toward an alliance with Germany. This tendency became even more marked after Hungarian political personnel acquired a decisive influence in Vienna. Great Britain, whose military and, above all, naval strength might have had an important influence on the outcome of a war, was currently refusing to enter into any contractual alliance in peacetime.

The successive French governments knew that English diplomacy was becoming increasingly alarmed at German hegemony in Europe. They maintained an attitude of utmost prudence vis-à-vis Great Britain, avoiding any challenge to its essential interests in order to obtain its support in the event of a diplomatic crisis involving the German Empire, and perhaps a military alliance if war should break out.

"The English fleet can't protect Paris," Kaiser Wilhelm II said. Only the Russian alliance was both politically feasible and militarily useful. The General Staff fully shared the conviction of successive French governments concerning this. Ribot, as Minister of Foreign Affairs, expressed the problem very succinctly. "This is the goal to be attained," he told his ambassador in St. Petersburg. "First obtain from the Russian government the promise that Russia and France will act in concert if peace should be threatened in Europe. Then obtain the simultaneous mobilization of the Russian and French Armies, without there being any need of a previous agreement, the moment that one of the countries of the Triple Alliance [Germany, Austria-Hungary, Italy] mobilizes its forces."

While the French government was seeking a defensive alliance, it also wanted a military alliance. The first Franco-Russian accord, signed on August 27, 1891, aimed at an understanding with respect to general policy and provided that the two countries should act in concert in a time of crisis. A military collaboration was envisaged in principle but received no preliminary definition.

Not until July 8, 1892, did Czar Alexander III extend an invitation to General de Boisdeffe, asking him to enter into contact with the Russian high command on the occasion of the annual maneuvers. General de Boisdeffe undertook to negotiate a military accord, and this was concluded on August 18. The first article stipulated that "If Russia is attacked by Germany or Italy, or by Austria-Hungary with the support of Germany, France will use all its available forces to attack Germany." Article II provided for the automatic mobilization of the French and Russian Armies in the event of the mobilization of the Armies of the Triple Alliance or of any one of them. Article VI arranged for the same duration of the Franco-Russian accord as had been allotted the Triple Alliance of Germany, Austria-Hungary and Italy.

This military agreement was the centerpiece of the Franco-Russian alliance, since it defined the circumstances in which the alliance would operate. It definitely established the defensive character of the alliance, since the mechanism could be set in motion only by the adversary's own action.

French diplomats and military men had yet to reach the end of their labors. It was not until December 27, 1893, that the Czar let it be known that the military accord could "be considered as definitively adopted in its present form." On January 4, 1894, the French government replied that the accord "was henceforth in force." The relief of French ministers and diplomats at seeing the conclusion of a negotiation that had gone on for two years and a half, and the satisfaction of the General Staff, once it could be assured that in case of war the French Army would not have to fight alone, were in complete harmony with the popular enthusiasm that had greeted the visit of the Russian squadron to Toulon the previous October.

If, after 1871, a kind of national unanimity existed with respect to the problem of Franco-German relations, the foreign policy of France outside Europe was several times critically examined. Later, two opposing schools of foreign policy came to be distinguished, one entirely centered on Europe, the other anxious not to harness French policy exclusively to the painful memories of the 1870 catastrophe and to ensure for France new possibilities of expansion on the globe. But from 1871 to 1880 there were few serious debates marking any differences among those responsible for French policy on the topic of colonial undertakings.

Everything worked together, during this period, to force on France a "policy of meditation," as Thiers called it. The recollection of certain of the Second Empire's foreign adventures, and especially of the war in Mexico, assuredly had a share in this. Moreover France was obliged to concentrate all its efforts on paying the indemnity of five billion gold francs, as required by the Treaty of Frankfort. Thus the country could not permit itself any scattering of its economic and financial efforts. Finally, French diplomacy was not unaware that any colonial expansion risked bringing the country into conflict either with Great Britain or with Italy, thus isolating it even more vis-à-vis Germany.

Only after 1880 did some political and financial circles come out openly for French expansion outside Europe. They had no doubt convinced themselves some years earlier that a bolder colonial policy was necessary, but in order to win support for their point of view they had to await French military recovery and the payment of the debts owed Germany. Even so, their outlook might not have aroused much response among the bourgeoisie if the serious decline of ground rents in the 1880's, the stagnation of the Bourse and the low rate of interest available for funds had not converted the totality of French economic circles to accepting colonial expansion as a necessity.

In 1882 a book appeared, the best doctrinal exposition of colonialism in the nineteenth century, which marshaled all the arguments in favor of a colonial policy. The author of this book, *De la colonisation chez les peuples modernes,* was the economist Leroy-Beaulieu. His doctrine was matched by the policy put into effect, between 1881 and 1885 by Jules Ferry, which was the object of violent attacks launched by the partisans of the "withdrawal inside Europe." When finally, in 1885, the news of the difficulties experienced by the French military in Tonkin forced Ferry out of the government, the violence of the campaign conducted against him might have given rise to the view that there existed, in French public opinion, a veritable divorce between partisans and adversaries of a colonial policy.

Jules Ferry was no less convinced than other French politicians that the risk of a new Franco-German conflict had constantly to be borne in mind. But since, like them, he eliminated the possibility of France's undertaking an aggressive war, he could see no way to give the idea of the *revanche* the least concrete content—not, at all events, before a series of alliances had been set up to limit the danger of German hegemony. Thus he shared the view that French policy should not be immobilized in its preoccupation with Franco-German relations. He cherished no illusions concerning the practicality of a genuine Franco-German rapprochement, and in 1884 and 1885, when Bismarck appeared to be seeking it, he refused to take seriously the advances made. He had, doubtless, to respect the marked reticence of French public opinion; but he well knew that the German aim was to obtain France's definitive acceptance of the 1871 frontier, and Ferry, like every other French leader, was opposed to this. He was, finally, filled with doubt as to Bismarck's real intentions, and suspected him of encouraging France's colonial policy only to estrange France from England. Germany might effectuate a sudden rapprochement with England, leaving France more isolated than ever.

Jules Ferry's opponents, the men who had attacked his policy in Indochina and brought about his downfall, did nothing to modify French colonial policy. When it turned out that the military difficulties in Tonkin had left intact the agreements reached with China, the positions that France had occupied in Asia were maintained, consolidated and extended. So it would seem that between Jules Ferry and his opponents lay nothing but a fine distinction in their estimation of the risks to which colonial policy might expose the diplomatic and military strengthening of France in Europe, as compared with Germany. After 1890 the opposition to colonial policy weakened considerably, in political circles and in public opinion. The Committee on French Africa, founded on November 18, 1890, brought together on its executive committee men from both Left and Right. Hostility to this policy was maintained only by some Radicals of the Left and by the Socialists. But these latter, prior to the Dreyfus Affair, occupied no important place on the French political scene.

CHAPTER TWO

FROM THE GOLDEN AGE TO THE DREYFUS AFFAIR

This continuity in the country's foreign policy eliminated the danger of any major clash between the state and the military. During the quarter century that lay between the defeat of 1870 and the first symptoms of the Dreyfus Affair, the French Army consistently took no part in the political battles that decided the destiny of the Republic. The tradition of political abstentionism had a long history. It was strengthened by the noninvolvement the Army had practiced in the revolutions that had swept away the great French Revolution's successive regimes, up to the collapse of the Second Empire.

The unanimous fervor that surrounded the Army helped to reinforce, alike in public opinion and among the military, the idea that the Army must in all circumstances hold itself aloof from political conflict. No one on either Left or Right had the least doubt that the majority of Army officers were conservative in outlook, if not downright reactionary. But the corps of officers was convinced that only the singleminded service of the State could ensure universal respect for the Army. The testimony of an anonymous colonel, in his book, *La Nation et l'Armée,* was most revealing of the state of the military mind at the height of the Dreyfus Affair. "Recall," he wrote, "the situation as it was some twenty years ago. In the eyes of all, whether military men or not, the Republic was essentially a government dedi-

17

cated to restoring the country. Even the generals who had grown up under the previous regime and had it to thank for their entire advancement, made whatever sacrifice of sympathy or gratefulness their patriotism demanded. . . . They rejected the notion that between the Army and the Republic there was bound to be a divorce based on incompatibility of temperament."

There were, actually, a few alarms. During the crisis of May 16, 1877, when MacMahon dissolved the Chamber of Deputies with the hope that the Republican majority would be defeated and replaced by a Conservative and Monarchist majority, the royalist sympathies of most generals awakened the fear that a Republican victory in the elections would be countered by a military coup d'état. In reporting, on March 8, 1879, on the elections of October 14 and 28, 1877, Brisson, a future President of the Council and Grand Master of the Masonic Order, declared that General de Rochebouët, President of the Council and Minister of War, had prepared a "coup d'état" against Parliament, which had a Republican majority. But the investigation revealed, at the same time—and it quoted numerous officers to this effect—that the Army cadres were not ready to obey any such orders emanating from Rochebouët. Freycinet, too, who was no less stoutly republican than Brisson, revealed in his reminiscences that "MacMahon, at a Council of Ministers held in 1878, declared incidentally that he had at no time considered taking a step in conflict with the constitutional laws, that he had indeed raised the question of a second dissolution, but quite independently of General de Rochebouët, so that the idea of a coup d'état must have been arrived at without the knowledge of the Cabinet."

Only the Boulangist crisis could, in actual fact, have made it possible for the Army to intervene in political controversy. The overthrow of the Republic, at the height of General Boulanger's popularity, would have encountered no concrete obstacle. Yet everyone knew, at the time, that only Boulanger himself could think of a coup d'état. The General Staff would not have taken such an initiative, and never even dreamed of it, since almost without exception its members were hostile to Boulanger. The testimony of General Galliffet leaves no doubt on that score. Galliffet had suppressed the Commune, and he was royalist in his personal sympathies—everything should have inspired in him a natural hostility to the republican regime. But he repeatedly warned the politicians most strongly attracted by Boulangism. On January 17, 1889, he wrote as follows to the Duc d'Aumale, son of Louis-Philippe, who because of his part in the Algerian War was well liked in the Army: "It is feared that your return to France [the government had just authorized this] might weaken the adventurer's chances. Permit me, *mon général,* to cry out to you: for the country and for the Army there could be nothing more shameful than the coming to power of a man whom the Army has expelled from its ranks. There is no graver danger for France. It is, then, the duty of every Frenchman to spurn this shame and to exorcise this danger."

Jean Jaurès, the Socialist leader, had been among those most vociferously opposed to the Army cadres' playing any political role. "The Army," he nevertheless declared, when writing at a later date about the Boulangist crisis, "was not the direct cause of the peril. . . . It gave no indication either of corporate discontent or of class ambition." He extended this judgment to the whole period, specifically stating that the military had maintained political neutrality. "The Army," he wrote, "is but an instrument. It has neither strength of its own, nor an independent will, nor an individual policy. . . ."

At the moment that the crisis provoked by the Dreyfus Affair was about to break, the Army, it is clear, had aroused no public controversy and was the object of the country's fervent enthusiasm. This attitude might be expected to have weakened with the lapse of time, but year after year it was reinvigorated by a literature that evoked memories of the 1870 defeat, by the homage paid to the memory of Alsace-Lorraine and by accounts of France's colonial epic. With every summer, July 14 returned and strengthened the cult of the Army. It was at this time that the traditional military parade took on its greatest glory, attracted the largest crowds and aroused the loudest demonstrations of patriotism. This was still the epoch when military service for the first time tore young Frenchmen away from the restricted horizons of village or suburb. For most of them, setting off for the regiment was setting off for adventure. Doubtless the adventure had the garrison for its setting, and was soon reduced to the regimental round. But for the young during the last quarter of the nineteenth century there was something about this sudden transformation of their entire existence that quickened the pulse.

"Every year," wrote Charles de Gaulle,

> 250,000 young men leave fields, factories and offices for the somber life of the barracks. When they arrive they are timid, anxious to do

well, and surprised at first to find that those already on the scene are helpful, that the beds are comfortable and that the soup is good. But immediately they are caught up in the cogwheels of military service. Training begins, with its long series of "classes" on foot or on horse-back, with exercises, shooting, marches, theoretical instruction, and periods in the gymnasium or riding-school. Beneath autumn rains or in winter cold the unhappy recruits learn to handle arms, carry their packs or ride. In springtime the horizon widens a little. The marches cover more ground, and sham fighting is carried out on variegated terrain. Summer is the season of long marches, of periods under canvas and of taxing efforts whose very intensity makes them more interest-ing. In the meantime there are countless reviews and inspections to go through, arms, accessories, tools and harness to be cleaned, horses to be fed and rubbed down, and also guard duty and innumerable chores. Dressed—none too well—in military attire, subjected to im-perious and interchangeable regulations, and involved in tasks that require no ingenuity, the soldier savors the full bitterness of being an anonymous gearwheel in the immense collective machine. All the same, his own happy-go-lucky attitude gives him strength. All the same, people show their liking when they see him march by in forma-tion, when on parade, or walking about the town, huddled up rather than martial-looking in his inelegant accouterments, long greatcoat, heavy boots, kepi with pompom, white gaiters and filoselle gloves. All the same, he has a hereditary sensitivity to the picturesque, un-expected and stirring features of army life, he sings on the march, concentrates on shooting practice, walks smartly on parade and yells loudly as he sets off on a charge.

This portrait was to remain valid for many a long year. But the century was not to expire before the occurrence of the first great crisis to shake the French Army. Since the 1870 disaster this Army had been called and truly was the "Ark of the Covenant," unassail-able and painstakingly sheltered from the violent political quarrels that marked the formation, triumph and consolidation of the Third Republic. Yet already, in the secret history that is made up of men's consciences and ideas and of slow social transformation, one might have glimpsed the first symptoms of crisis and foreseen that the "Ark" would be violated.

The Yearbook for the Class of 1868 at St. Cyr, the West Point of France, contains 89 names preceded by the nobiliary particle de out of 284 pupils. But five years later, in 1878, this figure had risen to 102 out of 365. Names may be read that had not appeared in a very long time, or never before: Clermont-Tonnerre, Ségur, Nompar de Gaumont, d'Humières, Metz-Noblat, Rouvroy de Saint-Simon, Rohan-Chabot, Noailles, Choiseul-Praslin, Villèle, Cadoudal, La Bourdonnaye, Galard, Féligonde, Bournazel, Kergolay, Gastines. The Constituent Assembly of 1871, on the other hand, contained seventy former officers (three-quarters of whom were also listed in the peerage book) whereas, after the elections of 1881, when the Right was snowed under by the Republican coalition, the number of officers elected sank to thirteen. Until the beginning of the twentieth century their number never exceeded thirty. Examination of these figures reveals the divergent developments underlying military society and political society. A deep division began to mark off the Army cadres from the political, administrative and economic personnel of the nation.

The Army's great prestige had attracted to a military career an ever-increasing number of men from the traditionalist aristocracy and from the conservative and Catholic bourgeoisie. The flocking to the colors, on the part of scions of these families, had a consequence whose ultimate effects would grow more and more serious. In the officers' corps, the proportion of former pupils of religious establishments increased with startling rapidity. Between 1847 and 1871, these establishments contributed 700 pupils to Saint-Cyr, but between 1871 and 1887 they provided 1,800. This was the starting point for an apparently irreversible process which continually strengthened the proportion, in the military hierarchy, of men with an aristocratic and religious background.

Until 1889, promotion in the Army was determined by a law that had been passed in 1832. Two-thirds of the officers were promoted on the basis of seniority, up to the rank of commandant; the remainder were freely appointed. But the execution of the law was entrusted to "classification commissions" made up of commissaries of Army corps or inspectors general who, in the last resort, possessed the widest powers in deciding on promotions and assignments. Thus advancement in the Army was largely dependent on a system very close to co-option. Personal liking, family ties and ideological and religious affinities tended to strengthen the proportion and influence of conservative and Catholic officers. This tendency developed very rapidly; and it came to be applied in a sectarian if not downright brutal fashion.

General du Barail, War Minister in 1873, forbade troops to accord military honors to soldiers or members of the Legion of Honor who

had a nonreligious funeral. Religious burial was, no doubt, customary
in France at the time; but the attitude displayed by the Minister—
aristocratic in origin and Bonapartist in sympathies, he had come
to be a sincere supporter of the Republic—is significant of the hostility, or positive horror, felt by the military hierarchy when faced by
anything that might smack of atheism or even anticlericalism. As
the Third Republic gradually assumed its true shape, this cleavage between the Army cadres and political circles inevitably widened. From
then on, everything would render the separation unavoidable.

It is essential that we should have a very concrete idea of the
political and social evolution that took place in the first twenty-five
years of the Third Republic, and understand how this evolution
appeared to the families who had traditionally provided the greater
part of the officers' corps.

The one subject of conversation in provincial châteaux and in
bourgeois residences situated in the elegant districts of Paris and of
the principal towns was the possibility of restoring the monarchy.
Families whose sympathies were traditionally royalist were buoyed up
by the hope that the country's misfortunes would at last permit the
return of the pretenders to the throne, the Comte de Chambord or
the Duc d'Orléans. Their portraits were displayed everywhere. Some
people even went on the "pilgrimage to Froschdorf" in order to do
homage to the Comte de Chambord, in whose favor the Duc d'Orléans
had just effaced himself. In military families the sons of Louis-
Philippe, particularly the Duc d'Aumale, were accorded universal
respect. But all these hopes came to naught, the dream faded. Monarchist deputies did, indeed, remain quite numerous up to 1881, but
with the almost routine successes won by Republican candidates,
most people already looked on their cause as doomed.

Soon, in every little town, the noble inhabitants of the château or
the conservative bourgeois clashed head on with the representatives
of the "new layers" of society. In the majority of cases, this confrontation ended with the rout of the former. As the town councils, mayor-
alties and deputies' seats eluded the grasp of conservative families,
these families felt themselves more and more excluded from real
political life, cut off from positions of power and permanently rele-
gated to the opposition, with nothing to cling to but their memories,
and a bitterness that soon turned to rancor. Admittedly some provinces
remained faithful to traditionalist political figures, monarchist or con-

servative, but this merely increased the sense of remoteness from the general forward movement that swept the rest of the country along to fresh horizons, new customs and ideas which, until recently, had been deemed revolutionary.

The conservatives would soon feel the full impact of the republicans' victory. Subprefectures, prefectures and Councils of State were peopled with republicans who were bourgeois to a man and conservative for the most part, but who were hostile to monarchical traditions, contemptuous of the old aristocrats, assured that the future belonged to a world forgetful of former nostalgias, and determined to free French society from the religious mentality and every trace of clericalism.

Thus the top levels of the administration were closed, from now on, to the representatives of aristocratic or bourgeois families who remained attached to monarchical and Catholic traditions. The landed aristocracy had participated only slightly in the accumulation of industrial and commercial fortunes. From now on, cut off from political power, squeezed out of the administrative cadres, and out of touch with economic evolution, a whole segment of society turned back on itself, menaced by its own decadence, its impoverishment and its rancor. Deprived of their traditional influence, conservative families had to look elsewhere for outlets that would match their sons' ambitions, talents or, more simply, their need to earn a living.

For the heirs of these families, the officers' corps provided almost the only setting in which their opinions and style of life would not make failure, and even exclusion, a certainty. This was the basic motivation that led so many young men of aristocratic origins and from conservative and Catholic circles to take refuge in an Army career, almost as though they were withdrawing from a world in which they no longer had a place. Paul Bourget, in his novel *L'Émigré*, would later describe this "retreat" by putting his own avowals in the mouth of his character, Lieutenant de Claviers-Granchamps:

In any case, I had no choice. . . . Every career was barred to the future Marquis de Claviers-Granchamps. Yes, barred. Foreign affairs? Barred. My father, at least, would have been accepted by the Empire. Today we are no longer desired. The Council of State? Barred. The Administration? Barred. Can you see a noble acting as Prefect of a Department? . . . The Army alone was left me. I studied at Saint-Cyr, though not without difficulties. There, at all events, I knew the joy of not being isolated, of feeling that I was a Frenchman like the others, of not being exiled from my own age, from my generation and my country, the joy of the uniform, of the comrades I rubbed elbows with, of the leader I obeyed and the subordinate I commanded. . . .

This tendency was constantly strengthened by professional and moral pressures. The suppression of the lifetime appointment of magistrates was regarded at the time, in Catholic circles, as the heralding of their own exclusion from the judicial professsions. The decree of 1881 ordering the dissolution and expulsion of certain religious orders aggravated the split between the republican state and the totality of families who cared about the interests, the rights and the protection of the Church.

To this were added economic motivations. The period extending from immediately after the war of 1870–1871 until the closing years of the century was marked by a long decline in prices. Wholesale agricultural prices, in particular, were afflicted by almost unrelieved weakness. The landed proprietors, among whom were to be found the majority of conservative families, grew steadily poorer. Ground rents sank at this time to some of their lowest levels. The bottom of the depression was reached in 1882, when a cyclical crisis of the whole economy aggravated the general drop in prices. The bankruptcy of a great Catholic bank, the Union Générale, caused many individual catastrophes in conservative circles. For the young men with this background the Army represented the solution of their financial difficulties —so much so that at the end of twenty-five years' development the Army had become one of the most exclusive bodies in the Nation.

During this long trend which seemed irremediably to condemn conservative circles to languish far from all power, one episode appeared nevertheless to offer possibilities they no longer hoped for. All of a sudden, at the height of the Boulangist wave headed by the popular figure of General Boulanger, former Minister of War, their electoral prospects grew bright. Thanks to the general's Jacobin nationalism and his denunciations of the opportunist bourgeoisie that had governed France for the previous ten years, the Republicans were meeting with one defeat after another.

Boulangism in its origins was doubtless much more the affair of the Radicals than of the traditionalist Conservatives. But the propagandist tone this leader adopted for his campaign, and the new nationalist tendency he represented, brought him nearer, first to the Bonapartists and then to the whole rightist bloc. Backed by monarchists and Bonapartists, with considerable support in the Army and the Church, Boulangism. it was thought, might eventually lead to the restoration of the monarchy.

These hopes were dashed with the collapse of the movement, but Conservatives did not forget the lesson taught them by the victories they had won in a long series of elections. The theses which Boulanger had utilized to win over public opinion were, in Conservative milieux, entirely new. The General had campaigned against the impotence of the parliamentary system, the ineffectiveness of governments that were constantly being defeated, the backstage intrigues and the disrepute into which the state had fallen at a time when the German menace should have imposed national discipline.

The rising Conservative generation had discovered the immense appeal that nationalism possessed for a great part of French public opinion. The watchword of "support for the Republic," launched by the Catholic hierarchy, had induced an increasing number of voters to switch from the old Monarchist candidates to moderate Republicans, whom they regarded as being more effective and more "modern," although not in the least alarming on social and religious issues. It was at this juncture that men were elected who, while they officially belonged to the Republican parties, owed the greater part of their support to former Conservative voters. In vain, Conservative families tried to prevent this loss of right-wing voters to the Moderate Republicans; the monarchy retreated ever further into a past that was cherished, it seemed, by no one. The young rightists who were just about to attain their political maturity realized that the longing for a monarch no longer stirred French hearts.

Another nostalgia moved voters both on the Right and on the Left, and Monarchists no less than Radicals. This was the longing for national greatness, military strength and patriotic discipline, for the strong state that could revive the Jacobin tradition, and with it the victories of the Monarchy and the Empire. An entire new generation would find a rallying point much less in any fidelity to the far-off memory of royalty than in the new nationalist climate which Maurice Barrès later depicted in his *L'Appel au soldat*. The new nationalism met with success, which the conservative tradition could no longer attain. The young heirs of monarchist families who were twenty-five or thirty years old in 1889 would remember this lesson a few years later when the Dreyfus Affair developed.

But while the Right was inconspicuously discovering nationalism, and convincing itself that only the Army could avert the unchallengeable victory of the Republic, a slow evolution on the Left was pulling in the opposite direction. A new wind was blowing in Paris and the large towns, where radicalism was in closest contact with intellectual circles. The liaison that would be formed between the political Left and the intellectual Left was the work of university professors, lycée teachers or schoolmasters, cultured primary school teachers or rectors of Academies. It was in this very milieu, several years before the Dreyfus Affair, that a new type of antimilitarism would grow up.

The year 1887 saw the publication of Abel Hermant's *Le Cavalier Miserey*, the first literary work whose theme was the criticism, bitter rather than violent, and melancholy rather than passionate, of military life. It created a kind of scandal, in the climate of unquestioning approbation enjoyed by the Army at that time, and in the quasi-religious atmosphere that then surrounded the military ethos. But the scandal was to be repeated. That same year the subject was taken up also by Henri Fèvre, in *Au port d'armes*. In 1889, in *Les Sous-offs*, Lucien Descaves told the story of a young noncommissioned officer pushed to the brink of suicide by the stupidity and ferociousness of the military universe. And one year later, in *Biribi*, Georges Darrien denounced the scandal of the Army prisons.

What was the meaning of this surge of antimilitarist literature? Many young intellectuals, brought into contact with the realities of Army life by their period of service, experienced it as utterly harsh and vulgar and as highly distressing, both morally and materially. Even those who had been excused under the terms of the law from wearing the uniform found it necessary, now that twenty years of peace had intervened, to react against the idolatry with which the Army was still regarded. The critical spirit, the rejection of all tradition and the cult of the individual, which were sought after in the universities, took issue with the brutal conformity, blind obedience to authority and unquestioning respect for superiors, whatever their limitations, that were cultivated in the Army.

The intellectual milieux reacted ever more strongly against the dogmas of French nationalism, and indeed against the most ordinary forms of patriotism. "Personally," Rémy de Gourmont wrote, in the *Mercure de France* of 1891, "in exchange for these forgotten regions [Alsace-Lorraine] I wouldn't give the little finger of my right hand, it supports my hand when I write, or the little finger of my left hand, I use it to shake the ash off my cigarette. . . . If things must be said clearly, well then, in a word, we are not patriots." His article bore the title, "The Patriotic Plaything." The *Mercure de France* asked for the views of intellectuals on "the idea of revenge." "I hope," declared Jules Renard in his reply, "that the war of 1870-71 will soon be looked on as a historical event of less importance than the appearance of *Le Cid* or of a fable by La Fontaine." Maurice Le Blond gave the assurance that in his youth "the idea of the *revanche* had almost entirely disappeared."

Through the intermediary of university people, this literature might meet the eye of a few deputies of the Left, either Republicans or Radicals. But they took good care not to present its theses to the electorate, antimilitarism being a luxury in which the cultivated bourgeois could indulge, but not candidates for the Chamber. There was, however, in this national unanimity on the subject of Army and country, a breach which those in political circles preferred to think about as little as possible. The Socialists, in France, were passionately antimilitarist. But whom did they represent, at that time?

After the crushing of the Commune, it was almost taken for granted that socialism had been banished once and for all from the French political universe. It was associated with the memories of the 1848 Revolution, and the Commune seemed to have been the last manifestation of its turbulent existence. "We have got rid of socialism," declared Thiers in a speech to his electors.

The future Marshal Lyautey showed extraordinary penetration in writing, as he did in November, 1878, shortly after graduating from Saint-Cyr: "As for the future, I vaguely feel that I can glimpse socialism emerging from the tempest." The century's closing years began to demonstrate how correct he was. Although split into four competing parties, in 1893 the Socialists at last scored a victory at the polls. Eighteen were elected, and to these must be added some thirty Independent Socialists, either former Radicals like Alexandre Millerand or Moderate Republicans like Jean Jaurès.

Who had voted for them? The Socialists' antimilitarism appealed to the workers. This is the area where they first succeeded in winning votes away from the Radicals, who until then had been the only serious candidates on the extreme Left. Antimilitarist sentiment was aroused in working-class circles by the whole history of their political and social struggles. Among the great historical events that made up the entire past of the working class, there were above all June, 1848, when the workers' revolt was crushed by the Army, and the 1871 Commune, which, once again, only the Army had been able to defeat. The blue-smocked workers had always, it seemed, been stopped in their advance by rows of uniformed soldiers. Apparently any government that saw itself threatened by a rebellious working class owed its survival to the Army.

The humanitarian dream, in French working-class milieux, was indissolubly linked with the Socialist ideal. After the first "communists," who had been contemporaneous with the French Revolution, Proudhon and Fourier once more took up this same tradition. Every working-class and Socialist militant was already convinced of what Georges Sorel was to write much later, in his *Réflexions sur la violence:* "The clearest and most tangible manifestation of the state that it is possible to have, and the one most firmly attached to its origins, is the Army." In the mind of the workers, and despite all doctrinal clashes between leaders and theoreticians, anarchism, socialism and antimilitarism were closely associated.

In 1897, the Congress of the C.G.T. (General Confederation of Labor), held in Toulouse, proclaimed the principles that were later adopted by the Congress of Syndicalist Unification, held in Amiens. "Antimilitarist and antipatriotic propaganda must become ever more intense and more audacious. In every strike the Army is for the employers, in every national or colonial war and in every European war the working class is the dupe and is sacrificed for the advantage of the parasitic, bourgeois employers' class. . . ."

These declarations would have surprised no one who had previously been keeping an eye on the frequent minor manifestations of working-class antimilitarism. The Federation of Labor Exchanges, which at the time had more members than any other workers' organization, had brought out a *New Manual for the Soldier* which it distributed in the barracks. The Army was denounced "not only as the school of crime, but also as the school of vice, cheating, laziness, hypocrisy and cowardice." In the people's theaters antipatriotic plays were performed, with violent tirades rounding out melodramatic scenes. They were called *A Béribi, The Red Strike, The Refusal to Obey, The Dragoon.* Particularly striking is the final scene of *The Last Cartridge,* which depicts soldiers who have just killed their officer, having realized at last that their obedience was a crime. Long before, the songs of the people had anticipated the dramatists' themes. The "Internationale" was already counseling:

> Crosse en l'air, et rompons les rangs!
> S'ils s'obstinent ces cannibales,
> A faire de nous des héros,
> Ils sauront bient que nos balles
> Sont pour nos propres généraux.

> (Raise your rifle butts, break rank!
> If these cannibals insist
> On making heroes of us,
> They'll soon discover that our bullets
> Are for our own generals.)

L'Almanach de la Chanson du Peuple published "The Absentee's Lament," less solemn in tone:

> Enfants, les soldats sont des bêtes . . .
> Enfants, les soldats sont des brutes . . .
> Tous les jours ne sont que des luttes,
> Le soir que vadrouille sans nom,
> Enfants, les soldats assassinent,
> C'est avec amour qu'ils chourinent,
> Quand ils se sentent les plus forts . . .

> (Lads, the soldiers are beasts . . .
> Lads, the soldiers are brutes . . .
> Every day is filled with struggle
> Every night, a disgusting spree.
> Lads, soldiers murder,
> They love to kill,
> When they know they're stronger . . .)

Only a widening gulf between the state and the working class could explain the vehement, desperate tone of these songs of protest. A new spectacle could be witnessed more and more frequently in workers' districts as the nineteenth century drew to a close. It became the usual thing to employ the Army in the event of a strike. Around the factories, which the workers had already left, troops were drawn up to defend the owners if a riot should break out, and they were at the disposition, also, of prefect and police. The first burst of rifle fire was heard at Fourmies, in 1891, and others were soon to follow, at Saint-Étienne and Châlons-sur-Marne, at Raon l'Étape, Draveil, Villeneuve Saint-Georges, etc., etc. In the workers' districts, uniformed officers could no longer venture into the streets without being insulted, and people sang:

Petit pioupiou
Ne tire pas sur nous
Nous sommes des frères de misère
Ne fais pas feu
O malheureux!
Tu peux tuer ton pèr', ta mèr . . .

(Soldier lad
Don't shoot at us
We're brothers in misery
Don't fire
Wretched lad!
You may kill your father, your mother . . .)

How much wiser it would have been if these complaints had been heard in the officers' clubs and at regimental headquarters. Then it might have been realized that already one segment of the population had completely broken with the Army.

CHAPTER THREE

THE DREYFUS AFFAIR

Drumont's anti-Semitic nationalist newspaper *La Libre Parole* announced, on October 29, 1894, that an officer of the General Staff had been arrested. Sensing a "big story," the paper cried its alarm. "Why have the military authorities kept silent?" Two days later the Agence Havas confirmed the report and under the headline "A Case of Treason" the *Figaro* gave the basic facts. "A French officer is suspected of having transmitted highly important documents to foreigners. . . . The truth," it declared, "must be made known." *La Libre Parole* could now cast aside all reticence: "High treason! Arrest of a Jewish officer: Captain Dreyfus."

Thus the Affair was born. Certain improbabilities might, indeed, have aroused skepticism. *La Libre Parole* had obtained its information from a note signed "Henry," but was this Major Henry of the Intelligence Service? The Affair was to be studded with fantastic episodes. The handwriting of the *bordereau* or memorandum listing the documents transmitted to the German Embassy resembled that of Captain Dreyfus. "His hand trembled" as Captain du Paty de Clam dictated to him from material similar to the intercepted *bordereau,* and Dreyfus was forthwith placed under arrest. A few years later the same du Paty, disguised as a "veiled lady," would give Esterhazy, the real author of the *bordereau* and traitor beyond a doubt, the "liberating document" designed to prove Esterhazy's innocence. From behind the drawn blinds of a horsecab General Mercier, the Minister of War, would survey the scene.

The Affair broke out just as the French were aiming at a more rapid mobilization of their own forces than was possible for the German Army. The mobilization plan had been prepared by General de Boisdeffre. There were to be 750,000 men in regimental depots, 400,000 garrisoning the fortresses, and 1,400,000 in the field. Equality with the German forces had almost been attained, and on either side of the Vosges the two nations were busy modernizing their armaments. The 220-millimeter mortar was already in use, two years earlier Captain Bacquet had designed howitzers of 120 and 155 millimeters, in the previous year the Lebel rifle had been perfected; and early in 1894, Deport and Sainte-Claire Deville had put the finishing touches to the famous 75-millimeter cannon. Every general staff in Europe was agog at these innovations, and kept urging its espionage network to provide as detailed information as possible.

"If I were to give you the names of the people in our pay in Germany," said Colonel Sandherr, head of French Intelligence, "you would become a Trappist." In practice, these intelligence services were often connected with the military attachés in the Embassies. These officers took their orders directly from the General Staff, and sometimes acted without even the Ambassador's being informed. For example, the military attaché in the German Embassy in Paris, Huene, had had to be replaced by Schwartzkoppen, after Boutonneut, a clerk in charge of records, confessed that he had revealed the secret of the melinite shell.

So there is nothing astonishing about the incidence of "spionitis." Between 1888 and 1894, six Frenchmen were convicted of espionage on behalf of Germany. In 1893 two French naval officers were arrested in Germany and, in 1894, Captain Romani of the French Army was accused of espionage in Italy. The wife of a French police inspector was arrested in Germany, that same year, and on November 16 two German officers were arrested as spies in Paris, while a certain Madame Millescamps was condemned to five years' solitary confinement. This seller of rosaries had "communicated plans involving the defense of the Territory."

It need scarcely be said that the nationalist press concerned itself clamorously with these affairs. Drumont had for several years been trying to link them up with his anti-Semitic propaganda. He had published a book called *La France Juive* in 1886, founded the Anti-Semitic League in 1890 and launched his paper, *La Libre Parole,* in

1892. He had at once begun the publication of a series of unsigned articles entitled "The Jews in the Army." No assertion was too preposterous for him. "They will become the Masters of France," he wrote, speaking of the day when Jewish officers would command the Army. "Rothschild will send for the mobilization plans, for reasons it is not hard to guess." Yet *La Libre Parole* had half a million readers, among them one hundred thousand priests.

The Affair would soon crystallize all the converging factors of the political crisis made increasingly unavoidable by the evolution of the parties over the previous few years. The Right tended to identify itself with nationalism, and this with all the more vigor since the Church's reconciliation with the Republic had induced many conservative rural voters to cast their ballots for Moderate Republicans rather than for "reconciled" former Monarchists. The Progressives, who made up Parliament's Right center, more and more frequently clashed with the Radicals on such matters as the proposed income tax and trade union regulation. But, bearing in mind the basic patriotism of the French public, they naturally feared what might come of any frenzied exploitation of the Affair by the nationalist Right. Everything, too, led them to believe that the General Staff's assumption of Dreyfus's guilt would turn out to be justified. One section of the Radicals would oppose another; one remained faithful to the Jacobin tradition of *la cause française*, while the other became increasingly aware that the Socialists were outbidding them for public support. Despite the acrimonious debates, one theme brought all the elements of the Left together. This was antimilitarism. Soon Briand would have to defend in a court of law Gustave Hervé, the author of the celebrated declaration: "I would like to see assembled in the main square of the district all the garbage and dung of the barracks so that solemnly, and to the sound of martial music, and with troops in full regalia, the colonel, wearing his plumed helmet, might plant the regimental colors in the filth."

For all that, the Dreyfus Affair aroused at first no particular interest on the Left or extreme Left. Why should they care? "Let him be shot if he is guilty!" proclaimed Leftist leader Jaurès, forgetting that in peacetime capital punishment did not apply to such offenses. More doctrinaire in his approach, Jules Guesde refused to concern himself with this dispute between sections of the bourgeoisie. The other Socialist and Anarchist groups felt the same hostility and contempt for Dreyfusards and anti-Dreyfusards alike.

Thus bourgeois liberals were the first to bestir themselves when the question of Captain Dreyfus's possible innocence was raised. Their attitude was fundamentally that of their ancestors, who had supported Voltaire in his championing of Calas and Sirven, in the eighteenth century. It was no easy matter for these liberals to obtain a hearing, since the antimilitarism current in Socialist circles and among the Leftist intellectual bourgeoisie had but slight impact on a public opinion that had remained basically patriotic and, as a consequence, was not at all ready to accuse the General Staff of duplicity.

The Army had at this time reached the point of maximum differentiation in its evolution away from the political and administrative domains. The memoirs of General Weygand reveal the general outlook in military families and officers' groups at the close of the century. He had decided on a military career in 1885. "They told me," he wrote, "that the Army was the thing for nobles without a fortune." He had earned a rebuke a few years earlier, at the Lycée Louis Le Grand, because one of his teachers had made a slighting reference to the career of his dreams, and he himself had "made an impertinent rejoinder." The future general had sensed at the time that "a sort of prejudice could be felt by some. . . ."

Who were they? Certainly not the antimilitarist Socialists and Anarchists, of whom the youthful Weygand knew nothing. Those who at once inspired his hatred were the "intellectuals." Many career officers already felt an instinctive aversion to professors or to the "red donkeys," those who professed liberal or republican ideas. They shared, too, the usual contempt of military men for politicians. Here is what Weygand had to say of General Boulanger, Minister of War at the time. "He gathered the instructors and pupils around him in the Cour de Wagram [at Saint-Cyr]. In the posture and with the voice of a tenor he spoke to us of many things, but not of the obligations that awaited us. He ended on a tremolo: 'Open, open wide, young men, your minds to the new ideas!' It was our first contact with a political general."

In actual fact, this military milieu was an almost perfect vacuum in intellectual matters. Weygand realized this:

> Something essential was missing in this regimental life. . . . We had no intellectual guidance. There were indeed, to raise us above the daily routine, garrison lectures, the winter assignments and the little speeches we had to give in the regiments. But there was no unity of subject matter, and the choice of topic was usually left to the individual. This aimless activity bore no fruit. No readings were

recommended us. Our libraries . . . were not enriched by any literature dealing with foreign military tendencies and doctrines, or with contemporary diplomatic history. We were left to our own devices and with no knowledge, despite our eagerness to learn, of the books we might most profitably have studied.

Yet at the disposition of these officers, or of those among them who had a real interest in their own time, was a rich source of material for study and reflection. This consisted of the twenty-year-olds who, one contingent after another, entered the regiment. One need only read Weygand's memoirs to understand what Lyautey meant when he spoke of those officers who knew all about the horses in their squadron, but not even their soldiers' names. Until war was declared, Weygand has nothing to say of the men.

The officers led a life apart. "La pension," the table reserved for lieutenants and second lieutenants, brought together in each regiment a few dozen officers aged from twenty to forty-five. "Not a word," declared Weygand, "was ever breathed of politics." Their contacts with the local bourgeoisie were limited by their meager resources: a second lieutenant received about 175 francs a month, paying 75 francs for his board and 40 or 50 francs for his room. His "visits" were all made in military circles or to the homes of country squires. If for pious practices one substitutes riding and a watchful eye on company drill, the existence of the junior officer was reminiscent, in the nineties, of monastic life.

It was among this conservative provincial bourgeoisie, the most closely connected with military society, that anti-Semitism was most rampant. So there is no cause for surprise that anti-Semitism should have met with so little resistance among Army men. When Dreyfus was finishing his studies at the École de Guerre, General Bonnefond, its director, deliberately lowered his grades, since he did not care to see Jewish officers, considered to be unreliable, serve on the General Staff. It can readily be imagined how the news of Captain Dreyfus's "treason" was received in officers' messes. The authority of the military hierarchy in its own domain was total; it was counterbalanced by no external influence at all. "Whatever the current political rivalries might be," wrote Weygand, "not a word about them reached our garrisons. . . . Unaware that it had so many hidden enemies, the Army was consequently quite unable to understand the upsurge of hostility it met with because of the Affair. . . . Once Captain Dreyfus had been convicted, we young officers, as remote from politics as we were from Headquarters, accepted his guilt. . . . It seemed to us monstrous, and therefore unthinkable, that officers belonging to the elite of the French Army could have concocted what was a lying accusation from beginning to end."

But a few days later, the Colonel of Weygand's regiment had brought together a number of young officers and "the Lieutenant-Colonel, a man of great merit . . . opposed his own counsels of prudence to the young officers' declaration of guilt: not everything was clear, it was better to reserve judgment. . . . It need scarcely be said that, upon leaving this hospitable prison, we used strong terms to characterize this view and this advice, which had failed to convince us." This was the atmosphere in which the Army's young officers were living. They refused to "talk politics" because they were all able to think the same, and any discussion would have risked casting doubt on sacred truths.

When the Affair broke out, General Mercier was War Minister in a Cabinet presided over by Dupuy. A Lorrainer himself, he had married a Protestant Englishwoman and was reputed to be a free-thinker. He had placed in charge of the École Polytechnique General André, an officer whose fidelity to the Republic was beyond reproach, and he "had given him constant support in the steps he took to counter the invasion of the clerical gangrene." He was a cold, methodical, resolute man. Previous to the arrest of Dreyfus, the nationalist press had made him a target: "This slug Mercier," wrote the former Communard Rochefort, a convert to ultranationalism.

But after the arrest, they sang his praises. He had decided to make the arrest on his own authority, and merely informed the President of the Council, the Keeper of the Seals and the Minister of Foreign Affairs of his action. This Minister, Hanotaux, had raised serious objections. Following his natural bent and, it may be, for reasons of his own, Mercier at no point abandoned his initial decision, "persevering in a line of conduct previously adopted." Dreyfus, he maintained, was "the king of traitors." By 1898 this freethinking general appeared to be on excellent terms with the doctrines favored in the most conservative military circles, and publicly deplored the "intellectual byzantinism" by which France was beset. Two years later, he had become a reactionary clerical senator.

The General Staff had for a long time past been subject to the authority of General de Miribel, who, although one of those responsible for Army reform, was himself a typical Army man. Under the system of promotion already described, the General Staff had filled the upper echelons with men from the same background, who shared the same ideas and were inspired by the same principles. Among these officers was the head of the General Staff, General de Boisdeffre. Another was the violently anti-Semitic Colonel Sandherr, at the head of Intelligence. Afflicted with creeping paralysis, he had to retire from active duty in 1895, one year after he had started the Affair. His chief collaborator was Major Henry, who was to commit suicide after confessing that he had made use of forgery in order to inculpate Dreyfus. Henry had been General de Miribel's aide-de-camp, and before the forgery became known was praised in the highest terms by General Gonse: "I answer for Henry as I answer for myself."

No political party, in 1894 and 1895, felt inclined to take up the case of the disgraced and convicted officer. The Moderates and Republicans, who were in power, were quite happy to remain neutral and were strongly disposed to accept the views of the General Staff. The Radicals, anxious to avoid being involved in a scandal which might bring shame on the Republic, took no interest in the Affair; nor did the Socialists, who on principle paid no attention to the disputes between bourgeois groups. The extreme Right, nationalistic and anti-Semitic, was of course delighted. On the extreme Left, the antimilitarists found it amusing. No one thought of asking whether General Mercier's precipitate arrest of Dreyfus had not been, as Hanotaux saw it, a "frightful" blunder. Dreyfus, in any case, was condemned to deportation for life, publicly disgraced, and dispatched to Devil's Island.

All, it might have been thought, was now over. In reality, all had just begun. Here and there, some indications of uneasiness were displayed. The Minister of Colonies, who had charge of Devil's Island, sent for the official who was to watch over the "traitor" Dreyfus and, "looking him straight in the eye," told him that the prisoner's guilt must be accepted without question, and that he was to be treated with particular severity. Barrès, who had witnessed the terrible ceremony of degradation, expressed to Colonel Sandherr his astonishment at Dreyfus's passivity and protestations of innocence.

"It's obvious," the Colonel had replied, "that you don't know the Jews. They're a race without honor or pride. For hundreds of years they've done nothing but betray." But at the Quai d'Orsay on that same day, Nizard, Director of Political Affairs, said to Paléologue, who was liaison man between the Ministries of Foreign Affairs and of War: "We haven't heard the last of this Jew." A week later Colonel Sandherr, now a paralytic, was replaced by Colonel Picquart as head of Intelligence.

Mathieu Dreyfus, brother of the convicted man, believed in his innocence. He had succeeded in interesting Bernard Lazare, the youthful author of a study of anti-Semitism and, after several failures, Joseph Reinach, a prominent political figure of the Left Center. They happened to know Félix Faure's doctor—Faure had replaced Casimir-Périer as President of the Republic—who passed on to them Faure's confidential avowal that Dreyfus's conviction had been obtained by irregular means. But while the judges were deliberating, the General Staff made available to them a "secret file" of which the defense knew nothing, and which purported to establish Dreyfus's guilt beyond a doubt.

Mathieu Dreyfus and his associates visited one politician after another, looking for some way of obtaining a new trial under normal conditions. Although they tried to act with discretion, some newspapers, among them *Le Journal, L'Avenir Militaire* and *Le Soleil,* printed accounts of what was going on. Dreyfus's lawyer, Maître Demange, made public reference to his client's protestations of innocence. This was enough to set the nationalist press once again on the warpath. *La Libre Parole* asserted that Mathieu Dreyfus and Hadamard, the Captain's brother-in-law, were plotting Dreyfus's escape. The paper was not to drop its campaign against the "overly lenient" conditions of his incarceration until the end of 1895. While the *Figaro* vainly asserted that it would be better to say nothing further about the convicted man, the anti-Semitic press would not abandon its prey—and this noisy preoccupation with Dreyfus apparently attracted new readers.

The campaign spilled over into the political arena. A deputy named Michelin introduced a bill that would have barred Jews from public office. In Paris and in the provinces identical themes were echoed by *La France, L'Impartial, L'Univers, L'Est Républicain, L'Autorité* and *Le Messager.* But this nationalistic and anti-Semitic campaign overreached itself, and the discreet steps taken by Bernard

Lazare, Mathieu Dreyfus and Hadamard began to undermine some people's convictions. In *L'Autorité,* Paul de Cassagnac contributed an article entitled "Doubt."

Strange rumors were now circulating in the military circles closest to Intelligence. Colonel Picquart, director of the Intelligence Service, had happened on a letter addressed by Esterhazy, who was notorious for his debts, to Schwartzkoppen, the attaché of the German Embassy. (This same attaché had been the intended recipient of the *bordereau* that had led to Dreyfus's conviction.) The letter and the *bordereau* were in the same handwriting. Picquart spoke of the letter to his superiors, who asked him to forget the whole matter.

A few days later Henry, one of Picquart's colleagues, most opportunely discovered the *petit bleu,* an express letter allegedly addressed to Schwartzkoppen by the Italian military attché, in which Dreyfus was actually named. Henry passed this on to his superiors, while omitting to tell them that the document was a forgery executed at his own request. The General Staff, with fresh confidence, judged that this piece of sensational publicity could put an end to the still hesitant campaign in favor of a retrial. Since Colonel Picquart had been ill-advised enough to question the authenticity of the incriminating documents, he was despatched on a mission that took him first to the provinces and then to Tunisia.

Just what was the situation, at this juncture? The campaign for a retrial had, so far, enjoyed but little success. Bernard Lazare had had to go to Belgium to find a publisher for his pamphlet attacking the propriety of the conviction procedure, since no French paper, not even the *Figaro,* which at the time was discreetly in favor of a retrial, would touch it. Yet there was to be a gradual, a most gradual evolution in people's attitudes. Scheurer-Kestner, a liberal member of the upper bourgeoisie and a securely established senator, was still very much alone when he undertook to defend Captain Dreyfus in Parliament, and Clemenceau still hesitated. "I don't know what is behind it all," he wrote, referring to the Affair, "but I regard it a formidable weapon in the hands of the parties."

The Socialists maintained their reserve. Millerand had only sarcasm for Reinach, one of the very few deputies favorably inclined toward Dreyfus. The foreign press expressed astonishment at the insignificant political repercussions aroused by the campaign for a retrial, and the facts cannot be gainsaid: when Scheurer-Kestner interpellated the government on the Affair, he was defeated by the massed

votes of his senatorial colleagues. In the Chamber, Castellin's interpellation was disposed of by 325 votes against only 153 votes for a
retrial.

At last, however, as 1897 ran its course, the climactic moment
approached when the whole nature of the Dreyfus Affair would
change, and considerably modify the relative strength of political
factions. A "new fact" was made known when a banker glanced at a
notice circulated by the "anti-Dreyfusards." In its reproduction of
the *bordereau* he recognized the handwriting of one of his clients,
Captain Esterhazy. Picquart, for his part, had reached the same conclusion. The revisionists had at last found the weak point in their
adversaries' case. The *Figaro,* relying on the dossier compiled by
Scheurer-Kestner, declared that it had in its possession "documents
demonstrating that this officer and the author of the *bordereau* are one
and the same." Referring to the famous document discovered *after*
the conviction and allegedly establishing Dreyfus's guilt beyond a
doubt, it spoke of "a ruse invented by the same persons who, after the
conviction of the former Captain Dreyfus, had an interest in strengthening the certitude of the government and public opinion that the
convicted man was guilty." On August 17, 1897, Esterhazy, the Dreyfusards' main target, was placed on the inactive list, and on November 14, Scheurer-Kestner felt strong enough to bring out a "public
letter" summing up the Affair. At the end of the month the press
reproduced letters from Esterhazy to his mistress, letters that hurled
splenetic insults against France and its Army.

The General Staff decided that Esterhazy should himself demand
to appear before a court-martial. Had not a "veiled lady"—who was
none other than du Paty de Clam, addicted to the dramatic setting—
entrusted him with a new document that irrefutably established
Dreyfus's guilt? Esterhazy, who based his defense on this "liberating
document," was triumphantly acquitted. This was the culminating
point of the nationalist campaign against Dreyfus. It also marked the
end of the Affair's first stage. The date was January 11, 1898.

On the very next day Emile Zola published his celebrated article
"J'Accuse" in Clemenceau's paper *L'Aurore.* After summarizing the
whole case, Zola directed his barbs against the military court and,
through the court, against the leaders of the Army.

The core of the debate was no longer the opposition of Monarchy
and Republic. Those who so eagerly exploited the condemnation of

Captain Dreyfus relied on the narrowest sort of nationalism, of course, but also on antiparliamentarianism, and on a widespread distrust of the alleged corruption and immorality of the Parisian political milieux and of those intellectual groups farthest removed from traditionalism. Through its assaults on "the Jews," "the traitors" and "the politicians in the pay of the Germans," this nationalistic, anti-Semitic campaign challenged the liberal, democratic and egalitarian outlook of Republican institutions. That alone would have explained even the most moderate Republicans' hastening to defend the regime. But not only the Republic was involved; there was the matter of the Army, and of its place in the Nation.

What the "anti-Dreyfusards" were striving for, in actual fact, was to identify the Army with nationalistic, anti-Semitic and anti-Republican views. As seen by the immense majority of Republicans professionally engaged in politics, who had been brought up to revere an Army which one day would carry out the *revanche*, the expansion of the crisis touched off by the Dreyfus Affair might have catastrophic consequences. If they failed to act in time, Republic and Army might soon be at daggers drawn, whereas until now the former had regarded the latter as its most respected, most stable and most glorious institution. The defense of the regime might involve a head-on clash with this instrument of national defense. The whole classical conception of the Republic, hammered out in its earliest years, might now be called into question.

In the final analysis, what really was at stake in the Affair, in these years 1897 and 1898, was not at all to prove the innocence or the guilt of Captain Dreyfus. This alone would not account for the zeal with which most military groups sought to defend the principle of Dreyfus's guilt, and the gulf that would soon divide the nationalist Right from the moderate and even from the most conservative Republicans. What mattered was to make it impossible for the nationalist opposition to attack the regime by systematically espousing the Army's cause, with the eventual design of serving the Army's ambitions; and also to make it impossible for the Socialist opposition to challenge the established form of the state and the bourgeois order by attacking the Army, symbol and pillar of the state, through the individual case of Captain Dreyfus. This is the fundamental meaning of the attitude adopted by the major part of the Republican political personnel from 1898 on, and the basic strategy which was already becoming apparent at the height of the Affair. In a few years this strategy would liquidate a crisis which, on the surface, had seemed to menace the framework of the military establishment, raised doubts concerning the Army's role in the Nation, and perhaps threatened to make of the Army something untouchable within Republican society.

It was at this point, just as some of the most representative Republicans in public life were about to intervene, that the French political scene was convulsed by the various episodes that made up the Affair. Verbal violence reached its apogee. The anti-Dreyfusards accused their opponents of being the tools of a syndicate which had all the "Jewish money" it needed to finance their campaigns. *La Croix,* published by the Assumptionists, spoke of "free-thought, the advocate of the Jews, the Protestants and all the enemies of France. . . ." Lucien Herr, librarian of the Ecole Normale Supérieure and one of the most representative men in intellectual circles to take up the cause of Dreyfus, bore witness to the "exaltation with which we lived" at this time. ". . . We were no longer mandarins . . . cut off from real life." The whole intellectual world entered the fray, with the inevitable division between the defenders of fundamental liberties on the one side, and the nationalists on the other.

Dreyfus had ceased to be thought of as a human being. He had become a symbol of the inalienable rights of man, while anti-Dreyfusism was simply the latest way of asserting that might makes right. Ever fewer were those who tried to remain above the conflict. Thirty-two Socialist deputies signed a manifesto declaring that they had "no interest in the fate of Dreyfus, a member of the enemy class," and *Le Père Peinard,* an Anarchist paper, could still speak of "the old exploiter Scheurer-Kestner, that senatorial codfish." But, on the extreme Left, Sébastien was ready to declare that "the Anarchists must not continue to remain altogether outside the movement." "Emotions are running so high," wrote *Le Petit Parisien,* a would-be impartial newspaper, "that every conscience is troubled." The historians Lavisse and Rambaud, whose names are joined on the title page of their collective work, took opposite sides, Lavisse for Dreyfus and Rambaud against. One of Caran d'Ache's famous cartoons depicted a family dinner in a bourgeois setting. "Above all else, let's not speak of it!" says the head of the household to his relaxed and smiling guests. The following cartoon, in which the dinner table has become a shambles and the guests are at each other's throats, bears the caption: "They spoke of it!"

Zola's trial crystallized all these passions and set the formula for all these views. "If the jury acquits Zola," wrote a nationalist paper, "the Army's General Staff will depart . . . an object of scorn, defeated, in no condition henceforth to command our regiments." Zola could be convicted for a single clause in one sentence of his article: each time that his lawyer asked a witness any question that touched on the fundamental problem, the presiding judge interrupted: "The question will not be asked."

Foreign spectators were appalled by the atmosphere of riot in which the case was heard, right up to the verdict of one year's imprisonment for Zola. "It would be rather mild to apply the term 'cannibalistic' to the scum that has invaded the courtroom," wrote a Belgian paper. The President of the Council, Méline, was almost alone in his attempts to declare that the Affair was closed. "At the present moment," he told the Chamber of Deputies, "there is no Zola case, no Esterhazy case, and no Dreyfus case. There is no case at all. . . . Whoever should choose to continue the battle can no longer lay any claim to good faith, and will be treated with the whole severity of the law."

Méline, actually, was merely anticipating what would soon be the main concern of the political personnel as a whole, the desire to dispose of the entire matter with the minimum of difficulties. But for the moment people were still at each other's throats, and the duels and the anti-Semitic outbreaks in Paris and Algiers made it plain that the fever had not yet abated, that nothing had been settled. The general elections of May, 1898, returned a Republican majority to the Chamber, with the result that the nationalist Right could no longer hope for any legal victory. This was to be the signal for a new attempt, on the part of Republican political leaders, to bring the Affair under control.

In the new Cabinet, presided over by Brisson, Cavaignac went to the Ministry of War. It was a significant choice. Descended from a long line of Republicans, Cavaignac was a Radical, but of the kind whose Jacobin predilections made the Army, for him, an object of veneration. As a man of the Left who at the same time defended military institutions passionately, Cavaignac could not tolerate any imputations against the rectitude of the General Staff. His first speech in the Chamber of Deputies was violently anti-Dreyfusard. But Cavaignac did not hesitate to refer, in his speech, to the documents whose fraudulence had been established by Picquart. Jacobin and militarist, he had the honesty to ask his collaborator Cuignet to re-examine the whole dossier of the Affair.

Then on August 30, at midnight, the Agence Havas issued the following release: "In the office of the War Minister, Lieutenant Colonel Henry was identified and identified himself as the author of the letter, dated October, 1896, in which Dreyfus is named."

This was the famous "liberating document" that had enabled the court-martial to acquit Esterhazy, although previously the *bordereau,* another essential document in the case against Dreyfus, had been recognized as the work of Esterhazy himself. The whole case against Dreyfus appeared on the point of collapse. The following day, after writing a letter to his wife in which he inculpated some unknown person—historians have yet to throw light on this—Henry committed suicide.

Cavaignac resigned. Nevertheless he had played a decisive part, and his own case remains typical. A Jacobin, he had not wanted the defense of the Army to provide the nationalist opposition with a "spearhead" directed against the Republic; a Radical, he was not desirous that the hostility of the extreme Left to the General Staff should become an assault against the Army in general. Other political figures before him had divined that Dreyfus's guilt would serve as a platform for the enemies of the regime, and that the nationalist campaigns would have to be countered, in order to defend the Republic and to avoid compromising both Army and state.

While Clemenceau, for all his passionate patriotism, was keenly aware that the anti-Dreyfusards constituted a threat to the regime—Poincaré and Georges Leygues, for their part, had foreseen as early as 1897 the way the Dreyfus Affair would develop. Both of them belonged to the new generation of Republican politicians. They had won their spurs at a time when the Republican regime was already established, and could readily understand that the regime's real foes were not the adherents of the monarchy, consigned to oblivion by public opinion as a whole, but the new nationalism. With their patriotism, their undoubted admiration for the Army and their concern for the requirements of national defense, they regarded with suspicion any attempted political exploitation of nationalism and militarism.

Their attitude was shared by the vast majority of Frenchmen. The Army had become a universal rallying point, a symbol of the Nation that stood "above all parties," and a "common possession" transcending all political vicissitudes. This conception of the Army implied not only its independence vis-à-vis the parties but, concomitantly, its strict neutrality, its remoteness from political conflicts and its unquestioning respect for the State and the regime, whatever the form of the regime might be.

From now on the Affair was to evolve on two distinct planes. Throughout the country, Dreyfusards and anti-Dreyfusards sought to win over public opinion, and they set up rival organizations in order to harness the opposing forces. On the parliamentary plane, less than three months after the Agence Havas had circulated Colonel Henry's confession, the Affair was already entering the phase of liquidation. On November 28, Poincaré mounted the rostrum in the Chamber of Deputies. The nationalist press had been asserting that every member of the government, at the time of Dreyfus's conviction, had seen documents offering irrefutable proof of his guilt. Poincaré had been a member of this government, under Casimir-Périer, and so was in a position to confirm or deny these anti-Dreyfusard allegations. Solemnly, "to unburden my conscience," he declared that neither he nor his colleagues had any knowledge of the documents mentioned.

Poincaré, from beginning to end of his career, had been intensely preoccupied with national defense and the exigencies of foreign policy. Yet he was among the first to disassociate himself, and a whole group of Moderate Republicans with him, from semi-involvement with a General Staff that had become enmeshed in falsehoods and even the manufacture of forgeries. Poincaré's speech plainly indicated that it was now time for the responsible political groups to wind up this Affair, with its deleterious effects on public life.

So much for the state of mind in bourgeois political circles, on November 28. On February 28 another happening would symbolize the Army's outlook and reveal its entire accord with the steps being planned by those with political authority. The state funeral of Félix Faure, President of the Republic, took place on that day. Had the anti-Dreyfusard nationalists sensed the change of climate? The national elections of the previous May had demonstrated that the bulk of public opinion was not with them. Now the attitude of Poincaré, Barthou and Georges Leygues, like that of many moderate newspapers, indicated that the most influential bourgeois groups would oppose any attempt at the political exploitation of the propaganda campaigns on the strictly parliamentary level.

The Republicans of the Center did not wish the Dreyfus Affair to bring about too close a rapprochement between Radicals and So-

cialists now that the latter, in the wake of Jaurès, had at last realized
that the Affair offered them prospects of escaping from their isolation
and enlarging their clientele. Thus everything seemed to herald
the imminent end of the great nationalist, anti-Semitic and antiparliamentary groundswell that had begun with the conviction of
Captain Dreyfus. Some anti-Dreyfusards felt that it was now or
never, that the risk had to be assumed. The troops were on their way
back from the state funeral, with General Roget leading them. What
an opportunity for a coup d'état!

Déroulède, the Rightist, founder of the League of the French
Fatherland, asked Roget to march on the Presidential Palace. The
general refused. His refusal made it perfectly clear that two distinct
factors characterized the military outlook. Military men were ready to
believe anything—and, within limits, to do anything—rather than see
the General Staff put to shame by the liquidation of the Dreyfus Affair. On the other hand, they remained faithful to the traditional
notion of the Army's political neutrality. While desiring, perhaps, the
victory of the nationalistic trend, they refused to act as its instrument;
while no doubt deploring the evolution of the Republican regime, it
did not enter their heads to overthrow the government.

The Affair would henceforth be liquidated at an accelerated pace.
Two months after Déroulède's abortive attempt, Freycinet gave up
the War Ministry. One month later the Supreme Court of Appeal
upset the 1894 decision. Dreyfus was brought back from Devil's
Island, and Zola returned to France. Simultaneously, after Poincaré
had failed to form a government in which, significantly enough, Louis
Barthou would have played a part, Waldeck-Rousseau took over the
reins.

Waldeck-Rousseau, like Poincaré, Barthou and Georges Leygues,
was typical of the Moderate Republican mentality that sought to
wind up the Affair without gravely weakening the Army's prestige.
This representative of the *grande bourgeoisie* had already denounced
the militarist spirit as a danger to the military spirit. To obtain the
backing of the extreme Left, he gave a Cabinet post to Millerand, the
Independent Socialist who, along with Clemenceau, Poincaré, and
Barthou, would dominate the French political scene for the next
third of a century. It has almost a symbolic value that this first Socialist in government should later, as President of the Republic,
invite Poincaré to return to power, so that he might put into effect

a more strongly "nationalist" foreign policy. The Waldeck-Rousseau Cabinet, in which Millerand held his first governmental post, had the task of checking nationalism and militarism.

The choice of General Galiffet as War Minister was no less symbolic. This grandson of Marshal Ney and of the banker Laffitte had earned the particular detestation of the extreme Left, for he had carried out the suppression of the Commune in 1871. In the Army, however, he enjoyed universal respect and exemplified very well the Army's virtues and defects.

The parliamentary debates that followed the formation of the Waldeck-Rousseau Cabinet gave another newcomer to politics the opportunity to carve out a place among the members of his generation; and he would continue in power until World War II was in the offing. This was Gaston Doumergue, a future President of the Council, who at this juncture proclaimed his support for "the policy of Republican defense."

The main concern of French politics from this time on was to be the maintenance of established institutions, both civil and military, the preservation of the Republic and the Army. This aim was reflected in the minutest details and would avail itself, when necessary, of every compromise. Thus Galiffet limited the "purge" of the General Staff to the transfer of two generals, at which the Army, it need scarcely be said, did not stir.

When Dreyfus was retried at Rennes, his innocence left not a shadow of doubt. But an acquittal would have been too grave a rebuff for the General Staff, which had proclaimed Dreyfus's guilt for the previous four years. The verdict was "guilty," but "with extenuating circumstances." In effect these words reversed the conviction, since in law there is no possibility of extenuating circumstances for the crime of treason. Galiffet would sum up the spirit that then prevailed in his famous order of the day: "The Army belongs to no party, it belongs to France." He was a soldier in the classic mold, an aristocrat and conservative who had little in common with republican psychology. However, he was the perfect spokesman for an Army which sought to embody the eternal aspect of the national ideal, as opposed to the conflicts between political ideas, and so it was fitting that he should utter the last word on the Affair. The famous phrase that concluded his order of the day was: "The incident is closed."

CHAPTER FOUR

THE HERITAGE OF THE AFFAIR

✠

The Dreyfus Affair might not have taken the particular turn it did, had there not been an imperceptible but constant diminution of Frenchmen's hitherto intransigent nationalism and militarism. Memories of 1870 had become blurred and the *revanche,* on which the older generation had pinned its hopes, was deferred to an ever more distant future. In their disillusionment, and weary of the demands that for thirty long years had been made on the Nation's young men, the French were ready—even prior to the Affair—to let the Army become the object of political controversy. Quite apart from the slow evolution that had led the Right to espouse nationalism, the Radicals to abandon their Jacobin tradition and the Socialists to diffuse an antimilitarist outlook among the workers, the country had been conditioned for the outbreak of the Dreyfus Affair by a transformation both more basic—since it had its origins in twenty years of peace—and more widespread—since it concerned all Frenchmen.

Prior to the Dreyfus Affair, as we have seen, there had been in the literary domain an initial revolt against the military mind. Public opinion turned with passionate interest to business and economic changes, to the defense or denigration of republican institutions, to financial scandals and the repeated ministerial crises. As the century closed, a long period of slowly rising prices spurred industrial expansion and consolidated the prosperity fostered by twenty years of peace. "Like the infanta weeping in the royal garden," wrote Charles de Gaulle, "the France of the nineties cultivated its melancholy while savoring its wealth." There was an unavoidable letdown in the efforts to achieve a military renewal.

The immense majority of officers had refused colonial service for fear they might miss the longed-for *revanche*. Most of them "believed at the time that they had a rendezvous with a destiny which, they hoped, would be sublime." But apart from the tiny number who found their way to the General Staff through the École de Guerre, and those attracted by the lure of an adventurous colonial career, officers familiar with the forced inactivity of peacetime service could only mark time in a profession devoid alike of prospects and of glory.

In the 1900's a man might remain a lieutenant for twelve or fifteen years, and captain for another fifteen or twenty. An anonymous colonel wrote a series of articles for *Le Temps*, in which he painted a humorous picture of the difficulties an officer faced in obtaining promotion:

> Most officers—I am speaking of those able enough to serve as generals of a division—become majors between the ages of 44 and 49. From this moment on they are constantly mindful of the age limit and struggle desperately to obtain the modest reprieve of two or three years that a higher rank would give them. We are heading for an almost universal rule that grants a man promotion to the rank of major four years before the captain's age limit is reached, to lieutenant colonel two years before a major must retire, and to colonel with one year to spare. And already there are many colonels who become generals *on the very eve* of retirement. . . . That is the picture of what awaits the best pupils of Saint-Cyr and Polytechnique and the best soldiers in the contingent—the elite, in a word—and that is how they will spend their time.

The above held true, furthermore, only for the officers trained in the *grandes écoles*. For the man who had come up from the ranks, the utmost limit of his career was to become captain rather than major.

There was nothing, on the material plane, to offset this growing torpor that beset the officers' corps, the increasing rigidity of military life, the melancholy of most officers and the bitterness of many, and the anger felt by the most enthusiastic or most fanatical. In his *L' Armée évolue*, which appeared in 1908, General Pédoya expressed the opinion that "an unmarried officer can just barely make ends meet, but the married officer can support his family with difficulty at best, and sometimes the situation is harrowing. Only a commanding officer with the entire confidence of those under him, or a colonel's wife who has made such good friends of the officers' ladies that they are willing to confide in her, could relate the full extent of this gilded poverty, and the suffering that sometimes lies behind it."

In his portrayal of *L'Officier contemporain*, Captain d'Arbeux sums up very adequately the steps that led from the idolization of the Army to the relapse into indifference, the moral and material impoverishment, and the loss of prestige which reached its nadir about 1905. "Ten or twenty years ago the officer with his mind set on marriage attired himself in dress uniform and white gloves in order to seek out his prospective father-in-law. Today he scarcely dares confess that he is an officer, and begs to be excused this youthful indiscretion."

The most decisive indicator was the number of young men between eighteen and twenty who decided on a military career. This figure had begun to drop, and within a few years would sink catastrophically. The number of candidates for Saint-Cyr, in 1897, was 1,920; in 1911 the number was 871. This represented a drop of 60 per cent in fourteen years. During the first ten years of the twentieth century the number of candidates at Saint-Maixent fell from 842 to 380; and, beginning in 1905, half of the young officers in the Engineers and Artillery resigned their commissions after leaving Polytechnique. Gravest of all was the fact that this marked distaste for Army life was not restricted to conservative bourgeois families, but extended to the levels of society which had looked on an officer's commission as a step up on the social ladder, and almost a claim to renown. Between 1900 and 1911, the number of noncoms who chose to re-enlist fell from 72,000 to 41,000. This was the most serious sign of the diminished prestige of the Army, and justified the gravest misgivings concerning the average value of the military cadres and the Army's over-all functional efficiency. The whole corps of officers might have wept, as did Psichari, himself an Army man, over the defeat of their youthful hopes: ". . . So much unutilized energy, so much potentiality and so little achievement, so many lofty destinies, so much promise and so much sterility, so much fiction and so little reality."

Only in such an atmosphere could the Dreyfus Affair have set in motion a groundswell that for several years would spread and intensify.

No other historic, social, psychological or diplomatic context could have produced it. Indeed, the military policy of succeeding governments between 1899 and 1905 would never have taken on the shape it did if it had not been above all else a reaction against the hitherto dominant trend to put the officers into a caste ruled by the representatives of the traditionalist aristocracy, marked by the influence of the clergy and harboring a thorough contempt for republican institutions. Those officers who refused to conform all had the same story to report: for twenty-five years the climate in the Army had been hostile to everything that deviated from an all-embracing conservatism, that is, from monarchist sympathies or a monarchist tradition.

"One dared not declare oneself a republican," General Pédoya wrote of this epoch, "unless one wished to be banished and left in the lurch, even by direct associates." And General Iung, one of the very few republicans among the officers, had this personal testimony to offer: "One is accused of politicking, if one has the effrontery to declare oneself a republican. . . . Only the man who himself has experienced these cheerless hours can have any idea of the furious tenacity with which some Army circles hound down, by every means, the unfortunate officers suspected of the least sympathy for the government. A whole book could be written . . . on the life of a republican officer, of a red donkey, under a republican regime."

One of these "red donkeys" was to become the chief instrument of the military policy that sprang directly from the antimilitarist sentiments aroused by the Dreyfus Affair. He had himself been subjected to ostracism by his traditionalist comrades. His whole activity was motivated by the desire to wipe out the caste spirit which he had witnessed and suffered under.

One month after General André had become War Minister, the chief of the Army's General Staff and the Vice-President of the Army Council were replaced. General Galiffet took a really major step by eliminating the promotion commissions which had made promotion, in effect, a matter of co-option. The initial consequence of this was a serious deterioration in morale.

The first punitive measures and the first spectacular promotions left no doubt in anyone's mind that the government was determined to eliminate the antirepublican, monarchist and clerical tradition from the higher levels of the Army. In every garrison officers began to spy on each other. It was easy to conjecture that the most ambitious officers would flaunt their republican sympathies, and that the most genuine republicans would seek just recompense for the long period of humiliation that some of them had had to endure.

Military life involves such close intimacy between officers of the same regiment, comrades of the same class and frequenters of the same clubs, that no officers could remain unaware of each other's political, social and religious affiliations. These, from now on—to quote Captain d'Arbeux—would play a major part in "promotions, and mutually exclusive cliques were formed, accusing each other of base flattery vis-à-vis political authority or of reactionary snobbery. Officers of every persuasion, in actual fact, had unhappy memories of this period. But for the moment all was bitterness, jealousy, and perhaps even hatred. The desire for advancement was too closely linked to intellectual and political preferences."

Captain d'Arbeux later declared that "conversions to a new ideal were both numerous and exceptionally violent! The neophytes burned what they had adored, gave up church attendance, flocked to the Masonic Lodges and paid homage to the Republic."

Some officers came to regard as suspect the generals destined for the highest posts. The men most anxious to end this hostility between the political authorities and the military did not dare defend openly an organization which was, they knew, basically antirepublican and rancorously disposed toward successive French governments. Matters could not have been more skillfully designed to break down the cohesion of Army cadres. "The officers are aware," wrote Captain d'Arbeux, "that they can no longer count on their leaders to defend them, as formerly they could."

This steady worsening of Army morale could not be neglected indefinitely, on the political level. Every bourgeois family with some member in the Army well knew by what conflicts the officers' groups were torn. They realized that on the outcome might depend not only a career but a man's whole existence. Two brothers from a prominent Burgundian family held the rank of colonel. One rose to be general while the other was suddenly retired, for no other apparent reason than his religious practices and the family's monarchist tradition. To the brother who succeeded in saving his career and obtaining advancement were attributed political compromises and ruses, and most of his former intimates ceased to speak to him. Such incidents were quite numerous, for several years. In a single regiment certain officers found no one to shake hands with them, duels were provoked, reports and complaints were despatched "through channels" on every matter of morale and promotion that might arouse unfavorable attention, and officers resigned from the Army. The number of inquiries into such incidents that the War Minister had to set in motion were twelve times more frequent in 1904 than in 1900.

That was the year when the crisis reached its peak, but by the fall a solution was obviously in the making. The elimination of the committees on promotion had been intended to wipe out the co-option by which, in practice, advancement was determined. But no other system was immediately developed that would have ensured a rigorous selection on the basis of merit and the destruction of the caste outlook. The views of the Combes government, in which General André was War Minister, could be summed up as the blunt intention to promote officers in accordance with the Minister's exclusive preferences. "Promotion, in the Army," General André declared, "is in the hands of Parliament." This meant, in actual fact, that new files on every officer were rapidly built up. It meant that General André had his personal staff see to the setting up of a vast information system. Fearing that these methods might encounter the disapproval of the officials at the Ministry of War, General André agreed, apparently, that the "fiches" or index cards should be kept at the headquarters of the French Grand Orient, the most powerful Masonic organization. The information was collected and noted on these cards either by officers who themselves were Freemasons, by other officers willing to help them or by Masonic officials.

Such procedures could not long remain hidden. The daily paper *Le Matin*, in the summer of 1904, accused General André, along with his parliamentary secretary General Percin and his orderly, of having organized within the Army a system of personal espionage enabling Catholic officers to be branded as such and denied advancement, while Freemasons and other officers who were outspokenly anticlerical were systematically favored. But these charges were not backed up by any proof. In the Grand Orient, the organization and actual writing of these "fiches" were in the hands of Vadecard, a man highly placed in the Masonic Order. The methods used, at the demand of the War Minister's staff, finally disgusted Bidegoin, Vadecard's assistant. About the middle of October he entrusted all the correspondence in his charge to Guyot de Villeneuve, a Deputy for Paris. On October 28, Guyot de Villeneuve set going the affair of the "fiches" by offering the Chamber all necessary proof. The text of the "fiches" made quite plain the political and ideological outlook that inspired the whole system. Most of the cards bore such summary indications as: "Goes to mass," "His wife goes to mass every Sunday," "His children are being educated by priests," "His brother is a Jesuit."

The way in which these "fiches" were used was placed beyond doubt by the letters that had passed between the Minister's staff and the Grand Orient. "As you can see," Captain Mollin wrote to Vade-card, "we have given great weight to the information you provide. The republicans have been preferred and the clericals neglected. . . . When these gentlemen come to realize what a real advantage it is to be a republican, they will change their ways, and at least will pretend to be republican."

The Combes government was doomed. This marked the beginning of a new attitude toward the military, replacing the one called into existence by the Dreyfus Affair. It was to last right up to 1914.

Thirty years of peace had inevitably had their effect. There was an unavoidable and increasing lull in initiative, in criticism and innovation. Every rank became steadily more lethargic, more weighed down by the dullness of routine and the worship of regulations. All this was intensified when the generation of leaders who had planned and executed France's military renewal, after 1871, were succeeded by a new generation whose theoretical training could not replace the lack of battle experience, the harsh memory of defeat and the support provided by a national climate highly favorable to the Army.

The revealing title chosen by Major Simon for the century's opening years, the period when he himself was a young officer, is *Le Formalisme*. "We spent whole weeks," he writes, "adjusting the straps of revolver holsters and the straps around canteens, seeing to it that the former should run between the first and second tunic buttons and the latter between the second and third tunic buttons. . . . On the range, what mattered was not to hit the target frequently but to adopt the precise posture that regulations called for, even if the marksman's physique made this uncomfortable for him. To allow the lefthanded soldier to put a rifle against his left shoulder would have seemed a grave infringement of discipline."

This decline in the intellectual value of the officers' corps was matched by a corresponding decline in the French military potential as a whole. The industrial revolution demanded a parallel revolution in military equipment. Within ten years chemical explosives, automatic weapons, new steels, the telephone, the automobile and the airplane would transform every problem of armaments, logistics, transport and communications.

The credits asked for by the General Staff and the services were at first looked at askance by the Ministers concerned, who hesitated to ask Parliament for funds to increase a military effort of which everyone had grown weary. This reserve shown by political circles with respect to the plans for re-equipping the Army was echoed by the Army's upper echelons. In 1909 it was still possible for the representative of the General Staff, addressing the commission of the Chamber of Deputies, to take very lightly the questions the deputies asked about German heavy artillery. "You talk to us of heavy artillery. Thank God, we have none. French strength depends on the lightness of its cannon." When the first machine guns were made available in 1910, the officer in charge of infantry expressed the opinion that "this device makes no difference at all." That same year, the exhibition of military planes led the commanding officer of the Army School to declare that "all this is just sport! For the Army, the airplane equals zero!"

Since 1870, French military efforts had sought to attain a fair measure of equality between the armed forces of France and of Germany. Fully aware of Germany's industrial strength and growing population, the General Staff had endeavored to preclude at least any catastrophic surprise during the early weeks of any future conflict. The number of men under arms had approximately kept pace, on a percentage basis, with the increase in German manpower. Yet, from 1893 on, the gap between the actual strength of the two armies kept growing, due to the increasing difference in the birthrate of the two countries.

The German Army's supplies of manpower were so great that the two-year period of service for "footsoldiers" and the three years for "mounted" soldiers were enforced for only about one-half of each contingent. But from 1892 on the German General Staff gave elementary military instruction to those who were not called up. The gap between the French and the German military potential increased ominously; it began to be realized that the frontiers could not be fully protected in case of war. It was with all this in view that the military reform of 1905 was instituted.

There was at this time such a close tie-up between military problems and political antagonisms that the debates on the bill presented almost a caricature of the traditionally opposed views of Left and Right concerning the professional Army and the "nation under arms." Lamarzelle, spokesman for the Right, demanded the creation of a force of 250,000 professional soldiers, of an "armée de choc" that could be used without delay and kept in fighting trim by intensive training. For the bulk of each contingent, a reduced period of service would suffice.

Jaurès, spokesman for the Socialists and a fraction of the Radical-Socialists, expressed the traditional hostility of the Left against the permanent Army and its caste spirit. He advanced the opposing doctrine. The Army, as he saw it, should have no other goal in peacetime than to serve as a permanent school for the totality of Frenchmen of an age to bear arms; and, in case of war, the immediate mobilization of all the trained contingents would provide the country with the manpower it needed.

But the great majority, both among the public and in every party except the Socialists and the extreme Right, were convinced of the need for a "protecting" Army and also for numerous, trained reserves.

The law that was voted through on March 21, 1905, reflected this dual concern. It set the period of military service at two years without exception, and the total period of availability at twenty-five years. In order to honor the principle of equal obligation and to eliminate the scandal of the "goldbrickers" who found shelter, during their actual years of service, in administrative jobs that had nothing to do with their military training, men not up to the requirements of combat were placed in an "auxiliary service" and allotted to physically undemanding positions. Future students of Saint-Cyr and Polytechnique had first to spend a year in the regiment. They made up the first category of reserve officers and had the rank of second lieutenant during their second year of service. The second category, the more numerous, was made up of the contingent's recruits or volunteers who were intellectually of a caliber to be officers. After one year's service, they took a competitive examination that qualified them to be reserve officers with the rank of second lieutenant at the end of six months. Thus they completed their final six months' service as officers.

In its application, however, the law of 1905 closely reflected the hesitation felt by the political arm when it considered the military effort demanded of the nation. The two periods of twenty-eight days each that had been envisaged for the most recent classes of reservists were cut down to twenty-three days, and later to seventeen. The reservists of the Territorial Army were called back for nine days, not thirteen, and the military authorities showed themselves increasingly indulgent toward all the excuses by which reservists sought to escape these "periods": harvests, grape-gathering, election campaigns and what not. Two years after the law had been passed, 3 per cent of the reservists did not answer the summons. The officering, too, fell short of the standards that the authors of the measure had hoped to achieve. In every regiment it was the least adequate or the oldest officers who were posted to the "supplementary cadres." As late as 1912, there were only four training camps able to handle large numbers of reservists: Châlons and Mailly in the east, Coetquidan in Brittany and la Courtine in the Massif Central.

What with the general indifference to the military effort, anti-militarism or distrust of the Army among a section of the public, and the intellectual, material and numerical weakening of the armed forces themselves, the military hierarchy was shaken. As General Langlois, one of the General Staff's chief theoreticians, put it: "We owe the truth to the country: the Army is threatened with disorganization."

Not until the Combes government had fallen was any systematic attempt made to dispose of the whole matter. But from then on a return to normal relations between the political leadership and the military hierarchy was gradually effected. Finally a deep reconciliation between Army and Nation would be achieved, the last stages being reached only in the period of armed watchfulness that preceded the explosion of August, 1914.

The liquidation of the Army crisis was made possible by the over-all transformation of French political life. The balance of political forces underwent a significant shift during the fifteen years that preceded World War I. Since their first notable electoral success, in 1893, Socialists of every shade had made a massive irruption onto the political scene. The fact that they helped to form the majority which for six years had maintained in power the governments of Waldeck-Rousseau and Combes no doubt favored this advance, since opinion on the Left could now look on the Socialists as a group that normally was counted among Republican parties. At all events, Socialist progress became more and more rapid. In 1890 the Party had 54,000 members; by 1914 this number had risen to 90,000. There were 830,000 Socialist voters in 1906; 1,400,000 in 1914. The number of

Socialist deputies rose correspondingly from 51 to 113 and then to 203.

This Socialist upsurge was the result of the long years spent in propaganda and agitation by the militants of the various Socialist groups which had been established in the last twenty years of the nineteenth century and which battled against police measures and the allied hostility of the state and the employers. Won over were a great many workers, certain peasant groups, and artisans who traditionally had been served by the Radicals. Only the economic and social transformation that had accelerated its pace since the 1890's could explain this success. The major capitalist powers had entered upon a new stage of their economic history with the "long-term" rise in prices that would continue until 1914. The accompanying growth in profits speeded up the rate of industrialization and accounted for a general, and very rapid, increase in industrial production.

For France it was a period of mounting wealth for every section of the bourgeoisie. Under the impact of industrialization large working-class centers were formed and the number of factory workers rapidly increased; a domain of activity and possibilities of expansion, such as it had never known before, were opened up for the trade union movement—already constituted on modern lines. The need for manpower in industry made it easier to hold out for higher wages. The larger numbers of wage earners increased the scope of the strikes. A militant spirit characterized all working-class milieux. The resulting social struggles occupied the center of the French political stage and brought about a realignment of the parties.

At Amiens in 1906 the C.G.T., the major working-class organization, officially promulgated its program. It was at this time, too, that there began the long series of strikes which was to have such a strong impact on French social conditions. The extent of this social unrest led to a whole series of major political developments. The hearing accorded the C.G.T. in working-class circles had a decisive effect on the attitude of the Socialist Party. The Party, henceforth, could never keep aloof from working-class activism that involved battles for rights, strikes, immediate violent combat against employers and, sometimes, against the state. The Socialists were also obliged to renounce any notion of accepting Cabinet posts.

The use against the strikers of the forces of public order, Army or police, gave rise to acrimonious disputes between the Socialists, the natural defenders of the strikers, and the governments whose aim it was to "maintain order." The antimilitarism of the Socialist parties was reinforced by the trade unions' antimilitarism, which for many years past had been much more violent and intransigent. At the Congress of 1906 all the workers' organizations, now associated in the C.G.T., voted through by 488 ballots to 310 the famous order of the day: ". . . Antimilitarist and antipatriotic propaganda must become ever more intense and more audacious." Clashes between soldiers and strikers maintained and whipped up the antimilitarism of the workers.

Each new international crisis provoked a pacifist response in the trade union organizations. At the peak of Franco-German tension in 1906, the C.G.T. organ *La Voix du Peuple* called on the workers "to refuse to take up arms in the event of war with Germany." In 1908 the Marseilles Congress decided, by 681 votes against 421, that "the instruction of the workers has to be undertaken from the international point of view so that, in the event of a war between the powers, the workers will respond by declaring an international strike." And in 1912 a special federal congress summoned to consider the danger of war adopted the following order of the day: "The delegates of the workers' organizations judge that wage earners obliged to go to war have this alternative only: either to take up weapons in order to go to the frontier and menace other wage earners, or to take up the battle against the common foe: capitalism."

While the Socialist Party accepted the more and more pugnacious positions adopted by the trade union movement, the entire non-Socialist Left reacted by developing a new line. Confronted by the competition of the Socialist candidates, the Radicals entered upon a decisive transformation. Many had labeled themselves Radicals only in order to stress their undaunted republicanism, at the time of the Dreyfus Affair. But on social issues they had nothing in common with the revolutionary doctrine of the Socialist Party. Ultimately, the coalition between the Moderates and the Radicals who rejected the Socialist program would bring about the political realignment that, in the ten years preceding World War I, would enable the Army crisis to be solved.

This insistence on a new political and social orientation and on the Army's moral and material rehabilitation was embodied in the group of men who, after the collapse of the Combes government, set the course that the new regime would follow. And they themselves adhered to the course they had once chosen. As early as 1905 and until long after World War I, this group completely dominated the history of the Third Republic. Ribot, not one of the

majority that had supported Waldeck-Rousseau and Combes, personally aided in welding Moderate Right and Conservative Center into
the new majority which would exclude the Socialists and the Radical
Left. Barthou and Poincaré, on the other hand, though they had
belonged to the "republican" anticlerical majority, were among the
deputies who brought about the fall of the Combes government.
Men like Messimy, who spent a long time as War Minister, and
Berteaux, who almost became President of the Council, represented
the fraction of Radical opinion which, having ridden to death its
anticlerical program, was unwilling to see the Third Republic veer
over to socialism and antimilitarism. Clemenceau remained faithful
to his deepseated Jacobinism by incarnating this desire for reconciliation among the Independent Socialists. When they had to choose
between party discipline, which in 1905 brought together all the
Socialist groups, and full freedom of action for parliamentary maneuver, they opted for the latter. Viviani and Paul-Boncour, unlike
Millerand and Briand, long remained close to Socialist circles. But
their concern for national defense nevertheless associated them with
the profoundly anti-Socialist Radical and Moderate majority that
was to rule, almost without interruption, until 1919. They looked
on themselves as no less Jacobin than Socialist, and believed that
socialism was not necessarily incompatible with the desire to maintain
the country's military strength.

These men came to power almost immediately after the fall of
Combes. The transitional figure was Rouvier, who had been Minister
of Finance under Combes and now succeeded him as President of
the Council. A banker, and personally active in a number of great
enterprises, he admirably symbolized the marked divergence from
Socialist policies that the parliamentary majority was anxious to
bring about. After Rouvier it was Sarrien who formed a government,
and the strongest personality in his cabinet was Clemenceau, Minister
of the Interior.

A few months later Clemenceau himself became President of the
Council. His first task was to take up the problems of social unrest.
The question had arisen whether government employees had the right
to form unions and go on strike. Clemenceau chose to defend the
traditional view of the relations between the state and its servants.
His lengthy polemics with Jaurès established a clear line of division
between the new political forces.

Later on, Briand adopted the same position when confronted by
the general railroad strike and the railroad workers' demands. The

characteristic feature of every government, between 1905 and 1910, was opposition to the demands of the working class. It was a striking break with the preceding period when, from 1898 to 1905, a coalition of "republican defense" and Jaurès's influence on the governmental majority had been decisive.

Now the Army could once more assume its normal place within the Nation and the state. Every time public order was threatened by working-class militancy, the government called out the troops against the strikers. On each occasion it could be seen ever more plainly that the government had to rely on the Army. Clemenceau had spent twenty-five years denouncing clerical influences in the Army and had supported every anticlerical measure. But now, in the interest of reconciliation, he did not hesitate to end these religious conflicts. The inventory of church property that was to have been made, after the legal separation of church and state, was impossible unless the Army were utilized to break down the doors of ecclesiastical buildings protected by crowds of pious Catholics. Rather than risk the resignation of far too many Catholic officers, Clemenceau called a halt to this stock-taking.

It was in this fashion that the general crisis in the relations between state and Army, a heritage of the Dreyfus Affair, came to an end in 1906. The solution, it is clear, was tied to the prospect of a reversal in French internal policy. This reversal came about in order to meet the "Socialist menace" and because the governments, in order to break successive strikes and resist working-class demands, had decided to make use of the Army. In this domain, therefore, the solution of the military crisis sowed dragons' teeth of future conflict. The Army had been deliberately employed against the working class. It was likely for a long time to remain, in the workers' eyes, the concrete symbol of bourgeois oppression and of the "iron law" imposed by capitalism and by the state that set out to protect it.

Thus once again the hostility between the Army and the industrial population was reactivated, tying in with a tradition that dated back to June, 1848, and to the Commune of 1871. Once again the workers in industry saw confronting them the uniforms of officers and soldiers. Once again the Army opposed them in defense of the social order. The consequences of this confrontation were too remote to be grasped either by the Army's leaders or by those with political authority. But between them a decisive bond had been established: they realized that they had emerged together from the long crisis whose starting point had been the Dreyfus Affair.

CHAPTER FIVE

MILITARY RENEWAL PRIOR TO WORLD WAR I

✠

It was indeed time. The French General Staff suddenly adopted the view, early in 1904, that the risk of war with Germany was much more serious, perhaps even more imminent, than had previously been thought.

A German citizen, who claimed to be a colonel and declared he wanted to revenge himself on the German General Staff, provided the French Command with information of considerable importance. The "avenger," as he chose to be called, made known the plan for the disposition of the German armies in case of war. Envisaged was the invasion of Belgium by the bulk of the German forces, which were to cross Belgian territory in a few days and attack from the rear the bulk of the French forces concentrated in Lorraine and along the Vosges.

The General Staff had no doubt that the "avenger's" information was correct. It did not, in actual fact, too closely correspond to the real German plans. Yet it indicated the main lines of the attack on the French forces via Belgium and the northern frontier. The high command felt ill at ease. They feared their own plans might prove entirely inadequate to meet the situation that could be created by a German onslaught at the very outset of the war. They realized, too, that the relative strength of the two armies was highly disadvantageous to France. And they wondered whether Germany, to clinch a victory, might not launch a sudden attack in order to fall unawares on the concentration of French forces. From 1904 on they repeatedly warned the government. A sense of urgency now prevailed among the military, and this motivated their persistent demands that the political authorities should end the crisis afflicting the Army on the twofold plane of morale and matériel.

The likelihood of war with Germany had never appeared really grave in the preceding period. The last decade of the nineteenth century had seen all the World Powers preoccupied with their colonial policies. International crises arose mainly out of the difficulties experienced in assigning precise limits to colonial empires in the final stages of the European penetration of Africa and Asia.

It was during these years that the French forward thrust threatened to collide with the British thrust, in the Indochinese Peninsula, East Africa and the valley of the Nile. The series of diplomatic crises that resulted ended with a victory, on balance, for the French claims in Laos and Siam, and with a compromise in the Niger basin. Only the Fashoda incident, in which a small French force met the British troops at the Sudanese strongpoint of Fashoda, seemed capable of provoking a conflict. The government, in order to create the impression that it would go to any lengths, started naval preparations. In London, similar steps were ordered. But within forty-eight hours semiofficial articles appeared in the daily papers, letting it be understood that the evacuation of Fashoda could be "reconciled with the national honor."

Thus it was plain that the French government would not allow the crisis to grow into war. The Dreyfus Affair was at it height. The country was morally no better prepared for war than it was in strictly military terms. Delcassé recognized the fact. "The problem is," he wrote in a private letter at the time of the Fashoda incident, "to harmonize the exigencies of the national honor with the avoidance of a naval war we are in no position to fight."

The General Staff had no illusions concerning the relative strength of the naval and colonial forces, in the event—the likelihood of which no French government entertained for a moment—of a clash with the British. But since the military accord of 1892, and with the Russian Alliance a reality, it was possible to envisage with less apprehension the outbreak of a war on the European continent. In each of the international crises provoked by the "parceling out of the earth" which was completed between 1895 and 1914, the government asked the leaders of the Army to state what reliance should be placed on the possibility of military action in determining French policy. Thus on each occasion the problem arose of the influence of the military on political decisions.

As we have seen, the Dreyfus Affair had created an atmosphere of distrust between politicians and military leaders. As one government gave way to another no less anxious to defend republican institutions against the nationalist and monarchist onslaught, no reasons could be found to treat with deference the views of the military. Their general outlook and political predilections were distrusted. Nevertheless, the Minister of Foreign Affairs and the head of the General Staff maintained a relationship much less exposed to internal strife, and the Army chiefs had several opportunities to underline the danger of a grave international situation, and this, possibly, served to check the great antimilitarist groundswell that followed the Dreyfus Affair. But what actually occurred on the international scene?

In November, 1895, a scant three years after the signing of the Franco-Russian military pact, the Armenian massacres ordered by the Turkish government led Great Britain to dispatch a squadron to the Aegean and threaten the Turkish government with a further advance into the Dardanelles and the Bosphorus. The Russian government let it be known that it was ready to "undertake the defense of the Straits" against any English incursion. On December 6, the Russian Minister of Foreign Affairs asked the French Ambassador what attitude France would take in the event of an Anglo-Russian conflict. In reply Berthelot, the French Minister of Foreign Affairs, promised Russia France's diplomatic support, should the situation result in the general liquidation of the Ottoman Empire. Otherwise, France urgently requested, the Russian government should adopt an extremely prudent attitude. Only a British attempt to win the shores of the Straits by force, in violation of the international treaty fixing their status, would lead to French military intervention.

The French position accorded with the military and political agreements signed with Russia, since no undertaking had been entered into with respect to Great Britain. But the constant preoccupation of every French government, right up to the 1914 crisis, was thereby made clear. France sought to limit the scope of the Franco-Russian Alliance to the sole danger of a conflict with Germany. Thus, on the first occasion that the Franco-Russian Alliance found a concrete application, French diplomacy adopted a line of conduct in perfect accord with the military policy followed by the General Staff. For one as for the other, the only risk of war to be envisaged was that of a Franco-German war.

Late in 1896, a rebellion broke out in Macedonia, followed by another in Crete. In April, 1897, the Russian government took the initiative in consulting the French government on the attitude that should be adopted by France and Russia, in keeping with their Alliance. The Macedonian rebellion, by raising the issue of the entire political map in the Balkans, might induce Austria-Hungary to decree a partial mobilization. This step, under Article 2 of the military convention of 1892, would automatically lead to the mobilization of the Russian and also of the French Army.

The French government had always feared the application of this second Article, but Czar Alexander III had made it an essential condition for the Alliance. Paris was obliged to agree, or the Alliance would never have become a reality.

Hanotaux, the French Minister of Foreign Affairs, now let it be known that no French military action with respect to the Balkans could be considered, since the drawbacks were so apparent and the advantages so difficult to discern. When, a few days later, he received the Russian Minister of Foreign Affairs, Hanotaux warned him against the German intrigues that would urge Russia in the direction of Constantinople, to act as a counterweight to Austria-Hungary. "The best service we could render Russia," said Hanotaux, "would be to observe a neutrality that would oblige Germany to do the same." On this occasion the French government was clearly trying to restrict the scope of the Franco-Russian Alliance to the single eventuality of a German initiative. The proposal made was that Russia, in case war should break out between her and Austria-Hungary, should so act that Russian interests would require no extension of hostilities. The Russian government could scarcely reject this line of argument, for Austria-Hungary was indeed so weak militarily that it would be in the Russian interest to limit the conflict.

But if France thus refused any military aid to Russia in the Balkans, she could not count on Russian support in the eventuality of a clash with the British in Africa, for had she not refused to include Great Britain in the pledges given with respect to Germany and Austria-Hungary, in the Franco-Russian military accord? "Besides," wrote Hanotaux to Montebello, the French Ambassador in St. Petersburg, "even if France should wish it, she could do nothing, because a war against England would be a naval war and France cannot commit herself to that. It is altogether impossible." Once again, France's foreign policy and her military policy fitted hand in glove.

Delcassé replaced Hanotaux as Minister of Foreign Affairs in June, 1898. He was to remain in office for seven years. All the Powers were mindful of the danger that the Austro-Hungarian Empire, because of the stirrings of the national minorities, might break into pieces. For France, this would have a particularly grave consequence. The Franco-Russian military accord was to have "the same duration as the alliance" between Germany, Austria-Hungary and Italy; the disappearance of one of the three would annul this Triple Alliance and, along with it, France's understanding with Russia.

Delcassé's objective was to give the 1892 military accord the same unrestricted duration as the diplomatic agreement of 1891. But Delcassé also shared the apprehension of his forerunners in office at the possible application of the military accord's Article 2. Even a partial mobilization of the Austro-Hungarian Army would inevitably lead to the mobilization of the French Army—and this, in its turn, to the mobilization of the German Army. If Germany should hesitate to support Austria-Hungary, French mobilization would eliminate all such hesitation. In view of this possibility France had to seek concessions from Russia. The French situation was rendered all the more crucial by the fact that Anglo-French rivalries in Africa might, in Delcassé's estimation, induce France to ask Russia at least for diplomatic support.

But Russia had not much reason to adopt a conciliatory attitude, in view of the opposition that she had met with from France at the time of the Balkan crises. Moreover, the series of events to which the Dreyfus Affair gave rise might well engender Russian skepticism of the value of the French Alliance, since the fury of the attacks directed against the General Staff would seem to presage a decline in the moral and material worth of the French Army.

It was in these conditions that Delcassé, in August, 1899, undertook to negotiate an agreement in St. Petersburg. On August 9, an exchange of letters gave concrete expression to the accord: "The Government of the French Republic and the Imperial Government of Russia, ever anxious to preserve the general peace and the balance of European forces, confirm the diplomatic arrangement of 1891 and decide that the military convention of 1892 will remain in force as long as the diplomatic accord, which was concluded for the protection

of the common and permanent interests of the two countries." Thus
Delcassé had attained the two principal goals he had set himself: the
notion of "the balance of European forces" applied to the possible
splitting up of Austria-Hungary and the eventual annexation by Germany of the German-speaking regions of Austria-Hungary, and also
to the revision of the political map of the Balkans. Furthermore, there
was the possibility, should a general war break out, of realizing what
Delcassé, in a letter to Loubet, President of the Republic, referred
to as "our views and hopes," or, in other words, the return of Alsace-
Lorraine to France.

More concretely, the Franco-Russian military convention of 1892
was now unlimited with respect to time, like the diplomatic accord
of 1891. France no doubt had assumed a greater moral obligation
to back up Russia in the Balkans than had been the case between 1895
and 1897. But the spirit of the Alliance remained unchanged, since
the military convention, which remained in force, envisaged only a
German act of aggression as bringing into play all the military clauses
of the Franco-Russian *entente*.

Between July, 1900, and February, 1901, the military took over
the task from the diplomats. The conversations between the two General Staffs, which went on for seven months, enabled the representatives of the French Army to stress their own chief concerns: it
offered them the opportunity to deflect the Franco-Russian Alliance
in the direction they desired. The French General Staff had always
thought that, in the event of war between France and Germany,
Germany would take the offensive and deploy the whole weight of
its forces first of all against France. So a Russian attack on Germany
would be required, compelling the German high command to keep
the greatest possible number of divisions on its eastern front.

The belief was held, by French military men, that it would all
be a matter of days. They wanted the Russians to take the offensive
on the fourteenth day after hostilities broke out. The Russians objected that the length and the inadequacies of their lines of communication made it difficult for them to mobilize their armed forces
rapidly. The Russians finally agreed to launch their attack on Germany on the eighteenth day after the declaration of war. To meet
this first offensive, the Germans would have to assign six or seven
Army corps to the eastern front. And on the twenty-eighth day of
mobilization, the Russians would throw in all the forces provided for
in the military convention, some seven or eight hundred thousand

men. As a counterweight a new loan was granted Russia, and
Delcassé arrived in St. Petersburg in April, 1901, to work out the
general conditions of this loan.

In another respect also the General Staff achieved the objectives
that the French government had envisaged for several years previously. It was decided, in the protocols signed by the two high commands, that even a general mobilization of the Austro-Hungarian
Army would not automatically involve the mobilization of the French
Army. Any military decision would depend on the two governments'
reaching an understanding. It was the General Staff that succeeded
in obtaining this revision, so long desired by French diplomats, in
Article 2 of the military convention of 1892.

By way of a *quid pro quo,* all the logical conclusions had now to be
drawn that were implicit in the preceding year's extension of the
Franco-Russian Alliance. Already in 1900 the first protocol signed
by the General Staff had dealt with the hypothesis of war with England. The terms employed gave perfect expression to the outlook of
the French military negotiators. "If England should attack France,"
this protocol declared, "Russia might confront England with a diver-
sionary move in the region of India. Reciprocally, if England should
attack Russia, France would concentrate 500,000 men along the
Channel, in order to threaten England with invasion." Being well
aware of the impossibility of waging naval warfare, the General Staff
committed itself only to land operations. Besides, it was willing to
consider only the hypothesis of an English attack, and left it to
the diplomats to determine in what specific cases the two governments would declare that they were faced by an act of aggression on
the part of Great Britain.

The Waldeck-Rousseau government, which came to power in 1899,
was entirely hostile to the idea of a conflict with Great Britain. It
was made up of Radicals and Moderate Republicans, the former being
strongly in favor of a rapprochement with Great Britain, while the
latter, although laying greater stress on French economic interests
in Africa and Asia, were nevertheless opposed to any idea of a war
between the two countries. Only the Right and extreme Right remained anti-British, but they had no influence whatever on French
politics. Perhaps their criticisms were motivated more by the wish
to accuse governments of the Left of sacrificing the "national interests" on every occasion than by any clearly defined political concepts.

In May, 1901, the governments were to ratify the protocols that their General Staffs had signed the previous February. The Russian government again manifested its attachment to Article 2 of the convention of 1892. It realized that, in the event of a Balkan war, any real French support depended on this and, in actual fact, that the French government would always seek to moderate Russian ambitions in Europe. Finally a new protocol was drawn up declaring that Article 2 was "maintained in the text of 1892." The only restriction expressed was that the French Army would not mobilize automatically unless Austro-Hungarian mobilization was general, and not partial. It is clear that the negotiators sent by the French General Staff were more vigorous than the diplomats in striving to limit French obligations.

The next two years saw an intensification of the character that the French government and General Staff had sought to impose on the protocols of 1900-1901. The Franco-British rapprochement was operating on every level. Only the risk of an Anglo-Russian conflict remained, but the economic and naval rivalry between England and Germany was beginning to modify British policy in its relations with other Powers. So the French government and General Staff could feel assured that they had attained their essential goal, that of increasing their military and political preparations for an eventual trial of strength with Germany.

But suddenly, in February, 1904, the situation took a turn for the worse. At the very moment when the General Staff came into possession of the "avenger's" revelations of the possibility of a surprise attack across Belgian territory, the Russo-Japanese War broke out. Thus the Russian Alliance was militarily paralyzed at the very moment when the danger of German aggression appeared, to the French government and to the General Staff, to be much graver and perhaps also more imminent than they had previously thought.

Delcassé's patient labors had led to the general withdrawal of England, Italy and even Spain from involvement in Morocco. This was the main compensation that the French Minister of Foreign Affairs had obtained at the conclusion of a series of compromises, which in any case were often favorable to France, on the totality of the colonial questions that had divided France and England. The British political and military "presence" in the Nile Valley was finally accepted by Paris, and the Moroccan affair, the last stage in the parceling out of the globe, would be settled in France's favor.

Spain had received promises concerning the north coast of Morocco and certain regions in the Sahara, and Italy could count on French support in its claims on Tripolitania and Cyrenaica. Only Germany had been left out of the feast. Germany might feel all the more tempted to challenge these arrangements, now that the Franco-Russian Alliance was paralyzed by the war in Manchuria. Early in March, 1905, the Russian Army was defeated near Mukden. At the end of that month the German Emperor, Wilhelm II, who had set off on a cruise on a carefully calculated date, paid a visit to the port of Tangiers. He delivered a speech in which he declared that he solemnly recognized the sovereign rights of the Sultan of Morocco, and he proclaimed his desire to see Morocco "remain open for the activity of all nations."

The French government was divided on this "Tangiers coup." Delcassé, assured of the support of all the European Powers, favored firmness. Germany, in his view, would have to propose negotiations, and France should not try to evade the issue, but should avail itself of whatever diplomatic backing it could count on. But Rouvier, the President of the Council, was very nervous about German intentions. He wanted to clear up the situation at once by initiating discussions.

On April 27, 1905, direct negotiations began between the President of the Council and the German government, the latter having already decided that its first objective would be the ousting of Delcassé from the French government. At the same moment, Delcassé began negotiations with Great Britain. The British Foreign Secretary, Lord Landsdown, had explained to the French Ambassador on April 22 that he could not tolerate "the German government's asking for and obtaining from the Sultan a port on the Moroccan coast." This was the chief fear in England at that time. On May 17 and May 25, the Foreign Secretary returned to the charge, and semiofficial conversations took place at the end of the month, hand in hand with the diplomatic negotiations. The English negotiators let it be understood that in case of war the British Fleet could disembark 100,000 men to the north of Hamburg. Nothing was officially decided, but it seemed that for the first time Great Britain had resolved to reach an agreement with France, laying down the course to be adopted if the Moroccan crisis should involve France in war. On May 30, Delcassé wrote to Paul Cambon, French Ambassador in London, that he was ready to undertake, personally and without delay, an unrestricted conversation with Lord Landsdown.

The next day Rouvier received the visit of a Counsellor in the German Embassy, Miquel, who complained of Delcassé's attitude since 1898 and spoke of the "disagreeable awakening" France would experience unless the situation changed. On the other hand he allowed a glimpse of a "modification of the German attitude," which would be made possible above all by a change in the conduct of French foreign policy.

"I cannot dismiss Monsieur Delcassé when Germany frowns," replied Rouvier; "people would never forgive me for it." But on June 2, he confided to two members of his government that Germany had threatened France with war, and that Delcassé's departure was the condition for the maintenance of peace. Four day later, at the Council of Ministers, Delcassé was disavowed by his colleagues, and he resigned.

His resignation was not followed by changes as sweeping as Rouvier had hoped. Germany had made known its demands to France, and these were rather stiff where its economic rights in Morocco were concerned. Then Wilhelm II sought to profit by Czar Nicholas II's discouragement after the defeats in Manchuria and the ensuing revolutionary disturbances, especially the sailors' revolt on the *Potemkin*. On July 10, he proposed a rapprochement between the two Empires, which could serve as the base for what in effect would be a continental alliance directed against England. At Björke he signed a secret treaty with Nicholas II. The Czar, however, was opposed by his Ministers, who were firmly attached to the French Alliance, and he was obliged to inform Wilhelm II on November 23 that since he had failed to persuade France to join the Treaty of Björke, Russia would not abandon her older ally. Germany had no further reason to spare French susceptibilities, and tension grew.

In the first phase of the Moroccan crisis, the General Staff could put its hopes in a prolongation of the Franco-German diplomatic conversations and could imagine that the Russo-Japanese War would not last or would end in a rapid victory for the Russian Army. Possibly it also hoped that a grave crisis with Germany would re-establish the unanimity in French public opinion, the patriotic fervor and the profound veneration of the Army that had existed prior to the Dreyfus Affair.

But the General Staff refused to take any risk. Ever since the "avenger's" revelations, early in 1904, the Army was haunted by the idea of France's being suddenly attacked by way of Belgium. They knew that the gap between German and French manpower had been increasing for the last ten years. And they feared that the French reserves, after the antimilitarism born of the Dreyfus Affair, would be insufficient to allow their adequate utilization. Those at the summit of the military hierarchy were thoroughly aware of the extent of the Army's moral and material decline.

On February 1, 1905, General De Négrier began to publish a series of articles in *La Revue des Deux Mondes*. The General had just retired, and had until then been designated as Supreme Commander in case of war. His articles were looked on, in political circles, as the first urgent call for a wholesale repudiation of the military policy that had been followed for some years previously. Only a few weeks away was the vote on the law that would reduce the period of military service to two years. General De Négrier uttered a warning against any reduction in manpower, and described the situation on the ill-defended eastern frontiers. He openly declared that the French Army would have great difficulty in standing up to a sudden offensive on the part of the German Army.

On February 20, 1905, General Pendezec, the head of the General Staff, addressed a note to the War Minister. He stated that he was conveying his own opinion, which was also that of several members of the Army Council. He declared that French troops might find themselves "at a given moment in no state to play their part efficaciously," that is, to provide the cover behind which the mobilization and concentration of the French armed forces could take place. A few days later General Pendezec warned Paléologue, Secretary General of the Ministry of Foreign Affairs, that in the event of war with Germany the situation of France would from the outset be extremely grave, since there could be no military implementation of the Franco-Russian Alliance: the Russian Armies had their hands full with the war in Manchuria. He took the matter up again on May 5 and told Paléologue bluntly that, in the event of Germany's launching a sudden attack, "we could not resist, in view of the inferiority of our armed strength."

Such was the feeling of isolation that permeated the General Staff, after the years of crisis the Army had lived through since the beginning of the Dreyfus Affair; its estimates concerning the utilization of the reserves were deeply pessimistic. Convinced, as were most of his colleagues, that during the preceding years antimilitarism had gained the support of numerous levels of the population, General Pendezec declared that a considerable number of reservists would not obey the call to arms and that, in the mobilizable reserves as a whole, one could expect a deficiency of 150,000 or 200,000 men. He repeated this, in the middle of May, to the Secretary General of Foreign Affairs.

When the conference of Algeciras opened on January 16, 1906, German demands had not varied, and still available was the diplomatic backing Delcassé had worked to obtain. In the meantime the war in Manchuria had ended. The Russian Revolution of 1905 was also over. To meet a catastrophic financial situation, Nicholas II had sent his Minister of Finances Kokovtsov to Paris, to negotiate a loan of eight hundred million francs. Rouvier gave him to understand that France could lend two hundred million at most, but would be able to do more if the Algeciras conference ended rapidly, with a favorable outcome for France. In this respect, Rouvier behaved exactly like all his predecessors in office, with respect to the Franco-Russian Alliance.

Toward England he acted exactly as Delcassé had before him. He tried to obtain not only the diplomatic backing promised in 1904 but military support also. During the first days of January, 1906, Colonel Huguet, the French military attaché in London, made what he insisted was a semiofficial visit to the head of the British Army's General Staff. He asked whether, in the event of a war between France and Germany over Morocco, England would support France. The British officer replied that he was not familiar with the intentions of his government and that it was not his task to declare what they were. But he was in a position to tell the French attaché that the question of a war with Germany over Morocco had been studied and that, should this war break out, England could immediately commit 100,000 men.

This was the starting point for a very far-reaching semiofficial conversation between the French and British General Staffs. The French aim, as it was expounded to the British, was to obtain a concentration of British troops in the north of France, opposite the Belgian border, so as to prevent the German Army's launching an offensive across Belgium. One hundred thousand men might be enough for the task, at least in the earliest days. This exchange of views struck the French government as sufficiently serious to merit a continuation at the diplomatic level. On January 10, Paul Cambon, the French Ambassador in London, was received by the British Foreign Secretary, Lord Grey, and proposed that semiofficial conversations take place between the General Staffs. A few days later this was agreed: at the order of their respective governments, the two General Staffs resumed contacts.

This was an extraordinarily important event for the French high command. The predominant concern in military circles had been the question of delays in mobilization, in the event of war. If England entered the war on the side of France, its support would be valueless unless the British Army could intervene at once in the area where its role could be decisive. The General Staffs were to reach an agreement on the measures to be taken in the event of a declaration of war.

On the technical level, the conversations went into the minutest detail. The places where the British troops would disembark were chosen. It was decided precisely where they would be quartered, in the region extending from Le Havre to Boulogne-Sur-Mer. An exact estimate was made of the railroad equipment necessary to provide for their movements in the north of France, facing the Belgian frontier, and the trains that would convey them were scrupulously inventoried. Finally, the concentration of British troops in the proximity of Belgium was worked out in detail.

Only by reaching a political agreement could the government round out what the military men had achieved, and on January 31, 1906, Sir Edward Grey explained the British position to the French Ambassador: ". . . Several members of the government are convinced pacifists who are opposed to any modification of Franco-British agreements. Besides, if England pledged itself in advance to intervene in a Franco-German conflict, the Entente Cordiale would become an alliance, an alliance requiring the assent of Parliament. But English public opinion is opposed to any alliance. . . . I leave the door open, and it is clearly understood that we will take up this discussion anew if circumstances oblige us to do so." Thus the diplomatic accords that Delcassé had negotiated two years earlier still remained in force.

They were adequate enough to provide France, during the whole duration of the Algeciras conference, with the backing of the main group of European Powers and of the United States against German pretensions, which were supported by Austria-Hungary. The political checkerboard had not changed since Delcassé's resignation. The conference ended by recognizing the "special rights" of France in Morocco, but left the final settlement of the issue still dominated by the German shadow—which would not disappear until 1911.

The General Staff could well be satisfied with the outcome of the Moroccan crisis. It had been definitively established that the indifference of successive governments to military problems, between 1899 and 1905, and the hostility of a segment of public opinion to the Army, had led to the weakening of French power. Alerted to the danger, from now on the attempt would be made in political milieux to raise the Army from the slough of the preceding years.

The Entente Cordiale had made it possible, early in 1906, for the General Staffs to reach agreements which, if England were the ally of France against Germany, would enter in force at once and would ensure the entire efficacy of the English intervention. Yet despite this the cornerstone of French plans remained the Russian Alliance. The General Staff could agree with Wilhelm II: "Paris can't be defended by the English Fleet." Consequently everything still depended, in the event of a German offensive against the French frontiers, upon the rapidity with which a Russian offensive could menace the eastern frontiers of Germany.

But what remained of Russian military power, after the war in Manchuria? In November, 1906, the head of the French General Staff, General Brun, met his Russian counterpart, General Palitzin, in order to clear matters up. According to the written record of the conversation, General Palitzin made no secret of the fact that, should war break out between France and Germany, Russian mobilization could be carried out only "with considerable delay"—and he even refused to say anything specific "concerning the time and the zone for the assembling of the Russian contingents destined to be employed against Germany." So nothing was left of the French General Staff's efforts to set the moment for a large-scale Russian attack against the German Army at about the fifteenth day after mobilization, and the protocol signed in 1900 was no longer applicable. Now the Russian high command refused to say what delays would be necessary before the promised offensive could be undertaken. The best that General Palitzin could do was to mention April, 1907, as the time by which the Russian Army would be sufficiently reorganized to form "reliable fighting units" on the eastern front. That was all. In July of the following year, or three months after the date indicated by Palitzin, the French military attaché in St.

Petersburg returned to the assault and asked the Russians how many days would be needed, after mobilization, to move over to the offensive. General Palitzin replied that he could not yet promise any offensive against Germany.

This was the situation in the interval that separated the first from the second Moroccan crisis, which began on May 21, 1911, when General Molinier sent troops to occupy Fez, where Europeans were being held by rebels who had revolted against the authority of the Sultan. The German government let it be known that if the French troops were not withdrawn, it would reassume its "liberty of action," and it decided to exact a "pledge." On July 1 the gunboat *Panther* lay off Agadir. The main point of the negotiations that got under way as a result of the "Agadir coup" was the compensation that might be offered Germany in exchange for its withdrawal from the Moroccan affair and its acceptance of French penetration in Morocco.

The French government understood that Germany was treating Morocco as a pretext for beginning fresh negotiations, and the decision was taken to agree to these, with the intention of haggling over the amount of "compensation" asked for by Berlin. On May 7, Caillaux, still Minister of Finances but soon to become President of the Council, in a confidential conversation hinted as much to Lancken, Counsellor at the German Embassy. On June 15, the French Minister of Foreign Affairs, Cruppi, told the German Ambassador that the government would be ready for "an exchange of views concerning both North Africa and the question of the Congo and the Cameroons."

The German aim, in sending the gunboat *Panther* to Agadir, had been to exact a pledge as rapidly as possible in order to obtain from the French government the greatest possible concessions. The British government informed De Selves, the French Minister of Foreign Affairs, that it would have no part in sending a squadron to wait offshore near Agadir. Thereupon, on July 6, the French government under Caillaux, who was entirely in favor of negotiations, decided to begin conversations with Germany, and on July 8 informed the German Ambassador that it could offer compensation to Germany in the Congo region. Negotiations were begun, but interrupted on August 6, since the German demands appeared excessive to the French. As had occurred during the Agadir episode, there were in reality two series of conversations taking place, one conducted by

Caillaux, the President of the Council, and the other, the only official conversation, by the Minister of Foreign Affairs, De Selves, who was aware that the other conversations were going on. On August 20, the German Secretary of State for Foreign Affairs, Kiderlen-Wächter, left for a holiday. The press circulated rumors that a rupture had occurred, and in view of the risk of war that seemed to loom ever nearer, the French government asked the British and the Russians to state their intentions.

On August 28, the Committe of Imperial Defense met in London. On that same day Sir Edward Grey warned Paul Cambon, the French Ambassador in London, that if the Franco-German conversations should break down, Great Britain would first of all propose an international conference. "We have decided," he explained, "not to take any more active steps before learning the German reply."

On the following day, August 29, the Russian Ambassador in Paris, Isvolski, made known the attitude of his government. He had been Minister of Foreign Affairs two years before, during the crisis caused by Austria-Hungary's annexation of Bosnia-Herzegovina. At that time the French government had urged on him the greatest prudence, and had maintained that the Franco-Russian Alliance could enter into force only when questions of "vital importance" for the two countries were at stake. On this new occasion Isvolski employed the very term that the French government had used; he declared that Russia would back France as soon as its "vital interests" were involved. In Paris, it was feared that this amounted to an evasion. General Dubail was sent to St. Petersburg to confer with the chief of the Russian General Staff, General Zhilinski. The latter, without repudiating the obligations of the Franco-Russian Alliance, frankly told General Dubail that the Russian Army could not sustain a war against Germany with any real hope of success "in less than two years."

It was during this period that Caillaux asked General Joffre, who headed the French Army's General Staff: "Do you consider that in the event of war with Germany we have a 70 per cent chance of victory?" Joffre replied in the negative. Six years after French governments had ceased to be influenced by the political and moral consequences of the Dreyfus Affair, and despite the fact that a military renewal had already been under way for several years, the man occupying the Army's top post still believed that war with Germany involved enormous risks. Once more the General Staff, to the extent that its views played a part in governmental decisions, had intervened in favor of the most prudent policy.

But in the wake of the Moroccan crisis, and of the extreme tension it had provoked in Franco-German relations, there remained a permanent atmosphere of uneasiness. It was clear to all the European governments that, since 1904, international relations had entered upon a particularly dangerous phase. Now that they had "parceled out the earth," the Great Powers confronted each other directly, and the demarcation of their respective domains had already stirred up a series of conflicts that might one day lead to a world war. This was the perspective in which from now on the General Staff would have to operate.

On January 21, 1912, Poincaré as President of the Council called together a special conference to discuss the various hypotheses to be considered in the event of war with Germany. Joffre, relying on the information at his disposal on the planned German invasion of Belgium, pointed out that the French front would be considerably lengthened, even if it were assumed that the encirclement of the armies in eastern France could be prevented. If, on the other hand, French forces went through Belgium right up to the German border, all risk of encirclement would be eliminated and the front would scarcely be any longer than if Belgian neutrality had been respected. So he proposed that the French Army should enter Belgium as soon as it became known that German troops, for instance, had been concentrated in the neighborhood of Aachen. Poincaré replied that in the face of international opinion France could not shoulder the responsibility of violating Belgian neutrality. Great Britain would be particularly sensitive on this score. "At all events," he added, "it would be necessary to ascertain that a plan of this sort would not lead the British government to withdraw its aid."

The French government had every reason to be disturbed. Not only did the Army's fighting strength continue to lag considerably behind that of the Germans, there was also little certainty about the speed with which the Russian Army could intervene against Germany, in the event of war.

Consequently, on April 15, 1912, as soon as the failure of the Anglo-German discussions on the limitation of naval armaments became known, the French government sounded out the British government on the possibility of widening the scope of the Entente Cordiale, which had been signed in 1904. The suggestion was made that, in lieu of a treaty which would be contrary to the tradition and the principles of British policy, an exchange of notes might round out the diplomatic agreement, now eight years old.

At the same moment the German government introduced a bill that would augment and speed up the construction of fighting ships. Great Britain met the challenge with a new program that provided for the construction, between 1912 and 1917, of twenty-one battleships instead of fourteen. But for the intervening years the British Navy would no longer have the predominance in the North Sea that the Admiralty deemed indispensable. The British government, accordingly, decided to recall for duty in the North Sea a part of the squadrons which normally were stationed in the Mediterranean, although it was realized that the protection of Britain's sea lanes might be weakened by this move. At the same time, Italy undertook the construction of a naval base at Tobruk and Austria-Hungary decided to strengthen its fleet.

In June the British Prime Minister, Asquith, the First Lord of the Admiralty, Churchill, and the Commander-in-Chief of the British forces in the Mediterranean, Kitchener, held a conference in Malta. They decided to start discussions with the French, and to propose that the French Fleet might reinforce the Mediterranean squadron and so compensate for the weakening of the British squadrons. The British government was well aware that in exchange France would "try to obtain something similar to a defensive alliance," as a telegram from the British Ambassador in Paris expressed it.

On July 17, Churchill informed the French naval attaché in London of the British intentions with respect to the Mediterranean. He suggested that the French Fleet should be as strong there as the Italian and Austro-Hungarian Fleets combined. The French government replied that this would require the transfer of the Brest squadron to the Mediterranean and that, in such a case, it would have to be assured of the protection of the French Channel coast in the event of war between France and Germany. It was at this point that the negotiations began which were concluded in November, 1912, with an exchange of letters in which the British government promised to take steps in common with France, should war threaten, and officially approved the agreements reached between the General Staffs in 1906. Finally, in 1913, a naval agreement was reached that reflected the British views.

In the eyes of the French General Staff, these agreements with

Great Britain offered substantial prospects of additional manpower and of naval aid in the event of war with Germany. But nothing in all this was sure. Besides, French military experts were uncertain of the value of British land forces.

Thus the question of a Russian offensive, launched as soon as possible against Germany's eastern frontier, continued to be of supreme importance. In reality, the Russian General Staff had been repeating since 1905 that it was in no position to honor the obligations that it had accepted in 1892 and again in 1900. On July 13, 1912, a conference brought together the chief of the Russian General Staff and the chief of the French General Staff, General Joffre. It was on this occasion that, after Joffre had explained French plans, the chief of the Russian General Staff gave him a written declaration that in case of war 800,000 men would be concentrated against Germany and would begin their offensive "on the fifteenth day of mobilization." This was everything the French General Staff had been hoping for, for the previous twenty years.

It was indeed high time to achieve these essential objectives. The German Empire began a military effort that threatened to bring about a significant shift in the European balance of forces. In March, 1911, Germany adopted the law of the "military five-year plan." The Army was increased by 5,000 officers, 3,000 noncommissioned officers, 15,000 men, 112 machine-gun companies, batteries and technical units. In May, 1912, there were added another 2,000 officers, 7,000 noncoms, 37,000 men, two Army corps, and new machine-gun companies and new artillery units. The funds earmarked for new material, which had amounted to about 100 million marks in 1904, rose to 160 million marks in 1905, 1906 and 1907; to 200 million annually up to 1912, and then to 430 million in 1913 and 1914.

On October 13, 1912, the German government, in a conference with the high command, decided to strengthen its armed forces to make up for the weakening of Austria-Hungary after the Balkan wars; it was to be foreseen that in the event of war the bulk of the Austro-Hungarian forces would have to be concentrated in the Balkans and so could provide Germany with no significant aid on the Russian front. This decision was recorded in a memorandum drawn up by the head of the General Staff's Bureau of Operations, General Ludendorff, and signed by the chief of the General Staff, General von Moltke.

On June 30, 1913, a new military law was accepted by the Reichstag. The manpower of the German Army in peacetime was raised, for soldiers alone, from 628,000 to 760,000 men by the end of 1913, and then to 820,000 men in October, 1914. The German Army would comprise 42,000 officers and 112,000 noncoms. In the spring of 1914 it would contain twenty-five Army corps in the field, eleven cavalry divisions and twenty-eight reserve divisions immediately utilizable in the front lines.

Simultaneously, the information reaching the French government concerning the German government's intentions became more alarming. In January, 1913, the French Ambassador in Berlin, Jules Cambon, and the military attaché, Colonel Serret, wrote as follows: "Little is being said any more of the rupture that has occurred in the Balkan equilibrium, and it is avowed that Germany must have great ambitions: 'we are a country in full expansion, we have more than seventy million inhabitants, we have the right to a place in the sun, we must have colonies.'"

In November, 1913, in a private conversation with King Albert I of Belgium, Emperor Wilhelm II said that the political situation was grave, that France was to blame and that "war is necessary and inevitable." The French government was at once informed of these remarks. In January, 1914, repeating an opinion that the German General Staff had been voicing for some months previously, the chief of the General Staff, von Moltke, wrote: "The moment is so favorable from the military point of view that nothing to equal it will ever come again," and he expressed the hope that war would soon break out against France.

Everything was now ready for making a reality of the total solution of the military crisis that had been set off by the Dreyfus Affair. There would be an over-all strengthening of the Army. The political realignment that had been achieved at the expense of the Socialist and trade union movement permitted the liquidation of all antimilitarist feeling at the very center of government. The calling out of the Army against strikers and the final exhaustion of the Republican parties' anticlerical program etablished a rapprochement between military and political personnel. The extreme Left, with its traditional antimilitarism, would remain out of power. No one in politics had any desire to see a resumption of the military crisis that had marked the first years of the century; all strove to put the relationship between Army and state on a normal basis. From 1906 on, the press repeatedly referred to the danger of a new conflict with Germany, and the country began to live on a footing of almost permanent alert.

This rediscovered ardor enabled the Army to mount the slope it had descended. The renovation of material, the increase in manpower, the reorganization of the high command, the improvement in officering, all this necessarily depended on the funds available for defense purposes. To a Parliament whose legitimate suspicions of the Army's upper echelons had been aroused, the sums asked had always seemed too onerous. "The credits asked by the various Ministers were never refused," wrote Joffre, speaking of Parliament, "but they were forced to ask only for what the Minister of Finances, in agreement with the parliamentary commissions, considered it possible to allocate to each branch." The Minister of War would reveal to the Senate, as late as July 14, 1914, that of all the credits requested by the Army between 1901 and 1911, one-third had been deducted by the governments even before the credits were discussed in both Houses. "The credits requested by the Ministers of War were never refused by the Ministers of Finances, no indeed! But very often, as the result of discussions that took place in the Council of Ministers, the War Ministers were persuaded to reduce the amounts requested."

So several years inevitably elapsed before the restoration of French military power was feasible. In practice, as always occurs under a parliamentary regime, the military credits were the object of bitter debate. In November, 1911, the General Staff had drawn up a program requiring 246 million francs for manufactures declared to be "very urgent," but the realization of which was to be spread over five years. In January, 1912, a new government cut down this program to fifty million, but in December of the same year the worsening of the international situation caused by the Balkan War made it possible to increase the armaments program to 450 million and in March, 1913, after another change of government, to 924 million. But this amount was reduced to 450 million, at the request of the Minister of Finances. The General Staff returned to the charge and had the War Minister present a program calling for 1,400 million. In December, 1913, a new shift in government allowed the War Minister to ask that the program of 1,400 million be voted through. Two weeks after the measure was finally passed by both Houses, war was declared.

In 1913, Parliament voted a general increase of pay for all ranks. In the same year the number of warrant officers who could be directly commissioned was doubled. But these decisions could have no immediate effect. In 1914 the French Army had still only 29,000 officers compared with 42,000 in Germany, and 48,000 noncoms against Germany's 112,000.

In 1905, Germany had begun to manufacture a rapid-fire 77-millimeter cannon, a 105-millimeter howitzer and a heavy 150-millimeter howitzer. On the French side, there was nothing to set against them but the famous 75-millimeter, which in the Army School was said to be "God the Father, God the Son and God the Holy Ghost." It was not until 1911 that Joffre was able to persuade the government that the Army arsenals and private industry should investigate the possibilities of a long cannon with a greater range than the 75-millimeter.

On mobilization day, the French arsenals had 2,500 automatic weapons against the German Army's 4,500, only 3,800 75-millimeter guns as compared with 6,000 77-millimeter guns in the German Army. Each German Army corps had at its disposition thirty-six 105-millimeter howitzers and sixteen 150-millimeter howitzers, while as Army artillery there was a large number of 210-millimeter howitzers and of long cannon of 100 and 130 millimeters. All this was modern equipment, whereas in comparison the French Army had no howitzers and was still using only some 155 Rimailhos and 120 Baquets, designed thirty years before. The situation was even worse with respect to siege artillery for which, according to the statement made by the Inspector General of Artillery in 1914, "nothing had been done for forty years."

The General Staff and the War Ministry showed more imagination where aviation was concerned. The early flights undertaken by Ader, Ferber and Wright were encouraged and investigated by the services of the War Ministry. Airplanes took part in the Army's annual maneuvers, in the very year that Blériot crossed the Channel. In 1910 a "General Inspectorate of Aeronautics" was set up in the Engineers Administration. In 1911 the General Staff formed military squadrons. Colonel Renard directed a service concerned with ballooning and personally supervised the construction of supple dirigible balloons, and on March 29, 1912, Parliament passed a bill organizing military aeronautics. In 1914 the French Army would comprise twenty-one Army squadrons, two cavalry squadrons, five dirigibles and four ballooning companies, twelve sections of which would man captive balloons, while another twelve would employ balloons in area protection. However, on mobilization the French Army would have only 136 airplanes against 220 available for the German General Staff.

French military leaders, aware of the increasing gap between France's armed might and that of Germany, needed to know exactly on what they could count, in the event of war. Since the General Staff's protocol of 1912, a Russian offensive was planned against Germany's eastern frontier, to be launched on the fifteenth day after mobilization. It was still necessary to know whether this offensive would be sufficiently effective and powerful to divert to the Russian front the greatest possible proportion of Germany's armed might.

In March, 1913, the nomination of Delcassé as Ambassador to Russia had as its main aim the strengthening of the Franco-Russian Alliance on every level, political, financial and military. The written instructions with which the government provided him envisaged in particular a fresh effort to induce Russia to increase her military potential. The real objective of the French government and General Staff was, if possible, to reduce the delays in mobilization and concentration of the Russian troops. Delcassé's representations proved successful. The year of his arrival in St. Petersburg, in 1913, the Czar's government voted through a military program that involved a very considerable increase in armaments and fighting strength. But the program would take four years to complete, and so develop its full effect only in 1917. The Germans naturally concluded that the balance of forces would be much more favorable for them in 1914 than in 1917.

The French General Staff realized this, too. It also possessed information on the military situation in Europe, if war should break out, of which the Germans knew nothing, and this information was far from reassuring. In 1913, the British Imperial Staff told the French that it would have to whittle down the obligations it had assumed under the secret military accords concluded between France and Great Britain. The grave disturbances that had broken out in Ireland forced the British government to reserve a part of its forces for that country. In these conditions, the British General Staff could send only five divisions, instead of six, to French territory. Furthermore, the French General Staff was constantly being reminded by the government that it was only a possibility, and not a certainty, that Great Britain would enter the war alongside France. As late as the early part of 1914, a note from the chief of the Army's General Staff stressed this: "We will act wisely by making no allowance for the English expeditionary corps in our plans of operations."

The ratio of forces was threatening to become catastrophic for

France. With two years of military service, the French Army had 540,000 men, and the German Army 850,000. No system of alliances and no increase in matériel could bridge this gap. From one day to the next, in the event of war, the enemy might cross the frontiers, with the French Army unable to do more than fight defensive actions offering small chance of success.

What could be done, if war should break out, to confront a German Army with twice the manpower and twice the matériel? A series of debates took place in the Army Council. The crux of the matter was how to provide greater "cover" for the French frontiers, so that reserves could be mobilized behind this shelter. To do this it would be necessary to strengthen the standing army. In succession proposals were examined that would extend the period of service to twenty-seven months, to thirty months and to three years. Briand addressed the same question to each of the generals who were members of the Army Council: "Do you believe that it is impossible to provide for the country's defenses without introducing a full three-year service period?" Each in turn replied "yes."

The three-year Bill was voted through on July 19, 1913. The general elections of 1914, with the traditional "republican discipline" holding firm, resulted in a left-wing majority dominated by the Socialists and the Radical-Socialists. It might seem that the three-year service law would be discarded. But Poincaré had decided to "fight for the law." He deliberately chose as President of the Council Viviani, an Independent Socialist. Viviani was informed of the warnings that the German Emperor had uttered in the presence of the King of the Belgians, in which he characterized a war as "inevitable and necessary." He decided to postpone any discussion of the period of military service.

War, at this juncture, was about to be declared. In purely military terms, the balance sheet of the political transformation that had occurred since 1905 had much on the credit side. This transformation would no doubt never have occurred so rapidly, nor in this precise form, if the defense of bourgeois society against the Socialist and syndicalist advance had not appeared in political circles to be the first desideratum of the new era. No doubt, too, these same political circles would never have evolved in this direction if the economic upsurge, business profits and general prosperity had not aroused in the French bourgeoisie a feeling of strength, vigor and even of pride that enabled them to face Socialist demands with the same energy they would apply to international difficulties. The return to issues of national scope, and the insistence on internal discipline, were tied up with the international crises provoked by the "parceling out of the earth," and by the repeated war alarms that marked the period between 1904 and 1914.

This historical movement was inevitably reflected in the profound change in public opinion, in Army circles and even among the intellectuals.

Between 1907 and 1914 there were nine Ministers of Foreign Affairs, eight Ministers of Finances, seven Ministers of the Navy, nine War Ministers and twelve Presidents of the Council. And, at that, some men occupied the same position more than once. During this period there were only two chiefs of the Army's General Staff, Brugère and Joffre. This stability, and the concentration of supreme responsibility in the hands of two men, served in itself to restore to the Army cadres the climate of calm and confidence that had so greatly suffered during the fury of the Dreyfus Affair.

Messimy, as Minister of War, not only appointed the General who would serve as Supreme Commander in the event of war to be Vice-President of the Army Council, a function that was already his; he also conferred on him the title of Chief of the General Staff (Chef d'État-Major Général), which gave him authority over the Army's General Staff. The first deputy chief of the Army's General Staff was appointed Major General of the Armies in the Field. The chief of the Army's General Staff would remain, if mobilization took place, attached to the Ministry of War and the government. Joffre, as Chef d'État-Major Général, had at his disposition, a "Committee of the General Staff" and a "Center of Advanced Studies," intended to prepare the chiefs of the General Staffs of the Army corps and of the Army. Each Army commandant had at his disposal, in peacetime, a chief of the General Staff and a chief of the Bureau of Operations appointed to serve in time of war. Finally, when Millerand became Minister of War, the post of chief of the Army's General Staff was attached to that of the Chef d'État-Major Général. However useful this reorganization of the high command may have been, its value depended entirely on the man whose abilities were thus called upon. In this sense, the decisions taken were to have immense consequences.

In 1910, when a new supreme commander for wartime had to

be named to replace General Fémau, the candidature of General Pau appeared the strongest, on the basis of the functions he had already exercised. But the Council of Ministers would have none of him "because he went to Mass." This crisis in the high command which had existed since the Dreyfus Affair, was not brought to an end until after the nomination of General Joffre, in 1911, as Chef d'État-Major Général. And with Joffre it was the Colonial Army which for the first time took over the highest military responsibility.

For the previous forty years, the officers who served overseas had led an existence totally unlike that of their comrades who remained in France. It is an established fact that, during the ten years that followed the defeat of 1871, almost all the best officers preferred to remain in metropolitan France rather than accept assignments to the colonial troops. For the great thing was to prepare the *revanche* against Germany. Many are the "memoirs" and novels written by officers who evoked the fear of being "out of it" when the long-awaited opportunity would finally arrive to do battle and retake Alsace-Lorraine.

In his series of popular novels that relate the story of a dynasty of officers in the nineteenth century, Captain Danrit brings on the stage pupils at Saint-Cyr in the 1880's who are amazed that one of their number should prefer the marines, which then constituted the main strength of the colonial troops, to the battalion of chasseurs or the cavalry regiment quartered in eastern France. Later on, it became clear that newly commissioned officers were motivated by a desire to find overseas the adventures that seemed ever to elude the grasp of those who remained in the Vosges.

Among the men who were fifty or sixty years old in 1910 there were very few who had of their own free will chosen to serve in Africa or China. Joffre had set off for the China Seas to forget his romantic sufferings. Lyautey had gone to Tonkin, on the advice of the chief of the Army's General Staff, General de Boisdeffre, so that people might forget the scandal caused in military circles by the publication of his article on "The Social Role of Officers." A special bond united those who had served in the Colonial Army, whether mere chance or some fluke of destiny had whisked them away from France, or whether they had foreseen, rather more promptly than their comrades, that military adventures would be found overseas at the turn of the century.

These officers had already a long tradition behind them. There can scarcely be any doubt that almost all of them, as they took part in the colonial wars, did it with a "clear conscience." On this point, they are in accord with the spirit of their time. In the conquering, triumphant bourgeois society that still ruled over nineteenth-century Europe, to conquer Africa or Asia meant to "civilize" them.

No one was hypocritical enough to gloss over the economic, commercial or strategic reasons that determined colonial expansion. The history of the world was being made by a few Great Powers, almost all of them European; and in this universal slicing of the cake, Africa and Asia were treated primarily as the "objects" of Great Power politics.

The spirit of adventure generally outweighed all other considerations, in the officers' eyes. But the best among them at once discovered the civilizing mission of colonial warfare.

Actual combat was relatively rare, and it interrupted long periods of tranquillity. The greater part of the Army, almost everywhere, was principally occupied in administrative duties, in supervision of territories, in building and pacification. Gallieni's "instructions," dated May 22, 1898, remained the charter of the Colonial Army right up to 1914:

> We must bear in mind that in colonial conflicts, which are, unfortunately, often forced on us by the unruliness of the population, we must never destroy except in the last extremity and, even when this is unavoidable, bring ruin only in order to build better. . . .
> Every time that warlike incidents oblige one of our colonial officers to proceed against a village or occupied center, he must never lose sight of the fact that his first responsibility, once the submission of the inhabitants has been assured, is to reconstruct the village, to set up a market in it and build a school.

Nothing better reveals the spirit that imbued the best officers of the Colonial Army than the meeting that took place in 1914 between Commandant Lyautey and Colonel Gallieni. The first referred to the second as a "despiser of conventions . . . hater of the whole striped bureaucracy." The first thing to strike the officers in the colonies was the magnificent contrast between their new life and the stultifying monotony of garrison existence, with its fear of shouldering responsibility or of incurring a reprimand, and the constant preoccupation with the list of promotions. "Here," wrote Lyautey from Tonkin, "you won't find a single little lieutenant, responsible for a post and in charge of reconnoitering, who within six months does not develop more initiative, will power, endurance and personality than does an officer stationed in France throughout his whole career. . . ."

Finally, in the ten years that preceded World War I, this whole generation of colonial officers came to occupy the Army's highest posts. Joffre may have played a decisive part in their advancement. He had a natural tendency to favor the officers from the overseas forces, for he knew that their service records, in the Colonial Army, were more outstanding or more convincing than the careers that the officers remaining in metropolitan France had tranquilly traversed. Gallieni acted in the same way. Little by little, the Army's upper echelons came to be populated by colonial officers.

Just before war broke out, if we except Joffre and Gallieni, most of these officers were not yet in positions of the highest importance. But after the first few weeks of combat, when the hour had come to make a pitiless selection among the general officers, Joffre gave most of the important commands to those whose careers had been spent overseas. Among them were Henrys, Guillaumat, Degoutte, Mangin, Gouraud and Franchet d'Esperey. In political circles there never arose the same prejudice against these men that still persisted against the generals from the "Jesuit warren"—against General de Castelnau, for example. Joffre had insisted that he serve as Major General of the Armies for the first three years of the war, but he was never named Marshal of France.

In 1891, *La Revue des Deux Mondes* had published an anonymous article that would remain a significant event in French military thought. The author of this article, "Concerning the Social Role of the Officer in Universal Military Service," was Captain Hubert Lyautey, then attached to the fourth regiment of cavalry chasseurs. His whole argument was summed up in the sentence: "The legal obligation to do military service is matched by the corresponding moral obligation to ensure that it shall produce the most salutary consequences from the social point of view." Lyautey observed that "the officer fights no more, or at least no more frequently, than any other citizen." He called on his comrades in arms to become the educators of the men entrusted to their charge. Otherwise, he declared, the Army would offer nothing to the millions of men who would have to pass through its ranks but "a weakened moral sense, a disdain for a simple, laborious life, and on the physical plane habits of intemperance and a vitiated blood."

Twenty years had to pass before the ideas expressed by Lyautey received official consecration. In 1901, General André, the War

Minister who incarnated, in the eyes of officers like Lyautey, politicking corruption and a sectarian Masonic spirit, nevertheless set out on the path indicated by the young royalist officer in his celebrated article published in *La Revue des Deux Mondes*. For the first time, he arranged that a course should be given at Saint-Cyr on the officer's social mission. Major Ebener taught it, and his outlook was to influence a long series of budding officers.

What was new about this was not the desire to give a greater human and educative value to the relations between officers and men. It was, rather, the spirit that imbued the advocates of the "social role of the officer." Lyautey, as a student at Saint-Cyr, had founded a group for social action at the same time his friend Antonin de Margerie was doing the same thing at Polytechnique. Both of them, along with another young officer, La Bouillerie, took part in the activities of the Workers' Circles that had been started by a former cavalry officer, the royalist deputy Albert de Mun and the future military attaché in Vienna, Major de la Tour du Pin. Nothing is more characteristic than the association of these names.

For this was the period when certain social ideas were stirring whose origins lay in the work of the Catholic sociologist Le Play. Embodying an outlook that was in reality more strongly traditional than reformist, these ideas took issue with the social egoism, optimistic and pitiless at the same time, of the liberal bourgeoisie that dominated French society. Among the old rural aristocracy or in some families of the provincial conservative bourgeoisie, the tradition lingered on of the obligations of the "castle" with respect to the "cottage," or, more profoundly, the tradition of protection and aid, of support and charity, inspired by a chivalrous spirit and Catholic morality. A natural evolution led the men imbued with this tradition to revolt against the irreducible wretchedness of the workers' districts in the large towns.

Frédéric Ozanam was the man who, better than anyone else, incarnated this evolution. His teachings had a profound effect in all conservative milieux. He was at the source of the whole Catholic social movement which undertook the first great effort to reconcile Catholicism and the modern world. The aristocratic, bourgeois and conservative families the most remote from business interests and from all industrial and commercial activities were, it so happened, those who provided the highest proportion of pupils in the great military schools. Thus the teaching of Ozanam, of Albert de Mun and of the Encyclical *De rerum novarum* found its most fertile soil in these groups of officers whose life brought them into contact with the realities of French people's lives. At the beginning of the century and, even more markedly, after the Army found it desirable to establish a cleavage between itself and the political turmoil of the Dreyfus Affair, this current of thought had a deep influence on the military hierarchy.

It seemed at the time as though the Army was trying to seek refuge in a moral austerity that might restore its lost prestige. This austerity, this return to a higher ideal, this refusal of the struggle of cliques and of political adventures, such was the countenance exhibited by the Army only a few years before World War I broke out. This new attitude signaled a return to the values appropriate to military life: indifference to money, the desire to serve, even in obscurity, the sacrifice of all the advantages that could be produced in a society growing steadily richer, and silent abnegation.

Throughout French society, indeed, a reaction was taking place against a system of values that had seemed unassailable up to the beginning of the century. The massive development of business, the robust health of the capitalist economy, the pride of the bourgeoisie which would deny any share of its own wealth to the workers it employed in its factories, in a word, all this self-confident prosperity was bound to provoke, in some, a reaction against a social climate so unfavorable to mysticism, to metaphysics, to the cult of ancient values that still had their charm for certain spirits. "In the domain of the intellect," wrote de Gaulle, "the advent of such men as Boutroux and Bergson, who renewed French spirituality; the influence that secretly radiated from Péguy; the precocious maturity of young men who felt that the reaper was at hand; and, in letters, the influence of a Barrès, who reawakened in the elite the sense of national eternity by revealing the bonds that united it with its ancestors, are both the effects and the causes of this restoration whose stippled outline can scarcely even be sketched by a contemporary, but which history will delineate with bold strokes."

At this juncture two young intellectuals of the Right, Henri Massis and André Detartre, using the pseudonym of Agathon, set out to investigate the attitude of bourgeois youth. The answers were characterized almost without exception by a kind of nationalist exaltation, by a strong desire for action, force and conflict. They range from a purely intellectual position to an apology for war itself. "Life is not a dialectic," wrote a student, "it is neither intellectual nor critical, but vigorous." Others thought that "France needs heroism to live" and saw "in war an ideal esthetic of energy and force." More concretely, a student confessed: "It is in the life of the camps and under fire that we will experience the supreme flowering of the French forces that dwell in us."

Symbols of the evolution of a whole generation of intellectuals, Charles Péguy and Ernest Psichari ran the gamut from the humanitarian and liberal outlook of the nineteenth century to the exaltation of faith, honor and sacrifice. This would receive its tragic incarnation in the trials of world war.

Charles Péguy, student at the École Normale Supérieure and a Dreyfusard, a poet who was the friend of Léon Blum and Jean Jaurès, would later celebrate the glory of the soldiers about to die, of the peasants who bent over their humble village earth, and of the mothers who lived only for their sons.

Ernest Psichari, the grandson of Renan and son of university people, enlisted in the Colonial Army after obtaining his *licence* in philosophy. He described his itinerary in his novel, *L'Appel des armes*. It expresses with all possible force the return of the Army to the austerity, to the bare essentials and to the purity of its old ideal. The hero of the book speaks of this as "the great force of the past . . . the only one which, together with the Church, remains virgin and unsoiled, untainted by the new impurity. . . . The Army can find in itself its morality, its law and its *mystique*." Even the minutiae of the book reflects these bare essentials. The hero of the novel lives in a hut of dried mud whose only ornament is a wooden shelf on which are ranged Bossuet's *Sermons*, Pascal's *Pensées*, the *Règlement d'artillerie de campagne*, a table of logarithms and Vigny's *Servitude et grandeur militaires*.

Charles Péguy and Ernest Psichari—these two men symbolized the need for meditation that would be felt by a segment of French youth, as though they sensed that they were growing up only to make a supreme sacrifice. Another little while and they would at last discover the meaning of their existence, of the thirty million years of military service that Frenchmen had spent under arms, silent, dreary years in which life seemed to ebb out uselessly.

Charles Péguy spoke to this whole youthful generation when he dedicated to Ernest Psichari his *"Ode guerrière,"* which winds up his greatest poem:

Vous qui avez un sabre, et c'est pour vous en servir!

(You who have a saber, a saber you will use!)

CHAPTER SIX

THE FIRST WORLD WAR

✠

On August 1, 1914, at about five o'clock in the afternoon, municipal employees and rural policemen put up a notice on the wall of post offices, schools and town halls. General mobilization was proclaimed for the following day.

In the days immediately preceding mobilization, anxious waiting gradually gave way to vertigo before the unknown. July 31 was the baptismal day of the entering class of Saint-Cyr. Jean Allard-Meus, a veteran of the previous class, recited these lines to the future officers:

> *Soldats de notre illustre race,*
> *Dormez, vos souvenirs sont beaux . . .*
> *Dormez, par delà les frontières*
> *Vous dormirez bientôt chez nous.*

> (Soldiers of our illustrious race,
> Sleep, your memories are happy ones . . .
> Sleep, beyond the frontiers
> You will soon sleep at home.)

To the thousand pupils of Saint-Cyr who heard this appeal for the reconquest of Alsace-Lorraine, it sounded like the final summons to action. One of their number, Gaston Voizard, called out: "Let us swear that we will go to battle in parade uniform, with plume and white gloves!" The oath taken by these youths, on the eve of the trench warfare that was to drag out for four years, is one of the last

93

pieces of bravura linking the old military tradition, made up of splendid gestures and pointless sacrifices, with the military epoch about to begin—an epoch of anonymous masses, heavy artillery, poison gas and millions of tons of steel and concrete. Jean Allard-Meus and Gaston Voizard were granted just enough time to experience this transition from one epoch to another, the former dying on August 22, 1914, and the latter on April 9, 1915.

The almost religious fervor of these young officers, who finally saw the moment arrive when the ideal of their adolescence would take on flesh, was matched by a more elementary popular reaction. The "Farewells of the Gare de l'Est" will always remain a kind of historical snapshot that reveals the collective blindness to the reality of modern warfare, and the extraordinary national discipline that then existed in every European country. "Whoever failed to see Paris, this morning and yesterday," wrote Charles Péguy on August 3, "has seen nothing."

Songs and warlike slogans helped to make the moment of leave-taking bearable. With no thought for the balance of forces and the possibility of defeat, the noisy conviction was expressed that victory would be easy and rapid. There were shouts of "To Berlin!" and "Down with the Prussians!" The enthusiasm of the crowd rose to delirium; the soldiers were pelted with flowers.

In the villages, the leavetaking was harder. There was no crowd, no band, no popular enthusiasm to hide the simple truth that the men were going. "They listened to the tocsin," relates an eyewitness, "as though it were the funeral bell." The anguished glance toward the morrow far outweighed patriotic fervor. "Who will finish the harvest?" the peasant families asked each other. "Will they be back for the grape-gathering?" In his *Travel Notebook* a sergeant, a university teacher in civilian life, noted that the young peasants who shared his barrack room were "sick at heart."

Four million men were immediately affected by the mobilization order. Needless to say, this represented an upheaval not only in every-day life, but also in the administrative, economic and social organization of the country.

Each individual Frenchman would now have the concrete experience of the "nation under arms," of the idea that for years had played such a part in the debates of military experts, the theories of sociologists and the hopes and fears of the politicians. Perhaps there had been an unconscious preparation for this vast collective upheaval that would standardize the lives of so many men, down to the last detail of their dress, their nourishment, their daily tasks, their waking and sleeping hours, even their vocabulary. "For several generations past," wrote de Gaulle in *La France et son armée,*

> the combined influence of universal suffrage, the equality of rights and obligations, and compulsory schooling, had tended to shape the whole nation in a single mold. Industry and urban life were eliminating local characteristics. Mass production was making the same manufactured objects available to all. The newspapers led people to concern themselves with the same topics. The mobility of capital created a wide range of interests. Parties, trade unions and sporting events gave a powerful push to collective feelings. Communications, travel and hygiene induced all to accept countless shared constraints. In short, this uniform, gregarious and hasty existence imposed by the mechanization of the age on all its contemporaries predisposed them to accept the surging mass movements, the enormous, scarcely varying clashes, that characterized the war of peoples.

This was no longer the day when wars could run their course without affecting everyday life, or the nation continue almost untouched by the maneuvering of professional armies. Nor was it possible any longer to consider the Army as separate from the Nation or the state. From now on the Army was made up of millions of ordinary citizens, no less than of professional warriors. Politics could not be pursued with slight regard for the outcome of the fighting, and that outcome would depend so closely on the economic mobilization organized by the government and on the alliances it had concluded, that military problems were entirely transformed. The arguments opposing a professional army to a militia were outdated, and officers were recruited from every mobilizable class.

Despite national unanimity, public opinion did not lose any of its delicate shadings and radical contradictions. "We, the soldiers of the Republic," wrote Charles Péguy in his *Cahiers de la Quinzaine,* "marched off on behalf of universal disarmament and the last of all wars." In the press of the Left and in Radical and Republican circles, the war that had just begun was being fought for "the right" and for "the liberty of peoples."

The French Republic was locked in combat against the old traditional monarchies of Germany and Austria-Hungary. France's Republican Army confronted an army of emperors, kings and princes. The violation of Belgian neutrality lent greater weight to the arguments advanced on the Left. Austria-Hungary had tried to crush little Serbia, and now the German Empire was violating "international law," repudiating all treaties and discarding any appearance of moral justification for its actions. On the Left, there was a ready and genuine fusion of the most elemental national or even nationalist feeling with fidelity to the old liberal principles that condemned the monarchies and favored the defense of small countries and weak nations.

Left-wing opinion soon adopted the notion that the war must lead to the liberation of the last nationalities oppressed by the German and Austro-Hungarian empires. After all, Austria-Hungary had exacerbated the crisis resulting from the assassination of Archduke Ferdinand in order to exert domination over the new Slavic peoples. Was it not logical to think that the defeat of these two Empires would lead to the liberation of all the nationalities that had not yet attained independence: Croats, Slovenes and Czechoslovaks? For France itself, the return of Alsace-Lorraine from German annexation was the only clear war aim. The idea of a liberal France doing battle against militaristic and oppressive monarchies was sufficiently popular abroad to induce 40,000 foreigners, Poles, Czechs and Jews of Central and Eastern Europe, to enlist at once, after war had been declared, in the Foreign Legion.

Republican France fighting for "the right" and for the freedom of peoples, that was France as most Frenchmen undoubtedly saw it.

Conservative right-wing opinion, with its monarchist and clerical tradition, would discover anew the visage of "eternal France," the France of Joan of Arc and St. Genevieve rising up against the modern "Huns." Now, perhaps for the first time in two generations, all these conservative families could love the whole of France without the restrictions, hesitations and disillusionment aroused by a secular, anti-clerical Republic. Nationalist and conservative opinion had long awaited the rebirth of this France that the war now brought them: unified, unmindful of the class struggle, and freed from the "altercations of the parties." Revealing in this respect are the letters sent home by the combatants who came from old Catholic and military families. Astonished and timid, first of all, but then delighted at finding themselves on close terms with "republicans," "freemasons" or, more simply, with primary schoolteachers and working men, they felt that they had been welcomed back into a national community from which they had been banned since their dreams of a monarchist restoration had faded, and especially since the great republican drive against the Church had begun.

The reaction of these young Catholic officers had perhaps an even deeper source. At the heart of the matter, France was perhaps working out its redemption for all the "faults" committed by Frenchmen since they had turned away from traditional values, the old order, religious faith, and respect for the political and social authority that had been spurned by the Republic. The priests in the trenches would dissipate numerous prejudices harbored by a considerable section of the French public against anything in the least clerical. The young scions of the old aristocratic and monarchist families, by their conduct under fire, would gain the admiration of their comrades of different social origins; they would win a renown that would put an end to their exile in the midst of the nation; and their families would later put it to good use in their dealings with the political and administrative world that so long had been closed to them.

The journalists of the Right had already begun to speak of the "pacifist ideology" and the "internationalist dreams" which, they maintained, had led France to the edge of disaster, weakened the indispensable national watchfulness and so caused the unpreparedness that accounted for the war's earlier reverses.

But these "internationalist dreams" were those of all the Socialists in the world, and especially of the French Socialists. The world of the workers was still resounding with the cry uttered by the old Swiss militant Grülich, at the Basle Congress, in the midst of the Balkan conflict: "War on war!" If one conviction was universally shared by every nuance of Socialist opinion, it was that conflicts between states represented a particularly debased form of the subjection of men by the capitalist bourgeoisies in their struggle for the world's wealth, whatever misery and bloodshed might be caused. "Humanity is accursed," Jean Jaurès had said, "if to prove its courage it is condemned to perpetual slaughter."

The moment that news arrived of the ultimatum addressed by Austria-Hungary to Serbia on July 23, the International Socialist Bureau decided to meet. During the four preceding weeks, the relative secrecy of the diplomatic steps taken had prevented international public opinion from clearly perceiving the danger of war. The danger of a world conflict did not seem imminent either in Socialist milieux, which had no share in the responsibilities of power, or in working-class circles.

The meeting of the International Socialist Bureau took place in Brussels on July 29 and 30. The Austrian Socialists warned their comrades that they could not oppose the decision of the Austro-Hungarian government to begin a war, if this decision was irrevocable. On the previous day, July 28, Austria-Hungary had declared war on Serbia, thus undermining any new English, Russian or French attempts to find a diplomatic solution for the crisis touched off by the murder of the Archduke Franz Ferdinand. Given the nature of the Czarist regime in Russia, the Bureau insisted on the importance of the role allotted the French and German workers. Theirs was the task, it was thought, to exert pressure on their respective governments so that Germany might restrain the bellicosity of Austria-Hungary, and France dissuade Russia from entering the war. On the evening of July 30, a public meeting against the war was organized. It was to be the last that would bring together all European Socialists before they were scattered by the winds of war. It was also the last time that Jean Jaurès would address them: the following day, in Paris, he was assassinated.

On that same day, July 31, the German Social-Democrats discussed the attitude they should adopt on August 4, when the Reichstag would have to vote war supplies. Those who counseled a negative vote numbered fourteen. Apart from a few deputies who recommended abstention, all the others had already decided to vote in favor. The only step taken was to send Hermann Müller to Brussels and Paris, in order to harmonize the attitude of French and German Socialists.

By the time that Müller had made contact with the French leaders, on the afternoon of August 1, Germany had already declared war on Russia and called on France to make her intentions known; the French government, in reply, had ordered general mobilization. The French Socialists made it plain that they would have to vote the war supplies if France was attacked. Müller thought that it was a difficult matter to distinguish between defensive and aggressive war, since the International Socialist Bureau had condemned the very principle of all war.

There was a lack of reality in this whole debate. The German Socialists had formerly been among those most insistent on the distinction between defensive and aggressive war. They could not deny that Austria-Hungary had taken the initiative by declaring war on Serbia, nor that Germany had replied to Russian mobilization by herself declaring war against Russia.

The French Socialists could draw no other conclusion than that war was certain and that the two empires of Central Europe had taken the risk and grasped the initiative. Doubtless they were unaware that, if France had decided to remain neutral, Germany would at once have demanded the occupation of Verdun, Épinal and Toul. Nor could they know that two days later the German government, eager to allow its General Staff to push through its plans in every detail, would itself declare war on France. Their proclaimed intention to refrain from voting for war supplies, unless France should be attacked, could have had no practical application.

So the following day, August 2, at the meeting of the Central Executive Committee of the Unified Socialist Party held in the Salle Wagram—this was the first day of general mobilization—there was no hesitation: if France was attacked, the Socialists would vote for the supplies. The next day, August 3, Germany declared war. On that day, the Social-Democratic Parliamentary Group of the Reichstag met. Their old leader, Karl Kautsky, although not a deputy, was invited to take part in the discussion. He first recommended abstention but, finding that the majority was opposed to this, asked that to the vote in favor should be attached certain conditions, especially "that the moment that the war became a war of conquest, the Social Democrats would oppose it energetically."

On the following day Chancellor Bethmann-Hollweg induced them to abandon this condition, and their declaration in favor was read at the opening of the Reichstag session. Only later did the Chancellor announce the violation of Belgian neutrality and the entry of Great Britain into the war. The Social Democrats were the first European Socialists to vote in favor of war supplies. They did it with no dissenting vote, those opposed bowing to party discipline.

Five days had elapsed between the first meeting of the International Socialist Bureau on July 29 and the decision reached by the Social Democrats on August 3. During this time the whole mechanism leading to the eruption of a world war had rolled implacably on, reducing to nothing the traditional protest of the Socialist and workers' movement against "capitalist wars."

In addition to this immense disappointment at realizing their own weakness, and the slight effect of their ideas and slogans, the French Socialists made, concurrently, a discovery that would have far-reaching consequences. They took the view that internationalism had arrived "too early" for the nations. No ideology had shown any real strength as compared with the elemental, passionate reactions of all the European peoples when faced by war. In every social class, among the workers no less than elsewhere, patriotism had swept all before it and its simplest and most spontaneous manifestations had been the most convincing.

The only way out for French Socialism was to support this war "for the right and for freedom," and to adopt the idea of republican France as the natural protectress of small peoples menaced by German hegemony, the idea of a war waged by the democracies against the autocratic empires, and which would be the last of all wars.

At Jaurès's funeral, one of the speakers was Léon Jouhaux, secretary of the organization that two years before had hurled its anathema against "militarism and patriotism." "In the name of the trade union organizations," he declared solemnly, "in the name of all the workers who have already joined their regiments and of those, of whom I am one, who are to leave tomorrow, I declare that we are going to the battlefield with the firm intention of repulsing the aggressor." At the Sorbonne, that sanctuary of the secular, republican educational system, and main theater of the struggle against clericalism and traditional dogmas, a patriotic ceremony brought together intellectuals of the most diverse views to celebrate their own *"union sacrée."* On August 26, two Socialists entered the government: Jules Guesde, who had introduced Marxism into France; and Marcel Sembat, whose book *Faites un roi, sinon faites la paix,* had prophesied that the Republic could not survive a conflict. Thus on all sides, in the national community created by the war, the Army became the highest and most perfect symbol of the *union sacrée,* reawakening the old fervor that had prevailed during the quarter century following the defeat of 1871.

The entire conflict was to amount to a prolonged attempt on the part of the states involved, of the peoples and the General Staffs, to adapt themselves to the unexpected strategic and tactical requirements of modern war.

Certain visual images are striking. Between Detaille's painting representing "The Maneuvers of 1877" and a photograph showing Poincaré at the maneuvers of 1913, there are far more points of resemblance than of difference. The uniforms are similar, and the packs practically identical. There are men on foot, wearing soft kepis, in a rural setting of haystacks and church towers; a few peasants or bourgeois are visible in the background. Almost forty years had intervened, but this is the same army, fighting in the open country and running on hillsides to attack the enemy with fixed bayonets, urged on by their mounted officers.

Two years later everything has changed. A photograph taken on the Yser shows a few men, helmeted and covered with mud, lost in a maze of trenches, in a universe made up of sacks filled with earth, with dim communication trenches and crumbled ravines. Another photograph, taken early in 1915, represents an "advance." No longer is there any running in the hills, but men crawling behind felled trees and over dead horses, on a terrain churned up by artillery barrage.

These contrasts convey the gulf separating the military conceptions current in peacetime and the realities of war that a few months, or even the first encounters, imposed on all. War cannot be tested out ahead of time. In the two opposing camps, the unexpected scale of combat took the governments and high commands by surprise.

Within two months, the French General Staff had to revise its theories utterly. The French plan, like the German, was based on an offensive strategy. It envisaged frontal assaults launched "by all forces in unison." One offensive would develop on the right, in the region bounded by the forest masses of the Vosges and the Moselle, downstream from Toul, and the other on the left, to the north of the Verdun-Metz line, the two attacks being connected by the forces active on the heights above the Meuse and Woëvre.

The German plan, on the other hand, based on the invasion of Belgian territory, aimed at overwhelming the French forces concentrated in Lorraine by means of a movement carried out by the left wing of the German armies. This was the plan evolved by the former chief of the German Army's General Staff, Count Schlieffen. It was readopted by his successor, von Moltke, who had nevertheless considerably reduced the strength of his advancing wing.

The two camps also had a different conception of tactics. For the French, the offensive should reach its climax in an attack, in which the question of morale would be of great importance. This idea found expression in the make-up of the French divisions, comprising 17,000 men, of which 13,300 were foot soldiers. The artillery was looked on as a supplementary force, a view which did not take into consideration the firepower of the German armaments, especially heavy artillery, and underestimated the effectiveness of defensive tactics. Several French military theoreticians had indeed warned the partisans of the *offensive à l'outrance* of the increase in firepower. Colonel Pétain was one of them, but the most prominent were Generals Lanrezac and Foch. The German doctrine held that within the over-all concept of offensive strategy the enemy's attacks or counterattacks must be resisted and broken up by the greatest possible firepower.

De Gaulle, on the basis of personal recollections, has described the actual clash of these two views on the field of battle:

> The first shock was an immense surprise. Strategically, the dimensions of the enemy's turning maneuver and the use made of the reserve units immediately upset our plan. Tactically, the revelation of his firepower instantaneously made historical relics of the current doctrines. Morally, the illusions that had served as a breastplate were swept away in a trice. . . . The mass of the troops were drawn up in a column. At first the men could imagine it to be a maneuver like any other. . . . Suddenly the roar of the guns aroused a feeling of crisis . . . the encounter with the enemy proved to be a brutal business, for the enemy, who had launched an attack before we had, adopted defensive tactics for the first clash. The troops were deployed ahead of time. Our "point" struck his "rake." The French vanguard thus made random contact with a firmly established line of fire. As a consequence, they were at once decimated and nailed to the ground. While he was waiting for them to transmit the information necessary to coordinate the over-all offensive, the divisional general saw his column caught at the head. Even had he wished to free himself, this would have been difficult behind a cover that had been badly shaken and that was calling for help. Besides, the idea scarcely occurred to him. The enemy was there. All that was required was to march upon him. The order, given forthwith, and transmitted at a gallop, arrived when the troops involved had already gone into action. . . . Suddenly the enemy's fire became precise and concentrated. Second by second the hail of bullets and the thunder of the shells grew stronger. Those who survived lay flat on the ground, amid the screaming wounded and the humble corpses. With affected calm, the officers let themselves be killed standing upright, some obstinate platoons stuck their bayonets in their rifles, bugles sounded the charge, isolated heroes made fantastic leaps, but all to no purpose. In an instant it had become clear that not all the courage in the world could withstand this fire.

The astonishment of these men who, in midsummer, 1914, encountered the enemy and discovered a war they had not expected, was shared at every level of the military, political and economic hierarchies. On both sides, furthermore, the military theoreticians no less than the economic experts had counted on a short war. In France, the extraordinary consumption of men and material in the combats of the first few weeks confounded the government and the General Staff, just as the enemy's firepower had confounded, between Scheldt and Vosges, the divisions in the vanguard.

This "industrial war" would soon effect a veritable economic revolution. Control of the monetary exchanges was established for the first time, most products were rationed, currencies ceased to be convertible into gold, the Army mobilized one-quarter of the active population, amounting to some four million men, while five million persons, men and women, worked in the factories and public services.

The human losses brought about a displacement of the population that had no parallel in all French history. There were 955,000 killed, wounded and captured in 1914, 1,430,000 in 1915, 900,000 in 1916, 546,000 in 1917 and 1,095,000 in 1918, some five million in all. The constant turnover in these human masses, made more difficult by the transfer of 1,500,000 mobilized men to agriculture and the armaments factories, made it necessary to call up 7,800,000 Frenchmen, or about one-fifth of the total population. No other state had to make a comparable effort.

But these manpower requirements became known only gradually, as the losses mounted. The need for material, on the other hand, at once became apparent and faced the government and the General Staff with a problem of life and death. By the middle of September, 1914, the average supply of shells had fallen from 1,400 for each piece of artillery on mobilization day to a mere 400. Behind the front lines, the stocks amounted to only 45 per piece. Daily production amounted to only 8,000 or 10,000. The loss of the Briey basin, and of the coal mines of Nord and Pas de Calais, struck a terrible blow against French metallurgical production, and the situation became so grave that Joffre ordered all 75-millimeter guns removed from the fortresses, and the scanty stocks to be found in the colonies returned to France. On September 20, 1914, when Millerand, the War Minister, informed the heads of the metallurgical industries of the seriousness of the munitions problem, there remained in all only 900,000 shells still to be fired.

There was a frightful gap between the means available at the time, and the requirements that would soon have to be met. In the following year, in the offensives of Artois and Champagne alone, the

French artillery fired one million 75-millimeter shells, approximately thirty for each meter of the front. Daily production of shells had to rise to 300,000. The General Staff had imagined, before the war, that the guns it already possessed would be sufficient for the whole duration of the war: 36,000 had to be added. On August 3, 1914, there were 3,000 automatic weapons in service; another 300,000 would be needed. As compared with 2,000 existing telephones, 350,000 had to be made; as compared with 2,000 batteries and 600 kilometers of cable, respectively 3,000,000 and 2,000,000 were made; as compared with 50 radio sets, 30,000 were made, and 300,000 accumulators. The French Army had entered the war with 136 airplanes and 500 spare engines. The Morane, Spad, Potez, Salmson, Breguet, Voisin and Farman factories had to build 35,000 planes and 180,000 spare engines. The Schneider and Renault factories, and the factories at Saint-Chamond, constructed 5,000 tanks. Since this industrial warfare descended upon a country whose active population was, comparatively speaking, the most seriously diminished and upon an economy deprived by the German invasion of one-half its coal, and two-thirds of its cast iron and steel, it brought about a collapse of France's vital and economic forces whose consequences would extend right up to World War II. The immediate result was to confront the governments with entirely unexpected responsibilities, which led to a reshuffling of duties among the different ministries, between civilian and military, between government and high command.

This difficult transformation was made even more grievous by the weight of old quarrels, the consequences of the rancor and distrust left by the Dreyfus Affair. The general conduct of the war required the closest cohesion between the political and the military arm, yet an outlook dating back twenty years was still held by men and groups who were, in addition, exasperated by their immense responsibilities and by the almost dramatic importance that their debates and decisions had assumed. The contrast between the breadth of the problems to be solved and the pettiness of personal quarrels or group rivalries was a further goad to passion, each individual attributing to the other the responsibility for internal quarrels that seemed scandalous, in view of the danger that threatened the country.

Almost immediately after the war broke out, there occurred a marked cleavage between the General Staffs, who were overwhelmed by work and absorbed in a task on which everything depended, and the political groups, who suffered from the sense of their own inactivity since responsibility for the conduct of operations had to be left to the military leaders. Their anxiety and their feverishness, as General Headquarters viewed the matter, reflected a lack of solidarity with the Army at war.

This split was worsened by the first defeats and the departure for Bordeaux of Government and Parliament. The rumor circulated, at General Headquarters, that some deputies were saying that Joffre had threatened to execute Lanrezac, who was at the head of the Fifth Army. It was known, too, that Clemenceau attributed the Army's setbacks to the "generals from the Jesuit warrens" and, in particular, to General de Castelnau. The normal reaction of the military men, when they heard these usually false rumors that had, nevertheless, a very precise connection with the political preoccupations of the moment, was to condemn outright all these "politicians" whose gossip could only "hurt the morale of the rearguard." After the victory of the Marne, the General Staff was astonished that the government did not make a greater propagandistic use of the successes gained. Joffre said he was painfully surprised at the moderate tone of the French communiqués which left him with "a rather sad impression." The very President of the Republic, Poincaré, remarked to General Headquarters that the professional officers did not put enough trust in the reserves, "although more and more they are becoming the vital substance of our armies." This reproach, while entirely justified for the years preceding the war, had ceased to be so after the Marne victory, when most of the reserve regiments had already been used in the front line. The General Staff was exasperated by this reprimand which, it felt, was no longer deserved.

The tension among the officers of the General Staff was heightened by the news that arrived from Bordeaux or that found its way into the press, concerning the life led by the parliamentary representatives in their temporary capital, while at the same time General Headquarters was submerged under a load of work. These rumors, though likely to be gravely exaggerated in military circles, were not entirely without foundation, since the President of the Chamber of Deputies, Deschanel, complained in Poincaré's presence of the somewhat loose morals common in political circles, during the forced inactivity to which they were condemned by their exile in Bordeaux. Briand must have shared the opinion of the military. "An unhealthy milieu!" he said of his parliamentary colleagues.

As soon as the two Houses had returned to Paris, a small group of political personalities, including Paul Doumer, Clemenceau, and Charles Humbert, launched a very vigorous campaign against Joffre. Paul Doumer especially, who in connection with colonial matters had often had to do with Gallieni, greatly admired him and was anxious that he should head the armies. "If I become War Minister," he confided to Foch, whom he was visiting at his headquarters, "I will replace Joffre, who is incompetent, and appoint Gallieni General-in-Chief." A whole group of politicians strongly reproached Joffre with having appointed to important posts a few Catholic generals, such as de Castelnau and de Langle de Cary, who were suspected of monarchism. They sought a counterweight in Sarrail, at the head of the Third Army, since he was deemed to be particularly "republican," perhaps even a Freemason.

An anonymous memorandum was put in circulation, in the spring of 1915, that violently attacked the person of the General-in-Chief. After a criticism of the conduct of operations, the author revealed the mental attitude of the political circles whose spokesman he appeared to be, when he took up problems of personnel.

> Joffre had to call on three retired generals, de Langle de Cary, Maunoury and Brugère, to command three of his armies. . . . It is true that if these generals' service records are examined, there is little compatibility with the Republic to be discovered. In the course of the campaign, General Joffre, finding himself compelled to replace army commanders or to create new armies, named as Army Generals Generals Foch, de Mauduy, Franchet d'Esperey, d'Urbal, Putz and Roques. An examination of the past of the first five at once throws a revealing light on their connections with the Republic.

This was followed by a defense of General Sarrail, which wound up as follows:

> . . . I believe it can be said that if General Joffre were unavailable for a period of two weeks and if supreme command were entrusted to General Sarrail, there can be no doubt that the Germans would be chased from the national territory, for there would be an entirely different conception of military movements, and a brutality of execution that would assuredly cost us less dear than the war of attrition under which we have suffered for the last five months. . . .

Clemenceau's paper, *L'Homme Enchaîné*, attacked the high command so virulently that in some prison camps it was the only paper allowed by the German authorities. This frame of mind was justified much less by any personal hostility to Joffre—who had been a Freemason—than by the almost irresistible suspiciousness of political men for any general.

This suspicion of the political loyalty of the top military leaders was shared by no one outside a small group of parliamentarians, a few dozen deputies and senators at the very most. One may wonder, too, whether their attitude was not determined less by any real conviction than by the fact that they were out of power. Former Council President Caillaux, one of those who had criticized Joffre most violently, was later accused and condemned, on the instigation of Clemenceau, who himself had been one of the harshest in his criticisms of the high command. Among the strongest defenders of Joffre were Jules Guesde and Marcel Sembat, the two Socialists in the government.

Public opinion was far from sharing the suspicions felt by a few politicial figures. The victor of the Marne was, naturally, one of the most popular men in France. People no longer made any distinction between fatherland and Republic, nor between Republic and Army. Fatigue, exasperation and anger would manifest themselves later, but they would arise for entirely different reasons than suspicion of the more or less dubiously "republican" outlook of one general or another.

Similarly, the problem of the relationship between the high command and the government possessed little interest for public opinion. The public knew nothing of the crises that stirred the narrow milieu of the political leaders and the Army chiefs. The evolution of popular feeling was decided by the actual incidents of combat. The burning of Reims Cathedral, the stories of "German atrocities," the popularity of King Albert I of the Belgians—"the knightly king"—the campaigns against the "gold brickers" who, far from the front lines, had found safe niches, the use of poison gas by the Germans on April 22, 1915, on the Flanders front and the general wave of horror that this inspired in public opinion, the heroic legend of some "aviation aces" like Guynemer—of such things was popular feeling made up, at least during the first three years of war. Not until the great campaigns alleging "defeatism" and "treason" would political life, as viewed by public opinion, once more assume its rights and reacquire real passions.

At a deeper level, the problem persisted of how to wage the war and how to organize the country for war, and this gave rise to the problem of the relations between government and high command.

The question of the high command in wartime had been raised almost by accident, in 1911. The interpellation of a right-wing senator, M. Provost de Launay, who asked the government what were the responsibilities of the Supreme Commander named for wartime command, and what were his connections with the civil power, was answered by General Goirand, Minister of War: "In time of war, the Supreme Commander is the Minister; the personage who bears this title is, in peacetime, only the Inspector General of the Army and, in wartime, Commander of the armies of north and east." This reply naturally evoked a violent reaction in one segment of Parliament, since it aroused the belief that this official position—which was in complete conformity with the laws in force—revealed a systematic distrust of the entire military personnel and, especially, distrust of the very idea that a general could really be Supreme Commander.

Since Monis, President of the Council of ministers, had been injured in an airplane accident, the government was unable to reply to its parliamentary critics by pointing out that a necessary distinction existed between the conduct of the war and the conduct of operations, and a feeling of unease persisted. Most ministers were of the opinion that General Goirand had gone too far in minimizing the role of the Supreme Commander in wartime.

One single voice was raised to justify the role of the government in the conduct of war and to distinguish this from operational responsibilities. The speaker was Paul-Boncour, at the time the youthful Minister of Labor. "I pointed out," he wrote later,

> that there would be not only a northern and eastern front, on which the personage entitled supreme commander was to serve. There might be an Alpine front. . . . There might be a Pyreneean front. . . . There would be a sea front and naval warfare. Although military aviation was still in its infancy, the perspectives were widening. Who would coordinate all that? . . . And who would decide when military operations and diplomacy had to be coordinated? Who would determine war aims? And, finally, who would see to the recruiting and industrial production for these armies and these fleets, with their manpower and matériel? And what about internal order, and the country's morale? . . . Who could stimulate this if it were not the men in whom the sovereign nation had placed its confidence?

He concluded by asking that, in wartime, the supreme responsibility should be vested in a limited government, a prefiguration of what, in the ensuing world wars, would be the "war cabinets." The skepticism of most ministers in 1911, who were men—of whom the Minister of Finances, Caillaux, may serve as an example—hostile to militarism in all its forms, shows that prior to 1914 few could imagine the vast range of modern warfare.

Everything depended on the nature of the war. If the only front was to be on the northeast frontier, the only military man with major responsibilities would be the officer at the head of the armies called on to fight there. His decisions would be so decisive for the life or death of the country, and his duties would be so overwhelming, that there would be no point in placing him under some superior military authority such as, for example, a technical counsellor of the government or a Chef d'État-Major Général. Such a duality would only lead to friction, arising all the more frequently and all the more violently since the only front concerned would be the northeastern front.

In the hypothesis that the war would be restricted to the clash of the French armies, with or without allies, and the German armies, along the frontiers, the only simple and straightforward solution was that adopted on the eve of war: a General-in-Chief, named in peacetime and then exercising the functions of head of the armies, would command the totality of military operations in the northeast. The government would see to the over-all conduct of the war. The relevant ministers, helped by general staffs stationed in Paris, would take charge of the recruiting and instruction of the forces, the manufacture and provisioning of matériel, and the economic and moral mobilization of the country.

This system functioned with the greatest possible efficacy until the beginning of 1915. At that time, the only problem that arose concerned the connections between the Allied armies on the northeastern front. The British government was not yet ready to admit that its armies should be subordinate to a French higher command. In practice, only the moral authority and the manpower at the disposal of the French commanding general ensured a solution of the abiding problem of Franco-Anglo-Belgian coordination.

Everything changed when, in February, the Allied governments decided to organize an expedition to the Dardanelles in order to occupy the entry to the Black Sea, to prevent the possible union of the Central Powers and Turkey (which had gone to war on their side), and to allow a more rapid and more regular transfer of supplies to the Russian Army. The operation was justified, therefore, exclusively on the plane of the over-all prosecution of the war.

Winston Churchill in England and Briand in France were the stoutest proponents of the venture. The French government was obliged, nevertheless, to consult the highest military authority in the country, Joffre. Joffre advised against the proposed expedition and made use of a single argument, which was indeed decisive. The French forces were insufficient to permit a diversion of any part of them outside national territory. The situation on the front, and the occupation by the enemy of about five Departments, required that all efforts should be concentrated in the northeast. He even went on to say that it would be impossible to assemble in the rear lines a main striking force that could be used at one point or another of the French front, let alone another front. "I need, from now to the end of the war," he declared, "all the men in the depots. In any case, to form new sections, there would at the present moment be neither officers, nor noncoms, nor artillery nor troop trains."

Joffre's advice would in actual practice have been given by any responsible French military leader occupying any other post. But this first occasion made it clear that, where the establishment of a second front was concerned—a problem clearly belonging to the over-all prosecution of the war, and not to that of operations—the government had not been able to turn to any other military authority than the general in charge of operations in the northeast theater.

The evolution of the war induced the governments to consider once again the idea of an expedition directed against the straits leading to the Black Sea. Some aid had to be lent the Russians, to compensate for the Turkish attacks in the Caucasus. And a military action in the region of the Balkans was also necessary to back up the diplomatic steps taken with regard to Roumania, Greece and even Bulgaria, which had not yet fallen in with the German plan. Joffre renewed his objections and the British Imperial Chief of Staff, Kitchener, refused to provide any intervention on land, seeking to limit the Dardanelles expedition to naval operations. Finally the two military leaders agreed to the governmental proposals. Four new English divisions were assigned to the northeast front, Australian and New Zealand troops would disembark at the Dardanelles, while two brigades of infantry, one regiment of cavalry and artillery units, under the command of General d'Amade, would embark early in

March bound for the Turkish coasts. But these forces turned out to be inadequate, and the War Minister asked Joffre for four additional divisions for the Dardanelles front. Joffre replied that many others would have to follow them, and that thus a dispersion of effort would have been permitted quite incompatible with the seriousness of the situation on the French front.

The failure of the Dardanelles expedition threatened to reverse the situation in the Balkans, which hitherto had been favorable to the Allies. On September 22, Bulgaria did indeed mobilize and entered the war on the side of Germany, Austria-Hungary and Turkey. Convinced that the Balkans offered a reliable base for future operations, the French and British governments decided, after they had assured themselves of the complicity of the Greek Prime Minister, Venizelos, to establish a fortified area at Salonika. On October 5, the 156th French Division and the British troops disembarked there, and General Sarrail, who had been named Commander-in-Chief of the army in the east, arrived on October 12.

This whole crisis revealed the unsuitability of the system of government and of command still in force to deal with the problems posed by the multiplicity of war fronts. At the same time it showed that a mere coordination was insufficient for the prosecution of war by a coalition. Already Joffre's opponents had used a technical criticism of the apportionment of military responsibilities as a lever to challenge the authority of the General-in-Chief. A second memorandum, probably inspired by General Sarrail or by someone in his entourage, and dated April 20, 1915, reminded its readers that "there is a commissar of the armies provided for by the Constitution and called President of the Republic. He is the natural intermediary between the Nation and the Army. He may order investigations and give advice. Only he is familiar with the diplomatic requirements . . . after nine months of warfare, he can no longer abdicate his rights. Let there be no mistake, he is now responsible."

This reminder of the constitutional prerogatives enjoyed by the President of the Republic did not correspond entirely to French political realities. The memorandum ended by declaring that "General Joffre has appropriate collaborators in the Army commanders and the Army corps, who are not only executants, but who must aid him to arrive at his solutions." This paid no attention to the functioning of a supreme command in practice or to the relations that the French commanding general had to maintain with the British and Belgian

Armies, which were engaged on his front but subject to their own governments.

The geographical extension of the war, with the successive interventions of the whole British Empire, of Japan and Turkey, made it necessary to strive for coordination. On June 23, 1915, Joffre, with the backing of his three Commanders of Army groups, Foch, de Castelnau and Dubail, explained to Poincaré, the President of the Republic, and to Millerand, the War Minister, the advantages of a unified conduct of operations carried out by the totality of the Allied forces. He summed up his view the following day in a letter addressed to the War Minister: "While the 1914 campaign opened with a war plan and a plan of operations . . . the present phase of the war, which is taking place in entirely different conditions, cannot be viewed in the same way. The relations of the Allies among themselves and with Italy . . . remain cordial, but the various armies are acting on their own account, with no over-all coordination. . . ."

He suggested that the French government should propose to the Allied Powers that the conduct of the war at the highest level be centralized in French General Headquarters, where over-all plans and directives would be elaborated. "With regard, more particularly, to the French theater of operations, in which the French, English and Belgian armies are active, the necessity of close, constant cooperation is plain. If it is thought better not to say that the French Commander-in-Chief gives orders, then at least it is indispensable, in order to win, that the heads of the English and Belgian armies should follow his instructions."

This note clearly reveals the state of mind that predominated in 1915. The northeast front seemed of such prime importance to France that the thought never arose that a centralization of the totality of operations undertaken by all the Allies could be effectuated anywhere else than at General Headquarters, which was responsible for operations on this front. But, at the same time, it seemed so difficult to limit the control exercised by each government over its own national army that the absolute unity of command on the northeast front could scarcely be openly demanded.

Joffre understood the difficulties that might be encountered. "Instead of demonstrating theoretically the necessity of over-all direction for the coalition," he wrote on June 29, "is it not better to take steps at once to obtain it? The matter is urgent. . . ." Joffre suggested a reform in the high command. The failure of the Dardanelles expedition had strengthened his position. The requests made for reinforcements by General Sarrail, since his arrival in Salonika, made it urgent that decisions should be taken on the capital problem of the allocation of forces and the coordination of the fronts. Joffre's solution was this:

> I will assume over-all command of all French armies, irrespective of the theater in which they are operating. To aid me in my task, so conceived, I would have at my side a general officer who would deal with current business, take my place during my absences, and be delegated to fronts where my activity as commander would require particularly close supervision. The War Minister would remain responsible for all internal resources (recruiting, instruction, manufacturing) and for the conveyance of these resources to the different theaters of operation, in keeping with the details of their utilization, with which I would provide him.

These measures were adopted. From then on, the government would have a military adviser for the totality of operations involved in the general conduct of the war. By naming Joffre to be commander of French troops in all theaters, the government had acquired this supreme military adviser whose responsibilities would normally be different from those of the operational commands on the various fronts.

In spite of the naming of an assistant, de Castelnau, Joffre remained directly responsible for the operations on the northeast front. This fact should have established some sort of equilibrium, in his mind, between his functions as Commander-in-Chief of all French forces and his operational responsibilities on the principal front. But since the French front traversed the national territory from one end to the other, it inevitably had supreme importance for the General-in-Chief, took up the bulk of his time and demanded priority in the allocation of manpower and armaments.

Personal factors served to make even worse the imbalance between Joffre's two functions. His whole renown rested on his victories on the northeast front: this was the front he knew and had made the object of all his concern, and of that of his General Staff, ever since he had returned from the colonies many years before. So the reform in the high command remained incomplete, falling short of the conclusions imposed by the geographical, political and economic ramifications of the war, with its multiple fronts. In addition, the reform left untouched the question of the unity of command between the Allied Powers, both on the French front and in the east.

However, the increased authority enjoyed by Joffre lent greater weight to the views he expressed at the meeting of Allied military representatives, held at Chantilly on December 6, 7 and 8. As the general in command of French forces on all fronts, he persuaded the representatives of the British, Belgian, Italian, Russian and Serbian General Staffs to adopt the principles that would determine the general conduct of operations during 1916. The main effort would be made on the two chief fronts, the Franco-British and the Russian, and there would be a synchronization of offensives on all fronts. Each offensive would be made ready within one month, at the most, and there would be a general launching of all offensives in the spring. Other decisions taken concerned the evacuation of the Dardanelles, the defense of the Egyptian frontier against a possible Turkish offensive, and the readying of Salonika as a fortified area.

But in February the Allied plans were forestalled by the German offensive directed against Verdun. Then began a long period during which unheard-of sacrifices were made, in order to deny the enemy a few hundred meters of terrain on a front only a few kilometers long. Until the Allied offensive on the Somme got under way, the horizon of warfare was limited to the Verdun trenches, where in a few months hundreds of thousands of corpses were piled up. Public opinion was stirred to an almost unbearable degree of nervous tension. There could no longer be any large-scale offensive, such as had been attempted in 1915—in return for very meager results. There was no longer any thought of freeing the invaded Departments. Victory, obviously, was remote—it was not even clear how the Allies' military effort could lead to any decisive operations promising victory. Verdun was to exhaust the German Army's offensive capacities. The Germans were unable to mount any considerable attack until the final assaults of 1918, after the collapse of the Russian front. But during the actual eight months' duration of the battle, while destiny seemed to hesitate, Verdun would hold out no prospect of victory for the French people in general, or for political personalities in particular. The only outlook for the French Army appeared to be defensive action; frightful bloodbaths reduced its manpower; the future, in military terms, seemed blocked. This was the situation when once again the problem of the organization of the high command was raised.

In March 1916, War Minister Gallieni addressed to the Council of Ministers a letter highly critical of all the activities of the high command in the previous eighteen months. It was an implicit reproach directed against the government for having allowed the high command to act as it had. The ministers realized this and refused to accept Gallieni's letter. Gallieni resigned. The crisis, which until then had been limited to the members of the government, now extended to Parliament.

The new War Minister was General Roques, a friend of Joffre's, and in response to queries of the parliamentarians he was unable to summon up all the authority that a prominent politician could have mustered. So he opted for flexibility, thereby encouraging an intensification of the criticisms to which deputies and senators were already highly partial, since they, like all Frenchmen, were appalled by the slaughter at Verdun, and exasperated by the apparently endless dragging out of the war. At General Headquarters, where a terrible state of tension had been created by the trial of Verdun, by the preparation and execution of new offensives on the Somme and by the crisis in armaments and manpower, the criticisms of the politicians stimulated an ever more vigorous reaction. These human factors weighed so heavily in the balance that they finally made it impossible to adopt the most rational solution.

His attention absorbed by the northeast front, Joffre could not force Sarrail, who was in command in the east, to put through the necessary measures to halt the retreat of the Serbian troops, and to compel the Bulgarian Army to concentrate along the Greek frontier. Yet this was the only way of drawing the bulk of the Austro-Hungarian and Bulgarian Armies into the southern Balkans and of covering the mobilization of the Roumanian Army, which was just about to enter the war on the Allied side.

Coming on top of the inextricable complications of the political situation in Greece, the violent animosity between Joffre and Sarrail paralyzed the armies in the east. The collapse of the Roumanian Army finally ruined the hopes that had been placed in an over-all reversal of the balance of forces on the eastern front. The disappointment was very strong among the Allies, but above all in France where Briand, President of the Council, had long foreseen that the only way of breaking up the immobility of the fronts was in the east, where the military and political weaknesses of Austria-Hungary offered an adversary who could more readily be defeated.

Briand rightly judged that the government had suffered by the lack of a supreme military adviser, freed of operational responsibilities on the northeast front, whose authority would have forced, among the various fronts, a division of effort in accord with the policy laid down by the government. At the same time, but without any illusions as to the merits of a change in leadership, Briand, who was naturally sensitive to the parliamentary atmosphere, saw that another reform of the high command would have the additional advantage of allowing a new general to be placed in command of the northeast front.

The situation was all the more critical for him, because in political circles there was no way of divining the frightful wastage of German forces after the failure of their attacks on Verdun and their defeat on the Somme. In Parliament, the overly schematic optimism of the official bulletins brought only weariness. Besides, on orders from the British government, which was appalled at the losses suffered on the Somme, the British General Staff had had to call off the offensive, whose chief weight it had borne since the beginning of the summer.

Briand tried to convince Joffre that there had to be a change in the organization of the high command. But Joffre, relying on the value of the successes he had won at Verdun and on the Somme, refused to accept any diminution of his responsibilities, which in his view he had discharged very well. He had just obtained agreement on the operational plans for 1917, and he was anxious to see them put into force. Briand confided to Joffre that certain political factions were particularly hostile to de Castelnau and Foch, overlooking the role that the former had played in the battle of Verdun, and the latter in the battle of the Somme. And he made known his intentions: A new General-in-Chief would be appointed for the northeast front. Joffre himself would retain his title as Commander-in-Chief of the French Armies, would be raised to the dignity of Marshal of France, would become supreme adviser to the government in all matters pertaining to the general prosecution of the war and would retain his authority over the generals in command on the various fronts.

Briand had thus arrived at the best possible theoretical solution of the problem of the relations between government and high command during a world war. Joffre must have realized this, since the first objections he raised against Briand's plan were essentially of a practical kind. He had, he declared, no real authority vis-à-vis the French government and the Allied governments except through the effective command which had been his for the last two-and-a-half years in the principal theater of war. Furthermore, since there was no unity of command between the Allied forces, a certain personal prestige was necessary to ensure that the instructions of General Headquarters would be followed by the British and Belgian General Staffs. Apart from Foch, who could not be promoted in view of the criticisms directed against him in political circles, he, Joffre, was the only man who had the indispensable personal authority. But Briand's view of things was difficult to challenge, and on December 4, Joffre let it be known that he would raise no objection, and spoke of resigning. Briand was able to tell Parliament that a reform in the high command would be carried out, and so disarmed the critics who were threatening the existence of the government.

The decisions based on the decrees of December 13 and 21, 1916, echoed those adopted one year earlier, on December 2, 1915. The problem was to organize two essential functions. One was that of the supreme military adviser of the government for the prosecution of the war in all theaters; the other was that of commander of operations on the northeast front. In 1915, the former had been sacrificed to the latter, since one man entrusted with both tasks would inevitably be preoccupied by his immediate responsibilities on the principal front.

In December, 1916, the opposite course was pursued. The two essential functions of the high command were clearly demarcated; but, under the influence of the personal criticisms directed against Joffre, the responsibilities that normally would be reserved for the government's supreme military adviser were enormously reduced. Joffre would have a mere consultative part to play and the government would be under no obligation to take his advice. He would simply have to transmit the decisions taken by the War Cabinet, which Briand had just established within the Council of Ministers.

Joffre took the view that the post that had been created for him had no inner consistency. On December 26, 1916, he submitted his resignation. While the reforms of December, 1915, had not gone far enough in reorganizing and differentiating the main tasks of the high command, those of 1916 went beyond what Briand had been aiming at and brought about the opposite of what he desired. Now, instead of having a military adviser whose competence and authority would have enabled the government to impose the over-all directives on those in charge of operations, there was a vacuum separating the government and the generals in command on the various fronts.

This vacuum had to be filled. Lyautey, who had become War Minister, thought that he himself could assume the functions that normally would be those of Commander-in-Chief of the Armies as permanent military adviser to the civil power. But this role was incompatible with that of a minister. During a session of the Chamber of Deputies, in March, 1917, he refused to give the explanations he was asked for. "You will allow me," he said, "not to follow you on the technical terrain, because even in secret sessions I state, with full awareness of my responsibilities, that this is exposing the national defense to risks. . . ." "All that remains to be done," protested an opposition deputy, Raffin-Dugens, "is to abolish Parliament." Taken aback and exasperated, Lyautey resigned.

The situation was now so grave that an immediate solution had to be found. It was hit upon on May 11, 1917. The post of Chef d'État-Major Général was created, with functions extending from the technical elaboration of operations to the recruiting and training of manpower, general services, the military organization of the territory and missions abroad. Pétain was first appointed, but on May 15 he replaced Nivelle in command of the armies of the northeast and was himself replaced by Foch.

This long crisis in command had serious consequences in the winter of 1916-1917. The deliberate limitation of the powers accorded the Commander-in-Chief of the French Armies and military adviser to the government had brought about Joffre's departure. This in its turn led to the postponement of the attacks that Joffre, in agreement with the Allied commands, had set for the first two weeks in February. To judge by the impression made on Hindenburg and Ludendorff, who had just taken over command of the German armies, these armies were in a critical situation in January, 1917. "The positions opposite which we had stopped in November," wrote Ludendorff, "were so shaken that they could not have resisted a fresh assault. If they had been pierced, they would have endangered those that stretched out to the east of Soissons and would have necessitated a retreat on a wide front." This anticipated withdrawal, which was decided upon by the German command, allowed the preparation of remarkable defensive positions and compelled the French General Staff to revise all its plans.

Nearly three years had been required to permit a rational solution to the problem of the relations between government and high command. Ideological prejudices, psychological rigidities and political calculations had all played their part. But these elements never took the upper hand, except at the worst moments when, late in 1916, Joffre was obliged to resign. Modern warfare, with its vast geographical sweep, and its human and industrial dimensions, had affected the whole apparatus of the state. At no moment was the Army as a whole in conflict with political authority. In the attitude of the General Staffs traces remained of distrust, rancor and bitterness. But, all in all, nothing in these quarrels had shaken the deep sense of identification between the Nation and its Army.

CHAPTER SEVEN

THE ARMY AND THE
RUSSIAN REVOLUTION

✠

A basic transformation was to lead, in the space of three years, from
the *union sacrée* of August, 1914, to the slump in morale of 1917.
The disputes in the General Staff, and the differences that separated
General Headquarters and the governments, had nothing to do with
this. Or, at the most, they were only a part of the network of events
that brought the Army to the very point of collapse. It was at this
juncture that a new idea came to occupy the minds of the military
cadres. No one could then realize how fraught with consequences it
would be, for it would shape the psychology of the officers' corps for
the following forty years.

The military hierarchy believed it could discern a great historical
lesson in the sequence of events that moved on from the decline in
morale, the widespread criticism of unsuccessful offensives and resistance to the most outrageous propaganda, to the first signs of revolutionary disturbances in Russia, the seizure of power by the Bolsheviks, the great mutinies of 1917 and the treason trials. The lesson
was that free criticism undermined the morale of the troops, introduced uncertainty into the general prosecution of the war and gave
rise to defeatism, while prolonged hesitancy on the part of the authorities prepared the way for rebellion and mutiny. Mutiny soon took on
the appearance of revolution, and revolution meant the collapse of
military strength, and the door open to the enemy. Revolution was
Communism, and Communism was treason.

In the history of World War I, what was uppermost was the profound identification of the Nation and its Army. The existence of the one was indissolubly linked to that of the other. The day war broke out, the Nation and the Army at once became acutely aware of the vital bond that connected them. The day the war ended in victory, the Nation celebrated its own courage when it celebrated that of the Army, and recognized itself in the heroic yet wretched, the glorious and tragic image presented by this Army, in which one million of the Nation's sons had just died. If we are to estimate correctly the dimensions of the crisis that shook the Army during the third year of combat, and which was to exert such a deep and lasting effect on the outlook of its cadres, we must not forget that it seemed to be a mere flaw in the fervent patriotism that united the Nation and the Army.

What Frenchmen could no longer stand, at this time, was the cleavage between the reality they were experiencing and the official image they were offered of this reality. In the patriotic exaltation of the summer of 1914, even the crudest and least subtle forms of propaganda could be accepted by a public passionately involved in the first battles along the frontier, still borne up by the hope of a speedy victory, and all the more ready to believe anything, since the very existence of the country was at stake.

A whole literature grew up, under the combined influence of the official censorship, nationalist conformism and the requirements of war propaganda. It blossomed in the press and in popular novels, in the fashionable drama and in transitory pamphlets, with its own mythology, vocabulary, morality and taboos.

It all began with the strange conception of the enemy that the newspapers sought to convey. His armed forces were said to be of little value. "The inefficacy of the enemy's projectiles," wrote L'Intransigeant on August 17, "is a universal subject of conversation. The shrapnel explodes feebly and falls in an inoffensive shower. The firing is very imprecise. As for the bullets, they are not dangerous. They pass through the flesh without tearing it." Besides, it was said, the enemy forces were badly supplied, and were actually short of food.

The history of "the slice of bread and butter" may serve as the finest example of the mythology that grew up in the first weeks of the war. L'Intransigeant reported it on August 16, attributing it to its Brussels correspondent: "An official communiqué quotes a carabinier, who has already taken several prisoners, as saying: 'I don't take along my gun any more, I set off with bread and butter. When the Germans see me, they follow it.' " Little by little, the portrait of the enemy soldier was rounded out. He was ferocious, cowardly and ugly. First he was called "Prusco," then "Alboche," then "Boche."

The Allied Armies, by way of contrast, were depicted as always invincible and always brave. The writer Henri Lavedan described the bayonet used by the French Army, and which had been baptized "Rosalie," as "impatient to plunge into the ass's skin it is piercing as it would pierce a human wineskin." The 75-millimeter guns, according to the newspapers, were "lubricated with sardine oil." As for the Russians, their "steamroller is on the march." In addition, the military correspondents recruited by the papers after the outbreak of war explained daily that every French offensive was a triumph and every German offensive a disaster, every French retreat a skillful maneuver and every German retreat a panicky flight. At the same time there appeared the first serial stories with patriotic pretensions: *Wilhelm's Woman Spy, The Poilus of the Ninth Regiment, Engaged to an Alsatian Girl, The Lads of the Field Battery, The Poilus.*

Between the picture that such a literature claimed to give of the war, and the experiences of the soldiers in the trenches, the gap rapidly became an abyss. Soon the whole press was suspected of printing eyewash. And this reaction, in its turn, ensured the popularity of papers that were hostile to official propaganda, that refused to print any idyllic, false descriptions of the fighting, criticized the military authorities and military justice, did not spare certain General Staffs and insisted on retaining their freedom to judge and their right to criticize. Daily papers such as *L'Œuvre* and *Le Pays* and, above all, *Le Canard Enchaîné,* voiced the exasperation of a large part of public opinion, especially among the troops. In 1916, after the Socialist conference held at Kienthal, the deputy Pierre Brizon started a new paper, *La Vague*. Protesting against eyewash (*bourrage de crâne*) and denouncing the bellicosity of governments and General Staffs, *La Vague* enjoyed an immense success by printing in its pages letters from soldiers. It was an outlet where the anger and disgust of the ordinary soldier could express itself with almost entire freedom. The General Staff did not demand that the paper be suppressed. It considered, quite on the contrary, that the paper served as a very useful barometer of the soldiers' attitude. This would seem to show that the General Staff was altogether sure of the discipline and cohesion of the troops, and perhaps less fearful than was the government of this voicing of complaints and discontent.

As the war went on, it was inevitable that the public should fail
to sustain the first high emotional pitch, and would begin to ask
questions concerning the reasons for a conflict that demanded such
heavy sacrifices. There was a clear connection between the protests
against the *bourrage de crâne,* this first healthy reaction to propagandistic excesses, and the initial steps in favor of a straightforward
definition of the "war aims." But it was impossible to demand that
governments and parliaments express themselves on the objectives
that France had in mind, which would justify the continuation of
the war, without at the same time raising the question of the usefulness and legitimacy of the sacrifices imposed on the country. It meant,
in the last resort, raising the question of peace.

Beyond a doubt, there was the almost universal conviction, in
political circles, that France would never have gone to war to take
Alsace-Lorraine. Yet now that the war had begun, it was felt that arms
should not be laid down until the lost provinces had been regained.
At no moment after August, 1914, did any government re-examine
this "war aim," the only one which French public opinion could regard
as unchallengeable.

The search for alliances had the unavoidable consequence of
increasing the number of promises made the new Allies. The negotiations pursued with Italy and Roumania, the necessity of preserving
the Russian Alliance, the plans to split up the Ottoman Empire, and
the competition between the warring factions to persuade Bulgaria
and Greece to enter the war, all obliged the French government to
multiply its promises, as the "war aims" of the Allies became ever
more numerous. But the campaigns that had been launched by the
most independent newspapers went on, arousing all the more approval
since the public was wondering whether there was no way out of this
interminable struggle. *L'Œuvre* and *Le Pays* were joined by *Le
Bonnet Rouge,* an anarchist paper belonging to Bolo-Pacha. Later,
after the foundation of *La Vague,* there appeared *La Vérité,* which
endeavored to unite Radicals, Socialists, syndicalists and anarchists on
certain fundamental matters. It called for a rejection of all *bourrage
de crâne,* criticized the administration and military justice, defended
individual liberties, and campaigned in favor of a definition of simple
and moderate war aims that might serve as the base for a rapidly
achieved peace.

All these papers, with the possible exception of *Le Pays,* were
journals of the Left. The right-wing press, on the other hand, was

unanimous in defending the necessity of a strict national discipline, and of a more universal mobilization of all the country's energies, refused to consider any compromise peace and sometimes referred to a future annexation of the left bank of the Rhine. In Parliament, similarly, the Right supported the government in power almost as a matter of principle, while tending to complain that the government was excessively indulgent toward men and papers who might be suspected of preferring a compromise peace to the continuance of the war until total victory was achieved.

Little by little there was a progressive lumping together of all those who demanded a definition of war aims and who envisaged a compromise peace, of the papers, men and groups who attacked the conformist and warlike outlook of the majority, and of those who were preparing to start a campaign against the continuation of the war. All would be condemned as guilty of "defeatism" and "treason."

The first cracks in the patriotic unanimity of Socialist opinion did not appear until after the battles of the Marne and the Yser. At the first meeting of the Socialist Parties of the Allied and neutral countries, held in London on February 14, 1915, Jules Guesde, who was at the time a minister in the government presided over by Viviani, explained the position of the French Socialists. "It is necessary first of all," he said, "to establish the fact that there can be no question of peace—a highly dangerous dream—until German imperialism has been vanquished. The duty of Socialists . . . is to continue the struggle to the end . . . a French victory will be the beginning as well as the condition of a Socialist victory tomorrow." But in May, 1915, the Federation of the Unified Socialist Party of Haute-Vienne, through its newspaper *Le Populaire du Centre*, reproached certain Party leaders with having written articles "very nearly blemished by chauvinism," and it proposed to the French comrades "to lend an attentive ear to every proposition of peace, wherever it may come from."

It was at the Socialist conference held on April 24, 1916, at Kienthal, that the peace slogan "No annexation" was first put in circulation. The French deputies who had taken part in the conference were subjected to extraordinarily violent attacks in the press and in their own party. Widely branded "German agents" and "traitors," they were threatened with expulsion by a fraction of Parliament. They were defended by a Socialist deputy from Aubervilliers, Pierre Laval, and were, in the long run, not penalized in any way.

It was on his return from Kienthal that Brizon decided to found his paper, *La Vague*. This provided a meeting place for the pacifist trend that had arisen in some Socialist milieux but had not yet met with any great response, a place to express the growing fatigue, weariness or even anger of countless soldiers worn out by trench life, who were appalled by the bloodbaths in which so many comrades had disappeared, and were exasperated by the rumors in circulation concerning war profits and the easy life that was being led, they believed, by those at home. This fusion would bear its fruits in the following year.

The winter of 1916-1917 was the coldest of the war. The front, practically immobile, witnessed feeble operations involving patrols and artillery duels, nil in their results but costly in manpower. A widening gap separated military and social realities, and the cumbrously conformist and resolutely optimistic picture which most papers, current literature and official speeches tried to impose on public opinion.

The accounts of the fighting published by the most important newspapers were read with horror by the millions of the mobilized, the wounded, and those who had emerged from the trenches and the large-scale butcheries of Verdun, Champagne and the Somme. Soldiers on leave were distressed to discover that people behind the lines had an entirely false idea of life in the trenches. They were revolted by the legends of the heroism and enthusiasm of the combatants and the weakness or cowardice of the enemy. And they were demoralized by the contrast between the 25 centimes per day allowed the ordinary soldier and the 10 or 15 francs earned by the workers in the armament factories.

The troops came to feel that the people at home were beginning to live a life unknown to them, in which they did not share and which they no longer understood. There was talk of the profiteers: industrialists who had Army contracts, everyone who exchanged his paper money for more lasting investments, business people who crowded around the factories and sold anything at all to the workers whose wages had never been so high.

Perhaps the combatants even succeeded, during their brief furloughs, in grasping the revolution that had taken place in the life of their wives. When the husband went off to war, each wife received 1 franc 25 centimes per day for herself and 50 centimes for each child. Women's financial independence, the new responsibilities they had to assume and the great mixing of social classes caused by the war rapidly disposed of the old constraints of life in society. In the towns, some women directed the factories of their absent husbands, and others were now working in the streetcars, buses and armament factories. In the middle classes, which were ruined by the stagnation in all judicial, intellectual and sometimes even commercial activities, the women had to find new means of livelihood. The combatants already sensed that, at war's end, they would not again discover the world they had known.

Their melancholy and their impatience, as they confronted the unending trial of the fighting, were made even worse by a new feeling: they realized that they were slowly becoming strangers in their own land. Perhaps it was then that there took shape, in the public mind, an idea that was to persist throughout the two wars. The Army came to be looked on as a kind of exile from the life of the Nation. The military world had no connections with the life of the country. Two universes were juxtaposed, the one civilian, the other uniformed, and they knew nothing and would continue to know nothing of each other. This feeling was not accompanied by any bitterness directed against the leaders of the Army or against the military professionals. On the contrary, the French conscripts first of all felt closer to their brothers in arms, irrespective of their social origin or their rank, than to those who had stayed at home, in a topsy-turvy and shameless world in which the marks of the old life and traditional ways could no longer be recognized.

But only a decisive turn in the war itself could convert this shrugging of the shoulders at the propagandistic eyewash, this exasperation at the politicians and war profiteers, into open revolt and mutiny.

In March, 1917, the Russian Revolution was not immediately understood by a large part of public opinion. The papers of the Left expressed pleasure that the autocratic empire of the Czars had given way to a liberal, democratic state. There had always been a certain embarrassment, in Socialist and Radical circles, at the thought that the principal ally was a country subject to one of the most reactionary regimes in the world.

But among the military, on the contrary, there was an immediate uneasiness. Most of the officers, with their traditional training and their conservative outlook, considered it impossible for a government to continue the war after it had permitted criticisms of the military hierarchy, and allowed indiscipline in the armed ranks and anarchy in the country. The French high command, well informed by the military attachés in Russia, was perhaps more keenly aware than the political leaders of the fragile condition of the Russian armies. In the course of 1916, weaknesses had become apparent in the Russian troops sent to France. In the month of August, the Second Brigade, which was being sent to Salonika, had mutinied and assassinated its colonel. Such facts had not been made known to the public, or even to Parliament, but the Grand Quartier Général had noted the symptoms of breakdown in the Russian armies, and was greatly concerned.

The French General Staff also looked on the new system of command of the Russian troops as absolutely insane. This was entrusted to a "Soldiers' Council," which was to abide by the majority's decision. The French military attachés reported that the offensive to be launched in April was a matter of passionate controversy. Weighing the lessons derived from the Russian experience, the General Staff clung firmly to the conviction that freedom to criticize the command, along with the weakness due to political intervention in military decisions, inevitably led to the degradation of the Army and eventual defeat.

On March 18, 1917, in the traditional parade celebrating the memory of the dead of the Commune, in front of the "Mur des Fédérés" at the Père Lachaise Cemetery, three uniformed officers, a captain—it was Marcel Déat—an infantry lieutenant and a second lieutenant of artillery marched past with the crowd of workers. As they went by, the spectators cried, "Long live the Red Army!" On April 3, the historian Élie Halévy, who was acting as sicknurse in a military hospital, wrote to a friend: "I don't know what soldiers you have come across, weakened perhaps by loss of blood. I myself have seen only the rebelliously inclined who constantly seek some way of finishing this massacre and who, finding none, brood on vengeance."

At Compiègne, on April 6, a final War Council was held, to consider the coming offensive. Painlevé, the President of the Council, would have preferred to await the reinforcements that might be expected from the United States, which had just entered the conflict. General de Castelnau, highly disturbed by what was going on in Russia, refused to express an opinion. Franchet d'Esperey and Pétain were skeptical about the prospects of success, but Nivelle, who had the operational responsibility for the northeast front, maintained his stand. The offensive was to begin, as planned, on April 16.

On that day, at six o'clock in the morning, sixty French divisions went into action. These assaults would come to naught in less than one week. On that very day, April 16, 1917, Lenin arrived in Petrograd, accompanied by several leaders of the Bolshevik Party. The whole stage was set for a revolutionary unheaval that would put the existence of the Army at stake, no less than the outcome of the war.

In 1914, the number of serious cases tried by courts-martial was 3,000. It rose to 14,000 in 1915, to 25,000 in 1916. In the first four months alone of 1917, there were 26,000 such cases. At the same time, the number of desertions rose from 409 to 2,433, then to 8,924, and in 1917 there were to be 21,871. On April 29, Nivelle explained that the German Army had only twelve reserve divisions left, and asked for the continuation of the offensive. On May 5, the renewed attacks were particularly costly in manpower. Since the beginning of the offensive, there had been 30,000 killed and 80,000 wounded. The hospitals had not been made ready for this frightful influx, and the Army experienced what was called at the time "a sanitary Charleroi."

On May 4, a company of infantry had suddenly refused to make an attack on the Laffaux mill; and it was reported that in the soldiers' quarters the number of signs was increasing with the words, "Down with the war! Death to those responsible!" The rumor circulated among the troops that Annamites, who had been recruited in Indochina in order to work in the arms factories of the Paris region, had killed the wives of several conscript soldiers, in the working class suburbs of Paris. On May 19, a battalion of infantry refused to attack, and scattered in the woods. The following day, the news got around that the soldiers had sung the Internationale in a divisional depot. On the 26th, four battalions refused to go into battle. On the 27th, another battalion, just as it was about to be sent to the front, broke ranks. The soldiers hastened to the station of Fers-en-Tardenois, and invaded the trains headed for Paris. The gendarmerie had to be used to quell the mutiny. On the 29th, two whole regiments decided to leave Soissons and march on Paris, in order to demand that the deputies and the government end the war. When the Grand Quartier Général drew up a balance sheet, it had to record that sixteen Army corps took part in the mutinies: 113 infantry regiments, 22 battalions of chasseurs, one Senegalese battalion, two units of the colonial infantry, twelve artillery regiments and one regiment of dragoons had rebelled.

For the General Staff, the situation assumed the proportions of a national crisis. During the few days marked by the gravest mutinies, a wave of strikes of a dimension unparalleled since the beginning of the war broke out in the main industrial centers. In Paris, the strikers numbered 100,000. They demonstrated in the streets, and to the slogans calling for reforms was sometimes added the rallying cry of revolutionary defeatism: "Down with war!" The military governor of Paris reported that the capital was filled with deserters. Potential deserters, according to the General Staff, were led astray as soon as soldiers on leave arrived at the Gare de l'Est. The industrial region and mining basin of Saint-Étienne were struck almost totally.

The Federation of Metalworkers launched an appeal to French workers calling for solidarity "beside the comrades of Russia and Germany, for an international action against the war of conquest." Thus this month of May, 1917, saw the coinciding of pacifist Socialism with the first signs of the Russian Revolution, of working-class resistance to war with the tragic weariness of the exhausted or rebellious soldiers. This coming together, as seen by the high command and the Army cadres, was the confirmation of all their fears and all their prejudices. The mutinies and the strikes demonstrated that the press campaigns against the General Staff, the agitation in Parliament concerning the conduct of operations, and the demand for "war aims" that would allow peace to be negotiated could lead to anarchy in the country, disorders in the streets and the disruption of the Army. This upheaval, following in the wake of the Russian Revolution, could bring about a general collapse and, soon after, defeat in war.

It is important to understand what the crisis of 1917 represented for the officers of the regiments stationed in the front lines or just to the rear of them. They knew the men under their command, since for months past they had shared with them the mud of the trenches, the rats, the vermin, the anguish before going over to the attack, the test of nerves under the pounding of the artillery. They knew that their units were sometimes at the end of their tether. They knew, too, that to emerge from shelter and advance unprotected toward the line of enemy fire required a flawless morale and entire obedience to superiors. This morale and this discipline had to be maintained, and imposed when necessary. But now the rumor was spreading that in neighboring quarters the men had refused to go up the line, that in one company there were five or ten deserters, that one regiment had to be pulled back from the front because the troops, at the signal to advance, had remained in the trenches.

The officers found that, all of a sudden, the whole foundation of the very existence of their units was threatened. They had to ask themselves if the real state of their units was not hidden from them, and whether the veil was not about to be torn into shreds. These were the same soldiers whom they had asked about their families, who shared their packs of cigarettes with their officers, who waited for the arrival of mail with the same impatience officers themselves felt, who lived in hope of the same leave, who had the same fears, used the same vocabulary and laughed at the same jokes. Might not these soldiers, tomorrow or perhaps at that very instant, refuse to obey, and turn their rifles on their officers? But the solidarity between the combatants of every rank was too great, the front-line camaraderie too strong, for these officers, however suspicious some of them might be at the "wrong spirit" of the men, to doubt for a moment the courage, the devotion, and even the decency of their own soldiers. What was the cause of this incomprehensible wave of anger and revolt, which suddenly seemed to sweep away the bravest of men, transforming them into mutineers or deserters?

In regimental quarters, in the mess halls where the officers of the same battalion came together, in the General Staffs of the divisions or Army corps, all the conversations fell back on the same theme. The "wrong newspapers" had disturbed people; some deputies had sent, to soldiers from their constituencies, letters that criticized the high command; soldiers returned from leave in the big towns and the workers' suburbs repeating "Socialist" slogans which the workers, who were too well paid, had picked up from trade unions that specialized in defeatism.

Besides, no one back home gave any serious thought to the war; money was circulating too freely in the hands of the "new rich" who set the tone, cared not a whit for what went on at the front, encouraged immorality and corrupted the deputies in Parliament. All of which led the officers to the final question: this disorder in the rear and rebellion among the troops, wasn't it what had already occurred in Russia; wasn't it a sign of revolution?

Pétain, who had replaced Nivelle at the head of the Grand Quartier Général, took measures to improve the soldiers' quarters, stepped up the frequency of leaves for the men and of periods of rest for the units, improved the food, distributed decorations more liberally, and carried out only twenty executions, although 118 had been condemned to death. But these measures would have had no effect if they had not been accompanied by an almost total stoppage of the offensives on the French front. The new Russian government, presided over since May

19 by Kerensky, informed the British, French and Italian governments that, while the Russian promise of 1914 to conclude no separate peace would be honored, it desired a return, as rapidly as possible, to a general peace "without annexation or indemnity, on the basis of the rights of peoples to dispose of themselves."

Simultaneously, the Kerensky government approved the initiative of the International Socialist Office, which had just issued an invitation to the Socialist Parties of the countries at war to attend a joint conference in Stockholm on the basis of these same principles.

On May 27 and 28, the National Council of the French Unified Socialist Party met to discuss the proposal. For the first time, it decided by a majority vote to send a delegation to Stockholm where, no doubt, there would be a delegation of German Socialists. General Pétain protested that in time of war it was intolerable that a political party should engage in negotiations with nations of enemy powers. The attention aroused by the Stockholm meeting could create the impression that peace might be established very soon, the continuation of the war would result in profound disappointment, and the morale of the troops would be affected. The government adopted this view, and refused to grant the Socialist delegates a passport.

For the first time, on a weighty and clearly defined issue, the General Staff had intervened to oppose a decision taken by a great political party. No doubt, 467 deputies had ratified the decision taken by the government at the request of the Grand Quartier Général. But there was now a flaw in the bloc formed in August, 1914, under the impulse of national unity. Pétain would most probably not have protested against the Stockholm meeting if he had not, at the same instant, had to deal with a wave of mutinies. But his actual protest showed very clearly that the whole military hierarchy had established a connection between the dislocation that seemed to threaten the Army and the Socialist tendencies in favor of a negotiated peace.

But in this same year, 1917, a new factor strengthened the *union sacrée* in its decision to continue the war. The United States entered the war on April 2, only a few days after the launching of the offensive whose failure would bring about the Army crisis. The American participation was an immense relief for every conscience worried by the exaltation of nationalistic and chauvinist feeling, and for all those who did not want the defensive war in which France was engaged to become a war of extermination. President Wilson proclaimed that he desired "neither conquest nor domination." He had

declared war on Germany only "in defense of law" against "the bar-
barousness of submarine warfare."

Thus it seemed that there was a universal consecration of this war
"for justice and liberty" which the majority of French people, and
especially left-wing opinion, were convinced they had been fighting
for since 1914. If the United States intervened on the side of France,
while having no territorial ambitions and no hatred of Germany, then
the Allied cause was just. It might be said that, in the French mind,
the American intervention not only guaranteed victory in the long
run, but served as a justification and as a tranquillizer of people's
consciences.

On January 8, 1918, Wilson enumerated his Fourteen Points. The
whole humanitarian and pacifist ideology of the French Left seemed to
find expression in them. There was such an unbroken connection between the struggle of the Left against right-wing nationalism, militarism and chauvinist delirium, and these principles of Wilson's, which
seemed to voice the ideology shared by all the Allies, that liberal
opinion and French left-wing circles could believe that once and for
all they had been shown to be justified in accepting the terrible political and moral constraints of the war. Everything was there: the condemnation of secret diplomacy, the freedom of the seas, the limitation
of armaments, the regulation of colonial questions "bearing in mind
the interests of the indigenous populations," the idea of a League of
Nations, the evacuation of the territories that the Germans had invaded, the independence of Poland, the liberation of Belgium, the
return of Alsace-Lorraine to France, the rectification of the frontiers
"on the basis of the line of division clearly distinguishable between
the nationalities," and, for the peoples of Austria-Hungary, "the greatest latitude for their autonomous development."

In left-wing circles it was felt that once Wilson's Fourteen Points
were adopted by all the Allies, they would ensure the victory, after
the war, of the liberal and democratic ideology as opposed to the
imperialisms, the military nationalisms and the autocracies. Some—
this tendency manifested itself among the minority in the Socialist
Party that was pacifist and sympathetic to the Russian Revolution—
hailed the triumph of the ideas they had defended at the time that
the invitation to the Socialist conference in Stockholm had been discussed. The rest, the majority of the Socialists and the Radical-
Socialists, thought that it was the justification of their fidelity to the
union sacrée, and of their rejection of the criticisms flung at them from
the extreme Left.

Public opinion on the Left was not particularly disturbed by the hesitation of the French government with respect to Wilsonian ideas. The people had no knowledge of the content of the secret treaties signed during the war. They had no sympathy for the Austro-Hungarian Empire and desired the liberation of all its nationalities. In university circles, those favoring Czech independence were particularly numerous. Furthermore, the resolution to eliminate once and for all the danger of any new German act of aggression was no less strong on the Left than on the Right. In this respect, it was felt that the French government could be relied on, when peace arrived, to ensure the safety of the country. The conclusion drawn from the United States' entering the war and from President Wilson's promises was, simply, that France's cause was just, that France was fighting "for the right."

To the high command and the military hierarchy, the events of May, 1917—the mutinies and wide-scale strikes—had offered proof in tangible form that the conjunction of defeatism and social disturbances could disorganize the country and the Army, and bring the country to the brink of defeat. At the root of the trouble, according to the military hierarchy, was the failure of the government to react against pacifist ideas, the press campaigns against the command and the conduct of operations, the corruption at home, and the indifference that appeared to have affected the whole administration of public affairs. From now on, military opinion readily reached the conclusion that the most trivial episodes of the war backed up its convictions. Léon Daudet's articles in *L'Action Française* and Clemenceau's parliamentary speeches reveal exactly the same tendency.

Malvy, the Radical-Socialist Minister of the Interior, was accused by Clemenceau of responsibility for the strikes and the mutinies. A friend of his, Almereyda, a former anarchist and Editor of *Le Bonnet Rouge,* was convicted of having been paid by the Germans to launch campaigns in his newspaper against the high command, against the military operations and in favor of a compromise peace. The business manager of *Le Bonnet Rouge* had also received handsome sums from the secret funds of the German Ambassador in Switzerland.

The indulgence shown Almereyda at the Ministry of the Interior brought about Malvy's resignation on August 31. At the same moment it was discovered that one of the chief French newspapers, *Le Journal,* was also in the service of "defeatist propaganda." The editor and his two collaborators had received twenty-one million francs from the German services and an intermediary, Bolo-Pacha, ten million. Nationalist opinion hesitated no longer to blame left-wing circles that showed excessive indulgence for certain Socialist groups, holding them responsible for too many weaknesses in view of the danger of treason. The espionage affairs infuriated people. After the discovery that *Le Bonnet Rouge* and *Le Journal* were involved, the woman spy Mata Hari was executed on October 13.

Three weeks later, the Bolshevik revolution in Russia justified all the fears that had been entertained in military circles. Socialism and the theme of peace "without annexation and without indemnity" had led to the weakening of the state and to revolution. Now this Russian collapse would allow Germany to focus all its efforts on the French front: revolution was treason. "The triumph of the maximalists in Petrograd," wrote the one-time passionate antimilitarist Gustave Hervé on November 10, "together with the Austro-German victory in Italy, ought indeed to inspire in our political leaders also the salutary notion of hastening a solution of the latent ministerial crisis in which we have been living for the past month." In *Figaro* of that same day, Alfred Capus came out in favor of a cabinet headed by Clemenceau. "The Unified [Socialist] Party has just pronounced its anathema against Clemenceau, whose eventual accession to power would be, it seems, a challenge hurled at the working class and a peril for national defense. M. Albert Thomas calls for M. Caillaux, cites him as an authority, and associates him closely with Socialist doctrine. In these circumstances there is no reason for astonishment that the Unified Socialists declare the scandals have been exaggerated and that M. Clemenceau is a national peril."

The chief organs of the conservative bourgeoisie established an equation between treason and the Left or, at all events, a particular Left that had been antimilitarist and pacifist before the war and that currently was suspected of being too indulgent toward defeatist campaigns, German maneuvers and revolutionary intrigues. So, while the entry of the United States into the war and the contribution of Wilsonian ideology to the Allied side strengthened, in almost all Leftist milieux, the conviction that this was a just war that had to be won, the political exploitation of the 1917 crisis heaped all the sins of the world on certain sectors of the Left.

At this time, *L'Echo de Paris* was the newspaper that officers read most frequently. Maurice Barrès's editorials set the tone in military circles. *L'Action Française* and *Figaro,* although they reached fewer people than did *L'Echo de Paris,* had as their most faithful clientele the conservative bourgeoisie from which so many officers came. In November, 1917, these papers named their adversaries.

They named Malvy, who had already been forced to resign. They named Caillaux, the former President of the Council, who was responsible for introducing the income tax in France and who had negotiated with Germany to settle the Moroccan affair—Caillaux the disdainful antimilitarist and the parliamentarian who, in the corridors of the Chamber of Deputies and the Senate, and also behind the scenes among the Socialists, was waging a campaign—clumsily, in actual fact—in favor of a compromise peace.

It was a victory for military and nationalist opinion when, on November 13, Painlevé bowed to the united opposition of Left and Right and resigned as President of the Council; a victory, too, when Poincaré called on Clemenceau, the implacable enemy of Caillaux, to form a government.

Clemenceau was the most representative figure of left-wing nationalism, the most characteristic of the Jacobins, the man who had always been in favor of the "hardest" policy with respect to Germany even before the war. His distrust for the conservative and clerical army cadres was matched by the most intransigent nationalism. His accession to power, in November, 1917, might have led to a renewal of the *union sacrée* in a fresh burst of patriotic fervor and, at the same time, to the general acceptance of a certain conception of peace, derived from the Jacobin ideal of the French Revolution and modernized by the new notion of the "right of the peoples to dispose of themselves."

But Clemenceau came to power at the height of the struggle against "defeatism." He had been supported by all who, under the cloak of national vigilance, sought to condemn the element of the Left that had been seduced by the example of the Russian Revolution and that, at all events, had decided to limit France's war aims to goals compatible with the democratic ideal. The current that swept Clemenceau into power might call into question the alliance of military opinion and left-wing opinion that had been sealed in August, 1914, and that lasted until the 1917 crisis, at the very moment when Wilson's Fourteen Points imbued the Left with the conviction that, by pursuing the war unflaggingly, it could remain faithful to its views. Confronted by these two divergent tendencies on which depended the future relations between the democratic spirit and military opinion, Clemenceau lent the whole weight of his personality, of his government and of his policy to the direction diametrically opposed to the Left. Maurice Barrès, in *L'Echo de Paris* of November 16, could already foresee that Clemenceau's government would mark the victory of the nationalist, military outlook over the pacifist strain running through the parties of the Left. "Today," he wrote,

> Messieurs Leymarie and Malvy have departed. Has their war policy disappeared with them? For three years catastrophic men have rummaged around in the services of national security and practiced the system of composition with the enemy. . . . It is the duty of the new government we are waiting for to hunt out, wherever it may be hid, each fatal virus and to destroy it. As for us, that we may play our part in this sanitary operation, let us definitively expose the true nature and the logic of the task that has been pursued by Messieurs Caillaux, Malvy and Leymarie.

Maurice Barrès was not mistaken. The tone of Clemenceau's speeches was sufficiently revelatory. "We present ourselves before you," he told the deputies, "possessed by the single thought of total war; the Frenchmen we were forced to hurl into battle have rights over us." Notice had been given that "total war" would justify the eradication of doubt, the muffling of the critics, the struggle against all those who, sincerely or not, demanded a peace that would not depend on "total victory." Those who wanted to avoid the pointless dragging out of the war had asked for a clear definition of "war aims" which the enemy could accept as soon as he had become convinced of his inevitable defeat. But Clemenceau at once announced: "You ask me for our war aims. My war aim is to be the victor." There was no clearer way of saying that the enemy could not learn the Allies' political intentions before being obliged to capitulate.

Public opinion was inevitably sharply divided, in view of the extreme attitude embodied by Clemenceau. In Leftist circles, where it was felt that patriotism should not serve as a cloak for warmongering, people repeated a stanza by Gassier:

> *Déjà drapé dans son linceul*
> *Clémenceau dit: je fais la guerre*
> *Hélas! pleure un humanitaire;*
> *C'est qu'il ne la fait pas tout seul.*
>
> (Already draped in his shroud
> Clemenceau says: "I make war."
> "Alas!" laments a humanitarian,
> "It's a pity he doesn't do it all by himself.")

From the military and nationalist viewpoint, the Bolshevik revolution was a confirmation, definitive and catastrophic, of the worst that had been imagined. Disorder, strikes, the breakdown of military discipline and defeatism could now be assumed to lead not only to a Socialist revolution but to the victory of the Bolsheviks, that is, to "peace at any price." The French General Staff and General Headquarters were aware that peace between Germany and Russia would result in the massive strengthening of the German Army on the French front. If American aid did not arrive in time, the worst dangers still lay ahead for the Allied Armies. It was not even certain that the front could be held.

The political circles closest to military opinion regarded the Bolshevik revolution as being above all the corroboration of all that had been said of the "weakness" of Leftist groups in their attitude to "defeatism." On November 17 *L'Echo de Paris* wrote:

> We have received our Lenins, the men who were needed to infect us. Russia, by the spectacle she is offering the universe, invites us to suppress all those who, so to speak, act Soviet, and everything that creates a mess. It's the same thing. Of course there is no possible analogy between morale in France and the uncertainties to be found in Russia, even before the throes of revolution. But all the same there is no sense in playing with such dangers, which have wiped out a great people in the space of a few weeks. Let Russia, as the Allies unfortunately are compelled to see and lament, be a warning, so that she may not be a contagion.

Father Sertillanges, whose authority in Catholic circles was very great, declared on December 11, in a patriotic address, that "French peace can no longer be a conciliatory peace, the peace of Stockholm or of the Soviets. It must be a peace reached through bitter warfare waged to its conclusion, the peace of power that smashes violence, the peace of the soldier."

The climate that had been created by the crisis of spring, 1917, and by the Bolshevik revolution that had just broken out, prepared the public to accept any measure that national vigilance would seem to require. The public, indeed, had been conditioned to accept this over-all identification of the pacifist Left, revolutionary Socialism, defeatism and treason. As the autumn of 1917 drew to a close, they all seemed to be involved in the same mysterious and fearsome conspiracy.

On December 12, at the request of the Paris Attorney General, Guillaume, proceedings were initiated against Caillaux, accusing him of being in touch with the enemy, of misuse of authority and of defeatist propaganda. Proceedings were also launched against Malvy. There was, in actual fact, no serious backing for the charge of communication with the enemy. Caillaux was condemned to three years' imprisonment only for "unwitting aid to the enemy," while Malvy, convicted of maladministration, was condemned to five years' exile. Both were later to receive amnesty and to regain their berths in Parliament. Caillaux became Minister of Finances in 1925. But, for all the fragility of the proofs of their guilt that the government had put together, nationalist and military opinion was provided with a mighty weapon by the decision to bring criminal charges against two prominent political personalities, both of the Left.

"During the first three years of the war," wrote *L'Action Française* on December 13, "France was betrayed by a gang whose secret leader was Joseph Caillaux, former President of the Council, and whose avowed leader was Malvy, the perpetual Minister of the Interior."

And Gustave Hervé, in *La Victoire* of December 16, had an answer for the Socialists and Radical-Socialists who appeared ready to defend Caillaux and Malvy against the violent attacks of the Right and extreme Right:

> Just as the Socialists, prior to the war, understood nothing of the war to come, nor of the seriousness of the Alsace-Lorraine issue, so today they have understood nothing of the Russian Revolution, nor of the obligation that rests on them to prevent a wave of Leninism from arising among us by publicly and solemnly repudiating every form of German Socialism's class struggle with which they have stuffed the skull of our working class for the last twenty years. Here they are, enlisting among the saviors of Monsieur Caillaux, out of hatred for Clemenceau, whom they have never forgiven for having been right so many times against our prewar German-style Socialism, and out of indulgence for the maximalists and defeatists in the Party, before whom they debased themselves two years ago. Here they are, upsetting the consciences of our Socialist working people by suggesting that the Caillaux affair is another Dreyfus Affair. And they wax indignant when they are told that, by this fantastic campaign, they are in danger of assassinating France.

Yet opinion, both in the population at large and in the Army, seemed little affected, throughout 1918, by the various political and juridical episodes of the struggle against defeatism that Clemenceau had undertaken. Paris was struck by the first shells fired from 100 kilometers away by "Big Bertha," which was to become one of the most famous guns of all time, and one of the most powerful recollections the French would preserve of the years of warfare. At the same time, the large-scale offensives launched by the Germans in the first six months of 1918 led to an exodus of the population, streams of refugees finding their way to Normandy, the Loire valley and Burgundy. The arrival of American troops in Paris revealed a new universe, inhabited by healthy young men who still had the freshness of the peace years so remote from the European peoples, morally and physically exhausted by the war. France's large towns became the most cosmopolitan cities in the world. They housed Americans, Portuguese, Englishmen, Indians, Australians, New Zealanders, Senegalese, Malagasy and North Africans. It seemed that the world had a rendezvous along the few hundred kilometers of the front, and that all humanity had finally come to succor France.

In view of all this, what importance could be attached to the protests of a Malvy, the sarcasms of a Caillaux, or to the daily parliamentary disputes between Socialists and government concerning a definition of war aims? A few months after the crisis of spring, 1917, almost nothing would have remained of the polemics and the accusations of defeatism and treason if, behind this treason and defeatism, there had not lurked, since the month of November, the specter of the Bolshevik revolution.

All the Allied governments had at once grasped that the seizure of power by the Bolsheviks would soon put an end to warfare on the eastern front. In the most powerful countries of the west, the daily press vehemently denounced the Bolshevik betrayal of all the undertakings entered into by the preceding Russian governments. At the same time, the papers provided a plethora of news items, true or false, about the violence that was accompanying the Revolution, the anarchy that was overtaking the Russian regime, the mounting famine and the bottomless pit of misery to which the Russian people seemed to be condemned. The military cadres reacted to the Bolshevik revolution just as did all bourgeois opinion, in France and the other Allied countries.

Bolshevism seemed to them, naturally enough, to mean the subversion of every traditional value: monarchy, bourgeoisie, state, Army, religion and fatherland. At bottom it remained quite incomprehensible, it would appear, to all bourgeois opinion, especially in France. The few attempts at an explanation that can be discovered in the newspapers and magazines, or in private correspondence, show that the Bolshevik cataclysm was accounted for by the hoary myths of the instability of the "Russian soul," and of the unbridled passions and mysterious furies of Dostoevski's characters by whom, apparently, Russia was peopled.

But for the military the Bolshevik problem had a more concrete and a more immediate impact. First it had to be estimated what effect the incidence of the Russian defection would have on the actual prosecution of the war. The Bolshevik government which had seized power on the night of November 6-7, on the 9th released a statement calling on all the peoples and all the governments at war "to begin discussions at once in order to bring about an equitable and democratic peace." It also specified that all territorial changes should be carried out only on the basis of a "free plebiscite." On November 21, the Russian Supreme Commander was ordered to begin negotiations with the Germans, and the Allies were asked to associate themselves with this. The refusal was immediate, and even the German General Staff was hesitant about how to proceed. Ludendorff, Major General of the Armies, telephoned General Hoffmann, the German Chief of Staff on the eastern front, and asked if it was possible "to talk with those people." General Hoffmann undertook to try, and on December 15 the armistice was signed between the Germans and Russians.

In the meantime, an inter-Allied conference held in Paris had discussed the Soviet initiative. The representative of President Wilson, Colonel House, proposed that in order to keep Russia in the war there should be a general revision of the war aims, "in a liberal spirit." The French government, overlooking the Russian suggestion that territorial changes might be carried out via a "free plebiscite," let it be known that it could not accept the re-establishment of the 1914 frontiers. Great Britain and Italy supported this viewpoint. Lloyd George, the British Prime Minister, proposed to relieve Russia of the obligations she had shouldered at the outset of the war. By permitting the negotiation of a separate peace, and so confronting Russia with the German demands, which would undoubtedly be considerable, the Russians would finally realize that their traditional alliances were the most reliable. The French and Italians rejected the British proposal. The Allied governments did not reply to the Soviet initiative, and announced that they would look into the matter of war aims with the "Russians" as soon as Russia had a regular government recognized by the people. Thus the Allied governments refused to recognize Soviet authority. But in military circles there were no doubts about the reality presented by the Bolshevik revolution.

With the consent of the General Staff, General Niessel, at the head of the French military mission, made contact with the Soviet War Ministry. The Soviets were asked to insert, in their armistice with Germany, a clause that would forbid the Germans to transport German troops from the Russian to the French front. The Bolshevik government agreed, and this clause actually figured in the armistice agreement, but the Germans refused to accept any supervision that would have established a check on its implementation.

Two days before the armistice was signed, on December 18, Trotsky suggested to Noulens, the French Ambassador, that discussions should be resumed on the Soviets' proposals of peace "without annexation" and with "the right of peoples to dispose of themselves." He demonstrated that these proposals would allow France to reacquire Alsace-Lorraine, since the inhabitants would certainly favor a return to France. Trotsky hinted that, if the Germans opposed this conception of the peace, the Bolshevik government would not hesitate to start a revolutionary war. But the French government under Clemenceau had not the least intention of seeking a peace based on principles enunciated by the Soviets. It did not even wish to recognize the legitimacy of their rule, and Trotsky's proposals received no reply.

Yet at the same moment, the representative of the French General Staff in Russia was trying to obtain a clear definition of the policy that France and its Allies would adopt vis-à-vis Russia. General Niessel could see three possibilities. The first, he declared in his reports to the French government, was to organize resistance to the Bolshevik revolution by backing up all the elements hostile to it. But he stressed the difficulties of such an undertaking, particularly in view of the lack of regular and rapid communications between the Allies and Russia. Or, he wrote, one might profit from the collapse of the Russian state in order to negotiate a peace with Germany that, in exchange for the ceding of Alsace-Lorraine, would allow the German Empire to obtain territorial compensations at Russian expense. This was the solution envisaged by Paléologue, the former French Ambassador in Russia. But General Niessel had two objections to make. Such a policy would be lacking in loyalty toward a country that had been France's chief ally before and during the war and, besides, since there would be nothing to stop German expansion to the east, Germany would ultimately be mightily strengthened both geographically and economically. The balance of power in Europe that had existed in 1914 would be completely overthrown, and to the advantage of Germany. A third possibility was to maintain contact with the Bolshevik government as well as with its adversaries. If the Russians should refuse to accept the peace terms that Germany sought to impose, a rapprochement could be effected with the Soviets, and they could be helped to go to war anew. In the opposite eventuality, the growth of resistance to the Soviets could be better prepared by relying on the national minorities, the Poles, Finns and Balts, for example, than by turning to the Russian monarchists who for the most part, in General Niessel's estimation, favored Germany.

All in all, the representatives of the French General Staff did not eliminate any possibility of some measure of collaboration with the Soviet regime, and they did not hesitate to call the government's attention to the difficulties that would be met with in applying the policy of deliberate support for the anti-Bolshevik groups. They even declared themselves, clearly enough, to be opposed to any solution that would leave Germany with a free hand in eastern Europe. Thus, in military circles, there seemed to be a greater concern about the risk of German expansion than any desire to crush the Russian Revolution at the first possible moment.

After a démarche undertaken by Trotsky, dated February 20, 1918, when the German-Russian negotiations had broken down, the French military mission succeeded in convincing Noulens, the French ambassador, to telephone Trotsky and assure him of the "military and financial support of France," in the event that hostilities between Russia and Germany were resumed. On February 22, the Council of the People's Commissars accepted "the aid of the brigands of French imperialism" against "the brigands of German imperialism." On the 23rd, General Niessel advanced his first practical proposals with respect to renewed hostilities, and at the same time advised the Soviet government to settle its difficulties with the Finns, Poles and Roumanians. But on the following day, February 24, the Council of the People's Commissars accepted the last German propositions.

Thus the French General Staff, attuned above all to the requirements of the war against Germany, had done nothing, in the course of the winter of 1917-1918, to urge on the government a deliberately anti-Soviet policy. The upper echelons of the Army had not taken an extreme position in the great wave of anti-Bolshevik feeling that

was shared by almost every element of French society and throughout
the political arena, except for a very limited section of the working
class. The question of opportuneness alone had dictated the General
Staff's moderate tone, when for the first time the problem of relations
with Soviet Russia had to be faced.

For the totality of military opinion, what mattered above all was
that the Bolshevik revolution represented the ultimate stage on the
path of defeatism and treason. What mattered was that social disturbances, rebellion against the high command and the undisciplined
behavior among the troops or on the street had led to the revolution,
which in its turn had brought about a cessation of the combat against
Germany. The mark that this left on military opinion would never subsequently be erased.

This was the time when deepseated and lasting myths were born.
The train that made its way across Germany, with the authorization
of the German General Staff, transporting Lenin from Switzerland
to Russia, became a historical symbol. This "armored train" would
remain, for more than twenty years, a kind of irrefutable proof, for the
military, that the Bolsheviks could never be anything else than German agents.

At the same time, the whole conservative and nationalist ideology
with which the military were so deeply impregnated induced them
to look on communism as the most acute form of social subversion,
and the deliberate destruction, not only of an economic system, a state
and an established order, but of the fatherland itself. Every officer
on active duty would regard as an incomprehensible scandal the adherence to the Communist International of the majority of French
Socialists in 1920. Henceforward, as seen through military eyes, there
would be in France a party dedicated to revolution, which would not
hesitate to "connive in treason, provided only that a defeat would
enable it to seize power."

With the great German offensives of winter and spring, 1918,
every Allied defeat was linked up, in all conversations, exchanges of
letters and official reports, with the mass transfer to the French front
of German divisions from the eastern front. The losses suffered by
the French Army heightened the dimensions of the drama, and the
blame was placed on "Bolshevik treason." In the early months of 1918
the French had as many men killed, wounded and taken prisoner as
in all of 1916, in spite of the slaughter at Verdun and the battles of
the Somme.

After the French once more began to gain the upper hand, the recollection of the crisis remained. There remained, also, this great "gap" in the east that appeared to have swallowed up civilization, religion and fatherland. The Russian Revolution, together with the victory over Germany of the coalition of the western Allies, was going to dispose of the old myth of the Franco-Russian Alliance for a long time, perhaps forever. Yet a whole generation of politicians, diplomats and generals had worked for this alliance, all the more passionately because they believed that on it depended security in peacetime and the longed-for *revanche*, if war should come. All the elements that had gone to form this alliance now were turned against revolutionary Russia.

The simple decree of the Bolshevik government reduced to zero the twelve billion gold francs that had been lent by France to the Czarist empire. Where had they come from, these twelve billion that constituted one-fourth of French investments abroad? They had been provided by the small or intermediate bourgeoisie, prudent and conservative in outlook, that had felt more confidence in the guarantees of the state than in the fluctuations of industrial prosperity, and had invested the money without fear, since the imperial government of the largest country in the world guaranteed the bonds. The investors may also have had the notion that they were performing a kind of patriotic duty toward their "Russian ally," as well as placing their money advantageously. And it was this same conservative, provincial bourgeoisie that provided the French Army with many of its officers. It was, in any case, the social milieu that appeared most familiar to an Army in which money was scarce and which, far removed from the main current of business interests, hoped to compensate for a meager pension by a cautious placing of its funds. If "Bolshevism was treason" in 1917 and 1918, after the war the Bolsheviks became "robbers." For a whole generation and a numerous social class, these new myths acquired an extraordinary power.

But the crisis of spring, 1917, appeared far distant now, and the presence of American troops pushed the Russian Revolution into the background. And then, victory lay ahead. "It was about midday on November 11, 1918," wrote a witness,

> that the signing of the armistice . . . was announced to the public. . . . I experienced, in Paris, that unrestrained joy and those hours of sublime folly whose waves rolled irresistibly over the town, when in the

middle of the day the cannon roared, the bells rang out wildly, the fronts of the buildings were covered with banners and the windows, filled with radiant faces, looked out on the deliriously happy streets. . . . This Paris began by tearing off the black veil which, since 1871, had covered the statue of Strasbourg in the Place de la Concorde. It was a splendid day in St. Martin's summer, with a slightly hazy sun and diffused light. In every city in the land, but in Paris more than anywhere else, people walked and ran in the streets as though crazy, laughing, crying, singing, shouting, gripping each other's hands and dancing wild fandangos. Anyone who wore any sort of uniform was loudly cheered or borne aloft in triumph. Strangers kissed each other on the mouth. Joy and delirium were everywhere. At every street corner and at the least opportunity, the Marseillaise resounded. That evening, the whole city was aflame, the whole city was dancing. . . .

In the solitude of the Élysée, Poincaré, the dry, austere President of the Republic, noted: "Joy, fever, delirium of Paris." Two days later he entered Metz with Clemenceau and Pétain, and that evening he wrote: "A day of sovereign beauty. Now I can die." One of those who has borne most eloquent testimony to this war, Jacques Meyer, confessed at the end of his book of recollections: "The war, *mon vieux*, was our buried, secret youth." History can relate subsequently that, for the French Army, old age had set in.

CHAPTER EIGHT

THE TREATY OF VERSAILLES

✠

Prior to the outbreak of war, the Socialist Marcel Sembat had issued a warning to the whole body of republican opinion. It was summed up in the title of his book, *Faites un roi sinon faites la paix* ("Make a King or Make Peace"). The idea was widespread, in leftist circles, that a victorious general might be the gravest possible danger to the Republic. This fear exactly corresponded to the more or less openly avowed longings of a segment of the Nationalist Right, reduced by its electoral defeats and political setbacks to cherishing the myth of the Soldier. Bathed in the glory of *revanche* the Soldier would use his sword, after victory had been achieved, to establish a new state.

But hopes and fears were largely forgotten, in this autumn of 1918 when Frenchmen were transported by the joy of a victorious peace, which had come to crown four years of unexampled hardships. The victory, moreover, could not be attributed to any one man. Despite the renown of Foch, who commanded all the Allied Armies in 1918, the public had not forgottten the part played by Joffre, the victor of the Marne, and by Pétain, the "healer" of the French Army. Perhaps Clemenceau's popularity was greater than that of any other political or military personage. His combative disposition and the actual violence of his words and attitudes gave him the dimensions of a real warrior. In the eyes of most Frenchmen, he who had incarnated the war effort now symbolized victory.

The prestige of the Army leaders at the end of the war was at a high point. France recognized its own image when it looked on its victorious Army, and the military leaders were refulgent in all the glory of a conquest that had demanded the labors of the whole country. Psychologically, public opinion was better prepared than at any other moment in the history of the Third Republic to comprehend the intervention of the military chiefs in the vital concerns of French politics.

With the German request for an armistice, on the night of October 3-4, the political questions raised by the war's imminent end at once began to tangle with the strictly military aspects of the armistice. In his reply to the request of the new German Chancellor, Prince Max of Baden, President Wilson was careful to associate the conditions of an armistice which would exclude any resumption of hostilities, with the conditions of a peace which implied that "those who up till now have been the masters of German policy" should be replaced by the "real representatives of the German people." Thus the American government itself subordinated the definitive end of the war to the political objective it regarded as essential, namely, a revolution in Germany.

The Allied governments were determined to impose on Germany an armistice that would make it impossible for her to begin war anew. "The main problem," wrote Colonel House, "was to determine precisely the conditions that would amount to a capitulation, without endangering the peace." This was the way in which the problem was submitted to the military leaders and, in particular, to Marshal Foch, the Allied Supreme Commander.

During the meeting at Senlis, on October 25, at which the Commanders of the French, British and American Armies were present, the Marshal proposed that Germany be required to hand over part of its rail equipment, in order to make the movement of troops impossible. He also proposed that the Allied troops occupy the left bank of the Rhine and the bridgeheads on the right bank. Clemenceau adopted Marshal Foch's arguments and obtained the approval of the Allied governments.

Colonel House addressed the decisive question to Foch. "Monsieur le Maréchal, from the strictly military point of view and putting aside any other consideration . . . would you prefer to see the Germans reject the armistice as it stands at present, or would you prefer that they sign it?"

Foch's reply was categorical. "One goes to war only for its results. If the Germans abide by the armistice as it has been signed, we are assured of its results. This being established, no man has the right to spill one more drop of blood." And on November 8 Foch said to Clemenceau, "This is my armistice, now you can conclude any peace you wish, I will be able to impose it. My task is over, yours is beginning." But Clemenceau was not able to conclude the peace "he wished." On November 4 he had accepted Wilson's Fourteen Points as the basis of the future treaty. From this moment on, French demands could only find a place within the framework which had been accepted even before Armistice Day and which had been imposed by the weight of the American contribution in the last phase of the war.

On November 27, at the government's request, Foch transmitted a first memorandum on the conditions of peace that could guarantee French security.

He was a member of the French delegation to the peace conference which included, besides Clemenceau and his principal adviser, André Tardieu, the Minister of Foreign Affairs, Stephen Pichon, and the Secretary General of the Ministry of Foreign Affairs, the Ambassador Jules Cambon.

Foch proposed that the German frontier should be at the Rhine. On the left bank of the river there would be set up states "relatively independent, and bound to the western countries by economic accords and by treaties of military alliance which would automatically place them at the side of France, if there should be any war against Germany."

A second note, dated January 10, 1919, insisted on establishing at the Rhine the "military frontier of Germany." This solution could only be obtained, Foch declared, if the countries on the left bank of the Rhine were independent, and entirely freed of German sovereignty. He no longer spoke of any military alliance with these states, but envisaged a permanent military occupation by the Allies, and a customs union with the western countries. On February 18, Foch made his position clearer. He expressed the view that Germany should be deprived of all sovereignty, not only over the left bank of the Rhine, but also over the territories occupied by the Allies since the armistice. This took in several bridgeheads on the right bank. As for the political stature of the Rhineland, after its separation from Germany, Foch said that he had no desire to make proposals, preferring to leave the problem to the outcome of the negotiations over the peace treaty.

Thus, from the standpoint of French security, he outlined a very clear policy on a point of capital importance: France should demand the political separation of the Rhineland from Germany. There could be no question of French annexation; Foch could not fail to be aware that such an annexation would conflict with the right of peoples to self-determination. Nor, doubtless, had he any illusions about the attitude of the Rhenish population. Abandoning, in his note of January 10, the notion of a military alliance between the Rhineland states and the Allied countries, Foch restricted himself to the principle of the political independence of the Rhineland, leaving it to the diplomats to work out the details.

Clemenceau made Foch's attitude his own. On February 23, he told Colonel House that the peace treaty should set up a Rhineland republic. He even insisted that it should be "prosperous," so that it might be sheltered from the temptation to rejoin Germany at a later date. On the following day Tardieu returned to the attack, expounding to Colonel House all the factors that worked in favor of the establishment of such a republic. Confronted, however, by the Colonel's skepticism with regard to the real feelings of the Rhinelanders, he suggested that a new state might have, to begin with, an independence with temporal limitations, after which the population could decide its lot in a plebiscite. This notion reconciled the principle of the rights of the peoples to dispose of their own destinies and the French demands with respect to the Rhine.

On February 25, the government expressed its official position vis-à-vis the Allies. A memorandum drawn up by Tardieu was transmitted to them, outlining the official position of the French delegation at the peace conference. This memorandum took up the position expounded by Foch. It was based on strategic considerations: Germany could bypass France's natural defenses in a few days by invading Belgium and Luxemburg; if the first battle was lost by the French Army, continental Europe would fall into the hands of the German Army, and it would then be difficult for the American and British forces to establish bridgeheads in Europe. Consequently the Rhine was the only possible frontier, not only for France, but for the whole group of western countries.

These factors were also of interest to the new European states in the east. Strengthened by the Rhineland glacis, Germany could exercise a decisive pressure on Poland and Czechoslovakia without the Allies being able to provide any help, particularly since there was now no Russian alliance to count on. Thus the only solution was the creation of a "buffer state" comprising the left bank of the river and the bridgeheads of the right bank. The independent state would remain under the supervision of the League of Nations. With regard to this essential element of the peace treaty, the highest military authorities in France and the government had an identical attitude which, furthermore, was in accord with the deep-seated aspiration of the whole country.

Convinced that they had indeed experienced the "last of all wars," most Frenchmen found little to interest them in the details of a peace treaty—their single concern, amounting to an obsession, was security. They readily agreed that the occupation of the left bank of the Rhine or, at the very least, the independence of the Rhineland, was the necessary condition of this security. The idea of "rounding out the national frontiers" by pushing them as far as the Rhine was traced back to the origins of the French state. Actually, this idea cannot be found in circulation under the ancient régime. It dates from the time when the Girondins were setting their mark on the French Revolution, and no government or regime had recurred to it after the collapse of the Second Empire.

Later on, when the time had come to reconsider France's military problems, de Gaulle would take the same ineluctable data as the starting point of his thesis, devoting the opening pages of his book, *Vers l'armée de métier*, to the problem of the northeast frontier:

> Just as a portrait may arouse in the observer the impression of a personal destiny, so does the map of France reveal our lot. The main body of the fatherland provides at its center a stronghold, a rugged massif of aged mountains, flanked by the plateaus of Languedoc, the Limousin and Burgundy; all around, immense glacis most of which are difficult of access for any threatening invader, being protected by trenches, the Saône, Rhone and Garonne, barred by ramparts, the Jura, Alps and Pyrenees, or plunging far away into the Channel, the Atlantic and the Mediterranean; but with a terrible breach in the northeast, that links up with the Germanic regions the vital basins of Seine and Loire. Though nature indicated to the Gauls that the Rhine was their limit and their protection, scarcely did it touch on France than it became remote, leaving the country exposed.
>
> It is true that the Vosges provide a broad partial rampart, but it can be circumvented by the Belfort Gap of the Salt Marshes. It is true that the banks of the Moselle and of the Meuse, supported on the one side by the Lorraine plateau, and on the other by the Ar-

dennes, constitute obstacles which although not negligible are lacking
in depth, so that one blunder, or surprise or piece of carelessness is
enough to lose them, and which the first withdrawal in Hainaut or
Flanders renders liable to a setback. Now it so happens that in these
lowlying plains there is neither a barrier nor a trench to which resistance might cling; there are no lines of surmounting heights, and
no rivers parallel to the front. Even worse, here geography organizes
invasion by numerous penetrating routes, the valleys of the Meuse,
the Sambre, the Scheldt, the Scarpe, the Lys, along which streams,
roads, rails undertake to guide the enemy.

Distressing when viewed in relief, the northeast frontier is no less
so with respect to its projecting groundplan. The adversary who attacks simultaneously in Flanders, in the Ardennes, Lorraine, Alsace
and Burgundy, is striking concentric blows. If he succeeds at one
point, the whole system of the French defenses crumbles. The first
steps forward lead him to the Seine, the Aube, the Marne, the Aisne
or the Oise, and then he need only make his way easily downstream
to strike at the heart of France, Paris, where all these rivers come
together.

This gap in the girdle of fortifications is the country's age-old affliction. Through it Roman Gaul saw the barbarians fling themselves on
its riches. There the monarchy stood up with difficulty against the
pressures of the Empire. There, Louis the Great defended his power
against the European coalition. The Revolution almost expired there.
Napoleon succumbed there. In 1870, disaster and disgrace took no
other road. In this fatal avenue we have just buried one third of
our youth.

There was an unavoidable conflict between the "Rhenish" conception of French security and the democratic ideal that had imbued the
entire ideology of a France at war, or at least the republican majority
in the country. Clemenceau, with his military and political advisers,
was simply trying to overcome this antithesis by throwing in with his
demands the idea of an "independent" Rhineland with supervision
vested in the League of Nations. This compromise opened the way for
others. On the Left, those most responsive to the ideals incorporated
in Wilson's Fourteen Points preferred to rely on the collective security
guaranteed by the League of Nations, on general disarmament and,
above all, on the disarmament of Germany and the substitution of a
democratic republic for the German Empire.

French nationalism was, actually, opposed to the Left's humanitarian and democratic ideal on one point only, the matter of what

territorial amputations should be practiced on Germany's western frontier. The Right looked on the political separation of the Rhineland as the only solid guarantee of French security against Germany. Here the Left ran up against the inherent contradiction between the desire for security and the nationality principle. Only the Socialists— or, at least, the Socialist majority—were directly opposed to the views of the nationalist Right, and placed all their hopes in the democratic future of the German Republic. The Radicals, Republicans and Moderates were on the lookout for any compromise that would reconcile security and principle.

This was, indeed, a serious matter. For the first time, perhaps, in the history of the Third Republic, a split had occurred in French opinion concerning the gravest problem of foreign policy: What must be done to ensure that France would never again be invaded?

It was in this political climate and this psychological context that discussions were begun between the Allies on the French proposals for the Rhineland. Early in March the British government announced its opposition to any policy of autonomy for the Rhineland territories. Lloyd George recalled that the basis of the peace treaty was to be Wilson's Fourteen Points, and that any such amputation of German territory was in conflict with the right of peoples to decide their own destinies. In Lloyd George's view, if Germany were divided, the attempt would be made later to re-establish national unity, and this could occasion another world war. Finally, he reminded his hearers that the whole tradition of English politics was hostile to long-term commitments on the European continent and that, in these circumstances, he could not accept the permanent military occupation of the Rhineland.

As for the American point of view, President Wilson expressed it in a cable sent on March 10 to his personal representative in Paris. "There must be no agreement, even provisionally, to the separation of the Rhineland provinces from Germany, and in no case may consent to this be given."

On the evening of March 14, the first interview took place between Wilson, who had just arrived in Paris, Lloyd George and Clemenceau. The last-named again went over the arguments contained in the note of February 25. Lloyd George set out to refute them, and when Clemenceau asked him to outline his own solution to the problem of western security, he made a new proposal. France, he declared, could have a guarantee of automatic and immediate aid, in the event of an unprovoked aggression by Germany. This was preferable, he went on to say, to the general guarantees provided by the Charter of the League of Nations, for this organization could not offer immediate aid to the countries attacked, whereas the American and British alliance could offer France immediate assistance.

Three days later, on March 17, Clemenceau let it be known "that he appreciated fully the offer made by Great Britain and the United States." But he asked for additional guarantees. Since the French Army would have to fight alone, at least during the early days of a new war with Germany, it would be necessary to demilitarize the left bank of the Rhine and a zone at least fifty kilometers in depth on the right bank. The Rhineland would also have to be occupied by the Allies on a temporary basis. Thus the essentials were settled. What followed were merely discussions of the supervision of German disarmament and of the duration of the Rhineland occupation, this being linked with the payment of reparations by Germany. The main lines of the treaty, with respect to the security provisions, were virtually decided.

Marshal Foch was informed of the decisions taken on the 17th by Clemenceau. Clemenceau explained that he had been unable to budge Great Britain and the United States from their rigid position, and that he had had to seek another solution. He stressed the value of the guarantees obtained, involving, as they did, the automatic intervention of the Allies in the event of war with Germany, and the permanent demilitarization of the Rhineland, after its temporary occupation. He concluded by invoking a strictly political consideration: the country would be unable to grasp a break with the Allies, in face of such guarantees, and there was not the least chance of having the original French views adopted.

Foch was surprised, apparently, by the rapidity of Clemenceau's change of position. President Wilson had been in Paris for only five days. Foch thought that the government had not really put up a fight, and had made no genuine attempt to convince the President. He expressed the objection that acceptance of the Anglo-American proposals was to "give up the prey for the shadow." The Rhine constituted a solid barrier, while the promise made by Wilson and Lloyd George "might be easier to make than to keep." The conversation between Foch and Clemenceau became rather heated, the latter accusing the former of "abandoning him," while Foch declared that he simply was abiding by the position he had expressed ever since the armistice was signed. It was not yet possible to speak of a rupture between the head of the government and the chief leader of the Army, but it could no longer be dissimulated that there was almost no line of approach shared by the two men.

For the first time the Army, with the voice of a Marshal of France, had had the opportunity to intervene directly in the delineation of policy, and to influence it in the direction desired by the military leaders.

While the occasion had been the Rhenish problem, the root of the matter lay deeper. For the overwhelming majority of the people, the Rhine was indissolubly connected with the idea of security. A great groundswell of opinion might support Foch, and suddenly bring about a major crisis in the relations of Army and state. The passionate determination to eliminate every threat of a new German invasion, and the prestige of the victorious generals, might lend additional force to this current. And this current might extend far beyond the narrowly nationalistic groups and provoke a head-on conflict with republican, liberal, humanitarian or Socialist opinion, which set store, above all, on international solidarity, the right of peoples to dispose of themselves, and the unchallenged sovereignty of civilian over military power.

In the last days of March, the crisis seemed ready to explode. Foch was determined to intervene on every possible occasion in favor of the original French attitude toward the Rhine, so that finally the Allies would be compelled to recognize how justified it was. On March 28, he seemed to be assured of weighty reinforcements, for Poincaré, the President of the Republic, wrote to Clemenceau to inform him that he was opposed to the agreement reached with Wilson and Lloyd George.

But Poincaré's views differed from those of Foch. He merely considered that the evacuation of the Rhineland at the end of fifteen years was "inacceptable." In his view, the payment of reparations and the occupation should remain connected as long as payments were being made, and not for fifteen years only. He thought it utopian to imagine that the Rhineland could be occupied anew—as had been provided for in the Allied compromise—once it had been evacuated, in the event that reparations payments were suspended. The reservations expressed by the President of the Republic concerned a very precise point and, at bottom, involved the economic and financial questions inherited from the war, not the fundamental problem of security. Nevertheless, he was considered hostile to the proposed treaty, and Foch believed that he could count on his backing.

The interview that took place between them revealed how far the Marshal was prepared to go in support of his thesis. Since Poincaré appeared to approve Foch's objections, the latter asked Poincaré to intervene directly. Poincaré replied that it was the task of the government to negotiate. Foch then invoked Article VI of the Constitution of 1875, which stipulated that "the President of the Republic negotiates treaties." Poincaré could only answer by pointing to the invariable tradition of the Third Republic, which vested the real executive power in the President of the Council and the government. Foch was well aware of this. What he was asking Poincaré to carry out amounted to a political revolution. He received a categorical refusal.

On March 30, he wrote to the president of the "Council of Four," which included Clemenceau, Lloyd George, Wilson and Orlando, asking to be heard "before the question has been decided any further." On the following day Foch presented two memoranda, one in defense of his own solution, the other explaining that any other formula would be "not only less certain, but also more costly." He declared that "to abandon the barrier of the Rhine would be an unthinkable monstrosity, because if this barrier were abandoned, it would give Germany the possibility of resuming an aggressive policy. As Commander-in-Chief of the Allied Armies, I consider that the Rhine must be the military frontier to be maintained in the future by the Allied Armies."

In the discussion that ensued, he stated that this did not amount to creating a new Alsace-Lorraine. "When I ask for the abandonment of the left bank of the Rhine, I conceive the possibility of leaving the territories to the west of the river in control of their own administration." In his conclusion, he endeavored to heighten the drama, and to round out the political and strategic arguments by appealing to war memories:

> There is no principle that obliges a victorious people, after it has won back in a defensive war the means indispensable to its own salvation, to hand back these means to the adversary. There is no principle that obliges a free people to live in the shadow of a continual menace and to count only on its Allies to prevent the disaster, when it has just paid for its independence with more than one million five hundred thousand corpses and by unparalleled devastation. There is no principle that can prevail against the right of peoples to exist, against

the right enjoyed by France and Belgium to ensure their independence."

According to the director of Clemenceau's military cabinet, General Mordacq, "Messrs. Wilson and Lloyd George paid only the most casual attention to these explanations, just on the side of politeness, and declared that it was pointless to insist, for they had made up their minds on the matter." No one supported Foch's view. On April 4, Albert I, King of the Belgians, took part in the discussions of the Council, but he too failed to support the Marshal. On April 6, Foch demanded that Clemenceau tell him if a definitive accord had been reached. The President of the Council answered that, although the negotiations were not entirely completed, it was already evident that none of the Allied governments would accept either the establishment of a political frontier on the Rhine, or the permanent military occupation of the Rhineland.

Foch then wrote to Clemenceau, asking that before obligations were assumed on which there could be no going back, the delegates should be called together so that they might be informed of the state of negotiations. On April 9, Clemenceau replied, stating that he no longer considered Foch to be a member of the French delegation. As Commander-in-Chief, Foch was "subject to the authority of the Allied Powers," whereas the French delegates "must be subordinate exclusively to the French authorities." But Clemenceau promised to summon Foch as soon as a "sufficiently clear formula had been provisionally agreed upon by the heads of government."

On April 17, the President of the Council had asked the Marshal to summon the German plenipotentiaries for the 25th, when they would be informed of the conditions for a peace treaty. Foch, in reply, expressed his astonishment that it had already been decided to convey to the Germans the text of the treaty when he himself, contrary to the promise given him, had not been consulted by the Council of Ministers before the final decisions had been taken. Nevertheless he drew up a proposed telegram which he sent to Clemenceau, so that Clemenceau might forward it to General Nudant, who was President of the Armistice Commission, and responsible for the relations between the Allied governments and the German government.

Clemenceau reacted violently to Foch's attitude. He complained about it to Poincaré, spoke of "insubordination" and, taking advantage of a worsening of the situation, summoned Pétain for the following day, no doubt in order to gain an insight into his frame of mind, in case it should be necessary suddenly to relieve Foch of his post as Commander-in-Chief of the Allied Armies.

On the same day, April 18, *Le Matin* printed an article that reproduced Foch's viewpoint and had clearly been inspired by him. The government received the information that the proofs had been corrected by one of his staff officers. Foch also granted an interview to the London paper *The Daily Mail,* in which he openly voiced anew his criticisms of the compromise project adopted by the Council of Four. The official censorship, which had not ceased its functions since the armistice, forbade the reproduction of the text in the French press.

Clemenceau had to meet the vigorous objections of Wilson and Lloyd George. He declared that he regretted Foch's intervention, just as they did, but that he was anxious to maintain the union of "the men of the victory" and "that one should not destroy the country's picture of them." Lloyd George and Wilson asserted that they had "the liveliest admiration" for Foch, but added that if he "should oppose the decisions of the government—no matter how great his renown"—they would not spare him, for at stake for them was a "fundamental question of constitutional responsibility."

On April 19, Clemenceau received Foch. He warned him against the maneuvers of newspapers and politicians and, apparently, raised the questions of the officers surrounding him, perhaps even naming General Weygand. Foch protested that he had acted in entire good faith in the telegram incident, and asserted that a Marshal of France, and military adviser to the government, had the duty to express his mind and make no secret of his feelings, but that he had never had any idea of disobeying in any way the orders of the head of the government.

On April 25, Foch was summoned before the Council of Ministers. He then asked "to be informed of the formula provisionally adopted by the head of the government." At this moment he thought that renewed pressure, perhaps in combination with a press campaign and the intervention of political personalities, might induce Clemenceau to abandon his intentions. Clemenceau objected immediately that the treaty would be deliberated upon by the Council of Ministers, that Foch was not a member of the government, and so had no right to be informed, at that time, of the decisions that had been reached. Poincaré, who was presiding, expressed the contrary opinion, that the Marshal should be informed of them so that he might give his views; whereupon the Council of Ministers would deliberate. Foch asked that minutes should be kept of the ensuing discussion. Clemenceau remarked that no minutes were ever kept of the proceedings of the Council of Ministers. But, since Foch's intervention was to take place prior to the actual beginning of the Council of Ministers, and in view of the risk that Foch might withdraw without having expressed his opinion, it was decided that Weygand, who had accompanied him, should take notes of the discussion.

All that it actually amounted to was a declaration by Foch of the importance of permanently occupying the Rhine; to do anything else was "to commit a crime of lèse-France." After this, Clemenceau asked him to withdraw, "together with persons outside the government." Later he was to send back to Foch the copy he had received of the minutes recorded by Weygand, stating (according to Weygand) that he "deemed it wiser to take no cognizance of it."

Not until the closing days of April did the Marshal come to know the exact text of the treaty. He at once addressed a letter to Clemenceau, protesting against the clauses of the treaty dealing with the Rhineland and giving him to understand that, unless they were modified, he would resign from his post as Commander-in-Chief of the Allied Armies. Clemenceau read this letter to Wilson and Lloyd George, and the three of them at once decided to replace Foch by Pétain, if the former did indeed submit his resignation.

But Foch opted for another course. On May 6, at a plenary session of the Peace Conference, and without having informed the head of any government of his intention, he asked to speak. His whole speech concerned the matter of the occupation of the Rhine. He noted that at the end of five years it would be necessary to withdraw from Cologne, which gave access to the Ruhr Valley, and that ten years later the whole Rhineland would be evacuated. "As the payments and reparations are to continue for thirty years," he said, "we will find ourselves in possession of more or less restricted guarantees for fifteen years, and, at the end of fifteen years, without any whatsoever." Evoking the possibility of a renewed occupation beyond the period envisaged, Foch remarked that this would depend on a decision of the Committee on Reparations whose jurisdiction, in his view, was inadequate.

Then he presented additional arguments in favor of the occupation of the Rhine:

> The occupation of the Rhenish territories is of value only because of the domination of the Rhine that it provides. By falling back, as has

already been said, we offer pledges, we open doors, we place ourselves in a position of inferiority because we are forced to occupy a country with no barriers and to defend it with much greater forces, that is to say, in a much more costly fashion. To maintain the occupation of the Rhine is the most economical and the surest formula. I may be mistaken, and that is why I have asked other military experts to associate themselves with me to re-examine this matter. How long should the Rhine be held? As long as one is anxious to receive guarantees, since there are no others. When payment shall have been received and the guarantees shall be sufficient, all that will have to be done is to withdraw the troops and leave.

Please note that I am asking for the continued occupation of the Rhine, and not of the Rhineland regions. It is on this point that there is a divergency of opinion. The objection is advanced that I am occupying a country: this is not so, I am occupying the crossings of the Rhine, and this requires only modest forces.

When the execution of the treaty shall be well under way, when the German lands shall reveal their unquestionable goodwill, when disarmament shall have been achieved, then the burden weighing on everyone, Allies and Germans alike, can be lightened by reducing the forces of occupation and this reduction, as you can see, will be achieved not by giving up a territory but by reducing the military manpower.

This intervention actually amounted to a retreat, as compared with Foch's previous attitude. He no longer insisted on the political independence of the Rhineland regions, and so left in obscurity the essential element of his notes written in November, 1918, and January and February, 1919, which had been at the bottom of the first proposals made by the French government. Besides, he now associated the problem of the carrying out of the treaty, and especially of the payment of reparations, with the continued occupation of the Rhine. All that Foch was doing was to make his own the reservations expressed by Poincaré, who had maintained all along that the occupation should last as long as the period of payment of the reparations.

By the date on which he was speaking, May 6, when the delegations of all the Allied and enemy governments had come together to sign the treaty, any discussion of Foch's views appeared belated, situated as they were between Poincaré's views and those that had been adopted by the Council of Four. The permanent demilitarization of the Rhineland eliminated the risk of a sudden attack against the frontiers. The guarantee of automatic and immediate assistance from the

United States and Great Britain assured France of massive support, and set against the dangers of a German aggression the certainty of a coalition of the three great western powers. The treaty stipulated that the evacuation of the Rhineland, in five-year stages, would be delayed if Germany did not fulfill its obligations. The continued occupation, or reoccupation, of the Rhineland territories would be legal, if Germany were guilty of gravely infringing the treaty, or if the guarantees it contained were to disappear—that is to say, the treaties of alliance with England and the United States. Had not Foch said, "When payment shall have been received and the guarantees shall be sufficient, all that will have to be done is to withdraw the troops and leave"? The feeling shared by all French ministers, and by most political personalities, was that Clemenceau had obtained all that he could obtain, in view of the irreducible opposition of the Americans and British to a political separation of the Rhineland from Germany.

It goes without saying that the Council of Four rejected the revision of the treaty asked for by Foch. Foch's surprise intervention in the plenary session of May 6 had, in any case, deeply shocked the English and American delegates. Bonar Law, a future British Prime Minister and one of the plenipotentiaries, declared: "If an English general took such an attitude vis-à-vis his government, he would be dismissed within fifteen minutes." "You know my views," Clemenceau replied, "but however much I regret the Marshal's attitude, we must not forget that he led our soldiers to victory."

This crisis atmosphere was still weighing on the Council of Four when the next day, May 7, the solemn objections of the German delegation to the clauses of the treaty obliged the Allied governments to envisage the hypothesis of a renewal of hostilities. So Foch was asked to prepare a plan for the invasion of Germany, and this was discussed by the Council of Four on June 16. But in the first two weeks of June, one of the major elements of the treaty, the occupation of the Rhineland territories for five, ten and fifteen years, was suddenly called into question by Lloyd George, who asked that the stay of Allied troops on the Rhine should be limited to eighteen months.

What had happened? From this moment on, American and British public opinion, but especially the British press, criticized the harshness of the peace terms imposed on Germany. On the Conservative side, there was the fear that the Germans might in despair affect a rapprochement with Soviet Russia, or even go over to the Bolshevik

Revolution. As for the Labor Party, it denounced the aggressiveness of French nationalism and the imperialist character of the clauses in the treaty that concerned the Saar, the Rhineland occupation, the "pillage" of German economic resources and the incalculable dimensions of the reparations. Lloyd George, who knew that the treaty had been hammered out after hard bargaining and that it would be extremely difficult to have it reconsidered, had a particular reason for asking that, at the very least, there should be a reduction to eighteen months of the occupation of the Rhineland.

The whole structure of the peace treaty had almost collapsed in the Rhineland in the last days of May. It was learned in Paris, on June 1, that a certain Dr. Dorten had tried to proclaim an independent Rhineland Republic the day before. It appeared beyond doubt that the French military authorities had helped him, while General Liggett, in command of the American troops at Coblenz, had objected. On June 2, Lloyd George and Wilson transmitted to Clemenceau the reports they had received from their own General Staffs. These reports concluded that the French authorities were responsible for the activities of the Rhineland separatists. Lloyd George at once demanded that the occupation of the Rhine should be reduced to one or two years, and to back up his demand he bluntly declared that the French generals "no longer hesitated to intervene openly in order to provoke the political independence of the Rhineland." It was no longer a mere matter of discussing the more or less deliberate interventions of Marshal Foch with the French government or the Council of Four. Now for the first time the political neutrality and the national discipline of the Army were in doubt.

The task of occupying the greater part of the French zone of occupation on the left bank of the Rhine, including Mainz, the capital of the Rhineland, had been entrusted to the French Tenth Army, headed by General Mangin. He belonged to the colonial cadres and had spent the greater part of his career in Africa. He was among those whom Joffre and Gallieni, themselves from the colonial army, had called on to take over commands at the outset of the World War. Coming from a conservative Catholic family, he represented rather well the generation of officers who had inherited the moral and intellectual traditions of the old aristocratic, traditionalist Army but who had breathed fresh life into them, owing to their experience overseas, and who no longer cared to restrict their horizons to the struggle "between officers' clubs and republican cafés." Joffre, although himself a Freemason, had noticed Mangin's talents and attributed to him a decisive part in the Verdun victory.

Mangin's experiences in the colonies had undoubtedly left a profound mark on him. He had certainly retained a relative indifference to the living conditions and to the psychology of the troops, and his zeal in pushing on with the most difficult and costly offensives had earned him, in 1917, the nickname of "the butcher." Perhaps he had also retained certain habits of independence toward political authority. In the wide spaces of Africa, the officers' freedom of action, where an administrative and economic role was added to their military functions, justified such an independence. At all events, he could not have acquired, in the African setting, a deep understanding of European political problems.

Mangin took a great interest in the Rhineland, "which," he declared, "has been entrusted to me, in part at least, by Marshal Foch." How seriously could one take the Rhenish particularism that Mangin thought he could discern on every side? Today it is possible to give a pretty precise answer. Since the amalgamation of the Rhineland with Prussia, in 1814, there had undoubtedly been a tradition of distrust—on the part of the Rhinelanders, who were more liberal, more western and more "bourgeois"—of the Prussians, and above all of the officials, who were authoritarian, respectful of hierarchies and more "military" in temperament. The fear that along with the rest of Germany they might have to pay dearly for the defeat of 1918 perhaps induced certain milieux to try to escape the burden by breaking away, at least provisionally, from the national community. It could also be thought that the *petite bourgeoisie* of industry and commerce might look on separatism as a means of protecting itself from the economic hegemony of the big Ruhr industrialists, of the German *Konzerne* whose authority and power had emerged strengthened from the war years, during which they had imposed the most rigorous economic discipline on the whole country.

As 1919 dawned, there were other reasons. The Social-Democrats had seized power in Prussia. Their first actions had been to counter clerical influence on the state and to attack the privileges granted the churches by the monarchy. This had aroused considerable apprehension in the Catholic circles of the Rhineland, whose members enjoyed a decisive political and moral authority.

Thus, in the Rhineland, those who were more anxious to see the continuation of the economic regime and of the social order than they were imbued with loyalty to the German fatherland could discover certain advantages in separatism or, at least, in political autonomy.

But these concerns could not be those of the great majority of the population, who for more than a century had been associated with other Germans in the Prussian state, for more than fifty years in the German Empire and for the four years of war with the common struggle waged by the whole of Germany against a coalition of enemies.

Mangin, who thought that he could everywhere see signs of separatist movements in the Rhineland, knew that Foch was at odds with Clemenceau, who, confronted by the intransigence of Wilson and Lloyd George, had at last abandoned the idea of political independence for the Rhineland. "Nothing is yet lost," he wrote to his wife on April 5, "despite our incredible blunders. Nevertheless, the treaty must allow the Rhinelanders to proclaim their desire for an independent republic."

Almost four weeks after the French government had decided to abandon the notion of political autonomy for the Rhineland, Mangin still continued to believe that this was not only possible, but indispensable. Aware of Clemenceau's decision, he still thought it possible to change it. No doubt he would not have adopted so unambiguous an attitude if he had not been convinced, at the same time, that the choice of the Rhinelanders, in conformity with the choice of peoples to decide their own destinies, would be to break away from Germany.

On April 6, Mangin summoned the leaders of the Rhenish separatist movement. "I have spent my day," he wrote, "talking with conspirators who show up in considerable numbers—too late, alas, for any immediate use to be made of their anti-Prussian feelings. They are very much disturbed at the thought that Prussia is going to remain." In the weeks that followed Mangin found nothing better to do than to bolster up the hopes of the Rhineland separatists, though he neither could nor would take the initiative. He was doubtless waiting for the result of Foch's interventions with Clemenceau and the Council of Four.

Toward the end of April, he had at last to bow to the weight of the evidence. The compromise solution accepted by Clemenceau and the Allies remained firm, the President of the Council had refused to bow before Foch's expostulations, and no one in Paris had the least hope of establishing a Rhineland republic. Only the development of a local movement, begun by the Rhinelanders themselves, could perhaps change the situation.

On May 9, at Aachen, Mangin met the chief Rhineland separatists. His estimation of these persons became, seemingly, less blindly partial. "One of them," he wrote, "a post-office employee, is intelligent." But he had no one else to speak to, and there was nothing for him to do but to explain what chances still remained of setting up a Rhineland republic. "The Entente," he told them, "knows nothing of the Rhinelanders, and the peace treaty speaks only of Germans because only Germany exists in its eyes. If the Rhinelanders want a special status in the German Republic, they must take the matter up with Germans. That is the attitude of the Entente. It can have no other."

Certainly that was the official position which should have been shared by the commander of the French forces of occupation. But Mangin went beyond this, and revealed his own views. "All is lost," he told them, "if the current attitude is maintained . . . but all may be saved if instead of a republic forming part of Germany an independent republic is demanded. The *'Los von Berlin'* must be total. Then you can take your stand on the Wilsonian principle that declares peoples free to choose for themselves. An autonomous German republic, you have said: add the word independent, and demand the right to be represented at the Congress of Versailles, speak without further delay. And I tell you that on my own account, for the scruples of the Entente are so great that it no longer passes on any orders to its representatives, so that you may have the greatest possible liberty."

Mangin found that his situation was becoming more and more difficult. The men he had encouraged and, perhaps, compromised in the separatist movement and who, in any case, plunged into the adventure with his support, might well be sacrificed the day after the peace treaty was signed. He hoped that the separatists would declare themselves openly and so present the French government with a *fait accompli*; that Foch would undertake, in Paris and on the political plane, what he himself would have done in Mainz on the local level.

The evening of May 12, Dorten, one of the principal leaders of the Rhineland Party, went to Mangin and asked "that the task should be made easier by ceding the basin of the Saar to the new republic. . . . The new republic would be separated from Prussia from the outset, but united to Germany." This would obviously be a decisive advantage for the partisans of autonomy. But Mangin realized that he was in no position to make any commitment concerning the Saar, and that Dorten was still playing on the words "autonomy" and "independence." "This is another point of view," he noted, "and a fascinating conversation, but it has not convinced me." The Rhineland separatists needed more substantial backing that they had so far enjoyed. By obtaining the unification of the Saar and the Rhineland, they would have an argument of great weight for the populations of the Rhine's left bank. After all, did not the peace treaty provide for the autonomy of the Saar, under the control of the League of Nations?

So they returned to the charge on May 17, in a three-hour conversation with Mangin. Mangin sensed that the foundations were far from sure, but there was no time to lose. The acceptance of the Versailles Treaty was being debated in Germany, and any attempt to thwart the Treaty would have to take place in a few days. On May 20 Mangin met again with the separatists, and the next day he felt bound in person to inform General Liggett, who commanded the American Army at Koblenz, "that the Rhineland Republic was about to be proclaimed in his zone and that he, Mangin, did not think that he had the right to prevent the Rhinelanders from expressing their will in his zone." General Liggett's reply—Mangin may have been familiar with his feelings—was both polite and firm. He "was personally very favorable and also most eager to satisfy General Mangin and to aid a project favorable to France, but he had orders to oppose any change in government."

President Wilson was at once informed of Mangin's activities. He protested to Clemenceau and received the assurance that the French government would not allow its policy to be upset by the private initiative of a general. Jeanneney, Under-Secretary of State for War, was despatched to the Rhineland to discover what role Mangin was playing. His report was severe and, on June 3, the government was to reprove Mangin, noting that he had intervened in political matters outside his competence and inviting him to limit his activities to his military duties.

But between Jeanneney's mission on May 25 and the government's note of June 3 lay a period of eight days which Mangin, while observing all possible discretion, decided to exploit without delay. "It's to take place tomorrow," he wrote on May 28:

> I have approved the proclamation to the people of the Rhineland. It's a great step forward as compared with the first proposal. Then I have sent an officer to explain the necessity of a first declaration, the birth certificate of a new state, in which it arrogates to itself diplomatic

representation, with the right to decide peace and war, treaties of commerce, etc. . . . Then would come the proclamation, and finally the notification to the Powers of the Entente and to Germany, and notification via Marshal Foch to the President of the Peace Conference . . . everything in a telegram tomorrow. . . . In a word, the matter appears to me to have gone too far for abandonment to be possible. I have been compromised to some extent in newspaper polemics, particularly in *Die Kölnische Zeitung,* but within limits, and there are enough errors in the news items to allow me to deny the whole thing.

But on May 29, the German government, informed of what was being plotted, made the solemn pronouncement that "any act having for its object the separation of Rhenish Prussia amounted to high treason punishable by forced labor." The separatists began to hesitate and looked fearfully to the future, although Mangin at once suggested to them the text of a new proclamation: "Twelve million Rhinelanders proclaim the Republic. The Berlin government condemns them to forced labor for life: who will carry out the sentence?" The commander of the Belgian occupation forces at Aachen asked Foch for instructions, since Foch as Commander-in-Chief of the Allied Armies was his military superior. Marshal Foch, whose staff certainly was fully aware of Mangin's activities, was thus officially informed of what was being prepared. He informed General Michel that he would send him instructions. Foch had only to turn to the Allied governments to know what their views were, and to pass on to Mangin and Michel orders reflecting this policy. But his instructions never arrived.

After forty-eight hours of hesitation, the Rhenish separatists made up their minds. Dorten proclaimed the Rhineland Republic and informed the Allies and the Berlin government officially. He established the site of the provisional government at Wiesbaden, in the French zone of occupation, where he was sure of protection. Apart from that, the rules of occupation forbade any manifestation; only the posting of notices was authorized. The French officials, both civil and military, asked for instructions. "I got out of this," wrote Mangin, "by saying that they should not refuse to enter into relations with a *de facto* government that had the future on its side." Simultaneously he organized the repression of the strikes that had been called, in Wiesbaden and Mainz, by German workers opposed to the secession. At this moment he put the whole French military and civil apparatus in the Rhineland, in effect, at the service of the "Rhineland Republic." But this was the last stage of his activity.

A telegram from the War Minister put a sudden stop to it. "I order you to take part in no conference, but to limit yourself strictly to the accomplishment of your military duties." Mangin could no longer maintain the Rhineland separatists. The deputy Doisy had visited him at his headquarters and congratulated him, adding, "All you have to do is succeed." "I have already been hanged several times!" he replied. He was not relieved of his command, however, until October 11.

On June 13, at the Council of Four, Lloyd George availed himself of the events in the Rhineland to argue for the last time that the duration of the Allied occupation of Germany should be reduced to eighteen months. Clemenceau saw to it that this request was rejected, pointing out that Mangin had been disavowed and had been forced to withdraw his support from the separatist movement. "My generals on the left bank of the Rhine," said Clemenceau, "favored a policy that was displeasing to us. I have put an end to it. Do not imagine that if I adopt the position I am now defending, where the occupation is concerned, that it is for opportunistic reasons. In the union of France, England and America, France too is indispensable."

On June 16, the Council of Four received Foch to hear him expound his plan for a war against Germany, in the event that Germany should finally reject the peace treaty. The main feature of Foch's plan, as it was reported by Mantoux, the Conference interpreter, at once led to a major political problem, that of German unity. In the opening moments of the Conference, there was a brusque return to the central problems that had earlier troubled the heads of the Allied governments. Foch's line of argument consisted in deducing the best possible strategy very precisely from a particular policy. "The regions traversed," he said, in speaking of his plan to march on Berlin—

> may offer difficulties of a special nature. As our advance proceeds, we must leave behind us occupation troops strong enough to maintain the respect of the population, that is, of sixty-five million inhabitants. It is not likely that we would meet with organized armies; consequently the force needed to smash them is unnecessary. But we must have occupation forces, because of the danger represented by the valor of the German population, if it is in the least stirred by patriotic feeling or by a nation with such capacities of organization. . . . On the other hand, this exposé serves to make clear the means available to weaken German resistance. If our maneuvers enable us to detach southern from northern Germany, at the same time as our troops are marching

along the valley of the Main, we will be confronted by only forty-five million, instead of sixty-five million men.

Foch did not seek to hide the political implications of the strategy he was proposing, indeed he stated them quite clearly. "A strategy of separation, aided by a separatist policy, would enable us to exert pressure on the head of the German organization in Berlin. The question is, are we prepared to treat individually with the separate States, the Grand Duchy of Baden, Würtemberg, Bavaria?"

Wilson and Lloyd George began by discussing the inconveniences of the "separatist policy" proposed by Foch, and pointed out that it would only be possible to deal with the States of southern Germany by remitting their share of the reparations. "One thing or the other," said Lloyd George, "either we deprive ourselves of what they must pay as integral parts of Germany, or, if we treat them like the rest of Germany, I don't see why they should come to us." Clemenceau objected at once that there should be no "mixing of politics with strategy," but stated that in his view Marshal Foch was greatly overstating the difficulties of an invasion of Germany, because he overlooked the efficacy of an Italian attack in the direction of Bavaria and of a Polish intervention in the east. Wilson, recalling the plan that Foch had proposed in October, 1918, before the armistice had been concluded, asked him if "anything had happened subsequently allowing him to modify his views?"

Foch might have replied by pointing out that the nature of the war might change completely, that one would not be confronted by organized armies but by a people practicing guerrilla warfare in the rear of the Allied Armies. In this state of affairs the necessity of a political and not of a strictly military solution would soon be made clear. But he limited himself to saying, in rather vague terms, that "the German organizations are not known to us; there may be some. The Germans may have manufactured matériel. German morale has certainly recovered. . . . The only way to eliminate southern Germany is to reflect on a separatist strategy, but if this separatist strategy is to produce any results, it must be completed by a separatist policy, imposing a separate peace and disarmament on the states of the south." And to induce the Four to make a clear decision and abandon their hesitations, he added: "I ask the governments not to seek only a single signature for the whole of Germany, but to have the treaty signed en route and so weaken the last resistance, which will be that of Prussia."

Clemenceau understood perfectly what Foch was driving at, and made such a brutal rejoinder that Foch's chief of staff protested against the terms used and left the meeting. Clemenceau had no trouble in exposing what he took to be a ruse on Foch's part. "Several weeks ago, Marshal Foch explained a plan to us and made no restrictions. He seemed to us full of confidence. What strikes us today is that he is asking for a political action without which, he says, he is unable to advance. . . . I cannot commit myself to this path. If the march on Berlin is impossible, we shall have to speak of it among ourselves and see what must be done." Lloyd George enlarged on what Clemenceau had said, recalling that three or four weeks earlier Foch, consulted on the means by which Germany could be forced to sign the peace treaty, had presented a military plan for which he had asked that a certain number of English and American divisions be maintained in Europe. He had received satisfaction. And now he let the success of his plan depend on purely political considerations. "I am afraid," said Lloyd George, "that the Marshal is mixing politics with strategy and allowing his judgment of political matters to create doubts in his mind concerning purely military questions. . . ."

It could not have been more politely asserted that Foch was altering the picture of the military situation solely to persuade the governments to deduce from it a new policy whose aim would be the destruction of German unity. Lloyd George stated this without any equivocation, after Foch had left the conference. "He wants," he said, "to return to the policy of the past, when France was aiming at the conquest of the left bank of the Rhine. . . . I fear that General Weygand's influence has much to do with this; I saw him constantly speaking into the Marshal's ear, telling him what needed to be said." Wilson had the same impression. "He has seen his projects collapse," he said, "and he does not want to help us to execute ours." And Clemenceau summed up: "It's Mangin's policy, on a larger scale."

On the evening of June 23, the German National Assembly decided to accept the Treaty. Foch's most recent plan for the division of Germany became completely irrelevant. In any case, on the very evening of Foch's intervention, on June 16, Clemenceau, Wilson and Lloyd George had envisaged replacing him by Pétain if hostilities should break out afresh. Only the fear that Foch's disgrace might encourage German resistance made them hesitate. The decision taken by Germany on June 23 put an end to the discussions of the conditions of the peace treaty. And, at the same time, it ended the crisis that had opposed to the government the highest French military authority and at least a part of the staffs.

All in all, the situation had lasted three months. Born on March 17, the day on which the French government had ceased to demand the political independence of the Rhineland, it ended on June 16, when the plans for "political separatism" proposed by Foch were categorically rejected by Clemenceau. But it could be considered virtually over on April 25, when the Council of Ministers contented itself with the guarantees of security provided by the promise of English and American alliances, the occupation of the Rhineland territories and their definitive demilitarization, and the partial but rigorously supervised disarmament of Germany. From this moment on, Foch's interventions were restricted to suggesting a better compromise than that reached in the month of April. The much more audacious steps taken by Mangin, with Foch's assistance, had to occur entirely outside the French political context, and they were nullified by the government's belated but categorical call to order.

The crisis had been serious, to the extent that it had clearly placed the government in opposition to several of the most illustrious Army leaders, at a time when they enjoyed immense prestige—equaled, however, by Clemenceau's—and with respect to the only major problem of foreign policy. Yet the crisis had been short. Everything occurred as though only Foch and his friends had supported his thesis and as though, once they had realized their isolation, they could but yield, after two or three more or less skillful maneuvers. There could be no question, even in the most conservative French political circles, of challenging some of the basic principles that Wilson, profiting from the influence of the United States in the Allied camp, had imposed on France. The right of peoples to dispose of their own destinies was, furthermore, very largely compatible with the objectives of French diplomacy, even apart from the question of Alsace-Lorraine.

Out of respect for the free disposition of peoples, and as though seeking to create a new European equilibrium, every tendency in French opinion was as one in desiring, on Germany's eastern borders, a strong Poland and a viable Czechoslovakia. In some sections of the

Right, a bias in favor of monarchist and Catholic traditions induced regrets for the vanished Hapsburg Empire. But French opinion was nearly unanimous in backing the Yugoslavs, Roumanians, Czechs and Poles. On the Left, in parallel fashion, the Danzig "corridor" was felt to be rather regrettable, in view of the desire to grant Germany a juster peace. But it had been Wilson, after all, who had wished to provide the new Polish state with access to the sea.

Thus there was a deep-rooted community of outlook concerning eastern Europe in the whole range of public opinion. Only the question of the Rhine could reawaken the old antithesis of Left and Right. The much vaunted right of the peoples could come into conflict with the requirements of French national security. Public opinion struggled, caught at the center of this contradiction, all through the discussions that preceded and followed the signing of the peace treaty.

Clemenceau had no difficulty in demonstrating that the question of the Rhine could only be solved by accepting a compromise. He began by noting the fact that absolutely no one had proposed that France should simply annex the Rhineland. Already, he declared, this politically independent or autonomous Rhineland, subject however to military occupation by the Allies, was a compromise solution. It was not necessarily the best, for if the Rhine is an excellent frontier, it is not impossible to cross it. The automatic and immediate alliance with the United States and Great Britain was a much better guarantee. And, in any event, the Rhineland was going to remain permanently demilitarized, and France would retain the right to reoccupy it, should the terms of the treaty not be fulfilled. Finally Clemenceau himself, the man who all his life had dreamed of avenging the defeat of 1871, spoke of Germany. "It is a country of sixty million inhabitants. . . . We have to live with them, even bear with them and try to get along with them. It is a question that can be solved in one way only, by getting along."

The whole of France's postwar policy was virtually defined, at bottom, in the parliamentary debate on the ratification of the Versailles Treaty. Almost everyone, except for a section of the Socialists, regretted the failure to provide lasting security along the German frontier. But everyone was resolved, at least in principle, to respect the right of the peoples to self-determination. Everyone was anxious to take every possible precaution against a German military resurgence, while realizing at the same time that one had to adjust to the fact that a powerful German state existed, and hoping that it would evolve democratically. Everyone agreed that France should belong to the League of

Nations and play the greatest possible part in it, but almost everyone was eager to strengthen the young states of eastern Europe and to maintain a firm alliance with England and the United States. Everyone wanted complete reparations for the damage inflicted on France, but no one knew exactly how France should set about obtaining payment.

The vote on the ratification of the peace treaty reflected this unanimity of bourgeois opinion. Foch's anxieties and Mangin's temerity had aroused no echo of any consequence in political circles. No groundswell could have stirred public opinion to back the direct intervention of the military leaders against the peace treaty. The skepticism concerning the solutions proposed, the alarm felt at the political "vacuums" that the treaty had created in Europe, were no match for the intense desire to escape at last from the endless discussions that had preceded the signing of the treaty, nor for the acute awareness that France could not, all by herself, impose her will. It was, fundamentally, the relative strength of the French and Allied forces that had dictated the main outlines of the peace.

In the spring of 1919, French political and financial circles were suddenly confronted by a new factor that would dominate international and internal matters for years to come. Great Britain and the United States had decided to abrogate the agreements that guaranteed the exchange rates among the Allies. At once the franc, deprived of British and American support, began to decline. Ruined and menaced with inflation, the country needed reparations from Germany as rapidly as possible in order to meet the "recoverable" expenses, those, that is to say, which matched the costs of reconstruction and of war damages. The battle for reparations dominated all French foreign policy, and was shared by every majority, every government and every party.

The battle could not be won without the backing of France's former allies. But it was clearly realized that the United States had no interest in the problem of German reparations. Great Britain, too, was eager to re-establish as rapidly as possible the system of international exchanges that had existed before the war, and would not support France to the point of threatening Germany's entire economic equilibrium, and Europe's along with it. Despite this latent difference in outlook, which was becoming more and more overt, the French leaders were resolved to seek a policy that would unite France with Great Britain, Italy and Belgium.

In October, 1921, the first difficulty arose. There had been an agreement between France and Germany to limit reparations paid in gold and currencies, replacing them by reparations in kind. This was thwarted by Great Britain, which feared the consequences of too close an industrial collaboration between France and Germany. At the same time, the British government intervened at the Washington naval conference to reduce France's habitual rank among the world's navies; it was decided that the French navy should be on a par with the Italian, and smaller than that of Japan, which itself was smaller than the American and British forces, which were to be equal. Thus the Franco-British entente was menaced.

On November 27 Germany asked for a postponement of the reparations payments. To induce France to accept a moratorium on the German debts, the British offered the guarantee of a British alliance against Germany that had been promised while the peace treaty was being negotiated but subsequently withdrawn when the United States had refused to ratify the treaty.

Briand considered that the moment had come to regulate both the political and the economic problems to which the war had given rise. He agreed to the summoning of a general economic conference of all European countries that would have prepared the way for the political re-entry of Russia into the "concert of nations." At the same time he wanted the guarantee of the British alliance "in case of an unprovoked German attack" extended to France's allies in eastern Europe, a request which the British had hitherto refused. He hoped at least to obtain an agreement that France and Great Britain "would concert their policies" in the case of German aggression against Poland and Czechoslovakia. What Briand actually obtained at the conference, which took place at Cannes in January, 1922, would be determined by the Dawes plan on reparations in 1924 and by the Locarno accords of 1925, guaranteeing the political frontiers. France might have obtained better terms then if the policy pursued between January, 1922, and November, 1923, had not awakened British suspicions and German resentment.

During this period the majority of French political parties tried to obtain more immediate and more bountiful results with respect to reparations by pursuing an independent policy based on military force. The industrial and commercial *grande bourgeoisie* realized that, without enormous German reparations made available very rapidly, France would be forced to devaluate the currency. The majority of the Council of Ministers decided, on January 11, 1922, to accept the responsibility of a rupture with Great Britain. Briand was recalled from the Cannes conference and was replaced by Poincaré. This was the starting point of a policy that wound up, on January 11, 1923, with the occupation of the Ruhr, with Italian approval and against the desires of the British government, which deemed this to be "disastrous" for Europe's economic welfare.

The "passive resistance" called for by the German government, from the very day that French troops first entered the Ruhr, at once led to the paralysis of the huge industrial basin and, in the rest of Germany, made it impossible for the Commissions of Control to carry out their function of supervising German disarmament. There was a trial of strength. Technicians had to be dispatched to put the mines and railroads in working order, while numerous units of Army, gendarmerie and police fought against acts of sabotage and took reprisals against the German strikers. The whole of French policy was at stake. The government could not remain indifferent to any loss, for economic and political disaster lay ahead. It was in these conditions that, for the second time since the end of the war, the problem of Rhenish separatism was raised.

Economic life was totally disorganized in the Rhineland. The run-away German inflation was ruining a segment of the population. The Rhenish populations had to bear the double weight of military oc-cupation and monetary catastrophe. Rumors were circulating that there was talk in Berlin of abandoning the Rhinelanders to their fate, with the idea of denouncing the Treaty of Versailles as a whole and, with the support of the British, conducting a policy of unlimited resistance to France and Belgium.

Thus the separatists were given a second chance. After Mangin's departure in October, 1919, Dorten had remained in touch with him. Mangin was still more or less convinced that if Foch had let him act freely for several months after the armistice it was because Foch was assured of Poincaré's support, but that Poincaré had not dared oppose Clemenceau. But now, in 1923, it was Poincaré who, as President of the Council, had the real power, and who could, therefore, put through his own policy.

Such was Mangin's frame of mind when, on April 5, 1923, he for-warded to Poincaré a "brief note concerning the establishment of a Rhineland Republic." Dorten traveled to Paris, and Mangin brought him into contact with several political and journalistic personages. Bunau-Varilla, editor of *Le Matin,* even assured Dorten that Poincaré was rather favorably disposed to the movement for a separate Rhineland. "Show your strength," he told him, "and you will be helped. As soon as things have got under way, Mangin will be sent you."

From this moment on, the separatists proceeded on the basis of a misunderstanding. Dorten was sure he would receive support as soon as the separatist adventure had been launched. Mangin and his friends had given him their promise. But they, for their part, had of course obtained no promise from Poincaré.

This misunderstanding on the French side was compounded by ambiguities on the German. The old partisans of independence for the Rhineland were joined by newcomers, Matthes and Deckers, who were more adventurous if not simply adventurers, and who at all events were risking everything. But other participants were "legalists," resolved to undertake nothing without the agreement, if not the complicity, of the Berlin government. Among these were Adenauer and Hagen.

On July 29, Dorten organized a great separatist manifestation in Cologne. Those taking part constituted an assembly and passed four resolutions. They were for the Rhineland Republic, for peace and reparations, for the immediate replacement of the Prussian administrative organizations by a Rhenish Council and Commissar and for a new Rhenish currency. Dorten anxiously awaited the French reaction. He noted with bitterness that the Paris press minimized the success of the movement, and that the French Minister of Foreign Affairs seemed to attach no importance to it. On August 12, he wrote to Tirard, the French High Commissioner for the Rhineland. "As for me, he declared, "in the current situation, with no authority like Mangin at my side, and, according to what you say, not even having the sufficient support of M. Poincaré, I might be unable to avoid ill-thought-out actions that could compromise the movement irrevocably." Dorten, it appears, was becoming aware of the misunderstandings that would lead to the final defeat of the separatist movement.

But the movement had been launched. He could no longer stop it, and perhaps he even hoped that it would gather sufficient strength to compel the governments to change their attitude. Mangin advised him to stress especially the economic arguments. So Dorten tried to draw up a project for a Rhenish currency that would free the inhabitants of the region from the fantastic nightmare of inflation that had befallen the mark. The "legalists," Adenauer and Hagen, practiced delaying tactics and finally accepted the proposal, passing the word on to Berlin. The lethargy with which they followed Dorten allowed enough time—and no doubt this was what they desired—for a new German currency to be created.

On September 12, a governing body was nevertheless set up, composed in the main of Dorten's followers. He was master of the situation to the south of the Aachen-Cologne line. At the same time a separatist putsch, inspired by the nationalists, however, was undertaken in Bavaria under the direction of von Kahr and with the support of Ludendorff and of Adolf Hitler's National Socialist Party.

In the interests of national unity, it was time that Germany, which was prepared to yield with regard to the Ruhr, should intervene. At midday on September 24, the Council of Ministers and the representatives of the occupied territories met in Berlin. Stresemann, the German Minister of Foreign Affairs, declared that "in view of the financial situation of the Reich and of the impossibility of obtaining consideration for its basic demands, the freeing of the prisoners and the re-establishment of the Reich's sovereign rights in the Rhineland and the Ruhr, the continuation of passive resistance can no longer bring about any improvement in the situation." Thus the separatist movement had played a part in shaping the government's decision.

It was clear, from this day on, that Germany was prepared to negotiate and that France, by backing Rhenish separatism, would soon be deliberately violating the most fundamental clauses of the Versailles Treaty. But it was in order to ensure respect for the Treaty that France had occupied the Ruhr. Any aid to Rhineland separatism would thus be at odds with Poincaré's basic policy. It might then be thought that separatism was virtually doomed. Nevertheless, it continued on the path once adopted. On September 30, the meeting of a Rhenish Diet at Düsseldorf provoked a reaction of the German police, which had abandoned its "passive resistance." Dorten was scandalized that he no longer had any support from the French press. He soon saw that Paris was about to drop the movement. But others more extremist than himself considered that, having now burned their boats behind them, and unless all was to be lost, the final steps would have to be taken and without delay. Deckers, in any case, believed he had the entire backing of the Belgian authorities. On October 21, in Aachen, he proclaimed the setting up of an independent Rhenish Republic. Dorten and Matthes met that evening. They agreed that the movement had no longer any assurance of substantial international backing and that it was high time to apply a brake. They decided to "save what could be saved" and to moderate their own supporters as best they could.

Tirard received Dorten the following day. "He asked me," wrote the latter, "now that everything was under way, to keep up the activity, and to associate myself and the whole movement with it. I voiced my anxiety, and he replied that the French government would lend its support to the activity; finally I agreed to collaborate with the express condition that first of all we should be given all desirable aid and, secondly, that the accession of the new government should be recognized *de facto*."

Thus the double game went on. Tirard was, no doubt, convinced that encouragement given the separatist movement might exert an effective pressure on the German government in the coming negotiations, just as it had played a part in ending the passive resistance. The French military authorities could not see, in any event, now that Germany had "yielded" in the Ruhr, why they should throw away a card that in their view had some strength.

Greater prudence prevailed in Paris—Mangin wrote to Dorten, advising him to exercise prudence—but in the Rhineland the Allied High Commission remained hesitant. It maintained the Prussian officials in office, although the Treaty of Versailles in principle gave it the right to replace them, but it took no steps to suppress the white, green and red banner of the Rhineland Republic. In Aachen the Belgian authorities, who had at first encouraged the separatist movement, now had the banners removed from public buildings. At this point Dorten wrote to Mangin that he was giving up, but Mangin replied, "You are the only responsible leader and this is now clear to everybody; for you to withdraw even for a moment would mean irremediable failure. . . . You must hold fast to the end and make every concession that does not compromise the victory of the cause. . . . It's hard, my friend, but I am sure of victory."

Had Mangin succeeded in convincing some French political circles that the separatist movement had an irresistible drive? However that may be, on November 23 Poincaré himself, addressing the Chamber of Deputies, declared that "it is still too early . . . to predict what will emerge from the occurrences that are taking place in the occupied regions, and in certain places, such as Trier and the Palatinate, the tendency to total independence appears to be very strong; while in the towns, which are least disposed to favor an entire separation, there is certainly a growing desire for autonomy. So we can expect, sooner or later, changes in the political constitution of the whole or part of the occupied regions."

What had occurred to induce Poincaré to emerge from his reserve? It was the fact that Dorten, convinced that his movement could no longer succeed throughout the Rhineland and that the extremists in Cologne and Aachen would have to face the reprisals of the German authorities, had turned to a policy of retreat. In Trier and in the Palatinate his followers were entirely in control of the situation. The corps of the French Army of Occupation was under the command of General de Metz, who was strongly in favor of a particularist policy. He had reached an agreement with Dorten to establish a state as independent of the rest of the Rhineland as of the whole of Germany. Dorten, with this backing, at once set up at Bad Ems a government that contained only his own friends, and that openly broke away from the rest of the Rhenish movement.

For the "legalists," who were only awaiting a favorable moment to resume relations with the Berlin government, this was a much more serious threat than the former Directory, composed in part of extremists and already abandoned by the Belgian and French authorities in the northern Rhineland. They got in touch with Tirard and proposed to him that a federated Rhenish state be constituted that would be superior to or would eliminate Dorten's, would exercise authority everywhere in the Rhineland and would finally come out for independence. The British authorities, as a measure of prudence, had always encouraged the "legalists," especially Adenauer. Tirard thought that at last he had the opportunity to escape from the impasse in which the help given separatism had placed the French authorities. He at once asked Dorten to desist in favor of Adenauer. Dorten understood very well what Tirard was aiming at. First of all the separatists would be replaced by the "legalists" who could then ensure the return in force of the German authorities. But Tirard had asked him to keep secret the proposed constitution of a Rhenish government under Adenauer. If he betrayed this secret and denounced Tirard's ruse, he would cut himself off from the French authorities. There was only one way out, to reduce his own government to zero, using it as an organ of liquidation. All alone, and without giving any explanations to his friends, he went about the dissolution of the separatist movement. Then he was invited to leave the region. Mangin, at this instant, was still writing to him, "You are a banner, you must stand firm."

The sequence of events would prove Dorten right. Adenauer had subordinated the setting up of his government to the creation of a Rhineland currency. He dragged out the whole matter, until finally Germany undertook a monetary reform. Then repression overtook the few adventurers or men of good faith who had compromised themselves in the separatist movement. On January 9, 1924, Heintz and Orbis were killed in Speyer. On February 12, some thirty separatists were trapped in the Primasens town hall, where they had taken refuge. German nationalist groups hurled hand grenades into the building. Finally they set fire to it and slaughtered all who tried to escape. The occupation authorities did not turn a hair. The separatist movement ceased to exist on February 17. As Clemenceau wrote, "There are recollections it is better to leave unevoked."

On November 23, the very day that Poincaré had referred in the Chamber to the independence of the Palatinate, he had also signed an agreement of economic cooperation with Stinnes, representing the Ruhr industrialists. German heavy industry, disturbed by the separatist movement, had preferred to wait no longer before undertaking to negotiate. As for the French policy that had been pursued since January, 1922, it had failed totally. The sums taken as reparations had fallen to 263 million francs for all 1923, as compared with 11½ billion in 1922, before the Ruhr was occupied.

At the same time, France was assailed by a terrible financial crisis. The Treasury bonds that had fallen due were no longer renewed, the new issues were not fully subscribed and the franc collapsed on the exchanges. Alarmed, business people and manufacturers asked that their reserves be repaid in government bonds, while importers, foreseeing a further decline in the currency, bought in advance the foreign currencies they needed for their future purchases. The monetary reform that had been put through in Germany led all the international speculators to turn to Paris. The collapse of the reparations policy followed in the Ruhr seriously aggravated the financial crisis that this policy had, initially, been supposed to cure, and Poincaré was forced to negotiate a loan with the Morgan Bank of the United States and with British banks. He had to use the Banque Lazare in order to re-establish the franc "technically" on the exchanges. France was back at the precise point in January, 1922, when Briand had attempted, in Cannes, to negotiate a general settlement of the economic and political problems that the war had left in its wake.

Poincaré, on November 30, 1923, agreed to rely on the findings of an international conference, from which the Dawes plan would emerge. Thus the unanimity of the political parties was re-established, willy-nilly, on the basis of a policy of understanding with Great Britain and collaboration with international capitalism as a whole, even if this meant extending concessions to Germany. The Ruhr affair had been the last occasion on which French policy, with the more or less tacit agreement of the government, had allowed certain military circles to go beyond that policy and bend it to conform with the goal they had set themselves, the separation of the Rhineland from Germany. The profit and loss account could be measured by the number of Rhineland separatists executed or assassinated after French policy had set off on a new course.

CHAPTER NINE

THE ARMY WITHOUT
A MISSION

✠

A woman wearing the Phrygian cap of Marianne, symbol of the French Republic, sends in her visiting card to the English and American statesmen who are compelling Clemenceau to abandon French demands. "Tell them," runs the caption of this cartoon of Forain's—a commentary on the Versailles Treaty—"it's the lady from Verdun." In another cartoon the same artist depicts a mutilated veteran banging his stump against the door of the international conferences. "I just came to inquire," he says, "whether or not I won." A little later, Gassier depicts two Yankees, cigar in mouth and revolver in hand, presenting their bill to a lean Lafayette. The caption is, "Lafayette, here we come!" These few cartoons indicate, better than any long dissertation could, the moral tragedy that France underwent in the twenties.

It was based on the misunderstanding that separated a country conscious of how fragile a victory had been won, and a world irritated by France's claims and its insistence on recalling the past, as though to deny the mobile present and constrain things to remain the same. France bathed in a halo of glory that was meticulously preserved. After the victory parades, the handing out of batons to the marshals and the march into Metz and Strasbourg, the memory of the sacrifices made became the cult of the past. There were ceremonies around the standards of disbanded regiments, that went to join the glorious taxis of the Marne and the standards taken from the enemy.

The Chamber of Deputies, after the elections of 1919, was to go down in history as the *Chambre bleu-horizon.* The majority, comprising almost everyone except the Socialists, adopted the title of *bloc national,* and on the lists of candidates the old hands at the game had judiciously blended men with the Legion of Honor, the Military Medal and the Croix de Guerre, those who had fought on the Marne and at Verdun, the severely wounded and ordinary soldiers.

Then came the dedications of monuments to those who had died in the war. Every week for years on end, in every Department, a minister, or at the very least a member of parliament, surrounded by worthy fellows displaying their medals, unveiled a stone or bronze group, in which around an allegorical France or symbolic Victory the sacrifice of the poilus was recorded for posterity. The speech inevitably repeated the same themes. France had saved civilization, the Army had fought for "the right," the whole world was indebted to France for the victory, no one would ever forget the sacrifices made by the participants. And these, as Clemenceau had declared, "had rights over us." The enemy of yesterday, it was proclaimed, must pay for the destruction he had wrought on French soil and, by way of conclusion, the vow was taken to act so that never again would France have to go through the same suffering.

This was the atmosphere in which France lived in the years that followed victory. The more justified these moral claims were, the more intransigently they were put forward. The national sensibility would remain marked by them for a whole generation. The "monuments to the dead," the bronze plaques on the walls of the churches with the list of the war dead, served to remind everyone of the holocaust of the "Great War." The whole of French society clearly believed that it had an immense moral credit balance compared to the rest of the world.

But France had some difficulty in recognizing this world, now that the universal hurricane had come to an end. France itself was no longer the mutilated country that "still remembered," even if no words were pronounced, the lost provinces of Alsace and Lorraine. Alsace-Lorraine was French once again, and the deepest source of inspiration for patriotism or nationalism, in prewar days, no longer existed. The great myth of the Russian Alliance that had buoyed up a whole generation of politicians, generals and diplomats had now disappeared in the Bolshevik uprising of November, 1917. On the new map of Europe, the French could indeed make out new friendly countries, but in the early months and even early years of the peace these countries attracted attention above all by their revolutions, their conflicts with each other and their monetary fiascos. To tell the truth, this new world appeared too far off or too unstable, too complicated and too unreliable for people to build on it new certitudes or reasons for security, or to find a framework in which to insert France's political future.

The "new age" was marked initially by shortages and poverty. All at once, the French ceased to exult in their renown and faced the spectacle of their indigence. When the monetary accord between the Allies was abandoned, in the spring of 1919, even before the treaties had been signed, there could be no denying the evidence: the franc, this *franc germinal* that had not changed since the French Revolution, no longer had its old purchasing power. The peace seemed to have removed the bolt in some mysterious trapdoor. At the beginning of 1919, the pound was worth 25.22 francs and the dollar 5.18 francs. By the end of the year the exchange rates were already 41 and 11 francs, respectively, and in 1923, 85 and 20 francs. The retail price index, with a base of 100 in 1914, rose to 285 in 1919; by 1925 it had risen to 453.

It has often been said that the French public mind revealed itself, after the war, as entirely unable to grasp the new situation of the economy and the financial problems to which the war had given rise. But the public did not lag very much behind the analyses offered by the experts. In actual fact, the economic upheavals caused by the World War had taken by surprise the whole of capitalist society. The French considered it outrageous that the country itself should have to pay the costs of reconstruction, although the Treaty of Versailles had solemnly affirmed this was Germany's obligation. Reparations represented the price that the entire world, after the victory, had agreed was due to France for the frightful sacrifices incurred. Why, then, should the Germans not be required to pay what they owed?

The Allied countries were so greatly indebted to the French dead on the Marne, at Verdun and along the Chemin des Dames. How could they fail to understand that it was their obligation to aid France in extracting from Germany the billions that were owed? "Our former enemies, massed against our frontiers," somber prophets wrote, "our former allies, massed against our finances." Events appeared to be in a hurry to prove them right. First France had had to "give up the Rhine," in exchange for the promises of an alliance made by Great Britain and the United States. A few months later these promises had become empty words, and France was on her own, without the alliances she had had in 1914. And then, on every occasion, Great Britain spoke in favor of a steady and immense reduction of the reparations to be paid by Germany. Our allies, it seemed, now preferred the former enemy. It was at this time that a new feeling took deep hold on the people of all social levels, a feeling that had no connection with the old colonial disputes. Now, the consequence of American bad faith and of British shilly-shallying was something tangible, vital and concrete: the devaluation of the franc was all the fault of the Anglo-Saxons.

This naive belief of the French in their own rights, and their economic ignorance and financial indolence—brought on by the exhaustion of resources and manpower—were matched on the American and especially on the British side by outmoded prejudices concerning "French imperialism," by unawareness of the real economic situation of France, and fears that had been long harbored, though now they had no justification, of any form of hegemony. Anglo-Saxon opinion made much of the most trivial fact that could justify its distrust of French intentions. Did not France maintain two divisions in Upper Silesia, a battalion of chasseurs in Memel, a staff of military advisers in Warsaw, and numerous influential missions in Belgrade, Bucharest and Prague? The British and American press apparently attached greater importance to this than to the enormous decline in French capital resources, to the state's domestic and foreign indebtedness, and to the destruction and flooding of the coal mines of Nord and Pas-de-Calais. Psychologically, the atmosphere was unfavorable for France in London and Washington, and this lent all the more strength to the economic and political arguments in favor of readmitting Germany into the "European concert of nations."

Thus the attitude of the Allies made it impossible for the French to obtain the reparations that might have slowed down the decline in the value of the franc. With this, the mechanism of postwar inflation was set in motion, and would not be halted until 1926. Socially, the victims would be recruited from the middle class, the small and middle bourgeoisie with fixed salaries or government bonds, and from old-line agriculture.

More than ever, this was the milieu that provided the military cadres. After the armistice, massive resignations deprived the Army of a considerable part of the officers who came from families of the upper bourgeoisie or the moneyed aristocracy. Various reasons motivated these withdrawals. Among them were fatigue, after the unparalleled effort of four years of war, the prospect of a long peace, which would offer no immediate goal for the military life, the gaps left in bourgeois families by the slaughter, the desire for a more agreeable and more comfortable life after all the misery that had been endured while in uniform, and the lure of rapid prosperity that the revival of business seemed to promise.

Those who chose to remain were those who could hope for no easy and advantageous reintegration in civilian life. The conscripts who had a less distinguished background, and who had succeeded in rising from the ranks, considered it a social advancement to be known as officers, particularly since, after the armistice, the Army was surrounded with renown and honors.

In the military hierarchy they became one with the heirs of the old aristocratic and landed families, the traditional source for Army officers, who scarcely glimpsed any other horizon than that of camp and uniform, and for whom the war had signified their acceptance by French society as a whole. All things considered, the Army was socially at one with the lower and intermediate bourgeoisie of the provinces, with the landed aristocracy that had done the least to adapt itself to modern economic conditions, and with the most conservative milieux, economically and psychologically speaking. Thus, throughout the twenties, the Army's outlook was primarily that of the French middle classes.

And these were the chosen victims of postwar inflation. Remote from the Paris Bourse, they had accepted the advice of banking advisers in making their investments, and had sunk six billion gold francs in Russian bonds. On the average, the purchasers of government bonds and other government issues had lost three-quarters of their capital before the currency was stabilized, whereas those who held common stocks had lost only one-quarter.

The middle classes nevertheless remained faithful to their old habits for a long time. Trusting in their conception of existence and of money matters, they were secretly convinced that victory and peace would soon bring about the return to the old norms of economic and financial life. But as Moreau, the governor of the Banque de France, declared, the saver of 1918 had lost 60 per cent of his capital by 1925.

This social milieu, so closely connected with the military cadres, had no trouble detecting those responsible for the decline. The enormous increase in taxes, between 1920 and 1926—it had been too long delayed and long remained insufficient to eliminate the budgetary deficit—provided fresh fuel for the age-long distrust of the state and the "fisc." The income tax was another sore point with small property owners. Not only were taxes heavy, these days, but they were accompanied by an intolerable "fiscal inquisition." For minor industrialists, for small and average business people, and for the farmers, this amounted to a permanent scandal.

Who, then, was to blame? Parliament, of course, and especially the deputies who, for demagogic reasons, let the deficit stand by voting all sorts of credits, with no thought for the taxpayer. Soon, the deputies and senators would be held responsible for all the disappointments that followed the victory; it was they who had let all that the Army had won in 1918 come to naught.

Confronted by the sudden drop in the franc, Poincaré himself, that intransigent patriot and honest guardian of the public purse, had been compelled to ask the Morgan Bank and the Bank of England for loans, and to request the Banque Lazare to intervene on the currency exchanges. Thus the selfsame British and American capitalists who had been thwarting the French reparations policy for at least the previous two years apparently were now in a position to endanger the national currency, then to bail out a government that had become more docile, and finally, as if by a miracle, to save the franc. It was not enough that the bankers of London and New York should decide to reduce German reparations payments, after having made the Versailles Treaty as moderate as possible in its treatment of Germany. It was not enough to have fought the Ruhr occupation and finally to have forced on Poincaré and then on Herriot the application of the Dawes plan. Now they had chosen to speculate against the franc, bringing the state to the edge of bankruptcy so that they could impose on it their own political and financial notions. What struck conservative opinion was the fact that a government so resolutely "national" as Poincaré's could do no more to withstand Anglo-American capitalism than the governments of the Left that came to power after the elections of 1924.

The antiparliamentary feelings of the conservative bourgeoisie—and of the military—had, of course, been exacerbated by the impotence displayed by the left-wing parliamentary majority which, between the summer of 1924 and the summer of 1926, had let inflation get out of hand. It was then that the conservative middle classes reached the conclusion that the parties of the Left were congenitally incapable of running public finances. The Left, having failed to choose between a policy of "confidence" and a levy on capital, and having failed to trim their projects in order to ensure a prior financial stabilization, found themselves in the crisis of June, 1926. They left to the Government of National Union, headed by Poincaré and including six former Presidents of the Council, the glory of "saving the franc." In the eyes of the modestly situated bourgeoisie, whose investments had a fixed rate of return, the Left became synonymous with financial chaos, antinational speculation, monetary panic and social spoliation. Only a step away lay a break between the actual parliamentary regime and a wide range of moderate or conservative opinion which, until then, had been loyal to republican institutions.

This new style of antiparliamentarianism strengthened nationalism. The English and American banks were still speculating against the franc, or so French people thought, unmindful of the fact that this speculation was swollen by enormous purchases of foreign stocks and currencies, and of gold, by small French investors who felt alarm at the rise in prices, the unbalanced budget and the decline of the franc. In the most ardently nationalist circles, this flight of the nation's funds, this abandonment of French issues in favor of anything foreign, was looked on as a kind of treason.

A new element, and of prime importance in the public eye, this treason was of no benefit to Germany, the traditional enemy, but served the big foreign companies, Anglo-Saxon for the most part, and international capitalism in general. In nationalist milieux, this rush to speculate in foreign stocks was linked to the continuing impoverishment of the holders of French government bonds, with the shrinkage of the old-line fortunes, based on bonds and other fixed-interest securities and on ground rents.

The drop in wholesale agricultural prices was a hard blow for all the families of landowners who sent so many of their sons to the military academies. The decline in their incomes persisted after the stabilization of the franc, until in the early thirties ground rents brought in barely half what they did in 1914.

Hand in hand with the social degradation of which those closest to the military felt they had been the victims went the conviction that

France was undergoing a moral degradation as well. Only a few short years after the heroism of the trenches and the apotheosis of victory, the whole intellectual current was involved in a sweeping criticism of the past. This was the time when dadaism and surrealism thumbed their noses at classicism, when the public became enamored of the American novel and when the rising generation, appalled by the horrors and uselessness of war, tended to reject totally the whole pre-1914 intellectual and moral heritage. The psychology that had been taught up to then in the French universities was revolutionized by the contribution of psychoanalysis.

Everything was changing in French society, which seemed swept along by a kind of universalized subversiveness: daily life was transformed. The men who were demobilized in 1918 saw strange new fashions grow up around them. People no longer danced to the old tunes, they drank cocktails, a fashion imported from America, dresses stopped at the knee and waists sank to hip level. In a universe it could no longer recognize, the traditionalist bourgeoisie beat a retreat. Impoverished, it looked askance at the new *joie de vivre* which no one, it has been said, can have known, if he did not experience these postwar years. It discovered new things to detest in the bitterness of the victory it considered spoiled, and in a society it judged to be drifting aimlessly. The Republic had let the currency be wrecked, Anglo-Saxon capitalism had betrayed France and the franc, to the greater profit of Germany. Everything alien had become inimical.

The entire Left, during the twenties, was fascinated by the birth and development of world communism, and debated endlessly on the possibility, or otherwise, of collaboration with the new party of the working class. But on the Right the nationalist paroxysm, the violence of the antiparliamentary movement and the series of bitter disappointments gave rise to new trends.

The final failure of the Ruhr occupation, Poincaré's appeal to the Anglo-Saxon banks and to the international financiers who authored the Dawes plan, wrote finis to a certain classical, "national" policy. In the ground that had been plowed by disillusion would spring up the first seeds of a twin economic and political nationalism which, from 1922 on, had triumphed in Italy under the name of "fascism." Nineteen twenty-four witnessed the Dawes plan, the first rescue of the franc by the great international banks, the victory of the "Cartel de Gauche" and the decision to evacuate the Ruhr. In that same year, almost symbolically, Taittinger founded the "Jeunesses Patriotes,"

a quasi-military organization that set out to gather the youth of the
Right around a flamingly nationalistic banner, and which denounced
the "traditional German enemy" as well as the capitalist powers, both
American and British, which were bending France, it was declared,
beneath a yoke of money.

Georges Valois, the editor of *Le Nouveau Siècle,* founded the
"Faisceau" (lictor's bundle), whose name revealed its Italian inspiration. He attempted to win over the traditionalist left-wing groups to
his ideology, which was both authoritarian and social, nationalist and
Jacobin. But by the time that he had launched his appeal for a "fascism
of the Left," the parliamentary Republic had already been saved by
Poincaré and his stabilization of the currency. When inflation was at
its worst, when the fall of the franc seemed to herald the ruin of the
conservative bourgeoisie, these conservative groups had not paid
much attention to the Faisceau that Valois had founded with the hope
of attracting youthful right-wing extremists. The Italian source of his
ideas was a handicap, in competition with Taittinger's Jeunesses
Patriotes. And French nationalism, in any case, had a master whose
doctrines were quite sufficiently vigorous to prevent right-wing opinion
from taking the path that Mussolini had traced out.

The war and the victory had been the golden age of "L'Action
Française." Nowhere else had nationalist febrility, the hatred of the
Boche and vigilance to spy out every form of defeatism and treason
found a more striking tribunal. With the French on the Rhine, with
French troops installed on the Vistula, the Oder, and the Danube, it
seemed that the old nationalistic dream so amorously fostered by
Charles Maurras and his friends had now become a reality. As, by
degrees, the concessions agreed to by successive Republican governments reduced the victory to simpler and more realistic dimensions,
as the illusions of 1918 faded in the harsh light of economic reality, as,
furthermore, the bourgeois Republic's inextricable imbrication in the
web of international capitalism stood revealed, the "integral nationalism" of L'Action Française met with a warmer response in the ranks
of a conservative bourgeoisie that was now bitter and disappointed,
proud but impoverished.

These elements found an outlet for their spleen in reading the
verbal acts of violence of Charles Maurras. Their bitterness was
voiced in the skeptical, disabused articles of Jacques Bainville. Their
anger at the "collective theft," as they called the inflation, found an
echo in the extravagantly vehement speeches of Léon Daudet. In

May, 1925, a Belgian periodical, *Les Cahiers de la Jeunesse Catholique,* conducted a referendum on the writers of the previous twenty-five years, and the replies showed that, for the larger number of the young intellectuals who had been approached, the greatest master was Maurras. The following year Poincaré stabilized the franc, and Pope Pius XI placed L'Action Française under an interdict.

This marked the beginning of the decline of Maurras's influence on Catholics and the conservative bourgeoisie. Yet until 1940, *L'Action Française* would remain the most influential organ of the nationalist Right, and lose none of its authority among the military, where the *nationalisme intégral* that it preached filled the bill precisely. From the Faisceau to the Jeunesses Patriotes, from *L'Action Française* to the Camelots du Roi, the authoritarian and antiparliamentary nationalist and antiliberal Right still practiced only a timid fusion of political and economic nationalism, although this expressed the secret longing of a bourgeoisie whose economic underpinnings were threatened and which tended to place on international capitalism all the blame for the woes that had beset French capitalism.

In 1925 one of the most popular theoreticians of the French bourgeoisie, Lucien Romier, already anticipated the end of liberalism in France. He set up against dying liberalism the nationalism he sensed to be "of all the west's popular ideologies, the one that reigns supreme." Besides, he asserted, "If the nationalist *mystique* . . . should disappear overnight, national states would have no surviving authority and would disappear, leaving nothing but conglomerations of interests."

Beneath Romier's elegant expressions it is easy to sense the heralding of Hitler's invectives directed against "international plutocracy." Romier demonstrated that the liberal state was but an ineffectual disguise of the universal reign of money. To restore "nationalist" vigor to the French state, he demanded that the governments be properly "tooled." This led him on to the strong state and modern technocracy, that would aim simultaneously at a popular policy, realizations in the economic field and national might, and so constitute a very much watered down and prudent form of the fascist regimes yet to come. After the collapse of 1940, Romier was to occupy a ministerial post in the last Vichy government presided over by Laval.

But, among the French bourgeoisie, these authoritarian and nationalistic tendencies did not survive the summer of 1926. The Poincaré experiment reassured the public mind concerning the viability of the parliamentary Republic. To a certain degree it even spared national susceptibilities that had been threatened by the plan of the Experts which, in 1925, had expounded the necessary solution of the monetary crisis.

The Experts, that is, the regents of the Banque de France, the inspectors of finances and the principal bankers, had maintained that budgetary equilibrium and the relief of pressure on the Treasury were inseparable from a renewal of confidence in the currency. To counter speculation against the franc, foreign loans would have to be obtained and, to that end, the agreement would have to be signed that provided for the repayment, by France, of the debts to America. Public opinion, exasperated by the necessity of paying to America almost as much as was owed to France by Germany, looked on the plan of the Experts as a kind of *Diktat* that international finance sought to impose.

The psychological shock that resulted from the government of national union that Poincaré had gathered around him, together with fiscal discipline and massive economies, reversed in favor of the franc the trend of speculation in currency. Poincaré was then able to authorize the Banque de France to negotiate its gold reserves at a rate below the official rate for the *franc germinal*. This *de facto* devaluation allowed him to lead the value of the franc gradually back to a level that reflected the level of prices and wages, and in actual fact stabilization was assured a few weeks after his return to power. There had been no need to seek further loans abroad, and an offer made by the Morgan bank was rejected at the end of the year. At the same time Briand, as Minister of Foreign Affairs, cultivated the "spirit of Locarno." In 1925, four years after he had endeavored to do so at the Cannes Conference, he succeeded in obtaining Germany's recognition of her western frontiers and the guarantee of these frontiers by Great Britain. He concluded, simultaneously, a defensive alliance with Poland and Czechoslovakia.

It was on these foundations that French policy moved in the direction of reconciliation with Germany, the anticipated evacuation of the Rhineland, the systematic recourse to the League of Nations and even the ideal of a European federation. French public opinion gave wide support to the twin policies of Poincaré in the country itself and of Briand abroad. And this was the moment when a kind of rupture occurred between the state of mind of a conservative bourgeoisie, reassured by the stabilization of the franc and the buttressing of the peace, and of an Army that continued to harbor the rancors that the rest of the nation had abandoned.

Military opinion, along with all nationalist opinion, had been deeply affected by the economic setbacks of the postwar period, by the failure of the Ruhr occupation, by the need to make concessions to Germany and the pressure exerted by the former Allies. It was all the more attracted to the new waves of authoritarian nationalism since they did honor to the Army and to the memory of victory. While the bourgeoisie found a substitute in economic reconstruction, the Army shut itself up within the melancholy of inactivity. Once the inflationary period had ended, the bourgeoisie set out to enjoy prosperity to the full, with all its glittering prospects and deceptive mirages. But the Army would find nothing to replace the general weakening of fixed-interest securities, of government bonds and landed property. The Army was a victim of the harsh financial measures, and no prosperity had come along to make up for inflation and devaluation.

This impoverishment came, too, at a moment when wartime tension had given way to a feeling that the Army had not known between 1861 and 1914, the feeling of being useless. Charles de Gaulle referred to this in his preface to *Au fil de l'épée*. "Our age," he wrote—

bears the stamp of uncertainty. All these rebuffs offered the conventions, estimates, doctrines, all these trials, losses, disappointments and, too, all these uproars, clashes and surprises have shaken the established order. The profession of arms, which had just transformed the world, could not fail to suffer at this, and lamented its own lost ardor.

This melancholy of the military organization outside the periods of enormous effort is, no doubt, a classically recurring situation. In the contrast between the make-believe activity of the peacetime Army and its latent strength, there is something disillusioning that those concerned cannot sense without distress. "So many unused forces," said Psichari, "so many destinies and so much sterility!" All the more strongly does this chagrin impregnate the soldier's soul in the years that follow battle. It seems that this sudden removal of tension breaks the spring, to release, at times, the deep, faint sound of lamentation with which Vauvenargues and Vigny have rocked us.

A wave of discouragement seemed to sweep over the Army. Painlevé, who was War Minister at the end of 1926, recognized how serious the situation was. "The Army," he said, "is at present the prey of a deep uneasiness. Its cadres are dispirited and look for an opportunity to leave the service. The youthful elite turns away from our military schools."

The shrinking purchasing power of officers' pay, in combination with the decline in the traditional family fortunes, led the rising generation to avoid a military career, and induced those who felt they could provide a better life for their dependents to leave the Army. The "reports on morale" covering the whole range of the military hierarchy stressed the officers' difficult financial situation. The situation was scandalous, in an era of "nouveaux riches," speculations on the Bourse and the enrichment of those who had bought foreign securities. Government employees not in uniform, who had trade unions to look after their interests, did decidedly better than the military. It became customary, in officers' families, to make up for the meager pay by supplementary earnings. The wives found employment. The newspapers reported that one officer was driving a taxi in the night hours and another was wrapping parcels in a department store.

The Army had suffered the consequences of its own victory, along with those due to growing financial difficulties. In 1921, the "blue-horizon" and intensely nationalistic Chamber, so close in its outlook to nationalist milieux, nevertheless reduced considerably the period of military service. Instead of three years, it would now last eighteen months. There can be no doubt that financial considerations played a decisive part in this new military legislation.

On the question of manpower, the eight War Ministers who succeeded each other between 1920 and 1926 were, furthermore, of the same mind as the Army's Chief of Staff, Marshal Pétain. In a speech at Béthune late in 1919, he had envisaged that the period of military service would eventually be reduced to one year. The government and the General Staff had gradually modified their demands, resulting in a steady diminution of the armed forces.

This diminution worsened the crisis of morale among the military and hastened the growing tendency, in the nation at large, to pay no attention to military problems. While the upper ranks were over-burdened with general officers and higher-ranking officers who had been promoted during the war, the intermediate and lower ranks of officers had such poor prospects that for ten years there was almost no promotion, while the most active and intelligent officers often yielded to the temptation to resign their commissions.

In Syria and in North Africa, the regiments were insufficiently officered. Whether it suited them or not, officers were ordered to take up posts in "the theaters of external operations." Either because they feared fresh adventures, after the trials of the World War, or because they wished to maintain family life intact, many preferred to resign. It was indicated that cheating had occurred, when the lists of these postings were drawn up. Only the monotony of garrison life in metropolitan France could reverse the trend and build up the prestige of the colonial troops, especially that of the North African regiments.

Yet the twenties witnessed a number of protests against this long degradation of the Army, on the moral, the material and the properly military planes. One of the most spectacular of these gestures was also among the most symptomatic. Written by "a high military authority"— it was, in fact, Commander Souchon—in 1929 a book appeared whose title reveals its outlook: *The Late French Army* (*Feu l'armée française*).

According to the author, the origin of the Army's decline, which had gone on uninterruptedly throughout the twenties, was to be found in the prevailing philosophy of life which embodied a conception of the Army he considered antithetical to the authentic and traditional military spirit. The enemy, he maintained, was materialism. For this he denounced the German influence as largely responsible. This influence, he wrote, "is so virulent that it manifests itself in the very terms that are used, in particular the impious expression 'human matériel.'" He regarded this as the source of an entire conception of warfare which had, finally, obscured the human aspect of military problems, with a "scientism grown heavily materialistic owing to the abundance of new mechanical devices. . . . The automobile has given headquarters the notion that the unforeseen can easily be parried. . . . The typewriter has also notably contributed to men's failure to understand, but above all it has supported the elements debasing the Command. . . . As for the telephone, beyond any doubt it is the most pernicious instrument ever invented."

This somewhat cantankerous and certainly paradoxical criticism of modern inventions as applied to warfare expresses a nostalgia that was not limited to the use of couriers, mounted squadrons and carrier pigeons. It was the anguished cry that emanated from a whole milieu that felt robbed of its culture, habits and traditions in the mechanized universe of the Army, as it had come to be since the outbreak of the World War.

The basic intuition of the author of *Feu l'armée française* was that the industrial revolution to which military society was committed inevitably led to a psychological revolution. He had, no doubt, good grounds for his protests. It was true that a brutal mechanical application of the rules, inherited from the latter period of the war, concerning the intensity and use of firepower, might prove to be dangerous for those whose duty it was to plan a future war. The worship of absolute rules was utterly hostile to the spirit of initiative, to strategical boldness and the search for new solutions that might be required by a further revolution in military techniques. Thus there was, perhaps, a healthy reaction to be found in *Feu l'armée française* against the "dogmatism of firepower" that the General Staff had adopted, as a result of the lessons learned in the opening months of the war. But the book was nothing more than a reaction. Looking backward, the writer cast a melancholy glance on the industrialized world, soulless, administrative and mechanical, that surrounded the Army and little by little was invading it. The very foundations of military society, it seemed to him, were threatened.

Furthermore, beyond this "materialism" of which he found the whole age guilty, he could see enemies who functioned on the political plane. He repeatedly denounced the "Internationals." Faithful in this to the prejudices of his own background, he did not even distinguish between the new Communist International born of the Bolshevik revolution and engaged in a world-wide enterprise of total subversion, and the old Socialist International containing the Social-Democrats of every country in Europe, who refused to follow the road traced out by Lenin. He pointed to the dangerous effect political propaganda might have on soldiers whose too brief period of military service might leave them incompletely assimilated in the military hierarchy. He suggested that since the war the connections between the General Staffs and political personages had become too close. In a word, he thought that modern society had contaminated the Army. His outlook was, in fact, that of a whole group of Army men whose considerable influence on the officers' corps was strengthened by the fact that the officers, having been victimized by the economic and social developments of the twenties, readily accepted any criticism of a government that apparently neglected both the officers themselves and a General Staff impotent to defend them.

The controversies concerning military policy would long be of this reactionary stamp, in the literal sense of the term. This basic handicap would continue to discredit, in political and intellectual circles, the most justified attacks, the most intelligent polemics and the most penetrating remarks. As a result, they remained ineffective. *Feu l'armée française* was the first example of this. The author rightly condemned a military standpoint that supposed the adversary to lack initiative and to move slowly—suppositions that were backed up by nothing. He regarded this habit as "the fundamental defect of every organization. The system works only if the French government is granted a certain delay. One would have to assume that in the future no one would take up arms without first politely giving two weeks' notice that he is forced to adopt these measures."

But he specified immediately, and so gave a particular political coloring to his critique: "There exists a comic conception of sociology, closely akin to the manias of elderly men whose lives are spent in textual exegesis, and who may sincerely believe that in the future no armed conflict will break out unless the legal proceedings that have previously been instituted at the tribunal of the League of Nations reveal that there is no peaceful solution. The antagonists will come to grips only after they have heard a solemn 'Proceed, gentlemen.' " On this theme, our author can never say enough. Not until General de Gaulle developed his great theses concerning motorized mechanical forces was there to be an end to purely negative criticisms of a military outlook which indeed was incompatible with the attacking spirit, strategic surprise and a capacity for making overwhelming ripostes.

Until then, the author's readers and friends were satisfied to keep on mouthing his notions of the "demilitarization of National Defense." They all thought the Army, with its dynamism and capacity for attack, was being engulfed in a vast economic and administrative system, and that strategic preoccupations would finally be absorbed in the still hazy idea of "war potential."

The book appeared to be so revealing and so disturbing that other "military authorities" set out to reply, in a volume entitled *The French Army Will Live (L'Armée française vivra)*, and dedicated to the author of *Feu l'armée française* as "an act of hope, after his cry of despair." The preface admitted that "career officers were generally grateful to the author of *Feu l'armée française* for having expressed with no less precision than subtlety what most of them had been confusedly thinking for several years past. . . ." *L'Armée française vivra* was bathed in the same climate of uncertainty. Its detailed suggestions, proposals and ideas gave no answer whatever to the sole question that should determine military policy: now, with the approach of the thirties, what should be the mission of the French Army? In the absence of a reply, and in accord with France's general policy in Europe, the country was launched a few years later on the long and distressing adventure of the Maginot Line.

This, then, was the Army, as the twenties drew to a close: public indifference, the longing for an authoritarian, conservative state that would ensure the Army's material and moral welfare, the decline of its power and the intellectual impoverishment of the Army cadres. The spirit of Locarno and Geneva had breathed on France. Ten years away from World War II, people dreamed of everlasting peace. "The hereditary enemy" had become almost a friend—and tomorrow, perhaps, he would be France's partner in the European federation of which Briand had spoken. What was the Army worrying about?

CHAPTER TEN

THE ARMY AGAINST COMMUNISM

✠

While French public opinion concentrated exclusively on internal problems and on relations with Germany, other occurrences tempted the General Staffs along paths with which, traditionally, they would have had nothing to do. It may be said that between 1918 and 1928, a twin evolution gradually transformed the Army's political and moral horizons. From the armistice to the Locarno agreements and the evacuation of the Rhineland in 1930, the German problem be came, little by little, less urgent, and soon ceased to be the daily preoccupation of the General Staff. Although it continued to occupy the first place when possible wars were envisaged, after 1925 it no longer represented any immediate threat. Whatever cleavage might separate public opinion, revolted by the notion of another war, and the military outlook, still dominated by its traditional vigilance and historical skepticism, the idea of a Franco-German conflict had grown quite remote.

For the high command new factors had come to occupy an ever more important place in military thinking. They all had one distinguishing feature: they sprang from the Bolshevik revolution. One after another, they brought the staffs into the world struggle against communism. At each stage of the Bolshevik revolution, the French high command played its part in the elaborating and sometimes in the execution of counterrevolutionary projects. In Russia, Siberia, Hungary and Poland, the Army sent its staffs, military missions and expeditionary corps to confront the same enemy, the Bolsheviks. The Army was to meet the same enemy in its own ranks, when occupying the Ruhr, and yet again in the French "Empire," where it was obscurely involved in revolutionary and nationalist movements and supported, inside France, by the French section of the Communist International.

Once the Bolshevik government had signed the treaty of Brest-Litovsk, nothing more could be expected of it. Quite the contrary, the government and the Grand Quartier Général expected the bulk of the German troops that had been fighting in the east to find their way to the French front. All that could be done was prepare to meet this eventuality.

There was one immediate problem, which would be the starting point for a long sustained French intervention in the Russian civil war. The Czech and Slovak prisoners, or deserters from the Austro-Hungarian Army, had formed a legion in central Russia, and before the outbreak of revolution it had been decided to employ it alongside the Russian Army. The leaders of the Legion now asked that it be transported to the western front. Clemenceau took a lively interest in the problem and instructed the French military mission in Russia to negotiate for the departure of the Legion. An agreement was signed with the Soviet government on March 26, 1918. The Japanese Army was to take charge of the Czechs at Vladivostok. So the Czechs began to make their way to eastern Siberia. Swelled by their fellow countrymen released from prison camps, their numbers rose to 60,000. But early in May, friction began to develop between the Bolsheviks and the Czechoslovaks. The Legion considered it wiser not to abandon its arms. It launched counterattacks, interrupted its march to the east and regrouped around the Trans-Siberian Railroad, controlling the principal railroad junctions.

At this point the Allies altered their plans. In early summer, 1918, the situation of the Bolsheviks appeared to be critical. Hoping for an intervention on the part of the Allies, 2,000 officers had risen in the region lying to the north of Moscow, on July 6. The Germans occupied the Ukraine, the shores of the Black Sea and part of the Caucasus. They were backing a counterrevolutionary army stationed in Estonia and threatening Petrograd. They had helped the conservative Finns to eliminate the Bolsheviks, while the Allies were still at Murmansk and held part of the railroad leading to Petrograd. The Japanese and Czechs controlled central Siberia, and were ready to extend help to the counterrevolutionaries installed between the Urals and the Volga.

In the meantime, in July, 1918, the Allies were bracing themselves to resist the supreme German offensive on the French front. They had neither the munitions, matériel nor manpower to undertake another action of any scope. Their main concern was, at any cost, to keep in Russia the million men the Germans had been maintaining there. They decided to disembark a small British expeditionary force at Archangel on August 15.

Later, since the situation in Siberia and the Russian eastern provinces seemed to favor the Czechs and the counterrevolutionaries, the Allied plan developed further. Masaryk, President of the Czech National Committee, passed on to the Allied General Staffs a message from the leaders of the Czech Legion in Siberia. "In our opinion," ran the message, "it is extremely desirable and also possible to reestablish a Russo-German front in the east." It was then that an Allied military mission was formed, with the task of proceeding to Siberia and taking in hand the Legion. The French General Janin was named to head the mission.

The War Ministry handed Janin his instructions on July 25. These dealt first of all with the relations he would have to establish with General Stepanik, who commanded the Czech Legion, and with the Japanese General Staff, which in principle was in charge of all the Allied forces in Siberia. But he was also given a long-range goal that ordered him to bring about "a developing movement of the Czech forces, in cooperation with the Allied forces that were intervening, so as to establish on the one hand an effective liaison between Siberia —their own base—and the Allied bases in the Arctic Ocean, and, on the other, with the groups in southern Russia that favored the *entente*."

There was, in principle, no ambiguity in these directives, which clearly set as their objective "to establish, against the Austrians and Germans, a line of resistance running from the White Sea to the Black Sea." The first goal that General Janin should endeavor to reach was the occupation of Irkutsk, which was still in the hands of the Bolsheviks, in order to ensure liaison between the totality of the Czech forces and the Japanese bases in far eastern Siberia. From there, the action would progressively extend toward the Urals and the Russian interior. Nevertheless, those who had drawn up the "instructions" sent to Janin—and Clemenceau was War Minister at the time—must have suspected that the means placed at his disposal might prove somewhat inadequate to achieve such ambitious goals. So he was advised also "to try to bring about the intervention of the Japanese on as large a scale as possible, and as far as the Urals." The Janin mission left Brest on August 30.

But it did not reach Vladivostok until November 16. The armistice had been signed several days before, and the whole aim of the Allied mission in Siberia had been altered by this. There could no longer be any question of re-establishing a front, in Russia, against Austrians and Germans. The one remaining problem was the struggle that set Czechs, counterrevolutionaries of various tendencies, and Japanese, on the one side, against the Bolsheviks on the other. At the same time, the attitude of the Allied governments inevitably evolved very rapidly. The permanent occupation of eastern Siberia by the Japanese, especially, would soon be looked on by the United States as a grave threat to the whole balance of power around the Pacific.

The Janin mission at once felt the effects of the radical change that had come about since November 11. On November 18, as did General Otani, Commander-in-Chief of the Allied forces—but whose authority was no longer recognized by the Americans—and as did the leaders of the American and British military missions, General Janin learned that the counterrevolutionary Cossack troops had arrested the members of the Bolshevik Directory—made up in part, however, of antirevolutionary Bolsheviks—that had been established in Omsk, and that Admiral Kolchak had succeeded them. Then he was informed by the Command of the Czech Legion that the Legion, grown tired already, wanted to know at once what attitude the Allies intended to take vis-à-vis the Bolsheviks. A quarrel broke out between Admiral Kolchak and General Semenov, candidate of the Japanese to head the struggle against the Bolsheviks. To make things even more complicated, the American government took official steps asking the Japanese government to withdraw, at least little by little, Japanese troops from Siberia.

General Janin informed the French government and, on November 26, he received fresh instructions. These were entirely unambiguous. Although the war was over, Janin was to continue to organize resistance against the Bolsheviks. "General Janin," these instructions declared, "must act as Commander-in-Chief of all western troops in Siberia to the west of Lake Baikal, whether Allied or Russian or other. . . . General Knox is associated with him to direct affairs behind the lines. As Commander-in-Chief, he will issue instructions concerning: (1) the organization and training of newly formed Russian troops, and also, (2) the matériel, provisions and reinforcements to be sent to the front." He was informed that the British government would provide military matériel for a force of at least 100,000 to 200,000 men. Finally, he was ordered to "explain to the interested parties, and especially to the Russians, that the support of the two governments [French and British] depended on the application of these measures." This was, then, a concerted plan of action against the Bolshevik revolution, the operational command being entrusted to a French general who was to be accepted by the counterrevolutionary forces, and with Great Britain supplying the material means.

General Janin arrived in Omsk December 13, where he was received by Regnault, the head of the French diplomatic mission, and made contact with Admiral Kolchak. Recalling the views of the Minister of Foreign Affairs, he reported that "Monsieur Berthelot was even more correct than he realized when he stated that the Admiral was too nervous to be a statesman."

Meanwhile, the Allied governments had decided to intervene in the Black Sea, both to stem the revolutionary contagion that might spread in the east after the capitulation of Turkey and Bulgaria and to protect Roumania which, by its annexation of Bessarabia, was now in direct contact with the Russian territories controlled by the Bolsheviks.

So an expeditionary corps was disembarked at Odessa, in November, 1918. It comprised 6,000 French troops, 2,000 Greek, 4,000 Polish, and several warships, and was under the command of Marshal Franchet d'Esperey, Allied Commander-in-Chief on the eastern front. His orders were to keep a watch on the shores of the Black Sea from the Roumanian frontier to Sebastopol, particularly when the evacuation from the Ukraine of the Austrian and German armies would leave Roumania without cover and allow the Bolsheviks to block the path of the Roumanian troops in Bessarabia. As for the Russian counterrevolutionaries, they could organize, arm and build up their strength under the protection of the Allied Expeditionary Corps.

Franchet d'Esperey seems to have been deeply disappointed by his contacts with the anti-Bolsheviks. General Denikin, who was in command of all the counterrevolutionary forces in southern Russia, was suspected of holding "liberal" opinions by his staff, made up of former officers of the Imperial Army. He had no political authority over the territories he controlled, or even over his own army. When the mobilization of all men able to bear arms was decreed, no one obeyed the order. Franchet d'Esperey, exasperated by the incompetence and the internal rivalries of the counterrevolutionary General Staff, began to feel alarmed.

Among the sailors there broke out a mutiny, which was to make André Marty famous. The Command decided to reduce the perimeter of the region occupied. The evacuation of Nikolaiev resulted in losses of matériel. Quite clearly the Odessa expedition was senseless, if left on its own. Either it had to be withdrawn, or enabled to function in the totality of anti-Bolshevik operations.

On March 25, 1919, the Council of Four, consisting of Wilson, Clemenceau, Lloyd George and Orlando, considered the question of the aid to be given Roumania in the event of a conflict with the Soviet Union. Marshal Foch was asked to prepare a plan of action.

To put an end to Bolshevik infiltration, Foch declared, it was necessary to establish a barrier in Poland and Roumania, to "clean out" the areas in the rear that might be "infected," such as Hungary and Lemberg, and see to it that communications were maintained via Vienna. As for Roumania, in particular, a whole series of measures was foreseen that would provide its army with the necessary equipment. The Roumanian troops would be placed, too, under the command of a French general, while in Vienna the Allied troops of occupation would be under an American general.

Wilson at once saw that Foch's plan went far beyond the objective initially assigned to him. He accepted the principle of aid for Roumania, and agreed to the evacuation of Odessa. The troops thus freed could help to defend the Roumanian frontier. But, he remarked, Foch had gone "much further" in his report. "Lemberg is mentioned in it. In the quarrel between Ukrainians and Poles, it is difficult for us to intervene without knowing more clearly what our position is with respect to the Ukrainians or Bolsheviks who are besieging Lemberg. To close the gap at Lemberg, at the present moment, would mean taking sides for the Poles against the Ruthenians. As for the idea of establishing a link between the Polish and Roumanian forces in order to confront the east, that is the prelude of a march on the east, and brings us to the question of military intervention in Russia.

We have examined this question more than once, and each time we reached the conclusion that we must not envisage a military intervention."

Thus Wilson refused to accept the plan suggested by Foch. He would not move beyond the stage of local acts of intervention, whose aim was merely to halt the Bolshevik groundswell, and turned down an over-all plan which, pushed to its limit, would switch the Allies from a "defensive position in Europe" to an "offensive inside Russian territory or in Siberia."

Lloyd George had already come to suspect everything the Marshal proposed. He asked ". . . if, when he spoke of establishing a barrier, he wished to take precautions against a military danger offered by the Bolsheviks, or against a danger of some other nature." Foch, in his reply, could not completely evade the political aspect of the question, but he was anxious above all to stress the defensive aspects of the plan, so as to forestall the criticisms of Wilson and Lloyd George. "Against an infectious disease," he declared, "a *cordon sanitaire* is established: a customs official is posted every two hundred meters, and people are not allowed to pass. Furthermore, if armed intervention is feared, a stronger barrier is erected. My opinion is that a barrier should be raised against both dangers, and this does not mean to prepare an offensive. . . . The whole system I have submitted to you tends to organize a barrier against Bolshevism; this is not an offensive, but a defensive barrier, behind which the necessary mopping-up operations can be carried out."

Foch was backed by the British Chief of Staff, Sir Henry Wilson, who asked the political leaders to wait no longer before "deciding whether or not they want military action against Bolshevism." But General Bliss, President Wilson's military adviser, thought otherwise. After the military men had left, Wilson persuaded Clemenceau and Lloyd George to reject Foch's proposed plan. Twice he referred to their uncertainty concerning the real feelings of the Allied troops. "Have we," he asked, "not only the troops we need, but . . . the public feeling that would back us up? . . . To try to stop a revolutionary movement by the use of armies in battle order is like using a broom to stop a tidal wave. Besides, the armies might be affected by the Bolshevism they would be required to fight. A grain of sympathy exists between the forces supposed to be fighting each other." While the American statesman knew very well what he did not want, he was, actually, far less sure of what he did want. "The only way to proceed against Bolshevism," he said to Lloyd George and Clemenceau, "is to eliminate its causes. This is, furthermore, an immense undertaking, and we are not even entirely sure what the causes are."

At all events, the heads of the Allied governments decided to refuse the only systematic plan offered them to counter Bolshevism, at a time when the combined activities of General Denikin in southern Russia, Admiral Kolchak in Siberia and the Allied expeditionary corps in Odessa, the Urals and Archangel gave the plan the greatest chance of succeeding.

The French high command had wanted to raise the struggle against the Bolsheviks to the level of a great international undertaking, under whose shelter every European country could be "cleaned out" and whose natural extension would be direct aid given the Russian counterrevolutionaries. After the Council of Four had reached its decision, all that the General Staff could do was to deplore the irresoluteness of the politicians and the predominant influence of Wilson on Clemenceau and Lloyd George, and then to draw the practical consequences. Marshal Franchet d'Esperey had Odessa evacuated on April 5, taking on board 5,000 men of Denikin's Army and 30,000 civilians, eager to remain out of Bolshevik hands. Two weeks later, Marshal Foch passed on to General Janin, in Omsk, a telegram from the Czechoslovak government demanding the repatriation of its citizens.

This month of April was the highest point reached by counterrevolutionary activities. Kolchak's troops were 110 miles from Samara and eighty-five miles from Kazan. Denikin had just reached an agreement with the Don Cossacks and was preparing an offensive which should have enabled him to join with Kolchak in June. But by the time he had pushed close to Saratov in July, it was already too late, for on May 2 had begun the series of defeats inflicted by the Red Army on the counterrevolutionary army of the Siberian front. By July, Kolchak's army was in confusion.

General Janin tried to prevent its becoming an utter rout. On July 28 he informed Prague that he was keeping the Czech Legion under his command, and would not withdraw as long as the counterrevolutionaries held Omsk, their provisional capital and the seat of his own headquarters. On August 28 he launched the final offensive, and in September met with final defeat. On November 8 he left Omsk for Irkutsk, prior to abandoning Siberian territory. Denikin, after reaching

Orel, 220 miles from Moscow, was forced back to the shore of the Black Sea, and another counterrevolutionary general, Yudenich, was repulsed outside Petrograd. His 20,000 men had been entirely fitted out and provisioned by the British General Staff in the region of the Estonian frontier.

French military circles placed the blame for the failure of the counterrevolutionary movement on the incompetence of government leaders who shrank from any substantial coordinated action, such as that proposed by Foch. The real reason for the opposition of Lloyd George and Clemenceau to the proposal was, above all, the desire not to hurt Wilson's feelings. When Wilson learned of Kolchak's defeats, he said to Lloyd George, "I am not so sorry any more that for a few months it's impossible to have any policy in Russia; it seems to me impossible to elaborate one in such circumstances." The British Prime Minister, no doubt realizing that the best opportunities for crushing Bolshevik Russia were slipping away, replied by mentioning "moral" considerations that could not fail to be preoccupying Wilson. "We have the duty not to abandon those we needed when the eastern front had somehow to be created, and public opinion would not forgive us if we abandoned them, now that we no longer need them." Perhaps it was to salve his conscience that he allowed the British General Staff to outfit Yudenich's army, which was, however, forced back into Estonia, where it was disarmed.

The Allied governments succeeded in achieving in Hungary what they had not dared to try in Russia. While they were deciding to reject Foch's plan of March 27, 1919, the Communists had been in power in Budapest for several days. This was the denouement of the situation in which the Provisional Government of the Hungarian Republic, under Karolyi, opposed the representatives of the Allied governments.

Hungary was in the midst of a social revolution. The failure of a Bolshevik demonstration on February 13, 1919, had led to the arrest of Bela Kun and the chief leaders of the Communist Party. But one month later, on March 19, new workers' demonstrations reversed the trend. And on March 20 the typesetters, throwing out the Social-Democrats who were in charge, placed Bolshevik leaders in command of their unions and decided henceforth to print only Communist papers.

On the same day Colonel Vix, chief of the French Military

Mission, with five other officers, called on Count Karolyi and handed him an Allied note, which had been drawn up by General de Lobit, of Marshal Franchet d'Esperey's staff, and which was dated March 12. After having referred to the decision of the Peace Conference to establish a neutral zone between Hungarians and Roumanians, and listing the incidents that had occurred between the two populations, the note laid down the limits of this zone, demanded that it be evacuated by Hungarian troops within a period of ten days, and authorized the Roumanian troops to advance to the eastern limit of the same zone, as soon as the Hungarians had retreated.

Count Karolyi was unwilling to accept this new amputation of territory that was almost entirely Hungarian. He preferred to hand over power to a government that contained the two workers' parties, the Communists and Social-Democrats, who had now resolved on their "complete unification." The chief personage among them was Bela Kun, the Communist Minister of Foreign Affairs.

The Council of Four, by presenting its ultimatum to Count Karolyi, had actually yielded to the twin pressure of the Roumanian government, anxious to exploit internal Hungarian difficulties and ensure territorial aggrandizement, and of the high command of the Allied Armies in the east, which clearly feared that the revolutionary contagion might affect all Central Europe and nullify the future decisions of the Peace Conference.

Immediately after Bela Kun had come into power, Marshal Franchet d'Esperey demanded the authorization to occupy Budapest, which Clemenceau refused. The Council of Four preferred to dispatch to Budapest a committee of enquiry, headed by General Smuts. Smuts's proposals, though much more moderate than the terms of the ultimatum presented by Colonel Vix, were not accepted immediately by the Hungarian Revolutionary movement. Thereupon the Council of Four, resolved to bring Bela Kun's regime to an end, informed Hungary's neighbors that it would no longer veto their armed intervention.

The Roumanians began their offensive on April 16, and the Czechs soon followed suit. Hungarian resistance accounts for the note sent by the Council of Four on June 10, summoning "the Hungarian government to halt at once all fighting against the Czechoslovaks, failing which the associated governments are determined to use extreme measures immediately to oblige Hungary to cease hostilities and to submit to their unshakable resolve to have their orders respected." For six weeks Bela Kun tried to induce the Allies to recognize his government by applying the terms of the armistice. But on July 6 semi-official releases let it be known that "the Supreme Council had agreed on the impossibility of reaching an understanding with the Bela Kun government," while, for their part, the Roumanian troops had not withdrawn to the demarcation line prescribed by the armistice.

Demanding that the Hungarians reduce the number of their soldiers to the level set by the armistice, the Council of Four took up negotiations with the representatives of the Social-Democratic Party and told them the departure of Bela Kun was necessary. He resigned on August 1. But on August 3, despite the promises that the Allies had given the Hungarian delegates, Roumanian troops entered Budapest, where the Social-Democratic government had just been overthrown and where the Archduke of Hapsburg was to arrive on the sixth.

The sudden return to power of the Hapsburg heir was quite unexpected. It was clear, however, that Archduke Joseph of Hapsburg could never have returned to Budapest without the backing of the Allied Armies' high command. When Bela Kun was overthrown, the Hungarian monarchists appealed to Marshal Franchet d'Esperey. They stressed the fact that only the restoration of a Hapsburg, first in Budapest and then in Vienna, could possibly turn Austria away from the idea of union with Germany, favored at the time by all the Austrian parties. They told Franchet d'Esperey that an Austro-Hungarian Catholic monarchy had the best chance of attracting Bavaria, which was conservative and Catholic also, and might perhaps seek to escape the Socialist wave that appeared to be sweeping across all Germany.

So Franchet d'Esperey's staff allowed the Archduke to return, and the monarchists received all the material facilities needed for their activities. The Archduke was proclaimed Regent, until at some later date the restoration became definite. But the restoration of the Hapsburgs was too fiercely opposed by the Czechs, France's main ally in Central Europe, for the French government to agree.

On August 26, Archduke Joseph had to leave Budapest. This was the last time that certain military milieux in France would attempt to challenge German unity, which had been approved by the Versailles Treaty.

By the end of 1919, the problem of French or British military intervention against Bolshevik Russia appeared to be settled. During the winter, the collapse of Kolchak's army reduced the forces opposing the Bolsheviks to those formerly headed by Denikin, which now, under the command of General Wrangel, had sought refuge in the Crimea.

The British government had offered to negotiate with Moscow on an amnesty. At the same time the French government, then headed by Millerand, proposed adequate financial and material aid for Wrangel, who agreed to support the offensive that the Polish Army was preparing to unleash in the Ukraine. Marshal Pilsudski, President of the Polish Republic, after rejecting the peace proposals advanced by Lenin, had just concluded an accord with Petliura, the former head of the Ukrainian government during the German occupation.

Millerand's main concern was the strengthening of Poland which, in the French system of alliances, was to take the place of Russia. A military mission was sent to Wrangel, to provide help in launching offensives that would coincide with those of the Polish Army.

But by the end of the spring of 1920, the successes of the Red Army induced the French government to take a further step toward military intervention against the Soviet Union. Since armaments, munitions and military missions no longer sufficed, an entire General Staff was now dispatched to Warsaw, headed by Marshal Foch's Chief of Staff, General Weygand. French military circles did not hesitate to take the credit for the reorganization of the Polish Army and the success of the counteroffensive, which forced the Red Army to evacuate Polish territory. This was the most spectacular of the long series of French military interventions against Bolshevik Russia. It was, also, the final stage. While military circles were celebrating "the battle of Warsaw" and stressing the part played by General Weygand and his Staff, the relics of General Wrangel's army were abandoning the defenses of the Perekop Isthmus. The French fleet took on board the 70,000 soldiers and 65,000 civilians who followed General Wrangel into exile, bound for Constantinople.

Thus for a period of over two years the Army had taken part in almost all the episodes of the civil war that had been touched off in Russia by the Bolshevik revolution. In Siberia, Odessa, the Crimea and Poland hundreds of officers of every rank had taken part in the General Staffs, military missions, expeditionary corps and in the Black Sea squadrons. A Marshal of France, Franchet d'Esperey, and General Weygand, one of the general officers best known in France and the immediate collaborator of Marshal Foch, had played a role. The Army's higher cadres, through the plans of the General Staff, the technical studies, the problems of logistics and provisioning, as well as through the dispatching of military advisers of every rank, had been involved as a body in the series of military interventions. For them, the world struggle against communism was not simply a matter of opinions, ideologies or class reactions; it had a direct connection with the exercise of their profession. It was of the "missions to be accomplished."

What confronted the General Staff now was no longer Russian but international communism and, more concretely, French communism. The equivalence that had been established in the military mind between the Bolshevik revolution in Russia and defeatism and treason in France soon manifested itself in a new guise after the founding of the French Communist Party. From now on, this was the incarnation of the enemy within. In this respect the outlook in French military circles was doubtless the same as that of the French bourgeoisie as a whole, and even of the entire Western bourgeoisie.

But with Army men, anticommunism was not a matter of political propaganda or the object of theoretical exposés; it was concrete and dramatic. It meant the surveillance of all those suspected of belonging to the Communist Party, disciplinary measures, transfer to special units, the exposure of regimental cells, the search for those who were distributing pamphlets.

Communist hostility to the great undertakings entrusted to the Army, from 1923 on, created in the officers' corps a specific anticommunism that bore no relation to the old, pre-1914 aversion to the Socialists. A political party, openly attached to an International which, in its turn, was associated with Bolshevik Russia, was directing its most violent campaigns of agitation against the main military operations ordered by the governments and carried out by the Army. Military men were left with the enduring impression that a certain segment of French public opinion, concentrated in the working class, but benefiting from the complicity of intellectual milieux, was guilty of permanent treason. This new feeling grew stronger throughout the twenties, at each decisive moment of foreign and colonial policy. On each occasion, the Communists as seen by the Army cadres were "the enemy within" and were made the object of the hatred directed against traitors, always stronger than that to which the enemy is subjected.

The Third Congress of the Communist International met in July, 1921. This was the time when France and Great Britain had succeeded in forcing on Germany a general agreement on reparations, and the first stage had just been fulfilled. It looked as though progress was being made toward a gradual settlement of the problems left unresolved by the Treaty of Versailles. A peace had been signed between Poland and the Soviet Union. A plebiscite had been held in Upper

Silesia. British diplomacy was determined to wipe out one after the other all traces of the war in international relations. The leaders of all the Communist parties in the world decided that "in order to hasten the victory of the Revolution, we must endeavor with the last ounce of energy to impose on the revolutionary struggle a single international direction." From then on, there would be one Communist strategy transcending the frontiers. The heads of the French Communist Party set themselves the task of demonstrating that, by tolerating the formation of an army of occupation filled with a nationalist spirit, the French working class was "nourishing its own enemy."

The Fourth Congress of the International called on all the European proletariat to mobilize against the application of the Versailles Treaty. Reparations were represented to be a crushing burden imposed on the German working class, while offering no benefits to the French working class. To combat the "mystification" so carefully maintained by the two bourgeoisies, the International called for "the fraternization of French and German soldiers on the left bank of the Rhine." Toward the close of 1922, the occupation of the Ruhr seemed to be imminent. The C.G.T.U., the trade union organization under Communist control, set up an "action committee" which aimed at stirring up French opinion against the government's plan. The committee proclaimed that "the occupation of the Ruhr is a crime against the French and German proletariat." It indicated that, on the French side, the occupation of the Ruhr would be met by strikes.

On January 3, 1923, 6,000 persons assembled at a meeting where Cachin and Treint spoke in the name of the French Communist Party, Monmousseau and Sémard on behalf of the C.G.T.U. and Rosy Wolfstein for the German Communist Party. "The French workers," declared the resolution that was passed at the end of the meeting, "announce that in common with their comrades from Germany and Austria they are ready to take all the concerted actions that may be necessary." In the heart of the Ruhr, at Essen, on January 6, there was a meeting of representatives of the French, German, English, Belgian, Dutch and Czechoslovak Communist Parties, and of the C.G.T.U., followed by meetings in Essen, Duisburg, Frankfurt and Stuttgart. On the 11th, French troops entered the Ruhr. For the first time since the mutinies of 1917, and those of Odessa in 1919, a political decision involving military action was confronted by the open and violent opposition of a segment of public opinion.

But on this occasion the opposition was headed by a political party acting in conformity with directives worked out on a supra-national level. This was no longer merely a trend of opinion or moral scruple restricted to certain milieux, or a matter of debates in Parliament. It was an attitude elaborated and adopted by a revolutionary party, connected with all the revolutionary parties in the world. Even more specifically, on the central issue of relations with Germany, a fraction of the French and German working classes proclaimed itself united in violent opposition to the policy adopted by the French government and executed by the Army. From now on the military hierarchy would no longer be confronted by vague press campaigns, anonymous tracts or the protests of intellectuals, but by resolute and clearly identified militants, who made no secret of what they were after. It was a head-on clash and, on the military side, embodied all the elements of a classical repression, with arrests, imprisonments and sentences.

The offices of *L'Humanité* were searched. The eight French Communist delegates returning from the Ruhr were placed under arrest. After an impassioned debate in the Chamber of Deputies, the government lifted Marcel Cachin's parliamentary immunity. Between January 10 and 11, the action committee against the occupation of the Ruhr was in permanent session. All its members were arrested. The same day that *L'Humanité* branded "the operation of pillage—and probably of murder—that Foch and Poincaré are preparing together," Communist meetings were held in Berlin, and sent "their fraternal greeting to the French workers and their arrested leaders. By their courageous struggle against French militarism, the imprisoned militants of the Communist Party and C.G.T.U. prove that they have nothing in common with Monsieur Poincaré's imperialism."

In March a "manifesto to the conscripts," launched by the Secretariat of the Jeunes Communistes, began to circulate among the soldiers in the army of occupation. "In no circumstances," proclaimed the manifesto, "will you accept the humiliating function of counter-revolutionary gendarmes. In no circumstances will your bayonets pierce the breasts of the rebelling German workers. . . . Set out for the Army in order to be the soldiers of Communism. . . . You will remain in close contact with the Jeunesses Communistes, which will wage an unceasing antimilitarist struggle, the extreme form of the class struggle."

Pamphlets were introduced into the barracks. The Command prohibited *L'Humanité*, but copies were read all the same, and the soldiers found reading them were brought before a court martial. In some regiments party cells were formed. Communist soldiers solicited subscriptions to help German Communists arrested by the occupation authorities. French soldiers were even observed at demonstrations organized by German workers. The attention of Maginot, the War Minister, was drawn to this Communist agitation in the Ruhr, and he went to see for himself. There were 135 arrests; a court martial held in Mainz condemned the Communist Party leader to ten years' imprisonment, three soldiers to two years, one other to one year, eleven German civilians to five years, and the rest to a few months.

French public opinion may soon have forgotten the men who were condemned by the Mainz court martial. But the officers of the forces of occupation did not forget the network of counterespionage they had had to organize in their own regiments against the Communists, after they had set off with the simple belief that their whole task was "to make Germany pay."

In Asia and Africa, the officers of the colonial army and of the North African regiments experienced the rebirth of nationalism in the colonized countries. In Indochina, the General Staffs kept an eye on the formation of a "Kuomintang" that sought inspiration in the Chinese revolution and whose long-term goal was the independence of Vietnam. The officers of the North African regiments shared an experience with their comrades on the General Staffs in Hanoi and Saigon, in the regiments of Annamite *tirailleurs* and with those, too, who officered the powerful expeditionary corps sent to the Levant between 1921 and 1925.

During this last year there was at last effected a fusion of the experience of the antinationalist struggle and of anti-Communist activity, in the Army's political history. It was an event fraught with significance. In the mind of the military cadres, from now on there would be an established bond between communism and anticolonialism. Communist agitation in the ranks, in the street and in Parliament was one with the great rebellion against French colonization which, after erupting in Indochina, Syria and Tunisia, would finally reach Morocco.

The Spanish Army had suffered a disaster on July 21, 1921, in the gorge of Aloual, where 12,000 men were slaughtered by the Riff tribes, who then made off with an enormous amount of matériel. Abd-el-Krim, who was at the head of one of the "confederated tribes of the Riff," continued the struggle against the Spanish occupation. At the news of the new successes achieved by the Riff, two leaders of the French Communist Party, Pierre Sémard and Jacques Doriot, sent a telegram dated September 10, 1924. "The parliamentary group and central committee of the Communist Party and the national committee of Communist Youth hail the brilliant victory of the Moroccan people over the Spanish imperialists. They congratulate its valiant leader Abd-el-Krim. They hope that after the final victory over Spanish imperialism, it will continue, in league with the French and European proletariat, the struggle against all imperialists, including French, until Moroccan soil is set completely free."

Shortly after this, a manifesto released by the Jeunesses Communistes announced, in unison with the Young Spanish Communists, the formation of an action committee against the Riff war and called on the "soldiers of France and Spain" to "fraternize with Abd-el-Krim." On February 4, 1925, in the Chamber of Deputies, Doriot read the text of the telegram sent Abd-el-Krim. "Peace will always be disturbed," he added, "as long as we have over there generals interested in fomenting trouble."

These statements actually aroused widespread opposition, including that of the Socialists. Painlevé, the President of the Council, was supported at the time by a left-wing majority. "These words," he replied, "reveal nothing but contempt for the Chamber." And Herriot, who was presiding, declared that "nothing in Monsieur Doriot's speech that might injure the troops' morale will appear in *L'Officiel*." But Doriot's words were translated into Arabic and circulated among the insurgents.

The war against the Riff involved the greater part of the colonial army and of the North African regiments, and even required the transfer to Morocco of a considerable contingent of troops from the metropolis. A year elapsed before Abd-el-Krim was forced to surrender on May 26, 1926. As soon as these operations had gotten under way, the action committee set up by the Communist Party, the C.G.T.U. and the Jeunesses Communistes issued a new proclamation. "The inevitable has happened. War has begun. . . . The occupation of Morocco has already cost the workers and peasants of France 12,000 dead and four billion francs. It has reduced millions of natives to veritable slavery. . . . Long live the independence of the colonial peoples! Down with war in Morocco!" On May 27, in the Chamber of Deputies, Doriot spoke once again. Herriot put through a vote of censure. The Communist deputies sang the Internationale. On July 4 a workers' congress meeting in Paris assembled, according to the Communist press, 2,470 delegates, including 130 Socialists and 160 members of the C.G.T. A "Central Action Committee" was formed, which was to turn to French workers and peasants as well as to the colonial peoples and to Spanish, Italian and British workers' organizations.

This Committee was presided over by Maurice Thorez, at that time a member of the Central Committee and Secretary of the northern region. Thorez appealed to the Socialist Party and the C.G.T. The Socialists did not answer but, in view of the spreading of military operations in Morocco and the outbreak of the Druse rebellion in Syria, they asked that the two Chambers be summoned. On September 25, Thorez let it be known that "the Central Action Committee, while having no illusions concerning the role of the bourgeois Parliament, is disposed to support . . . this demand that it be summoned."

This Communist campaign soon produced a reaction. The newspapers most widely read among the officers, such as *L'Echo de Paris* and *Le Figaro*, called on the government to take drastic action against the Communists. "The confidence of the entire world," wrote *L'Echo de Paris*, "will acclaim the government on the day, not far off, we trust, when it will reject all direct or indirect relations with these wretches and will let them feel, by other means than fine words, its firm determination to deprive them of every possibility of causing trouble. . . . Of all our enemies, the Communists are the worst. Whoever refuses to treat them as such is unworthy of our confidence." *Le Journal des Débats* took the same line. "What is required is to keep a watch on and strike down an enterprise aiming at disorder, managed from abroad, fostered by persons with disordered imaginations and carried out by adventurers from all countries who are planning to smash society."

The government acted as the bourgeois press desired. Briand, Minister of Foreign Affairs, and Schramek, Minister of the Interior, were authorized to contact European governments with a view to organizing a struggle against Communist propaganda. An agreement for the cooperation of all European police forces was finally drawn up by Jean Chiappe, Director of the Sûreté Générale. The propaganda calling for "fraternization" with the Moroccan rebels was illegal, and 165 Communist militants were imprisoned between the summer and fall of 1925.

Thirty years beforehand, the war in Morocco already foreshadowed certain essential features of the Algerian war. There were the same declarations of solidarity, made by the extreme Left, with the nationalist insurrection, the repression of the campaigns condemning the war and calling for aid for the insurgents, the rupture between the Europeans of Algeria, even those at a most modest social level, and the anticolonialist Left, the sympathy for this Left to be found in intellectual milieux, with men as little suspect of communism as Georges Duhamel and Henri Torrès placing their names alongside those of Louis Aragon and André Breton on a manifesto deploring "the spilling of blood in Morocco."

But for others, the Moroccan war was the last link in a great "revolutionary chain" that threatened France and the Empire with a fearful encirclement. Among their number were the military milieux concerned about developments in Indochina, Tunisia and Syria, and the few officers who, even in Paris, had surveyed the intense activity of colonials who had regrouped in the metropolis. Some, for example, between 1922 and 1926, had noted the articles, in the magazine *Le Paria,* by the anticolonialist militants who later became celebrated as Ho Chi Minh and Messali Hadj. Far more numerous were those whose recollections associated communism with the distressing pictures of police duties and courts martial during the occupation of the Ruhr.

This was the time when the military journals and the colonial newspapers most widely read by the overseas General Staffs and garrisons, whenever they dealt with Indochina, North Africa or the Levant, constantly evoked the frightful danger of "Communist subversion." Using the revolt of the colonial peoples and the "detour through Asia" that Zinoviev had heralded at the "Congress of the Oppressed Peoples of the Orient" held in Baku in 1920, this movement, it was felt, threatened all civilization. As the reverberations of the Great War against Germany gradually grew fainter, the military could already hear a new rumbling: the thunder of the revolution.

CHAPTER ELEVEN

THE TEMPTATION
OF FASCISM

✠

When prices crashed on the New York Stock Market on October 24, 1929, nothing seemed to presage the beginning of a new era in the history of the Western world. In France, perhaps more than anywhere else, the public was enjoying to the full the period of peace and prosperity that prevailed during the exceptionally long-lasting Poincaré government.

After the unparalleled trials endured in the war, the political and class conflicts of the postwar years and the ravages of inflation, French society had at last arrived, by the summer of 1926, in the haven of peace, of calm and prosperous tranquillity that had been its unvoiced longing ever since the mass slaughter of the Marne and Verdun, of the Somme and Eparges. Only a minority of the working class, tortured by poverty and inspired by the example of Communist Russia, had any thought of revolution. Elsewhere, political quarrels were restricted to the traditional maneuvers of the parties' "General Staffs," to electoral campaigns and parliamentary intrigues. The governments of the Right showed themselves every bit as prodigal of the public purse as any government of the Left could have been. Tardieu, President of the Council, put through a law creating forms of insurance for the working classes, and another that made secondary education free. Since Poincaré had retained Briand as Minister of Foreign Affairs, foreign policy continued to enjoy a kind of national unanimity that no doubt masked mental reservations, but which in the last resort depended on the weariness aroused by the numerous international emergencies that had for so long convulsed the world. People had rejected the ill-starred adventures of which the occupation of the Ruhr had been the prime example. Above all else they longed for peace.

In this social context, when all were satisfied with the re-establishment of tranquillity and with a prosperity now several years old, the Army had buried deep the seeds of crisis that still remained from the trials it had endured. In this era of European peace, how could one fail to understand the lack of interest shown by young people in the profession of arms? The nightmare of inflation, and the plunge into poverty, had left so deep a mark that no one would have dared to complain, now that stable prices, a full treasury and business expansion banished the spectre of want. Assured that Europe would never again be the site of military adventure, newly fledged officers opted for the overseas garrisons, the colonial army and the North African regiments. Thus, in their way, they adopted the vogue of travel that had taken hold of all bourgeois society and was reflected in an extensive literature, from Paul Morand to Blaise Cendrars.

Syria and Morocco, a few years before, had offered more opportunities for glory than service in Trier or Mainz. Among the young officers involved were Charles de Foucault, the Saint-Cyr graduate who later became a monk, and who was killed by Moroccan rebels on the fringes of the desert; Vieuxchange, an explorer, and the spiritual heir of Psichari, who disappeared in the Sahara; Henri de Bournazel, a lieutenant in the Spahis who soon became legendary. He was the object of a cult both religious and military, which attained dimensions equaling the homage paid Guynemer. Morocco became the outstanding and most recent symbol of the grandeur of colonial conquest.

There can be no doubt that reasons for profound uneasiness lingered deep down in the military mind, as the twenties drew to a close. But not until the whole of French society was in the throes of a crisis could there be any open rupture that would challenge the preciously preserved unity of the country and its Army, sealed by the bloodshed of wartime and consolidated in the exaltation of victory. The obscure travailings of the Army had to be matched by the collective distress of the Nation.

No one, on October 24, 1929, could have suspected that the crash on the New York Stock Exchange was the precursor of this encounter. No one could have foreseen that in a mere ten years a total situation would develop which would split Army and country, rupture the unity of the traditional state and yet, in the long run, be only the preliminary to a revolution that would convert the Army into a political force. The road that led to May 13, 1958, and the French uprising in Algeria, can be traced back to the stresses of the thirties.

The bourgeois, liberal restoration that had followed the war was everywhere submitted to a highly critical examination. The democratic ideology had already been challenged in a number of European countries; the number of dictatorial regimes was on the increase. In 1931, Yugoslavia; 1933, Germany and Estonia, with a consolidation of the regime in Hungary that same year; in 1934, Bulgaria and Austria. It was the turn of Poland in 1935, and of Greece in 1936. That same year witnessed the outbreak of the Spanish Civil War. The whole of central, eastern and Mediterranean Europe, with the sole exception of Czechoslovakia, had cast out the democratic ideology which, in French military circles, had so often been suspected of negating the 1918 victory. In the milieux of nationalists and conservatives, this return to authoritarian military and dictatorial regimes was regarded as a confirmation of their doubts with regard to democracy, and of their fundamental historical pessimism.

An accompanying phenomenon was the collapse of the hopes that had been placed in the League of Nations, the projects of a "European Federation" and the reconciliation between the old enemies. By 1930, Hitler's National Socialists were strongly represented in the Reichstag. In 1931 the "Manchurian incident" marked the first in a series of wars which have never since ceased. Where Manchuria was concerned, the most distressing feature was perhaps the failure of the League of Nations, whose decisions were not enforced.

Simultaneously, the economic crisis brought about the collapse of orderly exchange rates, and so led states to adopt extreme forms of economic nationalism, sometimes going as far as autarchy. From this time on, the fear never ceased to grow, both in France and abroad, among politicians, military men and economists, that this chronic "economic warfare" might one day be replaced by armed conflict on a world scale. As it was, violence erupted within the various countries. The new Spanish Republic was not established, in 1931, without disorders. Blood flowed at every election in Germany. Dollfuss used artillery to crush the workers' revolt in Vienna. Later he would himself be assassinated by the Nazis. The greater part of the world appeared to have abandoned legal and parliamentary methods. In France, those whose duty it was to prepare for war sensed that the days would come again when they would be called upon. Pacifism, the Geneva spirit, international reconciliation: in but a few years they had fallen to the rank of lost illusions, of faded myths.

Yet French society, which was left untouched by the economic crisis for a longer period than other countries, still seemed exempt, in 1932, from any temptation to turn to dictatorship, or to have recourse to violence. The 1932 elections offered nothing more drastic than some successes for the Radical-Socialists, and some setbacks for the Moderate Republicans. Herriot once more returned to office. But on this occasion there was too wide a gap between the harmless, routine functioning of parliamentary life and the drama of mass unemployment, peasant poverty and the ruin of the middle classes. Eighteen months sufficed to lead the country to the brink of civil war. February 6, 1934, marked the first great victory of the crowd against the majority in Parliament and against the orderly processes of republican institutions.

In the meantime, Hitler had seized power in Germany, and on every hand France could witness the spectacle of dying democracies and reborn imperialisms. While danger grew beyond the frontiers, within the country the successive ministerial crises and the financial scandals threatened to leave France weak and defenseless in a world that was already headed for another war. The military, professionally sensitized to the least indication of possible future conflict, were alarmed by this contrast between the slow dissolution of the aged Republic and the upsurge of the dictatorships. In another era, their alarm would have vented itself in representations made to government leaders and by a flurry of activity at the staff level, with the elaboration of new plans for mobilization and armed conflict. The needs of national defense would have re-established unity between the parties and social classes. But times had changed. Deep clefts were being formed in the public psyche. People were driven to despair by the tardiness of the state to counteract economic setbacks and mass unemployment, and ready to challenge everything: state, society, the economic organization, moral values, traditional philosophies.

The military hierarchy had long felt ill at ease in a world whose democratic ideology sided with pacifism to question the future and the necessity of a military establishment. But now, in the thirties, a new trend took hold of the collective mind, and associated itself with the deep-seated military suspicion of traditional democracy, the republican state and international capitalism. Thus an unexpected echo answered the Army's unvoiced temptations. A path was opened up that led from the crisis of capitalism to that of the bourgeois state, to the shaking of the Western world to its foundations. When everything had come to be threatened by universal subversion, then the Army could emerge from its former indifference to the political eddies. This would indeed be a revolution in the Army's outlook, but was it not being said on every side that the world was given over to revolution?

It is no longer easy to recall what this situation meant for citizens of the most advanced bourgeois society. All the ideas on which their conception of the world was based were now being brutally challenged. There seemed little sense in continuing to work, since nothing could be sold; in producing, since there were no markets; in discovering, since there would be no utilization. Why give birth to children, since they could not find employment? The immense effort of reconstruction and expansion, which had been accomplished at the cost of enormous effort in the postwar years, was now branded as vain. In the space of a few years, the thirties saw thirty or forty million men in the most advanced countries condemned to permanent unemployment and dire poverty. The whole social set-up was blamed by men horrified by this catastrophe that in two or three years had reduced production and the exchange of goods to a pre-1913 level. It seemed clear that the only outcome must be revolution and war.

A few lines written by Paul Reynaud strikingly depict the drama of a capitalist society staggering under these mortal blows:

> Deserted oceans, ships left unfitted in silent ports, no plume of smoke from the factory chimneys, long lines of unemployed in the towns, indigence in the countryside. The Argentinian saw the prices of wheat and cattle sink; the Brazilian, that of his coffee; the American, that of wheat and cotton; the Malayan, that of rubber; the Cuban, that of sugar; and the Burman, that of rice.
>
> Then came the day when riches were destroyed: the Brazilians threw their sacks of coffee into the sea and the Canadians their wheat into locomotive fireboxes. Like a man suddenly forced to leave his house, civilization appeared to be set on destroying the riches it had created before it disappeared. Men looked with suspicion on what

they had learned to admire and respect. . . . The crisis was even more widespread than war had been, and it lasted longer. The peoples grew economically isolated, but they were as one in their poverty.

For France the economic crisis came later and was less spectacular, but it was much more persistent. Only, indeed, in the year that preceded World War II did the French economy exhibit once more a certain dynamism. And this was too late. The other great industrial states, and Germany in particular, had long before made giant strides that France could no longer match.

The French could no doubt imagine, between 1929 and 1932, that they were being let off lightly. The high production costs of British industry had made Great Britain particularly vulnerable. The flight of foreign capital invested in Germany brusquely left the country without the means to fight off a depression of unparalleled severity and an unemployment rate that affected nearly one quarter of the working population. The United States, the first to be affected, offered the spectacle of a country whose previous prosperity left it all the more miserable, and whose high wage scales, high rate of investment and "miracles" of lending for purposes of consumption made the collapse all the more redoubtable.

For two or three years, French bourgeois opinion was tempted to think that France, better "balanced" and more "moderate," with a total income derived from industry, crafts and agriculture, and from large, intermediate and small enterprises, was being rewarded for its "wisdom." The illusion persisted even after 1932, and helped to keep a considerable part of French public opinion from favoring the most revolutionary trends, whether of Left or Right. The main effect was to cause the postponement of energetic solutions that cried out for adoption. But if the bulk of bourgeois opinion restricted itself to the arduous search for "safe" solutions and remained attached, as it had been for sixty years, to parliamentary institutions, by 1930 the indications of a new current of ideas were noticeable, and they rapidly multiplied.

Naturally enough, it was young people who were attracted to them. They had not had the same reasons as their elders to make a cult of the past. All they had known of the war was the disappointing aftermath of inflation, moral abandon and social breakdown. Against the glorious memories of the returned warriors they instinctively set up the less pleasant realities of the "infernal cycles of prices and wages" that marked the twenties and the less heroic impact of the greed for money and the commercial pacifism that went hand in hand with Locarno and Poincaré's return to power. Everything tempted young people to look more or less favorably on the revolutions to come.

The economic collapse, reflected in the collapse of traditional values, ultimately touched off the Army crisis. The young men swarming through the secondary schools, university departments and specialized institutions of advanced learning were like the young men who peopled the military academies and received their officers' commissions; they shared the same friendships, associations, discussions and reading. At the outset, only the younger military men were involved in these new trends of opinion. Later, as the economic crisis grew worse, with its revolutionary consequences and the threat of a social upheaval, the reserve or actual indifference they had hitherto exhibited would be abandoned by the older military cadres, who so far had remained attached to traditional values and conservative views. Their reactions would then accord with the much more violent outlook of the young officers, and this meeting of minds was to have an immense influence on the Army as a whole, on the eve of World War II.

The new ideas that stirred up people's minds in France, and above all those of the young, found expression in a number of periodicals whose contributors were later to be found in the most varied camps. They were called *Réaction, Combat, Esprit, L'Ordre Nouveau, Plans, L'Homme Nouveau*—and there were many more. Among the collaborators of *Réaction*, for instance, were Robert Buron, later a leader of the Mouvement Républicain Populaire, and Minister under the Fourth and Fifth Republics, and Jean-Pierre Maxence and Thierry Maulnier, disciples of Charles Maurras and of L'Action Française. Their first manifesto typified the state of mind of the young bourgeois with a conservative background, who suddenly had been confronted by the crisis in capitalism and the powerlessness of the traditional state in the face of economic collapse. "Order is neither the protection of strongboxes, nor the union of economic interests, nor the defense of those who have arrived. . . . What is required is to heed the lessons of the past, to return to the sources of life, and to react. Reaction in politics against democratic decadence, daughter of number and quantity . . . social reaction, against individualism, statism and the class struggle, in order to allow the development of the human person in his natural social framework. . . ."

In these lines can be read the double hostility aroused by liberal individualism, which is somewhat hastily equated with classical capitalism, and by socialism of a Marxist tinge, given over to the class struggle. The same twin hostility could be found among the Italian Fascists and the German National Socialists.

No clear distinction was drawn between those who desired merely to adapt Western democracy to a socialist economic set-up and those who, with their critiques of capitalism, really sought to undermine the republican state. In *Combat*, which numbered many intellectuals who had been influenced by Maurras, there was talk of "the bankruptcy of idealism and the threat of materialism." *Esprit*, later to take a firm stand on the Left, counted off its enemies: "Individualist materialism, collectivist materialism, and Fascist pseudo-spiritualism."

L'Ordre Nouveau numbered among its contributors those future specialists in European federalism, Robert Aron and Alexandre Marc, as well as a future journalist and Gaullist militant of the Fourth Republic, Albert Ollivier. *"L'Ordre Nouveau,"* a pamphlet proclaimed, "is preparing the revolution of order against capitalist disorder and Bolshevik oppression, against powerless capitalism and homicidal imperialism, against parliamentarianism and dictatorship."

Here again one encounters the equating of capitalism with the parliamentary regime and liberal democracy, and divines that the struggle against the "Bolsheviks" will take the form of an authoritarian state. *Plans*, with more substantial financial backing, boasted far more prominent contributors, including Honegger, Fernand Léger, Picart Ledoux and Le Corbusier. But among the others were one of the chief leaders of the agricultural movements under the Fourth Republic, Philippe Lamour, and a future Minister of Labor of the Vichy regime, Hubert Lagardelle. One remark to be found in the presentation of the first number might have been signed by the staff of most of these young weeklies and reviews. "The current drama of the industrialized West is essentially due to the artificial retention of individualist institutions as the framework of a collectivized economy."

L'Homme Nouveau was also anticapitalist. The fate of its editorial staff is characteristic of the confusion reigning in many minds in France, in the early thirties, before a definitive choice had to be made, one way or the other, with regard to National Socialist Germany. Marcel Déat and Paul Marion became Ministers in Vichy, Drieu la Rochelle supported collaboration between Germany and Vichy, Robert Lacoste took an active part in the Resistance and later played a prominent role in the Algerian war, Pierre Laroque was the chief author of the social security laws adopted after the Liberation, and Robert Marjolin became one of the most important officials in the organizations of the new Europe.

The same confusion is to be found among the authors of the "Plan of July 9," which, in 1934, appeared to voice the profound desire for a political, economic and social renewal that stirred the whole range of French intellectual opinion. The signatories included men like Paul Marion, who was Minister of Information for Vichy, but also P. O. Lapie, one of the first political personalities to join La France Libre; Roger de Saivre, who would be a member of Pétain's cabinet; and Louis Vallon, future member of General de Gaulle's cabinet.

The "Plan of July 9" took up many of the themes dear to *Réaction, Esprit, L'Ordre Nouveau* and *Plans*: hostility to liberalism, but also to the "totalitarian mystiques," the renewal of the state, anticapitalism, and sympathy for the corporate state. To all this were added more concrete political proposals, some of which certainly were nationally desirable (devaluation of the franc, for instance, which had to follow the devaluation of the dollar and the pound) but of which others, such as a Franco-German rapprochement, revealed either that the authors of the Plan had failed to draw all the consequences from Hitler's seizure of power or that they were willing to compromise with him. This general uncertainty was even more clearly shown by the political affiliations of some of the signatories. Some belonged to the leagues of the Right or extreme Right, the Jeunesses Patriotes or Volontaires Nationaux, while others were members of the Jeune République, which two years later would support the Popular Front. But many claimed to be apolitical and, if they had studied at Polytechnique, belonged to one of the most characteristic groups of the day, "X-crise." These were young officials of the top level or technicians working for large concerns, who had been struck by the impotence of capitalism in crisis, and had decided to improve matters by means of a technological reform of the state and the economy. Later they were to be found in every corner of the French political panorama. What they had in common with many officers of every rank was their training at Polytechnique, and this brought about many contacts with military circles.

Among the officers themselves, everything conspired to ensure that the most active, open-minded and intelligent would be highly susceptible to the doctrines that made up this new current of ideas.

They discovered in these doctrines the echo of some of the occurrences that had left their mark on the military psyche in the 1920's. There was the same detestation of the parliamentary regime and party impotence, the same hostility to international capitalism, to those banks that had already been accused of having "stolen the victory," and the same aversion to the moderate, classical parliamentary Right. The impression of decadence that overcame the intellectual bourgeoisie, when they surveyed the spectacle of the economy at a standstill, had been felt long before by the Army, embittered by the general indifference of the country, uncertain as to its own mission and in spontaneous reaction against the pacifistic spirit of Geneva and Locarno. Thus the fusion of military opinion with the movement of intellectual revolt in the 1930's encountered no obstacle.

But soon new cleavages would split French opinion. The grave worsening of the crisis, beginning in 1933 and 1934, the first diplomatic brushes with Hitler's Germany, the great antiparliamentary demonstration of February 6, 1934, the workers' riposte on February 9 and 12 and, later, the Ethiopian War gradually forced these men, who had been collaborating in the same reviews and the same manifestoes, to choose conflicting paths, some leading to an alliance with the Communists, the Popular Front and antifascism, and the others to a condemnation of the democratic state, to a total anticommunism and to the search for a French fascism, whose earliest manifestation would be a rapprochement with Germany and Italy. These distinctions were not drawn without hesitations and delays. The imperious behest of events was needed to clinch the matter.

For the bourgeoisie that still remained so deeply conservative and nationalist, and that was so terrified by the vitality of the workers' movement and by the revolutionary rise and spread of communism, there could be no question of placing the source of the maladies affecting French society where it really belonged, in the bourgeois ownership of the means of production and in the contradictions of classical capitalism. Even less could there be any thought of drawing the most extreme conclusion, that some form of socialism was absolutely necessary. Owing to the confusion made between capitalism and liberalism, this trend of opinion was categorized as simply anticapitalist.

A young writer with a past in L'Action Française and favorably disposed toward fascism, Jean-Pierre Maxence, looked back on the years of prosperity, 1928–1930. "Two years of capitalism. Nauseating years, nauseating enough to make one vomit." But it should not be overlooked that against this capitalism there was never any recourse to socialism. Recommended was the strong state, national discipline, corporatism and a form of statism. The Communists had no difficulty in seeing that this was an attempt to salvage capitalism, not to overthrow it. And antirationalism, in these same social and intellectual circles, like antimaterialism, was a way of attacking at the same time a bourgeois and a Socialist world. It attacked the liberal, victorious bourgeoisie of the nineteenth century, which was incorporated in democratic parliamentary regimes. It attacked, also, socialism of a Marxist hue, in which the revolt of the workers found expression. The invocation of spiritual values, and of traditional philosophies, was the intellectual form of a refusal to accept the revolutionary transformations that the economic and social situation seemed to demand.

This complex of ideas was, as a consequence, no less opposed to "Americanism" than to communism. "The cancer of the modern world," it was declared, in *Décadence de la Nation française*, one of the most typical productions of this time, "came into being far from the charnel-houses of the battlefields, on well protected soil, even better protected than is often believed. It is the American cancer. . . . The American cancer is the supremacy of bank and industry over the entire life of the age. It is the hegemony of rational mechanisms over concrete and felt realities, the veritable wellsprings of man's true progress . . . The Yankee spirit is nothing but the mass-produced exploitation, on a gigantic scale, of the most lamentable error that Europe has ever committed, the rationalist error."

How could the officers who had read *Feu l'armée française* fail to rediscover here the same excoriation of materialism and scientism that had already been offered to them in 1928? How could their old resentment of the "parliamentary mess" remain unaffected by the vociferous antiparliamentarianism of a whole intellectual generation, which found its best summing-up in an article published by *L'Ordre Nouveau*. "The idea, like the pig, is carried alive into the factory, Parliament, on a hoist—the Party—and emerges on the other side, in the form of laws no less numerous, varied and standardized than black puddings, hams and garlic sausages. The deputies and senators sterilize the ideas and feelings of their principals by means of methods every bit as perfectly time-engineered as the gesture of the Negroes who, in Chicago, bleed each pig as it makes its way down the line."

For the first time since the Dreyfus Affair, an intellectual and ideological climate was being formed that had come out of the economic collapse, had grown more powerful as the republican regime proved powerless to bring it to a halt, and was leading to a general arraignment of French institutions. There was bound to be a corresponding change in actual political life. This would be produced by the development of the parties and of international events, in the first five years of the 1930's.

In 1932, French politics was still following the line that had been laid down at Locarno. Now there was to be a conference on disarmament with, as its guideline, "equality of rights in the matter of armaments, in a settlement that would comprise security for all nations."

But on January 30, 1933, Hitler came to power, and in September of that year demanded the immediate recognition of the equality of French and German rights with respect to armaments. Great Britain, France and Italy refused. On October 14, Hitler announced that, in these circumstances, Germany was leaving the League of Nations and walking out of the Disarmament Conference. But he was eager to enter into direct negotiations with France and, on November 24, he proposed that the two countries should each have an army of 300,000 men, fully equipped; and he would accept a subsequent international control.

The government thought that to reach an agreement of such importance with Germany would give Hitler too much prestige in the eyes of the German public. In the fall of 1933, it did not yet appear certain that Hitler would be able to consolidate his position. Should he be granted an important diplomatic advantage, when he had just noisily broken with the League of Nations, and so sinned against the "spirit of Locarno"? The French government thought not. It was already hesitating between the policy of reconciliation and relaxation of tensions that had been followed from 1924 to 1932, and the distrust of a Germany which, since the recession, had turned away from its moderate political parties and permitted the National Socialists to come to power.

This hesitation lasted throughout 1933. On March 19, Mussolini had received Ramsay MacDonald, the British Prime Minister. Hitler's accession to power had led Mussolini to think that Germany would soon demand the revision of the 1919 treaties. He thought it preferable to seize the initiative, and to have recourse to Article 19 of the Pact of the League of Nations, which provided for such a revision.

He suggested that the question should be examined by a directory made up of the four great powers, Great Britain, France, Italy and Germany. MacDonald approved and Hitler, naturally, was very favorable. But Czechoslovakia, Poland and Roumania at once expressed their strong disapprobation.

France was caught in a dilemma between its obligations to these eastern states and the isolation that threatened, in view of the position adopted in common by Great Britain, Italy and Germany. Most French political personalities, despite their suspicions of the new German government, looked on this "four-power pact" that was suggested to them as the last stage in a line of policy that dated from Locarno. So the government thought it wise not to turn down the offers made but to deprive them of all practical validity by writing into the agreement the principle of respect for the rights of each state, "which could not be disposed of without their accord."

On June 7, the day on which the pact was signed, the French government informed the Czech government that in any frontier question the League of Nations would have the last say on the proposals made by the four, and would reach a decision in unanimity, including the states involved. This meant handing the question back to the states the least desirous of seeing any change in European frontiers. France, in short, had been unable to escape from the contradiction in which she had enclosed herself. The four-power pact was the last stage in a policy which until then had been supported by the major part of political opinion.

A twofold development was going to transform the data on the basis of which French opinion came to a decision on foreign problems. There would be no further question of granting Germany rights equal to those of other countries, nor of allowing its return into the "concert of nations." What mattered now was to defend the frontiers as they had been fixed after the Treaty of Versailles and to prevent an entire revision of the balance of forces in Europe, in favor of Germany. With the breakdown of the disarmament negotiations, the question arose of providing security for France and for the states threatened by the prospect of German expansion, by establishing a system of alliances solid enough to prevent Germany's forcing through a revision of the Treaty, and effective enough to compensate for the clumsiness and slowness of any appeal to the League of Nations.

These were the conditions that brought about a change in an

important fraction of French opinion, which since the 1920's had been favorable to European reconciliation and to a relaxation of tension with Germany. Two policies were envisaged. A "pacifist" trend preferred to make no allowance for the political developments that had transformed Germany and to go on with a policy of negotiation, compromise and appeasement. But a new trend, motivated by alarm at the German policy of the National Socialist regime, and at German rearmament, was convinced that a new era had dawned in international relations and that France was obliged to think out a new policy guaranteeing her security.

In similar fashion, the old-line conservative and nationalist current of thought, which had at first been very reserved about the Locarno Pact, now evolved and divided against itself. The rearmament of Germany and Hitler's policies were looked on, by some, as justifying their apprehensions, and they felt obliged to return to their habitual vigilance in face of the "German danger." Others, on the contrary, refused to give any absolute priority to the new problem posed by Hitler's Germany. Had it not, furthermore, by liquidating the Communist and Socialist opposition, freed Western Europe from a revolutionary peril that had seemed extremely grave, when millions of Germans were voting from the Left and extreme Left? Fascist Italy, too, had eliminated the Bolshevik peril after the First World War.

Right-wing opinion, the most indulgent with respect to the new dictatorial regimes in Germany and Italy, had no objection to a military effort, and its traditional sympathy for the Army led it to criticize the Radical governments which had too sharply reduced the military credits. But already, in their eyes, the precautions that had to be taken against the dangers of revolution far outweighed those required by the new German threat. A rapprochement with Fascist Italy appeared absolutely essential. An understanding with Germany seemed possible, and certainly desirable. But the idea of an alliance with Communist Russia, in face of the Hitlerite menace, was horrifying. This brought about the crystallization, the new political alignment which occurred in French opinion and lasted until 1939, after having received a brutal impulse from the events of February 6, 1934.

Born of the economic collapse and challenging alike the bourgeois state, capitalist disorder and parliamentary impotence, this new ideological trend was, to begin with, an intellectual movement whose influence scarcely reached as far as the administrative levels, either economic or military, of French society. It had no real hold on the population.

This was obtained only after the economic crisis had worsened in France, and affected most painfully the lower and intermediate bourgeoisie and the peasants, all the layers of society that were ruined by the depression, when the greater number of industrial, commercial and agricultural ventures were no longer profitable. The revolt of these sectors, latent since the beginning of the economic crisis, crystallized around the weaknesses and defects of the parliamentary regime. The financial scandals that were so numerous between 1930 and 1934 fed the rancor and irritation felt by an impoverished lower bourgeoisie against the "profiteers" of finance and of Paris politics.

Another little while, and there were to be manifestations, on the part of conservative and enraged, reactionary and honest citizens, with a march on the Palais Bourbon and shouts of "Down with the thieves!" The same critique of political and financial dishonesty, furthermore, developed at the same time in certain intellectual circles and in the conservative bourgeoisie. Emmanuel Berl, one of the most prominent essayists of that day, commented, early in 1934: "From top to bottom, rottenness is on the march and is gaining ground."

It is possible to find a "preliminary" echo of this remark in the literature put out by several organizations of war veterans. One of them, recruited in the main from soldiers or noncoms who had spent at least six months at the front and which later joined forces with the Croix de Feu, whose members had been awarded medals or been mentioned in dispatches, had already proclaimed to an audience of sympathizers in 1929, "It is with the help of men like you that the combatants will clean up the country and have their desires respected."

It was in areas where members of veterans' movements came together that criticism was most openly expressed of the political regime and parliamentary methods. This was symptomatic. For here was the intermediate ground between the military organization and French society. It was from these sources that the outlook of a certain small and intermediate bourgeoisie, traditionally nationalist, and with little understanding of international economic considerations or of modern political preoccupations, found its way into the officers' corps.

The 1930's were marked by the expansion of the most conservative, the most nationalistic and the most antiparliamentary veterans' movements. The Croix de Feu grew from 15,000 members in 1930 to 60,000 in 1933. At the same time, under the influence of its new leader, Colonel de La Rocque, the organization became much more strongly political. Even organizations whose political outlook was relatively timorous, such as the Union Nationale des Combattants, had many members: about 900,000, approximately the same as the Union Fédérale.

The despair that had overtaken the conservative lower bourgeoisie brought it close to the leagues of the extreme Right, which found inspiration in the new ideology, and this, in turn, was fostered in intellectual circles embittered by the ravages of the economic crisis.

A general convergence appeared to take place in the winter of 1933 to 1934. Common positions were established between the leagues of the extreme Right and the conservative *petits bourgeois* belonging to the veterans' organizations. Leading industrialists were also hostile to the parliamentary regime. *La Revue Hebdomadaire* published a series of articles by Mathon, President of the Wool Committee, that looked forward to the setting up, in France, of a corporate state. An article by François Le Grix predicted an imminent *coup de force.* Nothing simpler or more expeditious: the Chamber would adjourn *sine die,* and Paris would be in a state of siege, after demonstrations by taxpayers or the unemployed. "Perhaps," he added, speaking of the promoters of this *coup de force,* "this group will have to be ready a few weeks from now, and in places I cannot yet name. But I can assure you that it is gathering."

"The best minds," declared the financial paper *Le Capital,* "envisage the experiment of an authoritarian government on the lines of those in Italy and Germany." Gustave Hervé raised a question in *La Victoire.* "How can we rid ourselves of this impotent and corrupt regime? Who is the leader who will emerge in France, as he has in Italy and Germany?" One of the most important men in the electrical industries, Ernest Mercier, told the Assemblée du Redressement Français that "the only solution, which the circumstances will soon force on us, is that of an authoritarian government, backed up by an irresistible popular moral force. . . . This is the task to which we dedicate ourselves. And not one among us will call a halt until this has been accomplished."

"The country is nauseated and disgusted, and ready for fury

and acts of violence," declared Henri de Kerillis in *L'Echo de Paris*. Philippe Henriot, parliamentarian of the Right and a future minister in Vichy, expressed his opinion of the first violent demonstrations organized by L'Action Française: "This is the reawakening of the real France!"

The events of February 6 marked the coming together of every form of non-Socialist opposition, whether parliamentary, economic and social, nationalist, or fascist. While within the Chamber of Deputies the Right denounced the regime, the Croix de Feu gathered along the Esplanade des Invalides, the Action Française militants on the Boulevard Saint-Michel, the Jeunesses Patriotes at the Hôtel de Ville and the Union Nationale des Combattants on the Champs Elysées.

It was the extraordinary unanimity in hostility that gave this Paris rioting its strength, together with the additional opportuntiy offered by the resignation of the Daladier government. "On the morning of the 7th," wrote Jean-Pierre Maxence, who was both witness and participant, "the center [of Paris] was invaded by the crowd of those who had been shot at the previous day and by those who had been disturbed, indignant and revolted by this shooting. This time they were armed. Without any preliminary understanding, one man had brought his revolver, another a knife, while a third had a truncheon he had picked up on the 6th, in the street. The real day of revolution was not the 6th, but the 7th . . . Anything could happen. In the seventy years of the bourgeois Republic, no day had been so favorable to a decision, to action, to a revolutionary victory." As the morning slipped by, the most prominent militants in the leagues urged their leaders to attempt a *coup de force*. But these leaders had neither the inner strength that could have enabled them to act, nor the unflinching resolve to risk all now. "I do not choose," said one of them, "to take this responsibility in the eyes of history."

Throughout the 7th, attempts were made to persuade Marshal Lyautey to act. The idea was for him to place himself at the head of fresh demonstrations, bend the will of the President of the Republic and win the support of a number of personalities in the political parties. Colonel de La Rocque, leader of the Croix de Feu, opposed this solution. When the former President of the Republic, Doumergue, was asked to form a government, the crisis had clearly yielded to a parliamentary, not to a revolutionary, solution. But a French fascism had been born.

Between this fascism and the conservative bourgeoisie, through its spokesmen in the parliamentary groups of the Right, and among the Moderates and even the Radicals, a kind of permanent outbidding was now established. The pressure of French fascism did much to hasten the development of many in bourgeois political circles who, required to demonstrate their vigilance in face of the menace of revolution, paid ever greater heed to the warnings uttered by the extreme Right.

A whole segment of the Right wing gave priority over all other preoccupations, and in particular over the growth of the danger from Hitler, to the struggle against the Communist menace at home and abroad. Henceforward every rapprochement with Italy and Germany would be looked on with favor, whereas the detestation of these two dictatorial regimes tended to assimilate the campaigns against them carried out by the Left and the extreme Left. There were several stages in this process.

In the Doumergue cabinet, Barthou, the Minister of Foreign Affairs, was one of the last representatives of the great political generation that had governed France since the early years of the century. The moment that Franco-German negotiations on disarmament had broken down, he decided to work for a Russian alliance. This he favored in 1934, just as he had favored it in his youth, when the Third Republic succeeded in emerging from its international isolation by means of an alliance with the Czarist Empire. But he could neither challenge the Locarno Pact, nor appear to turn away from the spirit of the League of Nations. So he proposed concurrently to Germany and to Russia an "Eastern Locarno," embracing all the States situated between the Russian and German frontiers, namely Poland, Czechoslovakia and the Baltic States. All these powers would reciprocally guarantee each other's frontiers and would promise each other aid in the event of aggression.

Barthou foresaw that Germany, which had never agreed to regard its eastern frontiers as definitive, would refuse this proposal, and this actually occurred in September. That set the French government free to try for a direct alliance with Soviet Russia. The first stage was to be the admission of the Russian state to the League of Nations. It is significant that Herriot, Minister of State under

Doumergue, was entrusted with the negotiation of this first stage. Of all those who had worked for a policy of conciliation and relaxation of tensions with Germany, Herriot was among the number most disturbed by Hitler's policies, and most strongly resolved to oppose them. Similarly, on the conservative side, Barthou, the old nationalist, embodied the attitude of renewed vigilance with respect to Germany.

Russia was admitted to the League of Nations on September 19. This left the way open for a Franco-Russian alliance. When Barthou was assassinated in Marseilles, along with King Alexander I of Yugoslavia, on October 9, 1934, negotiations had already begun. On December 5 his successor, Laval, signed a "protocol preliminary to the diplomatic activity of France and Russia, with a view to the negotiation of the Eastern Pact."

With this, the Franco-Soviet Alliance became the central issue of all political struggles in Parliament, among the parties, in the press and even in the street. Laval himself, who feared the implications of the Alliance, delayed the formulation of the definitive text until May, 1935. To the pact of mutual assistance a signed protocol was added that made the application of the Pact depend on the League of Nations' certifying that aggression had occurred. This deprived the Alliance of its immediate, automatic character. As for the addition of a military convention, which in 1892 had been the main concern of the French government as well as of the General Staff, this was postponed until later. Finally, the ratification of the Pact was not asked for until February, 1936. The Pact had, in actual fact, become the main bone of contention leading to a realignment of the political forces in France.

Two tendencies confronted each other within every group, from the extreme Right to the Radical-Socialists, and even to the Socialists. Of the last-named, such representatives as Marcel Déat and Adrien Marquet, who would both become ministers under Vichy, left the Socialist Party as early as 1933, and envisaged an authoritarian regime and a rapprochement with Germany and Italy. Others who remained Socialists, such as Paul Faure and Charles Spinasse, sought to maintain the policy of international conciliation, even after Hitler's first bold strokes.

In December, 1934, La Voix du Peuple, a newspaper with a wide circulation and financed by the perfumer Coty, published, under the title "With Hitler against Bolshevism," a denunciation of "the short-sighted politicians imbued with false ideas, a hate-filled and anti-French sect in the service of the socio-financial International, who proclaim that Mussolini and Hitler have fearfully bellicose intentions that allegedly represent a threat for France." In the Moderate and Conservative groups, Goy, President of the Union Nationale des Combattants; Scapini, later to be Vichy's ambassador in the prison camps; and Tixier-Vignancourt, a lawyer of the extreme Right, opposed the Franco-Soviet Pact, whose Conservative defenders were Paul Reynaud, Georges Mandel and Louis Marin. Outside Parliament, the Bolshevik menace, worsened by the Franco-Soviet Alliance, was denounced by the leagues of the extreme Right, the Parti Populaire Français under the former Communist Jacques Doriot, and Colonel de La Rocque's Croix de Feu, later transformed into the Parti Social Français.

After the C.G.T.U. combined with the C.G.T. in 1935, the anti-Fascists made up three fourths of this great trade union organization. But several federations within the organization were led by men who feared an understanding with Germany and the maintenance of peace at any price.

In the press, also, a realignment took place, sometimes even inside the same paper. *Le Jour,* which was one of the papers most widely read in the Army, came out against the Russian Alliance and in favor of a Franco-German *détente.* The same views were expressed by weeklies of substantial circulation with considerable influence among the bourgeoisie. *Gringoire,* in particular, blamed English policy for the friction between France and Germany, and *L'Action Française* distinguished itself by abandoning its fanatical hostility to Germany, now preaching anti-Communist and anti-Soviet vigilance while expressing its customary suspicion of English diplomacy.

Other personages and groups went through a more complicated or more belated development. Henri de Kerillis, editorial writer for *L'Echo de Paris* and then editor of *L'Epoque,* was opposed to the Franco-Soviet Pact but remained passionately hostile to any concession being made to Hitlerite Germany. *La République,* a Radical newspaper, anti-Fascist and backing the Popular Front, changed its views in 1936, when it began a large-scale anti-Communist campaign and became more favorable to a moderate German policy. *La Flèche,* one of the most influential and most characteristic weeklies of the 1930's, and which also was anti-Fascist and favored the Popular Front, changed course after the outbreak of the Spanish Civil War. Its editor Bergery, who would later represent Vichy in Moscow and

Ankara, denounced the dangers of an internationalization of the Spanish Civil War, broke with the Communists and advocated a conciliatory foreign policy.

Xavier Vallat, a political associate of Colonel de La Rocque, made this declaration: "Whether you wish it or not, you will give Germany the illusion of being encircled." Another right-wing deputy, Montigny, was opposed to "France's seeking the first rank in this new clash between Germanism and Slavism." Philippe Henriot refused to place "French money and French soldiers at the service of the Revolution." As the electoral campaign of 1936 came closer, Henri de Kerillis, writing in *L'Echo de Paris* on March 23, denounced the foreign policy of the legislature that had just gone out of office. "Its majority of the Left and extreme Left tried to hurl France against Italy, and threw out Laval because he opposed this insensate policy. It ratified the Franco-Soviet Pact while neglecting the elementary precaution of considering the consequences of such a step, and while making no attempt to discover if we had England's agreement on the necessary countermeasures. If the country should return this majority to the Palais Bourbon, its insistence on pushing on with a philo-Russian policy at the behest of the Communists would rapidly lead to a worsening, which on this occasion would be fatal, of the external peril. The Popular Front means War!"

The propaganda of the right-wing parties stressed both the traditional national concerns and the fear aroused in a considerable segment of the middle classes by the alliance with Soviet Russia. A poster put out by the Centre des Républicains Nationaux reminded the passer-by: "The Popular Front, under orders from Moscow, ratified the Franco-Soviet Pact . . . with the consequences that Germany seized on this pretext to tear up Locarno, slight France, occupy militarily the left bank of the Rhine and prepare its positions in order to attack our frontiers." Another poster even more clearly appealed to the desire to reach an understanding with Hitlerite Germany, or at least to cause it no offense: "Remember Hitler's speeches! He clearly announced that if France voted for the Popular Front, and if it put in office a government favorable to Moscow, he would hurl himself at us in order to avoid encirclement by France and Russia. Of course, we are bound to protest indignantly against this interference in our internal politics. But must we overlook the warning? Must we neglect the threat?"

It was a natural reaction that the backers of anti-Fascism, of resistance to Hitler, of the Russian Alliance and the Popular Front, should discover the virtue of patriotism's traditional symbols. Edouard Herriot wrote a homage to the memory of Joan of Arc. Albert Bayet, a great leftist scholar, promised that the victors in the 1936 elections would no longer allow the emblems of patriotic feeling to be stolen from them. "We have suffered three thefts. We have let Joan of Arc be snatched from us, the tricolor and the Unknown Soldier. But, with the ardent awakening of the Popular Front, these great memories surged up anew. On July 14, 1935, the tricolor floated over the immense gathering of republicans. Communists saluted it, as did the great unanimous crowd . . . Just as it has turned once more to the flag of freedom, so the people will turn again to Joan of Arc. Then it will move on, in countless numbers, to express on the tomb of the Unknown Soldier its unshakable desire for peace."

There was, thus, a profound cleavage in the public mind concerning the essentials of French policy. Things took a decisive turn between the moment when the Franco-Soviet Pact was negotiated, and the moment when it was ratified. The initiative had been taken by a government backed by the Socialists, Radicals and Center parties; the Minister of Foreign Affairs, Paul-Boncour, was a man of the Left, strongly internationalist in outlook. The essential negotiations were undertaken under a cabinet that extended from the Right to the Radical-Socialists, and by a minister, Barthou, who was a Moderate Republican and a passionate nationalist. But by the time of ratification, almost all the Right stood opposed and, already, in the groups of the Center and Left, many had no desire to see it effectively applied. Among these was Laval, who had made the trip to Moscow to sign the document.

In conservative circles and for many segments of the bourgeois classes, during the winter of 1935 to 1936, resistance to Hitlerite Germany had not seemed the main requirement of French foreign policy. The events of the following spring and summer were to convince them that the real danger lay elsewhere. The triumph of the Popular Front would not have had the same effect on French public opinion if it had remained an electoral and parliamentary victory, although, for the first time, the majority included a powerful Communist party. But more than anything else it was a spectacle. And this spectacle was a frightful shock for all those who saw in it a revolutionary peril, the undermining of order and the risk of social upheaval.

Here, for example, is the description of the popular demonstration organized on May 24, at the Père Lachaise Cemetery opposite the Monument to the Dead of the Commune, that was printed in *Gringoire,* the most successful of the right-wing weeklies, with a circulation of 500,000. "During the whole afternoon the great cemetery was given over to bands of fanatics, utterly without restraint and with no respect for the dead. How many chapels were revoltingly defiled? How many flowers were torn up? How many poor dead folk were troubled in their slumber by the outcries, jeering laughter, low jests and coarse insults inspired either by a name engraved on a flagstone or a monument piously erected by a stricken family? Louts could be seen sitting astride crosses and bellowing the Carmagnole and the Internationale."

L'Echo de Paris, the paper so widely read by military men, voiced its indignation. "The Internationale, which not so long ago was a seditious song, has become an official hymn." Then, as sitdown strikes were carried out, and street demonstrations became more frequent, the conservative and moderate press sounded the alarm. *Le Temps* spoke of "these large-scale and unparalleled violations of order and of the most elementary public liberties." *L'Echo de Paris* announced that "the Paris street scene has changed. As the strikes spread more and more, the nervousness of the passers-by becomes more apparent. . . . Real Parisians were disagreeably impressed by the attitude of some strikers, by the puppets they had made and were hanging in effigy, the remarks they made, and the collections being taken by individuals with a red band around their arms and whose expression was often disturbing. Groups came together here and there, and rough words, and sometimes threats, were exchanged. . . . Paris has the very clear feeling that a revolution is already under way."

It was indeed a revolution whose initial stages were described by Pierre Taittinger—founder of the Jeunesse Patriotes, which was to be dissolved a few weeks later along with the other leagues of the extreme Right—in *L'Ami du Peuple:* "One need but see a President of the Council raise his fist before a human torrent, bellowing the Internationale, and see the ministers exerting themselves . . . pouring out their energies at popular meetings . . . to understand that . . . from now on it is the anonymous and irresponsible crowd, the passionate, blind, unbridled crowd, the crowd deceived by ten years of demagogy and soured by three years of crisis, yes, it is the crowd that exercises power."

The very children were enrolled in the revolutionary movement. "Is it not a crime," ask the prudent journalists of *La Croix* indignantly, "to teach such gestures to little children? Their little raised fists are all the more alarming, for they have time to grow. . . ." The "Bolshevik or Bolshevizing schoolteachers" were accused of training "the pupils, our children, in the school of the raised fist, the gesture of hatred." Instinctively, the conservative bourgeoisie returned to its old phobias, which included not only the schoolteachers, but also foreigners and Jews. "This is the immense flood," wrote Henri Béraud in *Gringoire* of August 7, "of Neapolitan filth, of Levantine rags, or dismal Slavic stenches, of frightful Andalusian indigence, of the seed of Abraham and the bitumen of Judea. . . . Crinkly-haired doctrinaires, furtive conspirators, green-tinged regicides, moth-eaten Polaks, the *gratin* of the Ghettos, arms smugglers, pistoleros on the bum, spies, usurers, gangsters, traffickers in women and cocaine, they all hasten on, preceded by their smell and accompanied by their bugs. They arrive from every side, ceaselessly, across the oceans and over the mountains, filling every train and every steamer. . . ."

Léon Daudet tried to outdo Charles Maurras in his denunciation of Jewish influences in France: "Thanks to the Republic, the regime of the stranger, we are actually subject to three invasions, the Russian, the German, especially the German Jewish, and the Spanish. The dregs of these three nations filter in and take up residence with us, in order to pillage, corrupt and assassinate. This filthy process, which is accelerating, heralds war. It dates from far, from the days of the traitor Alfred Dreyfus. The domination of the Rabbinic Jew, Léon Blum . . . multiplies the danger tenfold."

All this frenzied xenophobia, anti-Semitism and terror of "disorder" might have remained restricted to the extreme Right, if the panic felt at the phenomenon of the Popular Front had not lent them at the same time an extraordinary resonance. The word was repeated everywhere, "the Revolution" appeared to be at the country's very gates. This, at least, was the feeling of the threatened bourgeoisie, which itself had been dreaming for two or three years previously of the "order" re-established in Italy and Germany, and failed to see the good humor, naïve optimism, the unreasoning but agreeable generosity and the overflowing humanism which, all together, made up the spirit of the Popular Front.

During this summer of 1936, as "revolution" seemed to threaten France, it broke out in fact in Spain. Public opinion realized that the struggles of the parties might very well cease to be a matter of students' brawls, workers' mass meetings and press polemics, even the most ferocious. In Spain, it had all led at last to a civil war. This, like the Franco-Soviet Pact, served as a catalyst for the major trends of opinion in France.

The Popular Front could no longer hide the deep divergencies separating those who made it up. Among the Socialists and Radicals, the majority of ministers, parliamentarians and journalists were hostile to foreign intervention in Spain, although they knew that this prohibition would be respected by the democracies, and not by Germany and Italy. Some were inspired by a genuine fear that the internationalization of the civil war might lead to world war; others were motivated by the fact that for them the Popular Front had been a mere parliamentary majority, not an organization dedicated to total struggle against European fascism. But in the opposite camp the Spanish war acted like an alarm signal, pointing out that the revolutionary peril might lead the country tomorrow where Spain was today.

No doubt, it was not obligatory in all conservative milieux to accept as literal truth the allegations published by the curé de Saint François de Sales in La Croix. He maintained that "the Spaniards had all that was needed to be happy. Bathed in azure and with few wants, they could dream in the sunshine, live from their labors, nourish themselves on their own products and play the mandolin . . . Then, one day, sixty Jews arrived from Moscow . . . and lo and behold, this chivalrous nation bound itself hand and foot to serve a far-off Russia, which is not of its race, and from which it is separated by the whole breadth of Europe, and by countries of authority and tradition such as Italy, Germany, Austria and Poland." Nevertheless, the Spanish example greatly impressed Catholic conservative milieux, and especially the military, who were struck by the role that Franco's Army arrogated to itself as the only force capable of overthrowing the Republic. For military opinion, or at least for the segment most influenced by the conservative outlook and by the press of the Right and extreme Right, the Spanish war summed it all up: the "strong" State against the impotent Republic, social order against revolution, nationalism against proletarian internationalism, Christianity against materialism, Phalangism against a capitalism that in some mysterious fashion was allied with communism. Morality, religion and fatherland seemed to have come together once more under Franco's banner.

Better than anyone else, General de Castelnau succeeded in expressing the attitude of a certain milieu toward the Spanish war. His intervention acquired the value of a symbol. He was a Catholic who had never hidden his monarchist views, even during the Dreyfus Affair. Yet he was popular with the General Staff before 1914 because of his rather brutal frankness. Joffre, who had been a Freemason, insisted on having de Castelnau with him as Major General of the Armies, and it was he who took the measures that saved Verdun, at the time of the first German offensive. This old and celebrated, clerical and conservative general placed his prestige behind the military, Fascist rebellion. The tribunal he chose was *L'Echo de Paris,* which still remained the newspaper most read in the officers' corps.

"It is in the guise of the Spanish Popular Front," wrote de Castelnau on August 26, 1936,

> that on the territory of the Peninsula the battle is being waged between the Soviet Revolution directed from Moscow and those who have raised the standard of revolt against Soviet slavery. These are no longer, as formerly, two factions struggling for the prestige and the advantages of political power; today it is war between Muscovite barbarism and Western civilization. . . . It was the "Bolshevik front" that seized power and is conducting the war; this is revealed by the cruelties, the atrocities and countless crimes with which it bloodily daubs each of its days and each of its steps; it machine-guns, pillages, destroys, sets aflame; its antireligious fury especially knows no limits; it does not respect even the sacred domain of the dead. The civilized world has trembled with disgust and indignation at the sight of the poor Carmelite nuns disinterred, set upright in their coffins with a cigarette between their teeth, at the threshold of desecrated churches. . . . It is no longer a "frente popular" that governs, it is the "frente crapular!"

That summer, a poster could be seen, affixed to the walls, depicting the hammer and sickle, the outline of a factory and a battle scene, with the text running from top to bottom: "Just as in Spain . . . strikes yesterday . . . bombs today . . . war tomorrow . . . communism means war."

Beyond a doubt, the majority of Army men instinctively rejected the idea of civil war. But many officers were psychologically ready for it. Some were even preparing it.

The political involvement of the officers' corps presents, as though in a mirror, the composite and equivocal image of the whole intellectual and social drama of the 1930's. One can see the reflection of every bourgeois reaction and of every anxiety that traversed a threatened society: traditions and social standing swept aside by financial landslides, the search for a new doctrine to take the place of those that had been shattered, panic at the prospect of the revolutionary tide, the passionate hunt for a miraculous solution that would render revolution unnecessary while resolving the social crisis, and awaken mass enthusiasm while leaving every hierarchy undisturbed.

The vicissitudes of Army officers venturing on a new type of political activity formed the epitome of all the contradictions that beset the French bourgeoisie. Some of these men were forced outside normal service channels by the anguish they experienced at witnessing the weakening of the Army, the sclerosis of the General Staffs and the rise of a new German peril. Others thought they could discern, beyond economic depression and mass impoverishment, the revolution that would bear away all the institutions, principles and beliefs which, in their eyes, were the foundation stones of society and fatherland. Still others, fascinated by the German or the Italian example, thought that fascism provided the solution for French problems also, that nationalism could arouse popular enthusiasm and that order, authority, the hierarchical principle and social and national discipline alone could match the persuasive force of revolutionary socialism. The young bourgeois intellectuals were on a par with the officers who, in the remoteness of their garrisons, felt that revolution was imminent, and feared the approach of a general breakdown in which the Army would collapse. The little magazines of the extreme Right, which had a marked influence on the men who counted, or who would count, in industry, business and the upper levels of the administration, spoke of a "clean-up," sought to "sound the alarm" for those who were appalled by "the disorder" in politics and the economy, "the impotence" of the old doctrines and old institutions, "the decadence" of the liberal bourgeoisie and the classical capitalism that had nourished it.

One of the most original and most typical figures to be found in these officers' groups which had opted for political action was Commandant Loustaunau-Lacau. "One might as well jump into a tub of molasses and come out dripping with the stuff as try to deal with this structureless world of political haggling," he wrote, reflecting on the adventure in which he was about to engage. ". . . The twin goal I am proposing to my comrades . . . is to sound the alarm and clean up." The terms used are already identical. The ideas will often be identical also. The situation of Loustaunau-Lacau himself is highly significant.

In 1936 he was on Marshal Pétain's staff. Like most officers, he detested the political and parliamentary world with which his duties brought him into contact. He instinctively blamed it for the budgetary restrictions, the delay in the manufacture of matériel and the weakening of French military strength. In common with his generation, which has been obsessed by the dream of a *revanche* and which, from 1914 to 1918, had seen the dream come true in the trenches, he declared Germany to be France's hereditary enemy. He condemned equally pacifism, socialist internationalism, the spirit of Geneva and the frivolous illusions of French politicians. For him, all this was nothing but weakness, connivance or treason; communism was the worst enemy.

For a Loustaunau-Lacau, all was of a piece. The weaknesses, the pacifism and tolerant liberalism of the Third Republic's political personnel lent sanction to Communist subversive activities, since not to suppress the Communists was to protect and encourage them. Thus to defend Army "morale" it was necessary to dispense with official agreement, with government consent. The more the crisis favored the revolutionary tide, the more patent did government responsibility become, the more unbearable its inaction, the more reprehensible its guilt. So long as all that was required was to keep an eye on a few small groups of working-class agitators, easy to spot and quickly isolated, there was no call to go beyond the usual precautions and the surveillance customarily exercised by the officers in command of Army corps and units. But everything changed if the Communist audience included the entire working class and spread to other sectors of the population, so infecting future conscripts. This directly menaced the Army as well as the state. For the military mind, Communist subversion was but the final and catastrophic outcome of the old pacifist ideas preached by revolutionary syndicalism and Socialist propaganda: antimilitarism on the one side had led to the revolutionary impulse on the other. The reproaches that many officers addressed to the state were, actually, very simple. The papers of the extreme Left were allowed to attack the Army; no measures were taken against the Communist press and its campaigns vilifying all that was military; the utterances of Communist and even Socialist deputies encouraged breaches of discipline in the ranks. In his *Mémoires d'un Français rebelle,*

Loustaunau-Lacau attributes great importance to an episode which, according to him, took place early in 1936. Military maneuvers were being inspected by some parliamentarians on the Army Commission and one Communist deputy took exception to the poor quality of the soup being served the men.

But this trivial incident might itself have a symbolic value. Other matters also were discussed, during the course of these maneuvers. Loustaunau-Lacau, who was acting as guide to the parliamentary mission, was infuriated by the military theories that had apparently inspired the Command's choice of a goal:

> Eighty thousand men have been assembled in a rocky, mountainous corner of Provence to attack a few deserted pitons to the south of the Durance. I don't understand. I have just read documents that talk of armored divisions that can cover one hundred kilometers in a day. A commissary with five stripes delivers a veritable lecture on the mysteries of an army's rear echelons: "The commissariat is here confronted by a grave problem, that of water. There is no water in these mountains. We must provide three liters per man per day, and ten liters per animal; plus the wine. Water, gentlemen, wine, without which the machine grinds to a halt." It sounds like a street-hawker at his stand. . . Now we approach the divine. We are going to learn from the mouth of General Moyrand, who is in charge of the main advance, all the secrets of the maneuver. . . . That piton on the right will be taken care of by a 155-millimeter gun. That on the left, by the 155 and all the 75-millimeter guns available. . . . The fire looks after the advance, the infantry occupies. But no over-optimism, we will need four days . . . at the rate of 1,500 meters a day, it will take some time to reach Berlin. . . . Well or ill, I exceed my functions. Before they leave, I outline to the deputies the spectacle of our coming defeat, with squadrons of tanks and planes pouring across France, and I beg them to react.

In conclusion, he drew the moral contained in these maneuvers and in the soup incident. "We are confronted by two ills that are undermining the French Army, the outdated terrain-firepower concept of maneuver, and an insidious antimilitarism that saps morale."

Thus numerous officers expressed their traditional aversion for the weakness of the parliamentary regime, their fear of a mysterious—if not actually mythical—revolutionary subversion and their criticism of a high command bogged down in an outworn doctrine and overly subservient to the civil authorities. The hierarchical immobility of the

French Army between the two wars might be traced to the fact that the generals of 1918 were young enough still to be generals in 1939. Everything induced them to ponder for twenty years over the lessons of their victory, which was the pride of their existence and the source of their prestige. Pétain, who was idolized as the "Savior of Verdun," reigned over the Army until 1930 and maintained his influence at least until 1936. Weygand headed the military hierarchy from 1930 to 1935, deriving his sustenance from Foch's shadow. Gamelin, who succeeded him, was regarded as having originated the maneuver that led to the Marne victory. These are the best known, but they are simply examples, for all the upper rungs of the military hierarchy were occupied by men who had commanded brigades, divisions or army corps in 1918. Once arrived, they never left their posts, not only blocking advance but, even more importantly, making impossible any tactical research, any audacious theory or military innovation.

The overwhelming majority of officers belonged to units that had seen action in World War I. For the previous fifteen years they had seen their generals take root ever more immovably, while at the same time the prestige and strength of the Army declined. Some placed the blame on high command and civil power alike. Others, preserving their natural respect for the military hierarchy, condemned the political leaders for the weakness or incapacity of the generals. Referring to the situation that would induce him to undertake a more or less clandestine political activity, Loustaunau-Lacau was no doubt right when he wrote that "curiously enough, all the officers on the General Staff who saw military service in the 1914–1918 war with their regiments share this outlook, whereas the leaders whose passivity and lack of backbone we deplore were all on the General Staff in the war years."

Here we have the explanation of the conflict in many officers who, from 1936 on, abandoned the traditional political neutrality of military men. They rebelled both against the intellectual passivity of the high command and the absence of governmental measures to counter the dangers of subversion. They turned their backs on military as well as on civilian discipline. Their contempt for the generals' timidity would lead some of them to attempt a political exploitation of the coming defeat, operating within the Vichy regime. Others, inspired by the same basic spirit, would opt for dissidence with the Free French. Still others, who set little store on the virtues of clear thinking, and perhaps with an unavowed hankering after any form of underground activity, would try to utilize Vichy in order to continue the war against Germany, while nevertheless hoping that the end result would be a state inspired by the same principles as Vichy.

The antimilitarism displayed by the French Communists up to 1935 justified and increased the aversion that the Army cadres felt for them. It might be supposed that the Franco-Soviet pact, and the manifest desire of the Communists to give absolute priority to the democracies' struggle against Hitlerite Germany, would have weakened the habitual concern of the military men to detect any possible "subversion." But nothing of the kind occurred. Like the bourgeois, the military refused to believe in the patriotism of the French Communists. Since the threat of revolution had always been looked on as evil incarnate, no credence could be given this new paradox of revolutionaries turned patriots. With the arrival of the Popular Front government in 1936, the vast audience that now could be reached by the French Communist Party justified all the fears of the conservative wing. Surely the intellectuals of the extreme Right had told the truth, when they declared that the Republic might lead to communism, and liberalism to revolution.

The history of the Army's underground networks is revealing in this respect. Loustaunau-Lacau, who was one of the instigators, explained his outlook:

> When I decide to form "a secret renewal group," a grave decision and, I admit, a questionable one for an officer close to the high command, all the comrades I sound out will accept at once. I will not meet with a single rebuff, no one will hesitate or express the least objection. The twin goal that I propose . . . is rapidly adopted by my comrades. They have been brooding over it for so long! Civil and military opinion must be alerted to the necessity of adapting the Army to new strategic and tactical obligations. The Army must be purged of the cells that the Communist Party is constantly developing, with the objective of destroying discipline and wrecking morale.

The anti-Communist activities of the Army underground networks soon attained considerable proportions. "We are organizing ourselves," wrote Loustaunau-Lacau, "to have in every military district, every military unit, every air base and every armaments factory an officer who will gather information, and who will be seconded by a reserve officer, chosen by him, in the wings." These networks—which were civil as well as military, since the number of reserve officers equaled those on active duty—passed on information to staff officers sufficiently highly placed to influence postings, transfers and penalties. The highest rungs of the military hierarchy were often enough aware of the existence and activity of these networks. Marshal Pétain knew that Commandant Loustaunau-Lacau, who was on his staff, had founded the "Corvignolles" network, and that Captain Bonhomme, his aide-de-camp, belonged to it. He knew, too, that General Duseigneur, who had left the cavalry for aviation, belonged to another network headed by civilians.

In December, 1936, Commandant Loustaunau-Lacau established relations with Colonel Groussard, who headed Marshal Franchet d'Esperey's staff. Groussard formed a network inspired by the same concerns and set up on the same lines. Under his influence, the military networks tended to establish closer links with certain top military men. Regular reports on the activities of the Corvignolles network were addressed to Marshal Pétain and Marshal Franchet d'Esperey, to General Georges, who was then Chief of Staff of the Army, to several members of the Army Council and to several commanders of military districts.

In the fall of 1936 Marshal Franchet d'Esperey had had Colonel Groussard transmit to him a detailed report on the objectives, methods and recruitment of "la Cagoule." On March 3, 1937, he took it on himself to bring into contact Commandant Loustaunau-Lacau, head of the Corvignolles network, and the former naval engineer Eugène Deloncle, head of "la Cagoule." The two men decided to exchange the information collected on "Communist activities," and later Deloncle provided Loustaunau-Lacau with the list of officers who had joined "la Cagoule."

The name "Cagoule," as it happened, was given to Deloncle's movement by Maurice Pujo, editor of *L'Action Française*. Deloncle himself had for a long time been a militant in that organization. His temperament found adventure and violence attractive. Throughout his life he kept warmly alive his memories of 1914 to 1918, and he had indeed played a remarkable part in the war. Graduate of Polytechnique and a naval engineer, only slowly did he find the domain in which he could exercise his taste for underground activity, conspiracy and deeds of violence.

This domain was anticommunism. L'Action Française had disappointed him, with its literary bent, its stylistic exercises and permanent inactivity. Did he really believe that the French Communist Party possessed an underground organization, ever ready to overthrow the state, and that it must be opposed by forces set up on precisely the same

lines, clandestine at first but designed to meet any Communist action
with force? At all events he organized his underground movement,
the M.S.A.R. (Mouvement Social d'Action Révolutionnaire), at
whose peak was a committee, the C.S.A.R., which alone was informed
of Eugène Deloncle's real intentions. But the members of the movement were recruited for one purpose only, the anti-Communist
struggle.

It is most likely that Deloncle, by a series of calculated provocations,
sought to create conditions that would have forced the Communist
Party to turn to direct action, growing ever more violent, while the
state, in its turn, would have had to crush the Communists by an
increasingly brutal use of police and Army. This is the moment, it
would appear, when the M.S.A.R. would have intervened in the conflict, swamping the forces of public order and relying on the complicity of the police and military men.

Deloncle had some reason to believe that his plan could succeed.
The French police, and especially the Paris police, had long been
trained to repress the activities of strikers and workers' demonstrations,
and all in all were violently hostile to the Communists and the Popular
Front. For them, too, the Spanish War was an example. But as long
as legality was maintained, the police would be strongly disinclined to
condone anything that smacked of a plot or of subversive activity, or
that might cause disorder. Deloncle could count on a future alliance,
but not on any immediate complicity.

The leaders of the M.S.A.R. entered into contact with a certain
number of officers by means of the organizations of veterans, and by
friendships formed in circles close to L'Action Française. Apparently
as a precautionary measure, these officers were grouped in a separate
network. General Duseigneur, who headed it, maintained contact
with Eugène Deloncle. Marshal Pétain knew the part he was playing,
or at least divined what it was about: he could readily understand
that Duseigneur, who was in touch with "la Cagoule," and Loustaunau-Lacau, who headed "Corvignolles," had to be brought together. As for Marshal Franchet d'Esperey, he handed over one and
one half million francs to Loustaunau-Lacau for the expenses of his
network.

But the police were informed of Loustaunau-Lacau's activities
by a reserve officer, who had acted as his agent in Nancy, and he
was placed on the non-active list. Thereupon, with the agreement
of Franchet d'Esperey, the money was used to found two periodicals.

It is highly significant that one of them, *Barrage,* sounded the anti-Communist note, while the other, *Notre Prestige,* denounced the Hitlerite menace.

Soon the officers' networks would be on the horns of the dilemma thus implied, and a split became unavoidable. It is easy to see how these men, like the Army as a whole, came to adopt opposing paths after the armistice of 1940. Some, and some of the most prominent, were among the first to join the Free French. Lieutenant François Duclos is a case in point: he was the seventh "compagnon" to enlist under General de Gaulle. Founder of the first Free French network in the occupied zone, wounded in a parachute operation, arrested, set free, returning to underground activities, and then playing his part in the Liberation, he demanded to be tried in the "Cagoule" trial, which took place in October, 1948. He was acquitted, although before the war he had set out to purchase several vessels, on behalf of Deloncle, for use in transporting arms to the Cagoulard movement.

Among the officers in the prewar underground networks the fear of communism, and contempt for republican institutions, weighed much more strongly than the imperatives of national defense. This is clearly revealed by the steps undertaken between 1937 and 1939 by Commandant Loustaunau-Lacau, whose patriotism and passionately anti-German feelings cannot be questioned. He went to see Charles Maurras who, after a life spent in condemning the least gesture of appeasement directed toward Germany, supported the regime born of the capitulation and approved, at least on the surface, the principle of collaboration, while tirelessly condemning the "criminality" of Gaullism and resistance. He went to see Jacques Doriot, who welcomed him "with the greatest cordiality"—the same Doriot was to be the most vigorous partisan of a switch of alliances after 1940, and of armed collaboration with Germany. He went to see Colonel de La Rocque, head of the Parti Social Français, who, after having been arrested by the German police, solidly supported the policy of Vichy. He paid a visit to General Weygand who, in June, 1940, would be the most outspoken in favor of an armistice, the man without whom, indeed, the capitulation would doubtless never have been signed and who, in spite of his detestation of collaboration, had no hesitation in repressing every attempt at resistance or dissidence that attracted his attention, including Loustaunau-Lacau's own attempt. Basically, it was the political universe of Vichy that slowly crystallized around the Army's anti-Communist networks.

The social and moral upheaval caused by the great economic crisis had at last dug a ditch between the Nation and its Army, and this ditch would never subsequently be completely filled in. The date of this momentous break could be fixed as that summer day of 1937 when the members of the Army Council had to answer the simple question: "Are you in contact with the C.S.A.R.?"

After the arrest of General Duseigneur, and at the outset of the investigation motivated by the violent activities of "la Cagoule," suspicion was thrown on General Dufieux, Inspector General of the Infantry and a member of the Army Council. When Daladier as Minister of War asked the opinion of General Gamelin, the latter advised against having General Dufieux appear before an examining magistrate, and declared that he would personally answer for his loyalty. Since the information gathered by the investigators was quite disturbing, he suggested that, in turn, each member of the Army Council should appear before him and declare, on his honor, whether or not he had any contact whatever with the C.S.A.R. According to Gamelin, the word of these general officers would be sufficient proof of their loyalty. Daladier agreed.

Every member gave a negative reply to the question asked by the Generalissimo. Nevertheless, several of them knew of the existence of anti-Communist networks in the Army, and should have mentioned them in their answers, if only to draw a clear distinction between these and "la Cagoule." Some of them, including the two Marshals, Pétain and Franchet d'Esperey, had known of Eugène Deloncle's movement from the very outset, and were acquainted with its aims and methods. But no one breathed a word of it. Perhaps this lie marks the moral rupture between an important segment of the Army and the republican state. From now on, a more or less secret but unceasing activity would go on in military circles, and would remain hidden from the civil arm.

But the speedy transformation of the Popular Front into the old Radical Republic and, later, the signing of Nazi-Soviet pact, which mobilized the State against the Communist Party, calmed the fears that had induced many officers to join the networks. It could even be thought that the whole undertaking had no further purpose. But all those who had taken this clandestine political step remained at their posts in the Army. Their undercover leadership was not dissolved, their archives were neither made public nor entrusted to the civilian authorities. The shock of 1940 split up the networks, but by various paths their members came together once more, as the Army took up the struggle anew. "My Corvignolles comrades," wrote Loustaunau-Lacau, "so numerous, so brave, so devoted, whether in the field or in the reserves . . . your names will never be known and I, of all Corvignolles, will be the only one identified, because I was betrayed." Defending the illegal, clandestine activity into which he had led his comrades, Loustaunau-Lacau saw it as justified by the disaster of 1940 which judged and found wanting the state and the Army that Frenchmen had been willing to accept. "There, alas!" he wrote in conclusion, "is the justification of our efforts, questionable though they are for anyone who passively agrees that an officer's duty is to bow his head and keep silent in face of the catastrophe that is threatening to destroy his country." The officers who belonged to the clandestine networks of 1936 were already invoking this argument, which was used to justify every rebellion and every dissident act. With their own notion of how society—their society—should be defended, they were the first to step outside the limits traditionally imposed on them by their allegiance to the state. And, with this step, another phase in the history of the Republic and its Army was begun.

CHAPTER TWELVE

THE MARCH TO DISASTER

✠

Although it was not apparent at the time, the political involvement of the officers' corps was for France militarily the most significant fact of the 1930's. At the time, everything about the Army was most discreet; its activities went largely unnoticed by the public. The people looked on the Army with a mixture of irritation and confidence: irritation, because of the growing financial burden of the military establishment; confidence, because the reliability of the Army, its strength, its technical capacity seemed beyond question.

The readjustment in thinking required in 1940 was to be therefore all the more painful. Only in the distressing circumstances of that year would it become plain that a segment of the military had definitely gone political. It was only then that the critical situation of the 1930's would reach its true proportions and, along with the immediate consequences of defeat, bring up for examination the total relationship between Army and country. For the Army, 1940 was to be the point of convergence of the political situation that had crystallized in 1936, and the technical and intellectual doctrines that led to defeat in the field.

In January, 1931, General Weygand succeeded Marshal Pétain as Vice-President of the Army Council and Inspector General of the Armies—that is to say, the officer who would exercise supreme command in the event of war. Succeeding Weygand as Chef d'Etat Major Général de l'Armée was General Gamelin, who in 1935 took over both posts. But Pétain continued to serve on the Army Council after his retirement; he and Weygand remained, successively or simultaneously, the principal leaders of the Army up to the years immediately preceding the war. Furthermore, the prestige enjoyed by Pétain and the particular favor bestowed by Foch on Weygand endowed these men with unusual moral authority.

The aim of the high command from 1928 on was to finish building by 1934 the system of frontier fortifications. Tardieu, who succeeded Maginot as War Minister, was eager to associate the government with the disarmament plans being discussed in Geneva. The proposals he made to the League of Nations on February 5, 1932, had been drawn up in common by politicians and the military. The notion was to provide the international organization with a force to which France would hand over its most powerful armaments: transport aviation and bomber planes, guns, tanks, ships of the line and submarines or more than a specified caliber and tonnage. The whole scheme was buried by the League of Nations. Some months later France was compelled to face the acute budgetary problem that the economic crisis had hitherto spared the country, and this inevitably led to drastic cuts in appropriations for the military.

The successive disarmament plans that continued to be debated until the end of 1933 alarmed the military authorities, already disturbed by the reduction in credits and the information at hand on the secret strengthening of the German Army. "If fresh limitations of credits, manpower on matériel should be agreed on in Geneva," wrote Weygand to Paul-Boncour, the War Minister, "France would be in danger, and its defense seriously compromised."

But the governments were struggling with unbalanced budgets. In January, 1933, an over-all reduction of four billion francs was decided on, with two billion of this being lopped from military expenses, of which more than one billion was cut from the budget of the land forces. The Vice-President of the Army Council tried to oppose this. "The total effect of these measures," he wrote to his minister, "does grave damage to the life and training, as well as to the equipping and the fighting mettle of an Army which has just adapted itself to the one-year service period, which is in process of modernization, and whose manpower requirements still are confronted by alarming gaps." His objections were disregarded.

The effect of budget limitations on the Army was such that at one time the idea was entertained of cutting down the number of active

divisions from twenty to fourteen. However, Parliament would have
had to vote on an amendment to the law specifiying the country's
armed strength, and the government gave up the idea. In the draft of
the budget was a provision eliminating 5000 officers out of 30,000.
The following year, upon renewed examination of these provisions,
which would have deprived the Army of one-sixth of its cadres, it was
noted that 1000 officers' posts had already been suppressed.

Toward the close of 1933, once more the question arose of the
unavoidable deficit in the budget and the indispensable reductions
in credits. The General Staff began to panic. Intelligence maintained
that the Germany Army had twenty-one active divisions, backed up by
thirty or fifty reserve divisions. Yet the budget proposed for 1934
would reduce the number of men called to the colors to less than
200,000! Prior to the discussion of the credits by the Chamber of
Deputies, the Army Council was called together to consider the
matter. Its Vice-President, who was still General Weygand, pointed
out that "five divisions out of twenty, or one quarter of the peacetime
Army, could no longer be utilized as divisions in the field, that is to
say, so many reservists would have to be allotted to them that they
would simply have the value of reserve divisions." Eleven military
members of the Council, among whom were Marshals Pétain and
Lyautey, spoke against the government's proposal, while three approved, noting that this was actually a compromise reached several
weeks before by the military leaders and the ministers. On the following day the Chamber passed the bill.

The most severe downgrading of the military apparatus came in
1934. In February, after the riots of the 6th had led to the resignation of the Daladier government and its replacement by the
Doumergue government, Marshal Pétain became War Minister. He
received a report from General Weygand on the condition of the
Army:

> The Army today has sunk to the lowest level that the security of
> France can allow, in the present state of Europe . . . It just barely
> satisfies the needs of National Defense as set by the international
> political statute in accordance with which it was created and on which
> our security in part depends. Thus, if this statute should be altered
> to our disadvantage, of if the international contract from which we
> derive certain guarantees ceased to be respected, our military system,
> even if employed to its full extent, would no longer be substantial
> enough . . .

Weygand had summed up the effect of the reduction in funds on the armaments and the manpower of the Army. But he also referred to the political and moral consequences for the colonial Army:

> During the past few years there has been a very marked development in the state of mind of the North African units. This development is closely related to that of the whole Moslem world.
>
> It has already had consequences whose gravity is apparent to all. Thus, in spite of the economic crisis, there is a decided drop in enlistments (5,000 contracts fewer in 1933 than in 1932) and a drop, also, in re-enlistments. The soldier is more quarrelsome, and less devoted to his leaders. He is more sensitive to external influences; he mixes with the civilian population, a thing that formerly did not occur. Behind the appearances of discipline his mind tends to elude us. Grave incidents occurred last year in units stationed in France: the murder of a French officer by a native officer, desertions, and the presence of soldiers in revolutionary native gatherings.

Thus French military power had sunk to its lowest level at a time when the failure of the last attempts to achieve disarmament was leading to the conviction that France would henceforth have to attain security by its own efforts. Time was running out. Italy and Germany were openly demanding a revision of the treaties. The "vacant places," the number by which each year's contingent fell short of the previous year's, necessitated a reconsideration of France's whole military problem. In the month of May, except for Pétain who was in the Cabinet, all the military members of the Army Council (Marshals Lyautey and Franchet d'Esperey, Generals Walch, Dufieux, Mittelhauser, Claudel Georges, Belhague, Carence, Hergault, Gouraud, Billotte, Duchêne, Gamelin, Weygand) addressed to the government a solemn written warning which detailed the forces that Germany and Italy had at their disposition in case of war and reached the blunt conclusion. "In its present state, the French Army will be in no situation to face such a threat without grave risks."

The military leaders had begun to doubt the value of the instrument for which they were responsible and which, ever since 1918, had been their pride. While the French military effort had steadily decreased because of budgetary cuts brought on by the financial crisis, Hitler had come to power, all attempts to disarm had been definitively abandoned, the Saar had become German once more and Germany had re-established two-year compulsory military service. Even assuming that the troops and the command were exactly equal in merit, it was already certain that in a very few years the population increase and the industrial potential would tilt the scales in favor of Germany. De Gaulle pointed this out in his book, *The Army of the Future* (*Vers l'armée de métier*):

> For every Frenchman between the ages of twenty and thirty there are two Germans . . . We could never surpass the mass production of German heavy industry. As for metallurgy, Germany produces twice as much steel and four times as much metallurgical coke as we do normally. As regards the basic materials for the manufacture of propellents and high explosives, four times as much benzol, ten times as much cellulose and twelve times as much nitrate are produced by the great German enterprises as issue from our own factories . . .

No one could doubt that France, reduced to her own resources, could not face the new German menace, heralded by Hitler's assumption of power. Since the high command was aware of the stagnation, indeed the decline, of the military apparatus, it considered the problem of alliances to be at least as urgent as did the governments. During 1934, after the breakdown of the disarmament negotiations had wrecked the hopes that had been placed in the Four Power Pact, it became imperative for French diplomacy to escape from its isolation.

A rapprochement with Italy was first considered, since the assassination of Chancellor Dollfuss, in Vienna, had led Mussolini to fear the possibility of an Anschluss. In January, 1935, when General Gamelin became Vice-President of the Army Council (while remaining the Army's Chief of Staff), Marshal Badoglio passed on the word that he would be ready to envisage, with the French high command, steps aiming at military cooperation in the event of a German threat to Austria.

This was the beginning of the Franco-Italian negotiations that concluded with the Stresa conference. One episode stands out. On April 6, at a meeting of the Haut Comité Militaire, a limited organization of the Conseil Supérieur de la Défense Nationale, Laval as President of the Council asked whether, in the event of aggression directed against Austria and of the Italian government's asking for aid, the French Army could help by taking the offensive. Marshal Pétain declared that this would no doubt be difficult, since the Army was designed above all as a defensive force. General Gamelin, however, was of the opinion that the Army was strong enough to enter the field in accord with whatever decisions the government would take. Thus the question was raised of how well the French forces were adapted to the country's foreign policy. Two views had been expressed, but the man designated to be Generalissimo in wartime, Gamelin, had thought that to take the offensive was not beyond the capacities of the Army as actually constituted. The conclusion reached was that French and Italians should "exchange *sabots*," with an Italian Army corps intervening between Belfort and the Swiss frontier, and a French Army corps in the neighborhood of the Italian border with Yugoslavia.

The Ethiopian War was to ruin any prospect of a Franco-Italian alliance. But the General Staff continued to be concerned with the military consequences of a coalition between Germany and Italy, in the event of war. Since it was preoccupied by the possibility of a Franco-German conflict, it attached less importance to the meaning of the Italian attack on Ethiopia. Right-wing circles, and especially the conservative newspapers, were encouraged accordingly to look unfavorably on sanctions which would inevitably bring about long-term hostility between France and Italy.

Only the Russian Alliance could provide a major guarantee, on the military plane, in the event of war with Germany. As we have seen, Barthou, the Minister of Foreign Affairs in the Doumergue cabinet, had exactly the same attitude about this as his predecessors between 1871 and 1914. In his eyes, the Russian Alliance was the only real underpinning of French diplomacy. Barthou suspected that Weygand was opposed to any rapprochement with Soviet Russia. But Gamelin succeeded in persuading Weygand to express his approval of the Barthou project, with emphasis on the fact that "Russia represented the only eastern counterweight necessary vis-à-vis Germany." The two generals had a keen recollection of the part played by the Russian forces in 1914, when the Germans had to dispatch troops to the east just prior to the battle of the Marne, and again in 1916, when General Brusilov's offensive permitted the Allied offensive on the Somme.

Weygand and Gamelin declared that above all it was necessary to "avoid collusion between Germany and Russia, with a new partition of Poland as its principal aim." They insisted only on the precautions needed to prevent the Franco-Russian rapprochement from having repercussions on the "moral unity" of the Army. Thus the government had the support of the high command when negotiations with Moscow were undertaken. But the new French government under

Laval had taken care not to envisage any military agreement as an indispensable complement of the Franco-Soviet Pact, which was signed on May 2, 1935. On May 4, Léger, the Secretary General of the Ministry of Foreign Affairs, informed Gamelin that "for the moment there will be no question of the precise details of Franco-Russian military cooperation." Yet the General Staff seemed to have decided that the Pact should not remain a mere exchange of promises, devoid of real content. The Soviet government had invited the French to send a delegation to the Red Army maneuvers, and Gamelin sent General Loiseau. On his return, Loiseau stressed, in his report, the military excellence of the Soviet armed forces. "The technique of the Red Army," he wrote,

> is on a particularly high level . . . To achieve this level of armaments in three or four years not only demonstrates the success and power of Soviet industry, it also establishes the immense superiority of the Red Army over all other European armies, which are often forced, and for a long time, to use old matériel . . . The Red Army, at the present time, is probably one of the strongest armies in Europe, and this is a striking demonstration of the discipline with which the Soviet population consents to the sacrifices required by National Defense.

The General Staff spread this estimate about among politicians and journalists, prior to the debates concerning the ratification of the Franco-Soviet Pact. Knowing how weak France had become militarily after several years of deliberately pared budgets, the General Staff reached the logical conclusion that alliances must be sought to make up for France's deficiencies, compared with Germany, in population and industrial potential.

This was the situation when, in the fall of 1935, the Deuxième Bureau informed the high command that the German government was preparing to reoccupy the Rhineland, which in accord with the provisions of the Treaty of Versailles was still demilitarized. On October 21, the Army's General Staff warned the Ministry of Foreign Affairs that ". . . in view of the speed with which the German program [of rearmament] is being executed, the hypothesis of the Rhineland Statute's being repudiated must be envisaged by the fall of 1936 at the latest." On December 25 there came to light the actual steps being taken by the German authorities in the Rhineland to prepare for a military occupation. And on January 17, 1936, Gamelin explained the actual standing of the German forces to the High Military Committee.

This gave rise to two characteristic episodes. The government asked the General Staff under what conditions France could agree to the presence of German garrisons in the Rhineland. It was clear that the Laval Ministry was considering the possibility of a compromise, in the event of Hitler's ordering his troops to cross the Rhine and occupy the left bank, thus violating not only the Treaty of Versailles but also the Locarno agreements. A few days later, the French Intelligence services informed the General Staff that the German government, in order to justify its occupation of the Rhineland, would allege that the Franco-Soviet Pact was irreconcilable with Locarno.

The Laval government was overthrown, and Gamelin informed the new government, presided over by Sarraut, of the German justification of its intended move. The effect on the Ministry of Foreign Affairs, was considerable: did this indicate that the General Staff was engaged in altering its estimate of the Russian Alliance, and that it was seizing on the rumors of a Rhineland occupation in order to warn the government and clear itself of responsibility?

The public discussion that took place as a result of the debates in Parliament on the ratification of the Franco-Soviet Pact involved the whole future of French foreign policy. Those opposed to the Pact tried to throw doubts on its military value by having statements published in the papers that General Weygand had not been consulted during the negotiations. The Franco-Soviet Pact, by setting France on the path of general resistance to Hitler's policies, quite obviously embarrassed the conservative milieux which looked on the revolutionary menace represented by the Soviet Union and the Communist Party as being more serious than the danger of a new conflict with Germany. General Weygand, in military circles, typified this attitude. The prospect of a Popular Front victory in the elections to be held three months later, added to the possible consequences of the Franco-Soviet Pact, increased the risk that French policy might move in a direction diametrically opposite to that now sought by conservative opinion, both among the military and the politicians. The government was not blind to the situation: behind the warnings issued by the General Staff, it suspected that the military leaders closest to the Right had had a change of heart.

On February 27, General Maurin, the War Minister, reached an agreement with Gamelin on the measures to be adopted if the German

Army should enter the Rhineland. They estimated that the Army's peacetime strength would not allow any offensive, and that the "disponibles" (the inactive list), and those liable to be drafted in the frontier departments would have to be called up. Gamelin had already asked the generals commanding the frontier zones to prepare for a series of "localized but rapid" forward movements in the valley of the Saar.

Everything depended on the balance of French and German military forces. There were now 370,000 men under the colors in metropolitan France, among them 62,000 professional soldiers, 72,000 North Africans, Africans and other colonial troops, and 236,000 men of the current contingent. Of course, something far short of the totality of these forces was in a protected position close to the German frontier. But the mobilization plan prescribed the assembling of 150,000 men in 48 hours, of 385,000 men on the third day, and of 540,000 men on the sixth day. The supplies of arms, according to the Vice-President of the Army Council, ran between 90 per cent and 110 per cent of the theoretical level. No shortages were foreseen in clothing and munitions. On the other hand, the Army was gravely handicapped with respect to modern tanks and anti-tank guns, communications equipment, cross-country vehicles and optical apparatus. Aviation had 134 flights, with a total of 1500 planes, armed and equipped.

At the same time, the German Army was in a state of transition. Since compulsory military service had been re-established in May, 1935, the number of men actually under colors amounted to one million. This figure did not include the contingents normally liable to be called up and inserted in the professional Army that had existed prior to 1935, but elements of every class which, since 1920, had received no military training and which the German General Staff wished to instruct hastily. By March, 1936, the normal contingent of about 600,000 men had seen only four months of service and, apart from the 150,000 professional soldiers, there were 250,000 men of the untrained classes passing through a short service period and 100,000 men in the police garrisons. This enormous body of men could not possibly have great value in military operations, and thus German "cover" was inferior in quality to the French. As for armored forces, France had two light mechanical divisions and fourteen tank battalions, while Germany had three divisions, one in process of formation, for a total of twelve tank battalions. German aviation had 99 flights, comprising 1288 planes armed and equipped.

For the immediate future, the balance of forces was certainly in France's favor, especially in view of the total absence of trained reserves in Germany. Only in the longer run could German superiority in men and industrial power alter the balance of forces. These two factors guided the plans of the French General Staff. It judged that, conceived as a simple means of coercion, occupation of the Saar could be carried out by the covering troops, but that, if this led to a general war, they would need the support of the "disponibles." What the General Staff feared was to become involved in detailed operations while uncertain if a general war would follow, in which case the means would not be available to withstand the first great clashes. "Plan D," dating from 1932, envisaged the occupation of the Saar by three infantry divisions, one cavalry division and possibly a Senegalese brigade. But in 1936, after the re-establishment of military service in Germany and the premature occupation of the Rhineland, the General Staff considered that the same operation would need ten infantry divisions, one cavalry division and the nucleus of five Army corps.

On Saturday, March 7, German troops entered the demilitarized zone of the Rhineland. That morning a preliminary discussion took place in Paris. It revealed the state of mind that would continue to imbue the French government as long as the crisis lasted. Two ministers, Mandel and Paul-Boncour, favored an immediate riposte and, therefore, the assembling of the necessary military means. But no decision was taken, with the ministers as a whole examining only the general features of the situation. Sarraut, the President of the Council, asked Gamelin: "If we were alone in confronting Germany, with no allies, what would the situation be?" Gamelin replied that "at the beginning, as matters stand, we would have the advantage, but in a war of long duration the superiority in numbers and the industrial potential of our adversaries would inevitably play their part."

By late afternoon the first steps preliminary to the summoning of the "disponibles" were taken, but no decision to order partial mobilization had been reached, and the government continued to concern itself with the possible reaction of other states. On March 8, the government authorized the General Staff to assemble the active troops, but not to recall the "disponibles." That evening, Sarraut solemnly declared that France could not tolerate seeing "Strasbourg under German guns." But on that very day it appeared that the majority of the members of the government shrank from the series of military decisions that would be touched off by immediate intervention against Germany. General Maurin, the War Minister, did not dare give the assurance that the cover troops alone, reinforced by the "classes disponibles," would be enough to ensure success. If there was to be a clash with the bulk of the German Army, he explained, one must be prepared to go all the way, that is, to wage war. Most ministers were of the opinion that neither Parliament nor the country, with general elections only three months away, could readily be persuaded to accept the idea of general mobilization.

On the evening of March 10, Gamelin once more explained the position of the General Staff to the government. For a first operation of "obtaining a pledge," he would need a "strengthened cover," which meant the whole of the Army in the field and the three classes of reservists that were "disponibles." "We will enter Germany via the region the most advantageous for us. If our adversary resists we will see his reaction. If it is war we must proceed to a general mobilization without delay." A note dated March 11, drawn up by Gamelin and signed by General Maurin, actually envisaged only a partial mobilization for the "pledge-taking," or first French military reaction to the occupation of the Rhineland by the German Army.

No other plan of operations was later considered by the government. The decision was made to take the matter to the League of Nations, where France might count on the support of the other signatories to the Locarno Pact, and especially of Great Britain. All but two or three ministers looked on an isolated initiative by France as too risky.

According to the account of those who took part in these deliberations, there was scarcely any mention of the relative balance of forces of France and Germany, which might have motivated an immediate military riposte. Most ministers seized on the series of mobilization measures as a pretext to recommend a purely diplomatic response. But then, what was the point of imposing one or two years of military service on all Frenchmen, if they were not to be mobilized when the need arose?

Although the government had received a guarantee of Polish intervention, if France herself intervened, the General Staff was not at once informed of this. Yet the plans of action would assuredly have been simplified thereby. These facts serve to strengthen the impression left by all accounts of the government's activities, as well as by the attitude of most newspapers. In this opening round of the long series of trials of strength with Hitlerite Germany, French policy was influenced by a new situation: left-wing opinion remained convinced that collective security, the League of Nations and Franco-British cooperation were the best means of ensuring peace in face of the German initiatives, while right-wing opinion was more preoccupied with the revolutionary risks that might develop out of the formation of the Popular Front and be increased by the application of the Franco-Soviet Pact.

There were men, both on the Left and on the Right, who warned of the consequences of a lack of vigorous reaction to Hitler's policies. But in this spring of 1936, when the economic and financial situation of France had never been worse since the onset of the worldwide depression in 1929, and with the country only three months away from general elections, such men were a tiny minority. The government's attitude, at bottom, reflected that of the public. The General Staff had made no passionate demand for immediate military intervention in the Rhineland. Had it done so, it would have met with the fundamental reserve that reigned in political quarters.

From now on, the history of the Army takes place on two completely different levels. While the social and political situation, caused by several years of unresolved economic crisis, led a segment of the military cadres to a secret political involvement that set it in sharp opposition to the majority of the public, the military hierarchy as a whole continued to function in the rigorous framework of official policy. It even appears that it adapted its attitude, as closely as possible, to the outlook of each successive government.

Since the Popular Front owed its victory to a reaction against Fascist menaces, both at home and abroad, the government formed by Léon Blum in June, 1936, was the most warmly disposed to an increased military effort. On June 25 Gamelin sent to Daladier, Minister of National Defense and of War, a note that had been approved by all the members of the Army Council and by the two still living Marshals, Pétain and Franchet d'Esperey. This note, while stressing the results that had already been achieved by Germany, declared that by the end of 1936, and bearing in mind that the English, Belgian and Czechoslovak forces in their present state would normally be added to the French, the balance of forces might still be maintained by continuing with the military effort already under way, provided that one could be sure of Italian neutrality. But if there was no guar-

antee of this, if some French divisions had to be transferred to the
Alps and to Africa, and bearing in mind the permanent growth of
the German reserves, the balance would be destroyed. Gamelin's note
maintained that France could not greatly enlarge the number of men
under colors and concluded by saying that "from the single point of
view of the balance of forces on the ground" the General Staff deemed
it essential "to maintain our military agreements with Italy as the
consolidation of the Franco-Polish Alliance, whose effect would be
to compel Germany to immobilize on its eastern front a considerable
part of its armed strength." Daladier declared that he was in agreement with the conclusions of this note, and Gamelin submitted to
him a program for equipping the Army.

The essential features of this program were the adoption of "war
tempo" for the manufacture of tanks, artillery, anti-aircraft guns and
munitions stocks, compulsory advanced military training for at least
a part of the recruits, an increase in the number of professional
soldiers, the formation of three new infantry divisions and of two
tank divisions, the transformation of a third cavalry division into
a mechanized division and the motorization of ten infantry divisions
instead of seven. The program got under way with a first credit of
fourteen billion francs to be spread over four years, but this was increased later, both to speed up preparations for war and to compensate
for the rise in prices. All in all, 31 billion francs were spent on
armaments by 1940.

But no matter how considerable the French military effort might
be, it was clear that the imbalance between French and German
industrial potential would constantly increase the military imbalance
between the two countries. The General Staff knew that only a
system of alliances could keep the German Army in a position of relative weakness, should war break out. Despite this, during the two
years that separated the Rhineland occupation from the Anschluss,
military leaders put no pressure on the governments to add to the
Franco-Soviet Pact the military agreements which alone could lend
it any efficacy.

On coming to power, Blum, who had been in favor of the Pact,
discovered that the Soviet authorities were much more eager to reach
these agreements than were the French. The Red Army's high command had offered to give details of the Soviet Union's military and
industrial resources, and asked for the corresponding details concerning the French forces. The French General Staff was not anxious

to oblige. This was the moment when the social crisis unleashed by
the Popular Front's coming to power was at its climax. The atmosphere of Paris at that time was almost revolutionary. The General
Staff deemed it an unfortunate moment to pass on to the Soviet
government information concerning the state of the National Defense. Daladier, the War Minister, treated this reticence indulgently
—perhaps he even shared it—since he replied in rather dilatory
fashion to his President of the Council, who wanted the Soviet
initiative to be followed up. Then, in the fall of 1936, General
Schweissguth returned from the Red Army's maneuvers with a highly
unfavorable report, quite unlike the report presented one year earlier
to the French General Staff by General Loiseau.

Finally, in the winter months of 1936 and 1937, the Blum government gave up the idea of entering into serious military negotiations
with the Soviet Union. A warning had been received from Beneš,
President of the Czechoslovak Republic, that the Soviet General Staff
had secretly taken up contacts with Germany, and that it would be
dangerous to place any further trust in it. Beneš had had the confirmation of this information, obtained by Czechoslovak Intelligence,
thanks to the "involuntary indiscretion" of a German diplomat, Count
von Trauttmansdorff, who had come to him secretly with the proposition of a non-aggression pact. Subsequently, those who were formerly
responsible for German Intelligence declared that the dossier dealing
with contacts between Germany and the Soviet General Staff was a
pure fabrication. But at the moment the best-informed European
statesmen, including those who most readily would have welcomed
favorable accounts of Red Army strength, thought they had excellent
reasons to believe that the Soviet high command had "betrayed."
Furthermore, in the course of 1937, the Tukhachevski trial appeared
to prove that they were right, since it involved not merely a few generals—who might have been deliberately inculpated by certain special
services—but a large network of Soviet officers.

So a Franco-Russian military accord, on the lines desired by Léon
Blum, could no longer be concluded. By June, 1937, he was no longer
President of the Council, and his successor Chautemps, along with
Bonnet, Minister of Finances, and Delbos, Minister of Foreign Affairs,
was no fervent proponent of a genuine Franco-Soviet alliance. This
could readily be seen when, in the fall of 1937, Delbos made the
round of the European capitals but made no attempt to start negotiations that would have reconciled the Russian Alliance with the en-

gagements France had entered into vis-à-vis Poland, Roumania and, in particular, Czechoslovakia. At the beginning of that year, the Russian Ambassador in Paris, Potemkin, had actually pointed out to the President of the Council that, to be efficacious, the intervention of the Soviet forces in the event of German aggression would have to take place via the territories of Poland and Roumania, which separated the Soviet frontiers from the eastern frontiers of Czechoslovakia and Germany. Gamelin was well acquainted with the trend of Soviet thinking, and he held that it was indeed "militarily logical."

Yet he knew the political difficulties arising from the refusal of the Polish government to permit the presence of a single Soviet soldier in Poland, and he contented himself with noting that "a precise military agreement might not lead to the desired consequences." He wound up the explanation of the problem that he later gave by saying simply: ". . . however that may be, our attempt to enter into contact with the Soviets with the aim of establishing a military accord produced no result." It is clear that the General Staff exerted no pressure on the government to unfreeze the situation by persuading Poland to adopt an attitude more in keeping with the promise of aid that France had given. Léon Noël, the French Ambassador in Warsaw, tried to urge the French government along this path, but it appears that no military leader followed his example.

Yet the military leaders might well have been disturbed by the external situation of the country, now that the Rhineland had been occupied. Strategically, the state of affairs on the French frontiers was completely altered. The construction of German fortifications turned toward France already suggested that there would be grave difficulties for any future French offensive. Soon the Siegfried Line would constitute a defensive obstacle with which the General Staff would have to reckon. But, above all, Belgium's return to a neutral status in the summer of 1936 set brutal limitations on the strategic possibilities at France's disposal in the event of hostilities with Germany. Belgian neutrality, as in 1914, meant the possibility of a sudden attack directed by the Germany Army against France's northern frontier. It also meant that the French Army would have to give up any thought of starting an attack in the direction of the Ruhr via the plains of the lower Rhineland.

All that the General Staff had available, on the other side of the frontier, were the German territories situated between the Moselle and the Rhine, and traversed by the coal basin of the Saar and the massifs of the Harz and Hochwald. Quite apart from the strength of the French Army as a weapon of offense, it would have an inferior starting point, strategically considered, in the event of war. It was in these conditions that General Gamelin, toward the end of February, 1938, announced the imminent threat of the annexation of Austria by Germany, and told Daladier, the War Minister, what consequences in his view this annexation would have on the balance of forces in Europe. The Czech fortifications might be flanked by a German offensive starting from lower Austria, continuing toward Moravia and taking the Bohemian plateau from the rear. Germany might lend a hand to Hungary, and if Czechoslovakia were entirely occupied by the German Army, then Poland, enclosed between German territories on both north and south, would find itself in a catastrophic strategic position. Daladier shared Gamelin's view that the Anschluss might offer France an opportunity to call a halt to Hitler's policy. But the Italian Alliance could no longer be relied on, since Italy had worked hand in glove with Germany in the Spanish Civil War; Belgium would certainly maintain its neutrality; and there was no certainty that England would not bow before the *fait accompli*.

In the late afternoon of March 1, Daladier told the General Staff of the government's decision. (The government, incidentally, had resigned the day before.) France would do nothing without the agreement of the British government, and no immediate military measures would be taken. Gamelin suggested that a supplementary credit of 171 million francs be voted to extend the fortifications on the northern frontier and in the Jura. But the financial difficulty was still paramount, the economic problem remained to be solved, and his proposals led to nothing.

On March 15 a meeting was held of the Permanent Committee on National Defense, with Blum as President of the Council, Paul-Boncour as Minister of Foreign Affairs and Daladier still War Minister. At this meeting the French political and military leaders became fully aware of how dramatically France's position in Europe had weakened.

One pessimistic, disillusioned reply was followed by another. Thus Paul-Boncour explained that Great Britain wanted to know what could be done to defend Czechoslovakia, and turned to the generals. Gamelin, recalling the strategic consequences of the Anschluss, replied that French offensives against Germany "would aim at an already fortified zone, and would involve us in operations of considerable duration." When Blum declared that Russia would intervene, Gamelin pointed out that "the efficacy of Russian aid depends on the attitude of Poland and Roumania." General Vuillemain, Chef d'Etat Major Général de l'Armée de l'Air, made it clear that, even with respect to aviation alone, "Russian intervention on behalf of Czechoslovakia is very difficult, since the planes would have to fly over Poland and Roumania, so that these countries would have to decide what attitude to take . . . There are very few landing fields in Czechoslovakia, only forty or so, which German planes could soon render unusable." Gamelin added that even if it were possible to cross Belgium in order to reach Germany, "such a maneuver could not develop its full force if our troops, as must be expected, could not be withdrawn from their positions in the Alps and in North Africa." In its discussion of a possible intervention in Spain, where the Republicans were threatened with defeat by Franco, the Committee reached the conclusion that "it would be necessary to employ one million men, that is, to use the covering forces," that an operation against Spanish Morocco would require a partial mobilization in Algeria, and that action in the Balearic Islands would require the participation of land forces.

After Daladier had remarked that "one would have to be blind not to see that intervention in Spain would unleash a general war," General Vuillemain calculated that "within two weeks our air force would be wiped out"; Marshal Pétain added that "what counts in aviation is less the initial strength than the construction potential, and we do not have this potential"; and Guy La Chambre, Minister of Air, revealed that the rate of manufacture of planes in France was forty and soon would be sixty per month, whereas Germany was building 250 planes per month.

This was the state of affairs in the spring of 1938. A neutral Belgium, a Spain neutral but probably ill-disposed, a hostile Italy, a Germany already fortified and opposing the Czech Army, Russian intervention thwarted by Poland's refusal to permit Soviet forces on its territory, a Polish government hostile to Czechoslovakia and still on good terms with Germany. Yet, the French General Staff continued to study calmly the question of war with Germany, if the government decided to support Czechoslovakia. The possibilities were limited but it clung to them, and its attitude, throughout the Munich crisis, revealed an entire docility to the government's line of policy.

On August 29, Gamelin asked that the contingent to be dismissed in September should be retained, that a portion of the contingent just dismissed should be recalled, and that some units of the reserves should be called up. On September 2 Daladier, who had been President of the Council since April, acceded to this request. On the 12th, the Secretary General of the Ministry of Foreign Affairs, Alexis Léger, told Gamelin that there should be no possible doubts concerning the intentions of the General Staff. "It is being repeated in government circles," he added, "that your only solution is to launch an attack on the German fortifications via Lorraine." "By what other route could we attack," replied Gamelin, "if we can't go through Belgium? Should we force a passage across the Rhine, which in any case is fortified, and come up against the Black Forest?" That afternoon the Chef d'Etat Major Général, with the backing of General Georges, who had been designated to command the troops in the northeast, explained to Daladier what the French forces could do. Eliminating any operation involving Belgium, which would remain neutral, he showed that the French offensive would necessarily be restricted to an attack via the Saar. "So it would be a head-on clash," he said, "between the French and German forces. A rapid calculation shows that in the most favorable hypothesis, these forces would be equal at the outset . . . since we cannot use the forces in the Alps and North Africa, there would be some fifty to sixty infantry divisions on either side . . . So we must go over to the attack as soon as possible . . . But this, at the outset, would be a sort of modernized Battle of the Somme." This offensive was planned to get under way by the eighth to tenth day of warfare.

What else could the French General Staff do? Gamelin asked the French military attaché in Moscow to sound out Marshal Voroshilov on the possibilities of Soviet military intervention. But at once the question arose of passage for the Red Army through Poland—a simple matter, Voroshilov remarked, if Poland attacked Czechoslovakia, as apparently was intended. Ultimately Daladier did not let his decision rest on the opinion he may have formed of the balance of military forces. All historians are in agreement that he accepted the Munich accords because the British government had made up its mind, and Daladier thought it out of the question for France to go to war alone, if Great Britain were not to join in immediately afterward.

Was there something unavoidable about this series of withdrawals that allowed Hitler to seize Austria and Czechoslovakia, to surround Poland and destroy the whole system of alliances constructed by France in eastern Europe? Some men had foreseen this development even before the first moves in Nazi policy had been made. Basically, it was the Army that aroused their apprehensions. The line of argument was entirely rigorous: the French Army had been set up to maintain a purely defensive system, and if Germany attacked the countries of central or eastern Europe, we could do nothing to help them, except to mark time along the Rhine and the Saar.

One day in October, 1936—that very day the King of the Belgians announced that his country was returning to neutrality—Léon Blum, the President of the Council, received Colonel de Gaulle, one of the best-known opponents of the then current French military thinking. "First of all we spoke," relates the latter, "of what would occur if Hitler marched on Vienna, on Prague or on Warsaw. 'It's quite simple,' I remarked. 'Depending on actual circumstances, we will recall the "disponibles" or mobilize the reserves. Then, looking through the loopholes of our fortifications, we will passively witness the enslavement of Europe. Our present system forbids us to budge.'"

This interview between the old Socialist leader and the young tank officer, interrupted, it seems, by ten telephone calls, put in a nutshell the accusations that the French would later direct against their Army. The collapse of 1940 put an end to the respectful prejudices with which the country had surrounded its military machine since the 1918 victory. What had happened, during this shadow of a peace that had been maintained for twenty years, that could explain why the Army so totally failed in its mission that, in a matter of scarcely more than weeks, it disappeared beneath the onward rush of the German armored vehicles?

By the end of World War II, there could be no more doubt about it: the French Army had failed to grasp the military revolution brought about by the massive intervention of bombproof weapons. Huddling in its Maginot Line it had continued to believe in the permanent superiority of the defensive over the offensive, that lesson learned during the bloody and vain attacks that had exhausted its reserves between 1914 and 1918. While, *ex post facto*, the accuracy of this diagnosis cannot be doubted, a mystery nevertheless remains that has never been completely dispelled. How could the Army, at every level of its hierarchy, have failed to realize in time that it was on the wrong track and should push through with all possible speed "the revolution of the motor and of armor-plating"?

There is no mystery about the weakening and stagnation of the French military apparatus up to 1936. The grave undermining of the economy as a result of the First World War, and then of the depression of 1929, led to a steady, and more and more severe, contraction of the military effort. From this point of view the complaints of the General Staff, especially after 1932, were entirely justified. But at that moment Germany's massive rearmament effort was in its early stages. From 1936 to 1940, the French military effort was considerable. The figures tell the tale: in May, 1940, the number of tanks in the German Army and in the allied Armies was equal, about 3,000 on either side, those on the allied side being rather less fast but more heavily protected. Pieces of artillery were more numerous on the French side; fighter planes were about equal. The only real superiority of the German forces was in bombing planes. Thus we are thrown back once more on the differing conceptions of warfare.

The General Staff had made no secret of its view of things. For the fifteen years from 1921 to 1936, the Army based its activities on a basic document drawn up by a commission presided over by Marshal Pétain, Vice-President of the Army Council, and consequently Chief Commander in the event of war. This was the text entitled *Provisional Instructions Concerning the Tactical Utilization of Larger Units*, and it gave clear expression to the convictions of the General Staff. Affirming that "fire power had given a remarkable strength of resistance to improvised fortifications," it declared that the continuous front was invulnerable. The attack, it went on to explain, "is indicated only in favorable conditions after the assembling of powerful material means, artillery, tanks, munitions, etc. . . . Thus the attack is preceded by a more or less lengthy period of preparation, employed in gathering together this matériel and utilizing it." The use made of every weapon was conceived in terms of this basic concept. The tanks, for instance, "make it easier for the infantry to proceed by smashing the passive obstacles and the active resistance offered by the enemy." These are the only lines that deal with armored vehicles, and they sum up the French conception of tank utilization until 1936. The *Instructions* of 1921 leave no doubt as to their function: "They are destined to increase the offensive power of the infantry by facilitating its advance into combat." They must, furthermore, constitute a "subdivision of the infantry arm," whether they be light tanks "whose role is to accompany the infantry and to fight in close liason with it," or heavy tanks, "destined to clear the way for the infantry and light tanks, by using their mass and fire power to smash the resistance of strongly held points of support." Thus the principal task was still allotted to the infantry: "Preceded, protected and accompanied by artillery fire, and possibly aided by tanks and aviation, it conquers the terrain, occupies, organizes and preserves it." As for the role of aviation, the French conception excluded any participation of planes in ground warfare, of the kind the German Army would carry out in 1940: "By day, aviation proceeds to reconnoiter the troops, stationary, on the march or in combat, and so exposes them to artillery of every range; by night, it crushes them with its own fire."

Defined in 1921, maintained until 1936 and, to a great extent, even later, this conception was almost unanimously accepted in military circles. Even among the arms specialists most directly interested in the eventual utilization of armored vehicles, the doctrine of 1921 was held in honor. For example, when the General Staff, in 1931, envisaged transforming two cavalry divisions into light mechanized divisions, General Brecart, Inspector General of Cavalry and member of the Army Council, announced his opposition in an article that appeared in the October, 1933, issue of *L'Officier de réserve*. "These are dangerous utopias," he wrote. "We have no idea what this can yield." He begged military circles to bear in mind

> (1) That our cavalry divisions are a genuine force at the disposition of the high command, and that the suppression of these divisions in favor of automobile formations whose make-up, matériel and capacities have never been evaluated plunges us into a fearsome unknown in which we might meet with the gravest setbacks. Prudence bids us to maintain them as they are. (2) That a nation without gasoline supplies errs, not to say blunders, if it bases its tactics exclusively on automobile formations when it has no guarantee of the freedom of the seas and when certain weapons, such as aviation, tanks, and automatic machine guns are heavy consumers of gasoline and will absorb most of that available. Thus it appears logical to keep our cavalry divisions and our divisions provided with horses. (3) That a country possessing such marvelous breeds of horses as does France makes a mistake if it reduces the advantages to be derived from these different breeds. That is what will inevitably occur in France, with the gradual reduction of the cavalry . . .

General Brecart's ideas were largely adopted by General Weygand, Vice-President of the Army Council when, on January 14, 1935, he told the Council, with reference to the motorization program, "It is prudent to remain at the present level, and not to enlarge the program for the moment." It is in this same year of 1935 that Parliament, during a great military debate, was offered the idea of an armored division.

The notion was Colonel de Gaulle's, and it was backed by Paul Reynaud. Military leaders at once made their attitudes plain.

General Debeney, who was Chef d'Etat Major Général of the Army from 1923 to 1930, wrote that the "specialized corps" would be useless for an attack in the Rhineland. "The terrain is familiar," he explained, "very much parceled out, heavily wooded and densely populated. Is the mobility of this army to be utilized for a raid on the Rhine? In a region that has nothing in common with the plains of Hungary and Poland, where the roads continually pass through villages and the terrain, apart from the roads, is covered with trees and enclosures and traversed by deep ravines, the progress of the specialized corps will not be very fast: a few improvised obstacles would soon limit its possibilities of maneuver. These drawbacks are the least one can imagine. We will have a brilliant communiqué at the outset and, a few days later, a useless S.O.S." Writing again in the following year, and discussing the role of the armored divisions envisaged in Gamelin's program, he stressed that "the really effective support these divisions need in order to play a part in a large-scale attack requires a considerable mass of artillery . . . They will be wide, powerful attacks of the kind we launched during the Battle of France. It is simply a matter of amplifying them and inserting a heavy division . . . The tanks no longer enjoy the invulnerability they had in 1918."

General Weygand judged that the creation of an armored corps would threaten the Army's unity: "Two armies, not at any price," he wrote. "We already have a mechanized, motorized, organized reserve. Nothing need be created, everything exists." General Maurin, War Minister in 1935, informed the Chamber of Deputies' Army Commission that the creation of an armored corps "was useless and undesirable, and went against logic and history." Defending the conception symbolized by the Maginot Line, he declared that "when we have lavished so much effort on building a fortified barrier, who could believe us foolish enough to sally out in front of this barrier, in search of heaven knows what adventure."

The campaign was taken up in the press. A series of articles that appeared in the *Figaro* set out to demonstrate the uselessness and dangers of an armored corps. De Gaulle even quotes the following from a literary review: "It is difficult to treat with all the courtesy one would wish ideas that verge on delirium. Let us say merely that Monsieur de Gaulle was preceded, a number of years ago, by le Père Ubu,* who was also a great tactician, and with modern ideas. When

* A play by Alfred Jarry, *Ubu roi.*

we return from Poland, he declared, we will imagine, thanks to our knowledge of physics, a wind machine able to transport the whole army."

The same views persisted right up to the eve of the war. An article that appeared in *La Revue d'infanterie* in December, 1938, expounded the official doctrine on anti-tank defense:

> It can be estimated, on the one hand, that the first armored vehicles met with—Bren carriers—will never try to plunge deep into the body of infantry and, on the other hand, that even modern tanks can never conduct operations for and by themselves. Their mission still remains, in conjunction with artillery fire and the infantry's heavy arms, to aid in protecting and immediately helping the attacks. Thus it can be assumed that the depth of the forward rushes required of them will hardly exceed 1,200 meters . . . The tanks will no longer terrify the infantryman, for only surprise is fearful, and on difficult terrains an infantryman determined to defend himself fears no one . . . Now that the means of defense against the tanks are known and the technique of their utilization has been worked out, this obsession with tanks must cease.

Again, in 1938, the highest French military authority spoke out on the matter, and with the same conclusion. In his book *Une Invasion est-elle encore possible?* General Chauvineau, one of the most celebrated professors at the Ecole de Guerre, examined every possible hypothesis concerning the war to come. The preface of the book was written by Marshal Pétain, who backed it with his personal prestige. His view is expressed on every page of the book: "In France, the war of invasion at a rapid pace, which is also called a war of movement, has had its day . . . Today, when progress has multiplied tenfold the strength of the defensive, the nation that prepares for a short war is heading for suicide . . . If our neighbors have any notion of causing trouble on continuous fronts . . . the little flame they will stumble on will knock the vainglory out of them in a few weeks . . . As for the tanks, which were to bring a new epoch of short wars, their inadequacy is patent . . . It is the continuous front . . . which breaks the wings of offensive operations . . . The fear of the continuous front has become a factor for peace."

Pétain himself summed up the book's lesson: "In a word, General Chauvineau's views of the beginning of land operations are full of wisdom . . . This work may astonish and even perhaps scandalize the reader . . . It will remain the accomplishment of General Chauvineau to have demonstrated that the continuous front is based both on the lessons of history and on the technical characteristics of fortification defenses." He went on to make plain the inefficacy of armored divisions and the drawbacks of the tanks. "They are expensive, few in number and relatively slow to get in position . . . The time needed to enable them to function effectively can be used by the defender to bring up his reserves, and the narrower the front the easier this is . . . On land, the death-dealing barrage that opposes the passage of armored vehicles with caterpillar tracks exists; it is the obstacle of mines, together with the fire of anti-tank weapons." And he ends by asserting "the possibility for our country to be sure of stopping any enemy endeavoring to penetrate inside our frontiers."

This extraordinary blindness to the military revolution that was revealed by the 1940 campaign, this distressing picture in which intellectual conservatism rivals with presumptuousness, does not embrace all French military thinking between 1920 and 1940. The point might also be made that very few armies, before World War II, had foreseen and analyzed the "revolution of the motor and of armor plating." Here it does indeed seem that German military thinking had run ahead of any other. But in French military milieux, the General Staff's official conception, incarnated by a Pétain, a Debeney, a Weygand, always aroused a more or less spirited opposition. Almost continually, officers of more or less lofty rank felt the fascination of the new possibilities offered by an armored corps. In 1922 General Estienne, who during the First World War was looked on as "the father of the tanks," proposed a primitive type of armored division. In 1928 General Doumenc, who later became Major General of the Armies in the Field, proposed to the General Staff the establishment of armored divisions of exactly the type that the German Army would adopt a few years later. The year 1934 saw the publication of *The Army of the Future* (*Vers une armée de métier*) by Colonel, later General, de Gaulle. It looked forward to the creation of an armored corps, which would be a separate branch of the Army and would even be recruited in a different way.

This was the starting point of a campaign whose best-known spokesman was Paul Reynaud, which was backed by a segment of the press, and even echoed by some parliamentarians of different parties. Among governmental personnel, Colonel de Gaulle's ideas fitted in with the political views of Paul-Boncour, who made use of them to support his arguments in favor of an international police force to be placed at the disposal of the League of Nations.

The debate in 1935 that took up the suggested resumption of the two-year military service was the first occasion in which the totality of the French military problem was discussed. But the two Chambers, persuaded by General Maurin, the War Minister, of the superiority of the defensive strategy and of the excellence of the high command and its doctrine, neglected the suggestions voiced by Paul Reynaud and inspired by de Gaulle. Yet some measure of hesitancy became apparent at the summit of the military hierarchy.

On October 14, 1936, Gamelin presided over a meeting of the Army Council. "One must have the implements to match the technique," he declared. "The Germans have invented the Panzer division, which is the tool of a sudden attack followed by exploitation in depth . . . We do not have the instrument of attack . . . necessary for attack or counterattack in force . . . We need an instrument stronger than the Panzer division." But the Council as a whole did not share Gamelin's view. "In any case," he concluded, "the utilization of the heavily mechanized division must be studied."

On December 15, 1937, the question was again raised. "The moment has come," Gamelin declared, "to examine whether it is better to group with the general reserves the battalions of heavy tanks already existing or to be formed, or to bring them together in a large unit." Once again, the overwhelming majority of the Army Council was opposed to the formation of armored divisions. And once again the Council reached the conclusion: "As for the large armored units, the Council considers that, in the course of 1938, studies and experiments should be undertaken that will make it possible to decide on the eventual make-up of an armored division and on its possible utilization." On December 2, 1938, finally, after the Munich crisis, the Army Council noted that the experiments decided on a year earlier had not been carried out because of the partial mobilization of the Army, and settled in principle for the creation of two armored divisions. Each was to be limited, however, to four tank battalions, and the problem of their actual make-up was postponed.

Thus, in the interval separating the two wars, an almost unremitting struggle went on between the minority favoring a military revolution and the majority, satisfied with the General Staff's orthodox conceptions. But in one form or another the problem kept being posed, and on several occasions, particularly after the departure of General Weygand and the nomination of General Gamelin to the double post of Generalissimo in wartime and Chef d'Etat Major Général de l'Armée, there were excellent chances that the French conceptions might be radically revised. Thus, in addition to the decisions involving light mechanized divisions and armored divisions, the *Instructions on the Tactical Utilization of Larger Units* that appeared in 1936 re-established the principle, suppressed in 1921 by the Commission presided over by Pétain, that the offensive was the superior form of warfare.

> The offensive is the supreme form of action . . . Only the offensive allows definitive results to be obtained . . . A general localized defensive is the attitude chosen for the time being by a leader who judges that he is in no position to take the offensive over the whole or in certain sectors of his zone of activity . . . This attitude cannot bring about decisive results. As soon as the inferiority that has motivated it has ended, the leader must resort to the offensive in order to eliminate the enemy forces.

This was the right approach. But in the end the weight of these ideas, and of the men who were determined to push through the military revolution presupposed by the war of armored vehicles, remained insufficient. Vain were the increasingly frequent efforts made in the last years before the outbreak of war to break through the orthodoxy that had ruled for over twenty years. "In short," declares Fernand Schneider in his *Histoire des doctrines militaires,* "after a period of hesitation characterized by an effort devoted to the Maginot Line and the fortress troops, an attempt at motorization and mechanization was made, but unfortunately too late."

Between the two trends, revolutionary and orthodox, that divided military opinion, the means of arbitrament were necessarily complex. A strategy—and the doctrine of warfare derived from it—cannot exist without a policy, and this in large measure is a reflection of public opinion. Furthermore, in the Conseil Supérieur de la Défense Nationale, which included all the members of the government, as well as of the Army Council and the equivalent bodies for Navy and Aviation, where ministers were almost always present, the political leaders were in direct contact with the high command. There was a close organic bond between political authority and the Army. The state of mind on the one side could never be completely alien to that on the other side.

After the victory of 1918 the public lost interest in the problems of war and was distinguished by its passionate desire for peace. Military topics were no longer featured in the newspapers, and the debates on military matters in Parliament aimed at the steady reduction of credits. Everything was left to the marches along the Champs Elysées, the ceremonial parades in the Invalides courtyard and the veterans' ceremonies at the Arc de Triomphe. People consoled themselves with the idea that nowhere in the world was there anything to equal the French Army and its leaders. Doubtless the Army had to be called on to occupy Frankfurt and Duisburg, and then the Ruhr, and to watch over the plebiscites in Upper Silesia, Memel and Schleswig. It was sent to repress the Druse rebellion in Syria and Abdel Krim's rebellion in Morocco. But the public concerned itself less and less with all this.

Actually, the occupation of the Ruhr was the only episode that constituted an offensive on the part of France. The deepest urge of French policy was expressed by the one word, security. Since there was no urge toward new conquests or aggressive demonstrations, what else needed to be done but protect oneself against invasion and, if war should threaten, appeal to international opinion, embodied in the League of Nations? Here political opinion was at one with the most deep-seated and lasting recollections of the World War. For all Frenchmen who had served in the trenches, the anguish of the moment when they had to emerge from shelter and attack remained the veritable symbol of war's trials. The haunting memory of useless, bloody and ruinous offensives had long pursued the combatants, and it did not disappear with the return of peace. Public opinion was eager to grant the intrinsic superiority of any defensive strategy, since this harmonized with the fighting men's dreadful recollections and the pacific ideology of political circles. This ideology was no longer restricted to the Left. Since the failure of the occupation of the Ruhr, it was accepted more or less cheerfully by conservative opinion. Besides, the French nationalistic tradition, since France had recovered Alsace-Lorraine, had as its sole substance continual vigilance with respect to Germany, and all that this vigilance required was "the watch on the frontiers."

Hitler's coming to power, as we have seen, did not at once arouse awareness in the left-wing circles that might have been most upset by the intentions of the National Socialist regime. The threat of revolution at home and abroad awakened in the greater part of the Right a new indulgence for Germany, which had provided itself with an authoritarian government and in one swoop eliminated both socialism and communism. It was only very late that political conditions materialized which could have brought about a change in the public outlook concerning military matters.

On June 15, 1934, the process that would lead to war got under way. Hitler was in power, he had walked out of the League of Nations, the disarmament negotiations had been suspended. On that date there was an important military discussion at the Palais Bourbon. Inside the government, Pétain as War Minister incarnated the orthodox doctrine that favored the defensive. In any case, he was not the man who could have brought about a reversal in public opinion. Then Daladier began to speak. A former and future President of the Radical-Socialist Party, he had been overthrown by the riots of February 6. Since the Communists consistently opposed all military efforts and the Socialists, with rare exceptions, showed no interest in the problems of national defense, Daladier was the man best fitted to express the opinion of the Left on strategic and military matters. He had been War Minister in four successive Cabinets, and would remain uninterruptedly in this post from 1936 to 1940. He deliberately contrasted two systems, that of "the offensive as it was applied in 1914 . . . which, alas! almost wrecked our liberties once and for all, had the astounding reaction on the Marne not come about," and that of "defensive strategy." They are totally opposite, declared Daladier:

> It cannot be maintained that any system can be found reconciling two doctrines in such fundamental disagreement. The basic reason that induced us Radicals to vote these credits [for the fortifications on the northeast frontier] is the fact that we made our choice long ago, that we prefer the organizations in concrete, this powerful network of automatic weapons whose terrible efficacy against attacking troops has been revealed in war. From Dunkerque to Nice you have built a fortified network . . . You have heaped up these blocks of concrete on your frontiers, you have built these forts, these casemates, these carapaces, which can resist all guns known today . . . Now it is the cover that becomes the essential element. We have maintained this. We have so acted that this cover has become inviolable.

The conception expounded by Daladier had, at bottom, a great deal of internal logic. Since France wanted nothing of anyone, the essential thing was to protect the frontiers and, to that end, to construct a network of fortifications. This had become all the more advisable since the last war had revealed the superiority of the defensive over the offensive. This conception, which was widely accepted in 1934, still remained so in the winter of 1936–1937, when Daladier as War Minister opposed the formation of an armored division and defended the orthodox view of the General Staff. "If another choice were made," he informed the Chamber of Deputies, "our whole military organization and the psychology of the Army itself would have to be changed."

It is natural that this view should have found new defenders in the right-wing circles the most hostile to a firm policy vis-à-vis Germany. Thus, in the course of this same debate, Montigny, a member of the Chamber of Deputies' Military Commission and a friend of Pierre Laval's, agreed with Daladier and maintained that the only real mission of the French Army was to defend the frontiers. In any case, the future of the country should never again be risked in the hazards of an offensive campaign. But at the same time, on the Left, no overwhelming reason was found to take up the idea of a military revolution of the kind implied in the creation of an armored corps. Some, like Léon Blum, detected in this the dangers of a "professional army," which might prove a grave peril to the Republic. Some who favored Colonel de Gaulle's proposals took good care to specify that the recruiting of the armored corps had ceased to appear in the same light since the period of two years' military service had been adopted. Others, like Philippe Serre, deemed on the contrary that the armored corps would make it possible to limit the size of the national Army, and to replace it by militia whose period of service would be very short.

At all events, a reversal could come about only if the governments made a direct push for it. The public remained far too aloof from any offensive concept of warfare. The general outlook was well expressed in an article published by the *Mercure de France* in April, 1936, whose author was "General Three Stars." He pointed out that if it was normal for an aggressive Germany to equip itself with armored divisions, "France, pacific and defensive, could only be opposed to motorization." The only reason, actually, that could have led to an offensive strategy, and so to the search for an offensive instrument, was the obligation to support the countries of cental and eastern Europe, to which France had promised aid in the event of German aggression. It was incumbent on politics to dictate strategy, which in its turn would lead to a particular military conception of things. Everything, in reality, depended on the relations between the governments and the high command.

It cannot be said that ministerial instability had any major influence in determining these relations. From 1929 to 1940, two men only, Maginot and Daladier, occupied the War Ministry for most of the time. Paul-Boncour and Fabry, each of whom was War Minister on two occasions, were at the same time Secretaries General of the

Comité d'Etudes de la Défense Nationale. Pétain was a permanent member of the Army Council and General Maurin had also spent several years on this body. Apart from those already named, Tardieu, Barthou and Besnard were War Ministers for periods ranging from a few days to a few weeks. But while the continued presence of the same men in the top posts eased relations between the Army and the political arm, this was only one aspect of the problem. Perhaps the key of the historical enigma represented by the collapse of the French Army in 1940 is to be found in the remark made by General Albort to the French political personalities with whom the Vichy government had imprisoned him.

> No doubt it happened—though seldom enough—that you sent for the designated generalissimo and asked him this question: "What can we do, if . . . ?" This question condemns you. It shows, first of all, that you had no clear policy. And, secondly, it was most embarrassing for the man you addressed, for he felt that the responsibility was about to pass from your shoulders to his, and his reply was influenced by this. Confusion was born, and gave rise to mistakes and blunders.

Such, indeed, had been the procedure of governments, both when the Germans reoccupied the Rhineland and during the Munich episode. Gamelin was asked what he could do, after the German troops had crossed to the left bank of the Rhine. No one said to him, the government cannot tolerate this occupation; counterattack. The General Staff was not told that France would declare war on Germany if the Anschluss took place; when the issue arose, there was not even any discussion of a possible reaction. At the time of Munich, it was the same story. If the governments had had a clearly defined foreign policy, they could have informed the high command that, in such and such conditions, war would be waged. This policy would have enabled a strategy to be worked out. To apply this strategy, the suitable military instrument would have been sought for.

The make-up of the General Staff underwent very little change in the years immediately preceding the Second World War. Pétain, Debeney and Weygand insured continuity until 1931, Pétain even longer. The top posts in the Army continued to be occupied by the generals who had won in 1918. Their intellectual universe was that of the last campaigns of the War. Their main concern was to have available, in peacetime, the instrument that would enable them to apply the recipes that had given them victory. All this was very natural. Their prestige maintained them in power, whereas in normal circumstances they would have been replaced much more rapidly. Their authority was that of the victors. No such psychological factor had affected the relations of military and political milieux, prior to 1914.

The age limit, in practice, should have sufficed to limit the drawbacks of too long a period in the highest positions. But the War had permitted many promotions to be made which were justified by success. From 1919 on the General Staff's cadres were too numerous. They remained as they were with Pétain, the most representative officer of them all, at the peak of the hierarchy. The consequence was an extreme immobility in the officers' corps. Once the war had ended, prospects of advancement were practically nonexistent.

The direct effect of the losses incurred in the war was an additional factor, alongside this dearth of promotions, which led to the premature withdrawal of many officers whose experience and criticisms would have maintained a more keenly intellectual atmosphere in the Army. Thousands of lieutenants, captains and majors killed between 1914 and 1918 would have been colonels and generals in 1939. They would have formed the milieu whose activities, discussions, labors and studies would have provided the indispensable, normal foundation for a continuous renewal of military ideas.

The human impoverishment of France after the First World War affected the Army as much as it did the totality of the nation. And the officers' corps was impoverished in another way also: with the restoration of peace, the general lack of interest in military problems stimulated a plethora of resignations which deprived the Army throughout the twenties of perhaps its best and most intelligent elements. The first to leave were those who could find possibilities of more fertile action in the economic field. And, finally, the call to adventure and the thirst for renown, which explain the majority of military vocations, induced an increasing number of officers to seek beyond French shores the scope demanded by their vocations or their passions. Officers of every rank could find much greater satisfaction serving in Morocco, Algeria, in the Levant or in Indochina than in the fortresses of the Maginot Line or in the garrisons of the Paris region. So the best of them went overseas. But this did not lead to any systematic study of the requirements of modern warfare in Europe. The Army would one day reap the benefits of this centrifugal movement, but up to 1940 it was merely another element contributing to its inevitable decline.

CHAPTER THIRTEEN

THE WAR THAT FAILED

✠

Some dates are misleading. To speak of September 3, 1939, as the day on which France went to war against Germany might give the impression of a clearly marked historical limit. It is nothing of the kind. The Army, right up to the disaster that took place in the spring of 1940, maintained the same fixity it had had before hostilities began. Everything went according to pre-established plan, as though it were all a huge practice mobilization of the reserves.

The state of mind both of the Nation and of the Army remained what it had been, if not since the outset of the great economic crisis, at least since 1936. The necessary vigilance with regard to Hitler's Germany had a strong rival in the fear or even hatred felt for the Soviet Union, world communism and the French Communist Party. The Russo-German Pact provided a temporary escape from the dilemma in which almost all the political parties had let themselves be trapped. The dismay of those who realized that only the Russian Alliance could enable the Allies to counter the German threat effectively was matched by the relief, almost the joy, of those for whom Soviet Russia was an adversary at least as real as Nazi Germany.

The consequences of the Russo-German Pact dominated the French political scene, both at home and abroad, from September, 1939, to March, 1940, that is to say, from the first days of the war up to the German invasion of Norway. Almost the only measures the government found necessary to strengthen the morale of the Nation were the dissolution of the Communist Party and recourse to legal steps against the Communist militants and trade unions. This fitted in perfectly with the outlook of that segment of the Army which, since 1936, had deliberately shaken off the traditional political neutrality of the military. For the Army, as for political circles, now that the rightness of anticommunism had apparently been proved by the Russo-German Pact, anticommunism became one of the major aspects of official policy. Since the Franco-Soviet Alliance no longer existed and since the *union sacrée* of all parties excluded the Communist Party, an end had been made of the contradiction between the requirements of national defense and the thoroughgoing anticommunism professed in the totality of officers' milieux.

Revelatory is the haste with which the government set out to draw all possible conclusions from the Russo-German Pact. *L'Humanité* was seized on August 25, and again on the 26th. Yet on that day the Communist organ wrote, under the heading, "Unity of the French Nation Against the Hitlerite Aggressor":

> . . . this is no time for those who want to preserve the independence and the future of the nation to argue with each other on the possible interpretation of events . . . France must be placed on the best possible footing, able both to maintain a firm attitude and to fulfill its obligations to the menaced Polish ally . . . that is the un-challenged conviction of all Frenchmen worthy of the name. It is our conviction. The moment calls for the union of all Frenchmen. If Hitler dares to carry out the action he is thinking of, Communists will be in the front rank to defend the independence of all peoples . . . they represent a considerable human, material and moral force, which is ready to fulfill its obligations and carry out what it has promised.

At the same instant Marcel Cachin was writing to Léon Blum: "At this grave hour, the Communist Party declares that if Hitler declares war on France, he will find himself confronted by the united people of France, with the Communists in the first rank, to defend the security of the country. We declare that we approve the measures taken by the government."

It was of no avail. The groups that had been most anxious for a rapprochement with Nazi Germany saw to it that the unique opportunity offered them by the Russo-German Pact would be exploited at once.

On August 27, while the Communists were still solemnly affirming their eagerness to take part in the struggle against Hitlerite Germany, *Gringoire* printed the heading: "Will we continue to tolerate, in France, the Communist Party which is subsidized by Moscow, the ally of Berlin?" And a few days later the same paper declared that "Duclos must be judged by a military tribunal. He must suffer the fate reserved for spies, the death penalty. The case of Guyot is identical. Gitton and Dewez, like Duclos and Guyot, must be brought before a military tribunal, condemned and executed." On September 2, the Communist deputies voted for the military credits requested by the government. But one week later a decree deprived of the status of Frenchmen those whose attitude was deemed contrary to the national interest and, on September 26, the Communist Party was officially dissolved, together with "every association, every organization, every *de facto* group connected with it and all those who, whether or not affiliated with the Party, in the exercise of their activities obey the watchwords emanating from the Communist Third International." Parliament and press, in the following period, showed themselves even more set on repression than the government itself.

Crowding the heels of these anti-Communist measures were the reactions provoked by the Finnish War. It is noteworthy that the French government made no attempt to prevent public opinion, whipped on by the press, from expressing an unbridled hostility to the Soviet Union. Yet whatever worsened France-Soviet relations automatically strengthened German-Soviet relations. On December 3, just three days after hostilities had begun between the Soviet Union and Finland, the French Ambassador in Moscow, reporting a conversation he had just had with a representative of the Soviet Ministry of Foreign Affairs, let it be understood that already the Soviet government looked on the alliance with Germany as temporary. In Paris, no attention was paid to this information. The Finnish affair occupied as much space as the whole war against Germany.

"Public opinion was immediately inflamed," wrote General Gamelin."The natural reaction that condemned this new act of aggression, and the resentment aroused by the Soviets' reaching an agreement with Germany to crush Poland, were bolstered by a more or less overt campaign attacking the ideas for which Bolshevism stood. Among those who most ardently supported the idea of lending effective aid to Finland were the people who had been consistently opposed to the Franco-Soviet Pact." Paul Reynaud also expressed himself on the matter. "Those who in Parliament or in the country are most eager to fight it out with Stalin are the "pacifists," that is, those who three months earlier were looking for some way to avoid fighting Hitler. To-day they are not satisfied to have the German colossus to deal with, they wish to offer themselves the treat of adding the Muscovite colossus also."

Only a few weeks were needed to give shape to the projects for intervention. To begin with, matériel was dispatched, but in view of the advantage held by the Soviet troops along the Finnish shores of the Arctic Ocean, this was to be shipped via Sweden and Norway, which would give their tacit assent. This aid was far from negligible. France sent to Finland 175 planes, 500 guns and 5,000 machine guns, while England provided about 100 planes and more than 200 pieces of artillery.

The French and British governments and General Staffs were study-ing a plan of direct military intervention against the Soviet Union. Apparently no attention was paid to the fact that the U.S.S.R. was convinced that Finland would agree to the proposed terms. Over-looked, too, was the absence of any Soviet military preparation be-fore the beginning of hostilities; even after these began no degree of mobilization was carried out. Only the time required to concentrate the Soviet forces in the field along the Finnish frontiers could explain the slowness of the initial operations; the Russians did not launch a general offensive until early February, and in three weeks the war was over. Many French and British observers were impressed by the initial defensive victories of the Finns, and let themselves be persuaded of "Russian impotence." Gamelin passed on this judgment, which he attributed to "a person among the best-informed and most experienced" who wrote, on June 2, 1940: "Even if he wished, Stalin could no longer declare himself against the Reich. Besides, he would have nothing but his impotence to offer us. The card we must play is Russian weakness, not Russian strength."

It was in this climate that the idea of Allied intervention in Scan-dinavia was born, combined with air operations directed against the Caucasian oil fields. No one could be blind to the fact that such measures would lead to open conflict with the Soviet Union. General Gamelin no doubt did his best to disguise Allied intervention by first having the possibility examined of sending a Polish brigade or a brigade of foreign volunteers. But such expedients would have been quite insufficient if serious military operations were envisaged.

Apparently Gamelin felt it would be difficult to go against the current of opinion favoring the most audacious ventures. He took part in a military conference, held on January 31, to consider the Scandinavian situation. "Of course," he wrote later, "we could not send forces to fight on the side of the Finns without clashing with the Russians. If we wanted to do anything on these lines, we had to accept the consequences. I had, as is well known, my own views on this matter; but I did not believe I had the right, in this domain, to protest against a decision made by the government." The parliamentary majority, especially in the Senate, appeared to have adopted a determined position, and our Ambassador in Moscow, shortly before returning to France, wrote, "Russia is afraid of Germany and will do nothing against Germany, as long as that country remains strong. When it weakens, we will no longer have any need of Russia. So it is pointless to treat the latter with kid gloves."

Gamelin also cited the opinion of General Weygand who, placed in charge of the French forces in the Levant, would normally be required to work out the details for operations against the Caucasus petroleum. "For my part," said Weygand, "I consider it of prime importance to break the back of the U.S.S.R. in Finland . . . and elsewhere." This was written early in February. Less than three and one half months later, French military power would be wiped out.

What the British high command and, on the French side, the General Staff of General Gamelin were really trying to do was use the developments in Finland to intervene in Scandinavia, and so cut off Germany from Swedish iron ore. On January 16, in a note addressed to Daladier, Gamelin insisted "on the importance there would be, for us, in seeing theaters of operations open up that would prevent Germany, next spring, from unleashing against us operations of a decisive character." And, on January 19, the British war cabinet expressed the view that "the basis of all aid to Finland is to provide Norway and Sweden with effective support against a German reaction." So what was already being envisaged was, not the sending of troops to Finland, but the occupation of several Norwegian ports, using as a pretext the violation of Norwegian territorial waters by the German Navy. This was the outlook that carried the day, at the meeting of the Supreme Council on February 5.

A week later, the French General Staff was apprised of the first weakening of Finnish resistance. But the French troops needed for the Scandinavian expedition had already been assembled, and it was possible to embark the first brigade on the 26th. The halting of a German tanker in Norwegian waters on that same day provided the excuse the Allies had been looking for. The departure of the first elements of the expeditionary corps was set for March 13. That same day Finnish resistance broke down, and hostilities ceased at midday. Yet on March 15, at a meeting of the French Chiefs of Staff, Admiral Darlan, referring to the need to make the blockade of Germany more effective, could still insist that, "to deprive Germany of one of her chief sources of petroleum, we must consider operations in Transcaucasia . . . but that requires a firm policy vis-à-vis Italy and Turkey, and the decision to begin hostilities against the Soviets. It appears that operations against Baku could better be carried out by aviation. They could receive useful support from ground and above all from naval forces. The latter might take part by sending submarines to attack transport vessels in the Black Sea. That would require an understanding with Turkey for the free passage of the Straits and the setting up of bases . . ."

Thus, even after the Finnish War had ended, the highest authorities were still studying plans that would normally have led to war with the U.S.S.R. This country was deliberately consigned to the enemy category, on the same plane as Germany, against whom no offensive plan was considered from September, 1939, to May, 1940, except for the scheme to spread mine fields in the Rhine. This project was never carried out.

As has been said, the state of mind of the government and the high command remained what it had been prior to the outbreak of war. It was estimated that France and, even more decidedly, Great Britain, were undoubtedly lagging behind Germany in armaments and in manufacturing facilities for war. British and French industry had to be mobilized. Time, a great deal of time, was needed for this. The Minister of Armaments, Raoul Dautry, was to undertake so thorough a shake-up of industrial potential that manufacturing schedules were delayed by two or three months. During the meeting held in the presence of the President of the Council on August 23, 1939, with the heads of each Etat Major Général and their aides, the Ministers of Foreign Affairs, the Navy and the Air being present, Dautry had the opportunity to point out that "our bombing planes are not yet being turned out in large numbers; for that we must await the beginning of 1940."

But the most revealing document is the general study of the conduct of the war transmitted by General Gamelin on February 26,

1940, "after consultation, point by point, with the Commanders-in-Chief of the navy, the air, the Chef d'Etat Major Général for the Colonies, and with the services of the Ministry of Foreign Affairs." Reminding his readers that by the spring of 1940 the French and British land forces would amount to some 110 divisions on the northeast front, some ten of these being British, General Gamelin noted that "it is only by approximately the end of this year [1940] that all our larger units will have their full complement of modern weapons. Not until 1941 will we have available the heavy artillery and the new devices that at present are being envisaged, and are necessary for an attack on the Siegfried Line . . . The total number of fighter planes based in France and Great Britain will equal or exceed the number of the Reich's corresponding units. The Reich will continue to hold a decided superiority where bombing planes are concerned and, owing to the geographical situation, the possibilities of maneuver from one theater to another will remain more considerable." General Gamelin voiced the warning that "Germany will maintain, throughout 1940, a marked superiority in the means available." But he estimated that this superiority would be diminished and that "the spring of 1941 will probably see a reversal of the situation in favor of the Allies, if not with regard to manpower, at least from the point of view of armaments."

Although the war was already under way, everything went on as though it were still being prepared for. Despite mobilization, prolonged inactivity fostered a state of mind akin to that of peacetime. The severe winter, the discomfort of the quarters occupied and the boredom fostered by military inactivity turned soldiers' minds more to the matter of leave and the organization of leisure time than to intense preparations for combat. The test of fire had not yet done any winnowing among the officers, and their natural tendency was to maintain intact, with the minimum of alteration, the customary rules of garrison life. Since that time numerous works have attempted to recreate the atmosphere of these eight months spent in waiting. With the passage of time, the impression left is, quite irresistibly, that of an army of victims passively waiting for the day the enemy has decided to carry out the death sentence. It was no use General Gamelin's wishing this period to go down in history as the "armed vigil"—for the French it was to remain the *"drôle de guerre"* (phony war), when everything went on as if the world were still at peace, while three or four million persons had, thanks to mobilization, been granted "holiday leave."

French policy remained in part imbued with peacetime habits. Even the high command was not exempt. On September 11, 1939, General Gamelin was informed by Marshal Pétain that a ministerial reshuffle was imminent. "Pétain," Gamelin wrote, "had returned from Madrid, and he came personally to my command post. In substance, what he said was that Daladier would have liked to have him in the government, but Pétain himself was far from enthusiastic. 'Besides,' Pétain added, 'Daladier tends to place Monsieur Herriot in charge of Foreign Affairs, and I would not want to find myself beside him, in any combination. His presence would be enough to dispose Franco and Mussolini against us . . .' He asked whether I could not take steps vis-à-vis Daladier to obviate this solution."

A little later, a political personage warned Gamelin of "the existence of a peace offensive: Laval, Chautemps, Flandin, relying on the support of Marshal Pétain." In the spring, the Daladier cabinet was overthrown, as a result of large-scale abstentions by parliamentarians of the Right. Daladier was blamed, not for inaction with regard to Germany, but with having neglected the opportunity to intervene energetically during the Finnish War. The bargaining that went on prior to the formation of Paul Reynaud's government showed to what a slight degree the martial spirit had penetrated the world of politics. Though Léon Blum was a personal friend, and an out-and-out partisan of the relentless struggle against Nazi Germany, Reynaud did not dare offer him a cabinet post, considering him too "compromised" by memories of his leadership of the Popular Front. "To maintain the balance" he also refrained from iniviting Louis Marin who, as leader of the Republican Federation, was no doubt the most passionately anti-German of all the right-wing politicians. He gave up the idea of himself taking over the Ministry of National Defense and War, and kept Daladier. There was almost constant friction between the two, and this hampered the prosecution of the war for two decisive months. The exigencies of the political "blend" finally led Reynaud to assemble a very numerous and highly composite cabinet that seemed ill adapted to the requirements of a conflict in which the life of the nation was at stake. The parliamentary debate that followed the presentation of the cabinet was even less edifying. "It was a horrifying session," wrote de Gaulle.

After the declaration of the government had been read by its leader to a skeptical, depressed Chamber, those who took part in the debate were almost all spokesmen for groups or individuals who thought they had been slighted by the proposed combination. The danger in which the country stood, the need for a united national effort and the collaboration of the free world were evoked only to prettify the claims raised and the resentment felt. Only Léon Blum, for whom, nevertheless, no place had been found, spoke on a lofty plane. It is thanks to him that M. Paul Reynaud carried the day, though by the narrowest of margins. A majority of one expressed its confidence in the cabinet. Even at that, as Monsieur Herriot, President of the Chamber, was to tell me later, "I am not altogether sure that he had this majority."

Concerning the state of mind that reigned in Paris, in parliamentary circles, in the press and among businessmen, General de Gaulle's testimony is extremely revealing, for his connection with Paul Reynaud brought him close to the center of power. "Before returning to my post," he wrote,

> I spent a few days with the President of the Council . . . it was enough to give me an insight into the degree of demoralization that had overtaken the regime. In all the parties, in the press, the administration, in business and the trade unions, nuclei of very influential people openly favored the idea of ending the war. Informed persons asserted that this was the view of Marshal Pétain, Ambassador in Madrid, who was supposed by the Spaniards to know that the Germans would gladly come to terms. Everywhere people were saying that if Reynaud fell, Laval would come to power, with Pétain at his side. The Marshal was, indeed, able to persuade the command to accept the armistice. Thousands of copies of a folder were circulated, whose three pages bore a picture of the Marshal, shown first of all as the victorious leader of the Great War, with the caption, "Yesterday a great soldier," then as Ambassador, "Today a great diplomat," and finally as an immense, shadowy personage, "Tomorrow?" It must be said that some circles were much more anxious to look on Stalin, and not Hitler, as the enemy . . . As for the masses, left without guidance, and sensing nothing and no one at the head of the State who could control events, they hovered in doubt and uncertainty. It was clear that any serious reverse would submerge the country in a wave of fright and stupor that might leave nothing standing.

If there was no change in attitude, there was no change in military doctrines either. Just as before 1939, the high command rejected the idea of an independent striking force made up of armored divisions. Three mechanized divisions were organized and a fourth armored division, but instead of welding these into an autonomous mass, organized and commanded on the appropriate lines, all that was sought was to insert them in the formations available.

For one last time the high command had to examine a proposal that would have totally altered its doctrines and its plans. On January 26 General de Gaulle, who was then a colonel, sent "to the eighty leading personalities in the government, the military command and politics, a memorandum that tried to convince them that the enemy would take the offensive with a very powerful mechanized force, on land and in the air; that our front might thereby be broken at any moment; that, if we ourselves had no equivalent elements with which to riposte, there would be a grave risk of our being annihilated; that the creation of the desired instrument would have to be decided on at once; that, while arranging for the rapid manufacture of what was needed, it was an urgent matter to group together, in one mechanized reserve corps, those units already in existence or being organized which at a pinch could serve." Once again his suggestions were not taken up, even after the coming to power of Paul Reynaud, who formerly had shared de Gaulle's convictions.

The public, impressed by the lack of military activity and the official explanations provided, let itself be seduced into thinking that the victory might be won little by little and without fighting for it. "Can't you see," the editor of Le Figaro asked Colonel de Gaulle, "that we have already won a white Marne?" Léon Blum, reflecting on the possibilities available to the Germans in the west, asked: "What can they do against the Maginot Line?" All the notes written at the time by General Gamelin make it perfectly clear that he was convinced that Germany would launch an offensive against France in 1940, that this offensive would pass through Holland and Belgium and that, in any case, the German military potential would have a transitory but undeniable superiority. Yet he was convinced, also, that he could fight a successful defensive engagement. When for a few hours, in January, 1940, it was believed that the King of the Belgians, aware that a German invasion was imminent, would authorize the prior advance into Belgium of French troops, General Georges showed some hesitancy in thus forcing the start of operations on a large scale. But he recovered his poise and, in April, when Admiral Darlan proposed that Belgium be asked to authorize the Allied Armies to enter, he had the support of all the military leaders. They were convinced that, even if they wished it, the war could not be restricted to the maintenance of fortified positions or to the blockade. The estimate of the opposing forces revealed that some 100 Allied divisions on the northeast front would be confronted by 140 to 150 German divisions. The only reasonable objectives, in the view of the military leaders, were to obtain the backing of the Belgian divisions and the shortening of the front that would be effected by a "forward push" to the Antwerp-Namur line. But that depended, before all else, on the Belgian attitude, and the Belgians maintained their official neutrality, allowing only contacts between the General Staffs. The high command continued to rely on its own competence, its possibilities of maneuver and its rather blind confidence in the traditional military excellence of French soldiers.

At this moment in history, the man who for the last time embodied the universal belief in France's military might, and who presided over the conflict that smashed this belief for ever, was General Gamelin. It is impossible not to attribute to this man some of the traits usually associated with figures of a decadent era. As a young officer he had assisted Marshal Joffre during the greatest hours of the First World War. On the front he had taken over direct responsibility for difficult commands. He could not be accused, as was General Weygand, of being but the shadow of a great leader.

But these were only memories. The unctuousness of his manners, his velvety speech and brilliant intelligence made him the most civilian of the generals. In his youth he had believed in Dreyfus's innocence. Charged with responsibilities that brought him in contact with civil authority, he had maintained the best personal relations with most political leaders. He was the friend both of André Tardieu and of Paul-Boncour. When he first came in contact with Léon Blum, in 1936, both were delighted to discover their common interest in philosophy, and particularly in Bergson.

His own account of himself is enough to make the point:

> It has become fashionable to accuse me of being a philosopher. No doubt I committed a youthful indiscretion, that of writing, while I was still a captain, an *Étude Philosophique sur l'Art de la Guerre*. This brought me a cherished letter from Foch, whose pupil I had been a little while before, in the École de Guerre. Had not he himself preceded his Course in General Tactics with the dictum, "let us first learn to think"?

All in all, Gamelin enjoyed having this reputation, for he was quietly proud, like all military men, of the general culture of which warriors so often are supposed to be devoid. "In 1915, during the war, I was referred to in a newspaper as the 'leader of Joffre's Bergsonian entourage.' I am not ashamed to admit my immense admiration for Bergson, whom I regard as one of the greatest minds of our age, and on the intellectual plane I was deeply influenced by him."

But Gamelin was well aware that he was required to show other qualities than those of a professor, other virtues than those of a moralist and other capacities than those of a cultivated reader. "Yet I believe," he protested, "that as the head of the second brigade of *chasseurs alpins*, during 1916, of the ninth infantry division, from 1916 to 1918, and in the Levant, during the rebellion of 1925–1926, it was possible both to love meditation and to act. . . . May my readers permit me to evoke this reputation for them today, so that I may be pardoned for my philosophizing a little in front of them. . . ."

Gamelin was extraordinarily scrupulous about respecting the superior authority of the political arm and sought to leave the government at all times the master of its own decisions. Every time that he was consulted on the military consequences of one political attitude or another, his diagnosis was excessively qualified. It is perfectly clear that he hesitated between forcing the government's hand and an unwillingness to encourage dangerous illusions. The habit into which the governmental leaders had fallen of offering him hypotheses, and not informing him of decisions already taken, proved catastrophic. He was, furthermore, quite intelligent enough to realize that his opinions might be treated as decisive arguments, and he was both too hesitant and too scrupulous to orient them along the lines of a personal policy.

Among his peers, he may be said to have felt the same hesitation and the same scruples. He congratulated himself on having brought about a unanimous vote of approval for all the decisions taken by the Army Council, as long as he remained Vice-President of that body. This means that the Council's decisions concerning military doctrine and Army organization reflected the average view of the oldest generals. Thus every speedy and real change in French military conceptions was barred.

There is something tragic in this. General Gamelin was undoubtedly one of the French generals most favorably disposed to the offensive organization of the Army through the use of mechanical power. But he was not the man to force this through. To the end he remained convinced that the French doctrine represented the synthesis of all the possibilities of modern warfare; he believed that he had allotted both to prudence and to audacity their fair share; he was too fundamentally the heir of a military tradition to respond to the appeal of revolutionary innovations.

General De Gaulle pictures him as he was, five weeks before the disaster of May, 1940, in his headquarters at Vincennes:

> There he was, in a setting that resembled a monastery, with few officers around him, working and meditating, while taking no part in current business. He left the command of the northeast front to General Georges, which might be feasible as long as nothing was happening there but would certainly become impossible if a battle got under way . . . In his Vincennes hermitage, General Gamelin struck me as resembling a scientist, working out the reactions of his strategy in the laboratory . . . As I listened to him, I realized that by bearing within him a certain military system and lavishing all his industry on it, he had come to treat it as a faith. I felt, too, that taking as his example Joffre, whose close collaborator and, to some degree, whose inspirer he had been, early in the Great War, he had acquired the conviction that, at his level of authority, the essential thing was, once and for all, to center his will on a definite plan and, thereafter, not to allow any unforeseen circumstance to deflect him. Gamelin, whose intelligence, *esprit de finesse* and self-control had reached a high level, certainly had no doubt that, in the coming battle, he would finally win. It was with respect but also with un-easiness that I took leave of this great leader, readying himself in his cloister to assume forthwith an immense responsibility by staking all in circumstances I judged to be highly unfavorable. Five weeks later the thunderbolt fell. . . .

On May 13, the Meuse front was pierced. On May 18, Gamelin sent the government his last report on the military situation. On the 19th, he wrote his last "personal and secret instructions," which envisaged a twin counteroffensive in north and south against the rear of the German armored columns moving westward. On that same day General Weygand, whom Paul Reynaud had recalled from the Levant, agreed to replace Gamelin in the high command. The decree naming him was drawn up and left with the President of the Republic for his signature. "While this was being done," wrote Paul Reynaud,

> I unthinkingly opened for the first time that morning the drawer of the desk at which I had sat down, and in it I came on Gamelin's dossier. The first of the notes that made it up attracted my attention. The writer praised the young lieutenant with the face of a child who

had just left Saint-Cyr as first in his class. I had the letter to Gamelin rewritten, in order to add the government's thanks for the long, loyal service he had rendered the country.

The letter reached its destination at 8:45 in the evening. "If I say I slept," wrote Gamelin, "no one will believe me. I am the master of my nerves, to such a degree, I am sometimes told, that I seem to have no feelings. But not to this extent!"

General Weygand and General Gamelin were at opposite poles, with respect to character as well as in the domain of ideas. Yet it may be said that these two men incarnated the two panels of the diptych of which the French Army of 1939 was composed. On Gamelin's side were to be found the traditional respect for the state, the habit of silent industry, the striving to achieve a permanent synthesis between military preoccupations and political exigencies, and prudence and due deliberation in the development of strategic or tactical concepts. On Weygand's side were to be found the customary contempt of the soldier for politicians, a liking for flamboyancy, a fanatical attachment to traditions regarded as a sacred trust, a carefully preserved remoteness from political circles and from their influence, an almost insane reverence for the heritage of the past, a certain aristocratic attitude to the soldier's trade, and the hope, never to be abandoned, that one day the Nation would recognize itself in its Army, would set aside all political temptations and accord the Army its preference.

From the first day that General Weygand was appointed to the post of Army Chief of Staff, with General Gamelin the next in rank in that body, the latter constantly reproached him for his hostility—which though entirely verbal was extremely violent—to republican institutions and the personalities in French politics. Weygand, for his part, looked on Gamelin as a man eternally seeking a compromise, and always ready to bow to the decisions of the politicians, even when they went against the interests of the Army, without any attempt to oppose or even protest against these decisions. Unlike Weygand, Gamelin had successfully commanded larger units in the field, and he knew better than anyone else that Marshal Foch's former "right arm" had never been more than a good Chief of Staff and had never, anywhere, undergone his baptism of fire while confronting the enemy. Weygand was the best possible example of the longing to tilt against political authority that filled the hearts of so many officers morally and materially isolated in a society whose outlook and mores they often failed to share.

Gamelin, on several occasions, seemed to have sensed the military revolution that would be caused by the introduction of armored weapons. But he had neither understood it fully nor been able to impose it on a General Staff deeply conservative in its training and through long habit. Weygand, on the contrary, returned to head the Army only to observe the total failure of the military doctrine among whose chief supporters he had been. But he was able to exert his authority in his contacts with the government. He established the priority of his own political preoccupations over those of the government and of the leading personages of the regime.

It was the first time since 1919 that the high command would exert its full force in support of a policy, and this time the effort met with success. Before 1939, political activity had been a temptation for a mere fraction of the Army's cadres. Even then, it had always clung to a certain secrecy and the high command, at all events, had never concurred. But 1940 was to be marked by the direct intervention of the military hierarchy, on the very highest level, to exert pressure on and, eventually, against the government. It was paradoxical that certain Army men could use the defeat as an instrument of direct political intervention, and that only the defeat should have made this possible.

Immediately after the first setbacks, the military leaders grasped the exact dimensions of their error with respect to military theory and armaments. On May 28, having warned the government three days earlier that there might be a total disaster in metropolitan France, General Weygand decided to "place in the hands of the President of the Council a document, written and signed, explaining the gravity of the situation." He thought that it was "necessary first of all to underline the fact that, because of the introduction of a new factor into the struggle, there could be no valid comparison between the battles of 1914 and 1918 and those of the current war. This new factor was the Germans' combination of tank and plane and the doctrine of their utilization. Thanks to it, the exploitation of a local success could become immediate and lead to decisive consequences."

Ten days before that, General Gamelin's report on "the operations under way since May 10 on the northeast front" had already stressed that "the appearance of large German armored units, with their capacity for extended rupture, has been the great strategic factor of these last days. The massive, brutal usage the enemy has made of them has paralyzed all stopping operations, and repeatedly sprung the meshes of the chains spread out one after the other to stop them. The countermeasures could not be carried out with the necessary speed, owing to the lack of sufficient mechanized formations, although qualitatively our matériel, in numerous clashes, proved superior to that of the Germans."

So the French military leaders were lucid enough to comprehend that the revolution in doctrine accomplished by the German Army was enabling it to outclass its adversaries. General Gamelin, by May 18 and 19, had clearly seen the strategic idea that should have inspired the Franco-British counteroffensive against the rear of the German armored columns. Today there can be no doubt that his replacement by General Weygand postponed for four days the application of these orders for a counteroffensive—four days during which the Allied formation was so impaired as to exclude any possibility of a counterattack. But in any case the high command would not have had the weapons needed to carry out the plan. General Gamelin himself seems to have had few illusions about that. From this point on it was plain that the continuation of the war would lead to the German Army's occupying the entire national territory. Thus the high command would, instantaneously, have had to throw out all its notions concerning the conduct of operations and even of the techniques of combat. A form of warfare would have to be envisaged that involved aspects entirely unknown to the French Army—resistance, guerrilla tactics, the underground—and setting problems previously left unexamined, such as the large-scale arming of native populations, a strategy embracing the huge areas of Africa and the Mediterranean, and the subordination of military considerations to the search for new alliances, whether with the U.S.A. or the U.S.S.R. The government and the high command would have had to carry out this revolution in doctrine and strategy while deprived of the territorial base essential for the state.

After 1940, it became customary to look on France as one of the last capes of the European continent. But previously the French possessions in Africa had been regarded as an extension of metropolitan France. To move from one conception to the other would have required an intellectual boldness that lay within the capacities of many military and political leaders, but that was beyond the range of the oldest military men, for whom continental Europe provided the only framework for military operations.

To have continued the war outside France would have meant

accepting the prospect that the whole French apparatus of government would be, if not destroyed, at least helplessly exposed to German decisions. The whole bulk of French legislation might be jettisoned. There would no longer be the least guarantee of the validity of contracts, public or private, and similarly for property, the organization of society, and the customary practices in law and business. As long as the occupation lasted, there would be no assurance, anywhere in France, that the fundamental structures of society would be maintained. No one could know prior to the liberation of the country, what would happen to the social classes, to their income and style of life. For the first time in history the French population as a whole would be subjected to the arbitrary decisions of an enemy power, and for an indefinite period. A number of those bearing the heaviest responsibilities recoiled from this prospect.

This was the moment when General Weygand played his particular part. This 73-year-old whose surface vitality made him seem, in Paul Reynaud's phrase, "a fighting cock," was intellectually unable to conceive and to accept the new dimensions of a conflict that would be fought outside France, would cast the fate of several continents into the balance, and would radically break with the tasks traditionally asked of the French Army. Like all military men of the generation that had been victorious in 1918, he could not imagine that any other army was comparable to the French, except the German Army. Since the German Army had just won a decisive victory in France, he could not imagine that any other power might match it in armed strength. Thus Germany had virtually won the war. Weygand, like Pétain, was convinced of this, and there were many witnesses to report this certainty.

It is only fair to admit that, in the summer of 1940, no one could envisage an imminent defeat for Germany. The Russo-German Pact still existed, the United States remained anchored to its policy of neutrality, and Great Britain had lost, at Dunkerque, the larger part of its artillery and military transport vehicles. Before the German Army could be conquered, new forces would have to arise and do battle. The German Army would have to exhaust itself on many distant fronts before the coalition of new enemies could grind it in the dust. The occupation of France would be no transitional phase, it would last for a number of years. In the interval, there would be no state to ensure the stability or even the very existence of French society. This reflection linked up the military realities with social and

political considerations. It was a linkage that occurred first of all in
the mind of General Weygand.

On the evening of May 24, in a conversation with Paul Baudoin,
Under-secretary of State to the President of the Council and Secretary of the War Committee, Weygand expressed the opinion that the
one aim was "to raise France above the trials that have beset her, and
enable her, though defeated militarily, to get going again." On that
day the retreat of the British expeditionary corps toward the sea
sealed the impossibility of the counteroffensive envisaged by the high
command. Thus, four days after his arrival at General Headquarters,
General Weygand drew what were, in his view, the inevitable political
conclusions of military disaster. On May 25, in the War Committee
he repeated that it was his "duty to envisage the worst," and he stated,
in reply to Paul Reynaud who had asked him what attitude the government should adopt in the event that the German armies marched
on Paris, "that the government must not leave the capital." This
idea made sense only as a step in the direction of a more momentous
choice, the decision to negotiate an armistice between France and
Germany. The President of the Council had known of Weygand's
outlook since the day before, and so he took up the question of a
provisional refuge for the government. Should it be Tours, the Massif
Central or Bordeaux? It is noteworthy that, as late as May 25, some
of those who subsequently would be in favor of continuing the
struggle still failed to realize the actual dimensions of the choice before
them.

Lebrun, the President of the Republic, raised the objection to
Weygand's suggestion that the government remain in Paris, that the
government should be able to consider "in all tranquillity" the peace
proposals that Germany might make, if they were "relatively advantageous." He maintained that the government should leave Paris. The
political leaders did not yet see the necessity, in view of the fact that
no resistance could be made, of fleeing metropolitan France and taking
refuge in Africa.

General Weygand at once put forward, in reply to Lebrun's remarks, the argument that summed up his entire attitude, and to which
he returned again and again in the following three weeks. After Paul
Reynaud had interjected that France and Great Britain had the
reciprocal obligation not to conclude a separate peace, Weygand
declared that our Allies would have to be persuaded of the danger
facing France if the Army, having been totally annihilated, were no

longer in a position to "maintain order." He asked that the matter be raised at once with the British government. Pétain, concurrently, contrasted the huge sacrifices France had been willing to make with the relatively feeble efforts made by Great Britain.

Thus Weygand, the Generalissimo, had moved on from the military reasons that led him to credit Germany with a total victory, to the political and social reasons which, in his eyes, justified seeking an armistice. The War Committee's minutes for May 25 attribute to him this forthright statement: "We must, indeed, preserve the means to maintain order in the country. What disturbances might not occur if the last organized forces, that is, the Army, had just been destroyed?"

In the course of the next day he referred on several occasions to the same idea. In the morning he received General Paul Baudoin at Headquarters. "My point of view is," he told him, "that if the government wants to preserve intact the Army's morale, which is getting better day by day, and if it wishes to avoid a revolutionary movement's developing in Paris, it must declare itself ready to remain in the capital in all circumstances, keeping a hand on the control levers and assuming the risk of capture by the enemy." At midday, Pétain employed the same argument with Baudoin. "We must save part of the Army," he said, "for without an army grouped around a few leaders to ensure order, a genuine peace will not be possible." Perhaps the most significant episode of the day took place at four o'clock. This was the interview between Chautemps, Vice-President of the Council, and Paul Baudoin. According to the latter, Chautemps was "terrified by the situation" and wondered whether there was any use in continuing the struggle for long. He declared that France must group itself around Marshal Pétain, since "no civilian would have the necessary authority to negotiate, and that will have to be done soon." "I replied," adds Baudoin, "that General Weygand appeared to me to be a much stronger character than the Marshal. 'There can be no question of the General,' he replied quickly."

Chautemps's position, which would become quite patent from June 11 on, is all the more significant, since he was one of the most representative personalities of the Third Republic. Four times President of the Council—twice after the 1936 elections—and Vice-President or minister in a great many governments, he was above all else one of the outstanding men of the Radical-Socialist Party. At the same time he was assumed, and with reason, to be one of the highest Masonic officials. So he was not in the remotest to be suspected of sympathy for the Fascist States or for their right-wing admirers. His temperament, much more than any political doctrine, had prior to the war induced him to favor some understanding with Germany. All in all, he feared equally military adventures and the upheavals which would inevitably result from a new world war. It is in this frame of mind that he must have envisaged an armistice.

Perhaps, too, Chautemps thought that the conditions laid down by Germany would be "relatively advantageous," as President Lebrun had surmised at the meeting of the War Committee on May 25. Perhaps he thought that the momentary outcome of the war would soon be challenged by new developments in international relations. At all events he soon came to deem essential a solution that would keep a government functioning in France, guarantee the preservation of the state and assure the continuity of juridical, economic and social institutions.

Nothing in this respect is more characteristic than his discussion with Baudoin of the personalities of Pétain and Weygand. "There can be no question of the General," he had said. For Chautemps knew that Weygand was the man in touch with the most recationary groups, the contemptuous enemy of the Third Republic and the inflexible adversary of the regime's entire personnel. If the defeat were to enable Weygand to come to power, the Republic could not possibly outlive the war. And he did not want that to occur. He could agree to the diminution and partial disarmament of France, hoping that a government, a state, a society would be preserved, and making no distinction between them and the republican set-up within which they had functioned.

In the eyes of Chautemps and of his whole generation, Pétain was a "republican" marshal at least in the sense that he had never shown the least hostility to successive governments. Foch had clashed with Clemenceau; Franchet d'Esperey was reputed to be a royalist; Mangin had tried to carry out his own policy in the Rhineland; Castelnau had become a conservative, reactionary deputy. But Pétain had never stepped outside his role, had never shown the least liking for adventures or any political ambitions. While during the years immediately preceding the war some political propagandists had stirred up a campaign centered around him, this appeared never to have met with his approval. In left-wing circles the name of Pétain was often associated with the restoration of French morale after the crisis of 1917, and his desire to avoid mass slaughter was contrasted with the offensive spirit of a Joffre, a Mangin or a Foch. Thus a man with Chautemps's background inevitably regarded Pétain as the least dangerous of military men. For a state on its way to destruction, he constituted the least undesirable solution. He might turn out to be, for France, what Hindenburg had been for Germany between the two wars.

It still was necessary to overcome the opposition of those who favored going on with the fight, before the solution could be adopted that Pétain, Weygand, Chautemps and Baudoin had decided on as early as May 25 or 26. It is known that at two successive Councils of Ministers, held on June 12 and 13 in the Château de Cangey, General Weygand's passionate urging that an armistice be sought was brushed aside. And on the afternoon of the 15th another Council was still almost unanimous in backing the view of Reynaud, President of the Council. Pétain was instructed to win over Weygand, but Weygand on the contrary persuaded Pétain to return to his previous attitude in favor of an armistice.

When the discussion was resumed late in the afternoon, Chautemps for the first time expressed the view that only an official request for an armistice would enable the government to learn the precise nature of the terms Germany would lay down. If these conditions proved unacceptable the war could be continued, and otherwise the matter could be taken up with Great Britain. Paul Reynaud considered resigning but, at the request of his colleagues and after the intervention of the President of the Republic, he agreed to remain in office. He also agreed to get in touch with the British government, so that France might be authorized to ask Germany for the armistice terms. If these turned out to be unacceptable, then the government would leave Paris. At 11 o'clock on June 16, the presiding officers of the Senate and the Chamber of Deputies declared to the Council of Ministers that, in their view, "the President of the Republic and the essential organs of government should be put out of reach of the enemy, since otherwise there would cease to be any assurance of French sovereignty."

Marshal Pétain declared he was resigning, but was persuaded to remain, after Paul Reynaud pointed out that England had been asked for authorization to seek an armistice, and that at least one should wait for the answer. This answer took the form of two telegrams which required, as the indispensable condition for any request for an armistice, the sending of the French fleet into British ports. This was followed by the refusal purely and simply to free France of its obligations toward Great Britain, and then by a note proposing the creation of an indissoluble Franco-British Union. This last proposal was at once rejected by the Council of Ministers which then, while being incompletely informed of British stipulations concerning the French fleet, took up once more the suggestion that Chautemps had made the day before. It was in these circumstances, and without the Cabinet's having voted, that Paul Reynaud decided to resign.

Throughout all these comings and goings, General Weygand maintained an absolutely consistent attitude. Having expressed himself, on May 25, in favor of a Franco-German armistice, he intervened constantly and unhesitatingly until he obtained the agreement of the government. At the first Council of Ministers held at Cangey on June 12, he declared that cessation of hostilities was a *sine qua non* and that, if there were no armistice, he could no longer guarantee discipline in the Army. On the afternoon of June 13, he declared that England could not survive France's fall. On June 15, he spoke out against the cease-fire suggested by Paul Reynaud, as a means of limiting the sacrifices that the defeat was inflicting on the French population and on the soldiers. In this way he demonstrated that, in his eyes, the sufferings of the Army were not the reason that made a cessation of hostilities inevitable. His aim was to preserve both the military hierarchy and the state, for which he was willing to pay the price of an armistice with Germany.

By June 13, he perhaps believed that he had found a decisive argument in favor of his thesis: he dangled before the Ministers' eyes the spectre of a Communist coup d'état in Paris. At all events, the supreme argument with which he ceaselessly confronted those who wished to go on with the war was the need to maintain order in spite of the defeat. To his way of thinking, the regime was responsible for all the disasters that had befallen the country, and should take the responsibility of admitting the disaster by appending its signature to an armistice. But, beyond this political settling of accounts, he was looking forward to the maintenance, in France, of a civil and military hierarchy that would guarantee the permanence of a state and of a social order, whatever the conditions that Germany might impose.

This was the decision urged on the government. On the other side, a continuation of the struggle implied that the state would be put out of reach of the enemy's grasp. The adoption of this hypothesis meant that, while there could be no exercise of public authority on French soil, such a renunciation served to guarantee the freedom of public authority, its capacity to act on a world scale, and its independence of the invader. It was a question of the fundamental role allotted to state and government. Did the basic obligation consist in preserving order in the interior—which might justify the request for an armistice—or in guaranteeing independence with respect to the exterior—which required a continuation of the struggle outside France.

The same hesitation was to be found among military men as among politicians. The generals were certainly the most firmly convinced that the German Army was the world's strongest; if the French Army could not vanquish it, how could any other? And few politicians had the boldness of imagination necessary to envision prolonged resistance on a world scale to a Germany that dominated the European continent.

On June 5, the President of the Council had revamped his Cabinet to exclude those he considered most favorable to an armistice. In addition to General de Gaulle, the new Under-secretary of State for War, Paul Baudoin, Under-secretary of State for Foreign Affairs; Bouthillier, Minister of Finances; and Jean Prouvost, Minister of Information, entered the government. Three of the four showed themselves almost at once to favor an armistice. Doubtless Paul Reynaud preferred, when he chose them, not to ask for a clear statement of their attitude toward the continuation of the war, but it is remarkable that he found no way of estimating the probable opinion of most of his new ministers. Baudoin, Bouthillier and Prouvost represented one aspect or another of the French bourgeoisie: Baudoin, banking and business; Bothillier, the top level of the civil service; and Jean Prouvost, the most important newspapers. Reynaud thought that they would act as technicians rather than as politicians, and that they would be found to support him as their chief. Yet all three of them were among the first to speak openly in favor of an armistice.

The positions adopted with regard to the question of an armistice nearly always reflected the conflicting opinions on foreign policy that had marked the last years before the outbreak of hostilities. The backers of the Soviet Alliance were the most strongly opposed to a capitulation, while those who had been tempted by the idea of some arrangement with Nazi Germany were, in 1940, the most violently hostile to any continuation of the war. In 1935 and 1936, certain political groups had been restrained from accepting the Russian Alliance and all it signified by, above all, the fear that an "anti-Fascist" foreign policy might pave the way for an ideological war and, within the country, might strengthen the hand of the Communist Party and increase the risk of revolutionary upheavals. What made an armistice seem relatively attractive to them, in 1940, was the desire to preserve a state which would have its territorial base in France and a government which, at least in considerable measure, would remain master of the country's juridical, economic and social institutions.

This was Weygand's view. Did the other military leaders feel the same way? On several occasions Weygand insisted that he was speaking in the name of General Georges, Commander-in-Chief on the northeast front, and in the name of the Commanders of Army groups. But prior to June 16, when Paul Reynaud resigned, there was no indication of a general movement, among the totality of the military leaders, in favor of an armistice. Admiral Darlan, the Navy's Chief of Staff, while he took no part in the most important discussions envisaging a cessation of hostilities, expressed himself, and at times very violently, against the idea that the government should capitulate. His resoluteness brooked no compromise until June 15, only two days before the Pétain ministry was formed. The Admiral then foresaw a policy reversal and, recalling the advances that had been made in his direction by the entourage of Marshal Pétain at the beginning of the previous month, he agreed to enter the new government and from then on declared himself for an armistice.

On June 17, from Beirut, both General Mittelhauser, Commander-in-Chief of the troops in the Levant, and Puaux, the High Commissioner, informed General Weygand that they favored continuing the war. In Algiers, Governor General Le Beau was violently opposed to an armistice and declared that he could "answer for the feelings of Algeria, and General Noguès can answer for the feelings of Morocco." In Dakar, the Governor General of French Eastern Africa, the Commander of the ground forces and the head of the naval forces had decided to go it on their own after the signature of the armistice. Their decision was not reversed until June 24 with the arrival of the battleship Richelieu, whose Captain had decided to accept the armistice.

From Rabat, General Noguès sent word to the government in Bordeaux that North Africa opposed the capitulation and was eager to continue the fight. His attitude remained very firm until June 24 or 25. He was encouraged by the state of mind of the European communities in North Africa. They were unwilling to accept the armistice.

Also, General Catroux, Governor of Indochina and M. de Coppet, Governor General of Madagascar, sent telegrams to General Noguès, congratulating him on his decision to continue fighting.

This unanimity on the part of those occupying the principal posts in the Empire makes it clear that they regarded it as both desirable and possible to keep French Africa in the war. It is remarkable that in the meetings of the Council of Ministers held successively in Paris, Cangé and Bordeaux, no serious discussion took place of the possibilities of resistance in North Africa. Later, the weakness of the French forces overseas was invoked by those who favored the armistice. No doubt, some military leaders had pointed out the difficulties involved in transporting men and matériel from France to Algeria or Morocco. General Colson, the Army's Chief of Staff, objected to the transfer of two classes to North Africa on the grounds that there "would be no rifles for them." Similarly, Admiral Darlan is supposed to have stressed the lack of tonnage, in order to warn the government against entertaining excessive hopes.

It is true that, as late as June 15, he told Herriot, President of the Chamber of Deputies, that "Toulon must be defended at all costs to allow time for what remains of our aviation to fly off, and for the relics of our Army and government to embark for Algeria and reorganize there." Toulon, Darlan maintained, could successfully withstand a siege of several weeks. The example of Dunkerque was there to demonstrate that naval transportation could be carried out even in the worst conditions, and on a large scale. On May 31, 15,000 Frenchmen had been embarked, with a total of 120,000 being reached by June 4. Between June 14 and June 19, the British Army evacuated via St. Nazaire and Cherbourg 136,000 men and 310 guns. Twenty-four thousand Poles left for Great Britain by way of Bordeaux, Bayonne and St. Jean de Luz.

The forces that might have been embarked would not have been alone in defending North Africa. On May 20, 1940, there were eleven infantry divisions, one light cavalry division and two cavalry brigades in North Africa. On June 20 General Noguès put through an urgent request, via the French Embassy in Washington, for "10,000 rifles with 500 cartridges for each weapon, 200 anti-tank guns with 500 shells each, 50 anti-aircraft guns of medium caliber, with 1,000 shells each, 110 modern tanks with munitions; 50,000 aerial bombs of 50 kilograms." But a few days later the officers he had sent to France were placed under fortress arrest "for having had matériel embarked in spite of the orders given." An inventory made in late July, 1940, indicates that 1,817 military planes were available. But departures from metropolitan France were interrupted shortly after the armistice, although a considerable number of wings could have crossed the Mediterranean. In the Levant, French forces comprised 2,712 officers and 81,730 noncoms and men.

Finally, in a note dated June 7 and addressed to Paul Reynaud, his principal military private secretary, Colonel de Villelume, stated that there were "at the present moment in the interior, excluding territorial formations (625,000 men) and the older classes who have been sent home: (1) elements immediately capable of being recalled to the armies: 310,000 men; (2) elements undergoing training and which would be available on August 1: 180,000 men." He envisaged the immediate dispatch to North Africa of the 120,000 who had joined the ranks since June 8, and then of a second contingent of 234,000 men, recruited among the youngest classes or the deferred conscripts of the classes already called up. As for the forces in French West Africa that could be rapidly utilized, at the end of June, 1940 they amounted to 122,000 men and 20,000 native or supplementary guards.

It is easy to understand that the political and military leaders of the French Empire were convinced of their ability to go on with the war. The supremacy of the Allies on the seas was the prerequisite for this. It would have barred the transportation of powerful enemy forces across the Mediterranean or seriously handicapped any large-scale offensive starting out from Spanish Morocco—in the eventuality that Spain agreed to enter the war. Again, the time needed for a concentration of the German forces would have been long enough to permit the organization of defenses in North Africa. But, above all, the resistance of the French Army in France would have had an entirely different significance, if from the beginning of June it had been conceived as a vast delaying action serving to cover the transfer of a large part of the armed forces from France to Algeria and Morocco.

The message broadcast by Marshal Pétain on June 17 that the fighting was to end marks the beginning of a new phase in the history of the Army, and in the history of public opinion. The few courageous engagements fought by small groups of isolated French soldiers, in the midst of the universal debacle, were a prefiguration of what, over the course of the years, would be the French return to the struggle. The hierarchies had collapsed, and from now on there could be no blind trust in the state, its institutions or its leaders. From now on, the duty of the citizen had to be decided by the individual conscience. But in this old-established country whose social framework was regarded as one of the oldest and most robust in existence anywhere, no one was prepared for such an unprecedented test.

Nothing was more revealing in this respect than the behavior of those who opposed the armistice before it was signed and who, until Paul Reynaud resigned, may even have included more than half his ministers. They were supported by the President of the Republic, the presiding officers of the Senate and the Chamber of Deputies. With them were the Governors General of the colonies, the High Commissioner in the Levant, the Residents General in Morocco and Tunisia and the main leaders of the military forces overseas. But a few days after the armistice, and especially after the affair of Mers-el-Kébir, those who were resolved to go on with the war had been reduced to a handful. The number of political figures who left to join de Gaulle was quite insignificant. Before 1942, not a single ambassador went over to Free France. De Gaulle's entire military entourage was made up of a few generals, almost all unknown, and of a single admiral. The spirit of resistance seemed to have abandoned almost all the Empire's top military and civilian officials. General Noguès, whose attitude had been decisive in determining that of the greater number of governors and residents general, bowed to the repeated vituperative orders of Pétain and Weygand. Addressing representatives of veterans' organizations, who begged him to carry on the struggle, he justified himself by explaining that nothing could be done without the aid of the fleet, which had decided to obey Vichy.

The acceptance of the armistice by so many officials of the Empire followed the irreversible decision taken at Bordeaux. It did not precede it. Their choice was no longer between those favoring and those hostile to a request for an armistice. It was a matter of obedience to the state, or open revolt. Almost every Frenchman would eventually have to face this alternative. Everything was thrown into turmoil for the Army which, by definition, was bound to practice collective obedience, following the orders of its leaders and subordinating itself to the state. After the shame of the defeat, there began the tragedy of obedience.

Understood in this fashion, French military history may be said to have changed direction on June 18, 1940. As far back as one may go in the past, no trace can be found of the Army's openly opposing the state. Some generals may have lent their aid to some political maneuvers, but the military organization as a whole had never felt tempted to revolt, and had never succumbed. It had been the custom of Frenchmen to say that the Army—like the civil service—had served every regime with the same discipline and the same readiness. In the corps of officers, the reminder was voiced that the grandeur and servitude of military life directly implied the service of the state, whatever should occur. For France and the state were indistinguishable, as French history had exemplified on numberless occasions. The French state was one of the first in the world to exist as such.

In Italy and Germany, the officers for long had served rival or warring princes. Poles, Hungarians and Czechs had seen their countries disappear from the map for long stretches of time, and had found themselves serving the Czar, the Austrian Emperor or the King of Prussia. But in France the state was more deeply rooted than anywhere else. Its strength was increased by a homogeneous population and unbroken and relatively stable frontiers. In marked contrast with the succession of political regimes throughout the nineteenth century, the state had a permanence that guaranteed national stability. The Army was the symbol and instrument of this permanence. This was a dogma that nothing, it seemed, could ever shake. A province might be lost or an empire won, as the temporal authority of the day should decide; but the state remained. In this respect, there had been no fundamental change until the month of June, 1940.

The crisis that rent the Army little by little, after June 18, derived its gravity from its moral significance. Those who rebelled against established authority did so in the name of values transcending the traditional concepts of obedience and discipline. Later it would be pointed out that the state that established its headquarters in Vichy was entirely dependent on German good will and had, consequently, no real existence. That is true, but the fact can be established only by means of reasoning and argument. It was not any such analysis that motivated the overwhelming majority of the acts of resistance and rebellion that grew in number after the appeal broadcast on June 18 by General de Gaulle. They were an elemental revolt against capitulation, against the abandonment of the struggle while immense forces had not yet made any contribution. The feeling of honor was invoked to condemn obedience. Capitulation was judged to be dishonorable. Did not the teaching of the French Army forbid the laying down of arms before the soldier had exhausted "every means required by honor and the regulations"? No comparison can be sustained with the political revolutions that stud France's history. The issue was not the overthrow of a government that appeared detestable in order to replace it with another. Disobedience now did not merely challenge established authority; it overthrew the customary rules of the state.

For the defeat had left every hierarchy intact. In the immense bewilderment that afflicted everyone, civilian and military alike, the instinctive reaction of the Army officers was to take refuge in obedience to the "great leaders," in a blind adherence to discipline. And blindness it indeed was, a deliberate blindness. Since no gleam of hope could be discovered, hope must be mysteriously secreted in some ulterior motive or double game whose nature the humble executant could not possibly divine. Blind trust was, in 1940, the temptation to which the Army cadres were most commonly exposed. The unshaken position of the hierarchies made it easy to go on with the usual obligations of the soldier's calling. Government, the law courts, the police and the civil service were where they always had been: however the armistice might be judged, the state seemed to have survived. To rebel against the government, in these circumstances, was to rebel against the apparatus of the state.

Yet from the very outset this semblance was challenged, this fiction was unveiled. Whatever immediate practical consequences it might have, the appeal broadcast by General de Gaulle on June 18 had a basic historical justification. By calling for war to the bitter end, in spite of the orders of leaders who had "yielded to panic and forgotten honor," de Gaulle confronted the French with an alternative. Each individual now knew that obedience was not the only possible course. At each instant the other side of the alternative remained available: dissidence and resistance. It is meaningful in itself that this momentous gesture should have been that of an officer. Emerging from an organ of the state which by its very nature had the obligation to execute unprotestingly the duties set by the hierarchy, this officer cast doubt on the hierarchy, discovered elsewhere the sources of duty, and spoke in the name of values that transcended discipline and respect for the leaders.

Accordingly, we may look on June 18 as the initiation of an adventure that would traverse the whole war and find no end in victory. This adventure is still going on and may, indeed, never entirely cease. Each man now had to ask himself what he should do, and on what date or in what circumstances he should take up arms once more. War had ceased to be a collective destiny that imposed its iron law on the totality of a nation, on an entire army and an entire people. It became a matter for the individual conscience. The Nation virtually ceased to recognize itself in the state. The state might continue in Vichy for a longer or shorter period and the civil service and the Army remain faithful to the government; dissidence might be limited to a few regions or spread on every hand; the resistance might be organized sooner or later. In any event, the continuation of the war in Europe, the struggle against the invader, the natural desire to free the country, the impossibility of remaining passive while two thirds of France was occupied, would all inevitably lead the French, at some point, to rise against their government and to deny the authority of the state.

For the Army, the traditional instrument of constituted power, this trial was all the more harrowing since it involved the upset of its own values. As to every other Frenchman, the choice appeared to the Army officers in the guise of a conflict of conscience. One man did not hesitate, being unable to accept the idea that France should capitulate while England, the French Empire and the French Navy were still intact and able to fight. Another would get ready to break away, but would be disturbed by the first clashes between the British and French fleets. If the former Ally had now turned against France, there could no longer be any question of fighting along with her. Yet another was revolted by the handshake exchanged at Montoire in October, 1940, between Hitler and Pétain. Many believed that underground resistance would be possible, with the Vichy state serving as cover, only to discover that the "double game" reduced their efforts to naught and that they must break with the government. But this decision was taken in secret and sometimes changed nothing in its author's external circumstances. Such was the strength of their habits of obedience that in 1942, although they were eager to get back into the war, most officers hesitated to play any part against Germany and Italy until some proof was offered them that they could still remain faithful to Pétain, Vichy, legality and hierarchy. General Juin succeeded in offering them this proof, relying on a telegram sent by Pétain to Darlan and which, in actual fact, was couched in the vaguest of terms.

"Between 1940 and 1945," wrote Vincent Monteil, a former officer with the Free French,

> it was the officers who held in their hands the key of events, of the destiny of the fatherland, since everywhere they had taken charge of matters. Never to this extent had one seen so many things depend all at once on a few men—on their initiative, their faith, their imagination, their character, their sense of honor; or on their inertia, their doubts, their passivity, their spinelessness, their faithfulness to the externals of a deceitful discipline. To how many military leaders could

one not at that time have applied the words of Saint Paul: ". . . troubled on every side, yet not distressed . . . perplexed, but not in despair; persecuted, but not forsaken, cast down, but not destroyed . . ."? These were the officers whose acts allowed a Free France to exist, to receive the support of various territories and to re-enter the combat. Others bowed to the relentless machinery of the hierarchy of rank and function, and to the fascination and ready compromises of obedience without any risk—if not without remorse.

Since military men were the most inclined by their outlook, traditions and social ambiance to opt for "order," and for obedience to the new regime, it is among them that the conflicting urges besetting all Frenchmen were the most agonizing. The choice facing the officers was never a theoretical one: in Syria, Dakar or Madagascar, they had to fight on one side or the other. War forced on them a total choice, for no Gaullist officer could be satisfied merely to stick up for his opinions in arguments with his fellows. He had to abandon everything: the uniform, regulations, discipline, the hierarchy. He could not take refuge in inactivity, bad temper or scoffing, for Vichy demanded discipline and nothing else. Dissidence and the Resistance demanded irrevocable decisions and total commitments.

Once flouted, the authorities and hierarchies turned against the recalcitrant officer. Sometimes they had recourse to almost unbearable moral pressures. Thus Captain Frenay, who called his movement "Combat," received letters from his mother pleading with him to return to "duty," and wondering whether she should not denounce her son. No longer did a straight and narrow path lie ahead for the Army. There was only the confused and passionate search for the path of honor and patriotism. And each man had to go it alone.

In the history of the military consciousness, we have reached the age of the individual. The position occupied in the hierarchy, and rank and training, weigh no more heavily than character, ideas, ambitions and desires. The remainder of the Second World War was to be an individual struggle in which each man took part, at the moment he himself chose and in the spirit that was intimately his own, not as the result of a collective decision imposed by the State. But the age of the individual would not rapidly expire when the war was ended. Later, other men were to invoke values that outranked obedience to the state, and would let themselves be drawn to other acts of dissidence.

For the French Army, the age of the individual began on June 18, 1940. A full twenty years later, it had not yet ended.

CHAPTER FOURTEEN

TWO BLACK YEARS

✠

Under the terms of the armistice, the armed forces that the Vichy government could maintain in metropolitan France were limited to 100,000 men, this being the size of the German armed forces under the Versailles Treaty. The mechanization of the French Army was forbidden. Each cavalry regiment was restricted to a squadron of eight light armored cars, each artillery regiment to a single battery. There was to be neither heavy artillery nor armor, and very little anti-aircraft artillery. The air arm was largely neutralized, though in July, 1941, authorization was granted to build 600 planes. The Navy was treated much more leniently, being allowed to keep 60,000 men and most of its vessels which, however, had to remain in French ports.

Miserable though this embryonic Army was, with its anachronistic matériel, training that amounted to little more than zero and manpower wasted on routine tasks, strangely enough it was surrounded by a myth—one that was accepted by both the German and the French General Staffs. The Germans remembered their own 1919 Reichswehr, which, by means of its remarkable stockpiling, illicit manufacturing, intensive training and military research, gave birth with the greatest possible rapidity to the victorious Wehrmacht. The French saw in the German example a reason for hoping that the limits imposed by the armistice would soon be covertly infringed. In July, 1940, General Colson, who had ceased to be the Army's Chief of Staff and was now War Minister, wrote personally to the commanders of the military districts, asking them to camouflage matériel and supplies as well as possible. At the same time, the German espionage services kept a watch on the secret military activities in the free zone. A certain number of their agents were unmasked and held by the French services which thus, despite Vichy, kept their own warfare going. In all, some hundreds of officers and noncoms were passionately involved in the little game of covering up arms and matériel.

Military trucks and stocks of arms and munitions were scattered in the remotest farms, woods and villages, and in abandoned houses. The total of this hidden treasure was estimated, after the winter of 1940–1941, at 65,000 rifles, 9,000 machine guns and light machine guns, 200 mortars, 55 75-millimeter guns and a few anti-tank and anti-aircraft weapons. The Service de Conservation du Matériel, in order to have available a sufficient supply of military trucks in the event that hostilities should be resumed, searched for the thousands of vehicles that had been scattered in all directions after the collapse, and handed them over to eighteen trucking companies which were required to keep them in good order and to hand them back to the military authorities on six hours' notice. In this way 3,500 trucks or motor coaches were "hidden." Some ministers lent their support to these infringements, which though limited were genuine, of the military clauses of the armistice. At the request of the Minister of Agriculture, the forestry services helped in camouflaging these armaments. The Minister of Finances spread a part of the military expenses over the budgets of the civilian ministries or the overseas territories. He gave shelter to a "population service" which, allegedly carrying out statistical studies, collected all the demobilization cards and prepared a new plan of clandestine mobilization which envisaged raising from eight to twenty-four the number of divisions to be constituted in the free zone.

Inspector General Garmille, the man responsible for these operations, was arrested and died a prisoner. Finally, General Huntziger, the War Minister, accepted Colonel Groussard's proposal to form "protective groups" whose members would receive intensive training as section leaders. They would constitute a force readied in advance and able to intervene as shock troops the moment that war broke out anew. But the activity and the aims of these protective services were so evident to the police that the Germans soon saw to it that they were dissolved. It was in vain that Colonel Groussard had recruited his men among the militia of the old leagues of the extreme Right, and equally in vain that the militia, totally unaware of their leader's real aims, loudly proclaimed their liking for the Vichy regime. The protective groups at once awakened the suspicion of the German security services and also of the French milieux most strongly in favor of collaboration. This example, the most significant of all, should suffice to show the singularly narrow limits of the "double game" that most of the cadres sincerely hoped they could play within the framework of the armistice.

Looming over everything else was the twin subjection of obedience to the authorities and of recollections of past military glories. One might wonder if the Army was in any different plight from the rest of the country. For the country, too, had experienced the disaster of 1940 as an unveiling of the nothingness into which it might fall for all eternity. In the ghastly light of the defeat, each tried to blame the other for the harrowing trials that had just been undergone. Almost without exception, public opinion condemned the military hierarchy, or at least its upper echelons, which had failed to grasp the new forms of warfare, and had led public opinion astray with regard to the merits of the French Army, its doctrine and its leaders. There are countless testimonies to this universal contempt felt for the "old generals," all the more universal for being recent. Never in the past, and above all not after 1918, had the French doubted their own military prowess, the prowess of their Army with which, in the whole world, only the German Army could be compared. After 1940 there was no longer any question in the public mind of a blind confidence, of any degree of confidence, in the military leaders. Nothing could ever efface, in people's minds, the recollection of the rout that contrasted so cruelly with the praise, the respect, the consideration, even the fervor, that had been lavished on the band of generals, laden with honors, splattered with ribbons, their brows still encircled by the laurel wreaths earned in the dazzling victory of 1918.

This state of mind quickly made its way into the lower ranks of the Army. A myth had collapsed, that of the infallibility of the generals. Such a collapse was bound to have immense repercussions in the officers' corps. It explains how, in a space of two or three years, the great majority of the military cadres could tranquilly accept the cashiering of most of the military chiefs who remained in charge after the armistice. Even those who had not responded to General de Gaulle's appeal and who tried to reconcile their patriotism with obedience to the discipline imposed by Vichy, felt no common bond with these leaders who did not awaken their confidence and whom, in some cases, they despised. This "intellectual unruliness" would not spare the principal generals in the Italian campaigns, during the Liberation of France and in Germany. It fed on the minor scandals or dubious incidents that were to besmirch the early years of the Fourth Republic. There was to be a permanent rupture between the officers' corps as a whole and the military leaders. This rupture would play a major part in the Algerian War—and its origins are to be found in the events of 1940.

In military circles, there was no thought of shouldering the entire blame for the defeat. Heirs of a moral and political tradition that looked on a political regime weakened by crises and sapped by the menace of revolution as the enduring reason for the country's enfeebled state, most officers were inclined to believe that the outcome of the Battle of France was but the image of the country's preceding decadence. They yielded to this tempting conviction even while combat was still raging. The breakdown of some units, the terror of the ordinary soldiers when confronting the modern matériel in the hands of the German Army, the deplorable ease with which some soldiers let themselves be taken prisoner and the fear that overwhelmed many that they were about to "die for nothing" in a war that already was virtually lost—episodes of this sort aroused, in the officers of the professional Army, the impression that they could not fight because the men entrusted to them were unwilling to fight. But the public at large was often to believe quite the contrary. Many demobilized soldiers kept their memories of officers taking flight in automobiles, leaving the men they commanded to be captured. In any case, was it not the duty of the career officers to know what kind of war was going to be fought? Not merely did some reveal that they were cowards, all of them were guilty of incompetence. These accusations were to become so deeply incised that the victories gained between 1942 and 1944 would never quite eliminate the antimilitarism to which the defeat of 1940 had given rise.

Perhaps because it felt itself the target of this collective suspicion, the armistice Army could not condemn sufficiently harshly the attitude of the public prior to 1939. Military circles were the most eager to take up, with warmth and conviction, the great themes of Vichy's propaganda that the "search for pleasure" as contrasted with the "spirit of sacrifice" had been responsible for the country's unpreparedness for war, for its dissolution and defeat. In every garrison lectures were organized, and officers roundly denounced the Popular Front, the forty-hour week, leisure-time activities, the addiction to week ends and the love of comfort as having caused all the misfortunes of the country. With no clear realization that they were doing so, they attacked the whole struggle for social progress, and all the campaigns waged since the outset of the Third Republic to improve the lot of the population and, in particular, of the working class. In vain did they claim on occasion to have a "social conscience," for whenever they extolled the "moral order" that must be restored, they were attacking all the gains that had been won by the workers.

Nothing could be more typical of this attitude than the experiment of the Opne camp, which was initiated by the future Marshal de Lattre de Tassigny. He chose this site because of its barrenness and isolation, and because of the austere life that would necessarily be led there. De Latre had 300 young officers and noncoms construct, with their own hands, this officers' training school, which was intended to revitalize the spirit of the Army. The same concerns were, indeed, to be found in every effort to modernize the military apparatus after the victory. Here at least men of character were involved, who had the healthy desire to avoid conjuring up the memory of defeat and to turn toward the future. Yet even in this milieu, which assuredly was more energetic and more dynamic than that of the General Staffs, a moral critique served as a kind of preface to the effort undertaken. One of the first directives issued by General De Lattre de Tassigny said, in effect:

> The whole country had ceased to understand what effort means. This state of mind was indicated by the reduction of the work week, and a constant preoccupation with leisure. Discipline disappeared. The leaders were criticized, discussed and disobeyed . . . the goal that the Opne school sets itself is to give the young cadres a new spirit, to give them a doctrine and methods, to make leaders out of them. With no hesitation about abandoning the beaten track, and exempt from the influence of any routine outlook, it will renew our Army by providing it with young cadres, young not only in heart and mind, ardent cadres, tough but understanding.

The examples could be multiplied. Many corps leaders, in an effort to counterbalance the slackness to which they attributed all the ills that had befallen the country, imposed on their regiments a discipline much stricter than in prewar days. Did they realize that, by so doing, they exposed themselves to the criticisms and the irony of public opinion? Incompetent and licked, did these officers of high rank imagine that they now had the right to give lessons to and bully men who had no responsibility for the defeat? The most that these officers could plead, by way of excuse for their outlook, was that it was shared in other circles, for the directives issued by the Ministry of National Education to the teaching body had a similar inspiration.

Apart from this, the conviction of the General Staffs of the armistice Army was that the population must be convinced—in the free zone, at all events—that the French Army still existed. So at once large numbers of parades and military marches were decided on. Some were even more spectacular than in previous periods. The equestrian festival held on May 4, 1941, in the Nîmes Arena drew a crowd of 25,000 to this modest provincial capital. The finals of the Military Cup for Athletes, held in Vichy on August 24 of the same year, acquired the dimensions of some sort of national festival. Even historical panoramas were indulged in and, in many places, the population was asked to take part in the ceremony of hoisting the colors.

Here, too, the attitude of the military risked awakening the critical spirit. Why should the Army, after a total defeat, still make bold to march past? The irritation caused by officers who were looked on as pretentious became even more serious as the Resistance and Gaullism became more popular in France. Now the contrasting inactivity of the armistice Army was all the more shocking. Thus the least attempt to lend a respectable appearance to the troops that had remained in France often rubbed public opinion the wrong way and, far from attaining its objective, was met by shrugs or even sarcastic remarks. Sometimes the military parades, linked to the souvenirs of bygone battles, and arousing the idea of the *revanche* or the cult of Alsace-Lorraine which again had been lost, brought about an enthusiastic and genuinely patriotic reaction in the southern crowds. At such moments the Army awakened the belief, if only for a transitory moment, that it was there in order to fight again one day, one day soon.

In the meantime, it divided its attention between acts of camouflage and minor chicanery vis-à-vis the armistice commissions, and a barracks existence that to an ever-increasing degree found its inspiration in the Boy Scout movement. Since it could not imitate the German Army with respect to training, armaments and tactical and strategic experience, the armistice Army tried to ape the Germans in the physical preparation of the men. Training for sports, competitions, marches and excursions occupied an increasing place in military instruction. Many officers were detailed to work with the "Chantiers de Jeunesse," with several graduating classes of officers being enrolled in this organization and engaging in rural work. The very details of the activities of Boy Scout troops could be found in many regiments, as well as in the Chantiers: evening gatherings, camp fires, choruses, etc. In this atmosphere there was much talk of a renewal, of national restoration, but little mention of fighting. Fighting was postponed until later. Many hoped the day would soon arrive. But they kept this hope to themselves, and allowed themselves at most a few bold statements, or hunted for German spies, or kept the hidden matériel in good condition. The armistice Army, having chosen obedience, could continue to live only on the myth of the double game. The history of this Army, when all is said and done, is nothing but the history of a myth.

Four months sufficed to demonstrate with all necessary clarity that the logic of the armistice did not point to the preparation, methodically and in secret, of a resumption of combat. On October 30, 1940, Marshal Pétain actually declared that he was "entering today on the path of collaboration," and that this was an essential step, primarily in order to "lessen the dissidence in our colonies." On the very next day a conference was held in Paris to examine the details of a Franco-German collaboration "with a view to regaining from the English our dissident colonies in Africa." Vichy was represented at this conference by Laval, Minister of Foreign Affairs, Bouthillier, Minister of Finances, Huntziger, the War Minister, and Brinon, the government's representative in Paris. Considered was the hypothesis of a conflict between France and Great Britain, which might begin whenever Great Britain opposed with armed force the reconquest of the territories which had gone over to de Gaulle. This would require operations on a large scale since, by that time, disaffection had gained the upper hand in New Caledonia, the archipelagoes of the Pacific, the French possessions in India, the Chad, the Cameroons and subsequently all the French possessions in Equatorial Africa.

Before the armistice had been signed, Admiral Darlan had promised the British representatives to "bring about the geographic removal" of the fleet, and also to scuttle it, should the Germans attempt to seize it. But under the terms of the armistice the Mediterranean squadron, based on Mers-el-Kébir, was to return to a port in metropolitan France, and there to be disarmed. The English took the view that it would be at the mercy of a sudden move on the part of the Germans or Italians. They decided to attack it or compel it to sail in the direction of Martinique. Since Admiral Darlan had given orders to break off all connection with the British fleet, the British proposals were not examined, and an engagement began. The French Admiral would actually have agreed to sail for Martinique if he had received the British demands. From this moment on, the possibility of a Franco-British conflict had to be considered. Vichy rejected the hypothesis, but the decision to break off diplomatic relations was a first step in that direction.

After the armistice there was an alternative policy; either to go to war against Great Britain, as the logic of collaboration required, or to keep collaboration at a minimum and avoid as far as possible any danger of a Franco-British conflict. From the outset the "double game" in which the armistice Army found some comfort was in reality a triple one: it could lead to a war against the former ally, to a semi-neutrality blemished by military clashes with English or Gaullist forces and— but only as a third alternative—to a difficult and ambiguous preparation for renewed war against Germany.

The official propaganda put out by the Vichy government had, from the outset, oriented people's minds to the first and to the second of these hypotheses. Pamphlets that the Administration had circulated everywhere in French Africa explained that "Great Britain bears the entire responsibility for the disaster. The British forces, on Churchill's orders, abandoned the French Army in the midst of battle. This abandonment was intentional and fully desired. The cause of France must be forever separated from the English cause. . . ." In their search for an explanation of whatever lay behind the defeat of 1940, many officers and, doubtless, some of the public willingly accepted this interpretation. The recollection of war in France was strengthened, in certain circles, by the impression that the Mers-el-Kébir engagement produced. Everything was undertaken to whip up hatred against England. Psychologically, the climate favorable to collaboration had already been created by Pétain's declaration of October 30. It is here that the particular part played by the Navy in the history of Vichy— and of the Army—requires mention.

To explain this part, the centuries-old rivalry between the French and British Navies has often been invoked. But it is possible to attribute an excessive importance to this. In actual fact, there had been no conflict and no engagement between the two fleets since 1814. Since that time, the sailors of the two countries had often found themselves side by side. On land, the French marines were close to British troops in the Battle of the Yser in 1914 and in the Dardanelles expedition of 1915. French and British naval vessels shared the task of protecting convoys throughout the First World War, as they shared the task of hunting German submarines. Together they had carried out the blockade of Germany in 1939 and 1940; they fought side by side off the Norwegian coast and at Dunkerque. The most that can be said is that Franco-British rivalry went back to rather remote historical origins.

It is true that it must have been revived by several unfortunate episodes in the diplomatic history of the 1919–1939 period. At the conference on naval disarmament held in Washington in 1921 and 1922, Great Britain accepted equality between its own fleet and that of the United States, and succeeded in imposing the equality of the French and Italian fleets, whereas France's naval obligations were incomparably greater than Italy's. The same attitude of hostility to French maritime interests was revealed by the British representatives at the London naval conference of 1931. An Anglo-German naval accord reached in 1935 had openly accepted the abandonment of all the naval clauses of the Versailles Treaty, by the unilateral decision of British diplomacy, without any French agreement and without any moderation of intensive rearmament by Nazi Germany. Nevertheless, it appeared in 1939 that a close and loyal cooperation between the two Navies had been assured, and Admiral Darlan himself was greatly respected by the British leaders, particularly by Winston Churchill, First Lord of the Admiralty.

In the attitude of the French Navy, historical causes played a much smaller part than political reasons. The moral and psychological history of the naval officers' corps rather resembled a caricature of that to be found among their fellows on land. If the student body of Saint-Cyr was recruited in part on hereditary lines, that of the Naval School was much more so. The competitive entrance examination was much stiffer. Polytechnique and the École Centrale allowed young men of modest background to become Army officers in the best possible conditions, but not naval officers. Furthermore, the proportion of naval officers promoted from the ranks or emerging from the boatswains' schools was always negligible. Thus the social background of the naval cadres was necessarily very narrow and even exclusive.

The political influences that played a predominant part in military circles here ruled the roost; nothing else was known. There was no counterpart, in the Navy, to the plebeian Jacobin tradition which, although a minority phenomenon, nevertheless existed in the Army. The aristocratic, conservative and Catholic tradition outweighed all others. *L'Action Française* was the paper with the widest circulation. According to some, it was even the only paper tolerated in the mess-room of some units. A small number of naval officers did have the reputation of furthering their careers by maintaining solid political contacts, and they were regarded as "republicans" or even "Free-masons." Admiral Darlan was one of them—or, at least, that is what was often alleged in naval circles. These officers maintained all possible discretion with regard to their political contacts and sympathies; they accepted the rules and prejudices shared by all the naval cadres and displayed the strictest conformism, for fear of being cold-shouldered in a body that possessed considerable attractions and had undeniable merit.

Such was the state of mind of the Navy when the events of 1940 occurred. Nowhere else was the soil better prepared for the authoritarian and reactionary, antidemocratic and antirepublican ideology of the Vichy regime. Admiral Darlan had been among the opponents of capitulation, in the first political and military discussions to take place in June, 1940. When he went over to the position of Pétain and Weygand, his authority was not challenged in the Navy where, even more than in the Army, the respect for hierarchies was rigorous and imperative, with no questioning allowed. But, here as elsewhere, decisive as the habit of obedience was, concrete experience was probably even more decisive. The officers of the fleet had not witnessed the invasion of French soil; they had no direct experience of German occupation. They were not exposed to the immediate shock of seeing a hostile army occupy the national territory. This shock rapidly led to resistance in all its forms, among the French of the occupied zone.

The Navy was alone in experiencing the aftermath of the armistice, which meant the exchange of gunfire with the British fleet. With this the Navy had discovered an adversary, already described in the history manuals of the École Navale, and denounced every morning as "perfidious Albion" by *L'Action Française*. Here was the fountain-head of so many of France's sufferings, and a rival, too, with whom one could come to grips. It is impossible to exaggerate the violence of the attacks on England that filled the columns of the Vichy papers and provided official discourses with their longest lyrics. This was the time when the Vichy radio, speaking of the German raids on English towns, referred to them as a "nocturnal chastisement, inflicted on England by German aviation." Admiral Darlan himself set the tone for this propaganda by declaring, on May 5, 1942, for example: "Make the British pay as dearly as possible for acting like highwaymen. . . . Do not forget that the English betrayed us in Flanders . . . a day will come when England will pay."

In this atmosphere, everything called for a switch in alliances. There were the certitude of a German victory, the exploitation by Vichy propaganda of the first clashes between British and French forces, and the interest felt by some in taking up a position beside the victors, not the vanquished. The question arose as early as July 4, after the Mers-el-Kébir affair. Darlan and Laval came out in favor of an armed riposte against the British squadron as it made its way back to Gibraltar. Baudoin, who at the time was Minister of Foreign Affairs, feared the risks of an all-out war against England, and persuaded Pétain to restrict the steps taken to a rupture of diplomatic relations. Laval then made skilfull use of this concession to Baudoin's point of view. He gave Members of Parliament to understand, at the time he was soliciting their votes that would declare the Third Republic no longer in existence, that "we are not going to declare war against England." The two Assemblies were, naturally, astounded by this, since they had no idea that tension with Great Britain had become so serious. Thus Laval's assurances, so moderate in appearance, greatly relieved them.

But this was also the moment when Darlan decided to have the French ships halt any British commercial vessels they encountered, to have Gibraltar bombed from the air and to use the fleet to protect merchant vessels. He instructed his General Staff to work out one plan of operations against the British colonies in West Africa and another, in cooperation with the Italian air arm, to free the French squadron in Alexandria, where it had remained under the terms of an agreement between the British Admiralty and Admiral Godefroy.

Thus, a bare few days after the armistice had been concluded, the various paths open to the Vichy government had become plain: a switch of alliances, the mere execution of the armistice, or secret preparations for a resumption of the struggle. A group of officers in the Army's General Staff undertook to camouflage arms and equipment, and prepared a new plan of mobilization. The Navy's General

Staff studied the practical details for war with Great Britain. Weygand, like the majority of Vichy's administrative, diplomatic and military personnel, abided by the principle: "the armistice, nothing but the armistice."

As early as July 16, Vichy was offered the possibility of making a first choice between the different policies available. The German government, after Mers-el-Kébir, had granted two modifications in the armistice terms: the French fleet could make free use of coastal waters and the disarmament of French troops in Africa was postponed. In return it let it be known that "it expects that the French government, for its part, will provide the support it deems necessary to continue in an effective manner its struggle against England." What this meant in practice was putting at the disposal of the Wehrmacht airfields, ports, railroads and meteorological stations in North Africa. On July 17, the French ministers unanimously rejected Germany's demands.

Discussion began on the two replies that had been drafted, one by the General Secretariat of the Ministry of Foreign Affairs, the other by the minister's private staff. The first was an outright rejection. The second blended a negative reply with remarks that indicated the spirit in which this was done. "I am entitled to believe," the French Minister of Foreign Affairs would have declared, "that the demands of the German government confront the French government with an entirely new situation and raise problems of dimensions and of a gravity that exceed the competence of the Wiesbaden commission. I consider that only a new negotiation can provide a solution for these problems."

This was the text adopted by the Council of Ministers. The Vichy government demonstrated by this that, while it was determined to maintain intact the essential provisions of the armistice where the French Empire was concerned, it was always ready to negotiate a rapprochement with Germany. The increasing hold of the German authorities on the occupied zone, on the French economy and on the Departments of Alsace-Lorraine which had been officially annexed to the Reich, made naught of the hopes of those who had looked on the armistice as a means of maintaining intact the political, administrative and social structures of the state. The government, which had imagined it could return to Paris, found itself compelled to remain in Vichy. At the same time, the extension of the British blockade to the territories of metropolitan France threatened to asphyxiate the whole economy of France and its Empire. Was nothing then left of the basic principles of the armistice? At all events, and in case the German Army should find some pretext to occupy the free zone, Pétain gave Darlan oral permission to move to North Africa, while Pétain himself would remain in France.

A request that had been made to President Roosevelt to have the blockade lifted met with failure. In Paris and throughout the occupied zone, the German authorities supported parties and papers that waged a campaign against Vichy's attitude. The government, threatened on two flanks, limited itself to carrying out the clauses of the armistice, interpreting them in their widest, and even in a dishonorable sense. The first daily indemnities demanded by Germany, and which in the end were paid, were enough to support eighteen million men! Ninety soldiers of the Foreign Legion were handed over to the Nazi authorities, although it had been understood that only "those who had incited to war" would be asked for. A Rhenish separatist and two German agents of the Deuxième Bureau also had to be handed over, on Vichy's orders. The Commander of the camp in which they were interned allowed them to escape. Two German Socialist leaders and the industrialist Thyssen, not yet asked for by Berlin, were refused the exit visas that would have allowed them to escape internment and subsequent deportation.

At the same moment, the breaking away of the French territories of Oceania, of the Chad, of Ubangi-Shari, of the Cameroons and the Congo, gave rise to a new discussion in the Council of Ministers on August 30. Laval favored a declaration of war against Great Britain. Weygand and Baudoin were opposed, and Pétain agreed with them. On the one hand he tried to obtain a modification of the blockade, while on the other he informed Goering that he wished to meet Hitler. This initiative fitted in perfectly with the Führer's plans. He was eager to explore the possibilities of a vast operation against England's maritime communications in the Mediterranean and the North Atlantic.

On October 22, on his way to the Spanish frontier where he was to meet Franco, Hitler had a preliminary interview with Laval and, on the 24th, on the return journey, he met with Pétain at the same place, Montoire. On the 22nd, Hitler and Laval openly envisaged France's participation in the struggle against England. "It is in France's interest," the Führer had said, "if she wishes England to pay the costs of the war and not herself." But on the 23rd Franco, before promising to take part in a joint operation against Gibraltar, demanded that Morocco and the Oran region of Algeria should be handed over to

Spain. Hitler balked at this, since in his view, as he told Ribbentrop, "the Empire would probably go over *en bloc* to de Gaulle." So on the 24th Hitler was both less decided to go ahead and more demanding, where French intentions were concerned. Both Pétain and Laval rejected the idea of a new conflict that would involve France and England. Hitler evaded Pétain's questions concerning the future peace treaty and the immediate fate in store for the prisoners and the northeast Departments that were grouped under the military government of Belgium.

In the end there was merely a common public affirmation of the principle of Franco-German collaboration. Thus those who, in Vichy, were eager for a resumption of the struggle might deplore the new style of official policy, while deriving comfort from the idea that nothing irrevocable had been decided. Those who wanted a switch of alliances could tell themselves that the first step in that direction had been taken. And those who wished for nothing but the execution of the armistice terms could feel both disturbed and consoled by the realization that nothing concrete had emerged from the Montoire interview. The triple game would go on.

It went on, in the month following the Montoire meeting. A first Franco-German military conference took place on November 29, its subject being the reconquest of the colonies that had broken away. General Huntziger, who took part in it, had been instructed to let things drag on. But another conference was set for December 10. In the interval, negotiations between Jacques Chevalier, Secretary General for National Education, and Pierre Dupuy, Canada's chargé d'affaires in Vichy, resulted in a memorandum that would have maintained the status quo: an "artificial chilliness" between France and Great Britain, nonaggression on the part of Vichy with respect to the dissident colonies, the undertaking to deliver neither to Germany nor to Italy the fleet or any colonial territory, reserve on the part of the British Radio concerning French internal affairs, a moderation of the blockade, and eventually the opposition of the French forces if there should be any attempt on the part of Germany to invade the colonies.

This memorandum, of which London acknowledged reception and nothing more, sought at bottom to eliminate any occasion of armed conflict between France and Great Britain, and went no further. But the policy of active collaboration led in that direction. This contradiction in policy brought about the dismissal and arrest of Laval on December 13. A delay of only two months resulted, for Darlan, who was

Minister of Foreign Affairs from February 9, 1941, found himself in the position that Laval had occupied in December, 1940. The dilemma that confronted him was every bit as rigorous as before, and Marshal Keitel would put it in a very direct way when Benoit-Méchain came to discuss with him the setting up of German and Italian bases in Africa: "In the event that France failed to grant Germany the controls demanded in North Africa, she would be treated like Yugoslavia."

The operations in Iraq led Germany to ask for utilization of the airfields in Syria. On May 6 Darlan agreed to this. It was a first step in the direction of co-belligerence. On May 11 and 12, the Führer explained his intentions to Darlan. He let it be understood that if France collaborated in the German war effort, she could receive certain compensations in exchange for Alsace-Lorraine or the colonies ceded to Italy.

Aware of the coming German attack against Russia, Darlan may have thought that France would have no very important role to play in the next phase of the war. He declared, in any event, that "France is entirely disposed to help Germany win the war." Vichy appeared to be on the point of choosing between its three available policies. Darlan's account of his interview with Hitler, given at the Council of Ministers and passed on to the Governors General of the colonies, analyzed the choice the government had made:

> . . . if we favor English policy, France will be crushed, dislocated, and will cease to be a nation . . . If we try to carry out a policy of alternation between the two adversaries, Germany will cause a thousand difficulties in the exercise of our sovereignty, and will stir up trouble . . . The peace will be disastrous. If we collaborate with Germany, without going so far as to place ourselves beside her to make war against England . . . if we accord Germany certain facilities, we can save the French nation, reduce to a minimum our territorial losses, in metropolitan France and in the colonies, and play an honorable if not an important part in the future Europe.

On May 27, the protocols signed by Darlan and General Warlimont provided for the utilization by Germany of the Syrian bases, the passage across Tunisia of the German expeditionary corps in Lybia, the sale of a part of the stocks of the African Army, the subsequent utilization by the Germans of a submarine base in Dakar, and appropriate measures to reconquer the Gaullist colonies.

The application of the Darlan-Warlimont protocols would have meant the definite adoption of the policy of a reversal of alliances, but this irrevocable choice was prevented by the strong delaying action of those who favored the strict execution of the terms of the armistice. Once more, however, the entry of British and French troops into Syria on June 8 created another opportunity for Franco-German military collaboration. Germany offered to intervene in the air. This, indeed, had to be envisaged as soon as the resistance of the Vichy troops weakened. But on June 17 Darlan preferred to neglect the German offers, which would quite unavoidably have sealed a military coalition between France and Germany and directed it against Great Britain.

It was during this spring of 1941 that the Vichy government went as far as it was to go on the path of a reversal of alliances. Later on, it would be content to carry out the policy of passively applying the armistice terms. Each time that Germany would make new proposals for military collaboration, Vichy's reply would be to demand important concessions—too important, for the liking of the German government. The collaboration was maintained as a matter of principle, and publicly. In October, Pétain wrote to Hitler, on the anniversary of Montoire: "The victory of your arms over Bolshevism offers, even more than was the case a year ago, a motive for affirming oneself henceforth in works of peace for the construction of a transformed Europe."

But Hitler was interested in something more concrete, and he obtained the dismissal of Weygand, whom he regarded as the chief opponent of the reversal of alliances. All that Pétain received in exchange was the authorization to see Goering. The interview was inconclusive and, on December 15, Goering received in Berlin General Juin, the successor to Weygand in North Africa. He asked him to agree to the undercover provisioning of the German and Italian forces in Libya by means of Bizerte, and sought his promise of direct military aid in case Rommel's army should fall back on southern Tunisia. Juin passed on these demands to Vichy which, in return, asked for the almost total abrogation of the armistice clauses dealing with demilitarization in Africa. Germany was not ready to take this risk, and negotiations were adjourned. In the interval, on December 7, the United States had entered the war and, on the 13th, Darlan gave a solemn pledge, in the presence of the American Ambassador, that the German Army would never enter the territories of French Africa.

All in all, Vichy's policy would remain unchanged from now on, despite Laval's return to power in April, 1942. The government would be prodigal of concessions and would allow the German authorities to act as they saw fit in the occupied zone. On the path of resistance, the most that would be ventured were a few protests, almost always secret, while on the path of collaboration the most that would be conceded was the step-by-step adoption of legislation ever closer to Nazi concepts, but never involving active military collaboration. The most significant episodes, in this respect, occurred in September, 1942, when the British landing in Madagascar might have been the signal for a new trial of strength between certain Frenchmen and their former ally. Laval first authorized the Governor to negotiate with the English but withdrew this permission, after the Germans had objected. Nevertheless, the two whole months during which the Vichy authorities refused to yield resulted in a total casualty figure of two.

At the same time, the Vichy government agreed to the penetration of German missions into the free zone and into West Africa in order to track down the clandestine radio stations used by the French or Allied resistance networks. This would continue to be Vichy's line of conduct to the very end. It would not reach its utmost gravity until the militia, gendarmes and police, on Vichy's orders, entered the struggle against the maquis. But by that time the French Army in metropolitan France would have ceased to exist.

The Marseilles police, on November 6, arrested Commandant Faye just as he was about to send a radio message to London, and in this way learned that Allied troops would soon be disembarked in North Africa. The moment was approaching when at last the worth of the armistice army could be definitively established. At that time, two years and four months after the capitulation, not one shot had been exchanged between the forces that had remained under the control of Vichy and the German Army. But at Mers-el-Kébir and Dakar, in Syria and Madagascar, the French had repeatedly clashed with British forces, and sometimes with the Free French, in incidents that at times were costly in blood.

Until that time the "double game" appeared in practice to have functioned only to the detriment of the Allies, and of those Frenchmen eager to continue the struggle. Every justification attempted by those who favored the armistice, and in particular by the military leaders, rested on the hypothesis of a resumption of the war with reconstituted forces at some opportune moment, and in strategic conditions that would inflict the most losses on Germany. It was a notion that had motivated the labors of countless officers and noncoms who had everywhere tried to hide away matériel, and of the General Staffs and special services that had worked out the plans of mobilization and concentration. Thus, for instance, the second group of divisions had prepared a plan of operations involving the occupied ports of the Atlantic coast, in connection with possible Allied landings; and the officers in the entourage of General Giraud, after his escape, had envisaged a direct offensive from the valley of the Rhone to the valley of the Rhine, which would threaten the rear and the communications of the German armies occupying the center and west of France.

The Allied landing in North Africa took the French General Staffs by surprise. With the wisdom of experience, the resistance groups of Algeria and Morocco had taken good care not to contact the Vichy authorities, who would doubtless have arrested them, as they had arrested their forerunners in 1940 and 1941.

So neither in Casablanca nor Algiers nor Vichy had this move been expected; the information transmitted by the police and the special services had been neglected by Vichy's top dignitaries and generals. The officers with General Giraud ought normally to have been acquainted with the main trend of his intentions, in view of the role attributed to the General in the Allies' projects. They tended to believe that the landing in North Africa would be rapidly followed by the invasion of Europe, although it was clear that the conditions for a resumption of the struggle were unfavorable.

Nevertheless, the officers who for the preceding two years had lived for this day, and who knew in their hearts that only a resumption of warfare could justify their inactivity and erase it from people's memories, sensed that the moment had come. General Verneau of the Army's General Staff, who since 1940 had been directing the group of officers planning a serious resumption of the struggle, sent a secret order, using the only code that could still be employed. All Army units were instructed "to put themselves in a position, in the event that German troops should cross the line of demarcation, to remove troops and General Staffs from barracks and the main lines of communication. All munitions must be taken."

Only the generals and their Chiefs of Staff could decode this message. They passed on the word to all the regiments. Out of their hiding places came the automobiles, and the radios under camouflage since the armistice which were the only means of military communication. On this day, November 9, 1942, those who for over two years had done nothing but prepare more or less methodically for the armistice army's return to the field, thought that at last their activity had found its justification and that the moment of combat had arrived.

Yet it soon became evident, as the day slipped by, that the struggle, contrary to the expectations of many, would have to be resumed once more in the absence of any coordination with the Allies, and with no clear governmental directive. Laval set out for Munich to see Hitler. Pétain ordered the troops in North Africa to resist the Allied landing. In Algiers and Casablanca, French and Americans found themselves in combat against each other. In Montpellier, General de Lattre de Tassigny instructed his General Staff to prepare to install his division in the Corbières massif, giving them to understand that the struggle would be very rough, if not desperate. "By sacrificing ourselves," he said, "we will justify our existence, we will ensure the future, for the repercussions of our act of testimony will be immense."

The Army's General Staff left Vichy that same day and went to the farm of La Rapine, some thirty kilometers distant. General Verneau and forty officers established themselves there. The radio security service of the region had been functioning there since 1940, under Captain Leschi. Thus the conspirators were at the center of the communications network of the entire free zone. Leschi, by secret order of General Verneau, had equipped each military district with a high-power radio station mounted on vehicles. All through the night of the 9th and 10th, General Verneau waited for the news that the German Army had crossed the demarcation line. Whatever the government chose to do, he was ready on his own responsibility to give the order for resistance. By the morning of the 10th nothing had yet occurred, and the General returned to Vichy.

The decisive event of that day was Pétain's categorical refusal to accept the advice of those who would have had him leave for Algiers. From Germany, Laval released the news that Hitler had offered a full-scale alliance. The notion was rejected in Vichy, but so was the notion of resistance. There was no possibility whatever of playing off each of these rejections against the other; the only result would be the occupation, without a fight, of the free zone by the German Army.

On the morning of the 11th, General Bridoux, the Secretary of State for War, revoked all the orders given by General Verneau. The troops which were already on their way to their resistance area were returned to their barracks. A few measures sufficed to impose Vichy's authority beyond question. General Lafargue was relieved of his command. The gendarmes arrested Captain Quinche and some hundred men who were about to take off for the maquis. General de Lattre de Tassigny and three of his officers were also arrested. Everywhere else the armistice army allowed itself to be dispersed, giving up barracks and matériel without a struggle. Because it was so exceptional, mention is often made of the decision of Colonel Schlesser, commanding the Second Dragoons. He hid the regimental colors and ordered his officers to put on civilian clothes and to disappear into the surrounding countryside. They would soon be serving in the maquis, and the banner found its way to Algiers, where the regiment was re-established. Elsewhere a few rifle hammers were destroyed. That is absolutely all.

The hidden stocks of arms, on which so much care had been lavished, but which also served as an argument for so many in the "wait-and-see" brigade, finally found no useful employment. Scarcely anywhere did these arms find their way to the Resistance. The civilians who had agreed to provide hiding places were first of all left with no directives from the prefecture or the military authorities. Then they were told that the hidden arms must be inventoried and handed over. The Secretary of State for War formally forbade any illicit diversion of this matériel, and the bulk of French military equipment was indeed handed over to the German Army. It may be true that the belief was long cherished, in military circles, that Vichy would steer adroitly between a neutrality slightly tinged with a *pro forma* collaboration and the secret but energetic readying of a resumption of warfare. Now, however, the evidence was incontrovertible that only some of the most genuinely patriotic elements had seriously entertained the notion of ever re-entering the struggle. Vichy had never desired to abandon a neutrality that worked more or less in favor of Germany and was consistently hostile to the Allies.

Henceforth, the officers and noncoms who had belonged to the armistice army would have to make the decision that confronted every Frenchman after 1940. Each, on his own and totally alone, would have to find his way to active resistance. Only the officers of the special services and the Deuxième Bureau had no particular difficulty to overcome. They had always remained in contact with the British services, some had already worked with resistance movements, and their leaders left for Algiers the moment the Allies landed in North Africa.

From 1940 to 1942, the only important contact between resistance movements and military circles appears to have been the group that would soon produce the "Civilian and Military Organization." Jacques Arthuys, its leader, had been put in contact by the Deuxième Bureau with Heurteaux, a Colonel in the air arm and himself the Paris correspondent of the organization. This organization was a blend of underground and of police activity, which Colonel Groussard had tried to set up, with the aim of preparing to resume the struggle within the framework of the Vichy regime. They entered into contact with Touny, a cavalry colonel and the man who would succeed Arthuys at the head of the Civilian and Military Organization, and also approached Jean Mayer, Commandant of the reserve artillery, and Captain Rouzée of the cavalry. The first of these had already belonged, in the autumn of 1940, to a group of officers who collected information in the Departments of Normandy. The second provided perhaps the more important contact, since he presided over the "Réunion des Anciens de Saumur," and so was able to recruit innumerable agents among officers on active duty or in the reserves. In 1940 the Civilian and Military Organization, not yet known under that name, set itself up as a secret army headed by a General Staff provided with all the "bureaux" customary in every classical General Staff. But the contacts between the movement and military circles never developed. In October or November, 1940, General de la Laurentie, when sounded out by Rouzée, told him: "I hope for the victory of the English, and that is what we must work for." In September, General Riedinger took the place of Colonel Heurteaux. This was the sum total of the generals recruited by the Civilian and Military Organization, although it was, in social terms, the resistance movement closest to military milieux.

Nothing more was involved, until the end of 1942, than personal attitudes, individual commitments, deliberately adopted by officers who went against the general tide of opinion among the military. Obviously, those eager to fight at once, and unwilling to content themselves with preparing a fictitious resumption of the struggle by the Army as a whole, did their best to join Free France. Most of them had succeeded in this by 1940, or, at the latest, by 1941. They were undoubtedly in the minority. The Anglophobe propaganda of Vichy discouraged most of them. Of the 20,000 men in the Levant, only 2,000 chose to join the Free French when, hostilities having ceased, they were offered the choice of returning to France or getting back into the war. In France itself, only the dissolution of the armistice army provided all with the opportunity to make a definite return to combat.

The Army Resistance Organization was the instrument formed to channelize the Army's participation in the struggle. It was backed by the military leaders who had accepted the armistice but who considered it invalidated by the German occupation of the free zone. General Frère, the first head of this organization, had presided over the tribunal that had condemned General de Gaulle in 1940. He was arrested by the Germans and deported, and died while under arrest. These two stages of his existence sum up, in an almost symbolic fashion, the fatal dilemma in which most Army men had trapped themselves. His successor, General Verneau, had been the chief artisan of the secret preparations for a resumption of hostilities. After his undertaking collapsed on November 10, 1942, he continued to play his part clandestinely, and was the most active personage in setting up the Army Resistance Organization. His failure, inside the Vichy framework, and his undeniable achievements in the Resistance, cast a light both on the basic illusions and on the sincere hopes of the best elements in the resistance army. He too was arrested and died abroad. Only the third leader of the organization survived. This was Colonel Revers, with his aide, Colonel Zeller, both of whom would later become Chiefs of Staff of the Army.

The history of the Army Resistance Organization is basically that of its relations with the Resistance that was already functioning and had been at work for a long time. It had already had its sorrows, its successes, its leaders, its factional quarrels and its martyrs. Militarily, it already constituted a "secret army," brought about by the fusion of the Action branches, of the Libération, Combat and Franc Tireur movements, and it was headed by General Delestraint. For its part, the Front National had its armed organization, the Francs Tireurs and the Partisans. Everything put difficulties in the way of grouping the Army Resistance Organization with the others. Its members and their fellows in the other organizations had been kept apart by too many things: the inactivity of most officers between 1940 and 1942, the contempt of the Underground for the armistice army, the overlong subservience to Vichy shown by the greater part of the cadres, and the different habits of command and organization. Unvoiced political considerations also played a role. A very common notion among the officers of the Army Resistance Organization was, undoubtedly, that they should spearhead the resistance movements in order to put them out of commission the moment that liberation had been achieved, and above all to counter the extension of Communist influence and ward off "revolutionary excesses." In Normandy, for instance, Colonel Trutat spoke of this quite openly. His plan was to place officers at the head of most of the maquis groups and the networks active in the region, using as a pretext the argument of technical competence, and then to establish the unity of command on a territorial basis, to the advantage of the Army Resistance Organization.

To a certain extent he succeeded. But it can readily be imagined that almost everywhere the personal and psychological problems were the hardest to eliminate. Only combat, shoulder to shoulder, allowed recollections to fade and overcame the prejudices that divided the officers and the underground fighters of an earlier vintage. Besides, recruitment for the maquis had gone on spontaneously, without the combatants having any clear awareness of the background of their leaders. What counted was organization, supplies and armaments. There can be no doubt that the special services in London and Algiers favored the Secret Army and the Army Resistance Organization rather than the Francs Tireurs and Partisans. But these latter, on the other hand, owing to their dynamism and the aggressiveness of their cadres, found recruits more readily and took root in areas where, at the outset, the Communist Party had had no preponderant influence. This was true, for example, of the Massif Central and Brittany. There, too, the special factors that applied to underground and guerrilla activities weighed much more heavily than any political considerations. And little by little an over-all unification was effected at the topmost levels: the cavalry colonel Jussieu of the Combat movement took the place of General Delestraint at the head of the Secret Army, and later became Chief of Staff of the Comité d'Organisation Militaire et d'Action Clandestine—in which two members out of every three were Communists—from 1944 on. Their military adviser was the head of the Army Resistance Organization, the future General Revers.

But the participation of the former Army cadres in active resistance does not seem to have taken place on a large scale, despite the formation of the Army Resistance Organization after the armistice army had been dissolved. When, after the Liberation, the officers who had remained in France had to ask for reinstatement and give an account of their activities, 5,000 were definitively excluded. According to Pierre Dalloz, who had organized resistance in the Vercors, a region where many officers of the old Army were living, few of these officers felt much urgency about joining the maquis. "They had their habits," he wrote, "their apartments and families in town. Doubtless they sometimes lent a hand with training. But when some exploit had to be undertaken, our civilian camp leaders had to do as best they could on their own. This led to complaints and bitter criticism."

But all the officers who had taken part actively in the struggle found themselves in the Army that was organized anew after the Liberation. In this way they passed from the armistice army to the Army of the Fourth Republic, and so in their own persons testified to the continuity of the military organization and to the part played by the old-established Army in the struggle against the invader. They served as the amalgam bringing together all the segments of the Army. On the farther side of political vicissitudes, conflicts of conscience, psychological difficulties and moral crises, they were among those insuring the perennial existence of military society.

CHAPTER FIFTEEN

THE ARMY OF THE FOURTH REPUBLIC

✠

The enthusiasm of the crowds had ignited on the first day of the Liberation, in August, 1944. They came to celebrate the end of the occupation, to applaud the regiments that formed part of General de Lattre de Tassigny's First French Army and of General Leclerc's Second Armored Division.

Nineteen forty-five, the year of victory, was notable, among other things, for its many parades: June 18, after the armistice, July 14, November 11. The crowds, numerous at first but later somewhat wearied, discovered in the traditional setting of the Champs Elysées an Army whose uniforms were quite unfamiliar, since they had been heterogeneously derived from British and American models. There was a matériel to admire entirely of foreign manufacture; there were the initials of new units, new divisions and new weapons to ponder over.

These 1945 parades resembled but also differed from those which seventy-four years earlier had marched past Thiers and MacMahon on the Longchamps plain, after the disaster of 1870. Then, the people's ardor had gone out to an Army whose setbacks were lamented but which enjoyed universal gratitude and which, it was hoped, would carry out the *revanche*. Now, after the Second World War, enthusiasm was aroused by the rediscovery of liberty and the restoration

338

of peace in Europe, and gratefulness went to the troops whose victories had reassured the people, still haunted by memories of invasion and occupation. But the people were unable to assign any precise role to the Army.

After the defeat of 1870, and the loss of Alsace-Lorraine, the Army had provided a meeting ground for those of every political coloring and of every intellectual tendency. It was venerated as the shrine of national unity, respected as the symbol that promised a *revanche,* and cherished as the sole instrument that could shield the country from a new invasion. The prestige that surrounded it would last to the very end of the century. "France," Charles Maurras felt inspired to declare, "was monarchical, the Army was its queen."

But in 1945 the public mind occupied a position almost diametrically opposed to that of 1871. Laid waste by the invasion, the occupation and the combats of the Liberation, France had no thought of a new conflict and saw no need to prepare for one. In no circumstances could too large a part of the inadequate resources available be devoted to a military effort that seemed neither urgent nor even advisable. Not one of the political trends that shared public favor seemed to challenge the desirability of letting French military strength lie fallow. The authors of the Monnet Plan, who had been called together by the de Gaulle government, bluntly declared that there could be no question of reconstituting a powerful army before the preliminary step had been taken of endowing the country with a modern industrial potential. The following year, the same conclusions were reached by those who drew up the "Inventaire" of France's financial situation, in the report they submitted to Robert Schuman, Minister of Finances.

During the early years of the Fourth Republic there was a violent clash between the diverging conceptions of how military strength should be organized. The extreme Left maintained that everything should be built on the nucleus constituted by the cadres of the Forces Françaises de l'Intérieur. The old-line Right was interested above all in seeing to it that the officers' corps was purged with such strict moderation that its homogeneity remained intact, and in barring every level of the military hierarchy from invasion by Communist elements. For the Socialists, the main thing was to cut down the size of the Army as rapidly as possible, both with respect to those on active duty and the reservists. The government, for its part, was resolved to carry out a purge but anxious to avoid a total upheaval, and thus it tried to effect a synthesis between these conflicting aims. As long as the war went on, there had been a considerable measure of agreement as to the military objectives the country could reasonably set itself. But after the armistice, the political arm no longer knew what precise mission should be assigned to its military instrument. So all that could be done was to allow the General Staff to "dole out penury"—in the total absence of general directives or of any long-term line of conduct.

It might well be asked whether, transcending this hesitation about the military budget, armament programs and manpower problems, there was not a deeper reason to explain the sort of exasperated indifference with regard to the Army that characterized almost every nuance of public opinion. In 1940, for the first time in their history, the French had been confronted by the immediate menace of the country's utter annihilation; the very existence of France no longer seemed assured. Almost every social class was haunted by the feeling that the survival of the Nation might be challenged at any instant. In view of this basic insecurity, it seemed almost grotesque to maintain the existence of institutions that had formerly been looked on as exempt from criticism: compulsory military service, the famous military schools, the regiments with a glorious past, the arms factories once held in high esteem. Until 1948 or 1949 at least, public sentiment could only halfheartedly agree to support, at the least possible cost, a military apparatus in which all faith had been lost. Subsequently, the fighting in Indochina, and more particularly the cold war and the implications of the Atlantic Pact, modified the viewpoint of the French bourgeoisie—working-class opinion went a different road—but even so, all that was called for was a modest contribution to an international military effort whose main strength lay, as everyone admitted, neither in France nor in Europe but in the atomic arsenals of the American air arm.

Nevertheless, directly after the freeing of the national territory and the armistice of 1945, French governments and public opinion alike were most anxious to restore to France some measure at least of its international prestige. There could be no question of any official slighting of the Army's function vis-à-vis the Nation. A kind of cleavage took place that cut off semi-official opinion from official opinion. The former was well aware of the country's basic weakness, and of the modest military means that had been available since 1940, while after 1945 it proved barely possible to maintain even this level.

The latter, however, without distinction of political party, did all it could to stress the contribution made by troops in the various theaters of war, and was resolved to organize a new Army adapted to the new circumstances.

It was essential to pull together a military apparatus that had been scattered by the defeat and by the resumption of combat. Concretely, a very difficult amalgamation had to be brought about: that of the Free French forces and the African Army, of the Underground and the regular Army, of the cadres of the prewar hierarchy and those of the Forces Françaises de l'Intérieur. The history of the Army from the Liberation to the war in Indochina is, fundamentally, the history of this attempted synthesis.

Everything, it would seem, made it certain that the Free French forces would have the dominant role in the new French Army. Strong in the prestige derived from their radical opposition to Vichy, they could march boldly ahead of the cadres that emerged from the Underground and the Resistance Movements. Having fought for a full two years before the African Army began to do so, they were at least its equal in military efficiency, and their war experience could boast such glorious names as Bir-Hakeim, Kufra and Massawa. Thus they could serve as the catalyst for the composite groups that would make up the Army of the future.

The Free French had lived through a unique epic and, as a result, acquired a mentality all their own. General de Gaulle sought to define it: "A liking for risk and adventure so developed that it constituted an aesthetic, a contempt for those who remained spineless or indifferent, a tendency to melancholy and, consequently, to quarrelsomeness in periods exempt from danger, to be replaced in action by an ardent cohesion, a national pride pushed to a paroxysm by the misfortunes of the fatherland and by contact with well-equipped Allies, and, above all else, a supreme confidence in the strength and the wiles of their own conspiracy."

Two emotions outweighed all others: the consciousness that they had dared to break with the traditional subservience toward the state and the official Army, and the passionate desire to prove to the entire world that their country could not simply be equated with the defeat of 1940. This was reinforced by the sources of Free French manpower. As we have seen, the number of general officers who went over to the Free French prior to 1942 can be counted on the fingers of one hand. To which a former member of the Free French naval forces added: "As for the Admirals, one need but raise one finger. There was one out of fifty—Muselier."

Most of the others were young officers, for the most part little known before the war. One month after the appeal of June 18, the Free French comprised 7000 men. After the Syrian campaign they numbered two light infantry divisions, or some 12,000 in all. One year later, Free France counted 70,000 soldiers. Its Navy numbered 3600, but already had to lament more than 700 dead in combat and more than 1000 lost at sea on merchant vessels. Many men had gone through extraordinary adventures in order to enlist with the Free French. Some crossed the Pyrenees on foot, others made their way across part of Africa—like the former head of the Deuxième Bureau, Lieutenant Colonel Génin, who set out from Algiers to take part in the Eritrean campaign and was killed in Syria. This zeal found its counterpart in the heavy losses experienced in combat. Out of 211 men placed at the head of sections or platoons, 52 were killed. After four years in the field, the First Free French Division had captured 100,000 prisoners.

Contacts between the Free French forces and the African Army were difficult and even tumultuous, as can readily be grasped. The latter, embittered by two years of waiting, and disturbed by the renown that had been won during this interval by those who had fought at Bir-Hakeim, tended to pick a bone with the Free French concerning the rapid promotions conferred on their officers, and their general indifference to certain traditional forms of discipline, also the purges that were effected. Nevertheless, the resumption of combat by the forces in North Africa was so important a step on the way to liberating the national territory, that the sense of battles to be fought and victories to be won speeded up the amalgamation. Time would serve to heal many a wound and consign to oblivion the appalling clashes of 1940 and 1942. Those who had fought on opposite sides in the Syrian campaign, found themselves brothers in arms in Tunisia and Italy, and on the Rhone, the Rhine and the Danube.

Soon the Army as a whole, including the elements the least well-disposed toward de Gaulle, lost all desire to challenge the authority vested in such Free French officers as Leclerc, Larminat and Koenig, or General Vallin in aviation. Death alone, it may be presumed, prevented men of the caliber of Ornano or Brosset, who headed the First Free French Division, from playing a similar role. The subsequent career of a number of Free French officers shows that there was little difficulty in incorporating them in the traditional Army. General Vallin became Chief of Staff for Aviation. Leclerc was the first Commandant of the French Expeditionary Force in the Far East. Koenig was the second French High Commissioner in Germany. Dodelier was one of the private Chiefs of Staff of the President of the Republic. Jacquier became head of the Special Services. And among those who left the Army there was Pierre de Chevigné, who became Secretary of State for War under the Fourth Republic. In their hearts all officers, whether Gaullist or not, had come from the same social background and were happy to find themselves once more in the same military family, now that the Vichy regime had been liquidated and the final victory won.

With the Navy, the situation was different. No naval battle took place that could be considered analogous to the Italian Campaign and the Liberation of France, and which would have served to blot out the memory of the rupture of 1940. Nothing had occurred to make men forget that the overwhelming majority of the Navy's cadres had to the very end refused to make any use of their vessels, and that the naval officers had been the greatest beneficiaries of the Vichy regime, many of them having found their way into the Ministries, Prefectures and even police stations. At Dakar, in 1940, they had acted most vigorously in combating the English fleet and the Gaullist expeditionary corps. In 1941, after the Syrian Campaign, they had preferred internment in Turkey to a resumption of the struggle. In 1942, in Casablanca, they had been practically alone in putting up an energetic resistance to the American landing. In Bizerte, they had passively abandoned thirteen vessels to the Germans. In Toulon, they preferred to scuttle the squadron rather than join the French forces in Africa, which had already taken up arms again. Only after this last episode did the squadron that had been interned in Alexandria since 1940, and which had never had any desire to resume the struggle, at last consent to take a hand.

In such circumstances, the amalgamation of the Free French naval forces and the Navy that had remained unswervingly subservient to Vichy could not be effected without unpleasantness. The purge descended much more harshly on the Admirals than on the Generals. For years to come, the atmosphere of the Navy's wardrooms would remain painful. The destruction of the greater part of the fleet blocked promotion, and resentment had countless opportunities to express itself. The former Commander of the Free French Naval Forces did refuse to become the Navy's Chief of Staff, so as to make amalgamation easier. But with this sole exception the principal commands were reserved for veterans of Free France, such as Admirals Cabanier and Querville. Most officers had no prospect of rising higher than the rank of Lieutenant Commander, Commander or Captain. With the rarest exceptions, those who had not joined up with the Free French had no opportunity to make up for lost time.

In the Army, on the other hand, many officers who had seriously compromised themselves under Vichy were able to redeem themselves by their conduct in the campaigns of Italy and of France. The period of purges in North Africa was short, and limited to the highest ranks. The military cadres went over *en bloc* from one regime to the other and, their prestige heightened by the victories gained in the final campaigns of the war, came to constitute the bulk of the officers' corps. Sheer weight of numbers made it certain that they would play a far more important part in the Army than the Free French officers. An additional factor lay in the purging carried out among the officers who had remained in France and, later, in the practical application of the measures baptized "dégagement des cadres."

From 1945 until the time when the Indochinese War had its gravest consequences, the African Army made up the central core of the French Army and, in the main, constituted its cadres. The officers combined the prestige of victorious engagements, an experience of modern warfare, and a consciousness of military continuity that had been maintained from the beginning to the end of the conflict. In the history of the Army, it was an immensely important stage. The cadres of the North African regiments and of the colonial troops brought with them the spirit that had been theirs before 1939, perhaps even before 1914. Overseas, the military hierarchy had always felt much freer in its movements than in metropolitan France. Subordination to the civilian authorities, and the strict application of governmental directives, had never been practiced with the same rigor in Morocco, Senegal and Madagascar as in Paris, Metz or Strasbourg. Even the military leaders the most sincerely respectful of the state had always allowed themselves a certain latitude in their interpretation of orders. Everything led them to this: the ignorance that reigned in Paris with regard to the real conditions to be found in distant colonies, the difficulty of communications, and the interplay of military operations and political measures. Lyautey had often presented the governments with a *fait accompli*. Gallieni had anticipated the instructions of his Minister when he deprived the Queen of Madagascar of her throne. There was often no line of demarcation between military and administrative authority, and the responsibilities of the officers sometimes included the actual management of civil, economic or judicial matters, in the sectors under their control. All this had fostered a tradition and a spirit among the colonial troops and the North African regiments that was unknown among the regiments of metropolitan France

Despite the collapse of 1940 the French Army seemed to have maintained its authority intact in North Africa, or even strengthened it. The Vichy regime carefully preserved the appearances of military prestige. Its ideology blended in only too well with the political aspirations of the officers' corps. It echoed the unvoiced dreams of order, discipline and moral dictatorship cherished for a long time past by a military hierarchy temperamentally at odds with the liberties of the parliamentary regime, shocked by its impotence and embittered by its own material diminishment since 1918. The African Army was to pass on *in toto* to the postwar Army, the reactionary ideology adopted by the Vichy regime. For the African Army there was no break between the 1940–1942 period and the years that followed the return to the fight.

But there was also no moral concord between this Army and the country it helped to set free in the summer of 1944. The people were induced to overlook this latent cleavage in the joy of Liberation, in their renewed enthusiasm over an Army at last victorious, and in their pride at seeing important contingents of French troops among the powerful Allied forces. Nevertheless, an unbroken chain connected the Army that had been tempted by clandestine political activity at the time of the Popular Front, the armistice army and that of the Vichy regime, and the Army that had helped to free the homeland. In another few years, after the crosscurrents set up by the war had been eliminated, this would become plain.

The fundamental crisis had been covered over by the apparent amalgamation of all the French forces that had had a share in the war, whether from 1940 or from 1942, whether overseas, in a clandestine fashion or in the Underground. But in due time this crisis would reveal itself as more deep-seated than ever. The aftermath of the war revealed, indeed, that the causes were what they had always been, but they were mightily exacerbated by the political consequences of the occupation and the Liberation.

In 1944 communism was not merely, as it had been in 1936, one element in a parliamentary majority, and a magnet that attracted a large segment of the working class. Now it emerged as the party that had been most active in the Resistance, and the only one to have maintained the totality of its cadres unbroken. It had found a foothold in the government and made its way to the highest echelons of the Civil Service. It had won control over the great trade unions and seemed even to have acquired a footing in social groups and in regions from which hitherto it had been excluded. Moreover, the ideology of the Fourth Republic, liberal, yet impregnated with a certain kind of socialism, democratic, and suspicious of the traditional hierarchies that had compromised themselves under Vichy, was at the opposite pole from the authoritarian, conservative mentality of the officers' corp, which reigned more absolutely in the African Army than in any other part of the old Army. No understanding could easily be achieved between the cadres of the colonial troops and North African regiments and liberated France. The wounds left by the conflict between Vichy and Free France had not healed over before a new problem raised its head: that of merging into one body the regular Army and the Forces Françaises de l'Intérieur.

The collapse of the armistice army, after the occupation of the free zone in November, 1942, had not induced the professional army officers to move over in any great numbers to the Resistance and the Underground. Here was, perhaps, a great but wasted opportunity which might have placed at the side of the internal Resistance a considerable portion of the military hierarchy, just as the African Army found itself associated with the Free French. "One would have liked to see the Army, as its role required," wrote Colonel de Virieu, the former head of the Army's historical branch, "make a careful study of these procedures and codify them, so that clandestine training might have been effectively carried out. . . . But the Army lost the match, since it did not choose to step outside its normal functions, for the duration and only for the duration of these exceptional circumstances."

The majority of the cadres of the Forces Françaises de l'Intérieur were made up of civilians, who had enlisted with the simple desire to free the country. Now that the war was over, would these men not return to their normal occupations? Could it not be assumed that the fighters of the Underground, for whom patriotism and warlike activity had for a moment clasped hands, had no military vocation and felt themselves by temperament unfit to be career officers? If any attempt had been made to offer material advantages to those who might have been willing to enter the Army on a long-term footing, it is highly unlikely that many would have chosen to do so.

Nevertheless, in the summer of 1944, the Forces Françaises de l'Intérieur existed. It was to be expected that they would be used in the war effort until the enemy had been completely defeated, and particularly until the positions the enemy occupied on the national territory had been liquidated. The decision was taken to use the F.F.I. as a new army under the command of General de Larminat, against the Atlantic ports, which were held by the German Army. General de Larminat had been with the Free French, and had come into violent conflict with General Juin in 1943, when they shared the direction of the Army's General Staff. Since he was regarded as exceptionally intransigent with regard to any elements that had been associated with Vichy, he could not fail to be well-disposed toward the Forces Françaises de l'Intérieur from which his army would be derived. This body, however, which, with little in the way of equipment to help it, had had to fight unrewarding but very tough battles against German pockets of resistance, was demobilized almost to the last man after the war had ended.

The similar experiment undertaken by General de Lattre de Tassigny was much more considerable. De Lattre was passionately convinced that the injection into his army of the new blood represented by the F.F.I. could be of enormous value. He was fascinated by the adventurous and nonconformist but dynamic and youthful aspects of underground warfare. He had, too, absolutely no respect for the traditional forms of military bureaucracy. Of all the officers of the old Army, he was best fitted to bring about the fusion of the F.F.I. with the regular Army. He was entrusted with this task. The First French Army under his command comprised 250,000 men, at the moment of the Allied landing. He incorporated 137,000 men of the F.F.I. into it. Quite apart from the additional strength that this represented, de Lattre looked on the operation as a fascinating psychological problem. "Nothing more colorful and more ardent can be imagined," he wrote, "than the long, exciting effort to get a grip on this force, vibrating and tumultuous, without deforming it so that— though backed by puny resources—it might be induced to transcend itself without being annihilated. It was a struggle. A struggle against the routine outlook, against prejudice and intransigence. A struggle against indigence, anarchy and the easy way out. And it was a victory —perhaps no other has given me greater joy, because it was a victory for the spirit of synthesis and for French brotherliness."

The remarkable poverty of the French Army in 1944 and 1945 did, in actual fact, make it impossible to equip more numerous forces. There was assuredly a touch of demagogy in asking the government, as was done by certain groups that formerly had shown little interest in military problems, to decree the *levée en masse* of several classes. In a country whose industrial production had fallen to forty per cent of the prewar level, and without a single arsenal capable of manufacturing heavy armaments, with an almost total paralysis of communications and transport, so that of 18,000 locomotives only 4,000 remained in running order, it was futile to think of equipping a large army only a few months after victory had been achieved. These factors alone would have imposed a strict limitation of the number of men coming from the F.F.I. who could have been incorporated in the regular Army. The only successful example of amalgamation, that effected by de Lattre de Tassigny in the First Army, showed what difficulties had to be surmounted integrating 137,000 men. General de Gaulle has described this *tour de force,* and the strength acquired by de Lattre's army through this additional manpower. "De Lattre," he wrote, "playing skilfully with the reserves of matériel allocated in advance to his army, split up the contents among new elements. Finally, the ingenuity displayed at every level, whether in obtaining from American stores a little new matériel to replace machines declared to be beyond repair, in repairing these and then lining them up beside the replacements, or in taking over, with no concern for formal ownership, all the Allied armor, guns or vehicles that happened to be within reach of our soldiers, made certain supplies available. . . ."

But such practices, justified by the First French Army's enthusiasm for combat, could not alter the fundamental situation. Matériel obtained from the American Army alone could not enable the French fighting forces to be increased in strength.

If it is true that absolute necessity explains the very strict selection of the elements of the Forces Françaises de l'Intérieur incorporated into the Army, it is also true that the General Staffs looked on the practice as a kind of scandal and even a danger. The sort of training and instruction that filled the fighters of the Underground with pride appeared altogether inadequate to those who had been trained at Saint-Cyr, to the professional noncoms and to the generals of the old Army. The anarchical form of their incorporation was yet another reason to distrust them, in the eyes of the traditionalists. But no one could deny that the fighting spirit of the best-trained F.F.I. formations amply compensated for their lack of formal training. If they had been amalgamated with the regular troops, they would have had no difficulty in attaining the military proficiency of the other soldiers.

It was political reasons that outweighed all others in arousing the distrust of the General Staffs. The General Staff of National Defense, under General Juin, and that of the Army, which was headed by General Leyer, deliberately availed themselves of the distinctions between the Underground of the "Secret Army," the Army Resistance Organization and the Francs Tireurs and Partisans. The last-named, which formed the military arm of the National Front, were like the parent organization under Communist direction. Charles Tillon was their Commander and Professor Marcel Prenant their Chief of Staff. In actual practice, the members of the Francs Tireurs and Partisans were not recruited on the basis of ideological or political affiliation. Its members had joined them rather than other bodies for reasons of practical convenience: they were closer to their homes, or better armed, or better provisioned. But the General Staffs, fearing Communist infiltration, opposed their incorporation into the Army either as individuals or as a group. This ban extended even to the domain of honorific rewards, medals being very sparsely distributed among the former members of the Francs Tireurs and Partisans, while the fighters of the "Secret Army," with a different background in the Resistance, were treated with much greater liberality. It was the members of the Army Resistance Organization, coming from the Armistice Army, who received preference in the amalgamation of the F.F.I. with the regular Army.

The General Staffs saw to it that there should be no profound alteration, either social or moral, in the officers' corps. In this they were guided entirely by political reasons. They had, moreover, governmental backing, since the government, anxious to re-establish its authority over the entire national territory, made haste to discharge the "patriotic ministers" who had themselves emerged from the Underground. The surest guarantee of this appeared to be the presence of the regular Army in the zones where the power of the state seemed weakest. Thus a regiment of Zouaves was sent to the Bordeaux region, under the pretext of besieging Royan, still in German hands, but the real intention was to impress the population of the departments where the Underground still wielded a goodly share of authority. Similarly, a regiment of Spahis was posted between Toulouse and the Spanish frontier, where the Underground groups contained large numbers of Spanish Republicans. Even before the government had reached the least decision as to the future organization of the Army and its mission, it moved to utilize the Army to strengthen the internal authority of the state. The re-establishment of the central authority was, no doubt, of sufficient importance to justify such decisions fully, but, as things turned out, these measures were equally intended to check the more or less real danger of "Communist subversion."

The General Staffs successfully opposed any attempt to effectuate a renewal of the cadres, but they could not prevent the officers' corps from being subjected to a purge. They did what they could to limit this. In fact, the seeking out and expulsion of the men who had most seriously compromised themselves with the Vichy regime was always undertaken at the initiative of the ministers, never of the General Staffs. The number of victims of the purge in the Army amounted to 4000, a relatively important figure. Yet the most resolute partisans of severe sanctions against unworthy officers had to admit, later, that the purge had not truly changed the outlook of the military cadres. In the professional Army it was regarded as a kind of offensive launched from without and against which it was fitting to put up a last-ditch defense, the purgers having the status of enemies. One of them commented on the matter in the periodical *Esprit*:

> From the very outset, the purge was vitiated by two facts. The first was the humiliating obligation imposed on the officers who had remained in France to ask for reinstatement. Thus *a priori* they were looked on as guilty, while a prejudice in their favor would have been the only position that would not have wounded them. The second fact was the absence, in the Army itself, of the state of mind that would have favored a just purge. Yet it was normal that a place should be found for those who, with what means were available, had answered the summons issued by the cadres of the Resistance . . . A deep wound was caused. It has had no chance to heal since; among the officers who have been retained in the cadres, there is a group of outcasts, who are aware of their status.

Thus, we can discern the silhouette of the officers' corps as it was at the beginning of 1946. The additions coming from the Resistance were small, or entirely negligible. In almost every case, it had to be a man with a real vocation for the soldier's life, who would have joined the Army in any event, and whose sole preoccupation was to become one with the reigning outlook. The officers of Free France had no trouble in merging themselves in the whole, because they were very few in number and because, during the fighting, they had won the esteem of their comrades of the African and French Armies and now enjoyed the esteem of their fellow officers. Soon the return of the imprisoned officers and the arrival of young second lieutenants or lieutenants who scarcely had had to face the dilemma of Vichy and Free France, would rapidly help to diminish the poignancy of the conflicts inherited from the occupation and the war. The Army would rediscover a certain unity, thanks to the pride felt in the final victories that had been won, and in the new adaptations to modern conditions of warfare. No doubt, the "Grands Chefs" were surrounded by their own coterie, their private clan or even their clientele. But already, for the greater number of officers, and especially for the younger men and those lower in rank, all this was rather a matter for pleasantry than a source of conflict.

The consolidation of the Fourth Republic and the collapse, along with Vichy, of the whole authoritarian, antidemocratic, "Fascist" ideology, could lead to the disappearance of the remote causes of the political crisis that had not ceased to stir the Army since 1936. All would depend on the nature of the new regime and on its military policy. The consequences of the occupation had left so deep a mark on the officers' corps that the main concern was to close over the wounds, forget the conflicts, become one with the Nation and participate, in an appropriate fashion, in the reconstruction of the country. Yet, in spite of this, it was to take only a dozen years to set almost the entire Army against the Fourth Republic and propel it into political activity in rebellion against its own traditions of silence and political neutrality.

The history of this development would be inexplicable, if it were not first of all the history of a grave material decline. Everything began, in 1946, with the question of credits. The previous year it had been necessary to limit severely the civilian side of the budget, since raw material and industrial equipment were not available. There were, however, heavy military expenditures required for the continuation of the war and for demobilization. Thus, out of a budget of 390 billion francs, 173 billion was earmarked for military goals. But the government expected to take in only 154 billion francs. Clearly, any political leader would consider it essential to make drastic reductions on the military side.

A reduction of twenty per cent in the credits for national defense, passed by the Constituent Assembly, had very nearly provoked the resignation of General de Gaulle several days before. The Assembly agreed to reconsider its vote only in exchange for the promise that a bill dealing with the military organization of the country would be introduced that same year. As it turned out, no such bill eventualized and the credits were exceeded. The government that took over from General de Gaulle, under the leadership of Félix Gouin, tried to satisfy the general expectations of the political parties and meet the urgent need of budgetary equilibrium by endeavoring to reduce the military credits. It hit upon the worst possible device, a "dégagement des cadres" (the discharge of commissioned and non-commissioned officers).

The war had certainly left far too large a number of officers on active duty in comparison with the number of men in the ranks, inevitably far fewer than before the war. But this "dégagement des cadres" was in direct conflict with the fundamental terms under which officers had been commissioned. They felt that the State had gone back on its word, that it was depriving them of all security and disposing arbitrarily, not only of their lives, but also of their careers. It was a serious matter for officers for whom the Army was a genuine vocation, but it was even worse for noncoms, totally unprepared for a premature return to civilian life. The governmental measure prescribed that, in return for receiving a rather high percentage of their pay through the following ten years, 45 per cent of the officers and 40 per cent of the noncoms should leave the Army. The Army command itself was to take charge of the operation, applying the principles of age and professional competence.

For the Army, it was a dreadful moment. Each man's future could depend on the judgment of superiors who, in many cases, knew their subordinates none too well. Unavoidably, the divergencies of the occupation years played their part, also personal recommendations and political pull. In certain formations, the law was applied simply by drastically lowering the age of retirement. Elsewhere, those who wished to be excluded were asked to volunteer. The story is told of one Général Inspecteur d'Armes who entered his own name as the first of those to be separated from the Army. This state of affairs threatened to reduce the officers' corps to anarchy, and the noncoms to despair. The military cadres were to retain a lasting rancor against a state which had behaved like an enemy, and even against the high command which, in order to save what could be saved, had fallen in with the government's plans.

Catastrophic in its immediate effect, this "dégagement des cadres" was no less catastrophic in the long run. What it actually demonstrated was the powerlessness of successive governments to resolve the post-war military problem by tackling it as a whole. Only a few years later, the operations in Indochina were going to siphon off to the Far East a huge proportion of the available officers and noncoms. This brought about a shortage in the cadres left in metropolitan France, with a resultant decline, for years to come, in the value of the training given the conscripted contingents. It rapidly became almost impossible to recruit noncommissioned officers. Their average level of competence fell lower than ever before. Thousands of men who were earning a living in civilian life continued to receive a substantial part of their pay, and this at a time when the budget called for significant sacrifices. But the major victim of the "dégagement des cadres" was, perhaps, the quality average of the officers' corps. Just as after the First World War, those who chose to leave were often the men intellectually best fitted for technological employment, or for business or administrative functions. They were, in a word, frequently the best. This led to a grave weakening of the military cadres. Two figures speak eloquently of this: of the graduates of Saint-Cyr and Polytechnique, respectively 53 per cent and 65 per cent dropped out of the Army.

The average intellectual level of the Army cadres was declining at the very time the problems raised by modern warfare required a steady raising of this level. This development was to have incalculable consequences. It would strengthen the ascendancy enjoyed, in the Army, by small groups of officers, both in the higher and the lower ranks, who had acquired a general culture and a breadth of intellectual experience denied the bulk of their comrades, whose origins were more modest and whose training was more rudimentary. Without this thoroughgoing transformation in the make-up of the Army cadres, it would be impossible to explain the events of May 13, 1958, in Algeria and those that followed.

In 1947, while the cadres were being subjected to a painful winnowing, officers' salaries were equated with those of civil servants. A second lieutenant, after several years of service, had the index number 250, while an *"agent principal"* of the third class in Posts and Telegraphs had 382 and a surrogate judge had 310. A lieutenant colonel, after twenty-four years of service, had the index number 500, while a director of the second class in the customs had 600. Between 1900 and 1950, a captain's pay, stated in gold francs, sank from 161 to 95 francs. The awareness of this devaluation was made even more acute by contrast with the pay of officers in foreign armies. After the Atlantic Pact had brought together the Armies of the countries in the coalition, this became an easy comparison to make. In 1953 a Commandant (Major) in the French Army received 95,000 francs a month instead of the 120,000 he would have received in the British Army, 220,000 in the Russian and 280,000 in the American. This poverty might have been made more bearable by the existence of a stable family setting, which would have enabled the Army to derive some benefit from economic prosperity. But, from 1947 on, the French Army led a "nomadic" existence without parallel in all its history. There was one fortunate period, when the occupation of Germany provided a considerable part of the Army with comfortable surroundings, substantial allowances and good living quarters. But this did not last long, and soon the joys of occupation were restricted to a small number.

For the French Army, to live like nomads was almost a complete novelty. Before the war, only the colonial troops had to change garrisons frequently. But under the Fourth Republic the whole officers' corps lived in a state of permanent deportation. Many officers, after fighting in two or three campaigns between 1940 and 1945, spent some time in Germany and then spent two or three periods of twenty-seven months in Indochina, separated by training periods at the staff college or in schools of instruction, only to find themselves in Algeria from 1956 on. It has been calculated that, on the average, these officers between 1947 and 1959 spent eighty-eight months out of 144 outside France and apart from their families. The consequences can readily be grasped: constant moving, ceaseless interruptions in the children's schooling, lengthy separations and more and more frequent divorces. An officer remarked in 1957 that, for himself and his comrades, "there would have been no social crisis in the Army if we had found proper housing." That same year, an investigation published by the periodical *Réalités* reached the conclusion that another 52,000 apartments would have been needed to house the military cadres, and that twenty per cent of them lived in hotels.

This increasing poverty, amid the prosperity enjoyed by the country as a whole, constituted a grave source of division between the Army and the Nation. Such isolation had, for some officers, a certain romantic attraction. The echo can be found in the literature that would soon grow up around the war in Indochina. One of the heroes of Hubert Bassot's novel, *Les Silencieux,* admirably expresses this romanticism of a new kind:

> . . . I am not a bureaucrat; I do not make war from nine o'clock to twelve and in an office; I am not interested in paid holidays nor in family alllowances. I don't give a sh. . about the old age pension, since I'll certainly be killed before then . . . I'm not thinking of building a house in the suburbs or on the coast, and I have no garden to look after on week ends. I have neither the time nor the opportunity to enjoy all the advantages that have become my compatriots' sole aim in life. I have neither bitterness nor regrets . . . I passionately love my country and the profession that is mine. Perhaps it is the only and the last profession that lets me escape the nine o'clock to midday routine, the week ends and the automobile exhibitions . . .

But poverty imposes harsh constraints. Indigence would accentuate what had been set in motion after the war by pruning of the cadres and the general disinterest in military problems. In 1939, 2452 candidates presented themselves for Saint-Cyr and 762 were admitted. In 1951 there were only 587 candidates, of whom 334 were admitted. In 1954 the number of candidates had fallen to 360. The decline went on until 1956, when for the first time there was an increase. At this juncture one of the most characteristic signs of the Army's isolation, of the military clan's inbreeding, became clearly apparent. According to the Commission of Military Sociology, which questioned 10,000 officers who had attended Saint-Cyr, the sons of army men amounted to 30 per cent in 1937–1939, and to 44 per cent in 1954–1958. Of the 1956 graduates, 41 per cent were the sons of military men; of the 1958 class, 47 per cent. The increasing proportion of officers rising from the ranks or transferring from the reserves continued to lower the average social level of the army cadres. As the officers who had passed through the military schools became a small minority, those of bourgeois or aristocratic background became less numerous. Thus, in the Arme Blindée, the successor of the cavalry, favored by officers of noble origin, the number of officers whose names were preceded by the "de" sank between 1949 and 1958 from 38 to 32 per cent in the higher ranks, from 25 to 14.5 per cent among the captains, and from 16 to 6 per cent among the lieutenants.

No doubt, with the war's end a certain lack of interest in Army matters was inevitable. This was true of the entire country, and especially among the politicians, who tended to regard the usefulness of the military institutions as more and more dubious, the more the costs of upkeep rose. In the inflation that swept over France between 1944 and 1949, the military budget seemed the most likely place where indispensable economies could be effected.

But if the means available were necessarily limited, it was still possible to utilize them to the best advantage. In the short interval separating the Second World War from the war in Indochina, there was an opportunity to be grasped that might have been able to raise the Army to a level of unquestionable professional efficiency, though not to create a new spirit—this opportunity had been lost—or to give it a clearly defined mission—that would have to wait the cold war and the delineation of a colonial policy. Instead, all that marked this period was a serious setback.

One man's personality dominated the French Army at the time, that of General de Lattre de Tassigny. He held many a trump. He was one of the victors in warfare, and he belonged neither to the Free French minority nor to any of the groups most closely associated with Vichy. He was the only man who had succeeded in amalgamating the Forces Françaises de l'Intérieur with the regular army. His concern for the military prestige and his liking for military display found a response in the officers' corps. But his hatred of conformism, his detestation of routine and his contempt for the old military hierarchies also made him popular among civilians and even in circles of the Left and extreme Left, normally on their guard when the Army was involved. Perhaps even more unusual was the General's understanding of the press and his skill in utilizing it. He was by far the general best able to convince the Army that a radical transformation had to be put through and to persuade the country that it should aid in this transformation. Perhaps General de Lattre de Tassigny lost this battle as early as the spring of 1946, when the "dégagement des cadres" was decided on. For he lost thereby the confidence of many officers, who regarded with a like horror the government and the high command.

During the years of rigid budgetary restrictions that lay ahead, what should have been done was to build up an army of cadres. The path had been traced by the Reichswehr after 1919. If compulsory military service were to be regarded as indispensable, it would have to be short, because of lack of funds. So the problem was to provide the recruits with the most intense military training in the least possible time. Yet no important revision was undertaken either in recruiting practices or in the allotment of manpower. As one contingent after another was called up, beginning in 1946, no rational use was made of them.

General de Lattre de Tassigny had decided to set a new and modern stamp on the whole of military service. The principles that inspired him were unquestionably excellent in themselves: physical as well as military instruction, a liking for cleanliness and hygiene, and a rejuvenation of minds as well as of cadres. Yet the results fell far short of the excellence of his ideas. An exaggerated importance was attributed, in the programs, to the handling of arms, to gymnastics, to the upkeep of belts, gaiters and accessories. That would not have mattered, if there had been a long period of service. But for these contingents who were to spend only one year in the Army, the result was an over-all reduction in training and military instruction, and in the study of armaments and maneuver. Dangerous for the common soldiers, this system was disastrous for the corporals and sergeants. Physical presence and even the tone of voice finally came to count for more than technical and military proficiency. It may be said that, in several successive classes, the training received by the noncoms of the reserves was practically zero.

Considerable irritation and even fury was felt, in the officers' corps as a whole, to see every methodical plan of training and instruction sacrificed to mere appearance, in accord with a system in which paradoxes received more weight than genuinely new ideas. Reviews and inspections were made much more frequent, the hours spent in arranging for parades were greatly increased, and the officers were urged to develop themselves physically. This last was certainly useful in itself, but took away too much time from the officers' duties, and it must be admitted that General de Lattre de Tassigny made it impossible for a majority of the cadres to undertake the desirable and necessary rejuvenation of military methods. Just as he paid no attention to the need for intensive training during the brief period of service, so his plan to replace the old uncomfortable barracks by light camps open to nature and adapted for modern training had the drawback of being very expensive without being entirely indispensable. When the General was eased out of the post of the Army's Chief of Staff, budgetary exigencies at once asserted their predominance, and the few projects that had been undertaken were eliminated.

Because the modernization of methods of training had been ill conceived and unwisely applied, the impatience to return to the old-established customs, even when they were the least justified, gained the upper hand. The high command failed to realize that the Army, after the turmoils of war, had need of calm, rigor and method, and of clear and simple decisions, so that a normal, regular pattern might be re-established. Only in these conditions could the Army profitably absorb a thoroughgoing modernization of its institutions and regulations. In the eyes of most officers, the high command had discredited the best-inspired of the new ideas. The adversaries of innovation came to suspect any innovation whatsoever and to look back with a pointless and uncalled for nostalgia to the past. In his reply to a large-scale investigation of the Army undertaken in 1950 by *Esprit*, a periodical of a leftist tinge run by Catholics, a Saint-Cyr inspector wrote:

What are the future officers taught? Mathematics, history, mechanics, armaments. What about Man? The issue is scarcely raised. One might think that nothing had taken place since 1939. Neither the Chantiers de la Jeunesse, nor the Underground, where we learned so much about command and the exercise of command. Moreover, the problem of the Resistance, and the reasons that led us to step outside the directives coming from "the oldest, in the highest rank," are carefully disguised, with the pretext that it is not advisable to teach young officers that military discipline sometimes has its limits. And yet who can predict that, the next time also, there may not be the obligation to make a choice? In a word, I very much fear that the pupils leaving our hands will indeed be pupils, and nothing more! . . . I believe that there must be bold innovations, that the problem must be entirely reconsidered, and the admission made that the essential factors have changed. . . . In other terms, instead of "remodeling Saint-Cyr," what is required is to "create the modern school in which the officers of the modern French Army would receive their training." . . . I have known a day when such things occurred. But the latest classes to be graduated put an end to that, and it is they who have seen to it that the school became Saint-Cyr once again. . . . All that counted for these brainless lads was the return to the plumed helmet and the red trousers. . . . The Ecole Militaire Interarmes has become the Ecole Spéciale Militaire Interarmes, and on July 14 we will see its men file past in the uniform of our grandfathers. Always in the van of progress, as you can see! I am struck by the attention paid by the pupils to a past of which they themselves have had no experience, and by their fear lest the Army go in for "scouting," as they put it, and by the enthusiasm with which they welcome such trivial regulations as the requirement that officers wear the kepi. Well, they're young and like their rattles. . . . It is to be expected that they should arrive at the school with the desire to become Saint-Cyr men, but it is our task to convert them to the officer's vocation.

No more significant document could be cited. It was remarkable that an officer, clearly interested in innovation, should fail to see that, when these pupils arrived, they were eager to learn the modern forms of warfare and were also anxious that their future profession should maintain a certain standing in society. He failed to see that they could regard as irritating or even ridiculous an excessive addiction to gymnastics, corrective or otherwise, the perpetual lengthening of the combatant's obstacle course ("parcours du combattant"), the time spent in whitening belts and gaiters, the increase in the hours devoted to handling weapons, the whole system of instruction applied during General de Lattre de Tassigny's period of authority, which had indeed a "boy scout" atmosphere. Nor was the Inspector aware that his pupils, who had no desire to appear "poor" in a country under reconstruction, experienced an entirely normal exasperation at having to don an endless variety of graceless uniforms, the surplus stocks of every Army in the world. One military critic remarked at that time that the French Army was attired in "harlequin fashion." The Inspector was wrong, also, in thinking that the young second lieutenants in his charge would continue to neglect the morale and psychology whose absence from their programs he regretted. His condemnation of these programs as antiquated was fully deserved; a few years later all the students at Saint-Cyr would be taken to see factories, mines and research centers, and would attend courses in sociology and psychology.

But these young officers did not wait until the program of studies was reformed. More promptly than their former instructors expected, they discovered psychology and its applications, sociology and its laws, and the moral or national exigencies that must sometimes be allowed to outrank "the appearances of a pseudo-discipline." But they would make these discoveries on their own, and on the base of no genuine historical or economic culture. And these discoveries would be put at the service of the passions aroused in these young men by their experiences in Indochina and Algeria.

For a period of two or three years, the French Army felt that it no longer had a mission. Then, in 1948–1949 there was a return to a healthy position from the Army's point of view. The Brussels Pact, signed by France, Great Britain, Holland and Luxemburg, and then the Atlantic Pact, which embraced and went beyond its predecessor, would for a long time determine the destiny and destination of the military arm. At last the enemy could be named. The enemy was the Soviet Union, and also international communism. What a long-awaited victory for the officers who had belonged to the anti-Communist networks in the days of the Popular Front! Then their enemy had not been named the enemy of France, but now it was. The satisfaction of the great majority of officers was heightened by the fact that they saw in the Atlantic Pact and anticommunism the "posthumous" justification, on a universal scale, of their rupture with the suffering France of the Resistance. Their distrust had shown itself to be justified, since now the anticommunism which they had seen everywhere was being denounced as the major peril by the government and the new Allies, by the whole of Western policy.

It was indeed a kind of revenge taken by the Army on a state that had neglected, underpaid and humiliated it. It would be completed when, in June, 1950, René Pleven, the head of the new government, would announce an additional 80 billion in credits for national defense, after the Korean War had broken out. But the General Staffs had already begun to draw the consequences of the new foreign and military policies of the country. The very few officers suspected of sympathy for the extreme Left were separated from the Army or sent for good and all to a supply depot in Versailles. An alleged espionage affair, based on newspaper clippings, led to accusations against Captain Azéma, an officer stationed in Tarbes, in 1945. Use was made of this to launch a propaganda campaign that sought to identify the French Communist Party with a vast undertaking in the service of the future enemy. In the fall of that same year, the wave of strikes gave the government the opportunity to associate the Army with its internal anti-Communist policy. Reservists were called up; troops were employed against the strikers, just as during the great workers' crises of the early years of the century. Simultaneously, the military journals described the enemy to be fought, and in all international difficulties denounced the Soviet Union and communism as responsible.

Thus the argument was directed against an adversary who could wear the traits of the Russian Army's "Slavic imperialism," of the people's democracies in eastern Europe, of the Communist Parties, of organized labor, and of the nationalist movements in Africa and Asia

—above all, in Indochina. The General Staff directed that all the maneuvers carried out by the regular army and by the reservists should take place "in a climate of insecurity." This meant that the instructors should explain that the enemy would find support in France, and even have his partisans—who, to put it bluntly, would be the French Communists. The basis of every maneuver from now on would be a conflict between two camps, one being an assailant coming from the east, whose initial superiority would ensure significant territorial gains and who would enter France. It need scarcely be said that this was known as the "red camp."

It can be imagined how well these new perspectives fitted in with the outlook of the vast majority of officers, especially of those who, from 1940 to 1942, had not fought against Germany and were laboring under a kind of unavowed contrition. Not only did Germany henceforth cease to be the designated enemy of the French Army; the actual results of the Second World War, so favorable to the Soviet Union, allowed open criticism of Allied policy—including Gaullist policy—vis-à-vis the "Soviet peril" to which they had paid no attention.

The new orientation of military policy, on the basis of the Atlantic Pact, was to subject certain officers to harrowing conflicts of conscience. For some, it meant an immediate rupture between the mission of the Army to which they belonged and their own philosophy, ideology and political sympathies. They were not at all numerous, but their resignation or isolation would no doubt deprive the Army of elements thoroughly aware of how the modern world had been transformed. The Army could have made use of them, after the Algerian affair began. Their spokesman, in the *enquête* conducted by *Esprit*, was Louis de Villefosse, formerly with the Free French naval forces:

> It is not in accord with the truth to maintain that, in the view of our leaders . . . our present Army is an instrument of national defense. It is an instrument for the defense of capitalism against communism, and thus an army of ideological warfare, an army of civil war. . . . The evident truth of this is clearly realized in the General Staffs, which coldly include it in their estimates. . . . Today we would have but a handful of divisions to oppose a hostile army. But there is nothing secret about the studies published by our strategists in the military journals, where they endeavor to evolve an over-all doctrine, should war come. These studies devote an increasing place to actions whose aim it is to break internal opposition; they work out its tactics and define its aims: shock troops and mopping-up operations, filing teams

and teams to gather information; organisms for propaganda and to check on private correspondence, etc . . .

Few, in the active Army, shared Louis de Villefosse's apprehensions. They may have been somewhat more numerous among the reserve officers. The departure of officers with left-wing tendencies, few though they certainly were, helped to reinforce the conservative if not reactionary trend—anti-Communist, in any case—and weakened the Jacobin tendency, with its radical and republican connections, that had always found support in Army circles. This would have its effect when the time came for the most politically minded of military spokesmen to spread among the public their principles and their views.

There was, no doubt, a considerable number who, in this new military orientation of the country, sought in vain the echo of earlier beliefs. It was patent that traditional patriotism failed to explain the reasons for and the objectives of the Atlantic Pact. There was no direct conflict between Soviet Russia and France, and the war against communism pointed both to an external and an internal enemy. It could indeed be regarded as a kind of international civil war whose episodes, as long as they remained "cold," would consist in the progress of each country not only in armaments and manpower, but also in electoral campaigns, strikes, ideological quarrels and the struggles of the *maquis* in Africa and Asia. Where could one find the simple, splendid appeal of the fatherland which, in other days, had justified everything and provided a reason for everything? There can be no doubt that, at the bottom of their hearts, many officers were genuinely distressed to see the old myth vanish, its ideal and corporeal presence replaced by an implacable ideological war, abstract and bloody, and with more traitors than enemies to be discovered, since partisans now confronted each other, and not patriots. The investigation carried out by *Esprit* also bore witness to the moral crisis, evoked in a letter from an officer:

It seems that the "soldier's trade" has to be entirely rethought, in the light of recent happenings. . . . What needs to be discovered is whether, as it has now become, it still contains any of the elements which had originally turned our steps in its direction. Once there was a "grandeur" about the military career that enabled one to accept the servitude with enthusiasm. What remains of this grandeur today? We are no longer "the lords of the earth," no one imagines that, and the crowds that formerly were aroused by a military march past, the impressive symbol of a nation's strength and armed force, in 1948 pay no more attention to its progress than to a more or less well-arranged circus spectacle. . . . The Army of the cheap lithographs is no more, and we feel some melancholy at the fact. . . . On the other hand, it seems clear enough that one cannot be a good soldier without a superiority complex, without being absolutely certain of oneself as the invincible soldier of a great nation whose views are always coherent and whose intentions are always honorable. . . . In the same domain of ideas, in the event of a war we are no longer at all certain that we shall have to defend strictly national interests. . . . Today it seems that the only reason for killing is on behalf of one's ideas. "He who is not for me is against me"—and no one can be made to understand that who is not already possessed by the faith.

These are the vain laments of an outdated nostalgia. The Army, almost unanimously, gladly threw itself into the opening created by the Atlantic Pact and the cold war. How could it fail to do so? There it once again found a "mission," that is, the precious possession without which an army is led to doubt its own existence. But it also had the pleasant surprise, on its way, of finding that the too-long-awaited shift in public sentiment had occurred. It was in the years immediately following the war that one came upon the roots of the evolution that reached a decisive point in 1949 with the Atlantic Pact, and moved ahead at an accelerated pace after June, 1950, with the beginning of the Korean War. Public feeling did indeed seem to have run ahead, so to speak, of actual policy. The mainspring of the whole was anti-communism. The extraordinary success of a book such as Arthur Koestler's *The Yogi and the Commissar* bears witness to this, since it occurred in the middle of 1946, at the finest moment of the "tripartisme" that associated in the government and in the parliamentary majority Communists, Socialists and the Mouvement Républicain Populaire. The audience it found in left-wing intellectual circles heralded the coming break between Socialist opinion and the Communist Party. Later, Kravchenko's *I Chose Freedom* offered anti-Communist literature to a wider public. Long before the spring of 1947, when the Communist ministers were excluded from the government, the press had underlined with quite sufficient vigor the division of the world into two hostile blocs. The influence of refugees from eastern Europe in certain intellectual and political milieux had prepared many minds for the idea of a "Soviet imperialism." The occurrences in Prague, Warsaw, Budapest, Bucharest and Sofia formally established the incompatibility of the more or less reformist Left, incarnated in France by the Socialist Party, and the revolutionary Communist movement.

This split had been foreseen and accepted in the parties and political milleux which until 1947 had been willing to govern alongside representatives of the Communist Party. The bourgeoisie, including those of its political spokesmen most favorably inclined to the Left, were expecting massive aid from the United States in order to build up the country. For the Communists, American aid did not imply the risk of a political alliance. But all the other parties accepted or even desired a political guarantee, on the part of the United States, to bar any extension of communism to western Europe. In their eyes, this political objective was closely tied to the economic objective. The two, in theory, could have been separated, and in some left-wing circles, such as those which then expressed their opinions in the newspaper *Combat*, it was held that the obtaining of American financial aid could be achieved independently of any political coalition, in which the balance of forces would greatly favor the United States. But this notion had never been widely sponsored in the principal non-Communist parties. The Brussels Treaty, and then the Atlantic Pact, which marked the stages of their political evolution, necessarily led to military considerations.

When, in 1949, the Pact was signed, the daily papers of wide circulation and the reviews which were read by a cultivated public began to publish many articles that dealt with the armed forces of the two opposing blocs. A start was made at this time in contrasting the puny forces of the western armies with the irresistible power of the "175 Soviet divisions." In that same year, all China went over to the Communist camp. Russia exploded its first atomic bomb. In almost every milieu it was agreed that western military power must be built up. In France, the debates on the budget reflected the alarm felt in political circles. Orators put a kind of despair into their description of the nullity of the French Army, now that more than one third of its cadres and the best of its matériel were engaged in Indochina.

This change of outlook was converted into reality only by degrees. The Minister of National Defense from September, 1948, to October, 1949, was Paul Ramadier, who would leave the military with the recollection of a man who hunted for minor economies even in the most insignificant details. Only the Korean War succeeded in obtaining a substantial improvement in the credits made available to the armed forces in Europe. Then, too, the postwar inflation had come to a halt by January 1, 1949, and the level of prices and the size of the budget would remain relatively stable for eighteen months. It was the Korean War that would touch off inflation once again, and would rapidly erode the effectiveness of the new funds devoted to National Defense. In any case, the public mind had been considerably modified. From now on, non-Communist opinion would take military problems seriously, and follow with close attention the development of the balance of strength. Without having any illusions as to what France could do, henceforth military questions of every type would no longer be banned from its concerns.

One obstacle remained that might threaten this reconciliation of public opinion—in actual practice, bourgeois opinion—and military society. After the Brussels conference held in the spring of 1950, the American government openly raised the question of German rearmament. French political circles were hostile to this. The following September they still remained so, although France found itself at odds with all the other States adhering to the Atlantic Alliance. The concession had to be made that "the contribution of Germany to its own defense" would be studied. This was the starting point for the project of a European Army in which the Germans, who would be kept at the battalion level, would be submerged in a European military ensemble. This conception failed to stand the test of several months of negotiations, and finally the European Army became the "integrated" military force created by the Bonn and Paris agreements concluded between France, Germany, Holland, Belgium, Luxemburg and Italy. The internal crisis set going in France by the acceptance of a measure of German rearmament would not be wound up until August 30, 1954, when the treaty for a European army was rejected, and the beginning of 1955, when the existence of a German national army was accepted. French resistance to German rearmament was, indeed, in various forms, to last a full five years.

In the meantime, the fighting in Korea and Indochina had been settled. The Russians, almost immediately after the Americans, had exploded a hydrogen bomb. In Egypt, Tunisia, Morocco and even in Algeria the great battles for the decolonization of Africa were under way. When German rearmament became effective, in the second half of 1955, the international situation was markedly different from what it had been five years before.

In this long struggle that found a considerable part of French opinion opposed, in almost total isolation, to the rebirth of a German Army, the role played by the French Army was strange and significant. In Germany, the French Army had served first of all as a force of occupation. The "French Zone" had often been characterized as one of the few "sanctuaries" where, far from the alarms to which the Minister of Finances was subject, and sheltered from the criticisms of public opinion divided between indifference and irritation, the Army had been able to live relatively happy days. Numerous dwelling units, sufficiently spacious to lodge entire families without even omitting, it was alleged, mothers-in-law and grandfathers, automobiles requisitioned for the convenience of even the most modest subaltern officers, canteens whose abundance was in sharp contrast to the general wretchedness, dazzling parades of troops still inspired by the search for elegance that distinguished General de Lattre de Tassigny's staff— whether exaggerated or not, this legend, transformed into a memory, was substantially true. There is no doubt that the majority of officers preferred the German and Austrian garrisons to those in France.

After the First World war, the feeling toward Germany that predominated in the victorious Army was one of distrust. In 1945, however, everything was different. Germany no longer represented any danger, either immediately or in any foreseeable future. One should also bear in mind the effect on officers' minds of their actual presence in Germany. Witnesses of the unheard-of catastrophe that had befallen Germany, with towns and industries reduced to rubble, the men of the occupying forces could not have the same idea of the German future as the politicians, publicists and historians, who were haunted by memories of Bismarck, William II or Hitler. Here was an undeniable, overwhelming spectacle that turned into empty phrases the predictions of a Germany, reborn and dangerous, against which countless precautions should be taken. Thus a certain realism, along with a natural feeling of pity, made it impossible for the officers of the French Army of Occupation to take seriously the specter of a new German peril.

Besides, the German Army no longer existed. This traditional embodiment of imperial Germany had disappeared, and for the French Army, this meant the disappearance of the only enemy they had known. In its place, the officers of the occupation found only a people, reduced to wretched poverty in the towns, more fortunate in the country, but which everywhere sought to establish the best possible relations with the occupying forces, and was eager to prove in every way that it was not the barbarian monster that the Nazi regime had led others to suppose. For the great majority of French officers, contacts with the German population were neither disagreeable nor difficult. It seems that the anti-Germanism of a rather ferocious kind to be found in the political parties, from 1944 to 1947, had led the Army, with its repressed hostility to the Fourth Republic, to take the opposite tack, and to show a good will that did nothing to cut off all the material advantages of the occupation. Indeed, even in the earliest months, and long before French public opinion was ready for it, the Army could be found to have registered the first sympathetic shocks that heralded a reversal of alliances. The hundreds of thousands of refugees who had fled from the Soviet Zone or who had been expelled from Central Europe, the countless opponents of every stripe who emigrated from the new Communist States in eastern Europe, and the pitiable mass of "displaced persons," combined to create around the occupation authorities an atmosphere of violent hostility to the Soviet Union. As early as 1945 and 1946, conversations in the General Staffs and the mess rooms dealt with the problems posed by the Communist penetration into eastern Europe and Germany. Already the traditional distrust of Germany had become a thing of the past, though this was the ostensible reason for the occupation. The real reason for the presence and the build-up of the western Armies, and of French troops in particular, was to oppose a future Soviet "aggression."

The General Staffs had indeed realized, long before the politicians, that the question of German rearmament could not be eluded much longer. The contacts with the American high command would in themselves have been enough to enlighten the top echelons of the Army on the intentions of our Allies. The various "Plans," with which the American General Staffs were always most generous, let it be seen quite unambiguously that they looked on Germany's direct participation in western defense as an absolute necessity. It would be vain to seek, in the attitude of the French General Staff, any reaction comparable to that of Foch, in 1919, when he deemed that certain aspects of the Treaty of Versailles were dangerous. On the contrary, all occurred as though the majority of France's military leaders had concluded that Germany had ceased to be a possible adversary for France. At the most, they hoped that German rearmament would never reach a level approaching that of French forces, and that the main European commands, though available for German generals, would to the greatest possible extent be filled by French representatives.

This moderation on the part of the Army contrasted strangely with the bitterness exhibited by a large segment of French opinion in opposing German rearmament. The government which, in 1950, accepted the principle of this rearmament, did so only after the United States, supported by all the other signatories of the Atlantic Pact, had openly used pressure. It might be asked whether this pressure would ever have become a reality, if French opposition had been maintained. German rearmament without the agreement of France would have meant violating most of the treaties signed by France and its Allies since the war's end, and it is hard to imagine the American government accepting the disruption of the Atlantic Pact, since Europe would have been impossible to defend without French participation. But the French Government was unwilling to let things go so far, and American diplomacy, for its part, did not hesitate to make a very public use of threat.

The scheme thought up by several French politicians to make German rearmament acceptable was ingenious and even bold in appearance. Yet it was the gravest error committed by those who, either out of conviction or resignedly, favored the rearming of Germany. The first projects for a European Army had, at the outset, been inspired above all by the distrust felt by their authors at the prospect of a rearmed Germany. Jules Moch, as Minister of National Defense, could concede only that Germany should participate at the battalion level. Such a conception was lacking in realism.

The Germans would never agree to the project unless they were granted a basic equality of rights. Once the principle of German rearmament was accepted, arguments of military efficacy would weigh more and more heavily against the juridical barriers that the French government was trying to raise, in order to limit the scope of the plan. Soon there would be no limits to the rearming of Germany beyond those that the Germans themselves chose to set. Thus the project for a European Army, which had set out with the idea that the Germans would be grouped together only at the battalion level, soon acquiesced in their having "combat teams," that is to say, brigades and, finally, divisions. In the end, something very close to German equality was recognized.

This inevitable development turned all the hostility aroused by German rearmament against the European Army. Among the adversaries of the "European Defense Community" there would ultimately be found some of the authors of the first project for a European Army, including Jules Moch. Thus the policy adopted had not really disarmed the opposition. It had only worn it down so that, with negotiations having begun toward the close of 1950, the accords of Bonn and Paris were signed in May, 1952.

This was the occasion for the adversaries of German rearmament, who were unavoidably hostile to the European Army as it was to be constituted, to find fresh allies. These were the men who could not agree that German participation in western defense should be bought at the price of sacrificing French national sovereignty in one of its most essential instruments: the Army.

If military men had shown no great hostility to the idea of a re-armed Germany, it might be thought that a project leading to the dis-appearance of the French Army—at least in Europe—would have shocked them profoundly. Accordingly, the politicians who had staked their own careers on the European Army judged it prudent to limit the participation of the military in the negotiations. René Pleven, President of the Council in 1950, when the principle of German rearmament was accepted, remained in office until January, 1952, except for a brief interregnum when his Ministry, with no change in its composition, was presided over by Queille. Then, in March, 1952, he became Minister of National Defense, an office he still held when the accords of Bonn and Paris were signed. During this same period, Robert Schuman remained at the Ministry of Foreign Affairs. These two men, who acted as the French principals in the discussions leading to the European Army, provided the diplomats conducting the negotiations with a military adviser in the person of General de Larminat. He had had no personal authority in the Army and had occupied no important post before being despatched to aid the negotiators of the European Defense Community. Himself in favor of the project, he made reports at very long intervals on the progress of negotiations to the Conseil Supérieur de la Défense Nationale and to the Committee of the Chiefs of Staff.

The more time was consumed, the more the whole scheme appeared distasteful to the majority of the Army's leaders. It is noteworthy that the opposition of the main military leaders was not directed against the relative extent of German rearmament. What seemed intolerable to them was the disappearance of the French Army in an integrated European Army. The commands would be unified, the administration would be standardized, but above all the Army itself, losing its national personality, would be dependent on a body in which the French government would have no special authority. Furthermore, the French Army would be cut in two, since the overseas forces would not be integrated into the European Army. The number of generals actually in favor of the European Defense Community must indeed have been extremely small. In addition to General de Larminat, the only other well-known backer of the project who was mentioned was General Crépin, a future Commander-in-Chief in Algeria.

The opposition of the military never took an extreme form. The first version of the European Army project did not appear to be in the least dangerous. And, besides, the vehemence of Communist opposition to German rearmament in any shape whatever was an indirect argument in favor of Germany's making a contribution to western defense—at least in the eyes of military men, for whom anti-Sovietism and anticommunism had become basic principles. The attitude of the Army's chief leaders was not, however, entirely homogeneous. Several were decidedly in favor of a confederated European Army, in which each national army would keep its distinctness but in which, for example, the high command, and the Special Services for armaments and logistics, would be common to all. That did not mean that they accepted an integrated army.

But certain politicians sought to derive advantage from the ambiguity. Thus René Mayer believed he could affirm, while addressing the Congress of the Radical Party, that Marshal Juin favored the European Defense Community. The Marshal had, in actual fact, a rather more qualified view than most Army chiefs, but little by little he was influenced by their pronounced hostility. In January, 1953, he uttered his first public criticism of the project for a European Army, but this was very moderate, since he thought that it should be linked to "a general accord concerning its application, indicating what can be got under way at present and what must still wait." Before the year had ended, he repeated his objections in a more categorical way, in a lecture he gave in Brussels. However, it must be remembered that Marshal Juin was not only the principal military adviser of the French government, at least in theory; he was also the principal personage in the Army, and the Commander-in-Chief of the Central European Forces on behalf of the whole Atlantic coalition. This means that he had many reasons for avoiding too open an intervention in the quarrel over the E.D.C.

In any case, the General Staff was kept at a safe distance from all the negotiations that followed the signature of the treaties of Bonn and Paris, as it had been previously. At the same time military men were embarrassed by the accusation of "playing the Communist game," hurled by those who favored the E.D.C. against its adversaries. In actual fact, 1954 appeared on the calendar without the public's having any idea of the Army's feelings concerning a political decision that affected its whole existence, since it would be suppressed thereby.

The military leaders most hostile to the E.D.C., unable to express themselves publicly, asked several retired generals to speak on their behalf. In the great salons of the Hôtel Continental, one could hear several of the most illustrious generals in retirement, General Rovers, formerly the Army's Chief of Staff, General d'Anselme, formerly Inspector General of Reserves, and General Touzet du Vigier, formerly at the head of one of the corps of the First Army, condemn the E.D.C. in the name of the French Army's right to maintain its own existence. Finally, toward the end of March, 1954, Marshal Juin, no doubt encouraged by the fact that numerous opponents of the E.D.C. would be participating in the government, bluntly declared "that nothing could be gained through the treaty except by attaching to it a series of corrective measures which would state approximately the contrary, for its actual application, to what it expressly stipulates." The government, presided over by Laniel, who had the reputation for not exhibiting much energy in any domain, reacted by depriving Marshal Juin of all his prerogatives in the military hierarchy. But on August 30, after the Mendès-France government had failed to persuade the other signatories of the E.D.C. treaties to accept the amendment judged indispensable to ensure ratification, the National Assembly rejected, by a majority of forty, the project it had accepted in principle in February, 1952.

This E.D.C. affair was a highly significant experience for the Army. It had not tried to prevent German rearmament. When the treaties of London and Paris, negotiated by Mendès-France, provided for German rearmament, there was not the least indication of military disapproval. The E.D.C. challenged the very existence of the French Army. In spite of this, the military leaders had not at any time been consulted in any serious fashion by the governments. When it became evident that the Army's top leaders were opposed to the project, the only concern on the political side was to reduce this opposition to silence. Thus General de Larminat received permission to place his name and titles on a book that favored the E.D.C., while several general officers or high-ranking officers had to hide behind pseudonyms, in order to make their views known. The Army went through an experience in which its life was at stake, without being permitted to express itself or inform the country of its opinions. The only method it hit on was the slightly ridiculous appeal launched by a small group of retired generals. And when the only living Marshal of France dared to speak out, he was severely punished. Had Juin, then, no other way to express his opinion, since by statute he was the government's permanent military adviser? Later, this experience would bear its fruits: the Army would seek other ways to address the country and to convince the political authorities.

Less than ten years after the close of World War II, the French Army offered a rather lamentable spectacle. It was dislocated by the trials of the war and the occupation, morally cut off from a regime whose origins were alien to the Army, and materially reduced— almost to vanishing point—by the harsh limits imposed on its resources and on the credits voted. It was impoverished on the human plane, also, by successive waves of resignations or dismissals, intel- lectually weakened by the make-up of its new cadres, and soon to be deprived of its best elements, who would be dispatched to the Far East. Then it was hurled into the vast experiment of the cold war, which alone did something to restore its image in the public eye.

Yet the picture would not be complete if some light spots were not discerned in the enveloping gloom. It is true that, within a few years, the cleavages resulting from the armistice of 1940 were en- tirely forgotten. But not everything had disappeared of the urge to rejuvenate and modernize that had been felt so strongly in 1945: having cast off a number of illusions, military men would retain the conviction that they should not fall "one war behind." Best of all, perhaps, the Army was no longer at the center of political quarrels. Even in the disputes concerning the E.D.C., the Army as a whole was never a matter of controversy. All in all, after 1950 the situation was the same as in 1905, when the consequences of the Dreyfus Affair had lost all their venom. Then, the unanimity of the political parties had been achieved thanks to the requirements of national defense, only the Socialist Party and some elements of the Radical- Socialist Party remaining outside. On this new occasion, the unanimity of the cold war included the Socialists, some of whom contributed to build up the French military effort after 1950. Only the Com- munists were excluded and a few progressive or neutralist groups.

The Army did not fail to take advantage of these few favorable circumstances. The law of November 30, 1950, prescribing eighteen months of military service, had one original feature: it required that all conscripts should henceforth be subjected to "physical and psycho-technical selective examinations and tests." Thus for the first time a rational allotment of the young recruits was envisaged. There was, indeed, only a gradual use made of this important reform, which General Blanc, who had succeeded General Rovers as the Army's Chief of Staff, had spent several months in putting through. Nevertheless, the effect was considerable. The conscripts spent three days —or half-days, in certain cases—in a selection center, where they were examined by a psychiatrist and an orientation officer. A battery of fifteen tests established their general knowledge, professional qualifications, intelligence quotient and physical aptitude. The results were corrected and analyzed. The examinees who had an average score of seventeen out of twenty were considered eligible for training as reserve officers. Still required was the matching of skills and vacancies; it has been estimated that a fortunate union of one with the other was achieved eighty per cent of the time.

If the available human matériel was to be well employed, the conception of warfare had to be adapted to the atomic age. It was not simply a question of armaments, though it should be noted that, beginning in 1950, there was a whole series of impressive French achievements: the 15-ton light tanks A.M.X., the E.B.R. Panhard armored cars and, in particular, the famous ground to ground weapons SS 10 and S 11, the most extraordinary of their kind. The first studies undertaken by the Atlantic General Staffs revealed that the hypothesis of a nuclear war presupposed very light divisions, extremely mobile and with a great capacity for independent movement and superior fire power. The British Army was content to amputate, more or less, the manpower and matériel of its former divisions. Not until 1957 did the American Army create, in conformity with the new doctrine, "pentomic divisions" of which, several years later, only very few examples existed. The French Army was the first to draw the practical consequences of these modern conceptions of atomic warfare.

In keeping with General Blanc's directives and under the direct guidance of Generals Schlesser and Noiret, the latter having succeeded the former as the head of the Second Army Corps in Germany, a try-out was made with the "Javelot brigade," the prototype of future modern divisions. This was the model that served, between 1952 and 1954, for the constitution of the Seventh D.M.R. and the Fourth D.I.M. It was the last attempt to adapt to modern warfare made by the French Army before the Algerian adventure got under way. Symbolically, the first spectator to witness the annual maneuvers in which the new divisions took part was the Secretary of State for the Army in the Mendès-France government and Mayor of Algiers, Jacques Chevalier. Eighteen months later, these great modern units would leave *en masse* for Algeria, with an officering, a matériel and methods of warfare intended for atomic war and European battle-fields. In the jebels (mountains of Algeria), they missed their vocation.

General Guillaume, Chief of Staff of National Defense, and General Zeller, Chef d'Etat Major de l'Armée, tried to oppose this breaking up of the precious modern divisions that after several years' experimentation had been so carefully constituted. But the government, which had just despatched the contingent to Algeria, was resolved to sacrifice everything in order to attain its objectives. It demanded an immediate reconversion of the whole Army, and could not agree to the exceptions required if the modern divisions were to be maintained. General Guillaume and General Zeller handed in their resignations. And with this the history of the modernization of the French Army, with a view to fighting a nuclear war, came to an end.

CHAPTER SIXTEEN

THE EXPERIENCE IN INDOCHINA

"This revolution has remote origins," wrote one of the most celebrated journalists of the postwar period, writing of the French uprising in Algeria of May 13, 1958, and the events that followed. "The earliest episodes sink their roots into the ricefields of Indochina where the French Army caught yellow fever." On similar lines, countless commentators stressed, during the Algerian War, the importance of the trials undergone in Indochina in shaping the Army's outlook. The precise origin of French military theories on revolutionary warfare was discovered there, as were the doctrines of psychological action and the connection between politics and war.

The discovery, it must be said, came rather late. While the Indochinese War was still being fought, French public opinion paid little attention to the Army, except for the actual operations, or to its destiny, except for matters of manpower and manpower losses. Parliament debated the Indochinese War only at long intervals. The war did not become a central concern for Frenchmen until it was approaching its end, and especially when the battle of Dien Bien Phu raised it to its most tragic and spectacular dimensions. Previously public opinion, none too well informed of events in Indochina, since the press gave them relatively little space, could be stirred up only by the clash between official policy and the various recommendations put forward by those who favored negotiation with the Vietminh. These nonconformists were the Communist Party, a few neutralist news-papers, left-wing or liberal Christians and one single member of Parliament, Mendès-France.

If, then—directly for the Army and indirectly for the Nation—the Indochinese War was the starting point of a revolution, this revolution took place amid almost total silence and for a long while went on its way, vis-à-vis the public, shrouded in mystery. Today, when every-one agrees what revolutionary consequences the Indochinese War has had for the history of the Army, the outlines and the actual path of this revolution remain to be traced.

The trials undergone in Indochina affected the entire active Army, and especially the officers and noncoms between twenty and forty-five years of age. Only some specialists, some General Staffs and the ma-jority of generals remained unscathed. That line of demarcation al-ready begins to appear which, after 1954, would irremediably cut off the little world of the general officers, who would never get to know the Indochinese War in all its intensity, from the great majority of officers, of lower and higher rank, for whom it constituted their greatest military and human experience.

The Army found its way into the Indochinese adventure only little by little, borne on by an imperceptible but irresistible movement that, as the years slipped by, would convert these operations into the greatest colonial war in French history. In 1945, only 367 killed or missing were listed; in 1946, 2,828; 4,081 in 1947; 4,821 in 1948; 4,872 in 1949; in 1950, 7,150. That was the year when the Korean War began, and the first substantial shipments of arms from Communist China to the Vietminh had already transformed the Indochinese War into an international matter. The threshold had been left behind prior to which the "Vietnam expedition" could be characterized as a sort of long-drawn-out police operation whose aim was to consolidate the new political structures.

The same progression was visible on the level of the military credits made available for Indochina. They grew from 3.2 billion francs in 1945 to 308 billion in 1951. Beginning in 1950, the funds earmarked for Indochina represented between 40 and 45 per cent of the entire military budget. At the end of 1952, the forces assembled by France amounted to 175,000 regular troops, of whom 54,000 were French, 30,000 North Africans, 18,000 Africans, 20,000 Legionaries and 53,000 natives, to which must be added 55,000 *supplétifs*, 5,000 sailors, 10,000 aviators, 150,000 regular troops and 50,000 *supplétifs* of the Vietnamese National Army, 15,000 men of the Laotian and 10,000 men of the Cambodian Armies.

These figures show to what a degree that Indochinese War was, for the French, a matter that concerned only the Army's cadres, since the bulk of the manpower had been recruited overseas. But the loss of human life shows, on the other hand, what a sacrifice was required of the officers and noncoms who ceaselessly replaced each other on the Far Eastern front. Of the total of 92,000 killed, almost 20,000 were from metropolitan France, and nearly all of these were officers. Between 1945 and 1954, 800 Saint-Cyr graduates died in Indochina, 113 of these in the last six months of the war. It has been calculated that, over a period of seven years, one French officer was killed every day. Thus the regular Army bore the brunt of the war, and an appalling burden it was.

At the beginning of the Indochinese adventure, everything seemed to be a mere reflection of the differences to be found in metropolitan France. Only the defeat of 1940 can explain why the Japanese chose to intervene in Indochina. The Japanese General Staff had long known that the railroads connecting Chinese territory with the port of Hai Phong in the Gulf of Tonkin were being used to transport American matériel to Chiang Kai-shek's armies. General Catroux, Governor General of Indochina, had denied the Japanese the right to inspect the Tonkinese railroads. But on June 19, 1940, Japan sent him an ultimatum giving him twenty-four hours to accept the closing of the frontier with China, and Japanese supervision.

There was no military force in Indochina able to resist an act of aggression. On June 20, the American government informed the French Ambassador in Washington that the United States was unable to go to war against Japan. On June 27, at a meeting with the representative of the British General Staff in the Far East, General Catroux learned that Great Britain was in no position to offer him any military support, and on June 30 the British government confirmed that it had no desire to find itself at war with Japan.

The Vichy government dismissed General Catroux for having entered into contact with the British General Staff in Singapore, and replaced him with Admiral Decoux on July 20. On August 2, the Japanese demanded the right to send troops through Indochina and to exercise surveillance over all the airfields in the Peninsula. In spite of the recommendations of Admiral Decoux, who believed that Japan would not dare to attack Indochina, the Vichy government decided to accept the Japanese terms. To ensure total capitulation, the Japanese launched an attack on the garrison at Langson. From that time on, Indochina would be much more subject to Japanese policy decisions than to French authority.

At first, a conflict between these two forces appeared inevitable. Important elements of the Japanese General Staff did indeed favor the complete elimination of the French positions, to the advantage of the Vietnam nationalists. The Kempeitai, a blend of military gendarmerie and political police, was the basic instrument in this policy. It entered into an ever livelier struggle with the French Sûreté. During 1941 and 1942, military exigencies induced the Japanese government to leave untouched the French administrative apparatus, which could at least look after the public services and internal order. But toward the end of 1943 the Japanese Army began to arm the auxiliary troops recruited in the nationalist milieux with which it had been in contact for three years. Toward the end of 1944, these elements were already on the point of passing over to open insurrection against French authority, with the encouragement of the Japanese General Staff.

Since they could not possibly fight the Japanese the French military cadres in Indochina limited themselves to fighting, alongside the police, against the various nationalist groups that were supported and armed by the Japanese. Thus the traditional defense of the colonial positions became one, for the Army, with national resistance to the Japanese invader. The struggle appeared to have the justification of patriotism. But, in actual practice, what occurred was to make the future dialogue with the nationalists even more difficult.

The nationalists were still only a number of groups distinguished, in general, by their religious convictions and their traditionalism. The Vietminh became the main undercover force in Indochina, first with the support of the Chinese, who saw the Vietminh as an additional means of harassing the Japanese, and then in spite of Chinese distrust and the endeavors made to hedge it in with more "reliable" allies. Until the end of 1943, its determination to overthrow the colonial regime did not prevent the Vietminh from cooperating as closely as possible with the French Service de Renseignements, and its revolutionary Communist ideology did not lead it to neglect useful contacts with the American O.S.S. Until December, 1943, it issued numerous appeals to French patriots eager to take part in the common struggle against Japan.

Thus there existed common ground between the Vietminh and

France, and this might have been the starting point for a future entente between an independent Vietnam and metropolitan France. But on December 8 the Government of General de Gaulle in Algiers publicly declared its intention to re-establish French authority in Indochina, while saying nothing about the Peninsula's political future. The Vietminh, immediately sensing the danger, contrasted the desire for liberation that inspired the Allied powers and the spirit of reconquest that the French government was apparently manifesting. On August 6, 1944, the leadership of the Vietminh circulated among its cadres a document that described precisely in what circumstances the seizure of power would take place, once Japanese power had collapsed:

> In the interior, we will have to come to terms with the Gaullists and the Chinese. The Gaullists will be fighting in actual fact against the French Fascists, and the Chinese will rise against the Japanese and the French, as soon as the Chinese Army enters Indochina . . . Our goal is to create zones of revolutionary government, in order little by little to establish a single power everywhere in the country. The armed rebellion of our people will be unleashed during the last phase of the world war, when England, America and China will grab Indochina, when Gaullists and French Fascists will be at loggerheads in Indochina, when French and Japanese will be fighting and the Franco-Japanese Fascists will come to blows with the democracies . . . The Americans and Chinese will enter Indochina, while the Gaullists will rise up against the Japanese. Perhaps first of all the Japanese will overthrow the French Fascists in order to set up a military government. All these shadow governments, being weak and incapable, will topple, and Indochina will be reduced to anarchy. We shall have no need to seize power, since there will be no more power . . . But will England, America, the U.S.S.R., China and France allow us to retain our power and growing independence? Will not the recently formed de Gaulle government continue the old imperialist policy in Indochina? Or will not England, America or China replace France as the dominant power in Indochina? If it is easy to expel Franco-Japanese Fascism, will it be equally easy to retain power, once freedom and independence have been won?

Almost point by point, everything was to occur as the Vietminh had foreseen.

The first stage occurred less than three months later. The French Army in Indochina was seriously affected by the consequences that followed the events in North Africa and France itself. It could not

cheerfully abide to remain idle, and subservient to the Japanese occupation, when everything seemed to demonstrate the rightness of
those who, in 1940, had chosen to continue the struggle to the death
on every front against Nazi Germany, despite the capitulation of
Vichy. Perhaps another factor in the minds of some officers was the
desire to wipe out the memory of the frenzied anti-Gaullism of the
French authorities, during the governorship of Admiral Decoux. Until
the end of 1944, only some civilian groups, directed by Mario Bocquet
and Laurie Gordon, had resisted in any genuine way, and these had
been in contact only with the British and American special services.
At the conference held in Quebec in August, 1943, the Allied General Staffs decided to start subversive activities against Japanese occupation everywhere in southeast Asia. The French officers who were
responsible for liaison with the Allied command in the Far East offered to associate the cadres of the Army in Indochina with this effort.
Their offer was accepted. Thus a certain possibility of action was regained by French policy, enabling it to intervene in the Peninsula.

But the choice offered was indeed a difficult one. Given the undeniable intention of the Americans and Chinese to challenge the
French positions in Indochina—for different reasons and with different aims in mind—was it advisable to maintain to the very end the
French administrative and military apparatus under Admiral Decoux,
in order to prevent a dangerous vacuum at the time of Japanese
capitulation, and with the resolve to work out a new political statute
for the Peninsula? But since the French authorities had compromised
themselves during the Japanese occupation, could they possibly survive
this, and would it not be better to regain power in Indochina alongside
the Allies, enjoying the full prestige of struggle and victory, and if
possible in agreement with the Vietnamese who had been resisting
the Japanese?

The choice, as it happened, did not lie entirely in the hands of
the French. Japanese policy in southeast Asia, in the last phase of the
war, sought everywhere to strengthen the local nationalists and to
annihilate the bases of European colonization, so as to prevent the
return of the colonial powers even after the defeat of Japan. In Indochina, indications grew ever more frequent that the Japanese General
Staff would not tolerate for much longer the French administration
of Admiral Decoux, and would put in its place the Vietnamese nationalist groups it had been encouraging for several years previously.
Whatever the French might do, there was little likelihood that they

could maintain themselves in power to the very last day of the Japanese occupation.

Nevertheless, it was in the French interest that a trial of strength should be postponed as long as possible, so that aid from the Allies might play a part and the French Army itself not be entirely destroyed before it could take a hand in defeating the Japanese. But the impatience of the French officers to return to the conflict, the lack of prudence of the General Staff, and an almost total lack of discretion about what was being planned—despite the repeated warnings given by the Allied General Staffs and the French Services de Renseignements—tipped off the Japanese. On March 9, 1945, they moved, and within twenty-four hours the French Army in Indochina no longer existed, though several garrisons put up a desperate resistance. General Sabatier and General Alessandri saved a few thousand men, whom they led to the proximity of the Chinese frontier. Everywhere else massacres brought to an end the French administrative and civilian "presence" in Indochina.

These episodes would later have a serious effect on the state of mind of the Army, when more and more numerous military cadres were sent to serve in the Far East. The return to combat of the French Army in Indochina would not have the fortunate psychological effect it should have had. On the contrary, it was to be the theme of countless polemics. For some, especially those close to General Leclerc and Admiral d'Argenlieu, Admiral Decoux's regime had irremediably compromised French authority because of his collaboration with the Japanese. France had thus "lost face" in the eyes of the Indochinese peoples, some of whom had been able to fight Japan openly and who had thus gained the sympathy of the Allies. For others, the situation in Indochina was such that nothing could be done except to maintain the French positions against all and in spite of all, in order that no new power should take over. The attempts at resistance undertaken during the winter of 1944 to 1945 had ruined the prospects for this policy, it was held, and "Gaullist" activities were to be blamed. The imprudence had, in actual fact, been that rather of the General Staffs in Hanoi and Saigon, than of the officers despatched by General de Gaulle to India and China. Besides, there had been no means available to thwart the evolution of Japanese policy. But there would be no end to the arguments concerning the responsibility for the catastrophe of March 9, 1945. The officers present in Indochina during the Japanese occupation were driven to criticize violently the activity of the "Gaullists," since they thereby excused their own long inactivity. Just as their adversaries did, they turned to the attitudes adopted between 1940 and 1945 in order to find the origins of the Indochinese drama, which at that moment had barely begun.

The analysis circulated by the Vietminh proved extraordinarily correct. The Japanese had put a military government in the place of the "French Fascists." They had invited Emperor Bao Dai to form a government made up of the nationalists, their own clients. Then, exactly as had been foreseen, Indochina was divided into two zones of occupation, a Chinese zone in the north and a British zone in the south. Ten days after the official Japanese capitulation, the Vietminh had already become master of all Vietnam. On August 25, Bao Dai abdicated in favor of the Committee of Liberation set up by the Vietminh. The Vietminh then formed a provisional government, and on September 2 its President, Ho Chi Minh, proclaimed independence.

French policy, at this juncture, rested on nothing more substantial than a text and a decision. The text was dated March 24, 1945, and envisaged an Indochinese Federation in which five countries would be associated—Cochin China, Hanam, Tonkin, Cambodia and Laos—with a federal government presided over by the French Governor General, Indochinese and French Ministers responsible to him, and an Assembly in which the populations of Vietnam—that is, the representatives of Hanam, Tonkin and Cochin China—would have at most one half of the seats, and which would vote on legislation and the budget. But the only clear decision that General de Gaulle had reached was to have France take part in the struggle against the Japanese, since only in this way, he believed, could a foothold be regained in Indochina, whatever the political developments might be. Thus to the Army was attributed a capital role. As things turned out, it was not able to intervene until after the Japanese capitulation, since the Allies had refused to transport to the east the French troops offered by General de Gaulle. The British and Chinese entered Saigon and Hanoi before the French did.

It became plain at once that the problems of north and south were entirely different. In Cochin China, the French Administrator Cédile was parachuted in on August 22, on the 24th he entered into contact with the French who had remained in Saigon, and on the 25th a demonstration, that gave rise to no particular incidents, was organized by the Vietminh which there as elsewhere, and despite the power of the other nationalist groups, had placed itself at the head of the revolution. On the 27th, some French Communists and Socialists arranged a meeting between Cédile and the Vietminh representatives. Cédile spoke of the declaration of March 24, and assured the Vietnamese leaders that independence was already theirs; all that had to be done was to recognize it, and then useful negotiations could be undertaken with France.

But now the Vietminh and other nationalist groups came into conflict. These others reproached the Vietminh for having made contact with the French representatives. In order not to be swept aside, Giau, who was acting for the Vietminh, agreed to organize in common a mass demonstration in favor of independence, to be held on September 2. The demonstration got out of hand, and there were five killed and dozens wounded among the French civilian population, in spite of the attempt made by the Communist leaders to re-establish order toward the close of the day. The other groups found the behavior of the Communists open to criticism. And so the rivalry between the nationalist groups continued.

In view of the instructions he had received from the French government, Cédile could not enter into any profitable discussions with the Vietminh. The advisers who surrounded him in Saigon, exasperated by the incidents of September 2, urged him to take forceful measures, and pointed out the disorder to which the competition between the various Vietnamese groups had indeed given rise. He obtained from the British General Staff the means to rearm the French troops who had been imprisoned by the Japanese. And on the night of September 22 to 23 he reassumed control of the public buildings. Thereupon a segment of the French civilian population indulged in terrible reprisals against the Vietnamese population. The officers tried to ward off the worst, and were violently criticized for their pains. British intervention brought about a truce between the two sides on October 2. But disorders continued, and were stimulated by the rivalries already mentioned.

The French representatives could not step outside the framework of the declaration of March 24 and the instructions of the government. In any case, the native population appeared unable to respect the truce. General Leclerc arrived on October 5, and launched a vast operation covering the whole of Cochin China. By January, all the Vietnamese nationalists were thoroughly split. But General Leclerc's staff was fully aware that what lay ahead was a permanent guerrilla war.

During this "Cochin Chinese horseback ride," Admiral d'Argenlieu, who had been named High Commissioner in Indochina, arrived in Saigon. Those who took up positions around him were almost entirely civil servants, and they managed to convince him that a careful selection had to be made of the Vietnamese groups with whom France would be prepared to cooperate. Their point of view found expression in the declaration made by de Raymond, Admiral d'Argenlieu's political adviser, after the proclamation of independence and of the unity of the three Vietnamese provinces: "We abide by the statute of March 24. There is no question of taking into account the reunion of the three Annamite regions. What must be done is to re-establish the former State, and so permit the populations to express their views freely." This was the starting point of a policy that eliminated all negotiations with the independent, unified government formed by the Vietminh at the beginning of September.

But this government was not merely behind the resistance that opposed the reconquest of Indochina by the French, it was actually installed in Hanoi, and could be dislodged only by military action on a large scale. Such action could not be carried out, since there was a Chinese Army of 180,000 men in north Indochina. Thus the problem of the French return to Tonkin was both a Chinese and a Vietnamese problem. While negotiations were getting under way between France and China, General Leclerc's staff set out to examine the possibility of military intervention against Hai Phong and Hanoi. But this could lead to a general war everywhere in northern Indochina, and would once and for all place the Vietnam nationalists on the side of the Chinese. Then the problem would become international, and there could be no foreseeing its military and political implications.

It was the French Commissar in Tonkin—Sainteny—who convinced General Leclerc and most of the officers forming his General Staff that the only way out was through negotiations with the Vietminh. He had sounded out various representatives of the nationalist parties opposed to the Vietminh, and had even tried to establish contact with ex-Emperor Bao Dai. Everywhere he had found men without authority, or extremists even more intransigent than the leaders of the Vietminh. Also, the Franco-Chinese negotiations constituted for the Vietminh a threat of isolation that weighed in favor of discussions with the French. The arrival of reinforcements in Saigon would give Leclerc the possibility of undertaking military operations, if a political solution were not found. Everything favored contacts between France and the Vietnamese.

With this, a clash of policies arose, and the question was, which would come in first. Admiral d'Argenlieu was attempting to impose on Indochina the status outlined in the declaration of March 24, 1945, while General Leclerc was seeking agreement with the Vietminh on the political future of Vietnam. Even before General Leclerc could set the coping stone on his policy with the agreement of March 6, 1946, Admiral d'Argenlieu had set up a Cochin Chinese consultative committee. Thus the agreement of March 6 had to leave the question of the association of Cochin China with Vietnam to the choice of the populations. The competition of these two policies continued. While negotiations got under way at Fontainebleau between the representatives of the Vietminh and the French government, Admiral d'Argenlieu set up a provisional Cochin Chinese government, began negotiations with the Moi tribesmen and summoned an Indochinese conference at Dalat, with representatives from Cambodia and Laos, but none from the Provisional Government of the Republic of Vietnam.

Throughout this first phase of the Indochinese affair, at no time can the military authorities be found intervening to back a policy of force. General Leclerc, quite on the contrary, in his person embodied the search for a pacific solution. His General Staff, which included a number of men who later would occupy prominent positions in the Army, appeared to follow him without qualification. General Salan, for example, was the chief negotiator of the agreement of March 6. The future General Massu commanded the armored group which was the first to enter into contact with the Vietnamese People's Army. The head of the Bureau of Operations was Colonel Lecomte who, in Morocco, would be one of those mainly repsonsible for deposing Sultan Mohammed V and who would oppose that country's evolution toward independence. Colonel Mirambeau was, at the time, Leclerc's Chief of Staff. He was later to be one of the chief general officers to back the coup of May 13 in Algeria, and after the "Barricades" of January 13 he would be relieved of his command. It was he to whom Admiral d'Argenlieu said, on March 20, 1946, that the agreement reached with the Vietminh constituted another "Munich." Even General Valluy who, by the end of the year, would take on the responsibility of the first military operations launched against the Vietminh, was apostrophized as follows by Admiral d'Argenlieu, according to the Admiral himself: "I am amazed, *mon Général*, yes, amazed that France should have such a fine expeditionary corps in Indochina, and that its leaders should prefer to negotiate rather than fight."

The Admiral was surrounded by the top administrators of the civil service. The most active among them favored an over-all organization of Indochina with supreme authority remaining in French hands and relying, in Vietnam, on the traditional hierarchy of local bigwigs, mandarins and great landed proprietors. The history of French policy in Indochina during the second half of 1946 was to be that of the *de facto* coalition formed by Admiral d'Argenlieu and his advisers, and the political factions of the Right and the Center, supported by the central administration of the Ministry of France Overseas.

It is indeed impossible to separate the policy followed in Indochina from the vicissitudes of French internal politics. The elections of June 2, 1946, made of the Mouvement Républicain Populaire the numerically most important Party. Its alliance with the Communists and Socialists, in a "tripartite" government, distressed a considerable proportion of its electorate and earned it the reproaches of the right-wing opposition. This opposition could continually threaten to outbid the M.R.P., and this had a marked influence on most of the Party's leaders. The threat could be used with maximum effect in the field of colonial policy. While it was difficult for the M.R.P. to oppose the wage increases demanded by the trade unions and backed by the Communist Party, unless it wished to be regarded as reactionary, there was less inconvenience in adopting an intransigent attitude to defend "the French patrimony" against the demands of the Vietnamese nationalists. The temptation to do so was all the greater, since the representatives of the Vietminh who arrived to participate in the Fontainebleau conference made no secret of their contacts with Communists and Socialists. From this time on, negotiations with the Vietminh came to be classified as a policy of the Left, and as such were the target of criticism from Right and Center.

The whole history of French policy in Indochina was traced out in advance. In 1946, the Radical-Socialists and the Conservative groups, who made up the opposition to the "tripartite" government, took good care to exert the pressures on the M.R.P. that would bolster its resistance to the Vietnamese demands. In 1947, the same task was carried out by the Rassemblement du Peuple Français and the segments of right-wing groups that formed a middle ground between the governmental majority and the opposition. The results became apparent while the Fontainebleau conference was still going on. On September 14, all that could be agreed on was a mere *modus vivendi* extending the agreements of March 6, with no solution having been found for all the problems left in abeyance by those agreements. This meant taking grave risks. No later than November 20 a demonstration of this fact was provided, when the first serious incidents occurred in Hai Phong, in connection with the control of customs.

De Lacharrière, the head of the French civilian delegation sent to the Vietminh, tried to negotiate an agreement, in conjunction with General Morière, Commander of the troops in Tonkin. But, from Saigon, General Valluy, who had temporarily replaced Admiral d'Argenlieu, and Pignon, the High Commissar's political adviser, demanded that Hai Phong be evacuated by the Vietnamese People's Army and placed entirely in charge of the French troops. General Morière warned General Valluy that the Vietminh would certainly refuse to accept these conditions, and that the risk of civil war lay ahead. But General Valluy had informed Colonel Debes, who commanded the Hai Phong garrison, of his intentions. On November 23 the Colonel passed on General Valluy's ultimatum to the Vietnamese authorities and, on the 24th, fighting started. This became widespread, whereupon General Valluy drew up a new ultimatum, demanding the right to occupy the entire Tonkinese coastal region, and sent it on the 27th to the Vietnamese government, which decided to appeal to Paris.

But the French capital was without a government. The crisis touched off by the elections of November 10 had not yet been settled. Admiral d'Argenlieu, who was spending several weeks in France, insisted that the Vietminh was associated with all the other Communist Parties and entirely dependent on Moscow. The Indochinese affair was becoming more and more closely tied up with French internal politics, and Paris was less and less well informed about the real situation in Hanoi. A message sent by Ho Chi Minh to Léon Blum, who had just become President of the Provisional Government, was held up in Saigon: dispatched from Hanoi on December 15, it did not reach Paris until the 26th. In the interval, the Vietnamese Army had gone into action, and the Indochinese War had begun.

Early in 1947, the opinion of the military men as to the policy that should be pursued in Vietnam remained unchanged. General Leclerc,

who was dispatched on a mission by the Blum government, returned
with the conviction that only a massive military effort could deal
successfully with the Vietminh. He considered it necessary, therefore,
to pursue the policy he had previously envisaged vis-à-vis the Vietminh. At the same time, the determination of the military men in the
entourage of Admiral d'Argenlieu was strengthened by their conviction that the struggle against the Vietminh was but one aspect of the
struggle against the extension of communism throughout the world.
The Army's leaders did not, actually, take any part in evolving the
Indochinese policy of successive governments. They fell more and
more under the sway of the ideas propounded by the group which,
since the end of 1945, had been advising Admiral d'Argenlieu.

We can see how the contours gradually emerge more clearly from
the public declarations of French leaders, beginning in the first weeks
of 1947, that is to say, immediately after fighting had broken out.
The Minister for Overseas France had occupied the post for more
than a year, and should have been thoroughly conversant with the
reasons that motivated the agreements of March 6. Yet in January he
rejected the peace overtures made by Ho Chi Minh. "Such an appeal,"
he declared, "cannot be taken seriously. Quite clearly, this is a
propaganda maneuver . . . We can attach no importance to it . . . I am
convinced that those who really exercise power in the Vietnamese
government have no wish for an agreement." Admiral d'Argenlieu expressed similar convictions on January 2. "My conclusions are categorical," he stated. "It is henceforth impossible to negotiate with Ho Chi
Minh. We will find in this country personalities with whom we can
deal, and who also, no doubt, will be nationalists, but those others
have disqualified themselves. They have sunk to the depths." Pignon,
his political adviser, defined what the government's policy should be
on January 4. "One point seems certain," he said, "and that is the
impossibility of resuming negotiations with the government of M. Ho
Chi Minh . . . The importance of the nationalist idea among all the
levels of the Annamite population cannot be denied, and it must be
reckoned with. At the present time we cannot hope to separate the
masses from the Vietminh, except by showing in our words and deeds
that we are not endangering the nationalist ideal . . . Our objective
has been clearly set: we must make an internal Annamite issue of the
quarrel we have with the Vietminh Party . . ." And Moutet, after
his return from Indochina on January 7, appeared to have been won
over to these ideas. "France," he declared, "has no intention of going

back on its word, but it wishes to negotiate in entire confidence with the authentic representatives of the Vietnamese people."

This policy was to lead, by gradual stages, to the recognition of the independence of Vietnam for the benefit of a government set up by France in opposition to the Vietminh. It required the speedy granting of a theoretical independence to Vietnam, in order to endow with all possible prestige the government accepted by Bao Dai in 1949. After that date, the arrival of Chinese Communist troops on the frontiers with Tonkin would progressively modify the military factors of the Indochinese situation. The policy the government had opted for had an immense effect on the Army. Now it was no longer fighting for national goals, but to obviate the necessity of recognizing a Communist government as the legitimate authority in Vietnam.

Thus Indochina rounded off the long series of episodes which, since the economic crisis of the 1930's, or even since the Russian Revolution, had constantly pushed the Army along the path of direct opposition to international communism. Patriotic justifications had, indeed, gone entirely out of fashion. They were not to be found in governmental directives, or in the public declarations made by the high commissioners or the generals in supreme command, or in the press of France and Vietnam. The explanations offered to justify the interminable war the Army had to fight were of quite another kind: Vietnam was merely one front on which East and West had clashed, and the Army was defending the western world, Christendom and the "Free World." It was in the name of this interest shared by all the western powers that the governments would ever more vigorously solicit American aid And this aid came on the basis of the ever more frank and boasted avowal of Vietnamese independence.

But it was on the territory of the former French colonial empire that the Army had to assume the burden of this anti-Communist war. In Indochina it learned concretely that the continuance and success of the Army were tied up with the defeat of communism. Thus in the mind of French officers there was established a direct and unequivocal relationship between the warfare of a colonial nature, which had originally been undertaken to maintain the French positions, and the resistance put up by the western world to the plans of international communism. This attitude would be further strengthened, from 1950 on, by a comparison between the wars being fought in Korea and in Indochina. In Seoul, as in Saigon, was there not a nationalist "western" government that was standing up to its Communist foes?

The officers arriving from France, where they had seen the Army collaborate ever more closely in the Atlantic coalition, discovered in the Far East the same adversary that they were told they were confronting in Europe. In their minds there was no opposition, or even any essential difference, between the missions entrusted to the Army on the Rhine and the Danube, and to the expeditionary force in Indochina. In the one region, the task was to prepare for a conflict with the Soviet Union; in the other a conflict was already under way against an advance guard of the Communist forces. Everything conspired to convince the Army that Indochina was one of the hot spots in the cold war. In these conditions, any criticism directed against the war in Vietnam appeared to threaten the resistance being put up by the French Army, on behalf of the western world, against international communism. Criticism was in itself a sign of defeatism, and would soon be regarded as proof of treason.

For the Army, the history of the Indochinese War would soon become the epic of a band that had ventured to a far-off frontier, and had been forgotten by those who had sent it to fight and die. Its members would become alienated from their own people, after they had been insidiously betrayed, first by the opponents of the war, and then by the whole of public opinion, which was exasperated by the setbacks experienced, wearied of the financial burden, and disgusted by the stretching out of the conflict.

Enclosed within its war, the Army threw back rancorous glances on the country which seemed to have forgotten it. It had the almost corporeal conviction that the war in Indochina was being ignored by French public opinion. Each officer, on his return from the Far East, had the greatest trouble in explaining to his family, friends and acquaintances the nature of the strange conflict he had been waging, in which the relative strength of the forces involved appeared to have no effect on the real outcome of the engagements. The frightful sacrifices made by officers and men, in a harsh climate and against a faceless adversary—no one in France seemed to pay any attention to it. The press worked as one to maintain a relative unawareness of the real conditions in which the war was being fought; it was as if Indochina belonged to another world.

The soldier's feeling of malaise soon gave way to bitterness, revulsion and hostility. As their period of leave drew to an end, officers now sensed a kind of relief. Among their comrades, in the ricefields and on the high plateaux, they "belonged," they understood each other instinctively. But their own country had become foreign to them. Bertrand de Castelbajac, an officer in the colonial parachutists, describes in his *La Gloire et leur salaire* how a veteran of the Indochinese campaigns tries to make a return to civilian life:

> In succession, it was suggested that he sell apéritifs, nylon stockings, automobile accessories, perfumes and watches. He kept on refusing. He would have liked to find an occupation that had some other value than merely a means of making money . . . No, quite clearly he was not cut out for the struggle for life in the commercial civilization of the 20th century . . . There were the kids coming out of school, the women coming out of the grocery store, the cops waiting until they could go off duty, the messenger boy whistling on his bicycle, the car driver bursting your eardrums with his horn, and the retired people mulling over their bygone lives . . . You don't know these people, you scarcely see them. You have nothing to do with them, it's another universe . . . Thinking back on it, he had found the stay in France the most upsetting, for now he no longer thought of his "period in Indochina" but of his "period in France." Things made more sense in the war, there he felt at home, and elsewhere he was abroad.

In an investigation published in 1958 by *Le Courrier de la Nation*, a paper founded by M. Debré, a captain spoke of the outlook of his comrades in Indochina: "We turned in upon ourselves, we lived among ourselves, and we became as touchy and sensitive as men flayed alive. But how great was the despair we felt at being rejected by our country —and how great was our need of fraternity."

The ignorance—or indifference—on the part of the public was not without a certain official approval. Thus, for example, the government decided in 1948 that the citations earned by the combatants in Indochina would no longer be printed in *Le Journal Officiel*. In 1951 it was decided that the blood collected by the Office d'Hygiène Sociale could not be used for the wounded men in the expeditionary corps. Not until July, 1952, was a law passed that accorded the status of veterans to those who had served in Indochina, and not until the end of 1953 did this law become effective.

The Army cadres attributed a great deal of importance to the campaign waged by the French Communist Party against the Indochinese War. It was all the easier to do so in view of the fact that the bond uniting the party with the Vietminh appeared to exist beyond a doubt, and the Communist leaders, militants and press in any case made no secret of it. Most officers rapidly reached the conclusion that the Communist campaigns were comparable point by point to the defeatist propaganda the French governments had had to combat during the First World War. They could not understand why the same vigorous means of repression were not again being employed. The condemnation and the arrest of Communist militants appeared insufficient to them. The military security organization devoted much space in its reports to the psychological effect of the Communist campaigns. The least manifestation by dockers or railroad workers against the shipping of matériel to the expeditionary corps was noted. Sometimes the most absurd legends were mingled with the truth. In some officers' groups it was alleged that one could no longer risk a walk through working-class districts while wearing a uniform, and that hospital trains filled with men back from Indochina were the butt of hostile manifestations on the part of the Communists.

The Army's hostility was also directed against the few papers that disapproved of the Indochinese War. These papers were later included, as a matter of course, in every charge of treason that was raised. In 1954, in "l'affaire des fuites," launched with the hope of compromising the Mendès-France government, several journalists of the Left were accused of having handed over to the Vietminh the minutes of meetings of the Committee of National Defense. Soon, indeed, the entire press came to be an object of suspicion, if not of detestation, on the part of the military cadres. The concern for secrecy fostered this state of mind, and actual incidents sometimes provided a justification. The following example is cited by General Navarre, the last—and also the least popular—Commander-in-Chief:

> A top secret meeting between representatives of France and Vietnam . . . had just been held. The topics and the discussions had been kept absolutely secret. As soon as the meeting had ended, the correspondents of two newspapers sent off cables. They gave an account of the meeting that bore no resemblance to the truth, was a figment of the imagination of the authors and, it need scarcely be added, was of a highly startling nature. The investigation also revealed that, in order to save time, the cables had been filed barely half an hour before the meeting began to meet *in camera*. The cables were stopped, but I could obtain no disciplinary measures against the erring journalists.

General Navarre was, doubtless, exceptionally distrustful of the press, and had the same difficult relationships with journalists as with his own officers. But his view was probably that of many of the Army cadres. In any case, it bears witness to an extraordinary bitterness and to a sense that this was a real affliction. "A very important source of information on the Vietminh," General Navarre wrote, "was the press."

> This—and I am weighing my words carefully—was one of the curses of Indochina. It had developed deplorable habits . . . Thus a certain number of journalists, who openly boasted that they could "make and break generals," in order to obtain information and preferential treatment practiced downright blackmail, which was successful with some leaders too greatly concerned about their personal reputations . . . As a result there was to be found, in Indochina, a plethora of journalists who, with a few rare and all the more honorable exceptions, were meddlers devoid of real stature, and anxious above all to get hold of sensational information, whether true or false.

Many officers certainly failed to share these harsh views, but the same general frame of mind undoubtedly existed among a considerable number of Army officers.

The officers in Indochina plunged ever more deeply into a war in which the day-to-day reality of combat had no connection with the ideological justifications provided. They were highly suspicious of all that might be said about them, and took refuge in their own solitude, with the growing conviction that they were mercenaries in charge of other mercenaries, the men of the Foreign Legion, the North Africans, Africans, the fighters of the mountain tribes and the Vietnamese recruits. Commandant Monteil, in his *Les Officiers*, quotes statements that throw light on their outlook. "I am fighting in vain," declared an officer in 1949, "conscious that I am defeated, and beset with feelings against which I can do nothing—just as there can be no quibbling with military honor, when one is thoroughly imbued with it." At the end of that same year a commandant in charge of a unit, and entrusted with a particularly difficult mission, asked his battalion commander, "What is our goal? Mon commandant, give me a moral reason, even if it is only for my men." After a pause for reflection, the answer came: "Duty. You are soldiers." There were more than twenty dead that day, including an officer.

This uncertainty on the moral plane was matched by bewilderment on the technical and military level. In Indochina the Army found itself involved in a war that had no resemblance whatever to the campaigns of the Second World War, and the French military apparatus was shaken to its foundations. In his *Journal d'une fin de guerre*, an officer summed up the feelings of his comrades in the field, as they beheld the rules of the staff college and the careful administration of the traditional Army break down:

> This Indochinese War might have been, should have been, even for those who hated it and wanted none of it, the crucible of a new Army, modern in spirit and rejuvenated in its methods. Alas, the opposite occurred! What had been weaknesses in metropolitan France here became monstrous vices. No imagination and no initiative were tolerated—or nothing, rather, that rose above the level of the "talent of the interpreter"; the colonial cult of "residence" and a pious respect for the "period of command"; bureaucracy; paper work, uselessness or paralysis of the "services" (determined to be of no service); pathetic technical resources (the war is fought with one breakdown crane for the whole of Tonkin), with a handful of helicopters and mechanical equipment on the verge of collapse: the whole enormous machine is revolving to no end, or rather is not revolving at all. Of course the individual combatant is often magnificent, and there are born leaders, but it is all futile. We are fighting an outdated war, in false conditions, against an adversary who until now had no artillery, no aviation and no tanks. We can no longer camouflage ourselves. We have fallen into the worst habits. We have forgotten modern warfare, but we have not learnt guerrilla warfare, tomorrow's form of land warfare. Defeat in the field is nothing, compared to the illusions, the sclerosis and the *non possumus* which have turned Indochina into the grave of our Army.

This judgment is actually too pessimistic. For the French Army, the war in Vietnam was an incomparable experience. Soon countless officers would try to learn its lessons. At each stage of the war, new men were forged. There were recruiters of partisans, administrators of villages, leaders of commandoes, who had been dropped far behind the enemy lines with the task of equipping and training the upland tribes, the Thai, Nung and Tho, and with no future other than death or the end of the war, for there could be no thought of their returning home during the campaign. Even those who remained within the regular military system were the astonished but excited witnesses of experiments such as that of Colonel Leroy, who pacified a region containing 400,000 inhabitants by setting up his own militia for self-defense, supervised by village councils, and made a success of the undertaking on the economic plane and with respect to popular education. But such experiments were restricted and tended to bog down in this interminable war. As Ho Chi Minh had predicted, the Viet-minh tiger allowed the French elephant no respite. The French expeditionary corps, taking refuge in its melancholy and later in its despair, derived a bitter satisfaction from mocking its own efforts, foibles, weaknesses and vices. They felt not merely the irony and sadness of soldiers whose country has forgotten them, but also a dis-trust, merging into contempt, of the hierarchy on which they de-pended—the "generals."

The Indochinese War gave rise to an almost entirely new feeling in the military mind, that of a still purely verbal but scarcely concealed rebelliousness against the military leaders, who were more or less identified with the political leaders and judged, like them, to be responsible for the war's blunders and setbacks. The lessons learned and the principles officially proclaimed went for nothing in the rice-fields, the bush and the high tablelands. The Army was all the more disposed to react with anger and passion to the failure of its own regulations since each man had to bear, in his own person, its tragic consequences. Almost all the officers who served in Indochina could have made their own the words uttered by Colonel Lacheroy at the beginning of one of his famous lectures on revolutionary warfare:

I was about to set out for Indochina and I went to say goodbye to my leaders. One of them said this to me: "You are leaving for Indochina, fine, you are going to do your duty as a high-ranking officer. But bear in mind what I'm about to tell you: with your rank, at your age and with your previous training, you have nothing more to learn there. Nothing to learn on the strategic level, for you will be involved in an ant-like strategy that has been completely left behind by modern warfare. Nothing to learn on the tactical level, for you will be involved in outdated tactics closer to the wars of 1870 and 1914–1918 than to that of 1939–1945, outdated as that already is. You have nothing to learn even in the utilization of weapons, for that's a country where they are used quite inappropriately. I have been told," he said—for he had not gone there himself—"that armored cars were used in relatively small units, such as the squad." He was right, I used them in patrols. Now, a certain number of us have returned from this adventure and, looking back on this still recent past, we declare that no period of our military career has been so formative, because in no other were we obliged to such an extent to think through problems, to cross out the formulas we had been given, and sometimes to hit upon new ideas and new solutions.

This criticism of the doctrines promulgated by the General Staffs—not to say, this rebellion—would not have taken so grave a turn if it had been based only on personal, human and even moral objections. One must not minimize the effect on the military outlook of such a scandal as "l'affaire des Généraux." On August 26, 1949, the radio monitoring services in Indochina passed on the information that the Vietminh radio was broadcasting the report General Revers had written, on returning from his tour of inspection in Indochina. On September 18, more or less by accident, a copy of this document was discovered in Paris. It was established that General Revers had handed over his report to Roger Peyre, whose under-cover influence was enormous, and who had forwarded a copy to Van Co, the Paris representative of certain Cochin Chinese political milieux. Van Co had Vietnamese friends who were close to the Vietminh, and they had passed on a copy of the Revers report. In France this "affair" had immense political consequences. Certain politicians had tried to hush the matter up, claiming that the report contained no military secrets. But their real reason was that the pages which might have indicated who received the funds distributed by Van Co had been carefully eliminated. The "affair" had entirely different consequences in the Army. Most officers, though they had no doubts concerning General Revers's personal honesty, were scandalized to see how much more influence a man like Roger Peyre could exercise in political circles than could the Army's Chief of Staff.

It was to Roger Peyre that General Revers turned in such matters as the choice of the Chief of Staff of National Defense or of a general to command a military district, to obtain a hearing from the head of the government or to solicit funds for the expenses of a mission in the United States. It seemed that in every domain Roger Peyre was much the more powerful. Yet this man had a criminal record, and had been pronounced guilty of "national unworthiness." He appeared to be nothing more than a shady racketeer. If he had so much "pull" in certain circles, the politicians he dealt with were themselves displayed in no favorable light.

This was the first reaction to the news. It was followed by another, which concerned the general attitude of the military leaders vis-à-vis political authority. Many officers considered that General Revers should have had nothing to do with such a man as Peyre, and that the proper course would have been to denounce publicly his influence and his activities. Some aspects of the "affair" gave a distressing insight into the mediocrity of the situation, both material and moral, in which the men making up the high command found themselves. The Army's Chief of Staff actually wrote in these terms to Queuille, indicating that he would soon retire: "A measure of weariness accounts for this decision, but above all the realization that it is materially impossible for me to maintain my rank without reducing my modest resources to zero. The year will wind up with a drop of some 300,000 francs in my bank account, and in July I was forced to sell the only house I own, in Saint Malo." In the United States, he even had to borrow 300 dollars from a friend of Roger Peyre's. Thus the generals set the example of men who bore poverty, not with dignity, but with a sense of humiliation. This attitude struck most officers as shameful. They pitied General Revers more than they blamed him, but they tended contemptuously to lump together a political milieu that had no respect for the Army and generals who dabbled in it and got soiled.

This "affair of the generals" also had its repercussions in Indochina. After the cessation of all negotiations with the Vietminh in 1947, the search for a nationalist but non-Communist spokesman had led to the establishment of a Vietnamese State and to the restoration of Bao Dai. But this policy could only appeal to Vietnamese nationalists who had been assured that Vietnam would remain unified—and on this score Ho Chi Minh had met with a firm refusal—and that the country, at least in theory, would be independent. In this way, the gradual elimination was achieved of the earliest spokesmen hostile to the Vietminh, of those, that is, who had been discovered by Admiral d'Argenlieu in 1946: Cochin Chinese bourgeois liberals, civil servants or wealthy landowners. They had agreed to play the card of autonomy or even independence for their province, and now were not at all pleased at having to give way to the various governments formed by Bao Dai.

This political opposition did not remain restricted to Indochina; it took hold in France also. The Bao Dai regime, with its monarchical institutions, the corruption of some of its worthies and the intelligent, skeptical nonchalance of the Emperor himself, found little favor among the Socialists, who recalled that they had been for negotiations with Ho Chi Minh and had no desire to involve themselves in a "war on behalf of Bao Dai."

The political alternative was matched by a concomitant military alternative. General Revers's idea was to limit the activity of the French forces in Tonkin in the Hanoi-Hai Phong region, while concentrating all military effort in southern Vietnam so as to clean it out for good and all. With that accomplished, the attempt could be made to establish a political solution on a firm footing, even if it should be necessary to negotiate with the Vietminh. Implicit in this military alternative was the future fragmentation of Vietnam.

Thus the "affair of the generals" revealed the existence of close though sometimes mysterious ties between opposing political factions, rival generals and conflicting interests. The Cochin Chinese had their Socialists and their Radicals, who in their turn had their military men. Bao Dai and his associates had their Mouvement Républicain Populaire and their Rassemblement du Peuple Français, which in their turn also had their military men. This, naturally, is a very rough sketch of the actual situation, but the whole had quite sufficient consistency to impress most of the officers posted in Indochina. They would henceforth look on the war and the suffering it caused as a mere mask over a shady universe inhabited by piasters and the Parties' campaign chests, ministerial portfolios and the stars that denoted a general.

The expeditionary force would soon realize that the General Staffs, back home in France, were growing increasingly impatient of this endless war, which was hampering French military renewal. In 1950, the loss of the posts at Cao Bang and Langson, close to the Chinese frontier, led General Juin after a tour of inspection to envisage a retreat to the Tonkin Delta, with the abandonment of the mountainous regions in the north. This was the solution that General Revers was already seeking. General de Lattre de Tassigny reawakened in the expeditionary corps the élan it had lost, and genuinely won the defensive battle that allowed a provisional consolidation of the French positions in the Delta. But after his death in December, 1951, it became plain that the situation had not significantly changed. The Vietnamese National Army, to which he had given the bulk of his attention, still seemed utterly useless in combat. The expeditionary corps was largely tied up in the static task of defending the territories it was supposed to control. From across the Chinese frontier, the Vietminh was receiving an increasing quantity of heavy equipment.

In 1953 General Juin, who in the meantime had become Marshal Juin, could only confirm the conservative judgment he had expressed in 1950. General Salan had barely been able to follow the directives set by General de Lattre de Tassigny, abandoning the positions that were too advanced to be held by his limited forces. He was convinced that only a political solution could bring the war to an end. He preferred to limit the French military effort, while expressing the greatest skepticism about the real value of a Vietnamese National Army. His successor, General Navarre, was the first to present to the government a general plan of operations whose main feature was to remain strictly on the defensive in 1953 and 1954. The reason for his departure from this original plan was the attempt to restrict the invasion of Laos by the Vietminh. He dispatched part of his reserves to attack the adversary in the rear at Dien Bien Phu in the northwest of Tonkin. As General Revers had previously suggested, he thought it would be possible to clear the enemy out of central Annam, to the north of Cochin China. Such was the objective of the "Atlanta" operation, to which he held grimly, even after it became certain that the main enemy forces were going to attack Dien Bien Phu, and that a decisive battle would be fought there. When the moment came, he had at his disposal only three or four battalions as operational reserves.

Thus the Indochinese War was to be wound up with an undeniable strategic error, itself enmeshed in the uncertainty and hesitancy of French policy with respect to the "Associated States" of Vietnam, Laos and Cambodia. Like every vanquished army, the French Army sought the reasons for its defeat. It quite rightly went further than to examine the errors of strategy or tactics that the high command might have committed. Basically, what the Army wanted was a total explanation of the drama it had just passed through. It was beginning to discover the features of the "new type" of warfare it had failed to understand. This had not been a nationalist war, in Indochina. Almost immediately after the rupture with the Vietminh, the government had clearly announced that its aim was to establish an independent Vietnam. It was Communism and Communism alone that the Army had had to fight, and no national preoccupations were involved.

The Army, which had been abandoned by public opinion, was eager to find in France the origins of defeat. It would not place the brunt of the blame on the policy that had been followed. To do so would have meant reaching the conclusion that only negotiations with the Vietminh would have prevented war, and this conclusion was incompatible with anticommunism. Therefore the country's morale had to be found inadequate. Defeated armies prefer the "dagger thrust in the back" as an explanation of the enemy's miraculous victory. The French Army was no exception. The Communist Party, the "treason" of the politicians, the perfidy of the journalists who had declared themselves in favor of negotiation—there were culprits everywhere.

And how had the Vietminh succeeded in imposing its own form of warfare on the French Army? The methods had to be uncovered that had led to the defeat of an army incomparably better equipped, better officered and better trained. Many officers pursued this line of investigation with a veritable intellectual passion. Colonel Lacheroy was later to speak on their behalf. "It might have been thought," he declared, "that the military art would acquire a new form much less concerned than in the past with human values, and that we were heading for a 'press-button war.' Yet . . . in the last twelve years not a day has gone by without French officers and men dying for their country in some corner of the globe, and they were not confronted by any 'push-button war' but by varied forms of conflict, insurrections, ideological wars, etc. . . . or, in a word, revolutionary wars in which— more than at any other time and in any other form of conflict—human values revealed themselves to be preponderant." And he asked the question whose answer was being sought by all the officers who had served in Indochina:

> All the same, we had a certain superiority in command over the adversary confronting us. . . . We also disposed and still dispose of a marked superiority in infantry as well as in artillery and with respect to air, sea and armored forces, absolute supremacy, indeed, since our adversary had not and still has no planes, ships or tanks. And yet we were thwarted—that is the least that can be said—and we were not the only ones to find ourselves at much the same time in much the same circumstances. . . . In Indochina, as in China, as in Korea, as elsewhere, we see how the stronger appears to be defeated by the weaker. Why? Because the norms we used to estimate the opposing forces, the traditional norms, are dead. We have to examine a form of warfare that is new in its conceptions and new in its practices. This is the form of warfare we call "revolutionary war."

The enemy in this war, a whole school of officers asserted, was communism or, as they preferred to call it, Marxism-Leninism. This was the enemy that took up residence in the heart of every country, and fed on every economic, social or ideological conflict. It was backed, of course, by the individual strength of the Soviet Union. But the Soviet Union had no thought of intervening directly in the various episodes of the universal revolutionary war that it had inspired. In actual fact—and from this moment on, countless officers never tired of repeating it—the war had already begun. Everything tended to show that it would never take the form of an atomic conflict in which the U.S.S.R. would stake all on one throw. On the contrary, the Soviet Union found it much more prudent and more effective to instigate localized revolutionary disturbances throughout the world. As one officer put it, who wrote in response to an *enquête* organized by *Le Courrier de la Nation* and claimed to speak for a number of his fellows: "The Army has learned to identify the real adversary of the country it was defending. The threat, which for most French people, even the most lucid, remains far off and abstract, for military men has acquired the most immediate form, that of an invisible and omnipresent enemy less impressive for the real presence of his arms than for the strength of seduction or subversion exercised by means of propaganda or of undercover passwords." The real stake was the mind of the people. Everything became a weapon: the press, the trade unions, the radio and diplomatic maneuvers no less than the submachine gun, long-range gun or bomber. Colonel Lacheroy speaks of

> this total war toward which, alas, the world appears to be heading. Total, because not only does it mobilize in this war effort all the industrial, commercial and agricultural resources of a country, but also because it takes and utilizes in the war effort all the children, all the women, all the old people, all those who think, everything living, everything breathing, with all their capacity for love, for enthusiasm and for hatred, and hurls them into the war. This is the new factor. Total war, because it is a war that takes hold of souls as well as of bodies and bends them to obedience and to the war effort.

The implacable, rigorous and even apocalyptic elements in this analysis were ideally suited to seduce many minds. Yet it is remarkable that its propagators never in practice asked themselves the simple question: How had the Vietminh, for instance, managed to obtain the support of the mass of the population? That would have led them on to reflect on the nature of the economic ties between the former French Indochina and the homeland, and on the birth or rebirth of national feeling in Vietnam. But this new school of thought in the French Army was not looking for the reasons that explained the successes won in the type of warfare employed by the Vietminh. It preferred to think it was merely a matter of techniques. Nowhere was the question raised of the nature of the new nationalisms in Africa or Asia, or of their historical, economic, social or intellectual roots. Nothing was considered but the control of the populations by "parallel hierarchies," tricks of propaganda and terminology, the domination of the peoples' minds by terrorism, etc. The aim, basically, was to study all the methods of armed insurrection, all the procedures used by armed revolution, not to understand the motives of the rebellion and the source of the revolution.

The Army was already moving toward the acceptance of these new theories. General Chassin, a former Aviation Commander in Indo-china, published in October, 1954, in *La Revue Militaire d'Informations* the first studies of revolutionary warfare and, in particular, of the notions summed up by Mao Tse Tung in *The Strategy of Revolutionary Warfare in China*. Numerous articles on the subject were published by *La Revue de Défense Nationale*. During 1955 a mimeographed bulletin widely read by military men, *Message des Forces Armées*, published several studies on the matter. Soon the linkage of cause and effect was under way that would lead to the triumph of the new ideas. Since the adversary was to be found on the ideological, political, social and military levels, his doctrine had to be met by another with the same claim to totality and the same absolute seductiveness. In *Le Courrier de la Nation*, this was one answer to the *enquête*:

> In the current war of ideas that Marxism is waging against us, we cannot win unless we have truths to believe in and values to defend. Today every officer is convinced of this; formerly, the Nation needed warriors traditionally consecrated to the armed vocation. . . . At that time political preoccupations were pointless, for a narrowly specialized Army. But now that war has been transformed and has become a war of ideas, the character of the military man inevitably changes also. . . . He must be able to assimilate, expound and put into practice a coherent method.

"The drama of these young cohorts of officers athirst for the absolute," wrote Jean Brune a little later in *La Nation Française*, "and who have . . . understood that traditional nationalism must be fecundated by new notions . . . is, that they are cruelly tortured by the suspicion that only a substantial doctrine would enable them to embrace [their dream] and are desperately seeking for the elements of this, so far in vain. This Army made up of colonels who have been initiated into revolutionary warfare, and of captains and lieutenants confronted by human misery, hates this communism which, they realize, has been forcing them to retreat ever since Langson and Cao

Bang. It distrusts and doubts the value of capitalism, which seems to provide subversive propaganda with valid weapons. But, obsessed by these two rejections . . . it suffers at having nothing with which to challenge them . . ."

The stage was set for the great metamorphosis of the French Army. Another conflict would give it the supreme opportunity to revise its methods of warfare, and to try out its new ideas concerning the grip to be maintained on the populations wherein could be found, allegedly, the key to ultimate success. The stage was set for it to receive, in this final test, the stamp of theories and doctrines which, rolled up into one, would provide the explanation of everything, of its past failures and its coming victories, and which would irrefutably justify the seven years of war in Indochina and the future years of war in Algeria. These theories would at last establish an apparently unshakable connection between the universal struggle against communism, which was the goal of the Army's secret longings as well as being official governmental policy, and the new nationalisms that it had been or would be called on to fight. In this most recent stage of its long history, the Army would reach the apex of the curve that had led it toward political action. In the process, it would see its own unity shattered.

For the majority of the cadres there lurked in the background the painful and nostalgic recollection of the adventure in Indochina. Many officers retained the image of the Vietnamese people, to whom they generally attributed remarkable qualities. "I shall return from this country," wrote a colonel in 1947, "convinced that the only bond to be preserved is that of friendship . . ." They admired the extraordinary endurance of the peasants whose silent heroism won them over, these peasants who carried on their backs for hundreds of kilometers a matériel that the French Army would have transported by train or truck, and who had nothing to eat but scanty rations of rice. Yet they resisted every torture.

This admiration for the enemy was blended with feelings of solidarity, at first more or less unavowed but later very marked, with all the Indochinese who worked or fought alongside the French Army. There were Vietnamese, Cambodian and Laotian partisans, tribesmen and men from the high tablelands, guides, informants, simple soldiers, the inhabitants of the Catholic regions, and members of sects who, for reasons good or bad, had thrown in their lot with that of the French expeditionary corps. The remorse at having abandoned them after 1954 was one of the themes most frequently expressed, in every form, by military men. It was taken up again and again in newspaper articles and in periodicals, and in numerous personal records, whether volumes of reminiscences or novels such as Bertrand de Castel Bajac's *La Gloire et leur salaire*. It should not be overlooked that, with their insistence on the "dishonorable" aspect of this abandonment, many of the writers were stoutly attempting to discredit the negotiations entered into with the enemy, those persons who had always been in favor of negotiations and those who finally shouldered the responsibility for them. Their remorse was not of any unalloyed purity. It was based, nevertheless, on very genuine, sharply defined images, deeply imprinted and extremely painful. As a captain put it, in a article published by *Le Courrier de la Nation* and significantly entitled "The Yellow Malady,"

> Enclosed in our hearts is the picture of a crowd throwing itself into the sea to reach our ships, and the memory of all those who drowned, that day. The Méo . . . had worked with us the longest. One day they agreed to form underground groups, and in a few months they learned to use weapons, explosives and radio sets. With the armistice the order came to abandon these people along with all the others. This meant handing them over to the Vietminh, who would exterminate them. The radio sets of the Méo underground were still functioning after the armistice, and we can all remember the messages they sent us.

It counted for little, in the eyes of such an officer, that the vast majority of Vietnamese favored the Vietminh and, in any case, allowed it to triumph. It counted for little that the splitting up of Vietnam allowed the French Army's former brothers-in-arms to escape the Vietminh without leaving their own region or perhaps even their village. For him, as for so many officers who left Indochina, the bitterness of defeat was, quite naturally, the bitterness of all those who had participated in it, whatever their background, feelings or future lot. Remorse and regret blended irresistibly in the longing for a lost country, for a people left behind, for a horrible and devastating war by which so many nonetheless remained obsessed, and for a stage in the Army's history that has been called, borrowing the title of Tristan Corbière's volume of poems, "Les Amours Jaunes."

CHAPTER SEVENTEEN

THE ALGERIAN TRAP

✠

On July 3, 1954, the Secretary of State for War, Jacques Chevallier, delivered to the members of the Committee of National Defense his report concerning the effectives of the regular Army stationed in Europe and Africa who could be sent to Indochina—should the negotiations then being conducted in Geneva break down. Bearing in mind the government's obligations toward the Atlantic Alliance, the surveillance of military stores and the upkeep of matériel, the report stated that exactly 879 men were available for transfer to the Far East.

During the first seven months of that year, 100,000 men had been killed, wounded or captured in Vietnam, Laos and Cambodia, and 129,000 others had been sent in as reinforcements. Conscripts could not be sent to Indochina. They could, however, be sent to North Africa. But at the end of June, 1954, there were only 18,370 men in Tunisia and 54,000 men of the land forces in Algeria. For the whole of North Africa at that time there were 117,000 men in all.

This, then, was the French Army in the Maghreb, as the last stage of its career was about to begin. A few days later, Tunisia was to be accorded internal independence, and four months later, the Algerian rebellion would break out. After fifteen months the Conventions establishing the independence of Tunisia and Morocco would be declared, with the transfer of 400,000 men to Algeria.

The Army, back from Indochina, rediscovered in the Maghreb the memories of the preparations for the Italian campaign and of the disembarkment in Provence. They were distant memories, yet dear to most officers, for whom they summed up and symbolized the French Army's most considerable participation in the victory of 1945. North Africa aroused the memory of other eras and other traditions also, for it had been the cradle of one of the most original and interesting enterprises in French history.

This undertaking dates back to 1832, when the future General Lamoricière was put in charge of the "special bureau for Arab affairs." His task was "to maintain with prudence and success the relations with the tribes" and, after 1840, "to ensure the enduring pacification of the tribes by means of a just and coherent administration" and "to prepare the paths for our colonization and our commerce." This was the origin of the officers' corps which, by way of "Arab bureaux" and "native affairs" would create customs and traditions, indeed an entire way of living and exercising command. Few enough in number—186 in 1870, 300 at most in peacetime, and 600 including the *supplétifs*— they shared the common vocation that had led them to give up their former posts and to enter a universe dominated by tradition and by freedom of action at the same time. Each officer might be said to have followed his own independent policy, but all of them had received the same stamp and endeavored to carry through a particular conception of military and social action. Warned to beware of the caïd who "has his enemies and will try to convince you that they are yours," they often were regarded as a court of appeal against extremes of injustice and poverty. General Diego Brosset tried to tell the writer Vercors why he had chosen a career in the Army and how he acted. "Nothing," he told him,

> is more fruitful than constraints, and I have chosen those imposed by the uniform, first of all because it suits my temperament and also because it opens up for the right man an incomparable range of astonishing possibilities—perhaps only the Church could rival it in this—in which each man is offered the chance of personal fulfillment. And, finally, because it is also one of the few professions that accords you periods of wonderful tranquillity, genuine leisure, during which you can do what you want with your mind. I, for example, by the age of thirty had led several different existences, that of a French aristocrat, a Moroccan prince, a Berber nomad and a leader of Moroccan *rizzou*. I had an immense number of experiences in each of them, and there will be others.

It was in this frame of mind that, in Morocco, whole classes of officers concerned with "native affairs" lived out the adventure of soldiers who were administrators, builders and judges. The political doctrine behind their activity was as uncertain and veering as the whole of French policy in North Africa. Yet certain lessons learned went far deeper than the numerous directives dispatched from Rabat or from Paris. Such lessons, for instance, as that passed on by Colonel Berriau, when he stressed that the former Moroccan rebel "is not a criminal; he defended his native grounds and his independence. . . . The races that people Morocco are not inferior. They are different, that is all. . . . This implies, first of all, that we must have the desire and the ability to study the natives and understand them . . . to dismiss the usual solutions . . . to abandon the so customary practice of continual interference."

Marshal Lyautey was the master of Morocco for seventeen years. Thus his influence on the military cadres in North Africa went too deep to be forgotten after his departure. His clarifications and analyses would often be referred to. "We must take a direct look," he wrote,

> at the situation of the world in general and especially at the situation in the Moslem world, and not let events outstrip us. The declarations that have been diffused throughout world to the effect that peoples have a right to dispose of themselves, and the notions of emancipation and evolution, in a revolutionary sense, are not going to remain without effect. One must not assume that the Moroccans are, or for a long time to come will be, outside this general movement. . . . Here we really discovered a State and a people. . . . Nowhere else would stupidities and false steps be exposed more rapidly and more dearly. . . . There could be no worse peril than to allow European immigrants to commit imprudent actions that would be dearly paid for, or to let the seeds of discontent and distrust spring up among this people. . . . It would be an absolute illusion to believe that the Moroccans do not realize how they have been kept from any participation in public affairs. They suffer because of it and they talk about it. . . . A youthful generation is growing up among them that feels strongly and is eager to act. . . . If no openings are available—and our administration has distributed them stingily and only on a subaltern level—these young people will turn elsewhere . . .

But the military cadres did not invariably bear in mind these lessons. Most of them cherished the idea of an empire under French authority, built up by the Army and its leaders. Above all there lingered on the tradition of the Moroccan troops, of the ever "loyal" *tirailleurs*, of the

Spahis with their red cloaks and in particular of the *goumiers* and *tabors,* those purely Moroccan units, whose soldiers continued to live with their families and whose officers had the same training as the French officers in "native affairs." These *goumiers* had their own legend, and this became an epic, between 1942 and 1945, when they formed a highly important nucleus of the army that fought in Tunisia, and later of the expeditionary corps in Italy and of the First French Army in the Liberation campaigns. In 1955, after the endless Indochinese adventure, they numbered 15,000 men.

The heirs of a long North African tradition, the French military cadres still had much to say in the evolution and application of French policy in the Maghreb. In Tunis, after 1946, a military man, General Mast, was replaced by a series of civilians. In Morocco, on the other hand, Eric Labonne, a civilian, had been replaced in 1947 by General Juin, and he was to remain Resident General there until 1952. As his Director of Political Affairs he took, in 1951, General Boyer de Latour. Juin was replaced by General Guillaume, and not until the middle of 1954 did a diplomat, Francis Lacoste, take over the office. Until 1954, consequently, some of the Army's most prominent leaders were directly involved in the conduct of North African Affairs.

Yet this brought about no crisis between political authority and the military. After the exclusion of the Communist ministers, in the spring of 1947, it was in North Africa that the course adopted by French policy had its most immediate and its gravest consequences. The departure of Labonne, who was blamed for the prudently nationalist speech delivered in Tangiers by the Sultan of Morocco, marked the end of a liberal era. It seemed to be agreed, in Paris and in Rabat, that there would have to be a gradual return to a juster conception of the Protectorate, which would once more place in the hands of the Sultan and his government the management of internal affairs. In January, 1948, Chataigneau, the Governor of Algeria, was recalled to Paris, for he had been reproached, in financial and administrative circles, with having shown too great a sympathy for the Moslem community.

The first task of his successor, the Socialist Deputy and one-time Minister Marcel Edmond Naegelen, was to organize the election of the Algerian Assembly that had been created by the statute passed the previous year. He did this in such a way that the nationalist parties that had had the greatest success in the general elections of 1946 were now very weakly represented in the new Assembly. From this point on, the Algerian nationalists would be deprived of every legal means of expression and of action. From the outset, the path was prepared for those who favored armed intervention.

There could be no serious divergency between the plans of the governments and their implementation by the military, from the point of view of maintaining the political, military, economic and even administrative position of France in North Africa. All the governors and residents, however, complained of receiving no guidance from Paris. Robert Schuman, who was Minister of Foreign Affairs from 1948 to 1953, was absorbed in matters of European policy, and showed himself to be the most discreet of ministers, where Tunisia and Morocco were concerned. Later he complained of the difficulties experienced by those with overriding political authority in getting the men on the scene to carry out the decisions transmitted to them. This is an astonishing statement, in the mouth of a man who belonged to almost every government under the Fourth Republic up to 1956. He came to appear almost a permanent fixture, and he had immense influence in his party, the Mouvement Républicain Populaire, around which every parliamentary majority revolved. Marshal Juin and General Guillaume had no influence in political circles, and the former was even regarded with a certain distrust—inspired, it should be said, much more by his outspokenness than by his actual intentions. As for the Residents General in Tunisia, Messieurs Mons, Périllier, de Hautecloque and Voizard, the first was perhaps the most liberal, but the three others were named by Schuman himself, and he could easily have replaced them.

Mainly responsible, it seems, for France's North African policy was the very nature of the political regime. The almost total absence of directives from the government concerning Morocco, Algeria and Tunisia was no mere fluke. Such directives would have presupposed a policy. But from 1947 to 1951, and even as late as 1954, any choice would have split the parties making up the government and on each occasion provoked a new ministerial crisis. As long as North African problems were not too urgent and required no immediate decision, they were left outside the governmental purview. Too many other critical matters were clamoring for attention.

Except for the Communists and the anticolonial Left, the whole range of political opinion seemed blind to the possibility of a violent upheaval in the Maghreb. No warning could have induced the military to see any differently the future of countries to which they were attached by a tradition long in years and rich in renown. It was quite normal that those leaders of the Army who reflected on North African policy should have instinctively brushed aside any notion of the necessity of decolonization. In the early 1950's, indeed, the term was not in circulation, the idea was foreign to most men's minds. Here, as in so many other instances, the development among the military proceeded neither at a faster nor at a slower pace than among the politicians. Nothing could better exemplify this than the "general directives concerning our policy in Morocco" addressed to the corps of civilian inspectors, on March 8, 1951, by General Boyer de Latour, Secretary General for political and military affairs in Rabat.

This gentleman, a former officer for native affairs, who spoke Arabic and had a deep attachment to Morocco, particularly "the old Morocco," boasted in these "directives" of how the Moroccan leaders were attached to him, and of the confidence he inspired among the masses. He again stressed the need for the personal activity of French administrators and officers vis-à-vis the Moroccan population, using terms that no diplomat or republican member of parliament would have repudiated. "We must always remember," he wrote, "the celebrated phrase that made politeness the base of our relations with the Moroccans, and advised us to treat the Moroccan great lord, citizen and peasant just as we would treat any great lord, citizen or peasant in France. Each man's dignity must be scrupulously respected. We must banish every feeling of racial superiority, which is all the more improper since the Moroccans, like ourselves, are westerners."

The last word is significant. Since the Moroccans were "westerners," they were set off from the Arab world, to which they were linked by their language, their religion, their dynasty and the ethnic origins of many among them. In the view of such a man as General Boyer de Latour and of a whole school of officers specializing in Moroccan affairs, Morocco was to be kept as separate as possible from the developments of the Arab world. Even before World War II, some civilians and military men had been attracted by a "Berber" policy whose aim it was to "de-Arabize" Morocco. But this policy threatened the unity of the country and the authority of the Sultan. The Protectorate itself was called into question. Although they avoided such extremes, General Boyer de Latour's "directives" strongly underlined Morocco's occidental character:

> "The idea of a Morocco isolated or attached to an Arab league goes against all geographical realism, and is an absurdity that would not

stand up to the actual test. The Mediterranean is a geological accident and the Arab invasions are an historical accident, but the
Moroccans are westerners in the geographical and racial sense of the
word. . . . What a journalist recently referred to as 'the occidental
destiny of North Africa' is no idle construct but a concrete reality
of which the Moroccans and ourselves must become aware."

Such was the outlook imbuing French policy in Morocco in 1951,
and every measure promulgated necessarily bore its stamp. Thus the
re-establishment of the communes and the formation of local assemblies were intended to affirm the country's "originality"—that is to say,
its non-Arab character. Similarly, the attitude to be adopted with
respect to the young nationalists was inspired by it:

Vis-à-vis the Moroccan nationalists, a distinction must be drawn.
Nationalism is not a crime in itself, and the aspirations of the young
Moroccans must not be reprimanded; they must be understood, acted
upon and given satisfaction, insofar as order, the essential base of our
activity, is not thereby impaired. But nationalism becomes intolerable,
as soon as it becomes anti-French . . . our presence in Morocco cannot,
in any case, be looked on as an instance of mere colonial expansion.
This is a question of life or death for the French Nation and the
Empire.

If we omit the reference to the "western" character of Morocco
these remarks could have been made by the majority of the politicians
and highly placed civil servants of the Fourth Republic. They already
reveal some of the arguments which will later acquire their full
strength in the Algerian affair. "One has only to cast an eye on the
map," wrote General Boyer de Latour, "to understand . . . that the last
redoubt of European resistance is in North Africa."

This was the view of most political observers and of most military
experts. It was accepted all the more easily because, in 1951, the
fighting in Indochina and Korea dramatized the cold war, while a third
world war was a frequently envisaged hypothesis. The still recent
example of how Europe had been freed, from bases in North Africa,
had left its imprint on the General Staffs, and Morocco appeared an
essential element of western strategy. The French Army very naturally
came to the conclusion that in all conceivable circumstances its power
must be maintained in the Maghreb. This was the reasoning which
later would serve to justify the Army's intervention in the Algerian
political situation.

The ideas behind General Boyer de Latour's "directives" were, in

1951, being repeated in many newspapers and periodicals, and incorporated in official speeches. "The narrow nationalism propounded by the members of Istiqlal," wrote the general, "has now been . . . left far behind by the facts. At a time when airplanes can travel at more than one thousand kilometers an hour, these persons voice a nationalism that belongs to the stage-coach era. The concept of the Nation, as we ourselves have known it, is about to disappear, to be replaced by federations of powers in which Eurafrica will have a great part to play." Supranationalism, federation and Eurafrica: these notions were commonplaces for the political orators. They would have to be set aside, before the African nationalist movements could be understood and their irresistible character recognized. The politicians would perhaps find it easier to adjust to this than the military men, for whom independence meant the end of the Army's African traditions, the loss of the bases whose importance they had been taught to recognize, and the "abandonment" of regions that were familiar ground to a whole generation of officers.

The Army was sentimentally and passionately attached to French North Africa. For most officers, the Maghreb remained the "sanctuary" where the Army still was bedecked with the prestige of its noble institutions, whereas in France itself there was nothing but the dreary, impoverished existence in the garrison. These officers had been totally immersed in their Indochinese adventure, had had no opportunity to follow the first manifestations of North African nationalism. They looked on Morocco, Algeria and Tunisia as the firm, indisputable and undisputed bastions of French power in Africa—and, too, as the strongly defended bases of a strategic area indispensable to the western world. In the Navy, every school and every training course emphasized the importance of Mers-el-Kébir and of Bizerte to Mediterranean defense. In the air force, North Africa was depicted as the only French-owned region out of range of the Soviet bombers, and thus as supremely important in the event of world conflict. The presence of American military airfields in Morocco testified to this. In Indochina, officers of every branch and of every provenance had commanded North African troops: these, indeed, made up about half of the expeditionary corps' effectives. Everything combined to reinforce, in the minds of the military cadres, the conviction that French authority in the Maghreb was both natural and necessary.

The General Staffs were aware that in a very short period North African nationalism would present both a military and a political problem. Some of the Army's leaders sensed the dangers of new involvements that would swallow up everything that should properly be devoted to the nation's defenses: credits, officering, matériel and professional soldiers. Since the summer of 1954, a kind of cleavage had taken place between those who at any price wanted to avoid starting in Africa what had turned out so badly in Asia, and those who regarded the defense of the Maghreb as the first national imperative. The former judged that the Army's mission concerned before all else the protection of the national territory, now conceived as coextensive with the European peninsula. For the latter, this "watch on the Rhine," even if it had been transformed into a "watch on the Elbe," represented an outdated conception of national defense and even of western strategy. They held that there was no threat requiring the concentration of the French military effort on the European continent. Pointing to the political upheavals that menaced North Africa, they stressed the danger of an imminent collapse of all French military positions on the southern littoral of the Mediterranean. They still felt it was premature to allege too openly that the various nationalisms in North Africa were connected with the long-range schemes of international communism. Neither the part played by Bourguiba in Tunisia nor, in Morocco, the campaign for the return of Sultan Mohammed V could readily justify such a rapprochement. But one could already foresee that in the Maghreb, as in Indochina, the French military "presence" would be associated with the establishment of a western strategy.

It was the duty of the governments to find a policy. They could not, of course, remain unaware of military men's preferences, and they knew from past experience that these preferences matched the desires of the French populations in North Africa. While the administrative and financial cadres of the two Protectorates had played the decisive role, in 1951–1952, in breaking off the negotiations on the internal autonomy of Tunisia, and in the maneuvers that led to the deposition of Sultan Mohammed V, military personalities had also had a hand. Ever since 1951 Marshal Juin had favored the removal of the Sultan, if it should prove to be necessary, so that a particular policy might be forced on Morocco. Colonel Lecomte, Director of the Interior in the Residence General in Rabat, had himself given support to organized campaigns against Mohammed V. General Guillaume, who took over from Juin, although he tried to follow the governmental directives ordering him to maintain the Sultan on the throne, did nothing to hinder the plot that succeeded in replacing Mohammed V by Ben

Arafa. He also accepted the consequences of this, and so led the Laniel government to do likewise.

But if political leaders could see to what an extent their intentions were likely to be constantly thwarted by the men whose duty it was to carry them out, they should also have realized that this distrust might more justly be directed against the administrative personnel than against the military. Nothing, indeed, seems to have prevented governments from relying on military authority in order to put through their policy, whatever that might be. Mendès-France seems to have grasped this, when he asked Marshal Juin to accompany him to Tunis, where he was about to state his solemn intention of recognizing the internal autonomy of the Regency, and when he asked General Boyer de Latour to be the Resident General charged with seeing this new experiment on its way. Marshal Juin declared himself to favor Tunisian autonomy, expressing his approval publicly for the benefit of veterans' groups.

The General Staff, furthermore, had clearly seen what the military consequences would be of a policy that refused to provide any liberal solution for the Tunisian problem. It was haunted by the Indo-chinese precedent. Its basic preoccupation was to avoid experiencing anywhere else the dreadful setbacks it had met with in the Far East. Marshal Juin and the Generals Ely, Salan and Blanc had repeatedly told the governments that a purely military solution in Vietnam was impossible. They had the same conviction with respect to North Africa. But now there was a general officer who actually declared in so many words that only a liberal political solution could avoid the risk of a general war. General Blanc, the Army's Chief of Staff, after an inspection in Tunisia carried out between August 6 and 11, 1954, drew up on August 17 a report for the government in which he made no attempt to camouflage the dilemma in which France, according to him, found herself. "Tunisia," he wrote,

> on the eve of July 31, reached the stage that Indochina reached in 1945–46. As in Vietnam, the Tunisian people were divided into two great masses. One was strongly organized, was obtaining an in-creasing international audience, was awakening fear among the other Tunisians and organizing terrorist attacks against the French and their friends. The other was headed by leaders belonging to inchoate parties and with only politically backward masses behind them. To attempt to beat down this terrorism by force of arms—even with increased manpower—as it gradually extended from the *bled* to the

towns, without considering its sources both at home and abroad, that is to say, without resolving the fundamental political problem, would have led France to a new Bao Dai experiment and to a hopeless struggle, as was the case in the Far East. The disastrous experiment carried out in Vietnam has quite sufficiently shown, as had been predicted, the impossibility of mastering a popular movement by force, unless a heavy price be paid. To continue with the same mistakes would have undermined the whole French edifice in North Africa and threatened the position of France in Europe.

General Blanc openly recognized the efficacy of a policy based on negotiations with the Tunisian government, whose aim would be to establish the autonomy of the Regency. Thus the General Staff was firmly wedded to the line laid down by the political authorities. The resolution of the Mendès-France government no doubt had much to do with this, just as General Blanc, who had always been opposed to overseas expeditions, respected the limits of his position vis-à-vis the state.

Yet it should be realized that the support given by the military leaders to the policy initiated in Tunisia was fragile enough. One year after General Blanc had presented his report, the conference held at Aix-les-Bains cleared the way for Moroccan independence. The provisional character of the measure of autonomy granted at once became plain. Any intermediate stage between French domination and independence was bound to be short-lived. Less than one year after the ratification of the Franco-Tunisian accords on internal autonomy new agreements had to be made recognizing the total independence of Tunisia. And in Morocco, the Council of the Throne, which had been created to permit the departure of Sultan Ben Arafa and to block the return of Mohammed V, had but a few days of existence.

These examples had considerable repercussions in the Army. Those whose minds were best prepared to accept decolonization concluded that the liberal solutions, which provisionally barred the entire independence of the colonized countries, could only be stages on the way, and that they should be viewed as such. But for the others, that is, for the great majority, this meant that they should be rejected at any cost, in order to prevent the inevitable end, namely total freedom, from being achieved. They were, indeed, but the "antechambers of independence" and had, as a consequence, all the drawbacks without any of the definiteness of independence. All they really accomplished was to mask over the goal that was being aimed at. They fused into one "the lie" and "abandonment." After these experiences in Tunisia and Morocco, the Army's leaders hesitated to stake their authority in backing the ideas of association, interdependence or cooperation.

In the brief history of Morocco's rise to independence, between the summer and the fall of 1955, there was nothing to attract the military mind, nor to win friends for a policy whose aim was decolonization. The elimination of Sultan Ben Arafa, who had ascended to the throne only after the express demand of the French authorities, and the return to Rabat of Mohammed V, although this eventually had been solemnly excluded by the highest personalities in the State; the almost immediate disappearance of the solution that had been agreed upon after infinite trouble; the humiliation of El Glaoui and his followers, whose hostility to the Sultan could never have been expressed without the agreement and support of the French administrators—this was the balance sheet of the policy that had led to Moroccan independence. And the massacre of Europeans in Oued-Zem added a sinister note.

The revolt of the Riff tribesmen, the very day of Ben Arafa's departure, showed that even the most considerable concessions could not stem the tide of nationalism. For the officers in the small posts of northern Morocco, who were attacked on the night of October 1-2, and for those with the *tabors* and the regiments of *tirailleurs* who were fighting the Moroccan "Army of National Liberation," independence certainly did not bear the visage that it bore in Paris. There, the political milieux that had been most hostile to any liberal development discovered the wisdom, the prudence and moderation of Sultan Mohammed V, who was assuredly no partisan of a holy war or of a break with France. They became acquainted with the new Moroccan political personnel and found them to be neither terrorists nor guerrilla leaders but young men anxious to act as statesmen and to learn how to overcome the difficulties associated with an independence won in such brutal fashion.

Parliament ratified by an enormous majority the policy followed in Morocco, as it had ratified the Franco-Tunisian accords on internal autonomy. It was sensed, in Paris, that any other course would have led to a generalized war, of which the massacres of August and the revolt of October would have been only the first fruits. Public opinion had the deep resolve not to relive the Indochinese experience in North Africa.

Could military opinion share the same conviction? Between November, 1955, and October, 1956, almost normal relations were established between the French troops stationed in Morocco and the young state. They were affected only by the incidents of the Algerian War, which inevitably raised disputes concerning both troop movements and the utilization of bases. But gradually, as 1955 merged into 1956, the Army went over to its new task of aiding, instructing and cooperating with the new independent States of the Maghreb.

Martial recollections bound many Moroccan officers, civil servants and politicians to the French Army in which they had served. Even at the height of the crisis, in August, 1955, Moroccan opinion still distinguished the Army, which it was eager to respect, from the administration, which it distrusted, and above all from the police, which it had learnt to detest. Ten days after his arrival in Rabat, Gilbert Granval, the Resident General, set out to reverse the policy of stagnation that had been followed in the preceding years. "The Moroccans," he wrote, "are beginning to believe once more in the possibility of a dialogue with a nation whose true face they are re-discovering. Our Army has replaced the police in the Arab quarters and has once more taken over its protective role, and by its exemplary behavior, and its medical and social aid, it has already brought about a real relaxation of tension. The Legion has just been acclaimed in the medina of Casablanca . . ."

These are revealing remarks, coming from a man who at the same instant was being obscurely opposed by his own Director of the Interior and of Security, General Leblanc, and who, in Paris, ran up against the opposition of General Koenig, Minister of National Defense, and his Chief of Staff, General Lecomte. The Army no doubt looked on the Moroccan crisis as a test. But it had not agreed to accept official policy or, rather, the consequences of this. In Morocco, as in Tunisia, independence would prove to be the starting point for a new crisis confronting the Republic and its Army. The seeds had already been sown in Algeria. While the French officers in Morocco and Tunisia were becoming acquainted with the uniforms of the young armies improvised by the new States, other French officers were ap-prenticing themselves to a guerrilla combat from which they would later try to hatch a revolution.

Amid the splendors of the Moroccan Protectorate a certain original-ity had persisted, and this set its stamp on military life. The habits of direct administration had not suppressed—far from it—the particular relations established and maintained between French authority and the social hierarchies in Morocco. Morocco was not France. This was a very concrete matter for the officers who, outside their barracks, saw a very special style develop in the relations between their generals and the French General Staffs and the Sultan, his court, his feudal lords, and the tribes of his Empire. Besides, the officers concerned with native affairs had to some degree influenced all the military cadres in Morocco. The instinctive sympathy of the military milieu for the authoritarian and lordly traditions of old Morocco had strengthened most officers in their respectful though protective attitude toward the original organization of a country whose particular qualities they did not deny, but admired.

In other words, they were in no position to be able to understand and appreciate the awakening of a modern nationalism, rendered all the more suspect in their eyes because it challenged both French authority and Moroccan traditionalism. This nationalism arose, too, at the outset, among students and some bourgeois groups, and in the miserable, overcrowded quarters housing the proletarians and the unemployed of the big towns. Most French officers, proud of their own authority and attracted by Moroccan traditions, detested and feared this new Morocco.

In the summer of 1953, however, Moroccan nationalism spoke with the voice of legitimacy: the first requirement was to fight for the reestablishment of the Sultan on his throne. It is certain that at this time many officers failed to sense the irresistible force of this new trend. They had too long believed in monarchical authority, in the force of the dynastic traditions and in the value of tribal allegiance to the Sultan, to suspect that on this occasion nationalism would flow beyond the limits of the universities and the workers' quarters to win the adhesion of a great part of the Empire. On the other hand, the support given El Glaoui by the Residence, and the systematic utilization of certain tribes—the famous "Berber knights"—against Sultan Mohammed V and his followers, and against his return, too clearly showed that the Protectorate had renounced its own origins. It was now fighting against the unity of Morocco, which it had helped to rebuild or reinforce, and with its own hands it was creating the anarchy to whose disappearance it had previously contributed.

On the other side of the frontier, military society was entirely different. Algeria was the territory of the tenth military district, the other nine being in France. There one was subject to the Nineteenth Corps, whose origins went back to the first great military enactments of the Third Republic. The Army's function in Algeria was precisely that assigned to it in the homeland. Only the southern regions, with their haunting Saharan legends, still spoke of adventure. But in Constantine, Blidah, Cherchell, Sidi-bel-Abbès or Oran, garrison life bore an undeniable resemblance to garrison life in Pau, Montpellier or Valence. Admittedly, the troops had a different background, owing to the proportion of the native-born in the regiments of *tirailleurs,* Zouaves and *chasseurs d'Afrique.* But they could be found also in France or in Germany and, after 1946, the bulk of the North African units was blended with the rest and hurled into the Indochinese furnace.

The seven years of the Indochinese War had helped to make the Algerian garrisons resemble even more closely those of France itself. At the most, the bonuses and indemnities, the relative abundance of matériel and living conditions made life more agreeable. The prefects and subprefects, the town halls, the appearance of the European districts in the large and medium-sized towns, all contributed to an administrative and social atmosphere very close to that of France. Only a few General Staffs and a few specialized bureaux paid any attention to the traditionally "under-administered" regions where Algeria still appeared to be a wild, distant, scarcely conquered country, where political eddies and certain other symptoms gave a hint of future crises.

The atmosphere of 1955 might have led to the belief that Algeria would not for long remain unaffected by the upheavals that had occurred in Tunisia and Morocco. With the coming of Tunisian autonomy and Moroccan independence, many things that had appeared sacrosanct began to change. The history of French society with respect to decolonization still remains to be written, but it can be affirmed that in 1955 the French bourgeoisie as a whole was insistent, before all else, on not having to live through another Indochinese tragedy. The nightmare of Dien Bien Phu seemed to have left an enduring mark. Why not agree to the inevitable developments in Africa, where nationalism was not identified with communism?

The support of the leading newspapers, the agreement of the moderate political parties and the approval of the most influential elements in the *grande bourgeoisie,* suggested that there would be no further large-scale military adventures overseas. In France, economic well-being conspired with the political climate to create a general feeling of *détente.* Since early 1952, the stabilization of prices, the absence of new taxes, the rapid growth of industrial production and the impressive rise of stock prices gave the country a feeling of prosperity, equilibrium and expansion, which was justified by the increasing wealth of a considerable segment of the population. Inflation no longer disguised economic growth, which at last ensured the balance of payments. After the long years during which France had lived under the threat of monetary devaluation, the trend appeared to have been reversed.

In such an atmosphere, the bitter quarrels over the European Army and German rearmament seemed almost forgotten. The steps taken by the Faure government to get under way the negotiations that would lead to the Common Market and to Euratom met with no serious opposition. The prospect of a single European market was accepted all the more readily since this market had already been set up for coal and steel, without causing any catastrophe. Besides, nothing appeared to challenge the political independence of each state. As for German rearmament, this was all the easier to take, in the atmosphere of international good feeling that had reigned for two years past. The most solemn manifestation of this occurred in the summer of 1955 when Bulganin, Eden, Faure and President Eisenhower met at Geneva.

The Army, in its endeavor to reform its structures and to embark on a most intelligent and audacious plan of modernization, was working in harmony with public feeling. Its future, it now appeared, lay in the Javelot brigade, perhaps in atomic armaments. How far away was the time when French military opinion shuddered at the last appeals received from "Beatrice" or "Isabelle," the heroic bastions of last resistance at Dien Bien Phu! How far away were those "Amours Jaunes" that had attracted the heart and mind of so many French officers, whose whole existence was upset in this war among the rice-fields! From time to time, some newspapers published an item dealing with men who had belonged to the expeditionary corps in the Far East, when a few pitiful wrecks, dragged from political meetings to police stations, could still stir the consciences of Frenchmen or awaken bitter memories of the lost Indochina. But what remained of this adventure, now that the Sultan of Morocco, back from exile, received the submission of El Glaoui, the visit of the pretender to the French throne and even the homage of the French of Morocco, who had been his worst enemies?

But at this moment, when all seemed about to be forgotten, all was to spring to infernal life once more, from the depths of the Algerian *djebels*. The first reinforcements to be sent to Algeria since All Souls' Day, 1954, were just about to arrive.

In Algeria the Army was entering the last stage in the history of its imperial or colonial missions. No one imagined that Black Africa could be the theater of large-scale operations, and no one thought that, if Algeria were granted autonomy (or, *a fortiori*, independence), the African States could continue under French administration. The last fight would have to be fought in Algeria.

After the evacuation of Indochina, after Tunisian autonomy and Moroccan independence, the Army's horizon seemed doomed to shrink to the garrisons of France and Germany. For a whole generation of officers who, during the World War and then in the Far East, had known a life marked by departure, new surroundings, adventure and combat, the future threatened to be, not a return to the fountainhead, but a sort of bourgeois retirement in the outmoded setting of European barracks. Between two periods spent in Asia, Germany or Morocco, French officers twenty to forty years old had scarcely glimpsed anything of military life in France except its mediocrity and dullness. They had become aware only of the indifference or hostility of public opinion, the inadequacy or high cost of dwelling units and the low pay, all in marked contrast to the progressive enrichment of the bourgeoisie, the expansiveness of business and the rapid evolution of mores. A kind of anguish prevented the military cadres from accepting, without rancor or hesitancy, the idea of the return to an uninviting homeland. There was nothing political about such a feeling, which involved neither an ideological choice nor rebelliousness vis-à-vis the regime. But it forged a new link between the Army and the Algerian adventure.

Everything depended on the government's decisions. Jacques Soustelle, the Governor General appointed by Mendès-France, had arrived in Algeria in 1955 with the most liberal intentions, and he was responsible for the first plan envisaging political and social reforms. At the end of the year, after the massacres of August 20, which had been worse in Algeria than in Morocco, the government rejected the idea of federalism, which seemed to be the solution favored by the Socialist opposition. But the necessity, in the longer run, of some new policy was the reason put forward for dissolving the National Assembly. No path was yet barred. Numerous indications led the Army to believe that the path chosen for Morocco would soon be chosen for Algeria also. The Army had been impressed by the rapidity with which the obstacles had been overcome that had hindered the return of the former Sultan and the independence of the country, and was far from certain that in Algeria the authorities would stand up to nationalism and decide to employ armed force.

The government presided over by Guy Mollet had been accepted by a very large majority in the National Assembly. To deal with the Algerian affair it had a slogan, an idea and a man. The slogan dated from the election campaign, when Guy Mollet had spoken of "an imbecile war that has reached a deadlock." The idea was that of the "Algerian personality," which, vague though the formula was, implied a distinct status for Algeria that would take into account the specific character of the population and that seemed to promise autonomy but not complete independence. The man was General Catroux, one of the few general officers who had gone over to Free France. He had negotiated the granting of independence to Lebanon and Syria, he had drawn up a proclamation that gave voting rights to a whole category of Algerian Moslems, and had been sent by the Faure government to talk with the exiled Sultan in Madagascar. The Mendès-France government had named him Grand Chancellor of the Legion of Honor.

In vain, from the first moment of his being named Minister for Algeria, did this general with a liberal past affirm that "while the government intends to satisfy the demands of the Moslem community, it cannot in any circumstances transform the country into a national State, which inevitably would become independent. Nor can there be any question of placing the French in a minority position." The elected representatives of the European community, struck by the federalist overtones of the expression "Algerian personality," feared that in an independent Algeria a single electoral college would ensure the overwhelming predominance of the Moslem community in internal, and especially in economic and social matters, which would be under the sovereign sway of Algerian governmental institutions. Some of these representatives, including some looked on as very moderate, such as the Mayor of Algiers, Jacques Chevallier, and René Blanchette, who had practically a monopoly in the trade in esparto-grass and owned Le Journal d'Alger, could not accept General Catroux. "Despite our respect for the Grand Chancellor of the Legion of Honor," they wrote to Guy Mollet on February 3,

> it is our duty to inform you of all our fears relative to the dramatic consequences that might result from General Catroux's arrival, and to beg you not to subject Algeria to this new risk. . . . You will not have overlooked that the granting of the single college would eject the

French community from Algerian public life. Thus the only system
conceivable is one which would guarantee the community civil status
and its representation on an equal footing, such as you yourself have
recognized to be indispensable, along with economic status for the
community. That in itself implies the maintenance of the double
college.

On February 6 the government had to bow before the hostility of the
European minority; the President of the Council asked General
Catroux to resign. With that, the limits of official policy were pretty
narrowly drawn. Even if Algeria should be granted a certain measure
of autonomy, the statute could not in any circumstances allow the
Moslem majority to function as the majority. This preoccupation was
to handicap the secret negotiators sent by Guy Mollet to talk with the
representatives of the F.L.N. from March to September, 1956. It was
to inspire the first and second measures proposed, the following year,
to determine the status of Algeria. Nowhere does an examination of
the occurrences of February 6 reveal any trace of military intervention.
It was, in fact, a number of ministers who feared the outcome of the
day and the possibility of European demonstrations, who had suggested that reinforcements be sent to Algiers. No general officer, no
General Staff and no military group had intervened with Guy Mollet
when, in the Summer Palace, he received the public authorities and
delegations representing economic interests, trade unions or veterans'
groups.

As the demonstrations proceeded, maintenance of order was entrusted to the Compagnies Républicaines de Sécurité. Colonel Massu's
parachutists had to free the surroundings of the Palace, which was
threatened by the crowd. Once again, at this decisive moment in
French and Algerian history, though not for the last time, it was the
existence of a European community that exercised a decisive pressure
on the course of events by forcing the government to adopt its views.

The European community in Algeria was a kind of epitome of
French society. It had its businessmen, bankers and industrialists, its
veterans and trade unionists, its differences in class and background,
its Communist proletariat, its Socialist civil servants and employees,
its administrations and nationalized enterprises, its modest peasants
and large-scale farmers. Traditionally, the political representatives
were made up of a clerical Right, reactionary in tendency, which had
favored Vichy, and a Radical or Socialist Left, closely associated with
the parties in France, with Masonic connections, and influential in

the government and the main branches of the administration. Together, in Algeria, they owned the bases of economic power and controlled all political power. Independence or any degree of autonomy
that would have guaranteed the exercise of power by the overwhelmingly larger Moslem majority would have meant the end of this state
of affairs, and the certain overthrow of the social and economic structures of the European community. It was against this that the community rebelled, and against this that the government sought to
protect it, after the trial of strength on February 6, 1956.

Recourse to military means became unavoidable, although the
determination of the government had yet to be demonstrated. Whether
the rebels were to be reduced to submission, or whether the population
was to be blessed with a security that would be the reflection of the
political changes decided on in Paris, in any event the presence of
substantial armed forces in Algeria became indispensable. There is no
record of any disagreement on this score, when the dispatch of substantial reinforcements was resolved on. For the first time, the military
cadres and the classes liable to mobilization would be side by side,
fighting overseas in what would turn out to be the last colonial war.
The combatants were no longer only professional soldiers, men who
had enlisted of their own free will or Senegalese *tirailleurs,* foreign
legionaries or *tabors.* They were young Frenchmen, who were wearing
uniform as required by compulsory military service.

Thus the Algerian War became a task shared by the whole Nation.
It was clear that the Army, both officers and men, could not be treated
in the same cavalier fashion as the expeditionary corps in the Far
East. The rules of 20th-century warfare would of course be applied.
There would have to be ideological and moral reasons to justify this
conflict, in which Frenchmen would be taking part. These reasons
would have to be defined, expounded, defended, and not only the
Army but the whole country would have to be convinced. In this
undertaking the officers would have a major role, that of intermediary
between the State and the "Nation under arms" constituted by these
mobilized classes.

There was nothing new about this, for military regulations had
always instructed officers to watch over the morale of the men, for
which they were held responsible. But did the words now have the
same sense? Was this the age-old cult of the motherland? Was it
enough to rely on the traditional motivations of national solidarity and
patriotic sacrifice? For the insiders in politics, whether laymen or

soldiers, it was clear that the Algerian War took its place in the line of the wars waged to decide the destiny of the former colonial empires. Some were able to discern the difficult phase—but only the phase—that would lead to decolonization. Others estimated that the particularly long-lasting and intimate bonds uniting France and Algeria prohibited independence which, if it should occur, would merely be a curtain-raiser for social upheavals that would shake the whole position of the western world in Africa and the Mediterranean. But the great majority of officers had no political sophistication and did not seek to acquire it. Therefore it was natural that they should rediscover their traditional mission on Algerian soil: the defense of the national heritage. Some officers might be intrigued by strategic or political arguments; most of them clung to the simplest possible assertion, that of France's rights in Algeria.

Early in 1956, the defense of the population against rebel activity, and especially against terrorism in the towns, might have sufficed to endow this new war with the splendor of a just cause. But when it became apparent that really at stake was independence against the maintenance of French authority, only the clearest and most rudimentary formula could convince the least cultivated and least politically conscious of the military cadres, and enable them, in their turn, to convince the men that the State had been placed in their care. From the very outset the machinery got under way that would induce the officers' corps to believe in "French Algeria."

The recall of several contingents that had already returned to civilian life and, at the same time, the lengthening, in practice, of the period of military service, were the features that characterized the Army's new war footing. A few weeks later, the government obliged the high command to send to Algeria the officers trained to direct the modernized divisions in France and Germany. This meant the interruption, for a very long time, of all the attempts at adaptation that the Army had undertaken since the end of the Indochinese War. These two decisions set the stage on which the history of French military society would drag out for years to come. The principal scene would be Algeria. All the young men liable to be conscripted, and all the officers on active duty, would assemble there in order to fight the most considerable of overseas wars. The day was past when the French Army could be required to participate in the world competition to develop modern armaments, and in the military revolution that the Great Powers would have to put through, sooner or later. The

Army's horizon had suddenly shrunk, for nothing was visible outside the Tunisian frontier and the Moroccan frontier, with only Algeria in between.

The recall of the available classes posed an immediate problem for the military cadres. They had to get a grip on these newly constituted units, and see to the morale and general frame of mind of the men, as they were being dispatched to Algeria. The General Staff regarded with some apprehension an operation that had had no precedent since 1938. While half a contingent had been hastily recalled in the fall of 1947 to deal with the strikes, these men had been set free a few weeks later amid considerable disorder and without really having been utilized. The political climate, after the elections of January 2, 1956, did not appear to favor a direct, large-scale appeal to the Nation. The memory of the Indochinese War was still too close not to arouse the suspicions of a public that had welcomed calmly, if not with actual enthusiasm, the changes decided on in Tunisia and Morocco.

During the weeks that were required for mobilization to be completed, the General Staff was on tenterhooks. Many officers later referred to it as a veritable nightmare. The military hierarchy was overcome with alarm at the least rumpus occurring in a barracks, at any difficulty experienced in assembling and handling the soldiers who had been recalled, or at the least infringement of discipline. The General Staffs and the officers in charge were convinced that Communist agitators would try to exploit the very comprehensible discontent of the citizen soldiers, and would try to organize general resistance to the departures for Algeria. In Rouen and in Paris, and among some trainloads of men between Lyons and Marseilles, there were indeed incidents of some gravity. What the high command feared was that these incidents would, by sheer chance, degenerate into head-on opposition between the troops and their leaders, between the men recalled and the police and gendarmerie. The reports that recounted these incidents almost always blamed the Communist militants who had been mobilized along with the other conscripts.

In practice, their activities merged with those of left-wing student groups and Catholic militants, and it was impossible to distinguish the part played by one group or another. The only serious incidents reported occurred in regiments made up largely of workers. No political party, no trade union, and no religious or professional organization recommended any disobedience of military orders. How could the militants who had been mobilized get very far in exploiting the discontent of the conscripts. The Communist press and a few newspapers of the Left reported the demonstrations, and claimed that this proved the hostility of young Frenchmen to the Algerian War. But for the soldiers themselves these demonstrations could lead nowhere, since they did not go so far as to recommend disobedience to orders, or desertion. At the most, it was a matter of shouting pacifist slogans in the neighborhood of the barracks, or of slowing down the trains by pulling the alarm signal from time to time. After a bout of such activities, all that remained to be done was to follow the others and accept discipline once again.

These attempts at opposition were written off as a failure by the very men who had organized them. But for the military cadres, they constituted a grave warning. This was the concrete demonstration that the war in Algeria could not be fought until everything had been done, as a prerequisite, to convince the combatants that they were taking part in a just war. As the operations became ever more considerable, this need became more urgent. A troop of soldiers may be obliged to carry out security measures without having any deep convictions, but when 400,000 are permanently engaged in armed operations, this cannot suffice. Thus the officers' corps, practically unanimously, insisted on the need for a clear and definitive "war aim."

The Army as a whole was looking for a moral justification of the war it had been sent to fight. Each officer, for himself first of all, and then in addressing his men, sought an answer to the question: "Why have we been sent to fight in Algeria?" This was a kind of echo to the drama that had been lived through in Indochina, when no one could provide an answer to this same question, so fleeting were the policies, so lacking in precision the aims, and so obscure was the destiny of the country itself. But since the issue was basic, its consequences were felt throughout the officers' corps, from the highest to the lowest levels. And because, implicit in any moral justification of the war was a simple or simplified conception of French policy, this became the starting point for the "politicization" of the Army cadres. At the outset, the problem was more general and more deeply felt among the officers in the field than in the General Staffs, and among the officers in charge of platoons and the noncoms than among generals or colonels.

The first signs were not in the least furtive, on the contrary, they very boldly sprawled along the walls of every barracks in both France and Algeria. The new recruits had to be instructed in the kind of warfare they would have a part in. Large wallboards were set up in the classrooms, with clippings of newspapers that gave the latest news of the war, photographs of the life led by the troops in the remote outposts or in the native districts of the big towns, and a few summary facts about Algeria, its dimensions, population, resources, and France's economic or social achievements there. Soon there were photographs representing the "crimes" attributed to the "rebels." The "atrocities" committed by the fellagha were contrasted with French generosity, the uprightness of the Army, and the social instruments organized by the civilian and military authorities for the benefit of the native population. The officers lectured the men briefly on the Algerian War. The themes of these lectures were always very simple: the Army was there to re-establish order and tranquillity, and to maintain French authority. Algeria owed everything to what France had accomplished there. The native population had to be protected against terrorism. There could be no question of making war on the Moslem population, which was also suffering the consequences of the rebellion. The aim of the rebellion was to chase the French out of Algeria. The methods used were terrorism, assassination, arson and indiscriminate slaughter. The only aim of the war was to end this rebellion.

In view of their audience, the speakers had to remain simple and had to provide simple demonstrations. Instinctively, the military cadres had recourse to the most schematic presentation of extremely complex events or circumstances. The cause of France was just, therefore France's enemies were abominable. They wanted to chase France from Algeria, consequently the aim of the war was to maintain France in Algeria. These arguments had a logic that led far afield, since those who supported the rebellion were, indirectly, enemies, and these enemies were Tunisia, Morocco, Egypt, China and Russia. And those who, in France also, maintained that the Algerian rebellion was justified were necessarily "traitors."

Such a logic swept all before it, and to bring it to a halt the authorities would have had to repeat incessantly that the Army's only mission in Algeria was to create the conditions for a political solution whose details it was incumbent on Parliament and government to decide. Intervention would have been necessary at every instant, to permit the least deviation from the presentation of this sole, and simple, mission. Nothing of the kind was tried.

Thus the set-up for the future open conflict between the Army and the state was already under way and the military cadres were morally committed to the Algerian War. The massive utilization of the available classes of conscripts led them to harp on the moral or ideological justification for the war. There was such a justification, which had been solemnly avowed by the government itself at the beginning of 1956. It was to maintain France in Algeria, to protect the French community, and to defend the Moslem community against a rebellion whose crimes were publicly castigated by the highest personalities in the state. The total independence of Tunisia and Morocco, formally granted in the spring of 1956, proved that there were no halfway solutions between the maintenance and the total suppression of French authority.

Military men were profoundly moved by the episode of Captain Moureau. This young officer, posted in southern Morocco, where he was considered to be very popular, was seized and disappeared for ever, despite the steps taken in common by French diplomacy and the Sultan of Morocco. The incident, unique of its kind despite the political upheavals by which Morocco was beset, was enough to counterbalance, if not to wipe out, the initial efficacious and loyal collaboration between the Moroccan Army and the French officers placed at its disposition. Exploited in the press of the Right and by those who preferred war in Algeria, the Moureau affair became a symbol of the destiny allegedly threatening the Army, if Algeria should be handed over to the triumphant rebels. Yet there was still lacking, to ensure the politicization of the Army, the doctrine that would justify its direct intervention in public life and condemn its traditional neutrality.

That doctrine was to be found in military anticommunism—and in the "alliance" between communism and Arab nationalism. Born of the mutinies of 1917, and having grown larger in the General Staffs who worked out the plans for a war against the young Bolshevik State, this military anticommunism took on vigor and violence in the Ruhr, when the campaign against the French occupation was repressed, and again during the war against the Riff—indeed, even in the least noteworthy episodes of the repression exercised against nationalist movements in the French colonial Empire, where Communist complicity ever seemed to foment or support revolutionary subversion. This it was that decided many officers to plunge into underground political activity at the time of the "networks" in 1936. After World War II, anticommunism received official backing with the cold war, the Atlantic Pact, and the wars in Vietnam and Korea.

Now, among the military cadres, the habit arose of equating or even identifying Algerian nationalism and world communism. The first signs of this appear at the very beginning of the conflict. Jean-Jacques Servan-Schreiber, in his book *Lieutenant en Algérie,* speaks of the officers who preferred to save themselves trouble by calling the Algerian fellagha "Viets." Jean Planchais, the military critic of *Le Monde,* mentioned the general who never budged without taking along a map of the Mediterranean Basin on which a big red arrow set out from southern Russia and reached North Africa, "executing a flanking movement toward the south" around the Europe of the Atlantic Pact.

The General Staffs could not fail to realize that France's allies all desired a rapid end to the Algerian War, and that no one had denounced the F.L.N. as a Communist Party in disguise. The officers of the Army in Africa tended rather to associate Algerian nationalism with the Tunisian Néo-Destour or the Moroccan Istiqlal. While they knew nothing of the conflicts that separated the F.L.N. from the Algerian Communists, they encountered the latter nowhere in the course of the rebellion, and discovered them only later, in 1957.

But public opinion had already grown attentive to the international and ideological context of the conflict. In 1955, the leaders of the Algerian revolt had been denounced by French official propaganda, and by the greater part of the press, as narrowly linked with the Egyptian government and its special services. Documents, testimonies and archives discovered on dead or captured rebels had been produced in large numbers, with a varying degree of concern for authenticity and plausibility, but all of which went to prove the Egyptian origins of the rebellion. This was but the first step. The second was taken the following year, only three or four months before the arrival in Algeria of the first contingents mobilized.

The rapprochement that Guy Mollet had sought with neutral countries and, in particular, with Egypt, had failed. The nationalization of the Suez Canal was about to elevate hostility to Arab nationalism into a kind of official ideology. From this moment on the government itself, backed by all the political parties except the Communists and a few journalists writing for left-wing journals, would not be satisfied to blame Egypt for the Algerian rebellion. A new threat to the liberty of the world had been discovered: pan-Arabism. This was looked on as a return to the theocratic and totalitarian regimes inspired by certain Islamic conceptions, and also as a deliberate conspiracy to undermine the western positions in the Mediterranean.

A few Socialist newspapers vainly attempted to modify these conclusions by contrasting the western sympathies of President Bourguiba and the King of Morocco with Nasser's pan-Arabism. Yet these two, out of deference to anticolonialist solidarity, could not possibly express their dislike of Egyptian policy. Almost without exception, every politician and every newspaper compared Nasser with Hitler. Parallels were found between *Mein Kampf* and Nasser's *The Philosophy of the Revolution*. Pineau, Minister of Foreign Affairs, recalled how wrong it had been to let Germany remilitarize the Rhineland, and what a crime had been committed by yielding at Munich. Mitterrand, the Keeper of the Seals, compared the nationalization of the Suez Canal with German aggression against Czechoslovakia. Defferre, Minister for France Overseas, stressed the consequences that Nasser's action would have in Black Africa, and Robert Lacoste mentioned the repercussions in Algeria. It is significant that these two men can be mentioned in one breath, since the former had always advised that agreement should be sought with the F.L.N., whereas the latter had chosen to embody struggle to the death.

Egypt was supported by the Communist States alone. Every day the French press wrote of the arrival of new Soviet matériel to equip Nasser's troops. In the middle East, the alliance between the Communist camp and Arab nationalism appeared to be taking the most direct and concrete form, the most dangerous, also, for western policy. With tireless insistence, the French papers underlined the least details that could establish the reality of this alliance. The Cairo cinemas were giving free showings of films that dealt with the battle of Stalingrad, so that young Egyptians might learn the technique of street fighting. The teaching of Russian took the place of instruction in French and English. Nor was this campaign against the rapprochement of the Communist States and the Arab States limited to a few papers of the extreme Right. It was churned out daily in order to affect all segments of public opinion, the newspapers with the greatest reputation for moderation taking part in it, and Socialist ministers taking up the same themes in their speeches.

On the night of November 5 to 6, while French parachutists, released on Egyptian territory twenty-four hours earlier, moved on beyond Port Said, a new fact summed up and consecrated the *de facto* alliance between communism and Arab nationalism. "Fully resolved to use force against the aggressors," the Soviet government let it be understood that it could utilize the "terrible means of modern destructiveness" against France, Great Britain and Israel in order to help Egypt. In the history of military opinion, this date is perhaps more important than any other. It was, no doubt, not Soviet intervention but American pressure on the British government that induced the latter, and as a result the French government also, to give up their war against Egypt. The fact remains however that, for military opinion, a blow had been directed against the western positions by Arab nationalism and that it could not have succeeded without the support of the Communist camp. The Suez affair appeared, from this viewpoint, as the supreme example of international communism's new strategy. It was by the intermediary of nationalist movements, and in particular of Arab nationalism, that the western positions would be breached, undermined and finally destroyed. In the field vacated by the retreat of the western powers communism would one day stretch far and wide, whenever the weakness of its adversaries permitted or, simply, whenever the moment was deemed ripe.

In this decisive year, when the Algerian War was taking shape, the actual official policy of the government prescribed the contours of the doctrine accepted by the French officers who, some time later, would be responsible for the intervention of the Army in political life. Except for left-wing opposition, every political tendency had come together, in the fall of 1956, to denounce the nationalization of the Suez Canal as a defeat for the entire western world, to condemn the imperalist nature of Arab nationalism, and to assert that it was effectively allied with international communism. This is the source of the political ideology taken over by the Army.

Its official formulation was the contribution of several officers. There is nothing in the least astonishing in the part that was played by some of those who had been the most deeply involved in the Indochinese War. The experience they had gained there was more fascinating, more surprising and more revolutionary than anything the Army had experienced since the first World War. In Algeria they discovered a visage they knew well, that of countless enemies, indistinguishable from the population, who combined guerrilla warfare with urban terrorism and made no distinction between political and military action. In Vietnam these officers had learned the fighting value of ideas. Perhaps a secret hankering to discover, after a brief interval, the same adversary and the same type of warfare, had worked together with a predilection for situations already known, experiences already lived through and solutions already mulled over in their minds. The justification provided for the Indochinese War—the world struggle against communism—was again available to ennoble, with its vast ideological significance, the sordid daily struggle in the *djebels* and *casbahs*. Thus the Algerian War took on its full dimensions, those of a particular but immensely important war front, in the light of the universal conflict.

Everything was marvelously coherent. Communist expansion, after its setbacks in Germany, Greece and Korea, now found in Africa, as it already had in Asia, a huge area to maneuver in. The time had not yet come to set up Socialist regimes, but only to smash the western positions. This was the role allotted to nationalist movements in the Communist "plan." This African or Arab surface nationalism might deceive the naïve westerners, since communism did not present itself unmasked. Instead of falling into the trap, what was needed was to discover its long-term significance and foresee its ultimate consequences.

Nationalism, according to a dictum that became almost a password, was the antechamber of communism. From this standpoint, the least signs of weakness or anarchy in the new independent States of Africa and the Middle East fitted in very well with unvoiced expectations. If the Moroccan State seemed to falter, if the Tunisian economy appeared sluggish, if land reform broke down in Egypt, if revolution flared in Iraq—were not all these a converging proof that these nationalisms could never erect any substantial dike against the temptations and menaces of communism? Innumerable quotations discovered in the writings of revolutionary ideologues served to back up the theses dear to the Army's new theoreticians. They went back to the celebrated congress held in Baku, which had called on the peoples of Africa and Asia to rebel. They cited Lenin, who had predicted that the route to London and Paris would pass through Peking and Calcutta, and who declared that it would always be the Communists' duty to support an Afghan prince against a British Labor government. Stalin had given loftiest expression to the world strategy of communism when he affirmed as a principle the necessity of supporting, against the imperialist powers, the "bourgeois nationalisms" of the colonized States.

The intellectual history of the Army, from 1956 to 1958, is that of the widespread adhesion of the cadres to the theory that nationalism constituted the "advance guard of communism." This view lacked foundation in fact. Nowhere in the world had the nationalist regimes yet given way before Communist revolution. Nowhere in the western world, outside France, was this development regarded as inevitable. On the contrary, it was the practically universal opinion that the rapid granting of independence to former European possessions was the only means of weaning them away from the dangerous fascination of revolution. Such arguments should have been advanced against the view of the Army's new theoreticians. But to do that, the state would have had to concern itself with the morale and the intellectual demands of the military cadres. Besides, all political forces from the Socialists to the Right had come to the quasi-unanimous conclusion that the test of strength must be faced in Algeria, in order to prevent Algerian independence. The Army's theoreticians thus found few, among the politicians, to contradict them. And those who did oppose the Algerian War, were they not the Communists themselves, together with a numerically weak Left wing already noted for its opposition to the war in Indochina?

Nor did any contradiction make itself heard in the Army's own ranks. In the space of ten years, the social base for the recruiting of the military cadres had constantly become narrower. The officers' corps had never had so low a proportion of Saint-Cyr and Polytechnique graduates. Never had the candidates for Saint-Cyr come from so restricted a milieu. In particular, the numerous promotions of men from the ranks or as the result of competitive examinations reserved for noncommissioned officers had, markedly and lastingly, reduced the intellectual level of the officers' corps. These men, more and more left to themselves, and absorbed by the countless chores which since the end of the Second World War had come to be theirs, were ill prepared to understand the currents of new ideas coming from outside, and even less well prepared to accept the immense consequences of decolonization.

All seemed designed to assure a wide audience for the Army's new theoreticians. The experiences lived through in Indochina, the surface appearances of a certain strategy, the support given by the Communists to the Arab nationalist movements, the striking episodes of the Suez affair, all served to establish the soundness of their doctrine. Besides, in the middle years of this century, what enemy could a western state discover except the natural, permanent enemy—Communist subversion? For the Army of a bourgeois state, as for the bourgeoisie itself, could any other conflict be imagined than the one conflict in which everything would be at stake?

CHAPTER EIGHTEEN

PACIFICATION AND "THE MIND OF THE POPULATIONS"

✠

In Algeria, the adversaries encountered by the most humble French officer bore a remarkable likeness to the model displayed by the Army's new theoreticians. The F.L.N. itself invoked the Algerian revolution, it denounced imperialism and colonialism, predicted the equality of classes and land reform, and condemned the "wealthy colonists" and the capitalist "war profiteers." It set out to educate the population politically; its fighters were militants, its theory of war was a political doctrine, while its "politico-administrative organization" was strongly reminiscent of the "parallel hierarchies" that the Vietminh had set up, and whose redoubtable efficiency had impressed the French Army.

The teaching of the military theoreticians took on a remarkable vigor, since it corresponded too closely to concrete experience not to command overwhelming assent. By 1957, the presence of Algerian Communists in the F.L.N. networks in Algiers offered fresh "proof" of these "facts." Later on, throughout the world, surprise would be expressed that the French military cadres should so readily have accepted this crude view of the relations between communism and Algerian nationalism. But too many specious factors had hidden the real truth, too many signs had spoken in favor of a notion whose roots lay far back in the history and sociology of the Army.

So now it had come to war in Algeria. The enemy had been identi-

fied. The Nation had sent its young men to fight. Countless Frenchmen were risking their lives. On them depended the destiny of
Europe, the Mediterranean and Africa. The dimensions of the conflict were coextensive with contemporary history. But every war has
its own internal logic. It is serious enough when a professional army,
fighting alone in a remote theater of war such as Indochina, feels
that it has been abandoned by an indifferent people. It is altogether
insufferable when the army engaged in combat, through the incorporation of conscripts, is itself the "Nation under arms."

Military society believed that at last it was going to emerge from
its isolation. The country itself would shoulder the blame for its
previous hostility, indifference or hesitancy. Greatly overestimating
the part played by the public campaigns directed against the war in
Indochina, the Army attributed to them the origin of the country's indifference. On this occasion, the Army was prepared to demand that
such campaigns be repressed. "Treason" became one of the favorite
topics of conversation among officers. If the Algerian Communist
Party could be prohibited, why not its fellow Communist Party in
France? And if the country wanted to win the war against the F.L.N.,
why allow anyone to write that this body represented the Algerian
people and would have to be accepted as its spokesman?

The precedents set by the two world wars were invoked. The shade
of Clemenceau struggling against defeatism served to back the argument that all campaigns in favor of a negotiated peace should be
banned. The special powers accorded the government, vested in the
Minister for Algeria and transferred by him to the military authorities,
opened the path for the first open intervention of the Army in political
life. The censorship banned the Communist press in Algeria and
regularly seized the left-wing weeklies, and sometimes liberal daily
papers. For the same reasons the Minister of National Defense, in
Paris, frequently ordered similar seizures in France. Journalists known
to have been in contact with the rebels were arrested. Liberal personalities were taken to the police stations, questioned, and their dwell-
ings searched. But these special powers did not constitute a state of
war, and the situation in France remained distinct from that in Algeria. The contingents of conscripts did not suffice to bridge the gap
which separated French society and the military milieu.

It is noteworthy that the choice made by the government after
February 6, 1956, was not irrevocable. Algeria's fate had not been
determined once and for all. While the Army plunged into war, work-

ing out new theories and accumulating fresh resources, the political leaders sought for some way to end the war. The contacts made with the adversary in Cairo, in Belgrade and in Rome demonstrate how anxious they were to bring it to an end by making some allowance for the enemy's desires. The conversations begun with the Moroccan heir apparent, in September, 1956, were the first hesitant steps in the direction of a North African Federation in which Algeria would be autonomous, at the least. Though unable to estimate with any precision the prospects of success, the French government had not definitely barred a negotiated solution.

From this point on, a cleavage existed not merely between the Army's frame of mind and opinion in France, but between the war being waged in Algeria and the policy being adumbrated in Paris—or, perhaps, the absence of any policy coherently linked up with the pursuit of the war.

A striking demonstration of this cleavage was provided on October 22, 1956. Early that morning two officers from the military secretariat of the Minister for Algeria, Colonel Doucournau and Lieutenant Colonel Branet, proposed to the Secretary General of the Ministry, in the absence of Robert Lacoste himself, that the plane transporting five leaders of the F.L.N. should be forced to land at the airfield in Algiers. On the previous evening General Frandon, who commanded the Fifth Military District, which embraced all North Africa, had been informed by the French information services at Rabat of the flight schedule. The plane was transporting Ben Bellah, Mohammed Khider, Aït Ahmed, Lacheraf and Boudiaf to the conference in Tunis in which President Bourguiba and the Sultan of Morocco were to participate.

General Frandon informed General Lorillot, the Commandant Supérieur Inter-armes in Algeria, who took the view that it was the government's business to decide whether the plane should be captured. The two officers in the military secretariat strongly urged the Secretary General, M. Chaussade, to try to obtain a favorable decision. Neither the Minister for Algeria, nor the Minister of National Defense, nor the Secretary of State for Air could be reached. But at seven in the morning the Etat Major Général, having been briefed by Algiers, succeeded in contacting Abel Thomas, who headed the staff of Bourgès-Maunoury, the Minister of National Defense. The military were in favor of capturing the Algerian leaders, but Thomas referred the question to the Minister for Algeria. General Lorillot finally contacted Max Lejeune, Secretary of State for War, who agreed that the attempt should be made. Orders to land were transmitted to the French crew of the plane on which the Algerians were traveling. The messages were sent uncoded, so that the plan immediately became known to the General Staffs at the air, land and sea bases. The Army, thus alerted, could not fail to learn of the least decision taken subsequently by the political leaders.

The crew of the transport plane also received messages from every quarter, in which French officers with access to radio encouraged it to act as ordered. Robert Lacoste, when he arrived at the Algiers airfield later in the day, naturally had to take into consideration the Army's presumptive attitude. He decided to proceed with the plan, and declared it justified by the fact that France was at war in Algeria, and that the capture of the chief insurgents would doubtless have immense psychological consequences.

Guy Mollet, the President of the Council, and Alain Savary, the Secretary of State for Tunisian and Moroccan Affairs, were informed by the Moroccan Ambassador that "something was brewing"—the crew had informed the Moroccan airline of the orders received from Algiers. Mollet and Savary thought that the capture of the plane would have serious political inconveniences. But they were unable to contact Robert Lacoste, who informed Savary at 10 p.m. that the operation had succeeded. At 11 o'clock, at a meeting held at the Elysée, with the President of the Republic, Coty, Mollet, Bourgès-Maunoury and Savary present, Max Lejeune defended the decision he had taken as in keeping with the logic of the war that France was waging in Algeria. He was backed by Bourgès-Maunoury, and the government reached the conclusion that it would be impossible to set free the men who had been captured.

The matter was all the more serious since the government, on the eve of committing aggression against Egypt, had no desire to irritate Morocco and Tunisia. Savary had informed the heir apparent that France was displeased by the welcome accorded in Rabat to the leaders of the Algerian rebellion. But Guy Mollet hoped that a victory over Nasser would provide him with the requisite authority to negotiate a political solution, either directly or through the connections maintained between the Moroccans and Tunisians and the rebel leaders. This may have been an illusion. In any case, the "logic" of the war thwarted the government's political plans. At a critical moment, the desires of the Army had weighed heavily on political decisions. Yet the government had, throughout, maintained its freedom of choice.

The Army's job was to fight, and its problems were, in the main, military problems. Now, in Algeria, a new chapter began in the long history of the conflicts between an old-line Army and a people's rebellion. This amounts to saying that unsurmountable difficulties would be met with in Algeria, exhausting tasks and innumerable disappointments, of the kind that every army encounters when it is opposed by guerrilla forces. Many studies of this style of warfare had already been made. The military experts had analyzed its characteristics exhaustively, in the endeavor to find adequate countermeasures. The examples provided by World War II had conclusively demonstrated the relative impotence of regular armies in a type of struggle for which they were not constituted. The German Army had never functioned satisfactorily against the underground forces of Russia, Yugoslavia and France. The French Army itself could derive, from the Indochinese War, lessons of great value for the war it had now to fight in Algeria. Seven years of combat had revealed the helplessness of modern forces to deal with guerrilla bands methodically organized and systematically trained for the final showdown. Colonel Trinquier, who spent the World War II period in China and remained in Vietnam until fighting ended, summed up the analysis of guerrilla warfare in his book, *La Guerre Moderne:*

> Guerrilla fighting and terrorism are simply stages of modern warfare aimed at creating a favorable situation that will permit the formation of a regular army able to face and conquer another army on the field of battle. Thus the aim of guerrilla warfare, over a rather lengthy period, is not so much to win isolated successes as to oblige the forces of order to withdraw to more easily defended zones. This withdrawal will represent the concrete abandonment of the portions of some territories that the guerrilla fighters will be able to control. Consequently these fighters, at the outset of hostilities, will manifest themselves only in very violent minor actions, carried out unexpectedly but with prudence, so as to avoid losses. They have to remain widely scattered in order to be invulnerable. Their regrouping and transformation into large, regularly organized units will be possible only after they have gained absolute control over a vast area in which they can safely receive the substantial material aid required to constitute, train and utilize a regular army . . .

A whole generation of officers had already deplored the unsuitability of the French Army for fighting guerrilla forces in Vietnam. All that had been written about the French expeditionary corps in the Far East had evoked these troops blindly feeling their way through the ricefields or across the high tablelands, placing a desperate reliance on a few native guides but entirely at the mercy of a hostile population which kept the enemy posted on the Army's least movements. Blows aimed at empty space, and a do-nothing existence in isolated posts until the underground fighters one day concentrated their forces to win in a single onslaught—such was the dilemma of the French troops in Indochina. They gradually evolved "counterguerrilla" measures that tried to meet infantry with infantry, partisans with other partisans, and rapidly moving units with others that could move even more rapidly. But the expeditionary force always seemed to lag a step behind its adversaries. The partisans who had been armed on the high plateaux by the French General Staff had scarcely been organized and hardened for warfare, when the Vietminh poured out whole divisions from the *maquis* and hurled them at Dien Bien Phu. "A regular army," wrote Colonel Trinquier,

> with plenty of trained effectives and with an excellent supply of modern matériel finally showed itself unable to conquer an adversary who was practically unequipped and whose troops had in general received only rudimentary training. Implausible as this may appear, it is nevertheless a harsh reality that we must confront. A slave to its training and traditions, our Army failed to adapt itself to a form of warfare it had not been taught in the military schools. All its praiseworthy efforts, its sufferings and sacrifices succeeded in hampering our adversaries and in slowing down the execution of their plan, but proved in the long run incapable of keeping them from their goal. The Army usually expended its strength in a vacuum, and used up its considerable resources to no avail.

These criticisms rained down on the high command during the opening months or even the opening years of the war in Algeria. Here full scope was given to the revolution of minds that was under way in the Army. The hierarchy was under attack, it was accused of incapacity. The rebellion of the younger cadres, before turning against the state, tackled first of all the military *status quo*.

No other army in the world, it seemed, had made such a careful study of the armed insurrection that was now known as "subversive warfare" or "revolutionary warfare." The sum total of reflection, study and effort lavished on dissecting all the components of the Algerian rebellion was enormous, and many officers, even among those of lower rank, took part in one of the strangest enterprises known to military history. It was discovered that the secret guaranteeing the existence of the rebellion required the complicity of the population. This secret allowed the rebels to slip away and to form new groups that could not be identified. They enjoyed, as a result, the advantage of surprise and sometimes that of superior numbers, on the day and at the place where they chose to attack. These movements and regroupings in themselves posited the efficacious, silent assistance of the inhabitants. At every stage of this "rebel" activity this permanent fusion with the population of insurgent Algeria was noticeable. It was the "spirit of the populations" that guaranteed the existence and success of the rebellion, so that this spirit became the real object at stake.

Those who had cared to interest themselves in the history of communism in Asia had long known that Mao Tse Tung, in *The Strategy of Revolutionary Warfare in China,* had described the conduct that led to success in any armed rebellion. Military men made this discovery with a kind of enthusiasm that later would expose them to the absurd suspicion of having secret sympathies for "Communist methods." It was in the same terms that the theoreticians of communism had described the war that had confronted the Army in Indochina and which it would once more face in Algeria. The coincidence charmed many a simple mind, among the French officers, and strengthened the conviction that, whatever the latitude, it was always the same adversary and the same method of warfare.

This conviction would not, indeed, have been so deep-rooted and so entire if it had not found support in harsh experience. The most significant example of this is, perhaps, that recorded by Colonel Trinquier in his book: "In Indochina," he wrote,

> in the same region and with only short intervals, we were able to carry out anti-guerrilla tactics against the Vietminh, and then guerrilla tactics. This experience enabled us to see clearly the different possibilities at the disposition of the guerrilla fighters and of the soldiers in the regular army. When the French Army occupied the region of Than Uyen, on the right bank of the Red River, to the north of Nghia Lo, in the Thai country, the safety of the town and of its airfield was assured by a fortified post that had been installed on a rocky piton and was occupied by a regular company, with partisan support.
>
> But this safety could be highly deceptive, even in the immediate vicinity of the town, and on several occasions the Vietminh were able to fire on the planes as they came down on the airfield.
>
> In November, 1952, after the fall of Nghia Lo and the withdrawal of the regular units to the entrenched camp of Na San, the town of

Than Uyen, which had been evacuated by means of an aerial bridge, was occupied by the Vietminh, and was at that time some two hundred kilometers away from the nearest French troops, in Na San.

In the month of October, 1953, our native underground fighters from the right bank of the Red River, who had been recruited among the populations that had remained well disposed toward us, by their own unaided efforts succeeded in reoccupying, first of all, the region of Phong Tho and its airfield, then made a valuable foray against Lao Kay and, finally, seized the town of Than Uyen and its airfield, remaining in possession for seven months.

During this whole period, all those who arrived by plane in Than Uyen were struck by the fact that the post had not been reoccupied and that the field was never guarded. Nevertheless, the degree of safety was higher than the year before, when French troops had been in charge.

The regular troops had, indeed, used their eyes alone to watch the field and its immediate neighborhood from the post they occupied. Beyond this visual field of very limited dimensions, they were blind, and especially at night they could observe nothing. The Vietminh, aware of the limits of this circle, had no trouble in harassing us.

But our underground fighters, on the other hand, who had been recruited among the local population and lived with these people, kept an eye not on the terrain but on the Vietminh. They had slipped in their agents everywhere, first of all into the Vietminh units and then into every village, every house, and on all the tracks in the region. The entire population had been set to keep an eye on the enemy, and nothing could escape it.

The army cadres did not imagine that they could by some miraculous means obtain the aid of populations whose sympathy for the rebellion, whether genuine or obligatory, they had the opportunity to observe. Their first concern was to organize military measures that could decisively hamper the enemy in the two domains where hitherto his superiority had seemed unchallengeable: those of information and surprise. The French Army in Algeria achieved some remarkable things in that respect. The setting up of a grid was intended to cover the whole territory with a network of control and observation posts, to form a net sufficiently closely meshed to hamper the enemy's movements. At the same time, patrols and ambushes deprived the *maquis* of its initiative by spotting hide-outs, movements and zones of retreat. The adversary found himself obliged to skip out of one mesh, only to encounter the same difficulties in the next. In the spaces between the military posts, special intervention units "swept" the unsafe areas. On a larger scale, the general reserves carried out the work which, on a smaller plane, was left to the intervention units of the sectors and subsectors.

But if the grid, and the commandos and patrols, made it possible to detect the enemy's presence, only the rapid concentration of the requisite means could make it possible to surround and destroy him. This is where the factor of speed entered the picture, since it was necessary to prevent the scattering and "evaporation" of an enemy able to disappear in favorable terrain and amid a friendly population. The French Army sought to acquire this speed by the systematic use of air transport. In Algeria, the helicopter was utilized on a vast scale. The troops used for intervention, and the reserves, had found the way to solve the problem of distance, to overcome physical barriers and to challenge the enemy on his own ground. The advantage in speed of movement and of concentration passed to the Army.

The military achievement in Algeria is perhaps all that the Army has been given credit for, and all that is likely to remain. However, while it succeeded in depriving the adversary of his monopoly in information and surprise, owing to the rational utilization of the grid system, of reserves and means of transport, it changed nothing in the "mind of the populations," which came to be recognized as the essential weapon of the rebellion. The enemy must not only be prevented from profiting from the support of the population; the people had to be won away from the rebellion and their friendship gained. The Army set going a complicated machinery that led it to take general charge of Algerian territory and to redistribute the inhabitants. Colonel Trinquier had worked out the thetory: "A water-tight, inescapable perimeter will be created," he wrote, with reference to the villages that were to be brought under control,

> which will be protected by several blockhouses equipped with automatic weapons and able to defend the whole perimeter. The inhabitants of the nearest villages will gradually be brought inside the security perimeter. Most of them, indeed, will come of their own free choice. The inhabitants can leave the village only by gates at which all those leaving will be checked, and they can take with them neither money nor food. At night, no one is allowed to leave or to enter. . . . First of all we will proceed to the classic division into districts, islets and groups of houses, which will be numbered. Then we will carry out a precise census of all the inhabitants and of their

means of existence, especially of their livestock. . . . The inhabitants who can get to the village posts will do so; with our help, they will take with them all their means of subsistence, and in this way we will gradually increase the number of inhabitants who are supervised and protected. This different life, and especially the safety ensured the inhabitants in the protected perimeters will be a powerful attraction. . . . Whenever we have available the necessary means and manpower, we must set up new ones. It is only by methodical labor that we can progressively establish a strict supervision of all the inhabitants and of their means of subsistence.

From the start of the war until 1959, some two million Moslems were forced to leave their villages for regrouping centers, where the military authorities expected to supervise them closely and cut them off from all contact with the enemy. This extraordinary shifting of the population, which affected about one Moslem out of five, was carried out in accord with standards of security promulgated by the commanding officers. This operation took on such proportions and was sometimes carried out at such short notice that the civilian authorities became alarmed about its human and social consequences. The government's Delegate General, Paul Delouvrier, put an end to any further shifting of the population, after it became known that only some of these centers had been properly equipped to receive the inhabitants and provide them with an existence the conditions of which were sometimes better than those they had left.

For many officers, the sole aim of this operation had been to cut off the F.L.N. underground, and the collectors of funds for the F.L.N.'s political and administrative organization, from the source of their supplies and funds. But another aim was, more readily than could be accomplished in scattered centers of population, to provide economic and social benefits that would win over a people whose wretched poverty explained only too well its rebelliousness. This undertaking had, in the Army, an immense effect. For very proper motives it had induced the larger number of the military cadres stationed in Algeria to enter domains entirely foreign to the profession of arms. It awakened many a vocation, and also created fresh ties between the Army and Algeria, associating them much more intimately than any military victory or victor's rights could have done. Morally speaking it gave France the right, as the officers saw things, to remain in Algeria. In the long run, it reinforced the conviction that to give up the country would not only be a blunder, in national terms, but the abandonment of all the efforts that were being undertaken on behalf of the Algerians themselves.

At the outset of the Algerian rebellion, the tasks entrusted to the Army by official decree were limited to the customary duties required of the military overseas. General Cherrière, who was in command of the Algiers military district in 1954, actually stated that, immediately after November 1, the rebellion appeared to be very much like what had broken out in Algeria on a number of occasions since the French had first occupied the country. But as the techniques of warfare employed underwent an evolution, as the dimensions and importance of the struggle became evident, the Army's tasks too changed in character. This requirement was felt by officers of every school of opinion. It was no right-wing officer, but a liberal, Colonel Barberot, who wrote, in his *Malaventure en Algérie:*

> The Army, if its eyes are to be opened, must at all costs regain contact with the Moslem population, since this is the prerequisite for obtaining precise information and acting efficaciously. This resumption of contact demands that direct military action (intervention) and acts of pacification shall be carried out simultaneously. The authority which pacifies, on the one hand . . . and strikes, on the other, must be one and the same. This can be none other than the military. The former authority cannot carry out measures of pacification.

In taking over this role, the Army resumed an old tradition, handed down from a century of colonial warfare. The first systematic studies of pacification, as the crowning feature of the occupation, are to be found in the notebooks of Gallieni and in Lyautey's correspondence. The Indochinese experiment wound up in this fashion. The French Army had there learned that the enemy's political structures could not be regarded as apart from his military organization, and that in the turmoil of war they existed only insofar as they penetrated deeply into every layer of the population. Thus this aspect of the struggle in Algeria arrayed itself beside the need to consolidate the administrative framework of the country. Undeniably, successive governments, and especially in the years from 1956 to 1958, were all the more readily convinced of the value of these new forms of pacification because they had to fill in the huge gaps left by the lower-rank administration of huge territories.

The special powers granted the government and the Minister for

Algeria in 1956 aimed, in effect, at concentrating in the hands of the military an important share of the repressive and administrative powers. The setting up of the Special Administrative sections and the Urban Administrative Sections was inspired by this notion. This amounted to a totally new administrative apparatus which, quite apart from the old hierarchy of prefectures and subprefectures, covered the territory of the country with a mesh of new authorities. The officers who headed these Sections had total administrative responsibility for their sector, and indeed, in addition to the usual administrative chores —the keeping of records, registration, etc.—they broached economic, social and even educational tasks that set the seal of their authority on the whole life of the population. Their power had, in practice, very elastic limits, since they inaugurated or supervised medical programs, public hygiene, the starting of projects of public interest, the organization of the local police and the political activities in their sector. In theory the 600 officers employed in these Sections in 1956 were concerned only with regions that had been cleared of hostile forces, but in the fighting zones other officers had very much the same duties to perform. According to figures valid for May, 1957, the Army had discovered in its ranks 418 primary schoolteachers, who were teaching 23,000 pupils, and it had started 650 shops.

At the same time, the Army tried to set up in Algeria its own "parallel hierarchies," since experience in Indochina had revealed them to be one of the most effective means of keeping tabs on a whole population which otherwise, as an anonymous mass, could at any moment escape official authority. These "hierarchies" varied widely, in Algeria, depending on what the war required. In the large towns, where the main need was to keep an eye on and, if possible, to limit the F.L.N.'s underground activities, the main effort went to the recruiting of "delegates," for every building, every block and every district. But an attempt was made, at the same time, to get in touch with various groups in the populations by setting up new organizations: the "Veterans' House," for Moslem veterans; the "Women's Club," which was generally handled by a woman social worker; apprenticeship schools, whose supervisors came from a training center set up as the result of military instigation; and teaching centers, both administrative and military, for the heads of the *douar*.

These specialized institutions had nothing to offer the population as a whole, so another series of activities was devoted to information and propaganda. "Loudspeaker and tract companies," and ambulant officers, went from sector to sector teaching other officers the virtues and techniques of "psychological warfare" against an adversary and of "psychological action" on the population in general. Periodical publications, posters, films and radio programs were inspired and thought up by the General Staffs in Algeria. This new activity fitted in perfectly with the directives for pacification issued by the government and by the Minister for Algeria. It was not spontaneous. But it certainly added to and diversified the Army's tasks, to such an extent that the whole Army in Algeria discovered a new vocation. It endeavored to become the supreme source of inspiration for the whole population of the country. This was an extraordinary transformation, matching the radical change in the methods of warfare that the Army was trying out, for this final test of strength. "This Army," wrote Colonel Barberot,

> which in 1939 had regretfully agreed to give up its horses . . . to dirty its hands in the mechanism of its tanks and armored cars, and which had finally got used to the smell of oil and gasoline . . . now is involved in a war where in their turn tanks and armored cars will soon go the way of the horses in the Army's great retrospective museum. Now it is beginning to be convinced that it must look after the population, handle mercurochrome, antibiotics and sulpha drugs, supervise and count the population, give it work, talk of bulldozers, roads and bridges, highway construction and funds, teach the population to take care of itself, take a hand in local politics, etc. . . . that it has to be the Nation's maid of all work.

But maids of all work are not usually required to administer justice. The special powers accorded the government in connection with the Algerian War had, in practice, been entrusted to the Army. Henceforth it could not restrict itself to administrative and social tasks. In a struggle whose outcome depended on information, against an adversary who did not emerge into the open, police duties and the administration of justice had to be classified under the heading "maintenance of order." The Army could not escape the consequences of such a transfer of powers. Besides, colonial history from beginning to end is strewn with episodes that make no distinction between military power and police action, and go on to embrace the juridical function.

In this sense, the Algerian War was to be the last, probably, and certainly the greatest and most dramatic of colonial wars. It would subject the Army to the gravest and most distressing charges, those directed against its honor and, individually, against the honor of a great many officers and men. It is not proved that the practices used by the military men dealing with suspect populations and the interrogation of prisoners were very different from police practices in many countries. Be that as it may, the scandal of it all besmirched the Army, and all the more so since the Army had boasted of virtues quite incompatible with these practices. Myths as old as military society itself might be extinguished in an adventure that had taken on dimensions that no one could possibly have foreseen.

Nobody can estimate precisely the Army's degree of responsibility for all that took place in Algeria. The facts cannot be denied, and the number of such facts is extraordinarily high. Perhaps all that can be said is that, in every case, the attitude of each individual officer was decisive. It was a question of the man, not of his specialty or his origins. Police violence and the execution of prisoners were a function of the missions required of each unit, and did not depend on whether the unit belonged to the Foreign Legion, the parachute divisions or the regiments from metropolitan France. The struggle against terrorism appears to have given rise to many more of these incidents than the hunting out and destruction of underground fighters. The units stationed in the towns or in permanent posts carried out police activities that were much more serious and often much more reprehensible than did the units whose assignments were entirely military in nature.

The reason for this is that, in Algeria, urban terrorism was a much more important factor than in most popular rebellions. Even more than in guerrilla warfare, the Army had to deal with an enemy who was faceless and wore no uniform, and had no regard for the ordinary rules of fighting. In the Algerian *djebels,* as in the Indochinese rice-fields, the underground fighter had distinguishing marks, primitive though they were, and he became a sniper only if he hid his weapons and disguised himself as a peasant or a shepherd. In the towns, on the contrary, the Algerian fighter blended with the crowd, sometimes struck in ways that had not the least military justification, and escaped the consequences of his deed by taking refuge in the anonymity of everyday life. Everything depended on his arrest, in no other way could any glimpse be obtained of the degree of strength of the F.L.N.'s underground network, or the indispensable item of information be obtained that might throw light on the whole and lead to the defeat of the rebels. The struggle against urban terrorism had no other "front" than that of police repression.

In the winter of 1956 to 1957, it became clear that the ordinary police could not deal successfully with the F.L.N. network in Algiers. Its powers were transferred to the Army, and the Tenth Parachute Division, under the command of General Massu, took over. The battle of Algiers had begun. It involved the methodical, permanent supervision of the Moslem population, the setting up of a particularly severe system of security, and the interrogation of all suspects who might be able to provide the least item of information concerning the identity and activities of the terrorists. This would lead to extraordinary police action, and to a vigorous campaign that would arouse public opinion against the Army. For the first time in French history, military society as a whole was indicted for having infringed the most rudimentary moral precepts. It was a decisive moment in the crisis involving the relations of Army and country.

A number of officers set out to defend the practices used and to work out the theory. They refused to deny, hypocritically, the acts with which they were charged and which, they asserted, were a logical concomitant of this style of warfare. Colonel Trinquier reminds us of the horrors of terrorism, and deduces from them the means of defense they necessitate:

> The terrorist fights within the framework of his organization, and with personal disinterest, for a cause he judges to be noble and for a respectable ideal, like all soldiers in conflicting armies. . . . In an age when the bombardment of open towns is tolerated and when, in order to speed the end of the war in the Pacific, our Allies did not hesitate to eliminate Japanese towns with the atom bomb, no valid reproach can be made against him. Yosef Saadi, head of the autono mous zone of Algiers, made this statement after his arrest: "I dropped my bombs in the town by hand because I had no bombing planes to do it. But they caused fewer victims than the bombarding by artillery and by plane of the villages in the *djebels*. I make war, and you cannot reproach me for it." The terrorist has, indeed, become a soldier . . . but the aviator flying over a town knows that the shells of the anti-aircraft batteries may kill or wound him. . . . The foot soldier, wounded on the field of battle, has accepted the possibility of suffering in his own person. . . . None of them ever had the idea of complaining, of demanding, for example, that the enemy cease using rifle, shell or bomb. . . . The risks run on the field of battle and the sufferings endured are the counterpart of the glory to be gained. Now, terrorism claims the same honors but refuses the same corollaries. Its organization enables it to elude the police, its victims cannot defend themselves, and the Army cannot utilize its weapons,

since it remains permanently hidden among peaceful populations. But the terrorist must know that, when he is captured, he will not be treated . . . like a prisoner captured on the battlefield. What the forces of order that have arrested him want to do is not, indeed, to punish a crime . . . but, as in every war, to obtain the destruction or capitulation of the opposing army. So he will be asked for precise information about his organization. In particular, each man has a leader whom he knows; he is first required to give the name of this leader and his place of residence, so that an arrest may be made without delay. He will certainly not have the help of a lawyer during this interrogation. If he makes no difficulties about giving the information requested, the interrogation will soon be over; if not, specialists must force his secret from him and then, like the soldier, he must face the suffering, perhaps the death, that hitherto he has escaped. Beyond this, the terrorist must know and accept the fact as an element of his condition, and of the means of war that in full awareness his leaders and he have chosen.

There were very few who openly defended the inversion of all the principles and all the rules that have official backing—if they are not always observed—in civilized states. Many, there is no doubt, accepted or carried out these practices hoping that the sufferings of a suspect, who might perhaps be guilty, would obviate the sufferings of innocent persons. In 1955 a crisis arose between the military authorities responsible for "order" in Algeria and the political leaders who had entrusted them with this responsibility. Peacetime legislation was still in force, at least for the essentials. This prohibited or paralyzed the military operations, in the precise sense of the word, that the commanding officers deemed indispensable, if the rebellion were to be crushed in its early stages. This was admitted, in a book published in 1958, by Jacques Chevallier, who had been a minister in the Mendès-France government:

> The Algerian rebellion revealed how ill-fitted our judicial and legislative processes were to cope with an unprecedented state of affairs which forced us to undertake veritable military operations against French citizens (for the fellagha is a French citizen) in French Departments, in peacetime, and under a peacetime regime. The slowness and weakness so often deplored at the outset of the rebellion, and which were attributed to evil intentions, had no other cause than this impropriety of means, which compelled the responsible authorities to take illicit steps if they wished to act rapidly and effectively. This required of them the assumption of personal responsibilities that they sometimes refused to shoulder.

This incompatibility of means remained. The more the rebellion spread, the greater the dimensions of the repression. The way led ever deeper into a basic contradiction that could not be transcended. To seek information and uncover the population's acts of complicity vis-à-vis the A.L.N., the military arm of the F.L.N., meant, in one way or another, to attack the population itself, by suspecting, interrogating and tracking down an ever greater number of Algerians.

But the goal aimed at was, in principle, to detach the population from the F.L.N.'s political and military apparatus. The subordination of military activity to this political objective would have cut down the repression and this, on the other hand, would have eased the task of the rebels. Some officers tried to shake off this dilemma, which they could do nothing to abolish, by a sort of plunge straight ahead. If repression was necessary, in their view this was because its exemplary, rapid character constituted its efficacy, without which it ceased to be justified. Simply to overlook it was to admit that those involved at the lowest level had taken it on themselves to work out a system of repression and inquisition that was arbitrary, bloody and morally outrageous.

One man in particular boldly maintained these views before every body of opinion, military or political. His case is all the more noteworthy, since he had not been in Indochina and had had no previous personal experience of these matters. Colonel Argoud had the most brilliant prospects in the modern Army he had helped to think out and create. He was a specialist in armor and had been an organizer of the "Javelot brigade," the prototype of the atomic divisions that the high command decided to form, at the end of the Indochinese War. He set out to study the means of combating a war of subversion with the same intellectual passion he had devoted to the conditions of modern warfare. In his deposition at the trial that examined "l'affaire des barricades," he outlined his conception of justice in a period of revolutionary warfare:

> Confronted by the revolutionary triptych of underground organization, terrorism, and the enrollment of the masses, justice cannot utilize the customary means, for then it catches only the scapegoat and remains totally inffective. . . . Today [1960] just as little as a year ago, and a year ago just as little as in 1954, the justice that the French Army is allowed to exercise does not correspond to [my] definition of justice. It is profoundly unjust, since except in the rarest cases it strikes only the scapegoat. It is totally ineffective since, instead of the severe, simple, immediate and exemplary justice required

by the Moslem people and by the circumstances, we have had for six years, alas, a justice characterized by its culpable weakness, its intolerable sluggishness and its Byzantine complexity, a justice sometimes carried out almost *sub rosa*. . . . The terms I am employing I have heard on the lips of the highest military authorities and of some of the highest civil authorities in this country. . . . M. Patin [President of the Commission de Sauvegarde] entirely approved the affair in its essence. . . . M. Michelet [Keeper of the Seals] told me, "Mon colonel, you are right" . . . and all the more right, because I applied this justice myself. In command of a sector at L'Arbat, during the battle of Algiers in 1957, I was not eager to apply the justice put at my disposition, because I was responsible for human lives . . . and because, if I had applied this legal justice, I would have had the impression that I was failing in my task. Nor did I wish to resort to certain procedures, efficacious perhaps but irreconcilable with western ethics. So I decided, only of course after long deliberation, and with no illusions as to the drawbacks of the system, to mete out justice personally, accepting full personal responsibility. In other words, after a precise and scrupulous investigation, carried out with the help of the regular police inspectors, I ordered the assassins or the guilty men to be shot in the public square. I was running grave risks, as I well realized, and on each occasion I informed my chiefs. There was no reaction. I was able to conclude the operation successfully. Whereas at L'Arbat, from August 1 to January 1, 1957 . . . there had been practically one assassination or attempted assassination every three and one half days, after five months of this justice the country, in this respect, was pacified.

There is no lack of evidence that the conscience of many a military man was torn by these dramas of the repression. Sometimes it was a spectacular gesture such as that of General Paris de Bollardière, who had been an officer with the Free French, and who publicly refused to accept an "accentuation of the police effort." Many other refusals were adhered to, in the field, by obscure officers whose merit was all the greater, since the search for "information" and "efficiency" favored the speediest and most brutal measures. Many would have subscribed to the declarations of another veteran of the Free French, General Billotte, who wrote, in the fall of 1957:

One does not obey orders that are manifestly in contradiction with the rules of war, such as the massacre of prisoners and of civilians who have fallen into your hands and, consequently, are under your protection, torture, etc. As for torture, I categorically state that in any form and whatever its aim, it is intolerable, utterly improper and merits condemnation, and besmirches the honor of the Army and of the country. The ideological character of modern wars makes no difference; on the contrary, in such conflicts victory in the long run will go to the loftier ideology. One of the surest ways to victory—for it speaks directly to the hearts of men who temporarily are your enemies—is to be found in this very respect for human and moral values. Besides, the excuse that sometimes is offered, that one man tortured has perhaps saved a hundred lives on our side, does not hold water. First of all, there are very few cases in which a wretched prisoner possesses information of this importance. Secondly and above all, though it is a cruel obligation to meet, a leader, rather than accept a dishonorable practice, must not hesitate to expose his men, and even the population he is defending, to greater dangers. A leader without the moral strength to carry out such an obligation is not worthy to command French soldiers. The spirit of sacrifice is the soldier's cardinal virtue.

Every officer felt that he was involved in this question of repression. Countless private letters reveal that each man tried to face the problem as best he could, and that no one cold-bloodedly shrugged off the reproaches heaped on the practices current in many units. A number, knowing that they had withstood all temptations, were infuriated to think that the Army was being held collectively responsible for the illicit actions of some. Others passionately offered "the heat of action" as a justification and denied civilians the right, from their comfortable berths in the homeland, to judge the warrior. Most officers condemned as cowardly the attitude of the authorities, who left it to the Army to re-establish order, washing their hands of the inevitable consequences of their decisions and ready to let the whole military hierarchy take the blame for acts which they themselves had not had the courage to command.

The sense of outrage that came over the whole world, when the horrors of the repression became known, left military men feeling indignant, threatened and guilty. Indignant, they recalled that the Army had been begged to intervene, in order to stop the terrorism raging in the Algerian towns. Threatened, they foresaw that every arrest of a F.L.N. militant would become suspect, and that henceforth any operation could be investigated, so that the general suspicion directed by French opinion against the Army would weigh, too, on the individual officer. Guilty, they divined that one day there might be a settling of accounts and that then the weaknesses, errors and crimes, which in the event of victory would be overlooked, would become scandalous and unacceptable in any other circumstances. In this way dishonor would be heaped on defeat.

This fear never ceased to grow. As the months went by, the burden of the sacrifice that had been made rendered unbearable the idea of final disaster. It was already outrageous enough, in military eyes, that so much effort and so much bloodshed should have gone for nothing. The situation would be even worse if the harsh measures of repression, for which so many officers had accepted responsibility, should turn out to be futile. This state of mind became widespread, and led to the determination to accept no prospect of a solution that by degrees would lead to autonomy, a free association and independence. In that case, why was the Army induced to sacrifice the lives of so many officers and men? Why, above all, was it permitted to compromise itself by odious and sometimes dishonorable practices? The idea that the sacrifices that had been made and the dishonor shouldered should prove to be useless, though hard to accept in 1955 or 1956, was altogether intolerable in 1957 or 1958. At this stage in the Army's history, the precise machinery of the plots that were concocted mattered less than the moral and psychological climate in which the officers were plunged, after two or three years of warfare in Algeria. For it is this that explains why most officers welcomed any initiative that might dispel the nightmare of a war fought for nothing, of men dead in vain, and of disgraceful compromises that had no justification.

In the spring of 1958, the war was about to reach its dialectical conclusion. Everyone knew, said and wrote that this was no mere test of military strength. Everyone admitted that, when all was said and done, the decision lay with "the spirit of the populations." If they continued to approve the rebellion launched by the F.L.N., this would make all "pacification" impossible. The war could end victoriously only if they "swung over" in support of French authority. The expression, which was used at the time in every discussion of Algeria, seemed to put the problem in a nutshell: how could the Algerian populations be induced to "swing over"—if, indeed, this possibility existed.

There could be no prospect for it if negotiation seemed to lie ahead, for then the Moslem masses, believing that the future belonged to the F.L.N., could not compromise themselves by dallying with the French. This was the argument advanced by those who were opposed to all negotiation and appalled by the idea that the war might have been fought in vain.

Defeat, in particular—another term for negotiation, autonomy, and ultimate independence—seemed all the more unacceptable, now that the Army was coming to think the game was won. By the end of 1957, terrorism in the large towns had been virtually wiped out. To smother the underground groups, electrified barriers had been set up along the Moroccan and Tunisian frontiers, with the idea of preventing the passage of either men or matériel. The recollection of the aid given by the Chinese to the Vietminh had convinced the General Staffs that the enemy would never have had the means to win a genuine military success, had he been effectively cut off from the outside. If the Tonkinese frontier had been guarded, the Vietminh would never have had the artillery that made possible the assault against Dien Bien Phu. It could not happen in Algeria, if the underground were not supplied from its bases in Tunisia and Morocco.

The opening months of 1958 showed that this line of reasoning was correct. The command of the A.L.N. tried to do just what the Vietminh had succeeded in, four or five years before. It was time for its underground fighters to form large units and carry out large-scale operations, scattering once more in order to escape any counter-offensive. At the same time, relatively well equipped forces would have to come from the other side of the frontiers. The experiment was tried, and failed. The barriers proved too difficult to cross. The underground had to give up any thought of mass activity, and the rebels lost the military initiative.

For the French Army in Algeria, this was a decisive moment. From now on, it deemed that the enemy had lost in the field. The A.L.N. would never be stronger than at that instant; the war would not be lost. Or, if it were, the Army would not be to blame, for on the military plane it had won. Everything depended, from now on, on the political utilization of the victories won, and thus the final outcome of the war in Algeria would be decided in Paris.

The Army considered it as proved that the real base of A.L.N. strength lay beyond the frontiers. These new wars could not succceed, if no recourse were available to some "inviolable sanctuary." The "Manchurian sanctuary" had made it impossible for the Americans to occupy North Korea. The "Chinese sanctuary" had enabled the Vietminh to find fresh strength, put the French forces on the defensive and compel the government to negotiate. The "Tunisian sanctuary" had preserved the A.L.N. from total destruction. The French patrols could see through their binoculars, across the frontier,

the Algerian encampments on which they could not fire. Being pre-
disposed to simple convictions, military opinion attributed to the
existence of these Moroccan and Tunisian "sanctuaries" the prolongation of Algerian resistance.

This was a natural belief for the greater number of officers to
accept. It was quite spontaneously shared by even the humblest among
them. Consequently the military hierarchy, at every level, was prepared to avow that any negotiation would be treasonable, a "dagger-
thrust in the back" of combatants who, for their part, had accomplished their mission and defeated the enemy in the field. Concrete
experience in the strictly military domain also strengthened the conviction, whose popularity among the officers it is easy to understand,
that the war could be lost nowhere else than in Paris. All, therefore,
that need be done was for the government to want to win.

But the Army itself was in Algeria, and there it found itself in a
world hitherto unknown to most of the officers and almost all the soldiers. The hundreds of thousands of young Frenchmen who replaced
each other, contingent after contingent, on Algerian soil, first came
into contact with the European community. In most cases their
horizons never grew any wider. Thus the most frequent and most
fortunate attempts to enter into contact with Algerian Moslems did
not begin in the ranks. This was almost always done by officers, and
especially by those in charge of administrative or social matters. Their
opposite numbers were usually solid citizens, veterans and administrators of communes. Sometimes chance brought it about that a
friendship grew up with a Moslem peasant, storekeeper or minor
official. But from the very opening stages of the rebellion all possibility
of contact was lost between the intellectual cadres of the Moslem
population and the military cadres. Early in 1957 only two Moslem
doctors remained in the whole of Algiers. Repression had hit hard at
the "intellectuals" who were suspected, often quite justifiably, of
taking part in the rebellion by passing on information, collecting
contributions or functioning as propagandists. The barriers set by
social, cultural and linguistic differences could only have been
transcended by officers with a remarkable gift of human sympathy and
a great deal of intelligent curiosity. Some, nonetheless, succeeded in
developing a great affection for this Moslem people which, with its
poverty, pride and valor in combat was a worthy peer.

For every conceivable reason, the European milieu was the natural habitat for military men in Algeria. Back from their missions in the *djebels* and the isolated posts, officers and men found their way to the European quarters of the towns. There they met again with their comrades in the staffs and services, or in the units that maintained the urban grid system. Only in these surroundings could the Army, in its Algerian exile, find a climate like that of France itself, at least of southern France. There they could get to know the bosses in the little cafés, the girls in the dance halls and the fiancées they would marry, once military service had ended. For many Europeans, especially in the smaller towns, the Army was not merely their protector; the money that was spent supported many a minor enterprise. It brought new life to sleepy little towns, and a bustle that otherwise could never have occurred. Occasions for friction were not lacking, of course, and the soldiers thought that the storekeepers took excessive advantage of them. Certain differences in language and customs were bound to shock.

Sometimes the soldier felt inclined to remind the European that the Army was there on his account, and he had better not forget it. Sometimes, too, the treatment accorded Moslem employees was severely condemned, particularly on the farms and in industry. But there were limits to this severity. In the *bled*, the Moslem was always the suspect and sometimes the enemy. The same was true of the towns, during outbursts of terrorism. Language and mores were an insuperable barrier between the soldier from France and the Algerian Moslem. Where else could any compensation be found for the hardships of military life and of exile, if not in daily contact with the European community? Was there any more friction than with the inhabitants of French garrison towns? That is far from proven, since the soldier feels animosity against the storekeeper in any age and in any country. Until late 1958, at all events, businesses and business organizations would try to keep the demobilized soldiers in Algeria. The classified advertisements in the papers every day offered numerous possibilities of employment. Many European families tried to pair off their daughters with soldiers from France and to keep the latter in Algeria.

While actual conditions sometimes created difficulties in any relationship between the population and young Army men, everything on the contrary favored association between officers and European community. Fashionable and social connections played their traditional part. The General Staffs were in regular contact with the civilian administrators. This sometimes led to closer personal ties. For the young officers who after several periods spent in Germany or Indo-China had not yet settled down, Algeria offered plenty of the contacts that might lead to marriage. It was said of certain units stationed for a long time in the country, such as the Tenth Parachute Division, that more than one tenth of the officers were married to local girls. This contributed to form a social atmosphere that for several years would influence the attitude of the Army to the European community. And this had all kinds of subtle political effects. After a man had spent two or three years in Algeria, more counted in his eyes than the simple obligation to defend lives and property and to maintain French authority. For the Army, as for the whole of France, the Algerian drama had become almost the sole preoccupation. Its complexity, its numerous side effects and its economic and social factors did not escape military opinion. Being on the lookout for moral justifications for the war, the Army was anxious not to be identified with that "colonialism" which, it realized, had become detested throughout the world and was the constant object of attack on the part of international opinion and of the French political parties, of intellectual milieux and even of the most moderate press.

Most officers equated colonialism with economic oppression and social injustice. And this enabled them to skirt around the one basic problem, that of Algeria's political independence. How could they be colonialists, since they set the example, in their military existence, of austere living and of a certain concern for equality? In particular, recollections of the Far East haunted officers who, though they had been fought by the Vietnamese, yet felt a measure of liking for them. This sojourn in Indochina had left enduring traces on the military outlook. Many remembered corruption and rackets, fortunes speedily made in military supplies and by speculating in currency, the complicated maneuvers of major firms, the staggering wealth of some colonists and of some Vietnamese families submissive to French author-ity, and the poverty of the masses. Such recollections may have helped to restrain military intervention in French policy in Morocco, for there, as in Indochina, the suspicion was probably widespread that the sole support of French authority was provided by feudal lords whose wealth had dubious origins. There was nothing of this sort in Algeria or, at least, not after the political structures of the European community had developed during the earlier years of warfare.

Until 1955, the political tradition in Algeria was based on the power of the "preponderant" personages. Deputies and Senators came from the circles of the great colonists, the richest industrialists, owners of cork forests and fields of esparto-grass, shipbuilders and directors of land transport and shipping. They could exercise authority all the more easily in Paris, since they formed part of the established political groups, explained Algerian affairs to them and backed them with their funds and their authority. The Fourth Republic, like the Third, long bore the mark of this Algerian "lobby" which, in every party except the Communist, inspired French policy in the Algerian Departments and thwarted every reform that would have shaken the economic and political hegemony of the European community. This body was organized politically around its professional associations, the chambers of agriculture and of commerce, and the groups of employers and administrators. There the "preponderants" always played the main part. They took up the demands and voiced the fears of their more modest companions, the minor storekeepers, factory owners and farmers. These too were determined to thwart the political and social desires of the Moslem population. In this way, the economic interests of the most important and the most humble Europeans were closely linked. The "preponderants" would never opt for the path of political evolution which alone could ensure their survival, even in the event of Algeria's becoming independent.

The Europeans' standard of living was, on the average, below that of the homeland. Thus the social demands were the same as those of the least favored workers in the French economy. So it was quite natural that the Socialist and Communist candidates should do well in some popular districts of the Algerian towns. There was even some growth in support for the left-wing parties, in the period immediately after the World War, when the better-established political groups had to some extent compromised themselves with the Vichy regime. Another source of support came from the fairly numerous Moslems who still thought, in 1945, that assimilation offered them the greatest possibilities. But it was the Democratic Union for the Algerian Manifesto and, later, the Movement for the Triumph of Democratic Liberties, that received the Moslems' votes. Socialist and Communist voters consisted only of the inhabitants of workers' quarters in Algiers and Oran.

As the national question grew more and more acute, the Algerian Communist Party found itself in an increasingly difficult situation. Its attachment to the emancipation of colonial peoples aroused the suspicion of lower-class Europeans, whose supremacy was threatened

by the Moslem majority. On the other side, its refusal to give absolute priority to the demands of Algerian nationalism lost its votes
among the Moslems who had decided to seek independence before all
else. The first year of the war sufficed to remove any hesitation. The
Algerian Communist Party and the trade unions it dominated were
prohibited. The Socialist Party, being suspected of excessive sympathy
for Moslem aspirations, lost its electorate. The European community
was entirely wrapped up in the war, and ceased to give the "preponderants" the blind faith they had enjoyed in the past. The moment
had come for a veritable metamorphosis of the political structure.

The shipbuilders and the big colonists took a back seat. In the general elections of January 2, 1956, no change was made in the representation of the Algerian Departments, beacuse of the uncertain
conditions. Interchanges with a Socialist government presided over
by Guy Mollet forced the European community to find more popular,
and more representative, spokesmen. The most important part in Algerian political life soon came to be played by the heads of associations,
teachers, students and reserve officers. No doubt their means of action
and their financial backing had much in common with those of which
the "preponderants" had availed themselves. But this was a different
breed of men. The European community emerged in its true colors:
that of a population numerically inferior and physically dispersed,
but sufficiently strong and coherent in structure to present the image
of an individual people.

Its dealings with the Army were profoundly modified. The Army
was now confronted by an alive, dynamic society, whose passions
matched its sense of being menaced and which was all the more "nationalist" because it had to rely for its salvation entirely on the French
nation. The officers who for ten years had been fighting in the midst
of hostile populations, at last had popular support. For the first time,
the "crowd" was on their side. It was, of course, the European crowd,
but this in itself, if properly steered, advised and directed, could constitute a powerful arm. Many officers would never abandon it, for they
knew very well that in its defense they had come to Algeria. How
could they bridge the contradiction that required them to defend the
European community while winning over the Moslem community?
How could these two crowds be molded into one?

The extraordinary force of the idea of integration was primarily
due to the fact that it appeared to offer the clue to an insoluble problem. At the same time, it fulfilled the secret expectancy of the majority

of Europeans, for integration meant "French Algeria," the clearest, most elementary cause, fully capable of justifying a pitiless war in which hairsplitting and intellectual complexities would have no place. If one is to sacrifice one's own life and that of others, it is essential that the cause be simple. And if a solution appears that seems to resolve every contradiction, then its appeal is irresistible. Morality and patriotism are enlisted on the same side. A French possession will be saved, while nine million Moslems hitherto deprived of equality will now enjoy equal rights. In this way Republican Jacobinism joined hands with the national tradition. The minor European settlers, made up of storekeepers, workmen and students, attested as one man that there was no further thought of defending vested interests, a few huge colonial fortunes or a handful of privileges dating from another epoch. The miracle of integration was to gain the support of the Moslem crowd, since it would be carried out to Moslem advantage.

At this moment in the Algerian War, the dialogue between the Army and the European community attained, perhaps, a unique accord between the desires of the one and the ultimate hopes of the other. In Tunisia and Morocco, internal autonomy and interdependence had had too short a life. Military opinion had acquired a deep suspicion of any intermediate solutions that claimed to abolish French authority without frankly recognizing independence. European opinion instinctively shared this suspicion. Numbers alone would see to the political supremacy of the Moslem masses, if Algerian institutions allowed this factor to have its usual effect. Any government or Parliament ruling from Algiers and backed by ninety per cent of the population could make light of any barriers thought up by Parisian jurists to prevent the European minority's being "crushed." It would be the starting point for ceaseless new demands, and the instrument, too, for a continual deference to the Moslem masses, hitherto humiliated and neglected. The least measure of autonomy appeared to European opinion as but the starting point for an ineluctable movement toward complete independence.

The order of priorities in Paris, at the same time, was precisely the opposite. Some solution was being desperately sought that would lead the majority of the Moslems to turn away from the rebellion, while avoiding a definitive break between Algeria and France. The secret meetings with the F.L.N. leaders in 1956 had had no other aim than to discover if their agreement could be obtained for such a solution. The following year, *lois-cadres* were drafted that meticulously worked

out the apportionment of French authority and of autonomy. Some
looked on these steps as intended to interpose long intermediate stages
before full independence was, no doubt unavoidably, finally granted.
For others, it was an attempt to limit the damage done by allowing
the Moslems some share of power while keeping the essential prerogatives firmly in French hands. The Europeans of Algeria, under the first
hypothesis, had everything to fear, as they knew and stated. Under
the second, they could agree, but with all sorts of restrictions and an
insistence on additional precautions.

General Massu publicly expressed his displeasure at the defeat of
the first *loi-cadre,* but lower down on the scale officers could clearly
observe the futility of all intermediate solutions, which they themselves disliked and for which, clearly, the Moslems had no use. This
gap separating military and political opinion was to grow wider. In
Paris, the parties in power—from the Socialists to the Right—had not
yet reached the point of beginning negotiations with the adversary on
the political future of Algeria. But already public speeches, private
conversations and newspaper articles referred to the necessity of
"escaping" from the dilemma. Some myths had already evaporated,
such as the alleged responsibility of Egypt for the Algerian War, for
after the Suez operation and the barricading of the frontiers the rebellion went on. The draft law put through in the fall of 1957 seemed
without effect. International hostility to the Algerian War exasperated
but also alarmed the French bourgeoisie.

In particular, there had been a shift in internal politics. The Algerian conflict had, for a period of eighteen months, made it impossible
to form a majority of the Left with the backing of Communist groups.
But the government, under Socialist direction, was financing the war
by accepting fiscal burdens unparalleled in financial history. It had to
resort to loans exceptionally onerous for the Treasury. The consequences of the war with Egypt coming on top of the Algerian operations disrupted the balance of income and outgo, so that the reserves
built up in 1955—more than one billion six hundred million dollars—
had practically disappeared by the end of 1957. The moderate groups,
the M.R.P., Independents and Radicals, had returned to power in
October, under Gaillard. The first requirement was to prevent the
Algerian affair from imposing an intolerable strain on the French
economy. The problem of the Tunisian frontier would indicate the
limits of France's will to continue the war in Algeria.

The bombardment of Sakhiet-sidi-Youssef by French military aviation was, doubtless, a riposte to the numerous incursions on French territory carried out by units of the A.L.N. stationed in Tunisia. This turned out to be a morally disastrous business, for the attack took place on a market day and with children in a school believed to have been abandoned. So the Army was accused of breaking the international rules of warfare by attacking innocent civilians. The government's directives granted the troops stationed along the frontier the "right of pursuit." But a disagreement still separated the Ministry of National Defense in Paris and the General Staffs in Algeria. The former would agree only to land operations immediately following attacks that had originated on Tunisian territory. The latter objected that such operations would inevitably be long drawn out and of doubtful efficacy, whereas aerial ripostes would be much more expeditious and would have a greater punitive value.

The Sakhiet affair made French political milieux understand to what an extent the Algerian War was isolating the country. The reactions of international opinion and the Anglo-American diplomatic intervention whose "good offices" might lead to political intervention in Algeria, harshly exposed this isolation. There was some measure of injustice in the situation, for the initial responsibility for the incidents on the Tunisian border was unquestionably that of the F.L.N. and of the Tunisian government that tolerated its activities. The defeat of the Gaillard government in Paris was due as much to the sense of exasperation in political milieux as to any fear that was felt. The ensuing crisis marked Parliament's refusal to tolerate the rule of the most intransigent partisans of a French Algeria. It was becoming clear that some approach would be made to those "intermediate solutions" which, in the eyes of the military and of the European community, were but the first element in the process leading to independence. A parting of the ways lay ahead.

CHAPTER NINETEEN

THE SPIRIT OF THE 13TH OF MAY

✠

On the night of May 9 to 10, 1958, General Salan, Allard, Massu and Jouhaud sent a telegram to General Ely, Chef d'Etat Major de la Défense Nationale, and asked him to communicate its contents to the President of the Republic. "The Army in Algeria is disturbed," they declared, ". . . concerning the French population of the interior, which feels deserted, and the Moslem French who, in greater numbers every day, have been once more placing their trust in France, confident in our reiterated promises never to abandon them. The French Army, as one man, would look on the abandonment of this national heritage as an outrage, and it would be impossible to predict how it might react in its despair." The four generals begged General Ely to "call the attention of the President of the Republic to our anguish, which could be removed only by a government resolutely decided to maintain our flag in Algeria."

This telegram, it has been said, marked the "official entry of the Army into politics." The first significant feature about it is the names of its authors. General Salan was Commandant Supérieur Inter-armes in Algeria, General Jouhaud commanded the Fifth Aerial District, that is, the air force, General Allard commanded the Tenth Military District, or the land forces, and General Massu the Tenth Airborne Division, which occupied Algiers and its surroundings. Thus it was the summit of the military hierarchy in Algeria that cast off its reserve and intervened with the highest officers of the state, in order to inform them that the Army could no longer remain indifferent vis-à-vis the policy of French governments—even graver, that the Army's frame of mind would be so seriously affected by the idea of Algeria's being "abandoned" that there could be no telling how it would react.

These four generals were far from being considered hostile to the Fourth Republic. They actually were looked on with deep suspicion by the Army men most firmly resolved on political activity for working together either with those who were stirring up the European minority or with nationalist groups in France itself. It had not been forgotten that General Salan had been the opposite number of Giap, the Vietminh's Minister of War at the time agreement was reached in March, 1946, and that, of all the successive leaders in Indochina, he had been one of those least sure that a military solution could be reached, and with the greatest reserve concerning the Bao Dai regime and the "Vietnamese National Army." So he was assumed to have always been quietly in favor of negotiations with the enemy. His mission to Vietnam together with General Ely, when the Laniel government was in power, had resulted in a report highly pessimistic about the outcome of the war, and General Salan himself, it was said, had passed on this report to the press. Such was his political repute that, among those eager to see the war prosecuted more vigorously by a government "of public safety," his departure from Algeria was judged to be an indispensable first step. The previous year, in 1957, by sheer good fortune he had escaped an assassination attempt prepared by a European counterterrorist group whose leader, Dr. Kovacks, maintained he had been acting in common with a committee of political personalities including some of the principal foes of the Fourth Republic and of its Algerian policy. Among them, he declared, were Michel Debré and the Radical Deputy, Pascal Arrighi.

The truth of Dr. Kovacks's allegations was never established, but the plot alone was enough to demonstrate that General Salan had not the least connection with extremists in political milieux or in the Army. In other words, he was looked on as one of the generals most deferential to constituted authority, and who could be counted on to carry out the government's policy scrupulously. This was the man who, on April 25, when consulted by Pleven who was trying to form a government, replied that the only acceptable cease-fire in Algeria would require the A.L.N. to hand over its arms, whereupon a sweeping amnesty could be proclaimed. This was the man who took the initiative in sending the telegram of May 9 to General Ely.

As for General Massu, who had joined the Free French, he was indeed looked on as a Gaullist general, but above all had the reputation of being obedient. It was known that on several occasions the Minister for Algeria, Lacoste, had thought of turning to him to break up the demonstrations that the European activists were threatening to organize. It was known that he regretted the failure of the first *loi-cadre* for Algeria that had been proposed. The remark was often made that a Socialist government would never have entrusted him with full powers if it had felt uncertain about his loyalty to the Republic. No one, moreover, looked on him as politically interested, and his reputation was that of a military man with a taste for action and discipline. In the circles in Algiers that were preparing the surprise seizure of the public buildings and the revolt of Algeria pending the formation of a new government, the general view was that Massu would have to be arrested. Kept in ignorance of these plans were also General Allard and General Jouhaud, in spite of the feelings that the latter, himself of Algerian birth, might have been expected to have.

Yet these four generals who dispatched the telegram were certainly familiar with the state of mind of most of their officers. This is what they tried to make known, by passing on their warning with all possible solemnity. They feared, doubtless, that the ministerial crisis would give activist groups, both civilian and military, the opportunity for a trial of strength with Paris. But their own attitude and their hesitancy, on May 13, showed that they were taken unawares by the extent of the crisis in Algeria. Even if they did suspect it, they attributed its gravity exclusively to the moral distress of the Army cadres. At the time of the telegram, all they wanted was to call attention to a tendency which already seemed to them irresistible.

Although the undertaking was hatched in rather varying milieux and by rival groups, if indeed they were not downright hostile to each other, the actual processes to be unleashed on May 13 were conceived by all in identical terms. The European crowds had to be mobilized in Algiers, the territory had to be taken over by civilian and military authorities who would confront the government with the choice of disappearing or of setting up a government "of public safety." This would have the basic aim to proclaim Algeria an "integral part of France" and to achieve, by all means, a military victory against the rebellion. These processes presupposed, in the initial period, the active participation of some factions in the Army, so that the uprising in Algeria might be effective and total. They also presupposed the preparation of military intervention in France, in case the authorities should refuse to accept the dictates of Algiers.

These two conditions could only be met if a sufficient number of officers were convinced of the necessity of a *coup de force* in Algeria, so that all elements of the Army might agree to take part in this provisional revolt. It was essential, also, that the threat of military action in France should be so great that the General Staffs in France would at once refuse to call out "one part of the Army against the other." The first condition could be met, with the support of officers embodying the outlook of the new military generation. The second depended on the fact that in the Army there was no group, however insignificant, willing to oppose by force the group of officers who favored political action. Then the great myth of the unity of the Army could play its part. This is one of the myths that gives sustenance to military societies and which, in France, acquires additional strength the more it is menaced.

Many identical features marked the officers who were to play the chief part in preparing for May 13, and in the weeks to follow. First of all, there was the matter of rank: Puga, Goussault, Ducasse, Thomaso, Faugas, Trinquier, Godard, Vaudrey, Lacheroy were all colonels. They had played widely different parts: some, like Thomaso, had partcipated in almost every plot at the outset; others, like Lacheroy, had taken part in none; still others, like Godard and Vaudrey, failed to foresee all the political consequences of the demonstrations of May 13. But one thing they all had in common was a biography rich in experience of the Second World War, of years spent in Indochina and of the early years of "pacification" in Algeria. They were men whom war had exiled far from the homeland and whose long-drawn-out adventures had cut them off from the shared sensibilities of French opinion. They embodied the drama of an Army utilized in every corner of the world for wars of adventure in which neither personal conviction nor the will to conquer buoyed them up. In their own persons they felt the bitterness of being forgotten in their own land, while they carried out fearful tasks in Indochina or in Algeria.

Some had an experience even more intense than most of the Indochinese war. Colonel Vaudrey had married a Vietnamese woman, Colonel Trinquier had been one of those to organize the Méo underground. Colonel Puga and Colonel Faugas had a close view of

Moroccan developments and witnessed the reversal of opinion in most bourgeois political milieux, which came to favor independence for Morocco. Almost all shared the task of combating terrorism in Algeria. They knew that the Army had had to set aside its own rules, its morality and its traditions to carry out a mission entrusted to it by the government. Yet this mission might turn out to be the most futile of all, if negotiations with the adversary should promptly lead to Algerian independence.

Again, these were men who had had a professional preparation for violent action, far from the customary practices of political life. When, subsequent to May 13, ministers, civil servants or journalists got to know them, they were amazed to discover a type of man whose very memory had not survived in the Fourth Republic. During almost twenty years, these men had organized underground movements, raised up partisans, administered villages or even departments, organized secret networks, exercised police powers, hunted down traitors and suspects, built schools, set up drainage systems, changed their matériel three or four times and fought three or four different enemies. Their case was not exceptional, for many officers who had no part in the events of May 13 had gone through the same adventures. But the General Staffs in Algiers were made up entirely of men of this stamp. When they were removed from Algeria, others would replace them who were animated by the same will and motivated by the same passions.

When these young officers confronted their generals, it was a dialogue between two generations and two epochs. It was a striking contrast. Nothing, it seemed, could halt the men who had escaped from Dien Bien Phu, who knew the Tonkinese ricefields and the casbah of Algiers, who had practiced every trade, used every means and survived every trial. To get to know them was to realize the contempt, blended with a touch of indulgence, that they felt for the high command. In this respect, the officers of May 13 are the counterpart of their civilian fellow citizens. Like all Frenchmen, they acquired in 1940 a permanent skepticism concerning the competence and the character of most generals. In Indochina they felt themselves to be the victims of the tergiversations and discouragement of their General Staffs. They came to believe that the generals could never adapt themselves to the new forms of revolutionary warfare. The only leaders they respected were men, still young, who took a direct part in their combat engagements and, preferably, had exhibited some independence of mind vis-à-vis the civilian and military authorities. The Generals Lecomte, Massu and Gilles were such men. That is the reason, also, why they felt a profound respect for everything that recalled the Free French. In their ranks the Free French veterans enjoyed a special prestige. Jean-Jacques Schreiber, in his *Lieutenant en Algérie*, records that they were sometimes referred to as the "Commanders."

Against the ardor of these young officers, the generals at the peak of the military hierarchy set their prudence, their calculations, their admonitions. It is true that they employed these qualities vis-à-vis the civilian authorities also. When it was announced that there would be demonstrations in homage to the three soldiers who had been shot by the A.L.N., the four generals—Salan, Allard, Jouhaud and Massu—warned the President of the Republic. After the demonstrators and the instigators of the various plots had taken by siege the buildings used by the Gouvernement Général, General Salan once more turned to the Minister of National Defense, de Chevigné. He explained to him that the demonstrators had set up a Committee of Public Safety which they intended to constitute as "a mixed organization for vigilance to be presided over by General Massu." Salan had had to accept. "It was out of the question to order the troops to fire," he wrote, "for the crowd was made up in part of women and children, it was very numerous and increased from minute to minute. The inevitable consequence of any resort to force compelled us to accept these conditions. . . . My attitude was dictated above all by the desire to avoid any spilling of blood and by the desire not to determine the future. . . . But it is certain that the government's first decisions will be of capital importance During these hours and no one will challenge this impression—the whole population of Algiers had the feeling that it was defending the cause of Algeria as an integral part of France. . . . Any disappointment would create a tragic situation here."

This document sums up in advance the whole attitude that would be adopted during the next two weeks by the military leaders. In Algeria and France alike, it was the young officers who led the assault against the government and the regime, thus collaborating in the plans of action of the political factions. At the summit of the hierarchy, the generals pointed to the activities in which they themselves had no part, in order to exert the maximum pressure on the government. General Challe repeated *viva voce* to Guy Mollet, almost word for word, what General Salan had written on May 14. As a result his minister, de Chevigné, had him sent under escort to Brest. But the other military leaders used practically the same terms.

They did not all hope for the return of General de Gaulle to power.

General Ely and General Challe, for example, thought merely of a Government of National Union whose sole aim it would be to defend French Algeria. Only their collaborators, General Petit and General Beaufort, were downright Gaullists. But the Pflimlin government first tried to hold on to power and to block the military revolt in Algiers. It had counted on the support of the military hierarchy, but made no attempt to satisfy the demands voiced by General Challe and General Salan, or by General Ely. Thus it let the few days—or the few hours—slip by that permitted the backers of General de Gaulle to put him forward as the only solution, since a classical Government of National Union appeared to be impossible. When Pflimlin, the President of the Council, in his turn took up contacts with General de Gaulle, it was the latter who had the upper hand. Merely by keeping silent, he could let the planned military intervention take place in France, while if he was to stop it he required the assurances he considered indispensable for his return to power.

In the meantime, the machinery that had got under way in Algiers had placed the entire Army in the position that the instigators of May 13 had hoped for. The Army in France would never agree to fight the units coming from Algeria. The latter, for their part, were entirely determined to go over to action. In addition, the Algiers example had aroused the enthusiasm of many younger officers of higher rank in France itself. The contacts they had made with some Gaullist nationalist groups or with groups of the extreme Right had been enough to convince them that they would meet with complicity on every hand. Yet they received no encouragement from most of their generals. Only two generals in charge of military districts were willing to direct operations in metropolitan France. In Toulouse, General Miquel, who was allotted this role, hesitated up to the last moment to give the orders that would have overthrown the Fourth Republic and prevented the legal investiture of General de Gaulle as head of the government.

What the generals feared above all was resort to force. Almost the entire military hierarchy intervened so that a change of government might obviate the necessity for a revolt in France, on the lines of that in Algiers. These interventions had, as their first result, the removal of General Ely from his post as Chef d'Etat-Major Général des Armées. But he continued to inspire the attitude of the high command, and saw to it that unbroken discreet contacts continued between those who were preparing for direct military action and those who were begging the government to withdraw, leaving the way free for an authority to be constituted that would reconcile Paris and Algiers.

As negotiators, the Army chiefs were above all interested in saving the essential thing, the Army's unity. They attempted nothing else, from May 13 to June 1. The real drive and authority had already passed into other hands. They were the diplomatic instrument utilized for their dialogue with authority by the officers who had thrown themselves body and soul into the revolt of May 13. The investiture of General de Gaulle was a success for the high command, to the extent that it had been negotiated with the former government. It took on the appearance of a compromise between those who were anxious to preserve legal institutions, those who sought a change of policy in Algeria and those who, before all else, were anxious to avoid the risk of a showdown. But, all in all, the generals had served merely as the spokesmen of the feelings common to the whole Army; they had not inspired these feelings. They were no longer, in a certain sense, the Army's real leaders. The Army was no longer their mirror image. It may be said that their presence at the summit of the military hierarchy had disguised a reality brought to the full light of day by the events of May 13.

The summer of 1958 is the time when the features of the French Army were delineated, as it saw itself, as it wished to be and as it wished to be seen. Immediately after General de Gaulle returned to power, the few shadows were wiped out that had complicated the picture of a whole Army throwing itself into the crucial trial of May 13. There was no further mention of the reserve with which some generals or some groups of liberal-minded officers greeted the groundswell that seemed to bear aloft the State, along with the Army, on the evening of May 13. In any case, the first decisions of the new government legitimized the part played, at varying levels of command, by all who had stressed the danger of civil war and had persuaded the last rulers of the Fourth Republic to make way for General de Gaulle. General Ely was reinstated as Chef d'Etat-Major Général de la Défense Nationale, and General Lorillot was replaced by General Zeller as Chef d'Etat-Major de l'Armée. Since his retirement from active service in 1956, Zeller had been waging a campaign in the pages of the weekly *Carrefour* against any decolonization in Africa, and especially in Algeria. General Salan would receive the Médaille Militaire, the highest distinction an officer could be granted. A considerable number of promotions rewarded the main figures in the events of May 13. As yet, no discordant note was heard. The Army appeared to regard itself as a homogeneous body. Now that Parliament had agreed to accept General de Gaulle, the illegality was forgotten and only the success was recalled. An atmosphere of victory surrounded the Army—victory, no doubt, over the country's institutions, but the hope was cherished that in this way French authority in Algeria could be maintained.

In the history of the military outlook, July 14, 1958, has as much claim to be remembered as, for instance, July 14, 1871. Not that the Army once again had the unanimous affection of the Nation. But on that day—which, some would have it, was "one of the greatest July fourteenths"—exceptionally numerous and well equipped detachments made their way through Paris. There could be no doubt about the enthusiasm of the crowd, though this was directed toward General de Gaulle as much perhaps as toward the Army. Let one detail symbolize this confusion. For reasons of protocol, the new head of the government chose to inspect the fleet at Toulon; it was not he whom the troops saluted as they marched along the Champs Elysées. For the first time, there were many parachutists in the parade. They received the loudest ovation, for everyone knew the part they had played on May 13. It was, for them, a kind of popular consecration: they incarnated both the Algerian War and the weapon of the political revolution that had just triumphed. Were they being thanked for having helped to overthrow a regime that people despised? Or was the Paris crowd thus indicating its approval of the war and of the principle of French Algeria? This ambiguity would not last for long, where public opinion was concerned. Among the military, on the other hand, it would prove to be remarkably long-lived.

The summer of 1958 was one of those privileged moments when every hesitation is forgotten and no contradiction braves the light. The Army appeared to be an entirely flawless intellectual and social structure. All the military hierarchies took over the conceptions, hitherto defended only by a few officers, of subversive warfare and of the conclusions that the Army should draw from this. Now, in the General Staffs, in the staff college and in lectures to the troops, it could not often enough be repeated that what was at stake, in these new wars, was the "mind of the populations." The conclusion was reached that the Army should make use of the appropriate techniques in order to dominate this mind: psychological action on the populations to convince them that the French cause was just, psychological warfare against the enemy forces to split them up, demoralize or disqualify them. There were long descriptions of these methods, from the "in-

toxication" of the adversary by means of practices utilized by the
special services, to the use of films, pamphlets, posters and social
services. It need scarcely be said that Algerian nationalism was dog-
matically declared to be but the "antechamber of international communism." In Algeria, France was defending the west against the
F.L.N. From now on it would be heretical to state anything else. And
as it was deemed necessary to employ against the enemy the techniques of subversive warfare which, it was thought, had given him
victory in Indochina, the idea of the "parallel hierarchies" now
received official consecration.

It would no longer suffice to build up networks of informers among
the population, nor to provide support for the administration and
the Army from veterans' organizations and by carrying out social work.
Now the whole of Algeria must be covered by a parallel hierarchy
that would control the entire population. The task would be entrusted
to the committees of Public Safety. These included representatives of
every profession and every milieu of the European and Moslem communities. This pyramid was to provide solid support for French
authority, represented in Algeria by the Army. So that there should be
no misunderstanding about the role of these Committees, officers would
take part in their labors at every level. They would see to it that
the Committees followed the path traced out by the high command,
so that everywhere there would be the like civilian and military,
political and psychological, ideological and social action. Thus there
could be no renewal of conflict between civil servants and officers,
between European dignitaries and Moslem trade-unionists, economic
interests and social policy. Would not any disagreement be catastrophic, since the whole population had to be taken in hand with the
same coherence and forcefulness that the adversary was trying to
employ?

This extraordinary undertaking had a logic of its own. If in Algeria
the State, through its civilian and military instruments, was embarking on a vast operation destined to ensure the total maintenance of
French Algeria through the massive mobilization of the population
and its trained personnel, how could there be any doubts, in France,
as to its aims and methods?

The officers in Algeria looked on the resoluteness of France itself
as the prerequisite for victory. Any hesitation appeared to them to
explain the reserved attitudes that the Moslem population refused to
abandon. How could these Moslems be convinced that French

authority would tolerate no challenge in Algeria, if France did not as one man publicly and solemnly commit itself to the task? To permit the least doubt as to the intentions of France would give rise to the belief, in Algeria, that French policy might change and that, via concession after concession, the clear and simple idea of French Algeria would be abandoned in favor of the "intermediate solutions" which would inevitably lead to independence.

Fascinated by crowd psychology, many officers the most representative of their generation attributed an extraordinary efficacy to the irresistible force of simple ideas. They had observed that, in our century, independence is the strongest idea setting peoples in motion. So what France had to do was to oppose it with an idea of equal strength that could counterbalance the seductions of independence in "the mind of the populations." The arguments habitually used by advertising men here were pressed into the service of the most traditional, if not the most shopworn, national preoccupations. Can such difficult legal concepts as autonomy, federation and association possess the same crude attraction as the passionate demand for complete independence? No one, it seems, could be found to affirm it among the military. On the other hand, the complete integration of Algeria with France, with the grant of full civil and political rights to Moslems, the irrevocable recognition of their status as French citizens, could be the ideological weapon whose shock effect would "swing over" the Moslem masses and detach them from the F.L.N. Any qualification, restriction or mental reservation was, for many of these officers, a form of surreptitious treason blunting this supreme weapon for ensuring the political victory that would crown their military conquests.

The same logic led even further. If hesitancy in France could have such consequences in Algeria, how could it be tolerated in this age of subversive warfare? Political maneuvering, press campaigns, the movement of public opinion and diplomatic *démarches* could weigh as decisively as tanks, planes and guns. Above all, how could the Moslem population be allowed to think that French people, divided among themselves, might one day come to accept negotiations with the adversary? Military men now believed they had discovered the French political mechanism that menaced French Algeria. Its starting point was the support given Algerian nationalism by the Communists. The fact that this support was never overt made it all the more dangerous. It found shelter behind the mask of a campaign of ideas, instead of stepping over into illegality. In any case, the Communists opposed the war and called for negotiations with the F.L.N. in order to establish Algerian independence. Thus they provided the rebellion with unqualified political support.

But their audience, for all its importance, was nevertheless limited, and they could not sway public opinion as a whole. It is at this stage that the mechanism of political subversion, as the Army saw things, took on more complicated forms, thus enabling the opposition to a French Algeria to win over other sectors of opinion. In this activity the non-Communist Left played a major part. It spoke of national interest, economic realities and the right of peoples to dispose of themselves. It used arguments which affected the same people who might be won over by the spokesmen for a French Algeria. It easily fell together with traditional liberal views that deplored the continuation of the war, the rule of the military in Algiers, the diplomatic isolation of France and the financial burden of the conflict.

The military men who were involved to the hilt in political action believed they were confronted by a new and dangerous extension of the mechanism of subversion in France. For while the F.L.N. claimed to be the proper party to conduct negotiations, and were supported in this by the Communists, the selfsame conclusion had been reached by those bourgeois and liberal circles who failed to support wholeheartedly the integration of Algeria with France. They used various arguments; but is subversion not all the more menacing because of its protean ability to talk many tongues? If an industrialist declares that "the war is costing too much," is he not enrolled in the same political enterprise as the A.L.N. underground fighters, the clandestine networks of the F.L.N. and, even more globally, international communism? In this respect, military opinion was willing to make a distinction in favor of the F.L.N. This was an enemy one could sometimes respect; the others were traitors worthy of nothing but contempt. The hatred felt by the officers for this form of "treason" reawakened the old wound of resentment directed against the press.

Liberal opposition to the Algerian War found expression in several newspapers with which the military already had a bone to pick. These papers had also opposed the Indochinese War. They were suspected of having betrayed countless military secrets. The "affaire des fuites" was recalled. And their journalists were suspected, too, of hobnobbing with Communists. They unreservedly backed the F.L.N. or, at least, demanded that France negotiate with its leaders. These papers had also numerous Moslem readers and the articles they published were often referred to in F.L.N. propaganda. In the United Nations, the orators who demanded international intervention in the Algerian affair stuffed their files with clippings from these papers. This press was considered a true enemy, and countless officers made it the object of an especial hatred—though some, it should be said, maintained relations with these journalists out of a kind of intellectual coquetry.

But the mechanism of subversion in France, the military believed, was able to find expression in even more outrageous ways. The argument that the national interest required the end of the war was put forward by liberal bourgeois. But some Christian groups actually invoked moral and spiritual reasons to condemn the methods used in the war. In these campaigns against torture and extortion, many officers believed they could discern a political purpose. This was none other, of course, than the abandonment of French Algeria. Exasperated by the denunciation of crimes with whose reality they were all too familiar, but with respect to which they felt innocent or pleaded extenuating circumstances, all they could see was the campaign calling for negotiations with the F.L.N. They denied that there were any theological or even moral bases for this attitude. It was simply a means of gaining a hearing in traditionally patriotic or even conservative circles which, at all events, had never shown much interest in decolonization.

They may well have been not entirely wrong. The Catholic militants and the papers with Catholic backing which condemned repression in Algeria quite correctly stated that the methods used demonstrated the actual character of the war, which before all else was quite undeniably a popular rebellion. They reached the conclusion that force alone could not end the war and that, when all was said and done, Christian ethics spoke in favor of the Algerian people's rights. This logic infuriated many officers, most of them Catholic, who rejected the notion that Christian ethics might one day require them to abandon Algeria. They did not hesitate to range the humanitarian campaigns against the Algerian War among the methods of political subversion which, in their view, threatened France and the whole western world. Stretching from the F.L.N. fighters to the Catholics who raised their voices against torture, one vast chain—demonstrably, as they sincerely believed—linked up this underground coalition, making it necessary to treat it as one.

This portrait of the Army in the summer of 1958 has so far included a political doctrine, namely anticommunism "on a world scale," a method of action and of psychological warfare, Committees of Public Safety, the demand for the total integration of Algeria with France, and a passionate detestation of the myriad forms of "treason." Yet the picture would still be incomplete if no mention were made of the ideological and religious views with which numerous officers rounded out their conception of reality. Even prior to May 13 Georges Sauge, who had founded the Centre d'Etudes de Psychologie Sociale, had given his first lectures in the military schools and barracks. But later on his audience grew immensely. Claiming to know communism as only an ex-Communist can, Sauge depicted it as the universal, omnipresent, protean adversary which must be ruthlessly combated and which allows of no neutrality.

His views fitted in too well with a long military tradition not to arouse the strong approval of the officers. The General Staffs added to Sauge's standing by encouraging and inviting him. They asked him to speak to the students of Polytechnique and of Saint-Cyr-Coëtquidan. His lectures were printed in the *Bulletin des Anciens de Saint-Cyr* and in the *Bulletin des Anciens Combattants de la Ire Armée Française*. He spoke at the Staff College and at the School for Mechanized Warfare, at Saumur. He toured Algeria. To communism he opposed Catholicism, which he treated as a religious doctrine that led to a political doctrine. The simplicity of these asseverations accounts for their popularity among military men. To officers profoundly distressed by the campaigns against torture, the ideas of Sauge offered the balm of a religious justification for the Algerian War.

For others who were intellectually more demanding or more concerned with Catholic doctrine, the underground networks of the "Cité Catholique" provided a one-hundred-per-cent integralism with a marked predilection for political analyses. Captain Cathelineau, who was killed in Algeria in 1957, organized the first "Cité Catholique" cells in the Army. By 1959 there were a hundred of them. His bulletin, *Verbe,* became the organ, on a doctrinal and religious basis, of a philosophy that justified the political notions most widespread in the Army. Setting up Christianity against every form of "materialism," from Marxism to "naturalism," the theoreticians of *Verbe* condemned a liberalism which, they maintained, prepared the paths of revolution by destroying the natural and intellectual framework of society.

"Cité Catholique" enjoyed the official support of a number of highly placed officers. Participating in the congress of 1959 were

Marshal Juin, the Generals Weygand, Chassin, Touzet du Vigier and Frémiot, and the Admirals Auphan and de Penfentenyo. It had, naturally, a wider audience among naval officers and those of the mechanized forces, where the average intellectual demands were higher. The military chaplains, too, sometimes out of simple human sympathy, did what they could to protect the military cadres from the temptations of disquietude, if not of remorse. Some of these chaplains, including the best known, Father Delarue, served in the parachute regiments, and passionately preached the myth of the anti-Communist crusade of which, according to them, the Algerian War was the most glorious episode. These priests, going against numerous pastoral letters and frequent calls to order by the theologians most entitled to do so, lent the weight of their religious authority to condone the conduct of the Army in Algeria. On occasion they even denounced other Catholic groups as the accomplices of Communist subversion. In January, 1961, long after the political authorities had repudiated the spirit and the policy of May 13, Father Delarue still asserted, in the *Revue Militaire d'Information*, that "Christian progressivism, together with its militants, the worker priests, brings to communism the backing of the Faith."

With all these factors, religious, political and psychological, the French Army in 1958 is irresistibly reminiscent of a totalitarian organization, with a heritage of right-wing thought and adopting the practices of the Fascist States, forcing its policy on the country, and seeking to involve in the same totalitarianism institutions, parties, the press and public opinion. Yet the image would be incomplete if one overlooked a concomitant enthusiastic and simple-minded acceptance of the most daring social ideas. This is true, doubtless, only of some groups of young officers, most frequently found among the parachutists. But in the wake of May 13 their prestige was such that they set the tone for almost the whole Army. The authority of the colonels who had played so great a part in overthrowing the Fourth Republic was such that it was scarcely possible to contradict them. Perhaps this display of the most audacious social outlook should be regarded as a kind of defensive reaction against the accusation that the Army was "reactionary" and "colonialist." But it was also the final stage in a long evolution whose origins precede the Second World War, when capitalism seemed powerless to resolve its own crises. Impoverished and neglected, the Army had had little share in the great wave of expansion and prosperity enjoyed by the French bourgeoisie, once war and the aftermath of war had ended. In

Indochina, above all, it had had the misfortune to be on the side of the rich, feudal lords or great landowners, racketeers or great colonial enterprises, bankers or corrupt politicians. It had discovered the amazing strength that buoys up an army supported by the mass of poor folk surrounding it. With the conviction that only experience can give, most officers affirmed that the war in Algeria could never be won unless far-reaching reforms induced the Moslems to accept French authority.

They themselves set out to put into effect the needed reforms. The social, economic and educational tasks they took on offer testimony to their resolve. In military circles, it was customary to mock the old civilian administrations, with their conservatism and inertia, compared with the multiple achievements of officers who had to work with very limited means. Some went even further and spoke of the inevitable revolution. In this summer of 1958, when the Army had the feeling that it could accomplish anything in Algeria, there was no lack of officers to stress the urgency of total agrarian reform, to demand that land be distributed, that the forest lands be nationalized, and that French enterprises, preferably State-owned, should have the exclusive exploitation of the oil of the Sahara which, they hoped, would benefit all Algerians and the Moslems in particular. They wanted to show beyond a doubt that the Army had turned its back on social conservatism, and it became fashionable, in military circles, to talk of the experiments undertaken in Jugoslavia and Israel. Some did not even recoil from the idea of a national, Spartan, muscular, equalitarian and patriotic Socialism, which would lure away the working class from the Communist Party, and the Moslems from the F.L.N.

In the shorter run, the preoccupation of most officers was to condemn anything in the least reminiscent of the customary racialism of Algerian society. The officers of the Alger-sahel sector had organized fraternization between Europeans and Moslems, on May 16, in the Algiers forum. They were eager to see this symbolic gesture become a reality. They spoke out violently against the least verbal manifestation of racialism and insisted that Moslems should take part in all the activities to which May 13 had given rise. They became the most ardent advocates of the emancipation of Moslem women. It may be assumed that they alone believed that, by tearing the veils from the faces of young Algerian women, they had launched on its way a veritable social revolution.

Better than any other body, the parachutists incarnated the spirit of the Army after May 13, 1958. French opinion registered this fact with a mixture of amazement, curiosity and horror. Like every elite corps, the parachutists were surrounded by a legend that grew out of any proportion to their actual merits or demerits. To them were attributed every military success achieved and every heroic deed executed in the Indochinese and Algerian wars. But they were also blamed for all the excesses committed in repressing guerrilla fighting and terrorism, since 1956. The parachutists deserved neither this total praise nor these exaggerated accusations. But, like the shock troops of every nationality, they themselves cultivated a reputation that set them apart from the rest of the Army. Their garb alone was enough to distinguish them. Not without many a scuffle with the military administration, they had obtained the right to wear, outside the barracks, the trelliswork camouflage which originally had been intended only for operations and maneuvers. Without a tie, wearing berets, and in this uniform that looked like nothing ever seen before, they were already unique. Their *esprit de corps* and their eagerness to remain in an elite corps had led them to require of themselves a style of life in startling contrast to the gray uniformity of the French Army. Large numbers of them could be seen in the streets of Paris on July 14, 1958, all remarkably alike, with short hair and athletic bearing, walking slowly but with a slight undulation of the hips. It was obvious that, even in the most insignificant details of dress and vocabulary, the parachutists set store on appearing young, amazingly young.

Of all their officers, it is perhaps Colonel Bigeard who best exemplified the characteristics of the French parachutist of the 'fifties, and who most forcibly expressed their *esprit de corps*. "The men of the regiment," he wrote, referring to the Third Colonial Parachutists, "are handsome, proud and courageous . . . Our *paras,* we make real men out of them: healthy, sporting types, humane and well bred." Each adjective is important, but the most revealing is perhaps "handsome," applied to the young paratroopers. Any number of other military leaders would, like Colonel Bigeard, have stressed the value of physical training and the need for courage. It is less likely that anyone else would so calmly have listed handsomeness as a requirement for his men.

The reason for this is that in this military society that threw back a distorting image of French society, the parachutists were reacting against all forms of slovenliness, vulgarity and mediocrity—characteristics which they tended to attribute to a civilian world grown too peaceful, too prosperous and too prudent. A former *para*, Gilles Perrault, wrote a book to demonstrate the subtle bond linking the paratroopers' *esprit de corps* and that of the rebellious or delinquent youths to be found in every modern country. From this standpoint, it is impossible to equate the paratrooper units with the elite units which, in the French Army of former days, had prided themselves on being more than mere infantry regiments, as had the Chasseurs Alpins, the Zouaves and Tirailleurs. Their sole privilege had been to have taken part in more campaigns and to have suffered heavier losses. The best officers had preferred to serve in these regiments, and so helped to maintain their excellence.

More recently, however, all the units of the French Army had tended to become more alike, since the professional soldiers were a mere handful and since all the cadres served, in almost identical conditions, in Indochina. The parachutists, however, stressed their difference. They set out to be the successors of the shock troops who, during the World War and in the Far East, bore the brunt of the fighting. For the first time since the 1940 collapse, all the contingents of drafted men were taking part in a war, and it is in the context of this Algerian War that the prestige of the parachutists took on all its meaning. If they appeared particularly eager for battle, it was because the other units were not; if they fostered the love of renown and the spirit of sacrifice, it was because the rest of the Army had no liking for a weary, never-ending task. This consisted of police duty much more than of military assignments, and of long hours of guard duty, at a little post somewhere in the *bled,* followed by equally dreary hours of waiting. The atmosphere of apathetic resignation in which most of the young soldiers sent to Algeria found themselves plunged aroused, by contrast, the belligerent mentality on which the prestige and reputation of the parachute corps was founded.

This corps became, during the early years of the war, the symbol of the indignities and horrors of the repression denounced by the Leftist opposition. After May 13, when the parachutist regiments played an essential role, the distrust felt in all liberal and republican milieux was extended to all the airborne troops. These shock troops were baptized "the Fascist troops." Their reputation was embellished by legend. They were now depicted as embodying a dark romanticism in which the death longing was blended with unavowable political projects. Since there were two parachute regiments in the Foreign

Legion, which found its recruits above all in Germany and German Switzerland, all parachutists were summarily supposed to possess the dread qualities of Hitler's S.S. A less cursory glance reveals, however, that these parachutists had many purely French traits. Their easy-going, "bon garçon" outlook and the indulgence shown to the ordinary soldier was traditional in the French infantry—unlike the cavalry—and a certain mischievousness went as far back as the red trousers that had lasted until 1914.

Then, again, the parachute regiments maintained an equalitarian outlook that banned the least trace of racism. This had its origins, no doubt, in the celebrated pride of the elite units, for which the world was divided into two parts: the others, and themselves. Whether French, German, black or yellow, a parachutist was a parachutist first of all. The Indochinese War had strengthened this feeling. The number of recruits from France itself had been so low that Vietnamese, Africans, North Africans and Legionaries were also utilized. After May 13, the parachutist officers took drastic steps to ensure that Franco-Moslem "fraternity," officially proclaimed, should also have a few concrete applications. The example was set by their officers. General Massu, who commanded the Tenth Airborne Division, adopted two little Moslems, and Colonel Godard, whose name had come to symbolize, since 1957, the police repression carried out during the battle of Algiers, also adopted one. These officers were also the first to be attracted by the hope of establishing some sort of national Socialism in which the Army, reconciled with the people, would bring about a new social order miraculously wiping out class conflict, abolishing bankers and politicians, and disposing of the international trusts. It is true, furthermore, that in these circles much was said, in 1957 and 1958, of the social injustices inflicted on the Algerian Moslems, of the necessity for agrarian reform, equality of wage payments and the revolution which alone could bind the Moslems to France.

The unusual character of the parachutist regiments might have enabled one to predict their unhappy fate. It did not merely show up the lack of eagerness for combat that afflicted too many other units. It also revealed that the French high command was unable to deploy interchangeable masses of troops all equally qualified. Gilles Perrault has summed up this baffling dilemma of the French in Algeria:

> The following outline of the situation is too simplified to be fair but, subject to this qualification, it is correct. Today in Algeria, as

soon as, to use the customary phrase, contact has been made with the enemy—as soon, that is to say, as the first shots have been exchanged—the men stop advancing and sit on their backsides, for the waiting parachutists to arrive and launch the attack. For in these days it is the parachutists' job to take a piton. . . . Each man plays his part, and it is theirs to die. Thus degenerate fighting forces are more and more getting out of the habit of fighting. And the elite corps, which owes its origin to the general decline in military proficiency, makes the situation even worse.

Georges Buis, a military novelist genuinely liberal in outlook, was himself the embodiment of the loyal Army officer. Here are the views he attributed to one of the heroes of *La Grotte*, who has just sent for the parachutists to come and pacify his sector. "Whether you like them or not doesn't matter a damn to me. They suit me just as they are. There are not thirty-six different kinds of fighter. There are two. There is the tiny percentage who really attack, and the others. The *paras* attack."

The military consequences of this utilization of the elite corps, the parachutists, were unforeseeable and, in the long run, disastrous. In 1959, when General Challe, Commandant Supérieur Inter-armes, set out to eliminate the main underground groups of the A.L.N. by a series of hammer blows, he used the "general reserves," whose backbone consisted of the parachutists. The result was that the actual number of fighting men on the French side no longer had any relation to the total effectives of the Army in Algeria. Pierre Clostermann could even make this declaration from the rostrum of the National Assembly. "Today in Algeria," he said, "our combat troops never have the advantage of numbers, compared with the fellagha. I would even say that in practice there are more first-line fighters among the fellagha than there are shock troops on our side." Gilles Perrault described the inevitable consequences:

> On the tactical level, the method of "general reserves" has had almost identical results . . . in the Algerian *djebels* and the Indochinese ricefields. The spearhead is blunted in ceaseless combats, almost always successful. But when it achieves a victory at one point, the enemy takes over the lightly defended zones, where he need fear no serious resistance. . . This perpetual circulation of the "general reserves" . . . wore out the *paras* and the Legion during the entire Indochinese war, when they were deployed to the four corners of the country. Today this couple between them constitute our entire

"general reserves." No doubt the blows they inflict on the enemy have telling results, when this enemy is weaker, and has more difficulty in nursing his wounds. For all that, once the shock troops have left, after their fierce but brief onslaught, the basic structure is at once reformed. . . . So its military competence does not confer on the elite corps a superiority sufficient to outweight the numerical inferiority. They are not conquered, but they are lost in the crowd. . . . Sooner or later, this system of elite corps inevitably leads to military defeat.

The elite corps was the object not only of admiration but also of envy, which developed into jealousy. The more the parachutists set out to distinguish themselves from the rest of the Army, the more they isolated themselves. This led them step by step to the minority situation that could be glimpsed in January, 1960, with the affair of the barricades, and which became fully apparent with the coup d'état of April 22, 1961. But in 1958 they were still a representative, victorious body. They summed up the Army's drama and all its hopes. That is why their idiosyncracies, though they shocked their adversaries, also exercised an extraordinary appeal. At this exceptional juncture in the Army's history, their prestige and strength spoke of the power once enjoyed and now longed for; their gaiety gave birth to a dream of victory, and their willingness to sacrifice themselves awakened the old vocation of battle and death, inseparable from a military career. In secret, the whole Army could have repeated the celebrated prayer of the parachutist:

> Give me, my God, what you still have
> Give me what no one asks for
>
> I do not ask for wealth
> Nor for success, nor even health
> People ask you so often, my God, for all that
> That you cannot have any left
> Give me, my God, what you still have
> Give me what people refuse to accept from you
>
> I want insecurity and disquietude
> I want turmoil and brawl
> And if you should give them to me, my God
> Once and for all
> Let me be sure to have them always
> For I will not always have the courage
> To ask you for them

The Army shared, in its own way, the feelings that bound the parachutists to those in their ranks who were not of French origin. It also shared the vague revolutionary aspirations that attracted most of the young parachutist officers. In Algeria, the military cadres seemed to have been converted to an equalitarian outlook that stimulated their liking, which, however ambiguous, undoubtedly existed, for the Moslem population. We have already spoken of the ambiguity of their relations with the Europeans. Vis-à-vis the Moslems, it was another ambiguity. Distrust was certainly not extirpated, and at any moment the Moslem might appear as what he was: the enemy. This in itself was enough to poison any possible relationship between the Army and the Moslem community. Yet the greater number of the officers felt more liking for the Moslems, more affection, one might even say, than for the European minority. Poor, proud and brave, the Moslem bore a strange resemblance to the young officer who had come to "protect" him, when it was not necessary to fight him. Besides, the officer felt that he had a more essential role to play with respect to the Moslem population. On its behalf he could expend all his treasures of devotion, generosity and initiative which usually lay dormant, since his profession called on him to fight or to endure the routine of garrison life. Then, too, contact with Moslems stimulated his sensitivity to a quality that takes many different forms but which has always had the greatest possible importance for the soldier: loyalty.

In the old Army, up to 1939, praise was accorded the *tirailleurs* who remained faithful unto death to the person of their officers. Now loyalty came to acquire another meaning that was both wider and more ambiguous. The key to the war in Algeria, the military cadres believed, lay in arousing the loyalty of the Moslems to French authority, and this surely signified that, in return, France's loyalty was assured those who had sided with her. Once again the crisis of abandonment was being prepared, and this withdrawal was invoked by many officers to justify their disaffection or their acts of rebellion. Already a relationship in which the most passionate emotions found a part was growing up between the Moslem population and the Army. In a book aflame with fanaticism on behalf of French Algeria and hatred for those opposed to it, but attaining an extraordinary epic breadth, *Au lieutenant des Taglaits,* Philippe Héduy provides striking examples of this:

> A Captain of Dragoons reigned over the kingdom of Kpir, he was called Pêcheur. He was dry, lean and bony, like most of us, but he

had special reasons to bear marks in his flesh. . . . He had reached the end of his youth in Buchenwald. . . . Having escaped from the universe of the concentration camps, Pêcheur had dreamed of a world free and proud. . . . The freedom to which all were entitled was the freedom that Pêcheur, along with a victorious France, would give them. . . . He had become one of the most magnificent executors of pacification in all Algeria. . . . The sub-district of Kpir was next to ours, and we sometimes visited Captain Pêcheur. It was always an extraordinary spectacle and . . . a lesson in pacification. Pêcheur, who was a zealot of revolutionary warfare, had faith only in love, the demanding love that did not pardon acts of treason, the patient love that never tired of manifesting itself, disinterested love. Captain Pêcheur was in love. Between him and the Moslem population of his sub-district there was a spectacular liaison that set tongues wagging.

The testimony of Jean Yves Alquier, in his *J'ai pacifié Tazalt,* is equally impressive. He relates how he succeeded in winning over the population of his *douar* by undertaking as many economic and social projects as he did military and psychological ones. But the time came for him to leave Tazalt. One of the leaders of the community asked him to state frankly whether the inhabitants should come out once and for all in favor of French authority, whether France "would remain." Alquier, who was about to return to France, and who was familiar with political realities in France and Algeria, hesitated to give the pledge demanded of him. But other officers in his situation did not hesitate. That would provide them with a permanent reason or alibi for rebelling against the grant of independence to Algeria. They had given themselves a kind of moral pledge whose degree of sincerity it is impossible to estimate. Sometimes the dialogue between officer and Moslem was both simpler and more traditional, it was the exchange that always takes place between enemies who desire to esteem each other. "We thought of this war," wrote Colonel Bigeard, ". . . of our comrades killed in their onward rush or obliterated in their foxholes, and of the others who had killed them and who might have become our comrades . . . We felt no hate, and we looked after this one [a wounded A.L.N. fighter]. He had his law and we had ours."

This passionate identification of the Army with Algeria explains the vehemence with which its spokesmen always denounced the political opposition, whenever it tried to stir up French opinion against the Algerian War and its disastrous consequences. Curiously enough,

many officers equated the whole Nation with this opposition, perhaps
divining that one day French opinion would realize the uselessness
and harmfulness of the war. As these officers saw things, ignorance,
weariness and forgetfulness had formed a pact with subversion,
cowardice and treason. This vehemence was the premonitory rancor
of the vanquished, for these men, despite their eagerness to see war
crowned with victory, knew that they would not win. Philippe Héduy
gave their rebelliousness lyric expression. "Amid the pleasures of the
metropolis," he wrote,

the value of our struggle was diminished. Its meaning was forgotten,
so that we might more readily be forgotten. And we were not deluded
by the few outbursts of solicitude expressed by France for its Army,
by a few lines in the newspapers to lament three deaths, a few elegiac
editorials, a few tortuous party congresses where tears were shed over
this war that had become an abstraction and where hopes were
voiced for peace: a cheap electoral trick. We had been wounded in
our flesh, we had real dead to mourn over, we were no longer surprised at how little space was allotted our wounded and our dead,
our deeds and our sacrifices, in the newspapers, conversations and
reflections of the far-off homeland, and we felt that we were embarrassing people. We were spattered with blood and might soil
other Frenchmen, and the France of Pontius Pilate preferred to
wash its hands of all responsibility. Its great thinkers tended toward
what they called the Left, playing the silly game of political labels
and acting toward our enemies like mercenary fiancées. All of them,
university professors, students, writers classified as "of the Left"—for
those said to be of the Right were insignificant—and even the
comedians, ardently supported the cause of our adversaries. France
was upended, ass in the air and head down, for the men who guided
its destinies and tried to get it to think had been more or less the
same for fifteen or twenty years; it was they who had brought France
so low. In this posture the French snored away, heads down, the bats
of History, casting away their last possessions in a rapid, delightful
cadence. And the university professors, the students, the journalists
and the writers offered their cheeks to those who were striking us,
and brandished their ridiculous little fists and screamed like little
girls at us who were defending their freedom to scream. Who were
we to frighten little girls and arouse so much hatred? We were men
and sometimes wore a disguise. Handsome on parade and valiant
in war, we knew how to die. Those of us who fell amounted to a
reassuringly large number. It was consoling for the partisans of the
Left to count how many—how many of the officers they called

Fascists had, fortunately, disappeared on the colonialist fields of battle. Thus, at the very heart of a despairing France, there was a hidden joy at the death of all the lieutenants and captains killed in Indochina or in Algeria, and these people felt happier and more free.

Lieutenants dead in December, captains dead in July, officers counted off on the chaplets as the months slipped by, for what did you fight, and for whom? What had you sallied forth to defend in these unknown mountatins? What pointless chase, begun in the rice-fields of the Tonkin Delta, was being continued in the *douars* of the Constantinois? Some of us were still alive and we were now seized by panic, by a major tremor: had our dead friends died in vain for a useless and moribund France? We had been lunatics sent to die by cowards. By those who in 1940 had fled from war in a lamentable exodus and who now, twenty years later, were fleeing from the idea of war. Twenty years later there was another undisguised collaboration with the enemy which shocked no one and seemed natural, and intellectual ease was now to be found on the Left, as formerly it could be found on the Right. Yet, in the hope of a new Montoire [where Hitler met Pétain], the wolves, foxes and rats of collaboration with the F.L.N. multiplied their activities. They howled for peace at the price of defeat, the peace to which we were tending at the price of victory. They corrupted people's minds by opposing our adversaries' policy of force with a policy of comfort and tranquillity, for they were sure of being heard in this tired old country, which was ripe for the great Marxist horse trade.

In this dough made up of fat, lumbering Frenchmen, so difficult to raise, and so much worked by evil yeasts, there were ourselves. . . . We loved a brotherly Algeria, a hard but firm earth, that a useful blood might have fertilized. Now all this spilt blood, our blood, might have no more purpose than the flush of roses. So much blood poured out, and so much courage and so much suffering, Algeria traversed from end to end and paid for so many times over, so many officers killed, so many soldiers missing, so many mothers and fiancées, so many roses . . .

These cries of despair were not heard until later. In May, 1958, there was still nothing but passion and fury. Besides, only those were involved whose own sacrifices explained or justified their emotion. The other tendency in the Army was incorporated by the theoreticians of permanent war, and by those who favored a political mobilization of the Army and the military supervision of civilian opinion. They had a wonderful force at their disposition, the reserve cadres. The year

1958 was to be the beginning of a highly significant development in the instruction imparted to reserve officers and noncoms. The customary sessions devoted to the reworking, on paper, of the hackneyed theme of the deployment of larger units were replaced by courses on revolutionary warfare. From one end of the country to the other, before an interested and rapidly persuaded audience of many thousands of reservists, instructors began their lectures by propounding the axiom that "revolutionary warfare is one of the methods used by Marxism-Leninism in its pursuit of power." This was followed by the logically developed sequence of the usual themes. Algerian nationalism was the "antechamber" of international communism, association or autonomy was the "antechamber" of independence, negotiations inevitably led to the strengthening of the F.L.N., the campaigns against torture inevitably led to negotiations, liberal opinion was "objectively" serving the ends of communism, and so on.

Such was the hold exercised on the Army by these notions that the General Staff actually saw to it that they were circulated among the reservists. The high command had, apparently, no qualms and the Minister of the Armies, Guillaumat, a high official with no known political preferences, raised no objections. These, then, were the two aspects that characterized the Army in 1958, that of fighters appalled by the thought that one day their struggle might turn out to have been in vain, and that of the theoreticians—the same men, in some cases—who wanted to impose a logical order on the military apparatus, the apparatus of government and the Nation itself, in keeping with the notions born of their experience, their prejudices or their ideological preferences.

For the Army that had been revealed to the Nation by the events of May 13, the peak was reached in September, 1958. The referendum held on the 28th was the occasion of an immense military effort on behalf of a policy. Since French authority was to be exercised permanently in Algeria, and since this was the Army's supreme task, it openly abandoned its political neutrality. If the Algerian War was a political struggle much more than a military one, the referendum had to be regarded as the decisive engagement. French Algeria was at stake. No official qualifications came to attenuate the absolute validity of this act of faith. To vote "yes" was to vote for a French Algeria. There could be no ambiguity, for Algeria was made up of French Departments and would not be required, subsequently, to pronounce on the statute envisaged for the "States in the Community." Senegal and the Ivory Coast opted for this statute, which later permitted them to accede to independence.

Nothing of the kind for Algeria. After September 28, General de Gaulle would declare that Algeria had decided to work out its destiny "with France," just as he had declared prior to the referendum. The formula left many ambiguities standing, since it could be reconciled with integration and equally readily with a statute of association. In the electoral battle preceding the 28th, which the Army treated as though it were a military operation, things were made to appear much more simple. To vote "yes" meant, for the Moslems, that they were on the side of France, of a French Algeria. But thereby the Army, on behalf of the state, undertook to maintain French authority in Algeria indefinitely. The oath sworn to in the Forum, after May 13, was repeated in every *douar* by the entire military hierarchy. The referendum was presented as being a solemn, definitive contract. If the Moslems voted for a French Algeria, France, by means of its Army, pledged itself never to allow anyone to challenge this choice.

In the history of the Army, this referendum was even more important than the events of May 13. It is, indeed, quite impossible to allot responsibility to a few groups of officers embarked on an adventure that their leaders might repudiate, if it turned out badly. This time, the hierarchy itself was committed to the hilt. It would feel itself bound by the proclamations made before September 28. Nor did the government utter the least contradiction. The Army was not forbidden to take part in the debates on the referendum, and there was no disavowal of the officers of every rank who kept on repeating that "to vote 'yes' is to vote for a French Algeria."

The Army in Algeria was all the more ready to look on the referendum as a battle, since the F.L.N. had called on the Moslems to abstain from voting. So to persuade them to vote was to thwart the adversary. And why should the Army desist, since this was a vote for or against France and since it was the duty of established authority to guide the population? In Algeria, this was not the mere acceptance or rejection of a constitution. To vote "no" was to refuse a French Algeria. This was the meaning attributed to the referendum in the electoral campaign. The apparatus of the state, both civil and military, did all that could be done to induce the Moslem population to flock to the polling booths. Official directives required the secrecy of the ballot to be respected, but in practice it appeared that the masses were being invited to vote, and to vote "yes." The fate of the country was to be decided, and the military hierarchy, convinced that the armed struggle was inextricably involved in this political struggle, did not care to remain neutral. Since all was at stake, it had the obligation to participate.

Algeria, that September, resembled a totalitarian state in which the administration and the Army are the tools of the regime and its policy. There were astounding scenes, for Frenchmen who were accustomed to see the state respect the free interchange of political debate. The Army took over the task of putting up posters, transporting voters and of updating the registers. Meetings and lectures were organized all over Algeria by the military authorities. Officers acted as chairmen, and other officers spoke as though they were candidates in an election. It was the occasion for a vast public demonstration, in which once again the defense of Algeria was equated with the defense of the western world. Once again, those who favored negotiations were denounced as the agents of Communist subversion, and autonomy or association with France depicted as indirect paths leading to independence. General Salan, the Delegate General of the Government in Algeria, went everywhere in the country, and harped on these themes with all possible solemnity, thus lending them official sanction.

The evening of September 28 marked the apogee of the trend that had led the Army to intervene directly in politics. It was, so to speak, the apotheosis of the meditations that had begun in the ricefields of Indochina, of the trials undergone at each stage of the successive evacuations in Vietnam, Morocco and Tunisia. It was the apotheosis of the experiments that had been tried in Algeria, the apotheosis of May 13.

Nevertheless, this new, massive bloc that the Army had become already bore in itself the seeds of its future disaggregation. This would appear only gradually, as the ambiguities lurking in the compromise that had led to General de Gaulle's return to power came to the light. The prestige and glory that bathed the handful of men, civilians and military, who had been treated as rebels by the last government of the Fourth Republic, had created the impression that their victory was entire. But the contradictions remained, and this was but a compromise.

Algiers had called for General de Gaulle as the man who could ensure a French Algeria. The political parties had acceded to his return in order to eliminate the danger of civil war. Those responsible for May 13 preached the doctrine of integration. Neither Parliament nor General de Gaulle had publicly agreed to this. Nothing was said about it in the conversations that took place between the General and Guy Mollet, Antoine Pinay, Pflimlin or President Coty. General de Gaulle did not mention it in his speech of acceptance. This uncertainty concerning Algerian policy was even more significant than the General's ideas as to the procedures by which he could come to power, or than his promise to create a Fifth Republic within a parliamentary framework. Bourgeois opinion had not changed its views on the Algerian question. It was still anxious to lighten the financial burdens caused by the war, to maintain the principal French positions in Algeria, to bear in mind the existence of a substantial European minority, but to put an end to an interminable conflict.

Only the risk of an armed uprising had enabled General de Gaulle to return to power. Thus his historic and political role was implicitly laid out. He must avoid all risk of civil conflict while at the same time seeking for some way to end the Algerian War. The Army's intervention in political life, its dreams of economic and social transformation and the long effort presupposed by any attempt to integrate Algeria totally were not shared, much less approved, by French public opinion as a whole, and above all not by bourgeois opinion. Virtually, a new cleavage was now separating the Army and the Nation. This was much more serious than any previous rift, for on this occasion the Army was both guilty in the past, and responsible for the future: guilty of having broken with the traditional order in the state and of having sought to impose a particular policy on the Nation, and responsible for any ensuing setbacks, for the difficulties to be surmounted and the tempests it might have helped to unleash.

It might have been foreseen that General de Gaulle, by turning his back on a French Algeria, would not be opposed by a fissureless Army that would brook no rebuff. As early as May 13, the objectives and the unvoiced reflections of all officers were far from being identical, even among those who had played the major part in overthrowing the Fourth Republic. There could even be found among them almost the whole gamut of the political views most widely held in the Army. In France itself General Cherrière, who had animated one of the first groups meditating a change of regime, was openly hostile to the Republic. He represented the reactionary, antiparliamentarian extreme Right, which favored an authoritarian state and a corporate organization of the economy. His outlook was that of certain elements inspired by the monarchist tradition, in France and in the European community in Algeria. In Algiers Dr. Lefebvre, the theoretician of a corporate social order, was pretty much representative of the same trend, which was always in the minority but sometimes exercised a disproportionate influence because of its extremism. General Chassin, who was a friend of General Cherrière's, did not have any such precise social or political views. Historian of the war between Germany and Russia, formerly in charge of aviation in Indochina and coordinator of aerial defense in the Atlantic General Staff, he saw everything in terms of the universal war against communism, which was to be the sole task of the regime he envisaged as replacing the Fourth Republic. The officers working together with General Cherrière and General Chassin, such as Colonel Thomaso, shared their ideas but had no intention of themselves carrying them out. Most of them rallied to the support of General de Gaulle's candidature, when they came to regard him as the one man able to overthrow the Fourth Republic and bring about the integration of Algeria.

General Ely, Chef d'Etat-Major Général de la Défense Nationale, hoped that a Government of National Union would be formed and had no wish to change the regime. Two of his collaborators, however, General Grout de Beaufort and General Petit, desired the return of General de Gaulle to power. General Challe, Major General of the Armies, had favorable recollections of Guy Mollet, with whom he had worked out the steps necessary to launch the Suez expedition, and he turned to him now. He suggested that a Government of Public Safety should be formed, to inspire trust among Army men and to reveal a firm intention to defend Algeria. General Salan, in Algiers, did not rally to the support of General de Gaulle without considerable hesitation. Until the first days of May he had thought that Robert Lacoste, Minister for Algeria for more than two years, would be the man best qualified to head a government committed to a French Algeria. Familiar with the political milieux of the Third and Fourth Republics, he had never been a Gaullist, and his political reputation made him suspect in the eyes of the "ultras" in the European community. When he asked the Generals Allard and Jouhaud, and also Dulac, to announce together with himself that they favored the return of General de Gaulle to power, they did not agree because of any personal attachment to the one-time leader of the Free French. Faced with the resistance put up by the political parties to the developments in Algiers, and by their refusal to set up a Government of Public Safety, they considered that only General de Gaulle had the requisite authority to overcome this opposition, and that his prestige would calm the fears of the public. The only personage who responded to General de Gaulle's appeal out of personal attachment was Admiral Auboyneau, then in command of the naval forces of Algeria, who had been Chief of Staff of the naval forces of the Free French.

These men had one thing in common, the resolve to keep France in Algeria, and they saw but one method, to make Algeria French by integration. Apart from that, they had no political views in common, and no marked preference for any man or any regime, and had no clear conception of the means to be used to force through their Algerian policy. Thus General de Gaulle would have no great trouble in strengthening his power by chipping away at the seemingly solid block the Army had erected in Algeria by its assumption of authority over the administration, and by its supervision of the populations and the pyramid formed by the Committees of Public Safety. At an early stage, the Gaullist members of the "Algeria-Sahara" Committee of Public Safety succeeded in defeating a motion that would have called for the suppression of the political parties and the setting up of a corporate regime. Fourteen members of the Committee resigned forthwith. A wedge had been driven into the hitherto united front of the partisans of a French Algeria. Immediately after the referendum, the Army was ordered to "gain elevation" and refrain from intervening directly in the aftermath of the election. The spirit of this order corresponded too closely with the military's traditional distrust of electioneering not to be approved or, at the least, easily obeyed by most officers.

But those in whose view the Algerian War was condemning the Army to ceaseless political intervention were well aware of the risk that they might lose all control over events. To recognize the variety of opinions in Algeria might well smooth the path of the partisans of autonomy or association, and threaten the thesis of a French Algeria, which was supposed to remain an absolute dogma. This risk appeared all the greater since General de Gaulle had not repeated the remarks favoring integration that he had made everywhere during his journey in Algeria that June. At the same time, the offer of the F.L.N. to send representatives to France, with no preliminary conditions, to discuss the terms of a cease-fire, and the tone in which this offer had been made, awakened the suspicion that General de Gaule already looked on the F.L.N. as at least one of the formative elements of a future Algeria. Nor was any time limit placed on this offer, so it might be thought that it could be repeated later, perhaps with some modification. What now remained of the idea cherished by the men of May 13, that only the solemn proclamation of an irrevocable determination to keep Algeria "an integral part of France" could eliminate all hesitation from the minds of the population and ensure their opting definitively for France?

The General Staffs of the Army in Algeria did not carry out General de Gaulle's directives, or at best carried them out inadequately. Almost everywhere officers intervened in order to draw up lists of candidates all of whom favored a French Algeria. Their intervention was, indeed, often indispensable if the Moslems were to agree to register as candidates. Some officers even ran as candidates themselves. Some did so simply because they judged circumstances to be favorable. Among these were General Bourgund and General Noiret. Others were anxious to continue on the parliamentary plane the activities that they had got under way on May 13. Among these were Colonel Thomaso, elected in Bayonne, and General Miquel, who would have been in charge of any military uprising in France, and who was just nosed out in Oran. Some received orders to submit their candidacy, as did Colonel Broizat, Chief of Staff of General Massu, who wanted him elected so that he might guide the footsteps of the new Moslem deputies. But he was defeated in a Paris constituency. Almost everywhere in Algeria, electoral rivalries opposed only the former political personnel of the Fourth Republic and the members of the Committees of Public Safety. No one on either side challenged the concept of a French Algeria.

Four months later, in the municipal elections, things had greatly changed. Some extremist milieux toyed with the idea of abstaining. Several candidates boasted they had the "support of General de Gaulle" and refrained from any too direct allusion to a French Algeria. If liberals who favored negotiations with the F.L.N. declared they would not run, since there was no guarantee of the freedom of the ballot, the civil administration, under orders from Delouvrier, the government's Delegate General, begged them to do so. The state apparatus already had a great deal more homogeneity than at the end of 1958. Almost everywhere, outside Algiers and Oran, officers intervened in the preparation of lists of candidates. In smaller centers of population, the steps taken by the military authorities were, ad-

mittedly, necessary to ensure that there would be Moslem candidates.
Yet it was already realized, in the Army, that such acts of intervention
were frowned on by the government, which was eager to find moderate
nationalists who would more genuinely represent Moslem opinion
and who might be partners in debate, when the time came to provide
Algeria with a statute of autonomy or association.

Once more the ambiguity had crept in that was supposed to have
been banished for ever after May 13. With a meaningful insistence,
General de Gaulle refused to employ the expressions "integration" or
"French Algeria." On being elected President of the Republic, he at
once made a speech that looked forward, on Algeria's behalf, to its
"outstanding place in the Community." This was regarded as alluding
to an autonomous set-up akin to that enjoyed by such states in the
Community as Senegal, the Ivory Coast and Madagascar. The
partisans of a French Algeria did not fail to point out that the Constitution allowed these states to come out for full independence later,
so that the way would be opened for the secession of Algeria also. But
at the same moment the Prime Minister, Michel Debré, assured
Parliament that the Algerian Departments were an integral part of
France. The government did nothing to resolve this ambiguity, and
no directive was issued to put an end to the campaign waged by the
Army in favor of a French Algeria. There were still elements in the
Army sufficiently resolute to put an end to this ambiguity, once and
for all, by renewed political action.

A long series of transfers had made many changes in the military
scheme of things, since General de Gaulle's assumption of power.
General Salan now held the purely honorific position of Military
Governor of Paris. He had been promised the nonexistent and never
to be created post of Inspector General of Defense. General Allard
became Commander-in-Chief of French Forces in Germany, and
General Jouhaud Chief of Staff for Aviation. Colonel Lacheroy had
returned to Paris to direct the courses given to staff officers for the
reserve cadres. The Colonels Ducasse, Goussault and Trinquier were
removed from Algiers. But these changes did not seem to have any
noteworthy effect on the Army's state of mind. In the Algiers General
Staff, Colonel Gardes and Colonel Argoud, who had had no part in
the events of May 13, were determined to keep its spirit and policy
alive, and in Algeria they met with Colonel Godard and Colonel
Vaudrey, who had the same intentions. In Paris General Zeller, the
Chef d'Etat-Major de l'Armée, incarnated military opposition to any

evolution in General de Gaulle's Algerian policy. He used his authority to protect the propaganda efforts that officers were making in favor of a French Algeria. He was responsible for the new character given the training of reserve officers, who were henceforth required to know the nature of the subversive warfare waged by international communism and supported by Algerian nationalism and with the complicity, also, of liberal opinion. The Army continued to be markedly influenced by the men most determined to compel the state to maintain a French Algeria. The precedent of May 13 had shown that they could act and win. While General de Gaulle was the chief object of their distrust, they could imagine no other means to force a change in his policy than the methods that had proved so successful in the spring of 1958.

After September 16, 1959, many officers thought that the moment had come for the Army to intervene politically once again. General de Gaulle had not yet openly favored any of the three courses he recognized as being available for the Algerians, in their right to self-determination: full integration with France, association or seccession. At the most, the tone of his speeches might be taken to indicate that he preferred association, and this was also confirmed by almost everyone who had spoken to him personally. But the partisans of a French Algeria believed that one hope remained. All the government had to do was to declare itself for "Francization"—another way of saying integration—and to allow the Army to wage a campaign in favor of this choice in Algeria. All that was required was to deflect, not to break, General de Gaulle's line of policy. Most general officers approved this approach and made no secret of it, for they greatly feared a trial of strength that would have confronted them with the resoluteness of the head of state. But many officers among those most uncompromisingly faithful to the spirit of May 13 considered that the very principle of self-determination was disastrous. If the planned referendum were to be completely free, surely the partisans of Algerian independence would have the right to express themselves and to appeal for votes. Did not this mean legitimizing, in advance, the propaganda and the projects of the F.L.N.? General de Gaulle had, doubtless, condemned secession in vigorous terms but he had not excluded, quite on the contrary, the right of Algerians to take this path. The officers who looked on the political struggle as another aspect of the war at once reached the conclusion that the Algerian population would consider it a defeat for the Army, if the backers of total independence were allowed entire freedom of expression and action. Besides, was this not to disavow ahead of time all the propaganda that had been poured out during the previous two years or so in favor of a French Algeria?

Thus military opinion was already less categorical. One view was still firmly maintained, the necessity for a French Algeria, both by those who wished the government to declare itself in favor of integration and by those who wished this principle to be re-examined. But the former had no faith either in the necessity or in the possibility of convincing the head of state to abandon his policy. The others judged that some brake had to be applied to this evolution of Algerian policy which, they sensed, was tending to negotiation with the adversary. But their position was weakened by the fact that it allowed them no possibility of maneuver. A few verbal concessions on General de Gaulle's part would be enough to put them, ostensibly, in the wrong, and to show the rightness of those who still hoped, or declared they hoped, that official policy could be influenced. The history of the Army in the fall and winter of 1959–1960 must be comprehended in terms of this dialectic.

On two occasions the attempt was made to make fresh use of the same mechanism. In Algeria, the mobilization of the European community in vast demonstrations was to provoke the intervention of the Army, which would turn to Paris and beg it finally to express itself in favor of a French Algeria, as the only way of allaying distrust and of calming every apprehension. In France, political milieux partial to integration would do all they could to support this intervention of the military leaders, who would plead the cause of Army unity. In October, the partisans of a French Algeria had two trumps in their hand. In the National Assembly, a considerable number of U.N.R. deputies were to join forces with the deputies from the Algerian Departments, and it was estimated that this would pose a sufficient threat to the Debré government to force it either to back a French Algeria, with or without General de Gaulle's approval, or to resign. Then the way would be open for a new government that would have to be formed under the menace of civil war. Thus the situation of May 13 would have been recreated. At the same time, the presence of General Zeller at the head of the Etat-Major de l'Armée was an even more important weapon in the hands of the partisans of a French Algeria. He was due to leave his post on October 1—another reason for acting without delay—but the General Staffs would continue to be administered by officers who shared his ideas and who were equally suspicious of General de Gaulle. In a political enterprise in which the Army was to play a decisive role, the cadres seemed even more determined than they had been on May 13.

New colonels had taken the place of those who had left Algiers the year before. There were, for example, Colonel Argoud, General Massu's Chief of Staff, Colonel Gardes, head of the Fifth Bureau, and Colonel Crépin, who commanded the base of Ain-Arnat. The General Staffs of the Army and of Aviation provided them with a support their forerunners of May 13 had not had. The "carrefour" of the young reserve officers, those under thirty-five years of age, had just been held in Paris, and had come out in favor of Francization. Its thousands of members might form the supporting networks for a military operation that would pass over from Algeria to France itself. They would constitute the concrete link between Army and Nation.

The decisive moment had come for those who, disturbed by the threat of a new crisis, thought it possible to influence General de Gaulle's Algerian policy and to impose their own views. Their aim was to pick up the torch from those officers who were most acutely suspicious of General de Gaulle. Their attacks would be based on the most elementary and ineluctable considerations, which in their turn would become all the more threatening since behind them was the menace of military action. The highly placed military men who would inform de Gaulle of all this could use the prospect to arouse alarm.

This mechanism, which would be so successful in January, 1960, in the affair of the barricades, was set in motion as early as October, 1959. General Ely, Chef d'Etat-Major Général de la Défense Nationale, when he informed the head of state of the uncertainty and qualms that beset the Army, tried to obtain the assurances which, he maintained, would be enough to restore confidence among the officers. What they wanted was the definitive barring of any negotiation with the F.L.N. on Algeria's political future, permission for the Army to conduct the referendum and to continue suppressing terrorist activities, despite the government's policy of self-determination. Finally, they wanted the government to declare at once that it would campaign in favor of the "most French solution."

General de Gaulle took up these matters with General Challe, Commandant Supérieur Inter-armes in Algeria. He recalled that in his speech of September 16 he had repudiated the idea of treating the F.L.N. as the government of Algeria or as the opposite number in a dialogue with France. He gave the assurance that the Army would remain in Algeria while the referendum was being conducted, since no other body could see that it was carried out properly. As for the final solution, he was naturally in favor of an Algeria closely linked with France, but he reserved the question of deciding the precise nature of this bond. General Ely and General Challe looked on this assurance as sufficient. Their opinion was shared by General Gracieux, who commanded the Tenth Airborne Division, General Massu and Colonel Bigeard. It was enough to eliminate any possibility of political intervention on the Army's part, as this had been conceived by some officers more suspicious or more resolute than the others. The parliamentary echoes of the operation that had been projected amounted to very little. The nine resignations from the U.N.R. parliamentary group did not lead to the departure of the additional fifty deputies who, together with the bulk of the Independents, might have deprived the government of its habitual parliamentary support.

Yet the European population of Algeria was still available, and still ready for a test like that of May 13. In eighteen months the Gaullist elements had practically disappeared. The political organizations had hardened and the most extreme tendencies had gained the upper hand. At the same time, closer connections had been established with the General Staffs in Algiers. They, for their part, were eager to maintain control over such a substantial "striking force," since they knew by experience that this was the most effective way to exert pressure on the political decisions reached in Paris. And the leaders of the European community knew that they could have no power to influence decisions if they did not work as a team with the Army.

Thus another sort of double game came into being, similar to the situation that already existed within the Army, whose leaders served as intermediaries, with General de Gaulle on the one side, with the most headstrong officers, and those most bitterly opposed to the head of state, on the other. These officers were relying on the European community to serve as a threat or an argument vis-à-vis the Army leaders and, indirectly, vis-à-vis the government. In the meantime, the European political milieux waited for Army encouragement before taking any active step. This double game was obviously a very risky one, and at any moment the possibilities of self-deception were enormous. For example, the European political mileux had simply to construe incorrectly the encouragement given them by some officers. These officers had but to delude themselves concerning the efficacy of the pressure exercised by the high command on the head of state or on the government. The military leaders needed only treat too lightly the threat of a political mobilization or of an actual rebellion breaking out among the Europeans. And, finally, everybody might blunder at once. Each of these groups had to determine with entire precision when the threshold had been reached, beyond which there could be no hope of inducing General de Gaulle to modify his Algerian policy.

This threshold was judged to have been reached when General Massu was relieved of his command, after the *Süddeutsche Zeitüng* published the interview he had given their correspondent. It had been a conversation, not an interview. And General Massu had not been able to revise the text. Yet, despite several undeniable inaccuracies, the remarks attributed to the General reflected well enough the feelings shared by most of the military cadres. There was distrust of General de Gaulle, regret that he had not proclaimed a "French Algeria" and had done nothing to achieve integration, and irritation at the campaigns conducted against the methods of repression and at the legal restrictions hampering the officers who were required to stamp out terrorism.

General Massu's departure might not have had such grave consequences if the state of mind of the European community had not been so deeply affected by the wave of terrorism that was sweeping over the Mitidja and the Algiers region. Excitement had reached a peak among the militants of the political organizations, and the leaders of these groups, hoping for the encouragement of certain officers, were themselves pushed onward, borne aloft on a tide of opinion that made a trial of strength inevitable.

Another factor was the rivalry between the leaders of the European community. Joseph Ortiz, who headed the Front National Français, was in regular communication with Colonel Gardes, in charge of the Fifth Bureau, and with General Faure, who commanded the Tizi-Ouzou division. The General Staff of the Army corps in Algiers thought that it could control him by backing up his authority. But those immediately subordinate to Ortiz were in favor of a political revolution that would set up an authoritarian, corporate state in France. This movement used as its emblem the Celtic cross, as did "Jeune Nation," a small group of extremists in metropolitan France.

On similar lines, André Martel, who headed the small "Mouvement Populaire du 13 mai," was highly favorably disposed to violent action, since he wanted the Fourth Republic to be replaced by a regime modeled on those of Franco and Salazar. Finally, while conversations were still going on between Ortiz and the officers of the Algiers General Staff, the Deputy Pierre Lagaillarde, who had a great deal of influence in university circles, outdistanced them by giving the demonstrations of January 24 and the following days a breadth, discipline and moral force that would make it difficult to dispose of the affair of the barricades. Lagaillarde could not be swayed as easily as Ortiz, and by compelling the esteem of some officers he made it difficult for them to conduct their two sets of negotiations, one with Paris and the other with the barricades.

General Faure, whose reputation as a one-time plotter was a cause for mirth rather than alarm, had also strongly advised, on January 22, against any attempt at a rebellion. Colonel Argoud, Chief of Staff of the Army corps in Algiers, was fully aware that the Army as a whole was not ready for a clash with the government. So he too, on January 22, after consulting with his Staff and the colonels of the parachute regiments, advised against any action by the political organizations of the European community. But the excited state of Joseph Ortiz's lieutenants, and their rivalry with Pierre Lagaillarde, brought about the demonstration of January 24. A burst of fire, which was never clearly explained, caused the death of seventeen gendarmes and of nine demonstrators, thus making a trial of strength inevitable, though most officers, including the most fanatical, considered it to be ill-timed.

The machinery that had first been set in motion on May 13, and that had failed in October, began to function once more. Some dozen colonels, most of whom were parachutists, tried to use the resistance of the Europeans entrenched behind their barricades as a lever directed against General Challe, Delouvrier, General Ely or even Michel Debré, the Prime Minister, so that the government might find some legal pretext to abandon the principle of self-determination. Failing that, they hoped that the government might come out openly for Francization, making public the assurances that had been too discreetly given in October. The statements of Colonel Argoud are particularly valuable, for he had at first been hostile to any insurrection and when it did break out, in unfavorable conditions, he tried to use it to obtain every possible political advantage.

The first attempt was made when Debré arrived in Algiers during the night of Monday, January 25, to Tuesday, January 26.

"Monsieur Debré arrived at one or two o'clock in the morning," wrote Colonel Argoud.

> Some moments earlier, M. Delouvrier had asked to see me alone. I repeated . . . that this was a problem of confidence and that it could not be resolved by force . . . I was taken to see M. Debré. Knowing [that he] would grant me scarcely more than ten minutes . . . I had carefully prepared my statement so that it should synthesize everything as well as possible, and I uttered it in the most colorless way . . . "Well, *mon colonel*, what do you think of the situation?" was M. Debré's first question. *"Monsieur le Premier Ministre,"* I replied, "the people confronting you are absolutely determined. It's impossible to shoot. You cannot fire on Frenchmen who are shouting 'Long live French Algeria!' In any case, if you give me the order to fire I will not carry it out, and I will order my subordinates to disobey." I told him that it was a question of confidence. "The people confronting you, for reasons it does not behoove me to judge, have no longer any confidence in the government, neither the Moslems nor the Europeans. Unfortunately, too, for some months past they have no longer any confidence in the person of the head of state. This is the end result of fifteen years of lies and of one disavowal after another." . . . He interrupted me. "In your opinion, then, what is to be done?" *"Monsieur le Premier Ministre,"* I replied, "there aren't thirty-six different solutions. Everything must be done—and the Lord knows . . . French brains are able to find formulas on the legal level—to transform self-determination, to back out of self-determination." "And if General de Gaulle refuses?" "If General de Gaulle refuses, General Challe will have to try . . . to arrange things on his own." "And if General Challe refuses?" he asked, in a tone that had grown more and more peremptory. I grew somewhat impatient at this. *"Monsieur le Premier Ministre, in that event, it will be a job for the colonels, whatever their names may be . . ."*

That night, Debré heard the same thing from all the colonels; and used this as an argument in his efforts to persuade General de Gaulle to give the assurances that would satisfy the most seriously committed officers and enable the Army to re-establish its unity. But the head of state had no intention of changing his policy. So another attempt was made the following night, when a conference brought together in Algiers General Ely, Chef d'Etat-Major de la Défense Nationale, General Challe and General Gilles, Inspector of Airborne Troops and a former colleague of Debré's. General Challe's idea—he had refused, that afternoon, to allow the publication of a proclamation declaring that a "Committee of National Security" had been formed to set up once and for all a French Algeria —was inspired by the events of May, 1958. He wanted to mobilize the Moslem crowds to demonstrate in favor of the Army and of a French Algeria. But the following day this attempt failed, and Delouvrier, the government's Delegate General, had begun to consider leaving Algiers. He made up his mind to do so on Thursday evening, after appealing for reconciliation between the rioters and the Army, Algeria and the homeland, General de Gaulle and the European community. He asked the entire population to demonstrate its unity under the double aegis of General de Gaulle and of French Algeria.

Colonel Broizat and Colonel Argoud saw a way out of the crisis. They obtained the authorization of the Generals Ely, Challe and Crépin, who had succeeded Massu, to negotiate with Pierre Legaillarde and Joseph Ortiz. "Colonel Broizat," said Argoud,

> explained the situation to them as he saw it. He strongly urged them to . . . accept the conditions laid down by M. Delouvrier, and then told them his reasons for this. He said that it meant risking a split in the Army to continue, that the situation could not be maintained indefinitely, and that some of the officers were beginning to complain. "Why isn't this being settled?" they were saying. The unity of the Army might be at stake and . . . these officers had certain advantages [I myself was not entirely convinced of it]. I must say that for the time being M. Ortiz . . . did not seem entirely convinced . . . I tried to demonstrate that if he did not accept for the time being the conditions offered by M. Delouvrier, they risked facing absolutely different conditions the following day. At last we succeeded in convincing them. "All right," they said, "but General Challe and M. Delouvrier must commit themselves on three issues." . . . First condition: M. Delouvrier would declare that the attitude of M. Ortiz and M. Lagaillarde, throughout the week, had done much to strengthen the thesis of a French Algeria. . . . Second condition: General Challe and M. Delouvrier would undertake to do everything they possibly could to ensure that the solution of a French Algeria would carry the day. . . . Third condition: Self-determination would be reduced to two possible outcomes, independence or a French Algeria. Once more I picked up my pilgrim's staff and made my way to M. Delouvrier. . . . We embarked on a discussion of details, down to the last adjective and the last comma . . . I realized that the whole undertaking was done for, and one hour later M. Delouvrier told me that it was already seven o'clock, that General de Gaulle was to speak and that everything

must be postponed until the morrow. As I left his office, I knew very well that there would be no morrow.

This was, in actual fact, the last attempt made to change the course of the government's Algerian policy.

The speech delivered by General de Gaulle on January 29 marked at least the provisional outcome of the mechanism that had been set in motion, more or less haphazardly, on January 24. He eliminated any prospect of negotiations with the F.L.N. "The rebel organization . . . declares that it will not cease fighting unless, beforehand, I discuss with it . . . the political destiny of Algeria. This would amount to setting it up as the only valid representative and constituting it in advance as the government of the country. I will not do that." As for the future, he stated that "if one day the Moslems decided, freely and formally, that the Algeria of tomorrow must be closely united with France, nothing could give greater joy to the fatherland and to de Gaulle than to see them choose, between one solution and another, the one that would be the most French." To the Army, which he described as "engaged in winning the victory in Algeria," he promised that "when the moment arrives to proceed to consultation, it will be your task to guarantee its complete and genuine liberty." Finally he admitted that "the means to be utilized so that force may remain on the side of law can be of various kinds."

This, then, was the result of all the desperate *démarches* and passionate admonitions made and uttered by such men as Michel Debré, the Prime Minister, and General Ely, Chef de l'Etat Major Général. This, too, was the total achievement that could be claimed by the officers who, by their more or less calculated hesitancy, had allowed the trial of strength to take place and who had, in the event, paralyzed General Challe and General Crépin, Massu's successor as head of the Algiers Army corps, and the Generals Ducourneau and Gracieux, who were in command of the Tenth and Twenty-Fifth Airborne Divisions. Yet at the same time the policy of self-determination had been retained and confirmed. The mere fact that it had not been abandoned served to reinforce it. General de Gaulle had referred to the men responsible for the barricades as "agitators" and "usurpers." The tone of his speech, his insistence on the necessity for discipline, his condemnation of the "accommodating uncertainty of some military elements," and the assertion of his own authority, left no doubt concerning the future. Even his remarks about "the most

French solution" were weakened by other phrases. "As for the precise characteristics of one or another French solution," he had said, "it is my view that they must be worked out at leisure, once peace has been restored." This meant that he had every intention of remaining in power and would not yield to force, and also that he reserved the possibility of declaring to be "French" the choice in favor of association which, since the preceding year, could be assumed to have his preference.

Theoretically, the speech of January 29 renewed the assurances given in October, 1959. The consequences also were roughly the same. The military hierarchy as a whole decided to set about liquidating the affair of the barricades. It was Colonel Dufour, commanding the First Foreign Regiment of Parachutists, to whom the rebels capitulated. The Algiers General Staff saw to it that their enlistment in the Army should not be maintained. They almost all returned home. Joseph Ortiz, too, who had had very close connections with a number of officers, could not have escaped from the "barricaded redoubt" without military complicity. But, from the evening of January 29 on, almost all the general officers, like General Challe and General Gambiez, who commanded the Oran Army corps, had decided to content themselves with the few assurances contained in the speech of the head of State, and the officers' corps was ready to follow suit. "The unity of the Army," that myth indispensable for the Army itself, and which, as Colonel Argoud had correctly foreseen on January 22, would work against any attempt at rebellion, finally compelled the dismantling of the barricades. It was in the name of the "unity of the Army" that no general officer had been willing to order the "redoubt" to be taken by force. In its name, also, the officers most deeply involved in the affair of the barricades agreed that it had to be liquidated, and resigned themselves to what most of them regarded as the least deplorable compromise.

One man had become so identified with the myth of the Army's unity that he must serve as its tattered, pathetic symbol. Because he had unremittingly to experience the drama of the Army's impossible unity he was, in his own person, one of the most significant figures in French military history, perhaps even in the recent history of French society as a whole. This man was General Paul Ely.

Forty-five years in the service, twice Chef d'Etat-Major Général, three times kept on active duty beyond the normal date of retirement, Paul-Henri-Romuald Ely personified all the stages and all the conflicts

of French military society since World War I. As history would have
it, the civilians and the military men called on to decide such problems
as those of intercontinental rockets, atomic strategy, the struggle between East and West, and of decolonization and the revolutions in the
underdeveloped nations, had come to adulthood at a time when
the major forces confronting each other were the "blue horizon" of the
French Army and the spiked helmets of the German Empire. This was
true of General Ely, who had been born soon enough to take part in
World War I, to serve in the trenches as an officer and to receive a
wound in his right arm. For the officers of his generation the future
seemed simple, and their moral universe delimited once and for all.
It was the universe of the old French Army, with its conservatism
buttressed anew as a result of the recent victories, its traditions maintained by the almost clannish source of its officering, and its stout
loyalty to a state that had utilized it and now overwhelmed it with
honors. A major in 1940, Paul Ely was wounded again. He played a
very active part in the Organisation de Résistance de l'Armée, and was
arrested and deported, together with his wife. On his return to France,
after considerable physical suffering, the post to which he had been
allotted—the direction of the infantry, on the staff of the Minister of
the Armies—plunged him in the drama that was besetting the military cadres. The occupation and Vichy, Gaullism and the Resistance
had torn the officers' corps into passionately hostile segments. General
Ely was haunted by the fear of a new split in the Army and this, perhaps, was the determining feature behind his whole attitude during the
great crises of 1958 and 1960.

From 1949 to 1953, he represented France in the "Standing Group,"
the supreme rung in the hierarchy of the Atlantic General Staffs, on
which he served alongside an Englishman and an American. The
best elements of the French Army were active in Indochina, at that
time. There the adversary was not merely nationalist, he was Communist also. For the French government, and for General Ely who
represented it, the Indochinese War was to be understood as one of
the sectors of the world struggle between the western world and communism. General Ely never tired of repeating this for four years. It
was in this frame of mind that he was instructed by the government to
negotiate the conditions in which the American forces might intervene
in the battle of Dien-Bien-Phu. But it was the French government
that insisted on the question of American participation being studied
with all possible speed, since Georges Bidault, the Minister of Foreign

Affairs, seemed to think that this would be his trump card at the Geneva conference. General Ely, who became Chef d'Etat-Major Général des Forces Armées in 1953, returned from Indochina with the impression that it would be wise to turn toward a political solution. Quite unlike a number of American military personalities who considered it vital to prevent a Communist victory in Vietnam, at no time did General Ely recommend any intervention, on the part of the United States, that might have led to a general war. In May, he agreed to travel to Vietnam in order to take over the most painful responsibility that can be required of a military man. He was to assume command of an Army that had just been beaten and that had to accept an end to hostilities without any thought of wiping out the defeat. Every feeling of humiliation and of rancor had to be bottled up. This experience made of General Ely the only French general, perhaps, who did not belong to the generation of the fighters of Dien-Bien-Phu but who, nevertheless, shared their bitterness and their grief. He talked, one by one, with the officers who emerged from the Vietminh prison camps. He received their confidences, and became the "confessor" of the French Army. Then it was that he got to know the men who later, on May 13 and January 24, would seek to obtain in Algeria a *revanche* for the war that had been lost in Indochina, and would try to apply the lessons learned there.

At this time the character of General Ely took on its definitive cast. He is to be discovered at every turning point of the Algerian affair. This military man preferred civilian dress, the anonymous simplicity of bourgeois garb, to the five-star uniform befitting his rank. At the head of the French Army, he spoke in the modulated tones of a bishop decanting his episcopal wisdom. His fine white hands moved as though to convey every nuance of feeling of a sensitive soul and, under the white thicket of his brows, his bright eyes had a kind of candid simplicity. He wished to be, and soon became, the "conscience" of the Army. Recalled in 1956 to the post of Chef d'Etat-Major Général des Armées, he kept the habits he had acquired in Indochina. He insisted on seeing captains and lieutenants in private. As he collected their impressions, he saw how the spirit of the French Army was changing. Officers had returned from Indochina with the conviction that one may be beaten despite a crushing superiority in arms and manpower. They knew that, in these revolutionary wars that confronted France in Asia and Africa, the main consideration lay elsewhere: the real prize at stake was "the spirit of the populations."

A commission was appointed to draw up official documents dealing with the psychological aspects of this new warfare. The President of this commission was General Ollié, who would be General Ely's successor. On the basis of his report the Fifth Bureau of the Army was set up, its field of competence being psychological warfare and psychological action.

Occupying the position he did, General Ely knew how little trust the Army had in the intentions of the state, whereas the Army itself was involved up to the hilt in the Algerian War. He knew that the major concern of most officers was to avoid experiencing, once again, in North Africa, the traumatic retreat from Indochina. Their uncertainty as to the future of Algeria led them to question the value of their struggle, and, as time elapsed, and the sacrifices already made grew more burdensome, they found it more and more intolerable that no sure victory lay ahead. General Ely was so well acquainted with the frame of mind of the officers' corps that, when M. Pleven was trying to form a government, he went to Algiers. Minister of National Defense during the siege of Dien-Bien-Phu, Pleven had become an object of suspicion among Army men, and General Ely undertook to defend his reputation and to explain that Pleven was not personally to blame for the Indochinese catastrophe.

His own preferences, as it happened, were for a Government of National Union. He was all the more convinced of the need for one after his visit to President Coty, on May 10, when he transmitted to him the famous telegram from General Salan warning the President of the Republic that "the French Army as one man would regard it as an outrage if the national heritage were abandoned." Only by May 15, after General Salan had uttered his first "Vive de Gaulle!" from the balcony of the Gouvernement Général, did General Ely admit that only the return to power of General de Gaulle could preserve "the unity of the Army." Removed from the Etat-Major Général des Forces Armées by the Minister, de Chevigné, he advised General Lorillot to take over the post, for he was sure that all the military leaders would share his own feeling that the Army in France could not be ordered to fire on the Army in Algeria, and that, if the order were given, it would not be carried out. General de Gaulle's accession to power brought to an apparent end the crisis that had exploded on May 13.

In General Ely's view, the way was now open for the reconciliation of Army and State. He published, in *La Revue Militaire d'Information,* a long article that justified the role played by the Army on May 13. At the same time, he insisted on loyalty to the Republic as incumbent on military men, and also voiced the famous thesis according to which Communist infiltration in Africa was the most serious danger menacing the western world. For this Catholic had little trouble in believing that the supreme mission of the French Army was to play its own special part in the great struggle between the western world and communism. Like most French officers, he saw the Algerian War in this framework. In the endeavor to convince a civilian public, he reverted to the theme in an article published in 1960 by the periodical *Réalités:*

> In the strategic-cum-political struggle which today is of planetary dimensions, the permanent thrust of the Soviet world can take concrete form along three major axes pointing directly toward western Europe, toward the Middle East and, in a kind of rebound, toward North Africa . . . toward Black Africa and South America, and finally toward Southeast Asia. Actually, these axes of impulsion are the schematic representation of an action carried out directly or via intermediaries and which consists in diffusing over the zone a subversive ideology and in implanting the political, economic and social abscesses indispensable for this maneuver.

"Via intermediaries": the expression reveals the abyss separating the views of the French high command from those of every western government. While in every country the politicians and diplomats, and bourgeois and Socialist milieux alike, knew that the young nationalist movements had to be granted their due, if they were not to link up more closely with the Communist states, in the French Army the view was obstinately maintained that the African nationalist movements—the Algerian, above all—were the predecessors or antechambers of international communism. General Ely shared this conviction, and was afraid to see the western world give ground in any sector. The western world: his pen never ceased to trace these words. One senses that, as a Catholic, he would have liked to add the adjective "Christian." But he was writing in official publications and had to respect the "diversity of beliefs," so he adopted more prudent formulas. He writes, for example: "Our civilization, which is Christian in origin."

Everything predestined this man for the most grievous internal conflict when General de Gaulle, convinced that integration could not be achieved, turned his back on French Algeria and started the evolution that would enable him, on September 16, 1959, to recognize the Algerians' right of self-determination. It could have been foreseen, on that day, that a rupture between the Army and the head of state could scarcely be avoided, and would lead to new crises. General Ely was privy to the political maneuvers to be carried out in the middle of October. The parliamentary opposition would take over from the street demonstrations and from the general strike that would break out in Algeria. The Army would intervene as arbiter, and the Debré cabinet would have to resign, or to abandon self-determination.

There can be no doubt that this plan was that of a fraction only of the General Staffs in Algeria. In practice, only a group of parachutist colonels were really determined to go through with it. But once more that sacred myth, the unity of the Army, was endangered. General Ely turned to General de Gaulle. He stressed the gravity of the crisis that threatened. He begged him to give the officers in Algeria the assurance that their struggle had not been in vain, and that the government would not abandon its objectives. At his insistence, General Challe was received by General de Gaulle, who at least calmed him somewhat by his refusal of any political negotiations with the F.L.N., by announcing the struggle would go on and by declaring that he favored a "French solution." In preventing a clash between a part of the Army and constituted authority, General Ely's intervention had been decisive. All the same, it followed the line that he had traced at least since May 10, 1958, when he passed on General Salan's telegram to President Coty.

His task can be conceived of as double. Vis-à-vis the state, he had to plead the cause of the Army's unity and, vis-à-vis the officers, that of respect for the state. General Ely felt that this double imperative was tearing him asunder, as it was tearing the Army. The last crisis took on the dimensions of a *via dolorosa*. The Chef d'Etat-Major Général was haunted by the fear that some new incident would be caused by the successive stages of General de Gaulle's Algerian policy, provoking a desperate reaction on the part of those military cadres the most ardently attached to a French Algeria.

Prior to January 24, his anguish did not awaken the least sympathetic tremor in the head of state. De Gaulle seemed convinced that the Army did not suffer from the torments of which General Ely had spoken or that, at all events, the majority of the cadres would get over them. He thought it normal that a minority of officers should be in contact with the extremists in the European community but

that the Army as a whole was loyal, and would not let itself be mesmer-
ized by a small activist minority. General Ely, on the other hand,
believed that the officers' corps in a body was attached to the idea of a
French Algeria. Throughout the day of the 25th, he kept urging
Debré to go to Algiers. He foresaw that the Prime Minister would be
informed time and again that the Army had no intention of clashing
with the Algerian French unless it were sure that this would be on
behalf of a French Algeria. He was not mistaken, and Debré returned to Paris convinced that this was so. But General de Gaulle's
firmness made it necessary to find some way out that would reconcile
respect for the state and the feelings of many officers. The search for
a solution became, for General Ely, a test of actual physical endurance.

In the course of the week, his colleagues saw him go almost without
sleep, hastening from the Elysée to Matignon, constantly receiving
general and high-ranking officers, jumping on a plane for Algiers, and
talking things over for a whole night with General Challe. Finally
Debré informed him that, while General de Gaulle refused to modify
his policy, he maintained his rejection of any negotiations in which
the F.L.N. would have to be treated as a government, and that he
would allow those responsible to find, in Algiers itself, some means of
disposing of the affair of the barricades. General Ely decided to content
himself with these assurances. He was able to give the Generals Challe,
Gambiez and Ollié the guarantees they were waiting for. The three
generals had only to turn to their general officers and persuade them
that it was time to end the crisis. General de Gaulle's speech of
January 29 dealt harshly with the men at the barricades, but approximately all the guarantees mentioned by General Ely were to be
found in it. Perhaps the only remaining ambiguity concerned the
"French solution" that the head of state would himself prefer.

Two months later, on the last day of General de Gaulle's "mess-
room jaunt" through Algeria, General Ely heard the words pronounced: "Algerian Algeria." He could no longer overlook the fact
that all General de Gaulle's adjurations, promises and tranquillizing
measures had had no other aim than to stifle little by little the Army's
opposition to the policy of the head of state. But General Ely had made
his decision. A French Algeria was no longer possible, he had to obey;
and soon the whole Army would understand. It was in December that
the illusions of most were dispelled. The day of the 10th possessed a
certain symbolism. The Algerian sky was particularly overcast. General
Ely, who during the early hours of General de Gaulle's second day

in Algeria had remained in his shirtsleeves, now drew his coat around him. There had been disquieting news from Algiers and Oran. Two hours later the first columns of Moslem demonstrators, bearing the colors of the F.L.N., would march through the street of Belcour in Algiers. In a hangar on the Blida airfield, 400 officers were listening to General de Gaulle:

> The Algerian question now presents itself in a form totally unlike the former situation. There has been this rebellion, after many others, and this rebellion is not over. . . . The population of Algeria has acquired a consciousness it did not previously have. Nothing can prevent this. This rebellion is taking place in a new world, in a world that has no resemblance to the world I myself knew when I was young. It gives no pleasure to a man of my age and my training to tell you that . . ."

That evening, General Ely knew that most of the officers had reached the same place on the road as he himself had. Two months later he silently withdrew from his post as Chef d'Etat-Major Général de la Défense Nationale. Perhaps it seemed to him that the drama of Algerian policy had ceased to convulse the Army, and that it would no longer yield to the temptation to rise against the state. He left just in time to avoid experiencing, at the summit of the military hierarchy, the coup d'état of April 22. All in all, he had merely anticipated the evolution of Algerian policy under General de Gaulle. He had merely sensed that one day the Army would have to accept this policy, though with rage in its heart.

CHAPTER TWENTY

THE DEFEAT OF
FRENCH ALGERIA

✠

Hesitancy, on the part of the military authorities, had allowed the affair of the barricades time to develop. After January 29 their renewed determination put an end to it. The Army had to some extent played the role of an arbiter. Many officers estimated that General de Gaulle himself had had to reckon with this, and that his speech of January 29 showed it. A few weeks later, while on what was called his "mess-room jaunt" in Algeria, his repeated stressing of the Army's operational tasks showed that he was still anxious to calm the anxieties of the officers' corps. It could be thought at the time that he realized that the Army's "arbitrament" had worked in his favor in January and that he would not too brutally brush aside the political demands of most Army cadres.

These demands were summed up in a single formula, "French Algeria." But General de Gaulle had launched another formula, "Algerian Algeria." In the provisional outcome of the affair of the barricades, equilibrium was maintained between the "assurances" given and actual repression. This equilibrium was to be broken, from June on. The breakdown of the Melun conversations seemed to set the limit to any concessions the French government could possibly make to the F.L.N. But the clarifications given by General de Gaulle during his trips to Normandy and Brittany showed that he already conceived of an Algerian State, associated with France, in a much bolder way than ten months earlier, when he delivered his speech of September 16 on the subject of self-determination. Finally, on November 4, he spoke of an "Algerian Republic."

Even before this evolution could be observed, the events of January had immediate consequences whose effect on the military in the longer run would be immense, and especially on those most hostile to the head of state. The whole mechanism of the Army's repeated interventions in political matters would be challenged. These interventions had begun with the political mobilization of the European community. The failure of the affair of the barricades seemingly put an end to them. Most of the Algerian political movements had been banned. Some of the most prominent personages had been arrested or had fled. The officers who had had the closest ties with the European settlers had been transferred to France. One of these, Colonel Gardes, had even been accused of complicity in the affair of the barricades, though finally he would be acquitted.

The military milieux most devoted to a French Algeria were convinced, however, that the idea could not prevail unless it were backed by a substantial body of opinion in France itself. The recollection of January 24 strengthened this view. In the face of General de Gaulle's resoluteness, almost no serious opposition had arisen. The colonels had no doubt been caught unawares by an operation they had neither altogether foreseen nor entirely committed themselves to, so that no parallel movement in France had been prepared, to fan the rebellion. But public opinion as a whole was behind the head of state. About the only exception to this was the group of "Independents and Peasants," in obedience to its chief spokesman, Roger Duchet, who had grave reservations concerning General de Gaulle's Algerian policy. Indeed, it was among their colleagues in the National Assembly that the Algerian deputies found most sympathy, when they tried to stir up French opinion while the affair of the barricades was still raging. For the partisans of a French Algeria, this was the only favorable sign on a distressingly hostile horizon.

The immediate result of the affair was a profound cleavage, if not a definitive break, between the European community and military milieux, even those most wholeheartedly committed to defending a French Algeria. For days on end, the Celtic cross on the French tricolor, the symbol of Joseph Ortiz's Front National Français, had floated over the barricades. Around Ortiz could be found such men as Doctor Joseph Perez, Doctor Lefebvre and Professor Lambert, all right-wing extremists who favored a corporate social order and an authoritarian state, and demanded the suppression of political parties and most of the established liberties of the republican regime. In the atmosphere surrounding the European community in Algeria, it was natural that the most extreme partisans should appear to be the most energetic, aggressive and lucid, and that they should attract the greatest following. But, by this very fact, Algerian activism deprived itself of any support in France itself. Its authority could not extend beyond the European quarters of Algiers and Oran. Across the Mediterranean it met with nothing but disapproval and condemnation. French public opinion was bound to react violently against the very symbol of the Celtic cross.

There is no reason to be astonished that some officers should have felt an irresistible kinship with this Algerian activism, and with its totalitarian spirit. What was more commonplace in the daily talk of messroom and General Staff than the condemnation of political parties and the regime itself? What was more frequent in military milieux than a repugnance for mediated solutions, political intrigues, dubious compromises and a suspect tolerance? Personal relations sometimes contributed an emotional bond that intensified and prolonged the connections between officers and European activists. The latter were recruited above all among the lower classes. The officers were not confronted by the dubious and highly suspect image of the old colonialism with which they were sometimes reproached, when they saw the men of the Unités Territoriales, the shock troops of the barricades, or the clients of Doctor Perez, who almost all lived in the workers' quarter of Bab-el-Oued, or the student friends of Lagaillarde. The men of the barricades were neither rich colonialists, nor shipbuilders, nor bankers, nor newspaper editors, nor business men half of whose fortune was safely tucked away in France. The Army cadres felt closer to the European populace in Algeria than to the prosperous, peaceful citizens of metropolitan France, so forgetful of its soldiers.

But the lesson of the barricades could not be overlooked. French public opinion found Algerian activism intolerable. The cause of a French Algeria could even be compromised. The Army could not be mobilized around the Celtic cross; it could not risk being reproached with affection for a new "Fascism." At the same time, this activism could not be reconciled with the attempt to win Moslem support for the cause of a French Algeria. The day that the men of the barricades tried to persuade the Moslems to demonstrate on their behalf, their entire failure had shown how utterly unable the European milieu was to overcome the hostility of the Moslem masses.

This was far indeed from May 13 and the simple demand for a Government of Public Safety, far from May 16 and the Franco-Moslem fraternization so cheerfully organized by the General Staffs in Algiers. Without the Army's help, there was no hope of saving the flickering cause of a French Algeria. Again, without substantial backing in France itself, there was little hope of inducing the Army to risk any fresh political intervention.

This was the starting point for an undertaking that, in various ways and with limited success, would induce some of the military cadres to seek a number of new allies in the fight for a French Algeria. The old mechanisms, which all involved the mobilization of the European community, had to be replaced by another technique that would have Paris, not Algiers, as its center. It was hoped that the exigencies of Europe and of Atlantic solidarity would come to the aid of a French Algeria. French political milieux would constitute the "troops" and so replace the European crowds in Algeria, hopelessly compromised in the affair of the barricades.

In February, most of the officers who had been heavily involved in this affair—the Colonels Argoud, Broizat, Godard and Bigeard—or who were the most irreconcilably at odds with the head of state, such as the Generals Faure and Mirambeau, were transferred to France. In March the Army, reassured by the statements made by General de Gaulle to confirm its operational missions, did not react against the new idea of an Algerian Algeria. In May Si Salah, who headed Willaya IV, the military district of Algiers, made contact with the French General Staff and then went to Paris, where he was received in the Presidential Palace. It appears that he was trying to negotiate a cease-fire between the A.L.N. and the French Army. These conversations led to nothing, and some military leaders placed the blame on the new measures envisaged by General de Gaulle, though everything seems to indicate that Si Salah failed to convince any of the main leaders of the A.L.N. But the overwhelming majority of the officers knew nothing of these dealings.

On June 14, another speech by the head of state let it be surmised that the conversations with the F.L.N. might extend beyond strictly military matters to embrace political considerations. It may be that the first meeting between the representatives of the F.L.N. and of the French government was responsible for the breakdown of Si Salah's attempt. In any case, it did not succeed.

The government sought to minimize the importance of the conversations with the F.L.N. The Prime Minister's office put out a very cautious explanation on the very first day of the talks at Melun. Here is a note that was signed by Debré himself:

> It may possibly be learned, on Monday morning, that the reply of the leaders of the rebellion to the most recent appeal made by General de Gaulle is not entirely negative. The present instructions have the aim—in case this eventuality should materialize, and arouse a great deal of interest—of laying down the general directives you and your subordinates should utilize in replying to the questions that may be asked you, or on your own account, in order to guide the reactions of public opinion and of the press.
>
> I. The fact that the rebellion has not, once agan, replied in the negative to an offer made by General de Gaulle is a success for France.
>
> This success is due to the Army's efforts; hermetically sealed barriers, constant activities against the rebellion—labor of pacification. The Nation has not stinted its support for the Army, and the Army has labored nobly.
>
> This success is due to the acceptance of this policy by the majority of the Moslem population and by almost all the population of metropolitan France.
>
> This success is due, finally, to the clarity of the aims laid down on September 16. "Self-determination," that is to say, a free choice, excludes any desire to dominate on our part. If, during the whole period of tranquillization, we must act in such a way that the overwhelming majority of Algerian population understands the necessity for the union of France and Algeria, it nevertheless remains true that the final consultation will be free. Why, then, should the fighting be prolonged unless, on the side of the rebels, there are ambitions that dare not avow themselves openly?
>
> II. General de Gaulle's speeches need no commentary. They determine the tone and the framework of the discussion that could begin.
>
> The "cease-fire" requires discussion. I remind you of the words used in the speech of June 14 last: "Once more I turn, in the name of France, to the leaders of the rebellion. I declare to them that we will wait for them here in order to discover with them an honorable end for the fighting that is still dragging on, to determine the disposition of the arms and to provide for the future of the fighters."

Subsequent confrontations may be envisaged. They presuppose the end of all rebellion. They would then bring together the representatives of all political trends. Furthermore, and this is essential, Algeria requires a long period of tranquillization.

It is a fundamental requirement that the Army remain in Algeria. If it were not for the French Army disorder would reign, and civil war would not be extinguished. The French Army is indispensable so that the two communities may reach an undertsanding, and for the development of the economy and for liberty.

III. In the event that discussions should begin and as long as they should last, it is advisable to adopt an attitude both prudent and serene.

A prudent attitude: for the leaders of the rebellion are allied with bitter enemies of France and the western world. These enemies desire to see any conversations fail, and so will try to establish unacceptable conditions.

A serene attitude: France is on the right path, I mean the path of success, and can obtain this in different ways. It goes without saying that, being eager to end the fighting as soon as possible, we will do everything necessary to bring about a cease-fire, but under no circumstances should the impression be aroused—which would be false —that peace is dependent on the discussions that might begin, nor that it would be a catastrophe if they failed.

IV. Complementary directives will be given you if events should call for it.

The Melun conversations took place without causing any marked degree of alarm in Army ranks. The discreet outline of the future Algerian State, evoked by General de Gaulle during his trips in the provinces, did no more than confirm what was already known in the Army and elsewhere. The head of state wanted to establish a more or less sovereign Algeria which would be associated with France. This might be highly upsetting for the partisans of a French Algeria, who were still in a strong majority among the Army officers. But it is unusual for political regrets or disappointments so to disturb Army circles that they would accept the enormous risks of dissidence or rebellion. For that, some moral shock was necessary that could passionately move or exasperate the majority of the officers, including those least eager for political action. Such a shock was administered in the summer of 1960, when the country let itself be induced to accept the idea of an "Algerian Republic" without the Army's thinking of offering any opposition. The case of the deserters and absentees took on as much importance, in military eyes, as the campaigns against torture, prior to May 13, 1958.

It seemed that the problem had not again arisen since the spring of 1956. Four years later, officers still remembered as though it were a nightmare the recall of the demobilized classes, the demonstrations at the Gare de Lyon and the mutinies at the Gare de Rouen, with soldiers marching past in protest against their departure. Numerous reports recorded the resistance shown by those who had been recalled and how their attitude had infected those called up for the first time. Every day catastrophic incidents were to be feared, as the men poured into the stations or after the trains had started on their way. But everything soon returned to the regular round. Since that time hundreds of thousands of Frenchmen, contingent after contingent, had made their way to Marseilles and Algiers. Nothing, it appeared, had ever occurred again. But this was only the surface. Between 1956 and 1958, "Comités de Jeunes" organized more or less clandestine networks. Their importance was certainly more than negligible, for a bulletin to maintain liaison between them was published pretty regularly, as well as pamphlets, posters and communiqués distributed locally or regionally. In 1956, 1957 and 1958 there were even "national assizes" that brought together most of the "Comités de Jeunes." They were not in the least interested in stimulating absenteeism or desertion. Apart from the usual but rare cases of conscientious objectors, who were inspired by personal motives, all that was aimed at was to awaken the sympathy of other Frenchmen for those who were setting off to fight a war in which too many people seemed to have no interest.

Fundamentally, these were young men who were aware of the numerous campaigns of opposition to the war in Algeria, who knew how uncertain and hesitant the political parties were and who were appalled at the idea of being nothing but victims. The committees disappeared after May 13, and there were no more soldiers' demonstrations. The country grew accustomed to the war while, at the same time, General de Gaulle's policy aroused great hopes. Henceforth any initiative would be purely individual. Some who set off for Algeria hoped that at least they could oppose the worst excesses and, by their actual presence, show Algerians that they had friendly feelings. Others, fearing that they would be swept along by the mechanism, chose to desert, just as they were to leave for Algeria, or to neglect the mobilization order. They were but few, and these gestures took place in a kind of secrecy that was not abolished until the Communist Party started its campaign on behalf of its militants Liechti and Magnien, who had been imprisoned for their refusal to fight the A.L.N.

This era is described in a book called *Le Déserteur,* whose author used the pseudonym "Maurienne." Three young conscripts in particular, one of whom is a reserve officer, realize that they cannot bring themselves to take part in the war and try to discover, in practice, their own solution. To serve a prison term for disobedience can touch off only a very minor movement of protest, which would be weakly supported by an "aid committee" and would soon fade away. For the public, their case would be scarcely different from that of the conscientious objectors. So they decided to desert. Their choice would be that of most objectors to the Algerian War. For many, however, this was but a first step, and the logic of their attitude would soon lead them to take a position on the side of the F.L.N. The author of *Le Déserteur,* while still in uniform, wanted to help the Algerians. He relates how he confided in a man he knew to have contacts, and how he was immediately utilized to organize illegal crossings of the frontiers.

This evolution from desertion to support of the F.L.N. is pretty close to the metamorphosis undergone by *Vérité pour,* a clandestine bulletin fairly well known in university circles. The first numbers, which were published in September, 1958, simply called for resistance to the Algerian War and against the threat of Fascism, in terms that were similar, though more violent, to those used by the newspapers of the Left and extreme Left. Then the stress was placed on the most direct forms of opposition to the war, such as help for Algerians subjected to police repression, and on disobedience and desertion. Beginning early in 1960, *Vérité pour* no longer distinguished opposition to the war from the defense of absentees, nor this from active support for the F.L.N. The instigators of *Vérité pour,* particularly the young university teacher Francis Jeanson, had known from the outset what they were aiming at. Deeming that the struggle against colonialism required them to take the side of its victims, they had never forgotten that they must inevitably move on from opposition to clandestine activity, illegality and rebellion.

Most of the young absentees had not followed the directives of any party, Church or trade union. They had made up their minds alone. Whether young Communists, young trade union militants or young practicing Christians, they were most often motivated by an extremist ideology or by the dreadful example of comrades who had set off for Algeria determined to "keep their hands clean," and who had returned morally wrecked by the experiences they had passed through and almost physically changed, having been unable to keep any of the promises they had made themselves. A kind of shame stigmatized them. Even the small number of actual deserters could, indeed, not be explained were it not for an atmosphere in which disobedience to the state seemed to have become much more frequent. Significant in this respect is a pamphlet dated March, 1960, which was distributed in the southeast:

> it is clear that disobedience pays. The disobedience of the "ultras," made easy by our own passivity, the disobedience of February 6, 1956, when the Republican Front forgot its promises. And the disobedience of May 13, 1958, set up the Fifth Republic. That of January 24, 1960, exposed the Gaullist ambiguities. . . . We in our turn must disobey, organize resistance and generalize our refusal. All forms of disobedience, resistance and refusal are good.

One month later, the problem of the absentees was raised in the public forum. Beside his own article in the weekly *Carrefour,* Georges Bidault printed a call for desertion and for aid to the Algerians that had been put out by a committee calling itself "Jeune Résistance." An article in *L'Express* gave the entire history of the underground movement opposing the Algerian War. This aroused an extraordinary sense of scandal. It was the first time that the question of military duty was publicly debated, except for the special cases of conscientious objectors. The emotions aroused had all the more difficulty in dying down, since a movement of support for the absentees began to grow around the "Jeune Résistance" committee. The committee now had supporting networks in Switzerland, Italy, Belgium and Great Britain.

The trial of a network helping the F.L.N. began on September 5, 1960, in the Cherche-Midi prison, in a climate of veritable moral crisis. Known as the "Jeanson case," it provided a platform for all the partisans of direct, illegal action against the Algerian War. With the violent incidents that occurred during the trial, the presence on the witness stand of Paul Teitgen, a former General Secretary of the Algiers Prefecture, a letter from Jean-Paul Sartre, and the presence among the public of many personalities in the fields of letters, the arts and the performing arts, this was one of the most spectacular episodes in the controversies concerning the Algerian War that were arousing public opinion. The day after the trial had begun, on September 6, 121 intellectuals—soon to be followed by dozens of others—published a manifesto on "the right to disobedience in the Algerian War," in which they declared that they understood those who, being opposed to the war, took illegal steps.

In the Army, this was the signal for a veritable moral rebellion against a government accused of complacency when confronted by acts of "treason." Overlooking the legal guarantees that made it difficult for the state to react severely against the mere expression of opinions, military men were infuriated by the thought that the most elementary principles of duty to the state could be challenged with impunity. They sensed, actually, that beyond the most striking episodes of the campaign against the Algerian War there lay the weariness and irritation of public opinion as a whole, which had been waiting for the previous two years for General de Gaulle to end the war. The bitterness of the Army was proportionate to its feeling of isolation. It judged that the abandonment of Algeria had already taken place in people's minds if not in official policy. It compared the relative indulgence shown by the State to the "121" and the imposing list of transfers that had revolutionized the officering of the troops in Algeria, affecting all the officers suspected of too passionate an attachment for a French Algeria.

The transfers, nevertheless, had done almost nothing to diminish the Army's political disapproval. General Crépin, who replaced General Challe, revealed himself to be no less attached than his forerunner to the defense of a French Algeria. The Fifth Bureau, which dealt with psychological action, had been suppressed in February, 1960, only to be replaced by a "Bureau d'Etudes et de Liaison" under Colonel Jacquin. This officer had to be transferred from Algiers, for exactly the same reason as in the case of so many others. The affair of the absentees was all the more an issue in the eyes of the military, since it enabled them to give vent to a brand of polemics they were thoroughly familiar with. They already detested the milieu of atheist writers, amoral women novelists, cinema actresses and Leftist professors that was grouped around the manifesto of the 121.

The "Jeanson case," with its scandalous atmosphere, aroused the indignation of the partisans of a French Algeria, and especially among the military. The Centre d'Etudes de Défense Nationale, to which many reserve officers belonged, voiced their displeasure. "They denounce the unworthy maneuvers of certain Frenchmen in favor of a rebellion, such as the act of downright treason committed by the 121 signatories of the 'Manifesto for disobedience in Algeria,' and the scandalous scenes that occurred during the trial of the Jeanson network." General Salan, as President of the Veterans Association of the French Union, now that he had left active service and was living in Algiers, emerged from his silence. Condemning the backers of disobedience and those who with impunity had done harm to the national heritage and its defenders, he stated his attitude on the issue of Algeria's future:

> No authority whatever has the right to abandon a territory where French sovereignty is exercised. No one has this right, and no one has received such a mandate from the country, particularly where Algeria is concerned, which is made up of Departments and Communes and is a territorial collectivity of the Republic, under the terms of Article 72 of the Constitution. I do not hesitate to affirm that the national reaction of May 13 and the referendum that followed it established Algeria definitively as French soil, by the free and unanimous will of its inhabitants.

As September wore on, the passionate indignation of the officers' corps at last came together with the calculations and long preparations of the few elements in the Army who, drawing a lesson from the affair of the barricades, had sought new paths for the Army's political intervention—the last hope of those who favored a French Algeria.

January 24 had clearly shown that the rebellion of the European community could not shake France itself, and was even less capable of reversing the State's Algerian policy. Algiers could no longer manage without Paris, and Paris had remained deaf to the appeals coming from Algiers. So public opinion in the homeland had to be influenced, if the partisans of a French Algeria were ever to break out of the isolation that was gradually closing in on them.

It would appear that the attempt was made by political personages, to begin with, and not by military men. In France, the opening months of 1960 were difficult ones for the government. Agricultural and social problems were causing parliamentary eddies, and the parties seized the opportunity to become active, in some measure, once again. The various forms of opposition that had fallen silent during the affair of the barricades, when General de Gaulle appeared to have public opinion solidly behind him, took ever clearer shape in the following months.

The great hope entertained at that time by the adversaries of General de Gaulle, and especially by those who opposed his Algerian policy, was to unite in one coalition the partisans of a French Algeria, the right-wing opposition, the supporters of a classical parliamentary regime and the milieux of the Left least favorable to independence for Algeria. This attempt took on concrete shape in June, when the National Assembly was voting on a motion that demanded the release from detention of Pierre Lagaillarde, Deputy for Algiers. In favor were 165, while 268 rejected the motion. The opposition grouped around the banner of a French Algeria had never obtained so many votes in the National Assembly.

At the same time this opposition, now at what would prove to be its maximum strength, came together in the colloquium that took place in the Vincennes town hall. In addition to most personalities of the Right, present were the former President of the Radical Council, Bourgès-Maunoury; a former Secretary of State for Air, Laforest, who was also a Radical; the former Socialist Minister for Algeria, Robert Lacoste; the former Socialist Minister for the Sahara, Max Lejeune; and a number of persons with Radical tendencies such as Patrice Brocas and Jean-Paul David, the former President of the Ligue de l'Enseignement; Albert Bayet, the President of the Confédération Générale des Cadres; André Maleterre; and one of the leaders of the "Force Ouvrière" trade union confederation, Lafond. Never again would the camp of those in favor of a French Algeria extend so far to the Left.

At the date on which the Vincennes colloquium was held, June 20, the arrival of the F.L.N. plenipotentiaries was being awaited at Melun. Public opinion was so openly and so overwhelmingly in favor of these negotiations that even the political milieux the most hostile to independence for Algeria hesitated to express opposition to the policy of General de Gaulle. But the partisans of a French Algeria would for some time longer cherish the hope that they could find support in all the political or social mileux hostile to the head of state. The affair of the barricades had left its mark on them, and they would never again compromise themselves with Algiers extremism, with the Celtic cross of Joseph Ortiz and the corporatism or monarchism of Dr. Lefebvre and Robert Martel.

The European political milieux, endeavoring to create an organization that would not be branded "Fascist," as were the former activist groups, founded the Front pour l'Algérie Française, a single movement without any ideology and without a doctrine. Its backers tried, in this way, to escape the risks of division and of rivalry that had resulted in the clumsy and inopportune outbreak of the affair of the barricades. This organization claimed to represent the totality of political opinion in the European community, and to give it a discipline and a structure it had never previously known.

In military circles, the officers most deeply committed to a French Algeria had the same concern. They tried to carry out, vis-à-vis the General Staffs in France and in Germany, what the political personages were trying to achieve through the parties and trade unions. The great number of transfers that had followed January 24 favored this shift in the political activity of the officers, late of Algeria, from one shore to the other of the Mediterranean. The experience of the barricades had left a deep mark on a great number of military men who had been influenced by the principal colonels of the Algiers army corps. The recollection of their isolation led them to think that the cause of a French Algeria must become that of the military hierarchy as a whole and that, in any case, it must cease to be a domain reserved for a small group of superior officers, whose greater notoriety made them all the more vulnerable. The publicity that had seized on their names was no less embarrassing than the jealousy directed against them in the Army. Most of them were parachutists, and they were affected by the rivalry that set their regiments against all the others. Scattered throughout the garrisons of metropolitan France and in Germany, they tried to break out of their isolation. The evolution of General de Gaulle's Algerian policy showed that their suspicions had been justified, and so increased their authority among the Army cadres.

Thus a rapprochement became possible between two groups. One group consisted of the die-hard officers who, completely without confidence in the head of state, had tried to force through a change in policy if not a change of government by means of the trials of strength that took place the fall of 1959 and in January, 1960. The other group consisted of the more moderate Army leaders who had done no more than utilize this threat in an attempt to influence, as much as possible, General de Gaulle's line of conduct. Now they had the impression that they had failed and they too found a lesson in their disappointment. They tried to redeem their caution and hesitancy, perhaps they even felt some measure of remorse when they considered the officers who, in October, 1959 and in January, 1960, had more boldly committed themselves. At the same time these officers tried to shake off their isolation and establish contacts with the military hierarchy. This twin development led to a joining of forces. The history of their efforts marked the closing months of 1960 and continued until April 22, 1961.

Since 1956 General Valluy had been the over-all commander of the Allied "Center Europe" Forces, with headquarters at Fontainebleau. He left this post and retired from active service in May, 1960. He then published a series of articles in the *Figaro* and a little book that promulgated the same theses. He came out vigorously in favor of integrating the French forces in the Atlantic defense community, and so attacked General de Gaulle's attitude. This revealed that a considerable number of the French General Staffs were at odds with de Gaulle, who preferred to keep the bulk of French military fighting strength at the sole disposition of the French government. General Valluy insisted, at the same time, that this was a permanent, universal struggle against communism, and stressed the danger of revolutionary subversion in Africa. He paid his tribute to the "psychological weapon" while declaring that he was for the maintenance of French positions in Algeria and for a closer alliance between France and its Atlantic Allies.

This was the signal, in the Army, for the development of a trend of opinion linked with a political maneuver. The French officers on the Allied General Staffs were naturally aware of the attitude of their American and British counterparts, and knew that these men, in accordance with the policy of their governments, frowned on the prospect of unceasing warfare in Algeria. There were frequent differences of opinion, in the General Staffs of Roquencourt and Fontainebleau, between those—almost all French—who wished France to remain in Algeria, and all the others who were distressed that western policy should be compromised, in the eyes of the leaders of the new States in Africa and Asia, by this Algerian affair. The French officers suffered greatly at their inability to convince their colleagues. They failed to move them by evoking the threat of Communist infiltration which, they asserted, would soon occur in Algeria, once the French Army had left. It was equally useless to point out that Algerian territory formed part of the zone embraced by the Atlantic Pact, and to mention the strategic importance of the western Mediterranean and the value of the base at Mers-el-Kébir. They may have had some slight success with American officers annoyed by General de Gaulle's

demonstrations of independence or disturbed by some symptoms of
Communist influence in Africa. But it was clear that the western
General Staffs, like their governments, continued to hold the view
that the continuation of the Algerian War could do more than anything else to strengthen the ties between the Algerian nationalists and
the "Peoples' Democracies."

Could the integration of the French forces in the Atlantic defense
community make any change in the basic factors behind this sterile
discussion? Some thought so, in French military circles. Soon a plan
was suggested that was to be the object of many a conversation in
the General Staffs, at least until December, 1960. The idea was a
simple one. By moving toward Algerian independence, General de
Gaulle in the longer run was "playing communism's game," but he
was also doing so by opposing the integration of French forces with
the Allied forces. If his policy could be upset all along the line, American desires would be satisfied. The United States would no doubt
continue to deplore, for a while, the elimination of Algerian independence. But the Americans would soon have to recognize that the
continued presence of the French Army on the other side of the
Mediterranean was in harmony with western interests. They would
be especially pleased by the other aspect of this switch in policy,
namely the integration of French forces in Europe, which they had
so persistently asked for and which General de Gaulle refused to accept. For those with a more calculating turn of mind, this was to be a
deal. But in the eyes of many officers, the defense of the west was
all of a piece, so that the strengthening of the Atlantic Alliance went
hand in hand with the maintenance of a French Algeria. This latter
feature was, they believed, the prolongation of the front established
by the western powers in Europe, or even the extension of a unified
Europe whose virtues struck them all the more forcibly, as their hostility to General de Gaulle's policy grew ever stronger.

General Valluy was the theoretician of these views, before becoming their publicist. Summing up the "mortal danger" that the "Communist menace" constituted for the west, he arrived at these
conclusions:

Between 1949 and the present the Soviets have attained the following goals: (1) The expulsion of western forces from the Far East,
not yet completed but total in the long run. (2) Increasing difficulties
in North Africa for the whole of the Free World. (3) Interference
and then deep penetration in the Middle East and the eastern

Mediterranean. (4) Dissemination of centers of rebellion followed by the creation of new sympathetically disposed States throughout Black Africa (Guinea, Congo) and Latin America (Cuba). (5) Economic difficulties and loss of economic potential in France and Great Britain. (6) Immense loss of prestige for the United States.

He imagined the following dialogue as taking place between two military men:

A. As for Algeria, it does indeed seem that the choice between self-determination and integration is unacceptable, since self-determination inevitably leads to autonomy and autonomy inevitably provides a door half and then fully open for meddling from Moscow. It is not I who insist on the inevitability of this, but the partisans on either side, and the recent evolution of the new nations shows that they are right. . . . France has no right to take this risk and Europe—Europe, I say, and not its Mediterranean sector—has no greater right to allow France to run this risk.

B. And integration?

A. The word should be abandoned, since it covers varied intentions. But however it may be named, this "association" is so dubious on the legislative level as well as with respect to capital investments, labor, technically trained personnel, the economic substructure and the costs of education that, already a heavy burden on France, it threatens to become overwhelming and disproportionate.

B. But no less necessary!

A. Precisely. What forty-five million Frenchmen cannot manage might perhaps be achieved by 150 million Mediterraneans. And even more readily by 250 million western Europeans—I dare not add, by 250 million Atlantic citizens. France has the qualifications to serve for some years as the "Administrative Officer" or "Managing Director" of this corporation with limited but no less ineluctable liability. Just as Belgium could have done in the Congo and England all over the place in Asia Minor and Africa, if their pride had not led them to act as if they were alone in the world! To provide solid backing for our action in Algeria, we must involve our allies in it, and not continue to desire for ourselves alone a role that can only be played by all Europe.

With this, all the concepts commonly accepted in military milieux had been brought together. All contradictions appeared to have been surmounted. The defense of Europe was associated with the defense of Algeria, and the struggle against communism had attained its full dimensions and formed a perfect chain, in its passage from the south to the north of the Mediterranean. Nothing could be more revealing than the personality of the man who had built his theories on the Army's various causes for alarm. A participant in World War I and in the Syrian and Moroccan campaigns, General Valluy had not been a Gaullist between 1940 and 1942. He represented the outlook most frequently met with in military milieux. Marshal de Lattre de Tassigny's Chief of Staff and then in command of a division, he symbolized the resumption of conflict, and the victory, of the Army in Africa. Having played an active part in the renewal of hostilities against the Vietminh, in December, 1946, he inevitably had the same recollections of Indochina as other Army men. Since 1952 he had belonged to most of the great Allied General Staffs. Since he spoke with the authority of a man who knew international military problems, he could not be suspected of a passionate but blind attachment to the Algerian affair, and he had neither age nor experience in common with the young colonels of May 13 and January 24. Through him the traditional Army, the Army that was integrated in the Atlantic coalition, found a voice. His testimony suggested that, once General de Gaulle had been removed from power, it would be possible to work out and apply a policy that would satisfy the Allies, build Europe and preserve a French Algeria.

If General Valluy had no desire to be the man incorporating this policy, perhaps it was because of his familiarity with French opinion in the fall of 1960. At that time, political and military circles seemed headed in opposite directions. Convinced that General de Gaulle was gradually moving toward independence for Algeria, the General Staffs had reached the outlook that a small number of colonels and general officers had wished them to adopt in October, 1959 or January, 1960. The military leaders who had retired, and some who were still active, debated together in order to draft a manifesto expressing their common hostility to the Algerian policy of the head of state. General Crépin had just used terms, in public, that would not have been disowned by the activists of May 13. One of his predecessors, General Salan, had vigorously expressed his views, and after going to Spain let it be understood that he was willing to assume entire liberty of action, during the next episode in the Algerian drama. The other forerunner, General Challe, who had taken over from General Valluy the command of the "Centre Europe" Allied Forces, did not hide his distress vis-à-vis those who begged him to act. Some exchanges between military men took on a more precise character, and various

ways were discussed of getting hold of General de Gaulle. But another
dream had already evaporated, the dream of a great political coalition
extending from the extreme Right and taking in certain Socialists, on
a broad base formed by the partisans of a French Algeria, those who
favored European integration and those who wanted a return to the
classical parliamentary regime.

The large audience that listened to the campaign for a negotiated
peace with the F.L.N. made it clear in what direction public sentiment was turning. The Socialist Party, the great trade union organizations, the students' unions and the youth movements now made
common cause with the extreme Left and the liberal Left, which long
before, though without wider support, had called for negotiations.
When General de Gaulle spoke on November 4 of a future "Algerian
Republic," those who objected were, as always, a majority on the
Right and a minority among the Radicals, and isolated figures in other
sectors of opinion. The Army men who had tried to convert the defense of French Algeria into a much wider political operation had to
abandon their pretensions. Only one man, General Challe, fell heir
to this phase in the history of military opinion, when the idea of a
French Algeria was blended with a certain conception of Atlantic and
European policy. Nothing else could be foreseen, as the fall of 1960
neared its end, but a return to the old mechanisms which, since May
13, had been utilized by the Army in order to further its political goals.

The two words, "Algerian Algeria," uttered on November 4,
marked the beginning of the crisis. The resignation of Jacomet,
Secretary General of the Administration in Algeria, almost touched
things off. If his example had been followed by a large enough number of other highly placed functionaries, a group of colonels would
have taken over the controls of the administrative apparatus and
Algeria, for all practical purposes, would have rebelled. Jacomet's
gesture remained isolated, but the alarm had been sounded in the
military milieux most determined to fight a last battle on behalf of a
French Algeria. This time, the idea was again adopted of mobilizing
the whole European population, through an appeal to its one organization, the F.A.F. It was planned that six parachutist regiments should
intervene "to prevent the spilling of blood," and that at least a part
of Algerian territory would rebel. In Spain, General Salan and his
principal collaborators would form a kind of provisional government
with which Paris would have to negotiate.

These projects were so little disguised that the authorities came to hear of them. One of the officers who was destined to play an important part, Colonel Dufour, commander of the First Foreign Parachutist Regiment, was removed from his post, as was one of his collaborators, Captain Martin. Convinced that the insurrection would break out shortly, Colonel Dufour postponed his departure as long as possible. To speed up his departure from Algeria, the Ministry of the Army named Lieutenant Colonel Guiraud to succeed him. Colonel Dufour left his regiment, taking the regimental colors, and disappeared. He actually remained in the Orléansville region, where he made contact with the officers whom he knew to be ready for the political and military operation that had been planned.

Most officers were unwilling to express themselves or showed themselves to be hesitant. For the government, on November 16, announced that there would be a referendum to ratify the principle of self-determination, which would be started on its way by means of provisional institutions. There could be no doubt that the country as a whole would give a favorable reply. So any previous rebellion would appear to be a refusal to abide by the verdict of universal suffrage, and a confession that the cause of French Algeria was not that of the Nation. To revolt, subsequently, would seem a direct challenge to the country itself. The hesitancy of the officers, at the beginning of December, simply reveals that they were coming to realize that they were in a blind alley. Confronted by a brutal dilemma, they realized that at last they must decide, with death in their hearts, to accept the will of the state.

But the most resolute among them had not yet given up. General de Gaulle's arrival in Algeria, on December 9, offered them a last opportunity to adapt their plan to new conditions. It is remarkable to observe how this plan once again fell back on the old mechanisms that had functioned on May 13 and January 24. Now the European demonstrations would be touched off by General de Gaulle's voyage. These, it could be foreseen, would be met by a Moslem reaction— inspired, indeed, by official encouragement, for the aim would be to show that the head of state awakened Moslem enthusiasm. In this clash between the two communities, the Army could not stand idly by. It would be forced to intervene and, in repressing the Moslem riots, it would have the European crowds on its side. It would have "swung over" to them. On this occasion, General Salan could at last leave Madrid and take over the political aspects of the operation. Best of all, it might prove possible to get hold of General de Gaulle, and his presence on Algerian soil facilitated this.

These December days marked one of the most important stages in the history of the Army during the previous fifteen years. Involved in the successive episodes were to be found some of the personages most prominent in the Army's Algerian drama. Some were colonels who bore the whole weight of the Indochinese trials, of the recollections of May 13 and of the debates of January 24. In the company of the head of state could be seen the meager silhouette of General Ely, the Army's "confessor." General Jouhaud had just left his command and was back in Algeria, where he had been born. He was waiting in the shadows for the day when he might again establish contact between his former comrades and his European compatriots. In Madrid, General Salan was waiting for the signal that would call for his return. From day to day he expected to find himself in the Algiers forum where he had once given the decisive impulse to the revolution of May 13. He was endeavoring to unite in his person the two trends characterizing the military opposition, the insistence on European solidarity and the fanatical devotion to a French Algeria.

This scion of a provincial republican family found the right tone, when he assured his Spanish hearers that "the future of Algeria is of vital importance for Europe. The Soviets would soon take over in Algeria, if France should leave." Since he had remained in contact with many persons in French political life and was now the man of the hour for the Algiers activists, this former head of the Deuxième Bureau of the General Staff for the Colonies thought that all the strings were in his hand. He did not have the feeling that he had cast aside the prudence which everyone attributed to him. Between the French political parties, the Army and the European community in Algeria, he thought he had sufficient room for maneuver, and could find the path by which everyone could return to legality, when the rebellion had attained its goal.

His calculations were matched by the determination of the European crowds to turn General de Gaulle's Algerian trip into a trial of strength. Algeria, on the eve of December 9, appeared to be keeping an armed vigil. A lugubrious autumn threw a gloomy light on a country traversed by riots and strikes. On December 9 and 10, the streets of Algiers and Oran were filled by European demonstrators who clashed intermittently with police and gendarmes. Telephone calls and telegrams bore the news to General de Gaulle and his retinue, who were winding up their tour. By the second day the moment had been reached, the moment eagerly awaited by those who hoped for a military outbreak, when the two communities began to come to blows. The Army would soon be able to intervene. At the same instant, the head of state uttered, in the presence of the officers gathered before him, the words that summed up the choice they had to make, even if it was a cruel one:

> The Army serves no clan, no faction and no interest. The Army serves France, and that is all. If it did not set the example it must set, that of service, this scandal might perhaps suffice to strike a mortal blow at the soul of the country. . . . The soul of France is with us, and I repeat that the entire country has confidence in you, beginning, *Messieurs les officiers*, with myself.

On Friday, December 9, Moslems had gotten in touch with several officers of the "Urban Administrative Sections" and told them that they were going to stage street demonstrations. In accordance with the directives issued, these officers gave their consent, and informed them that the watchword must remain "Algerian Algeria." Exasperation had indeed reached a climax in the Moslem districts of Algiers. The forces of order were concentrated in the heart of the town, and intervened neither in the outlying zones nor on the borders between the European and Moslem districts.

On the evening of the 10th, the first columns of Moslem demonstrators marched down the streets of Belcour. They displayed the green and white emblems of an independent Algeria. During the night, several parachutist regiments arrived in the town. On December 11, the destiny of the Army was at stake. The Moslem rioting became remarkably widespread. The greater part of Algiers was decorated with green and white flags and with nationalist watchwords. After years of oppression, the Moslem crowd literally let its too long suppressed nationalist fervor explode. Back from the *bled*, the parachutist regiments discovered that in Algiers the flag of the enemy was waving, the enemy they had been fighting for five years past. Arson and destruction had apparently turned the town into a battlefield. At some points, the police and gendarmerie were barring the rioters from the center of the town. But these forces did not level their weapons against the crowd, and permitted the first great nationalist demonstration to take place since the Algerian War had begun.

In Belcour, at the corner of the Rue de Lyon and of the Rue Albin-

Rozet, a symbolic incident occurred. Colonel Masselot, who commanded the Eighteenth Regiment of Parachutist Chasseurs and was accompanied by several of his officers, asked Commissar Gavoury to disperse the Moslem rioters and to remove the green and white flags. If not, the regiment would intervene. The request was refused. This brief interchange indicated that a decisive development had taken place in the Algerian affair. There was no longer any attempt to deny or even to challenge the authority of the F.L.N.; at the most the European and Moslem communities might be prevented from clashing. There was no longer any attempt to wage war or to proclaim French authority; at the most it was desirable to maintain order.

Thus, on December 11, the parachutists who had been called the "spearhead" of the Army in Algeria, had a preview of the unavoidable end of a war they would have liked to continue until victory was attained. Outside Algiers they would continue to ferret out the A.L.N., to destroy the underground groups and crush the "rebellion." But in the center of Algiers they were forbidden to carry out this assignment; French authority recognized the F.L.N. in the streets, before recognizing it around a conference table. At several points the parachutist regiments were used to throw back the Moslem crowds, who were already confronted by armed Europeans. But on December 12 these regiments were withdrawn from the principal sectors of the town. They had not got their hands on the control levers and had not even tried to do so. The Army had not "swung over" to support of the European community which, appalled by the Moslem riots, had retreated. The mechanism of a military rebellion had not functioned. French Algeria was a lost cause.

The happenings of December, 1960, presaged the end of the war. The Moslem crowds had needed only a few hours to demonstrate that an "Algerian Algeria" was necessarily an independent Algeria. This would be set up on the basis of negotiations between the French government and the F.L.N. The December riots made plain what the course would inevitably be. By forbidding the Army to suppress the adversary, the government had chosen to talk with him. Less than six weeks later the first meeting took place between the accredited representatives of the French government and of the provisional government of the Algerian Republic, M. Chayet and M. Saad Dallab.

It was clear to all that in the future the European community could no longer play its old part. By its recourse to street demonstrations, it had provoked the Moslem reaction, and this would be the pattern for the future. Thus no attempt to prevent Algerian independence could count on the intervention of the European masses, which could only lead to fresh Moslem demonstrations. The mechanism of the political outbreaks of May 13 and its successors had had its day. Offered one last opportunity to intervene on behalf of the European community and against the Algerian policy of the head of state, the Army had remained aloof and maintained a silent discipline.

There was another significant episode. At Cherchell, officers had intervened so that the Moslem crowd might freely demonstrate in favor of an "Algerian Algeria." But those who had seen how the parachutist regiments had jumped out of their trucks, in the Algiers streets, only to watch the progress of the Moslem demonstrations, could sense that this decision to obey would be accompanied by acts of indiscipline. Those who saw how they reacted to the order that forbade the suppression of the demonstrations could easily imagine that, in spite of everything, many officers would still prefer rebellion.

April 22, 1961, was the precise counterpart of December 11, 1960. The essential characteristics of the *putsch* had been predetermined by the aftermath of the days filled with Moslem riots. Only a few regiments had felt inclined to intervene against them. In their isolation, they could not pick up anew the task of ensuring order in Algeria and so missed their last chance to re-establish military authority over the whole administrative apparatus in the Algerian Departments. These regiments alone were involved in the attempted coup d'état on April 22.

The handful of those eager to repeat, in December, the operation of May 13, 1958, was matched by the tiny handful of those acquainted in advance with the details of the *putsch*. This provided the remarkable degree of secrecy that was maintained to the very eve of April 22. But it also indicated that the plotters were increasingly isolated among their Army comrades. Among the instigators of April 22, we find the names of men whom May 13 or January 24 had made famous. Colonel Argoud and Colonel Broizat had been extremely active during the affair of the barricades. Colonel Godard and Colonel Vaudrey shared responsibility for the Sûreté Nationale during the year that followed May 13. Colonel Lacheroy had been the spokesman of the first Committee of Public Safety, after having worked out the theory of resistance to subversive warfare. Colonel Masselot, who commanded the Eighteenth Parachutist Regiment of the Marines, was one of the officers who would have wished to reassume control over Algiers on December 11. His regiment took part in the *putsch* of April 22, as did the First Foreign Parachutist Regiment, which had stood opposite the barricades from the evening of January 24, and to which the insurgent leaders capitulated, a week later.

Few men, few soldiers, and always the same: for the Army in Algeria, struck by the spectacle of the enormous Moslem crowds bearing along the green and white flag of the F.L.N., was present at the disappearance of a myth, one that had been indescribably dear to officers' hearts. This myth had declared that the Moslem population was warmly attached to France but was paralyzed by the threats voiced by the F.L.N. networks or by the underground fighters in the Willayas. Now there could be no question of inducing Moslems to parade through the streets of Algiers or Oran to display their support for a French Algeria, integration and fraternization. The officers now knew that, in the least significant locality in the country, they might from one day to the next be confronted by Moslem rioters just like those of December. They could no longer feel that they had the least freedom of action. They discovered the pointlessness of the four or five years of pacification which, they had hoped, would lead to a victorious outcome. They were, however, not in the least inclined to believe that only negotiations with the enemy could solve the Algerian situation. Most blamed the veering course followed by the government for the irresistible drive for independence that had come into the open on December 11. They worried about the safety of the Moslem soldiers who had fought alongside the French Army. But their attitude was already that of men whose sole thought was to save from the disaster what could be saved—honor, friends and cherished symbols.

The referendum of January 8, 1961, finally convinced the military that people's minds had turned irresistibly toward the acceptance of an Algeria separated from France. All the partisans of a French Algeria were hostile to the "yes." The seventy per cent of the ballots that favored General de Gaulle's policy made their failure official.

The government had mobilized the military hierarchy to bring out the Moslem vote. Categorical, highly official directives stated that the Moslems should be advised to vote "yes." Many officers took refuge behind a neutrality that actually demonstrated their hostility. But the whole weight of the military hierarchy, backing up the steps taken by the civil administration, nevertheless ensured an overwhelming percentage of favorable votes in the Moslem constituencies. The European community, on the contrary, voted "no."

The unadorned electoral statistics condemned the idea of a French Algeria. The official issue of the referendum was the principle of self-determination and the setting up of provisional institutions designed to effectuate this. The referendum did not, in itself, require the opening of negotiations with the F.L.N., nor did it exclude them. But everyone realized that a policy of integration would be dropped once and for all. French Algeria, which in practice had been a dead issue for months past, was officially executed on January 8, 1961.

For the Army, the lesson of January 8 rounded out that of December 11. Those among the officers—and, no doubt, this still meant the vast majority—who had not wished to renounce Algeria had now witnessed how Algeria renounced them. One month after the great Moslem riots, they could foresee that any continued struggle on behalf of a French Algeria would cut them off from the French Nation also. The military leaders, who had a better insight than the officers of lower rank into the evolution of public opinion, realized that there was no possibility of reversing the trend that would lead to a dialogue with the F.L.N. Countless retired generals voted "no," and sixteen of them, who had held commands in Algeria, put out a manifesto to herald the fact. But generals on active duty had known, ever since December, that a military victory was not to be had. They were convinced that a French Algeria could never be restored. Even a change of government, even a change of regime could no longer prevent the negotiations that had now begun, so deeply did the country desire an end to the conflict.

Thus the planners of a new coup d'état could find no backing among the generals holding important commands. No defection was to be noted in the Etat-Major de la Défense Nationale, nor at the head of the General Staffs of the Army, Navy and Aviation. In Algeria, neither General Gambiez, the Commandant Supérieur Inter-armes, nor the commanders of the Algiers and Oran Army corps supported the coup d'état. General Gouraud, who was in command of the Constantine Army corps, did so only after hesitating for forty-eight hours and under the immediate pressure of several regiments under his command. The *inspecteurs d'armes* remained loyal to the government, as did the commanders of the military districts in France. General Nicot, Major General for Aviation, at first refused when he was asked to provide transport to Algeria for General Challe, who was to take charge of the coup d'état. General Bigot, commanding the Fifth Aviation District in Algiers, adhered to the plot only after he had been assured that the whole Army would follow General Challe, and this induced General Nicot to do likewise. General Petit, struck by the success that the coup d'état met with in it first twenty-four hours, accepted the post that General Challe offered him. On April 23 and 24, several generals were on the point of following his example, but the hesitation of the officer' corps was so marked that they withdrew in time to be able to proclaim their loyalty to the state.

This hesitation on the part of the Army in the field had been so clearly foreseen by the organizers of the coup d'état that they had appealed to retired generals to head it. Once again, the choice of men reveals the isolation of these partisans of violent action against established authority. The participation of General Jouhaud was indicative merely of the anguish felt by the European community in which he had his origins, not of the state of mind current in the air force whose Chief of Staff he had been. The name of General Zeller had always been mentioned, whenever any conspiracy was discussed, since the founding of the Fifth Republic. He would have played a decisive role, if the political operation planned for the fall of 1959 had taken place. Chef d'Etat-Major de l'Armée, he had succeeded in confiding the key posts to officers who shared his views, and he had considerable influence throughout the military hierarchy. Eighteen months later he served the coup d'état simply as an asset, not as a guide.

In December, 1960, General Salan would have been at the head of another operation, conceived on the same lines as those of May 13 and January 24. On the last day of the April *putsch,* he suggested that the same means should be used, and that the massive interventions of the European community should be ensured by forming anew the Territorial Unities and by the mobilization, on the actual scene, of several classes. But the other generals did not desire General Salan's participation in the coup d'état. For his presence would have given it a political significance they preferred to avoid. Salan's connections with the European activists who had taken refuge in Spain, his unpopularity in the Army and the personal attacks to which he had been subjected made him a liability rather than a help for the authors of the *putsch.* But the "Organisation Armée Secrète," which had taken over from the defunct "Front pour l'Algérie Française," had relations with some of the officers planning the coup d'état. It saw to it that Salan could reach Algiers.

Salan, however, had no influence as long as the *putsch* lasted.

During these four days, the only important part was played by General Challe. He was an aviator, and belonged to the least conservative of military milieux, the one most affected by the modern passion for technique and the most deeply imbued with democratic procedures. Major General of the Armies prior to May 13, he was too familiar with the French political atmosphere to have any illusions concerning the authoritarian, corporate state favored by the officers closest to the Algiers activists. He had had excellent relations with Guy Mollet's Socialist government, and had been his collaborator and adviser in preparing the Suez expedition. So he had not hoped from the outset that the crisis of May 13 would lead to the return to power of General de Gaulle. Like most French generals, however, he quickly came to favor this, when it appeared that nothing else would preserve the Army's unity by eliminating the danger of civil war. He was both a Gaullist and a supporter of a French Algeria, as long as the two could be reconciled. He firmly believed that General de Gaulle could be induced to modify his Algerian policy, and that the most important thing was to avoid any crisis akin to May 13. On January 22, 1960, at the meeting of the Committee on Algerian Affairs that followed the dismissal of General Massu, he thought that he had been given serious reassurances, or at least he tried to persuade himself of it. On January 24, he agreed to the demonstrations organized by Joseph Ortiz and the Algiers activist movements, since he viewed them as a valuable warning for the government. Yet on January 26 he refused to associate himself with the demands that a group of colonels wanted him to pass on to General de Gaulle, in the name of the entire Army. On January 29, he tried to convince his officers that they could rely on the few assurances that were to be found in the speech delivered by the head of state. The affair of the barricades convinced him that in no circumstances could French Algeria be defended with the help of Algiers activism, which was universally regarded, in France, as Fascist. Besides, he was willing to believe that the association formula preferred by General de Gaulle was also a "French solution." He tended to think that what mattered was to win an incontestable victory in the field. Believing in the excellence of his plan and in its success in practice, he saw victory as near and certain; for him it was within reach.

When General Challe was relieved of his command, he felt that he had been robbed of the fruits of the undertaking he had started on its way eighteen months before, and which he had hoped to see through to the end. Personally, he was filled with bitterness against General de Gaulle. Morally speaking, he had already broken with him. At Fontainebleau, where he took over from General Valluy the post of Commander-in-Chief of the "Centre Europe" forces, he found himself in the midst of that body of military opinion that had always been opposed, not only to General de Gaulle's Algerian policy, but also to his Atlantic and European conceptions. He listened attentively to the criticisms voiced in the Allied General Staffs against the political and strategic independence that General de Gaulle was intent on preserving. He, too, imagined that a reversal in Algerian policy could coincide with a general rapprochement between France and her Allies in the Atlantic Pact. And for a long time past he had believed that Algeria was but one front in the universal war between East and West. In May, 1959, he already remarked, at a meeting of reserve officers, that the Algerian War was only the "prefiguration of a continental conflict . . . on a battlefield so vast it might extend in depth from Brest to the Urals . . ."

But General Challe, unlike many of the other generals who had these same convictions, had a passionate attachment to Algeria. He had been so strongly affected by the Algerian affair that he decided to ride roughshod over all considerations of prudence, ethical scruples and technical feasibility to undertake a coup d'état. Regrets for a lost victory and disappointment at his failure to rise to the summit of the military hierarchy, combined with a particular view of western strategy, would not in themselves have propelled him into dissidence and rebellion. Personal passion had to play a part also.

Perhaps the starting point may be found in the "Jumelles" operation, carried out in Kabylia in late spring, 1959. General Challe, who had been trained as an aviator and was accustomed to staff work, became personally acquainted with infantry warfare in a rebellious *djebel*. He had all that was needed to become a remarkable tactician of modern warfare and an outstanding specialist in the utilization of technical weapons. But here he was in a tent set up on rocky soil, on hills that sweltered in the sun. Kabylia was far removed from the luxurious setting inhabited by the Allied General Staffs which, with their extraordinary equipment and gigantic installations, seemed to belong to another world. Challe discovered a universe he had never known in which dwelt young colonels without inhibitions and with no excessive respect for the hierarchy, aggressive and sportingly inclined, whose gaiety was bolstered up by their youth and their remarkable competence. Their good humor, "go" and simplicity greatly appealed to the General, who had at last stepped down from the heights to which his rank had previously restricted him.

The colonels explained their conception of revolutionary warfare to General Challe, and what steps should be taken to meet it. For a general officer of his classic background, this was a kind of revelation. When some of these young colonels later begged him to head a rebellion of the Army in Algeria, his refusal was soon overcome. When he asked Debré, the Prime Minister, for premature retirement, he could not let slip the opportunity to indicate an Algerian policy. "Let France give up its atom bomb and accept Atlantic integration," he told the Prime Minister, "and the United States, as a *quid pro quo,* will help us to keep Algeria." Thus he represented a marked trend in military opinion.

General Challe had no intention of once more using the mechanisms employed on May 13 and January 24. While he may have regretted the fact that he had let the affair of the barricades go by without having seized the opportunity to reverse the government's policy, he remained convinced that the activism of Algiers, which bore the taint of "Fascism," was seriously damaging the cause of a French Algeria. If the French in France were to be persuaded that Algeria could still be held, all association with the crowds of Algiers and Oran would have to be avoided. General Challe, to the very end, forced this idea on the organizers of the coup d'état of April 22. The still vivid recollections of the December disturbances made it all the easier for him to do this. It was realized that European demonstrations could at any moment touch off Moslem reactions of incalculable dimensions and destructiveness.

This seeming wisdom was but a sign of powerlessness. The *putsch* was to have no popular backing. The European community would remain inactive, and the hostility of the Moslem masses was assured from the start. No sympathy was to be awaited from public opinion in France. The plotters were, in reality, appealing to the Army alone. And the Army would vainly look around for the least indications that the uprising was gaining ground. It would find itself confronted by established authority, the country, a call to order and an appeal for loyalty, and the exigencies of discipline. For Army opinion, the failure of the *putsch* would consist less of any moral condemnation of the rising than a total skepticism concerning this last, desperate effort to revive French Algeria, which for a long time past had been irremediably lost.

Every incident in the military coup d'état, from April 22 to 26, goes to show that the Army cadres could not shake off their hesitancy. The same uncertainty marked the exchanges between General Challe and the military leaders whose collaboration he solicited. General de Pouilly, for instance, who commanded the forces in Oran, was certain from the very first that the *putsch* would fail. He explained his views to his officers, and convinced them he was right. His whole attitude was based on this analysis, which proved to be correct. But he had no desire to order out his regiments against those of General Challe. They had been in the same class at Saint-Cyr, they knew each other well and held each other in high esteem. All that General de Pouilly would undertake would be to try to convince General Challe that the whole thing was hopeless. General Arfouilloux, whom the government wished to appoint to head the Army corps in Algiers, as a replacement for General Vézinet, who had been captured by the rebels, dispatched officers to examine for themselves the situation in Algiers, and to report whether General Challe had any real chance of success. General Gouraud, who commanded the Army corps in Constantine, vacillated between the behests of established authority and the attractions of the coup.

One reaction was very common, on the part of officers asked to take part in the *putsch*. This was a blend of sympathy for General Challe's project and of conviction that it was doomed to failure. In Oran, all the officers took General de Pouilly's attitude as their guide. In Sidi-bel-Abbès Colonel Brothier returned from leave and revoked the orders of his substitute, who had gone over to the dissidents. The Second and Eighth Regiments of Marine Parachutists refused to have anything to do with the *putsch*. The First Regiment of Parachutist Chasseurs did take part, but its colonel remained loyal. The same was true of the Second Foreign Regiment of Parachutists.

It could be seen from the very first day that the military cadres were not answering General Challe's call. Even before the first signs of opposition in metropolitan France or among the ranks, the officers did not believe that the coup could succeed, and most of them adopted a waiting attitude. General Challe's only genuine support came from six or seven parachutist regiments and they, and they alone, continued responsive to his orders right up to the end. But on the second day of the operation, the soldiers shook off their customary taciturnity and displayed their opposition. It was a haphazard effort, to begin with, with the tying up of telephonic communications and with transportation difficulties, orders that got lost and files that disappeared. The men in each unit made contact with the officers they knew to be faithful to General de Gaulle. Almost everywhere these contacts were the outward and visible sign that the draftees were hostile to the *putsch*. Thus the officers remaining loyal could feel that there was real strength behind them. They kept hammering this fact home, in their debates with officers who had gone over to General Challe, and it made it all the easier for them to resist pressure. Within two or three days the drafted men, backed up by the official radio, the press and the political parties, came to realize their strength. They endeavored to learn their officers' real intentions. They contacted neighboring units and tried to organize resistance to the coup.

Had these soldiers felt very differently on May 13 or January 24? Probably not. But peace appeared to be so close, in April, 1961, that this military coup d'état took on the aspect of an outrageous attempt to prolong the war. General de Gaulle's firmness and the vigorous reaction of public opinion in France reminded the draftees of all the major demonstrations against the war that had been organized during the previous year by trade unions, student bodies and youth movements. The young soldiers modeled themselves on the young civilians at home who, after prolonged inactivity, had gradually mobilized in favor of a negotiated peace.

It still remained for the soldiers to give concrete expression to their disapproval of the coup. They utilized the opportunity offered by their officers' disunity. If the military hierarchy had been passionately united, these various manifestations of dissent could no doubt have been crushed. But there was skepticism, uncertainty and pessimism concerning General Challe's chances of succeeding. The least sign of justification for these fears was eagerly noted, and used as a reason for remaining loyal to the state. These fears were confirmed by the attitude of the draftees, and all the traditional arguments calling for Army unity and respect for the hierarchy were invoked by those who favored obedience to the government. If the coup were not soon abandoned, it would menace military discipline. The men would grow distrustful of their officers, and would keep a sharp eye on them. Several cases were already known of officers who had gone over to General Challe having been arrested by their men. This could lead to the breakdown of the Army. French Algeria was clearly such a hopeless cause that it would be folly to sacrifice on its behalf the very existence of the military establishment. The Army and the Nation had reached an imminent parting of the ways, and most officers grasped the fact that this coup was a frontier that they were unwilling to cross.

While the events of December had heralded the failure of April 22, this in its turn prefigured the impossibility of any dialogue between the Army and the O.A.S. [Organisation de l'Armée Secrète]. The latter, incidentally, had drawn a valid lesson from the four days that the *putsch* had lasted, and warned the French troops in Algeria not to act as though they were forces of occupation. The first pamphlets were distributed early in May, and they were categorical in tone. Some elements in the European community already looked on these soldiers from France as enemies, whose function it was to provide established authority with the assurance it could lead Algeria toward independence and the assumption of power by the F.L.N. The European community felt that it had watched idly as the last chance to reverse the trend slipped away.

The mechanism of the *putsch,* since it called for no civilian participation, had left the clandestine apparatus of the O.A.S. practically intact. This organization, however, could no longer rely on the military complicity it would have had, but for the failure met with on April 22. The events of December had led the political organizations of the European minority to abandon all mass demonstrations. Taking refuge in clandestine activity, they founded the Organisation de l'Armée Secrète, which soon took over all the practices of underground warfare. Deeply rooted in the population, it would survive every blow, right up to the cease-fire. But the nature of the struggle involved it ever more in activities that precluded any future intervention of the Army on its behalf. The resentment that the European community felt for the soldiers from France was already creating numerous psychological barriers between soldiers and civilians. The terrorist activities of the O.A.S. completed the job by wounding the feelings of the majority of officers and awakening their sympathy for the Moslem community. The traditional reflexes favoring order, authority and hierarchy also helped to make impossible the rapprochement desired by the leaders of the O.A.S.

With the failure of the *putsch,* these leaders lost many of their military contacts. Within a year, some dozens of rebellious officers had been tried and condemned, usually with a suspended sentence, about eighty were declared "unattached" and about one thousand resigned. The majority of the officers most passionately involved in the cause of a French Algeria were eliminated. The Army as a whole had the same attitude with regard to the O.A.S. as toward the organizers of the coup d'état of April 22: while reluctant to condemn them it refused to commit itself, and oscillated between sympathy, disapproval and passive complicity.

But with the intensification of O.A.S. activity, and with the date for the cessation of hostilities coming ever closer, the military cadres were obliged to take a definitive stand for or against the state. After the failure of April 22, it was certain in advance that they would obey. Now the importance could be seen of the officers, long overlooked, who had always been hostile to any political intervention on the Army's part. Some were the heirs of the republican, Jacobin tradition whose roots plunged deep in French military history. But such officers were few. Others, far more numerous, found inspiration in the memory of the Free French. Inevitably, they were greatly distressed by the authoritarian, totalitarian aspects of the officers most fanatically attached to a French Algeria. Their Gaullism exempted them from the secret longing for revenge nourished by some cadres who had previously backed Vichy, and who were no less instinctively hostile to General de Gaulle in 1960 than in 1940. Sometimes officers were surprised to hear their colleagues on the Algiers General Staffs deplore the Algerian War and regret the failure of France to grasp the necessity of decolonization. Yet others, with a humanitarian and liberal conception of their mission, were revolted by the political tactics and police procedures used without scruple by those responsible for May 13 and by the plotters of January 24.

Such officers played a discreet but not insignificant role in aiding the government of General de Gaulle to get a new grip on the military cadres. Some of them had been meeting, even before 1958, in discussion groups the most important of which seems to have been "Rencontres." They were all agreed that the reputation of the Army as a whole might be irremediably threatened, if no opposition were offered by military men themselves to the attitudes expressed in the outbreaks of May 13, January 24 and April 22. Concretely, they wished to participate in the struggle against the O.A.S. The names of Lieutenant Colonel Rançon and Major Poste, who fell in this struggle, did more to efface from the public mind the recollections of the military uprisings than any lengthy historical and sociological explanations could possibly have done.

At the time of the cease-fire in Algeria, the military apparatus was gradually settling down to a definitive obedience to the state. A number of gestures served to symbolize this decision. In Algiers and Oran, some officers made contact with the leaders of the F.L.N., in order to prevent any general clash between the European and Moslem communities as a consequence of O.A.S. terrorism. In the Ouasenis region, other officers persuaded the Bachaga Boualem, an old enemy of the F.L.N., to reject the suggestions of Colonel Gardes, who wanted to establish an O.A.S. underground group in the territory of his tribe. Here and there, shots were exchanged between soldiers and O.A.S. activists. Soldiers were killed. On March 26, the *tirailleurs* units who had the job of keeping order, fired on a crowd of European demonstrators. Whatever the precise details of such episodes, their meaning was clear: from now on there would be no political intervention by the Army on behalf of a French Algeria.

Yet the psychological reality was far removed from the reality of fact. An object of grave suspicion, the Army had regained neither the confidence nor the esteem of wide segments of public opinion. It still remained under the shadow of the accusations made against it during the previous four years. It had been held in a vise of distrust ever since its appearance on the political scene had profoundly modified the national existence, and it could not break loose from this. The topic of an Army purge had become a favorite theme for the parties and newspapers of the Left. The most casual remark made by a general was analyzed in detail. The transfers and postings of officers were endowed with political significance, even when they had none.

Many officers thought there was nothing to be done but keep silent. They were determined to free the Army from any political domination, and knew that the aftermath of the Algerian drama would for long weigh heavily on the military cadres. At all events the withdrawal from Algeria, however long postponed, would be a rude test. They were anxious to meet and endure this test without its being made even more unbearable by a flood of criticisms or by vain calls for rebellion. If the wounds were to close, they would have to be isolated from ceaseless polemics.

But no secretiveness could hide the fact that military society was profoundly disturbed. If the Army was suspect, there were reasons for this. After long years of warfare in Algeria, it had been asked to draw the most radical conclusions from decolonization; it would be required to use force against the partisans of a French Algeria. This political surgery seemed out of the question, in the opinion of most officers. Active rebellion was barred, but they could continue to move down the slope of passive complicity. It is not certain that this benefited the Eurpean community in any way. What is certain is that, by adopting this attitude, the Army contributed to its own distress. All complicity risked punishment, and this fed the Army's bitterness and rancor. The state's comprehensible distrust found expression in a close watch over declarations and attitudes. The idea quickly arose, on the basis of one incident and another, that a system of espionage had been introduced. Thus a kind of ostracism was still meted out to those officers who had been the most loyal and the most clearsighted, and who had most rapidly realized that the Army should not so closely identify itself with the cause of a French Algeria that it would rise against the state.

A rash of resignations gave the impression that the Army was in process of liquidation. In some military milieux, the evacuation of Algeria and the end of the Army were equated. The object of distrust and embittered by failure, they felt a morbid delight in thinking that the disappearance of a French Algeria might herald the downfall of the west. Then this personal bitterness could be submerged in universal catastrophe. In the meantime, the officers who adopted this outlook enclosed themselves in an isolation from which they looked down contemptuously on the whole of French society, which was guilty, in their eyes, of having renounced all effort and chosen the illusory tranquillity of a withdrawal to continental France. Many officers remained self-exiled by their refusal to see that what had been tried in Algeria was an impossibility—the responsibility for this being that of successive governments, at the outset, and not the Army's. They sought the poisoned pleasures of martyrdom and solitude. Regarding themselves as persecuted, they could blame everything on the state and on society, the oppressors, while all dignity, honor and loyalty were their own. They also cultivated and spread around them a remorse that fitted in well with their regrets. Indeed, even the officers the most remote from political involvement were disturbed by the memory of the Moslem soldiers they had commanded and whose lot might be frightful. In this way the refusal to accept the inevitability of decolonization for Algeria was decked out in the appearance of virtue, and the recollections of brothers in arms took the place of the struggle to maintain French dominance in Algeria. Perhaps this nostalgia, in the case of many, was associated with an unavowed sense of shame at having played a part in useless acts of repression and police violence.

Mention must be made here of the new appearance of the Army, sociologically speaking. The officers, as we have seen, came from very humble circumstances. The percentage of Saint-Cyr and Poly-technique graduates had shrunk considerably. And, conversely, promo-tions from the ranks and via the school for noncoms had become much more numerous than before the war. Thus the military milieu had been transformed. There were now families that had achieved upward social mobility by the presence of an officer in their midst. This milieu was, in the main, that of the agricultural or storekeeping *petite bourgeoisie*, and the families of noncoms now became the fami-lies of officers. This increased the isolation of the military in French society. For now the roots lay in classes that had remained outside the immense economic transformations that had taken place in France in the previous fifteen years. Thus Jean Planchais, in an article pub-lished by the *Revue Française de Sociologie*, could refer to a certain "military Poujadism." And indeed, in military circles today, as with certain groups of storekeepers, artisans and small farmers, there is the same rejection of modern economic transformations, the same fear of the risks of change, the same suspicion of all the revolutions of our day, which explain the immense electoral success enjoyed, in 1956, by the Poujade movement.

Again, one must often distinguish between the military milieu and the officers themselves. After the failure of April 22, the wives of officers set up small groups for mutual aid and comfort, in order to help the families of the arrested officers. A strange atmosphere of undercover activity and persecution surrounded these undertakings. People outdid each other in claiming to be menaced by disciplinary measures, denunciations and forced retirement. Some officers' wives agreed to act as O.A.S. agents. This was but an extreme form of the passionate refusal to accept Algerian independence. It was only a rearguard action, but it revealed how fearful a whole group of military men were of the new situation they had done all they could to pre-vent and with which they wished to have no dealings. This oppressive climate bore down on the officers' corps.

The military cadres themselves are today perhaps more ready for the future than are their families and the milieux from which they come. Certain transformations took place in seven years of fighting in Algeria. New vocations were discovered. More recent classes of officers entered the Army.

Today, most officers of lower rank have had no part in the Indochinese War. Thus they do not share the feeling of being abandoned that so affected their elders. They are not attracted by ideological warfare or by the prospect of actual conflict with communism, and they are exempt from the "yellow loves" to which so many older officers look back nostalgically. These younger men even feel less bound to Algeria than the older men did to Indochina. Much testimony awakens the impression that the same affection was rarely felt by officers for the soil of Algeria and the Algerians that had been aroused in them by remote Indochina. They seldom cared for the European groups. The Moslem population appeared to them more ineradicably foreign than had the Vietnamese and Cambodians. Marriages between French Army men and Indochinese women were not exceptional, whereas almost no marriages were entered into with Moslem women. Perhaps, too, the officers who knew only the Algerian War do not feel the same need for revenge as do those who made their way out of Dien-Bien-Phu. The French Army suffered no catastrophe in Algeria, on the strictly military plane. It was left with no inferiority complex. Psychologically, it should be more readily able to face new assignments.

Many French officers have declared, during these last years, that the most modern form of warfare the Army ever experienced was the fighting in Algeria. No doubt the notion was often entertained that it was no less old-fashioned to imagine that the next general war would be atomic, than to believe, in 1939, in a warfare of unbroken fronts. At the same time new classes of officers were emerging from the Ecole d'Etat-Major, the Ecole de Guerre and the Institut des Hautes Etudes de la Défense Nationale. Many officers spent long periods in the inter-Allied organizations. Others took part in the maneuvers of the western forces in Germany. Finally, aviators and naval men were more interested in modern warfare than in psychological action or the splitting up of populated areas into grids. Thus the great movement of transformation, the first symptoms of which could be seen in the Army of 1954 and 1955, had never entirely ceased. It had been kept alive in many minds, and all that was required was to translate it into military reality.

This is what General de Gaulle wanted the Army to look on as its essential task, once the Algerian war was out of the way. By stressing that the modern weapons used to equip the Army would remain entirely under the control of the French state, he proclaimed that the traditional idea of national defense would be adopted once again. His intention was, no doubt, to provide the country with an instrument that would permit an independent foreign policy. But in this way the Army was also linked more closely with the Nation, its metamorphosis was connected with that of civilian society, and the opportunity was provided for French officers to find a place once more in French society, from which they had too long remained separated.

General de Gaulle met with two types of opposition to these plans. The officers who had most strongly favored a French Algeria regarded them as a maneuver to turn the Army's attention away from the Algerian drama and to obliterate any sense of shame that fresh withdrawals in North Africa might cause by arousing the hope, among military men, that they might become a great modern Army. The officers closest to the Atlantic General Staffs regretted France's failure to place its defense effort within the framework of western defense and to share in this division of labor, which would call on France for a more limited and more effective effort. Political preferences played a part in these attitudes; the officers most strongly opposed to General de Gaulle were the most enthusiastic about European integration and listened with the maximum of docility to one or another of the American generals.

Whatever the precise form of the "dissuasive force" that General de Gaulle desires, inevitably it will represent a new stage in the existence of the Army. Nothing indicates that there is any thought of a sort of twofold military apparatus, with some of the cadres required to deal with modern weapons and others being utilized in units of a traditional type. Atomic artillery would not present any radically new problems, compared with other artillery and, in any event, all the Army cadres should be familiar with its characteristics and tactical effects. The aviators required to drop atomic bombs would not need different training from that given other bombers, and the actual manufacture of these weapons would of course be a matter for the armaments factories, not for the troops. Thus the whole Army will be obliged to undergo a thorough modernization. On the human, practical level, the lessons of the Indochinese and Algerian wars must be learned, while an over-all revision of customs and concepts will be needed with respect to logistics, armaments and tactics.

History has shown that the evolution of the military arm cannot be separated from that of civilian society. As long as France is putting through an immense effort of economic renewal, while the birth rate has increased to a remarkable extent, with staggering effects on the old structures of society and the professions, it can scarcely be imagined that the officers' corps alone could remain untouched by any conception of modernization. For the first time since 1830, the Army's effectives will all be on French soil. A historical change of such importance must of course impose serious strains on men's outlook and customs. Perhaps the example set by civilian society has never had so much impact on the future of military society. Prosperity, expansion, forceful industrialization and job security should provide the Army with a firm enough base to banish the temptation of any moral and social self-exile, by which military men would condemn themselves to rancor, decline or revolt.

By embarking on the path of modernization and seeking to bring about a revolution in military concepts, the young officers would be modeling themselves on a society filled with enthusiasm for techniques and productivity, turned away from values and abstract ideas, and contemptuous of the past, but looking forward to the future as an era of wealth, security, statistics and well-being. These officers would be at one with their age.

But our century has other forms of vertigo. The call to catastrophe can start off deep resonances. From Indochina to Algeria, the road of defeat may lead to a horizon of universal tragedy. Revolutions aflame in Asia and rumblings in Africa may fascinate the men who thought that in Hanoi, and later in Algiers, they were defending western civilization. They would thus see their own withdrawal as the prelude to the end of the civilization whose heroes they envisaged themselves. Possessed by a dream of cosmic decline and making an unavowed cult of despair, such officers, with their attachment to tradition, loyalty, honor and the bygone days, are also men of our era, in which philosophers contemplate nothingness, writers speak of an absurd universe and moralists abandon hope, to describe the death of ideas. Yes, they, too, are the children of this century.

CONCLUSION

✠

Have we reached the end of an age? Has the adventure that began in the 1930's played itself out, with the settling of the Algerian War? Today there are numerous indications that the Army's longest and gravest crisis has come to an end. Finding a lesson in its sufferings, it may now be effectuating a silent return to its normal place within the state. If the Algerian War was the occasion for all the issues separating the Nation and the Army to come to a head, the restoration of peace, eliminating the causes of this friction, may finally permit that meditative calm in which psychological wounds can heal over.

But the Algerian War was not the origin of the opposition between the Army and the state. It was only the final stage of a long process which began before the Indochinese War and even before the Second World War. The roots are to be found in those years when bourgeois society was shaken to its foundations, in the 1930's, when it seemed that there was no way out for the western world than to opt between alternate forms of an inevitable revolution.

Today nothing remains of the anxieties that convulsed bourgeois France of thirty years ago. We seem indeed, far removed from the climate of economic depression, social disaggregation and ideological and moral uncertainty characterizing the great crisis that began in 1929. For the past eighteen years the French economy, for all its monetary difficulties, has been passing through every stage of a seemingly

553

irresistible expansion. There may be some trouble in keeping the different sectors in balance, but no one has any doubts concerning the validity of the basic processes involved. We blandly toy with the notion of limitless growth. The least delay or least weakening in the established rate of expansion strikes us as scandalous, so confident is the bourgeois France of 1962 in the economic weapons at its disposal. It may be that this serenity has been achieved only at the price of a painfully acquired indifference to the destinies of Africa and Asia. In any case, there seems little reason for military society to find any attraction in the notions of illegal activity and civil war, which had such a seductive force in the days of the Popular Front and the "Cagoule."

Each fresh class emerging from Saint-Cyr reduces the percentage of officers whose life has been marked for ever by the choice they made between de Gaulle and Vichy, between the Army in Africa and the Free French. Today these conflicts belong to history. The Indochinese War has also receded into the past, and the fate of Africa has ceased to set Frenchman against Frenchman in unbridgeable antitheses. Practically everywhere relief was expressed that the task of decolonization had proceeded so smoothly in the immense regions of French Black Africa. There may still be lengthy arguments concerning the economic consequences and estimates of the effect exerted, for good or ill, on the African states with respect to their industrial progress, social structure or cultural level. But all this leaves public opinion unaffected, and military society, reflecting the outlook of French society as a whole, no longer believes that its own destiny is tied to the political future of Black Africa.

This is true also where Morocco and Tunisia are concerned. Those who were most violently hostile to their independent status may no doubt garner some bitter and trivial satisfaction from the political and social troubles that sometimes convulse these states. But this is only the last relic of the imperial dream, and of the recollections of greatness and renown associated with the era of the two Protectorates. The Algerian wound has not yet healed over, but the Army has already turned away from a venture that had been passionately pursued and, so to speak, lovingly preserved against all vicissitudes, but which had one day shown itself to be hopeless. Oblivion has been preferred to vain regrets.

Military men have emerged from their Algerian trials as from a gigantic nightmare. No clear historical insight is possible for them, after so many officers have been killed, wounded, convicted and left destitute, while many others have resigned. There may be some unvoiced realization, on the part of the Army cadres, that "French Algeria" was an impossible undertaking, entirely at odds with the spirit of the age, the irresistible upward surge of nationalist feeling and the population increase among underdeveloped peoples. But experience was gained at too high a price. Political maturity does not spring directly from the disappointments and setbacks that have been suffered, nor from inner distress and conflict. Time must elapse before awareness can be attained.

The French Army now has this breathing spell at its disposal. The return to France of the legions from Algeria writes *finis* to overseas adventures, and the great cause of the threatened and defended "Algerian province" has vanished into thin air. Distrust, wariness and the spirit of rebellion henceforth have nothing to feed on, in Army life. Now, it may be thought, is a time for meditation, for silent, methodical labor, and during this time wounds can gradually heal over as the old dreams fade into oblivion.

But is this really the last word in the last chapter of French military history? Let us recall the origins of the great chasm that threatened to cut off the Republic from the Army. For the military to have recourse to illegality and political activity, it was necessary that French society as a whole should be shaken to its foundations, and that the crisis should grow until it came to appear tangible, imminent and dramatic, and to present all the perils of revolutionary subversiveness. This turning point was reached in the 1930's. The haunting fear of communism succeeded in doing what had been accomplished neither by the Dreyfus Affair, nor by the "affaire des fiches," nor by the First World War, nor by the problem of the Rhineland.

The new enemy, communism, over a period of twenty years, had exhibited a visage of many aspects, ever different and ever the same. From the 1917 mutinies to the military tribunals in the Ruhr, from the campaign against the operations to subdue the Riff to the revolutionary nationalisms of Annam and Algeria, everywhere it was international communism by which the Army considered itself confronted. And it believed, too, that this same enemy was around the corner in France itself, nesting in the social hopelessness and economic distress of the thirties, and denounced as the sole fearful adversary by demoralized bourgeois thinkers. The Army judged that the occasion had arrived to abandon all neutrality, and many officers yielded to the allure of political action. They were merely the first to do so.

At the price of a dictatorship invoking moral order and social discipline, Vichy would have for ever banished the redoubtable specter of Communism; therefore the attraction of such a regime was, among the military, practically irresistible. But, in exchange, they would have had to give up the most elemental patriotism and accept the most undeniable servitude. There was no bridging this contradiction, and in the most favorable circumstances it took, at the most, two years to crumble under the stress of reality.

While the Fourth Republic was aureoled with the prestige of the Liberation and of victory, it nevertheless was terribly marred, in the eyes of the military, by one thing: the share taken by the Communists in setting it up. Feeling utterly remote from such a regime, the cadres fell back on their bitterness, their inner conflicts and their poverty. No popular fervor buoyed them up, and they even lacked all sense of mission, at a time when postwar history indicated a path to salvation that would have fulfilled their secret longings.

Then, in the universal clash between the west and the Communist world, the Army once more found a role to play. For the Army, this war had a grim reality; the corpses of 2,000 officers remained in Indochina. It discovered the real nature of this war, that what was at stake was the mind of the populations; the battle took the day-to-day form of political, social and ideological struggles. The Army had fought, in the Far East, a lonely, murderous war, which was forgotten by Frenchmen and neglected by the state, and hidden away by the governments themselves. Many officers were resolved that in the future the Repulic should pay proper respect to the tasks set the Army.

The lapse of time throws a clearer light on the main lines of the debate that separated the more moderate and more bourgeois partisans of Algerian independence, based on negotiations with the F.L.N., and those, especially among the military, who sought to prolong the defense of a French Algeria. The former wanted to reach an agreement with Algerian nationalism, lest the nationalists compromise themselves irremediably with international communism, and lest its inevitable victory be a purely revolutionary triumph. The latter looked on Algerian independence as but the first step in the general undermining of Africa. To accept it was to open the door to revolution; the only recourse against this greatest of all dangers was to integrate the Algerian Moslems in the French Republic. Any intermediate solution, it seemed to the military, would inevitably lead to secession and, ultimately, to communism. Through all the vicissitudes of the Algerian

War, as during the era of the clandestine networks that were set up in 1936, and as in the ricefields of Tonkin, the French Army had tirelessly fought the same adversary. As one trial succeeded another, it had discovered that there was no fundamental distinction between armed conflict and the political battle. No one could seriously challenge this identity.

Is not the same conflict to be found in Europe as in Africa, in France as in Algeria? On their return from Algeria, the legions are called on to face the same adversary. It is within the framework of the still functioning Atlantic Pact that each new phase of the permanent, organized tension between the western world and communism must be located. This is, of course, a diplomatic and military alliance which sets the Army no other task than the methodical, coordinated preparation of a hypothetical war. But who today will deny that the outcome of this undeclared war depends above all on the social struggles and political convulsions by which the states on every continent are being shaken? Having withdrawn to the tip of the European peninsula, the French Army might be satisfied to watch these events, attentively, no doubt, but in silence. And, at that, it would be necessary that the waves of revolution should stop short of French shores. There can be no illusion on this score: any risk of social revolution in France would entail the risk of renewed military interference in the political domain.

Is there any other possibility? Only if there should be a return to missions of purely national interest, to the single imperative of national defense. Only if an era should be reborn when patriotism once again becomes the supreme law, and an age summoned up from the distant past when the Army's only reason for existence would be to serve the fatherland. But can there be any such return, now that all the great states of the west have subordinated their national interests to the collective preservation of their economic concepts and their social structures? The Republic must remain bourgeois, lest the Army cease to be Republican.

✠